AUTOMOTIVE COMPUTERS AND DIGITAL INSTRUMENTATION

ROBERT N. BRADY
Vancouver Community College

A RESTON BOOK
PRENTICE HALL, Englewood Cliffs, New Jersey 07632

Library of Congress Cataloging-in-Publication Data

Brady, Robert N.
    Automotive computers and digital instrumentation.

    "A Reston book."
    Includes index.
    1. Automobiles--Electronic equipment. 2. Micro-
processors. 3. Automobiles--Instruments--Display
systems. I. Title.
TL272.5.B64 1988   629.2'549   87-36027
ISBN 0-8359-0263-3

Editorial/production supervision and
  interior design: Tom Aloisi
Cover design: 20/20 Services, Inc.
Manufacturing buyer: Bob Anderson

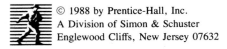 © 1988 by Prentice-Hall, Inc.
A Division of Simon & Schuster
Englewood Cliffs, New Jersey 07632

Printed in the United States of America

10 9 8 7 6 5 4 3 2 1

ISBN: 0-8359-0263-3

Prentice-Hall International (UK) Limited, *London*
Prentice-Hall of Australia Pty. Limited, *Sydney*
Prentice-Hall Canada Inc., *Toronto*
Prentice-Hall Hispanoamericana, S.A., *Mexico*
Prentice-Hall of India Private Limited, *New Delhi*
Prentice-Hall of Japan, Inc., *Tokyo*
Prentice-Hall of Southeast Asia Pte. Ltd., *Singapore*
Editora Prentice-Hall do Brasil, Ltda., *Rio de Janeiro*

Contents

4

ENGINE/VEHICLE SENSORS   78

5

ELECTRONIC FUEL-INJECTION SYSTEMS   114

6

ELECTRONIC IGNITION SYSTEMS—COMPUTER-CONTROLLED   147

7

GENERAL MOTORS ECM SYSTEMS   169

8

FORD EEC SYSTEMS   226

Preface

Advances in technology have a way of making the skeptics "eat their words," so to speak. The electronics explosion in the automotive field since the 1980–81 model year have allowed the Jules Verne type of visionaries to bring to fruition the concepts and ideas that were frowned upon by many of their associates. It wasn't that long ago that skeptics were saying disc brakes and fuel-injected engines would never find much commercial use outside of a racing circuit.

In the passenger car field today, there are very few manufacturers who are not employing fuel injection, either in the TBI (throttle body injection) or MPFI (multi-port fuel injection) format. As of 1988, both Ford and General Motors no longer employ carburetors on their passenger car engines. All are offered with either TBI or MPFI designs. What might have been considered pure gadgetry a few years ago is now accepted as a necessary part of the on-board electronics package that has been made possible by modern electronics wizardry.

From the minute drivers decide to enter their cars, electronics technology takes over. Keyless entry through a pre-determined code offers the owner the ability to access his or her vehicle without the conventional key concept. Once inside the car, and with the ignition key inserted, the operator can adjust the seat to his or her favorite position by the touch of a button. A synthetic voice then advises the driver to fasten the seat belt, while the on-board computer automatically runs through a digital diagnostic check of the electronics system.

When the engine is cranked over and fires, electronics under the hood and in the car controls the distributorless ignition system, the fuel injection system, and the exhaust gas oxygen sensor. This fine tuning of the air/fuel mixture results in minimal pollution of the atmosphere. This scenario occurs just a scant 20 years after the initial debut of the electronically fuel-injected VW squareback, with its then feared "black box" syndrome.

No longer does the driver have to sit for five minutes in cool weather to ensure that the engine will not stumble and stall. Electronic fuel injection/ignition and the various engine sensors allow immediate forward movement of the vehicle without any of these conditions occurring. During the closed-loop operating range of the engine (computer receives a voltage feedback signal from the exhaust oxygen sensor), a perfect or stoichiometric air/fuel ratio of 14.6/7 : 1 can be maintained under all conditions.

Power availability from an engine, which is now in many cases only one third the size of its predecessor V-8, is available through electronically-controlled turbocharger wastegates. Aftercooled engines are commonplace in the 4 cylinder and V6 turbocharged engine configurations.

Future designs may produce electronically operated intake and exhaust valves so that actual engine valve timing can be varied at will to produce an engine power rating and performance curve to suit different operating environments and conditions.

Electronically controlled transmission shifts are now commonplace in automatic type transmissions, while anti-skid braking devices are being offered in increasing numbers on all models of passenger cars and light duty (pickup) trucks.

Once underway, the operator can select a temperature-controlled passenger compartment environment with the mere touch of a button, again made possible through the world of electronics. Relaxing to the stereophonic sound of a favorite radio station or cassette tape, the driver can also resort to a touch screen map layout to decide the fastest route to a target destination.

Electronically controlled suspension systems will automatically trim the ride quality as the vehicle moves from one type of road surface to another. Should the driver decide to put in some spirited driving maneuvers, optional electronically controlled active suspension systems and four-wheel steering can help him control the vehicle's actions with precision. These are just some of the features available to the general public on passenger cars today.

Should the operator of a vehicle not be mechanically minded and fail to carry out service procedures as required, then the on-board computer, working in conjunction with the various engine and vehicle sensors, will gently remind the driver through a flashing instrument panel warning light that there is something not right in one or more systems. In other cases, should a faulty operating condition exist, then the on-board computer will revert to a predetermined program and allow limp-home capability of the engine/vehicle, albeit at reduced operating performance.

Maintenance and troubleshooting of electronic systems can either be easy or very tough. In order to make it easy, it is imperative that the mechanic/technician be trained in the basics of electricity and electronics so that he or she understands the concepts and design of the various vehicle circuits, and how they interact with one another. In addition, the technician must be aware of the various diagnostic tools and instruments that are commercially available, where to use them, and how to connect them into a vehicle circuit safely.

The on-board computers used in cars and trucks are capable of self-diagnosing problems occurring in the systems, and these computers will retain stored trouble codes in memory. The codes can be accessed with the use of special diagnostic readout instruments. Some upscale vehicles can be made to flash these trouble codes on the instrument panel. Others can relay these trouble codes through the flashing Check Engine Light on the instrument panel. If a diagnostic readout tool is not available, using a simple jumper wire across two contacts of the ALDL (assembly line diagnostic link) will initiate the self-diagnostic readout procedure of the on-board computer system.

It is also important that the mechanic/technician develop an attitude of respect for the electronic system and components on the vehicle, and not approach a troubleshooting task with a negative or ''black box'' syndrome mind set. The electronics era is here to stay, and it will not disappear. Therefore, learn to appreciate its contribution to the successful operation of the total vehicle.

This textbook will provide the reader with a good grounding in basic electricity and electronics, and an introduction to the concept of operation of the on-board ECM and BCM (electronic control module and body control module) computers and various sensors that form the basis of control for all of the various engine/vehicle electronic systems.

Special diagnostic tools and equipment are also shown and their function is described so that you, the reader, will know when and where to use such instrumentation. A description of how all of the various electronic systems now used in passenger cars operate and interact with one another is given in a straightforward manner so that you can understand and appreciate what might create a problem in a particular system.

If you had reservations about approaching an electronic system malfunction before reading this book, you will gain insight and, hopefully, confidence in your ability to approach and extract systematically the stored trouble codes from the on-board computer. Doing so will lead you to the general area of where the vehicle problem lies.

Both the major domestic and import vehicle manufacturers' cars are discussed in this book. This approach allows you to appreciate just how similar all these various electronic systems actually are.

No attempt is made to duplicate the information contained in all of the various manufacturer vehicle service manuals. These manuals contain specific information for all systems on their vehicle models, as well as detailed and often lengthy diagnosis procedures that must be followed in order to pinpoint a particularly tough electronic system problem. Use these service manuals to assist you, but first learn where to locate this information; and don't attempt to bypass a procedure, for otherwise you may miss completely just where the fault is located in a system.

I am confident that this book will provide you with a solid foundation on which to build and develop your own skills and expertise on electronic systems and on-board computers. If you couple this electronic information and theory with a systematic *Hands-on Approach* to the daily problems that you encounter in servicing and troubleshooting, you will quickly be able to assimilate both the *How* and *Why* of operation of any vehicle electronic system.

Keep in mind, however, that although you may suspect that the problem lies in the electronic system, the first thing you should do is to check under the hood for such things as loose, crimped, or misrouted vacuum lines, loose or corroded electrical fittings, burnt wiring, etc. The problem with an engine that lacks power, stalls, and runs rough can be caused by a simple item, such as a dirty air filter or a plugged PCV valve. Therefore, keep in mind that you should check these easily accessed mechanical items before you condemn the electronics system.

The growth of passenger car electronics has shown a quantum leap in the past couple of years, and will continue to improve the operating efficiency of both the engine and associated vehicle components. Therefore, it is here to stay.

The fact that you have chosen to read this preface is testimony to the importance of electronics in helping to maintain and service today's passenger cars and trucks. I'm sure that you will find this book both interesting and informative, and it will prepare you for more detailed exposure and learning as you progress through either your studies of automotive technology or as you attempt to increase your knowledge of what you already know about the on-board computer systems in passenger cars.

I wish you well in your pursuit of excellence. Without the thousands of dedicated individuals such as yourself, the proper maintenance and successful operation of today's passenger cars and trucks would be impossible!

Robert N. Brady

NOTE: *Included at the end of Chapters 1, 2, and 19 are a number of basic system review questions. These questions are used in these particular chapters, because it is important that the reader have a good understanding and solid foundation of the principles of both basic electricity and electronics prior to proceeding into the operational characteristics of the on-board vehicle computers. Questions in Chapter 19 deal with general operation and safety-related items for vehicle theft deterrent systems, so that the reader will be aware of the methods required to isolate such a warning system prior to servicing the vehicle.*

Acknowledgments

A book of this scope and detail can never be written without the strong support and assistance from numerous companies who have contributed sales literature, brochures, and technical information. The following companies and individuals therefore deserve special mention for their time, effort and, most of all, encouragement in helping me to produce the finished product now before you.

1. AC Spark Plug Division, General Motors Corporation, Flint, Michigan. Mr. John V. Dinan, Jr., Director of Public Relations.

2. Allied Automotive, Autolite Division, Fostoria, Ohio. Mr. Jeff Davis, Product Planner, and Mr. Harry P. Wertheimer, Manager, Oxygen Sensor Engineering.

3. ALLTEST Auto and Truck Diagnostic Equipment, Hoffman Estates, Illinois. Mr. E. M. Parr, Vice President, Sales and Marketing.

4. American Isuzu Motors, Incorporated, Whittier, California.

5. American Motors Corporation, Detroit, Michigan. Mr. D. R. Linderman, Supervisor, Service Publications.

6. Cadillac Motor Car Division, General Motors Corporation, Detroit, Michigan. Mr. D. D. Wright, Group Leader, Electronics/Diagnostics.

7. Chevrolet-Pontiac, Canada Group, General Motors Corporation, Warren, Michigan. Mr. R. A. Monticelli, Technical Service Activity.

8. Chrysler Motors. Mr. J. L. Freeman, Manager, Service Publications.

9. CTS Corporation, Elkhart, Indiana.

10. Delco Electronics, Subsidiary of GM Hughes Electronics, Kokomo, Indiana. Marilyn Y. Grant, Manager of Public Relations.

11. Delco Remy Division of General Motors Corporation, Anderson, Indiana. Mr. K. J. Pitcher, Director of Public Relations.

12. Digital Automotive Systems Incorporated, Garden Grove, California. Mr. Ric Erdman, P.E., President.

13. John Fluke Manufacturing Company Incorporated, Everett, Washington. Mr. Mikio Ishimaru, Corporate Patent Counsel.

14. Ford Motor Company of Canada Limited, Oakville, Ontario. Mr. W. C. Rowley, Technical Training Supervisor, National Service Office.

15. Industrial Optics Products/3M, St. Paul, Minnesota. Mr. George A. Gregori, Market Development Supervisor.

16. Kent-Moore Tool Group, Sealed Power Corporation, Warren, Michigan. Andrea W. Kolton, Advertising Manager.

17. Mechanical Engineering Publications Limited, Bury St. Edmonds, Suffolk, England. Mrs. Judith Constantine, Senior Co-ordinating Editor.

18. Motor Age Magazine, Chilton Company, Radnor, PA.

19. NEC Electronics Incorporated, Mountain View, California.

20. Nissan Automobile Company (Canada) Limited, Mississauga, Ontario. Mr. J. L. Black, National Consumer Support Manager, and Mr. G. M. Roadley, National Technical Operations Manager.

21. Oldsmobile Division, General Motors Corporation, Lansing, Michigan. Helen Jones Earley, Public Relations.

22. OTC Division, Sealed Power Corporation, Owatonna, MN. Mr. Douglas R. Snorek, OTC Cummunications Group.

23. Robert Bosch Corporation, Broadview, Illinois. Mr. Robert E. Rodriguez, Production and Communications Manager, Automotive & Diesel Products.

24. Society of Automotive Engineers, Incorporated, Warrendale, PA. Mr. Antenor R. Willems, Director, Publications Group.

25. Toyota Canada Incorporated, Scarborough, Ontario. Mr. N. Bess, Technical Training Manager.

About the Author

Robert N. Brady has been involved in the automotive and heavy-duty truck and equipment field for 29 years, having served a recognized five-year apprenticeship, and having worked as a shop foreman, service manager, and fleet maintenance superintendent. In addition, his experiences have included positions as National Service Trainer (Canada) for Detroit Diesel Allison Division of GMC, as well as a Field Service Representative.

He has taught for 18 years at Vancouver Community College, ten of those as a Department Head of the Diesel Mechanic/Technician Program, specializing in Commercial Transport Mechanics, Heavy-Duty Mechanics, and Diesel Engine Mechanics.

He has developed technical training programs for a number of major companies in both the automotive and heavy-duty truck and equipment fields, and acts as a technical consultant through his own company, HiTech Consulting Limited.

This is his fifth book for Reston/Prentice-Hall, with other publications being, *Diesel Fuel Systems*; *On-Highway Trucks, Power Trains and Suspension Systems*; *Electric and Electronic Systems for Cars and Trucks*; *Automotive and Small Truck Fuel Injection Systems, Gas and Diesel*.

He is a certified automotive mechanic/technician as well as a heavy-duty truck and equipment mechanic/technician.

He is a member of the Society of Automotive Engineers Inc; and currently, he sits on the governing board of the British Columbia chapter. He is also a member of the Association of Diesel Specialists, NACAT (National Association of College Automotive Teachers), the Canadian Vocational Association, and the Vocational Instructors' Association of Vancouver Community College.

CHAPTER 1

◆

Fundamentals of Electricity

No discussion of computers or solid-state devices can be considered prior to understanding the basic concept of magnetism and the flow of electrons within a wire. In this chapter, we review the principles of electricity to assist you in understanding the close links between conventional electrical flow and circuitry, before moving onto a discussion of electronic devices.

The modern electrical system used on passenger cars, commercial, and heavy-duty equipment is an intricate system that supplies the necessary electrical energy to operate lights, horns, radios, stereo tape decks, heaters, windshield wipers, defrosters, air-conditioning systems, powerseats, and the vehicle ignition system on gasoline engines. In addition, the electric starter would not be possible without the use of a battery, which itself requries a generator or alternator to keep it in a state of charge. All of the other fancy factory options, or after market add-ons, would be of little use without the electrical system.

Considering the little attention that it often receives, the electrical system does a remarkable job in maintaining trouble-free operation throughout its life. When electrical problems occur, they can usually be traced to a lack of maintenance, or improper service procedures.

Although the reader may have a limited knowledge of electricity, most people do understand the typical fresh-water system that is found in the normal family home and office. Everyone has probably used a garden hose at some time and has found that with no nozzle on the end of the hose outlet, and with the hose tap turned on, a large volume or quantity of water flowed from the hose, but with little pressure. This can be likened to quantity or volume is an electrical system, only it is commonly called amperes or amps when discussing electricity. In the water system we commonly refer to this quantity or volume as gallons per minute, or liters per minute.

If we were to place our thumb over the end of the garden hose, or to screw an adjustable nozzle onto the hose end, then we would be able to effectively control the quantity or volume flowing from the end of the hose by manipulation of this adjustable nozzle. In either instance, what we actually achieve is a reduction in quantity or volume, but a definite increase in the force of water leaving the hose. This then is pressure, which in an electrical system is known as *voltage* or *volts*.

We can still have pressure in water flow without placing our thumb or the nozzle over the hose end. However, this pressure remains reasonably constant, and is developed at a city pumping station in your community by the use of mechanically driven water pumps. It is not variable as with the adjustable nozzle on the hose end.

City water pressure will force water through the street pipes until it meets a resistance at your house such as a closed water tap or faucet. This water flow (volume) is the same as the current pushed through an electrical circuit, which will also meet resistance in the form of lights or other electrical accessories in the system. All substances offer resistance to flow whether they are water pipes or electrical wires. The size and length of these pipes and wires will vary the amount of resistance present in any given circuit. This resistance in an electrical circuit is known as ohms.

Therefore the main properties that we are concerned with at this time are:

- Quantity or volume expressed as amperes or amps
- Pressure expressed as voltage or volts
- Resistance expressed as ohms

When considering any electric system, remember these three properties.

The water pump at the pumping station supplies the pressure and, in effect, becomes the battery in the electrical system. The battery stores electrical energy both in the form of amperes and volts, in quantities determined by the actual physical size and design of the battery. We will discuss this later in the chapter dealing with batteries.

An understanding of the actual relationship between the three properties listed so far—current (amps), pressure (volts), and resistance (ohms)—will assist you in future discussions related to any electrical system.

Common electrical terms include:

- **Volts:** Unit of measure for electrical pressure or force, commonly measured by the use of a voltmeter.
- **Amps:** Unit of measure for current flow, measured by an ammeter.
- **Ohm:** Unit of electric resistance that opposes current flow, and causes heat to be created by this resistance (friction) to flow. Measured by the use of an ohmmeter.

CONDUCTORS

In the typical water system, we use pipes to carry the flow throughout the system; in an electrical system, we use wires for this same purpose. These wires are usually made of copper, since it is reasonably inexpensive and plentiful in supply. Aluminum wiring has also been used, especially in house wiring and commercial buildings. However, in automotive and heavy equipment, copper is used extensively for wiring, since it has proven to be less troublesome than aluminum and stands up better under the types of operation encountered by these electrical systems.

Most metals, in fact, are good conductors of electricity, with silver, copper and aluminum being the most widely used. When flexibility is desired in a wire, copper wiring may be composed of a large number of very small strands of wire.

The size of the wire used can have an adverse effect on the resistance created when electricity flows through the wire. This can best be explained by considering Fig. 1-1.

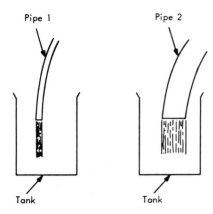

FIGURE 1-1   Pipe size versus flow rate and resistance.

In Fig. 1-1, water is directed through pipes of two different diameters, namely Pipe 1 and Pipe 2. You can appreciate that since Pipe 2 is larger than Pipe 1, the tank immediately under Pipe 2 will fill up much faster than the tank under Pipe 1. The reason for this is that obviously we can direct a greater volume or quantity of water through Pipe 2 in the same time as that for Pipe 1 because of the larger diameter of Pipe 2.

Both pipes will create a resistance to water flow. However, since Pipe 1 has a smaller diameter than Pipe 2, Pipe 1 will have a higher resistance to the flow of water through it.

The flow of electricity is caused by the movement of electrons within the wire. The greater the electron flow within the wire, the greater the quantity or volume flow will be in a given time period, much like the gallons or liters per minute flowing through the water pipe. The electrical flow, as you may remember, is measured in amps.

If we now consider Fig. 1-2, which of the three wires shown would have the greatest resistance to current or amp flow?

If you said Wire A, you were correct. Which wire in Fig. 1-2 would allow the greatest current or amperage flow? If you said Wire C, you were correct.

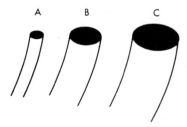

FIGURE 1-2   Wire size versus flow rate.

USE OF ELECTRICAL ENERGY

To systematically evaluate how electrical energy can be used in a system or circuit, let's compare the simple water wheel system to that of the electrical one through the use of basic line diagrams.

One of the easiest ways in which water power can be used to provide work output is that of the old mill wheel, where water from a river or stream was used to drop over an embankment and drive a large water wheel or paddle wheel. A shaft running from the center of the wheel was then connected to a millstone, which was continually rotated by the water wheel.

If work was required from a water wheel, however, with no river or stream close by, the only way to achieve this was to use a pump driven by some means to direct water to and against an impeller which was then continually rotated by the water pressure produced in the pump. Such an example is shown in Fig. 1-3.

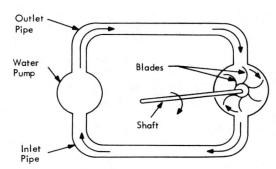

FIGURE 1-3 Sealed water pump system.

Although Fig. 1-3 shows a sealed system, it is only because this system requires less water than an open system, which would continually require a steady water supply.

In the simple Fig. 1-3, the pump creates the flow within the system to drive the shaft. As the pump rotates, it will create not only flow (quantity or volume), but also pressure because of the sealed system, and resistance is created through the effort required to drive the shaft and by the size of the piping.

If we now substitute a similar arrangement, but use electrical components, we would have the view shown in Fig. 1-4.

In Fig. 1-4, we have substituted wires for the water pipes, a storage battery in place of the pump, and a light bulb in place of the shaft connected to the load. In Fig. 1-3, the water flow and pressure rotated the shaft, while in Fig. 1-4, the current being pushed through the wires by the voltage causes the light bulb to glow. Remember that the battery contains both quantity (amps) and pressure (volts); therefore, the battery has replaced the water pump. The system shown in Fig. 1-4 is also a sealed system similar to Fig. 1-3, with no means of recharging the battery at this time. Current flows out of the battery to the light bulb, and then returns to the battery.

In Figs. 1-3 and 1-4 we called the systems a sealed system; however, in an electrical system, the more common

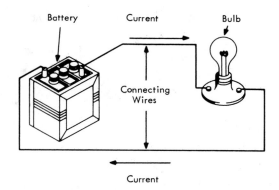

FIGURE 1-4 Basic electrical system.

term used is a closed circuit, because there can be direct loss of electrical energy other than that which is used to light the bulb.

If we were to break a water pipe, or cut a wire, then there would be a loss of energy. In this condition, the shaft in Fig. 1-3 would no longer rotate and, in Fig. 1-4, the light bulb would no longer glow. Such a condition in an electrical circuit is commonly called an open circuit, meaning that there is a loss of electrical energy.

The word circuit is derived from the simple word circle. In other words, in order to complete the circuit, the current must be capable of flowing around the circle from the point of origin and back again to that same point.

In Fig. 1-4, the light bulb is an energy-absorbing device, since it requires current to keep it lighted. In turn, the current or amps are forced through the circuit by the electrical pressure or voltage. Anything wired into an electrical circuit that uses current is, therefore, part of the electrical load placed upon that circuit. The greater the number of accessories wired into the circuit, the greater will be the current requirements or amperage needed to operate them all.

In addition, as we add accessories to the circuit, these current-carrying devices will offer greater resistance to the flow of electricity, and will, in many instances, require additional voltage to overcome this added resistance.

BASIC ELECTRICAL SYMBOLS

In Fig. 1-4, we showed a battery, wires, and a light bulb. This was done for clarity and for ease of instruction. However, this is not the way that such a circuit would be shown in normal electrical terminology and layout.

An easier and less involved method is shown in Figure 1-5. Note that the battery terminals are shown by two different symbols. These are used to differentiate between the positive and negative terminals.

The positive battery terminal can be a large $\top$ or a plus sign (+).

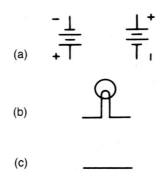

(a)

(b)

(c)

FIGURE 1-5 Electrical symbols: (a) battery, (b) light bulb, (c) wire.

The negative terminal is shown as either a short ⊥ or a minus sign (−).

Other commonly accepted and used electrical symbols are shown in Table 1-1.

RESISTORS

All conductors will offer some form of resistance to the flow of electrons (current/amps) through the wire. This resistance is caused by the resistance of both the wire and the circuit resistance. A resistor therefore is an electrical component that can be used to add or alter a fixed amount of resistance to any electrical circuit.

By adding a resistor to a circuit, therefore, we decrease the current flow. For example, Fig. 1-6(a) shows a simple circuit with no resistance other than that offered by the wiring and a single light bulb. This arrangement allows four amps to flow through the closed circuit. However, in Fig. 1-6(b), we have installed a fixed resistor to the closed circuit, which will therefore decrease the current flow from the previous four amps shown in Fig. 1-6(a) to only two amps as shown in Fig. 1-6(b).

Resistors which have more or less resistance can be used to suit the situation as desired in the circuit. Therefore, in Fig. 1-6(b), the light bulb will not glow as brightly as it did in Fig. 1-6a because of the lower current (amperage)

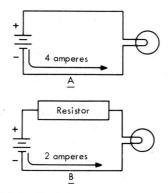

FIGURE 1-6 Resistance versus current flow.

TABLE 1-1
Commonly-used electrical symbols.

A.	⏚	ground AC source
B.	—Ⓥ—	voltmeter
C.	●	connected wires
H.	●	
D.	⊃	unconnected wires
F.	┼	
G.	(AC GEN)	generator
I.	⎓⎓	electromagnet
E.	—√√√—	variable resistor
P.	—√√—	
J.	+⊣ⅠⅠⅠⅠ⊢−	battery
K.	—•⁄•	SPST switch
O.	—•⁄•	
L.	—√√√—	fixed resistor
M.	—(MOT)—	motor
N.	—Ⓐ—	ammeter

flow. As the value or amount of resistance is increased, the current flowing through the circuit must decrease. Thus, by employing different resistors in a circuit, we can change the value of a fixed resistor, change the voltage source, and control the amount of current (amps) flowing in that circuit. The symbols for resistors are shown in Table 1-1.

The fixed (non-variable) resistor is used throughout automotive and heavy equipment circuits to limit the current

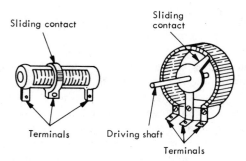

FIGURE 1-7 Variable resistance.

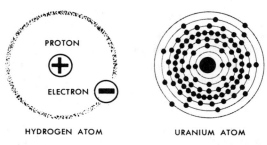

FIGURE 1-8 Hydrogen and uranium elements.

flowing at any given point. However, there are resistors available that can be adjusted in position by use of a sliding contact to provide variable resistance to suit a variety of conditions. To vary the resistance of a variable resistor, a sliding contact connected to an insulated hand-adjusted sliding contact allows you to dial in the resistance to suit almost any condition within the circuit. A simple variable resistance is shown in Fig. 1-7.

INSULATORS

When it is necessary to prevent a loss of electrical energy by a bare wire (for example, one touching a metal object), the wire must be covered by a material that will not allow any external flow of current. Materials such as rubber, plastic, glass and wood are examples of good insulators, since all of these materials have a very high resistance to the flow of current.

Without this insulation in an electrical circuit, you would get a severe shock when you touched or handled wiring. The insulator also protects other components from short-circuiting or creating an open-circuit by coming into contact with one another.

GENERAL THEORY OF ELECTRICITY

In its simplest statement, electricity can be said to be the flow of electrons from one atom to another atom within a conductor. All matter is composed of atoms, and these atoms are so small that they are invisible to the naked eye, and even to powerful microscopes. The atom is the smallest particle into which one of the elements can be divided while retaining its properties. The elements combine in many different combinations to form various kinds of matter found on earth. The elements hydrogen and oxygen, for example, combine to produce water. Again, combined, sodium and chlorine produce salt. All atoms have a center or core made up of particles known as protons, around which other particles called electrons rotate. Both of these types of particles become extremely important in our more detailed study of electricity.

Let's start with what is known as the simplest of all elements, hydrogen. The hydrogen atom consists of two particles; a proton which is a positive charge at the center of the core, and an electron with a negative charge circling the proton. We will compare this hydrogen element with the very complex one of uranium. Figure 1-8 shows the typical arrangement of protons and electrons of both these elements.

The uranium element contains 92 protons (+) in its core, and 92 electrons (−) in an orbit about its core. Between these two are the remaining elements, each having an atomic structure that differs from its two neighbors by one proton (+) and one electron (−). Other well-known elements are nickel with an atomic number of 28, copper with an atomic number of 29, and zinc with an atomic number of 30.

Since we frequently deal with copper in the electrical systems in wiring, connectors, etc., let's look a little more closely at this element. Within the copper atom are 29 protons (+) and 29 electrons (−). The protons are concentrated at the core, while the electrons are distributed in four separate shells or rings, with each shell or ring located at a different distance from the core of the atom.

Figure 1-9 shows the basic core of the copper atom with the 29 electrons clustered around it. You will notice that the two electrons in the ring closest to the core remain equally spaced from one another, the eight electrons in the second ring from the core are equally spaced, and the 18 electrons in the third ring also remain equally spaced from each other. Also note that the outer ring contains only one electron.

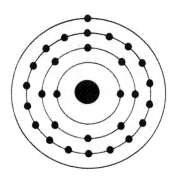

FIGURE 1-9 Copper atom.

Any element that has less than four electrons contained within its outer ring is a good conductor of electricity, while elements with more than four electrons in this outer ring are known to be poor conductors of electricity. From our earlier discussions, you may recollect that any element that is a poor conductor of electricity is called an insulator. Those elements that contain four electrons exactly in the outer ring are classified as semiconductors, which we will deal with later in this book. Any conductor with less than four electrons in its outer ring makes it rather easy to dislodge these electrons from their orbits by use of a low voltage. This action will therefore create a flow of current (electron flow) from atom to atom.

In summation, remember that the proton is positively charged, while the electron is negatively charged. Opposite charged particles are attracted to one another. Therefore, opposing electric charges will always attract. The negatively charged electron (−) will be pulled towards the positively (+) charged proton.

Because of the electron movement that exists around the core of the atom, it is not at all uncommon for an atom to lose some of its electrons. These electrons that leave the atom's outer rings are generally called free electrons, and they tend to gather in the same place, creating what is known as a charge of electricity. When these free electrons begin to move, say along a copper wire, a certain number of these electrons pass a given point on the wire in a set time period; in other words, we have a certain quantity or volume flowing or moving within the wire. The electrical term for quantity or volume, from our earlier discussion, is current, which is measured in amperes or amps. Electricity, therefore, is flowing in the wire at this time. The free electrons moving along the copper wire will always move away from areas of many electrons into areas where there are fewer.

ELECTRON FLOW IN A COPPER WIRE

If a negative (−) charge were placed at one end of a copper wire, while a positive (+) charge were located at the other end, the condition shown in Fig. 1-10 would result.

As we already know, when electrons (−) flow through a wire, a current is created which is measured in amperes. The number of electrons required to produce one ampere is 6.28 billion billion passing a given point in one second.

Figure 1-10 illustrates the flow of these electrons within

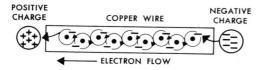

FIGURE 1-10 Electron flow in a copper wire.

a typical copper wire. For simplicity, we will show only the single electron contained within the outer ring of the atom.

The positive charge at the left side of the wire attracts the electron, thereby causing it to leave its atom. The loss of the electron now makes the atom positively charged, and the atom exerts an attractive force on the outer ring electron of its neighboring atom. This reaction causes a chain reaction to occur along the length of the copper wire, with each succeeding atom giving up its electron to another atom. Because of the great number of electrons flowing, electricity is created.

The negative charge at the right-hand side of the wire shown in Fig. 1-10 provides a repelling force equal to the attractive force created by the positive charge at the other end. Electron flow will continue within the wire as long as the positive and negative charges are maintained at each end of the wire.

VOLTAGE

In earlier discussions, we described the voltage as being similar to water pressure. It is this electrical pressure, then, that pushes the current or amperes (electron flow) through the wire.

In Fig. 1-10 we saw how electron flow was initiated in a wire; the unlike charges at each end of the wire have potential energy due to their capability to move electrons through the wire because of the forces of attraction and repulsion.

The potential energy between the wire ends is called voltage or electromotive force (EMF). We can produce voltage by various means. In automobiles or heavy equipment, we generate this voltage by chemical means within a battery. Voltage can also be produced through friction and mechanical energy, as in a generator or alternator.

A typical vehicle battery of 12 volts has a potential voltage of 12 volts between the positive and negative terminals (posts). With no current absorbing devices connected to the battery posts, there is still a potential energy of 12 volts. Voltage can exist on its own without the presence of current (amperes), but current cannot exist if there is no voltage present to push it along through the wiring.

In a battery, the voltage is limited by the strength of the charges between the positive and negative terminals or posts. Therefore, the greater the lack of electrons (−) existing at the positive (+) end or post, and the greater the excess of electrons at the negative post, the higher the voltage will be.

In Fig. 1-4 earlier we showed a battery supplying power to a light bulb. If we were to substitute a generator in place of the battery, the generator when driven would supply a continuous flow of current (amperes) through the light bulb.

In effect, the battery or generator pumps electrons through the wiring to the light bulb and back to the source of supply, which can be either the battery or generator.

RESISTANCE

Earlier we discussed that if water is forced through a pipe, some resistance to flow would exist because of the friction created between the surface of the pipe and the water. When electrons are forced through a conductor such as a copper wire, resistance will also be created because of two conditions. First, each atom resists the removal of an electron due to the attraction exerted upon the electron by the protons (+) in the core of the atom. Second, collisions are always taking place between the electrons and atoms as the electrons (−) are moving through the wire. Such collisions create resistances which buildup heat within the conductor when the current is flowing.

We mentioned earlier that the electrical term for resistance is the ohm. An ohm can be defined as the resistance that will allow one ampere to flow under the force or pressure of one volt. The electrical symbol for the ohm is Ω, which is similar in shape to a horseshoe. The number preceding the horseshoe indicates the total number of ohms; therefore 10Ω indicates a total resistance of ten ohms. The symbol for resistance is defined by the Greek letter omega (ω) in addition to the horseshoe shape shown.

TYPES OF ELECTRICAL CIRCUITS

The basic types of electrical circuits that we are concerned with in automotive and heavy equipment are either series of parallel circuits. Certain applications, however, sometimes employ a combination of both of these, and are therefore known as series/parallel circuits. One example of the series/parallel circuit is the use of batteries for both starting and charging; through the use of a series/parallel switch, two 12-volt batteries can be tied together in series to produce 24 volts of cranking power to the starter. Once the engine starts, the automatic operation of the series/parallel switch allows the generator to charge the batteries at a rate of 12 volts.

Prior to looking at several examples of series and parallel circuits, Fig. 1-11 depicts the simplest form of a basic electrical circuit. A battery supplies the energy for the system (volts and amperes), and a resistor (load) offers a fixed resistance in the circuit.

Also shown in Fig. 1-11 are an ammeter and a voltmeter to measure both the current (amperes) and voltage in the circuit respectively. Take careful note that the ammeter is placed into the circuit, and not across the battery. If the ammeter were placed across the battery, damage to the

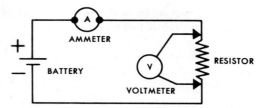

FIGURE 1-11 Basic electrical circuit (*Courtesy of Delco Electronics Corporation, Subsidiary of GM Hughes Electronics*).

ammeter would result. The voltmeter, however, can be placed across the circuit at any two points to obtain a voltage reading.

CURRENT FLOW

In the early years of electricity, it was assumed that current in a wire flowed from the positive source of the voltage to the negative terminal of the source after having passed around the circuit. However, in the year 1897, this theory was proven to be totally incorrect. Scientists discovered and proved that, in reality, the current flowed from the negative terminal, through the circuit, and back to the positive source.

Since that time, both theories have been used. For example, some companies in the industry choose to use one theory, while others choose to use the other theory. These two theories are known as:

1. The conventional theory in which the current flow is considered to be from positive to negative.
2. The electron theory in which the current flow is considered to be from negative to positive.

The conventional theory is widely used and accepted within the automotive industry, although some major manufacturers of heavy-duty equipment prefer to use the electron theory. Again, either theory can be used.

BASIC ELECTRICAL FLOW

There are two theories commonly used to answer the often-asked question: Does electricity flow from the positive battery terminal to the negative battery terminal, or is it the other way around?

1. What is referred to as the conventional theory depicts the electrical flow as from the positive to the negative battery terminals. This theory is most often used in discussions and accepted as standard practice.

2. The electron theory, however, maintains that the flow is from the negative battery terminal to the positive battery terminal; this fact was discovered as long ago as 1897.

Since either theory can be used, although the conventional theory is most often followed, most manufacturers state in their manuals which of the two should be used when studying their electrical systems. History records that 2500 years ago the ancient Greeks knew that amber rubbed on cloth would attract feathers, cloth fibers, etc. Since the Greek name for amber was elektron, the term electron was coined in our language, meaning basically the property of attraction. Electrons are negatively charged.

Many manufacturers of heavy-duty trucks, etc. prefer, however, to use positive ground systems over negative ground systems for reasons given in the following sections.

POSITIVE VERSUS NEGATIVE GROUND ELECTRICAL SYSTEMS

A discussion of electrical systems invariably involves the question of why one system is a negative ground system, and another is a positive ground system. Most North American built cars are negative ground, while many imported vehicles are positive ground. Similarly, many trucks and heavy equipment are positively grounded.

The main reason that positive ground electrical systems are more widely used on heavy-duty trucks is that in the electroplating of the vehicle during manufacturing, the plating material is attracted from the positive anode to the item to be plated, which is the negative cathode.

If, for example, during manufacture of a heavy-duty truck you could dip a negative ground vehicle into the electrolyte in a plating tank, the positive electrical system consisting mostly of copper (wiring, etc.) would immediately start to plate itself over to the negative structural and steel portion of the vehicle. You would end up with a copper-plated chassis, but no electrical system!

If we were, however, to dip a positive ground vehicle into the same plating tank, the material flow would be from positive to negative; but you would not end up with steel-plated copper. When you removed the positive ground vehicle from the tank, it would certainly be nice and clean, but otherwise undamaged.

The situation just described can be compared with the conditions that the average heavy-duty highway truck is exposed to in wet and winter-type weather. Salt placed on the highways to melt snow and ice becomes a very efficient electrolyte. During high-speed winter driving, this spray totally envelopes the entire vehicle in a manner similar to the tank situation described herein. Severe corrosion will

result to the electrical accessories on the vehicle if the negative pole of the battery is grounded.

Heavy-duty truck manufacturers have found that the positive ground electrical system practically eliminates the worst types of corrosion or electrolysis affecting the electrical system. To further explain the disadvantages of the negative ground system, consider that all of the steel structural parts of the truck are negative or cathodic. The energized electrical system, copper wires, terminals and switches, solenoids, motors, etc., are positive or anodic. The voltage differential between the steel parts and the copper electrical system is approximately 14 volts.

When the negative ground vehicle is exposed to moisture (in particular to salt-laden moisture through salt de-iceing), the condition that exists is similar to that of an electroplating bath in which steel items are being copper-plated. The positive copper anode in the electrolyte bath is ionized and attracted to the negative steel. The same situation exists on the negative ground vehicle with the result that the electrical system deteriorates.

On a positive ground vehicle, the action is reversed. However, due to the large mass of steel in comparison to the small amount of energized copper in the electrical system, the effect is insignificant. The advantage of the negative ground system is that if you can totally seal out any entrance of moisture to the electrical system and accessories, then the system will function extremely well. However, the configuration of heavy-duty, on-and-off highway trucks is such that this approach becomes rather impractical due to their operating environments. Many generators and alternators on such trucks are open in order to allow the passage of cooling air through them. The salt fog, drawn through the radiator by the vehicle movement or the engine fan, circulates through these devices, causing electrolytic corrosion of all energized surfaces that it comes into contact with.

When two dissimilar metals meet at a junction in the presence of salt-laden moisture or liquid, the resulting galvanic action generates a voltage which will electrolytically cause ionic material transfer. The voltage generated is dependent upon the electrode potential between the two metals. In the case of a typical truck, copper has a voltage potential of plus 0.347 volts, and steel has a voltage potential of minus 0.340 volts. Therefore, the voltage generated at the junction point becomes, in effect, 0.687 volts.

Electrolytic activity supported by the typical 14 volts of the vehicle electrical system is 20 times the galvanic 0.687 volts, or 20 times as severe.

The negative ground electrical system was developed because, years ago, few electrical accessories were in use on vehicles other than the basic ignition system and some running lights. However, with the advent of the transistor, research was increased to apply it to automotive use. The car radio was an ideal place in which to use this device. The first transistors were of the germanium PNP type, which were more easily applied to a negative ground system than a positive ground system because of their makeup. This development generated a swing away from the previously positive ground systems on both cars and trucks. Little information was available about the problems that could develop with the negative ground system.

Since the PNP germanium transistor was developed, major advances have been made, and silicon transistors are now widely used.

The negative ground system on passenger cars and low mileage vehicles presents no major problem, and it may be economically impractical to change over to positive ground. However, on high-mileage trucks that are in operation 24 hours a day, seven days a week, where high maintenance-free mileage is expected, and where road failures caused by electrical system problems must be kept to a minimum, many heavy-duty truck manufacturers favor the positive ground electrical system, rather than the negative system.

OHM'S LAW

There are a variety of calculations and formulas that are needed and used when designing electrical circuits and components; however, it is not necessary for the automotive or heavy-duty mechanic to be familiar with these.

It is extremely helpful, though, to know the relationship among amperes, voltage, and resistance within an electrical circuit, because if any two of these are known, one can calculate the value of the third. When adding components to an existing circuit or when wiring a new circuit, the application of this principle ensures that each component within the circuit will receive the current necessary to operate at peak efficiency.

For example, if the resistance within a circuit is too high, then certain components will not operate properly, or operate at reduced efficiency. In addition, one must know the total current draw (load) in the circuit in order to calculate what size battery is required, and also what capacity of generator is required to ensure that the battery will maintain its full-state of charge under varying conditions of load. The wrong-size wiring can also produce a high resistance to current flow. If we know how to calculate the necessary current (amperes), voltage, and resistance demands of the circuit, we can establish all the demands to be placed on the circuit. We can accurately establish this through the application of Ohm's Law.

Ohm's Law is an expression of the relationship among the current, voltage, and resistance in any circuit. The formula for Ohm's Law is arrived at by substituting the letter I for amperes, the letter E for voltage, and the letter R for resistance. Sometimes the letter V is used in place of the letter E for voltage. We will use the more common E designation.

From these letters, we establish the following formula:

1. $\text{amperes} = \dfrac{\text{volts}}{\text{ohms}}$ or $I = \dfrac{E}{R}$

2. $\text{volts} = \text{amperes} \times \text{ohms}$ or $E = I \times R$

3. $\text{ohms} = \dfrac{\text{volts}}{\text{amperes}}$ or $R = \dfrac{E}{I}$

To demonstrate how effective the application of this formula is, let's look at some examples of simple circuits, both series and parallel.

SERIES CIRCUITS

In a series circuit, all current leaving the source of supply, such as a 12 volt battery, must flow through each component of the circuit in sequential order. A simple example of this are the three light bulbs connected in a series circuit, as shown in Fig. 1-12. Here the current leaves the negative battery terminal and returns to the positive battery terminal by one direct path through the circuit, having, of course, first passed through each light bulb in series.

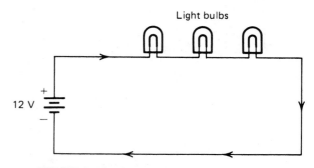

FIGURE 1-12 Basic series circuit flow path.

In the arrangement shown in Fig. 1-12, no switches are shown. Therefore, the light bulbs would glow constantly. In order to be able to switch them on and off at will, it is necessary to insert a switch somewhere in the circuit. Figure 1-13 shows how this could be done.

To re-emphasize the difference between an open and a closed circuit, Fig. 1-12 is known as a closed circuit, because current can continually flow to and through the light bulbs, and back to the battery.

In Fig. 1-13, the control switch is shown in the open position, which will prevent current from flowing to and through the light bulbs; however, the battery still has a

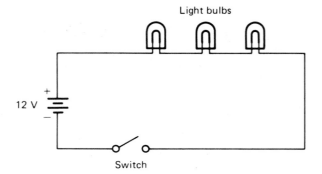

FIGURE 1-13 Series circuit with switch control.

potential voltage (electromotive force, or EMF) of 12 volts, although no current is flowing.

As mentioned earlier, each accessory or electrical component in a circuit uses current, but it also creates a resistance to current flow. This resistance will vary between accessories, and Ohm's Law allows us to calculate just what this resistance is.

To show the Ohm's Law formula at work, the following examples are given.

EXAMPLE 1 (SERIES CIRCUIT)

Calculate the amount of current flowing in the circuit shown in Fig. 1-14.

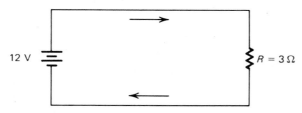

FIGURE 1-14 Example 1: series circuit current flow.

The Ohm's Law formula for finding current is amperes = volts/ohms or $I = E/R$. Therefore, $I = 12/3$ or 4 amps of current.

EXAMPLE 2 (SERIES CIRCUIT)

Calculate the total resistance in the circuit shown in Fig. 1-15.

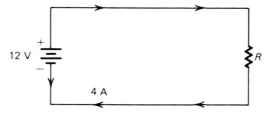

FIGURE 1-15 Example 2: series circuit resistance.

The Ohm's Law formula for finding resistance is: ohms = volts/amperes or more simply, $R = E/I$ ($R = 12/4$) equals 3 ohms.

EXAMPLE 3 (SERIES CIRCUIT)

Calculate the total voltage in the circuit shown in Fig. 1-16.

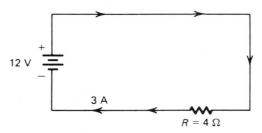

FIGURE 1-16 Example 3: series circuit voltage.

The Ohm's Law formula for finding voltage is: volts = amps × ohms; therefore, volts = 3 × 4 which equals 12 volts.

When more than one resistance is present in a series circuit, the total resistance is simply the sum total of all of the resistors. If three different light bulbs were wired into a series circuit, and they all had 4 ohms of resistance to current flow, then the total resistance would be 12 ohms. If one light bulb had a resistance of 3 ohms, the other a resistance of 4 ohms, and the last one a resistance of 5 ohms, then the total resistance to current flow would be 12 ohms.

In a series circuit, regardless of the number of accessories wired into the flow path, the current flowing is the same at all points of the circuit. If two light bulbs of 4 ohms resistance each were wired into a series circuit, then with a voltage source of 12 volts, one and one-half amps would flow through each light bulb: $I = E/R$ or $I = 12/8$ = 1.5 amps.

If we were to double the voltage, yet use the same two light bulbs, then the current flowing would now be 3 amps.

In each of the two situations just mentioned, the same amperage that flows through the light bulbs will also flow through the battery.

When more than one accessory is used or wired into a series circuit, the voltage (electrical pressure) must give up some of its potential energy to force the current through the resistance of the accessory. Therefore, a percentage of the source voltage is used up as it passes through each accessory (load). An example of this is given in Fig. 1-17.

The source voltage or potential energy of the battery is 12 volts, with 10 volts being required to force the 2 amp current through the accessory resistance of 5 ohms, and the remaining 2 volts being used to force the 2 amp current through the accessory with 1 ohm of resistance.

The previous examples characterized the value of using

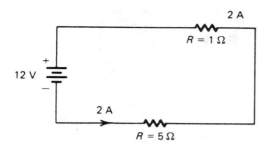

FIGURE 1-17 Volts, amperes, and resistance relationship in a series circuit.

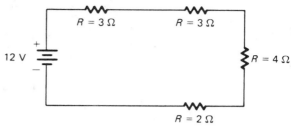

FIGURE 1-19 Series circuit with four resistors.

Ohm's Law; however, in addition to calculating what an unknown quantity is in a series circuit, we can also use:

- An ammeter to measure current,
- A voltmeter to measure voltage,
- An ohmmeter to measure resistance.

These gauges can be used independently, or can be bought in what is known as a VAR (volts/amps/resistance) meter, or what is more commonly called a multimeter. By use of a selector switch on the face of the meter, either amps, volts, or resistance can be measured.

Figure 1-18 shows a simple series circuit; with the placement of both the ammeter and voltmeter into the circuit; the ohmmeter can be placed across any two points in the circuit to establish a given resistance at any point.

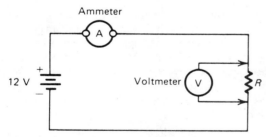

FIGURE 1-18 Voltmeter and ammeter placement in a series circuit.

Figure 1-19 shows a series circuit with four resistors (accessories) wired into the system. Total circuit resistance is established by adding all of the resistance together; the current flowing is $I = E/R$ or 12/12 or a current flow of one amp. An increase in resistance through an accessory will cause a higher voltage drop to occur in the circuit, while a lower resistance through an accessory results in a smaller loss or drop in voltage through the respective accessory.

From the basic information we have learned so far about a series circuit, we can state three known facts related to this type of electrical circuit:

1. The current (amps) that flows through each resistor (accessory load demand) will remain the same.
2. The amount of voltage required to force the current through each resistor will be proportional to the actual resistance within that resistor (accessory); therefore the voltage drop across each resistor or accessory will be different if the resistance through each accessory is different.
3. The amount of voltage loss or drop through the circuit will always equal the source voltage; for example, if a 12 volt battery is the source voltage, then the voltage drop in the circuit will be 12 volts.

In addition to the three facts listed above, we can also list several other known specifics about the series circuit that we have learned about so far. These will quickly allow you to recall some major aspects of these earlier discussions.

1. Total circuit resistance is the total of all resistors in the system.
2. Total series resistance must be more than the largest individual resistance.
3. If an open exists at any one component, then the entire circuit will be open, and no current can flow.
4. A short across part of the circuit will cause increased current in the wire between the short circuit and the voltage source.

PARALLEL CIRCUITS

In the series circuits that we just looked at, the current flowing in the circuit followed one path only from the battery post, through the accessories, and back to the opposite polarity battery post.

In a parallel circuit the current leaving the battery can flow through more than one path before returning back to the opposite polarity battery post or terminal. Figure 1-20 shows the layout for a simple parallel circuit.

The three main facts related to a parallel circuit that distinguish it from the series circuit are:

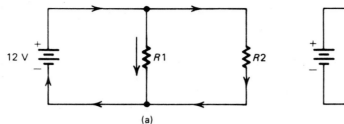

FIGURE 1-20   (a) Simplified parallel circuit; (b) parallel circuit with four resistors.

1. The voltage across each resistor (accessory) is the same.
2. The current (amps) through each accessory or resistor will be different if the resistance values are different.
3. The total of the separate currents (amperes) equals the complete circuit current.

To calculate the amps, volts and resistance in a parallel circuit, we can always refer to Ohm's Law. However, let's look at some typical examples of calculating various unknown quantities in a parallel circuit.

EXAMPLE 1 (PARALLEL CIRCUIT)

In a parallel circuit with two resistors, you find the total resistance by using the following formula:

$$R = \frac{R_1 \times R_2}{R_1 + R_2},$$

where R represents resistance.

What is the total resistance of Fig. 1-21?

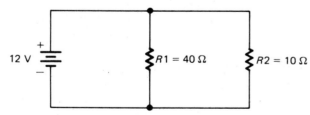

FIGURE 1-21   Calculation of total resistance in a two-resistor parallel circuit.

By application of the formula shown above, we simply replace the R_1 and R_2 portion of the formula with the values of each resistor. We therefore have resistance

$$R = \frac{40 \text{ ohms} \times 10 \text{ ohms}}{40 \text{ ohms} + 10 \text{ ohms}}.$$

The result is now $400/50 = 8$ ohms. Therefore what we have proven is that the total resistance in a parallel circuit is less than that of any individual resistor.

EXAMPLE 2 (PARALLEL CIRCUIT)

What is the total resistance of Fig. 1-22?

Figure 1-22 shows four resistors (accessories) in parallel. These accessories will each require a given current to operate them, so we can refer to these as branch currents since they are all attached to the main supply as branches are attached to a tree trunk.

Ohm's Law for finding current is

$$\text{amps} = \frac{\text{volts}}{\text{resistance}} \text{ or } I = \frac{E}{R}.$$

Therefore in Fig. 1-22, with four branch currents, we would, in effect, have $I = E/R$ four times, or $12/6 = 2$ amps, $12/3 = 4$ amps, $12/4 = 3$ amps, and $12/4 = 3$ amps to give us a total battery current of $2 + 4 + 3 + 3$ to equal 12 amperes. The circuit resistance together, however, would only be equivalent to one ohm because Ohm's Law for resistance is $R = E/I$, or 12 volts/12 amps = 1 ohm. We can calculate this actual circuit resistance by the following method:

$$\frac{R_1 \times R_2}{R_1 + R_2}$$

for the first two resistors, and repeat this same formula for the next two resistors. We therefore have

$$R = \frac{6 \times 3}{6 + 3} = \frac{18}{9} = 2 \text{ ohms}$$

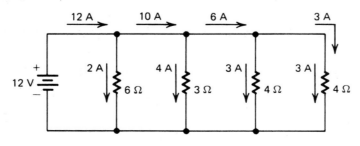

FIGURE 1-22   Calculation of parallel circuit resistance with four resistors.

for the first two resistors. In the next two resistors, we have

$$R = \frac{4 \times 4}{4 + 4} = \frac{16}{8} = 2 \text{ ohms.}$$

Remember that the total circuit resistance in a parallel circuit is always less than that of any individual resistor. Therefore, the two-ohm equivalent resistor in parallel with the other two-ohm equivalent resistor will be equal to

$$R = \frac{R_1 \times R_2}{R_1 + R_2} = \frac{2 \times 2}{2 + 2} = \frac{4}{4} = 1 \text{ ohm.}$$

Total circuit resistance then in Fig. 1-22 is one ohm.

As we have seen so far, parallel circuits provide more than one path for the current to flow. Therefore, a break in one path (open circuit) will not prevent current from flowing through other parts of the circuit, unless the break existed in the wire before the current reached the individual branch wires. If, however, each branch circuit was to be fitted with a switch as shown in Fig. 1-23, then each circuit or branch could be opened or closed when desired.

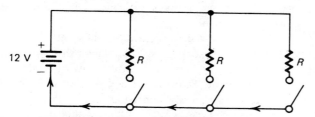

FIGURE 1-23 Parallel circuit resistance, with three switches controlling resistors.

Remember that in a series circuit, since the current only has one path of flow, a break in the wire (or the installation of a switch) would result in all accessories losing current flow because of the wire break (or if the switch were to be placed in the off or open position).

Because it is desirable in automotive and heavy equipment installations to have independent control of each accessory to suit conditions, the parallel circuit is usually used. The series circuit is used for certain circuitry to provide, for example, greater starting voltage by wiring two 12 volt batteries together. Parallel circuit wiring is also commonly used in house wiring.

VOLTAGE DROP

The total voltage drop in a series circuit must equal the source voltage. In a parallel circuit, the voltage drop across any component is the same as the source voltage.

To ensure that you understand this concept, look at Fig. 1-24, and establish the source voltage for both the series and parallel circuits shown.

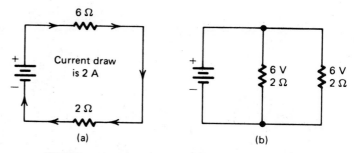

FIGURE 1-24 Calculation review: (a) series circuit resistance; (b) parallel circuit resistance.

In Fig. 1-24(a), we see a series circuit with two resistors or accessories. What is the source voltage?

Fig. 1-24(b) shows a parallel circuit. What is the source voltage?

The correct answer to Fig. 1-24(a) is 16 volts. The answer for Fig. 1-24(b) is 6 volts.

EXAMPLE 3 (PARALLEL CIRCUIT)

From Fig. 1-25, establish the total resistance in the circuit; also find the current flowing.

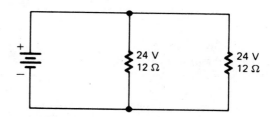

FIGURE 1-25 Establishing resistance and current flow in a parallel circuit.

Remember that total resistance in a parallel circuit is less than the resistance of either of the resistors; therefore to solve Fig. 1-25, we simply use the formula for resistance calculation in a parallel circuit:

$$R = \frac{R_1 \times R_2}{R_1 + R_2}$$

$$R = \frac{12 \times 12}{12 + 12} = \frac{144}{24} = 6 \text{ ohms.}$$

To find the battery current we refer to Ohm's Law which states that current = volts/ohms, or $I = E/R$; therefore, $I = 24/6 = 4$ amps.

SERIES/PARALLEL CIRCUITS

As mentioned earlier, series/parallel circuits are used in certain instances rather than a straight series or single parallel circuit. Figure 1-26 shows a typical series/parallel circuit.

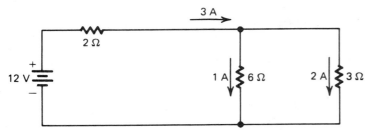

FIGURE 1-26   Typical series/parallel circuit.

Note that Fig. 1-26 shows current flowing from the battery through a series (one path) accessory first, where it then flows to two other accessories in parallel.

The total current flowing in the circuit is equal to the total voltage divided by the resistance total. To find the total resistance of Fig. 1-26, follow the same sequence as you would in finding the resistance in a parallel circuit first, plus the sequence required to find the resistance in a series circuit.

We therefore have

$$R = \frac{R_1 \times R_2}{R_1 + R_2}$$

$$R = \frac{6 \times 3}{6 + 3} = \frac{18}{9} = 2 \text{ ohms}$$

for the parallel part of the circuit.

The resistance for the series part of the circuit is shown as 2 ohms. Therefore, if we add these two resistances together, we have a total circuit resistance of 4 ohms.

From Ohm's Law we can now find the current flowing in this series/parallel circuit; current = volts/ohms is $I = E/R$ or $I = 12/4 = 3$ amps.

The circuit is arranged as follows. The voltage drop across the series resistor is voltage = amperes × ohms, or $E = I \times R$, which is E = 3 × 2 = 6 volts.

Source voltage remaining after passing through the series resistor or accessory is six volts, which will pass through both branches of the parallel part of the circuit.

The current flow through both of these branches is arrived at simply by Ohm's Law where, current = volts/ohms or $I = E/R$ to give $I = 6/6 = 1$ amp. Current flow in the second branch is also shown and is arrived at in the same fashion: $I = E/R$ or $I = 6/3 = 2$ amps.

Total current flow through the parallel branches is therefore the sum of both, which is 1 + 2 = 3 amps.

COMPARISON OF CIRCUITS

Having now looked at and studied the series, parallel, and series/parallel circuits, we can conclude from the examples and calculations that each system would offer a different resistance to current flow because of individual design. In summation, we can say that the resistance to current flow in similarly designed circuits of the three types discussed would be as follows:

1. Series circuits offer the highest resistance to flow.
2. Parallel circuits offer the lowest resistance to flow.
3. Series/parallel circuits offer medium resistance to flow.

CONDUCTOR PROPERTIES

Earlier in this chapter, we discussed the basic makeup of what is classified as a conductor of electricity. Because some degree of flexibility is required in the conductor (wire) used in both automotive and heavy-duty equipment applications, we mentioned that instead of using a solid strand of wire, we most often find a large number of very small strands of wire.

Small-strand wire is generally used because current flows on the surface of the conductor; therefore, more surface area is exposed than that of a one-piece solid wire with the net result that there is lower resistance with the stranded wire than with a solid one.

Based on the earlier discussion of how resistance is created, it makes sense to select a conductor that will offer a minimum amount of resistance to the flow of current in the electrical circuit. Selection of a wire with too high a resistance can dramatically affect the current flow to the accessories and can cause heat buildup within the wiring and lead to potential fire damage.

Because of its plentiful supply and relative low cost, copper is widely used for wiring in electrical systems.

The amount of resistance in any copper wire is caused by the following:

1. Wire length
2. Wire diameter
3. Wire temperature

Using a length of wire that is unusually long is not only a waste of wire and money, but also increases the circuit resistance to current flow. Doubling the length of a wire will double its resistance. Also, using a wire that is too small in diameter will similarly create added resistance to current flow. Again, if the cross-sectional area of a wire is doubled by using a wire twice as large, the resistance will be cut in half for the same length of wire. Therefore, select a wire of the smallest size that will not cause excessive voltage drop throughout the circuit.

Let's consider a typical example of a circuit with a given wire size. Figure 1-27 shows a simple electrical circuit with a parallel wire arrangement to two headlights.

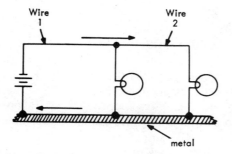

FIGURE 1-27 Establishing circuit resistance in a parallel light circuit.

The wires shown have a known resistance of .25 ohms each; each headlight has a known resistance of 2 ohms. What is the effective circuit resistance?

To calculate the circuit resistance, we substitute the formula given earlier in parallel circuits:

$$R = \frac{R_1 \times R_2}{R_1 + R_2}.$$

Therefore the effective resistance through the two headlights is:

$$R = \frac{2 \times 2}{2 + 2} = \frac{4}{4} = 1 \text{ ohm.}$$

The total resistance of this circuit, however, is the 1 ohm through the headlights plus the resistance of each piece or length of copper wire. Each wire has a resistance of .25 ohms, for a total circuit resistance of .25 + .25 + 1 ohm + 1.5 ohms. The current flow is $I = E/R$ or $I = 12/1.5$ = 8 amperes.

We mentioned that voltage drop is a factor in an electrical circuit because of resistance, and which, can cause problems. Let's calculate what the voltage drop would be in this circuit. Ohm's Law for voltage is, volts = current × resistance. Therefore, we have $E = I \times R$, or $E = 8 \times .25 = 2$ volts, or a total of 4 volts for both wires. This is a poorly designed circuit, because having started with a 12 volt source at the battery, we have only 8 volts left to operate our vehicle headlights. Since the sum of the voltage drops must equal the source voltage, we have 8 + 2 + 2 for a source voltage of 12.

Eight volts would provide a very dim headlight indeed. The answer to our problem is to select a wire having resistance values to allow adequate voltage across the load (accessory) for proper operation: in this case, a high enough voltage for proper illumination of the headlights. The size and resistance of wire can again be likened to the size or diameter of a water pipe shown in Fig. 1-1 and to water pressure.

Although you may not be thoroughly familiar with wire sizes yet, consider that the wires used from the vehicle battery to the starter motor and vehicle frame (ground or

earth) are much larger than the wiring used for the accessories. This explanation is easy to understand when we consider that the starter motor requires very high amounts of current or amperes to crank the engine for starting.

Remember that current or amperes in electricity is the equivalent of gallons or liters per minute in a water system. Therefore, the smaller the wire, the smaller the flow rate at the other end for a given pressure (voltage).

We would be unable to supply the high amperage requirements to the starter motor with small gauge wiring, and moreover we would burn out the smaller wire through overheating (electron bombardment and heat buildup).

TEMPERATURE EFFECT ON WIRE

An increase in temperature creates a similar increase in resistance. Consider a length of wire ten feet long having a total known resistance of 0.4 ohm at 70°F (21°C).

At a temperature of 170°F (76.6°C), the resistance increases from 0.04 ohm to 0.05 ohm per foot.

Wire Gauge Sizes

Copper wiring used in both automotive and heavy-duty equipment is classified by a wire gauge number which denotes its size, resistance, etc. This is shown below.

WIRING RECOMMENDATIONS

Copper wiring used in automobiles, trucks, and heavy-duty equipment is basically broken into two categories: wire used to carry current for lighting and accessories, and wire required to carry larger currents such as that required for starting motors from the battery.

The following tables show the recommended SAE (Society of Automotive Engineers) and AWG (American Wire Gauge) stranded wire specifications.

Recommended conductor construction (AWG strands)

SAE Wire Size	Class I No. Strands/ AWG Size (in.)	Class II No. Strands/AWG Size (in.)
6	37/21 (.0285)	7 × 19/27 (.0142)
4	61/22 (.0253)	7 × 19/25 (.0179)
2	127/33 (.0226)	7 × 19/23 (.0226)
1	127/22 (.0253)	7 × 37/25 (.0179)
0	127/21 (.0285)	7 × 37/24 (.0201)
2/0	127/20 (.0320)	7 × 37/23 (.0226)
3/0	—	7 × 37/22 (.0253)
4/0	—	19 × 22/23 (.0226)

Note that the lower the wire number, the larger its size.

Metric wire strand size

SAE Wire Size	Metric Size, mm²	Class I No. Strands/mm Size	Class II Size
6	13.0	37/.66	—
4	19.0	61/.63	—
2	32.0	127/.57	7 × 19/.57
1	40.0	127/.63	7 × 19/.63
0	50.0	127/.71	7 × 19/.71
2/0	62.0	127/.79	7 × 19/.79
3/0	81.0	—	7 × 37/.63
4/0	103.0	—	7 × 37/.71

Wire gauge sizes from 4/0 up to 6 are generally used on vehicles and equipment that require large current-carrying capacities, although Size 4 is generally the minimum size that would be used for battery cables.

The following tables show the accepted wire size recommendations required for vehicle lighting and accessories.

Recommended construction

SAE Wire Size	Class III No. Strands/ AWG Size (in.)	Class IV No. Strands/AWG Size (in.)
20	7/28 (.0126)	—
18	16/30 (.0100)	65/36 (.0050)
16	19/29 (.0113)	—
14	19/27 (.0142)	—
12	19/25 (.0179)	—
10	19/23 (.0226)	—
8	19/21 (.0285)	—
6	37/21 (.0285)	7 × 19/27 (.0142)
4	61/22 (.0253)	7 × 19/25 (.0179)

Metric sizes

SAE Wire Size	Metric Wire Size mm²	Class III No. Strands/mm Size
20	0.5	7/.31
18	0.8	19/.23
16	1.0	19/.28
14	2.0	19/.36
12	3.0	19/.45
10	5.0	19/.57
8	8.0	19/.71
6	13.0	37/.66
4	19.0	61/.63

Wire gauge Size 14 is widely used on automotive applications for lighting and accessories.

WIRE COLOR CODE

The recommended colors of wire cable should match as closely as possible the following colors as set forth by *The Color Association of the U.S. Inc.*, Ninth Edition.

Stripes can be used where additional color combinations are required. The stripes shall be applied longitudinally along the cable. Black or white stripes are recommended, but other colors may be specified.

TECA Colors, Ninth Edition

Color	Nom.	Dark	Light
White	70003	70004	
Red	70180	70082	70189
Pink	70098	70099	70097
Orange	70072	70041	70071
Yellow	70205	70068	70067
Lt. Green	70062	70063	70061
Dk. Green	70065	70066	70064
Lt. Blue	70143	70144	70142
Dk. Blue	70086	70087	70085
Purple	70135	70164	70134
Tan	70093	70094	70092
Brown	70107	70108	70106
Gray	70152	70153	70185
Black	None	—	—

In addition to the wire sizes and color codes, wires are further identified as to their specification types by the following abbreviations:

Type GPT	General Purpose, thermoplastic insulated
Type HDT	Heavy Duty, thermoplastic insulated
Type GPB	General Purpose, thermoplastic insulated, braided
Type HDB	Heavy Duty, thermoplastic insulated, braided
Type STS	Standard Duty, synthetic rubber insulated
Type HTS	Heavy Duty, synthetic rubber insulated
Type SXL	Standard Duty, cross-linked polyethylene insulated

ELECTRICITY AND MAGNETISM

In an automobile or piece of heavy-duty equipment, the battery or batteries can supply the reservoir of electrical energy required to operate all of the electrical loads (accessories), including supplying adequate power to the starter motor to crank the engine.

The battery alone, however, can only supply this source of energy as long as it retains a sufficient state of charge to overcome the circuit resistance. If some means is not used to recharge the battery as it is supplying this electrical load on the circuit, eventually the battery will lose this source of energy. We all know what then happens—the battery in our car goes flat!

Batteries today are constantly kept in a state of charge by the action of either a d.c. generator or, more commonly, an alternator which develops a.c. current. The letters d.c. mean direct current, and the letters a.c. mean alternating current.

Both the generator and alternator rely heavily on the principles of magnetism to produce the necessary electrical energy required to keep the battery or batteries in a constant full charge condition.

Because the theory of magnetism is so important to these two units, let's study how magnetism and electricity are related to the needs of the system.

MAGNETISM

For well over a thousand years, sailors have used the compass as a means of knowing their approximate location. The basic use of the compass was derived from the fact that fragments of iron ore called lodestone were found to attract other pieces of ferrous metals, such as other pieces of iron ore. Furthermore, if a long piece of iron ore or an iron bar were to be suspended in the air, one end would always point towards the earth's North Pole. Naturally, this end was therefore called the north pole while the opposite end was referred to as the south pole. In a compass, the needle will always swing into a north/south pole position, because the earth itself is basically a giant magnet.

An iron bar that exhibits magnetic properties is commonly called a bar magnet. You may recall from basic science tests that you conducted at school with bar and horseshoe-shaped magnets that they are both capable of attracting other metal objects to them without having to come into actual physical contact with these objects. A good demonstration of this fact may be given by sprinkling iron filings onto a table top, then placing the magnet in the vicinity of these metal filings. The result is that the metal filings are pulled against the magnet as by some unseen force. This attraction occurs because a magnetic field of force exists around all magnets.

A simple method of establishing what these unseen lines of force look like can be done with the use of a magnet placed underneath a sheet of paper, then sprinkling iron filings onto the paper. By lightly tapping the paper, the iron filings will arrange themselves into a clear pattern around the bar magnet as shown in Fig. 1-28.

The area around the bar magnet that attracts the iron filings is called the field of force or magnetic field. The strongest field of force is created next to the two poles of

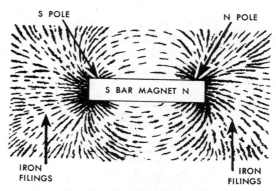

FIGURE 1-28 Magnetic attraction of iron filings. (*Courtesy of Delco Electronics Corp; Subsidiary of GM Hughes Electronics*)

the magnet, with the lines of force leaving the north pole and entering the south pole. When two bar magnets are placed opposite one another as shown in Fig. 1-29, unlike poles will attract one another, while like poles will tend to repel one another.

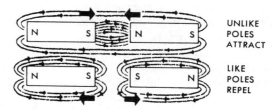

FIGURE 1-29 Like and unlike magnetic poles. (*Courtesy of Delco Electronics Corporation, Subsidiary of GM Hughes Electronics*)

MAGNETIC THEORY

Magnetism can be further simplified by the use of two commonly known theoretical models:

1. Any magnet consists of a very large number of minute magnetic particles, which will align themselves with one another to form the magnet. This concept is shown in Fig. 1-30(b). If, however, these particles have no particular arrangement, then the bar will be nonmagnetic, and the minute particles will be as shown in Fig. 1-30(a), not aligned.

2. The second theory of magnetism deals with the electron which we discussed in some depth earlier in this chapter. You may recall that the electron has a circle of force around it; therefore, anytime that the electron orbits align themselves in a bar of iron so that these circles of force are added together, the bar of iron will also become magnetized.

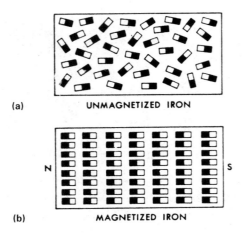

(a) **UNMAGNETIZED IRON**

(b) **MAGNETIZED IRON**

FIGURE 1-30 Unmagnetized and magnetized iron. (*Courtesy of Delco Electronics Corporation, Subsidiary of GM Hughes Electronics*)

CREATING A MAGNET

Not all iron bars are magnetic, and, of course, we would not want them to be. How can we create a magnetic bar from one which is not magnetic?

One simple method is to stroke the nonmagnetic iron bar with one which is magnetic to induce the necessary realignment of the particles within the nonmagnetic iron bar.

Another method is to place an iron bar into a strong magnetic field so that the lines of magnetic force within the field will pass through the iron bar and will induce the particles to realign themselves so that the bar will become magnetized. Figure 1-31 shows this process of magnetic induction.

In Fig. 1-31, the North and South Poles of the magnet can be readily identified by placing the large magnet in suspension on a piece of string and allowing the magnet to rotate of its own free will to the North and South Poles of the earth.

Although we can magnetize an iron bar by these two methods, the specific composition of the iron bar will de-

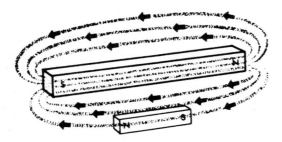

FIGURE 1-31 Magnetic induction. (*Courtesy of Delco Electronics Corp, Subsidiary of GM Hughes Electronics*)

termine just how much of the induced magnetism will remain after it is removed from the force field of the original magnet. If the iron bar retains this magnetic force with no loss over time, it would be known as a permanent magnet.

Uses of permanent magnets are very common, one example being in a generator. Other uses of such magnets are in starter motors, and in meters such as voltmeters and ammeters.

ELECTROMAGNETISM

Although magnetism has been used for well over a thousand years, it was not until the year 1820 that some relationship was found to exist between both magnetism and electricity.

A small experiment showed that when electricity flowed through a wire, and a compass was placed over the wire, the needle of the compass automatically swung around to place itself perpendicular or crosswise to the wire. From such an experiment, it was concluded that as the only force that could cause the compass needle to move would be magnetism, then the current flowing in the wire obviously created a magnetic field around the wire.

To obtain a more positive understanding of how these lines of magnetic force emanated from a current-carrying wire, a further simple test was conducted, in which the wire was placed through a hole in a piece of cardboard, as is shown in Fig. 1-32.

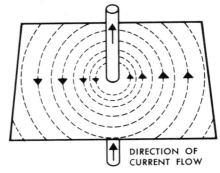

DIRECTION OF CURRENT FLOW

FIGURE 1-32 Field strength (magnetic) versus distance. (*Courtesy of Delco Electronics Corporation, Subsidiary of GM Hughes Electronics*)

With iron filings sprinkled onto the cardboard, current was then induced through the wire; the result was that the iron filings arranged themselves into concentric circles around the wire.

The concentric circles of iron filings were very heavy near the wire, but became less heavy the farther away from the wire they were. This allows us to conclude that the force of the magnetic field decreases as you move away from its center or core. Magnetism produced by passing a current through a wire is known as electromagnetism. This electromagnetic field will exist along the total length of the wire.

If we were to wind a length of wire into a coil, then pass a flow of current through the wire, we would create a magnetic field around the coil of wire with both a North and South Pole similar to a bar magnet. Figure 1-33 shows such an arrangement.

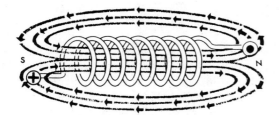

FIGURE 1-33 Current flow of magnetism in a coiled wire. (*Courtesy of Delco Electronics Corporation, Subsidiary of GM Hughes Corporation*)

The strength of the magnetic field around the coil would be dependent upon the number of turns in the coil, and upon the amount of current flowing in the wire. Therefore, the strength of the magnetic field depends on the ampere-turns of the coil. In order to establish the polarity of the coil ends, we can use what is known as the right-hand rule for coils. This is done by holding your hand as shown in Fig. 1-34, with the thumb extended in the normal direction of current flow, which will also be the North Pole of the coil. Should the current flow through the coil be reversed, then the polarity of the coil ends will also be reversed.

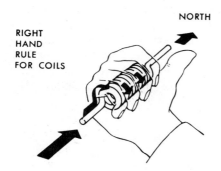

RIGHT HAND RULE FOR COILS

NORTH

DIRECTIONS OF CURRENT FLOW

FIGURE 1-34 Establishing polarity by the right-hand rule method. (*Courtesy of Delco Electronics Corporation, Subsidiary of GM Hughes Electronics*)

One additional method which is often used to increase the magnetic field of a coil of wire is to simply insert an iron core into the middle of the coil windings as shown in Fig. 1-35. The use of iron in a magnetic path can increase the magnetic strength by as much as 2500 times over a coil that simply has air in the center.

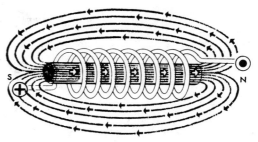

IRON CORE INCREASES FIELD STRENGTH

FIGURE 1-35 Iron core increases magnetic field strength. (*Courtesy of Delco Electronics Corporation, Subsidiary of GM Hughes Electronics*)

Because iron is a much better conductor of magnetic lines than is air, the addition of the iron core to the coil shown in Fig. 1-35 creates a considerable increase in the magnetic field when current flows through the wire.

In effect, the coil with the iron core has now been transformed into an electromagnet. Such an arrangement is typical of the system used in a generator to create the strong magnetic fields required to produce a steady output of electricity. (For general information, a coil without an iron core is usually referred to as a solenoid.)

The resistance that a magnetic circuit offers to lines of force, or flux, is commonly called reluctance. The effect of an air gap on the total reluctance of a circuit is very important. As we mentioned earlier, air has a poor conductibility compared to iron. Therefore, air will also have a higher reluctance than iron. Doubling the size of the air gap in a magnetic circuit will also double the reluctance of the circuit, and the field strength will be reduced by half.

One common application of the electromagnet is the use of the large steel circular weight used on the end of a crane for picking up scrap steel. When current is directed through the coils within the weight, the steel weight becomes magnetized and allows steel to be picked up. When the current through the coils is cut off, the reduced magnetic field allows the scrap steel to be deposited or dropped from the end of the weight.

CREATING ELECTRICITY FROM MAGNETISM

With a good understanding of magnetism, we can now look at how electricity can be produced in a wire through the use of magnetic lines of force. If we move a conductor, such as a piece of copper wire through a magnetic field, a voltage is induced in the wire. Such a condition is called electromagnetic induction, and is commonly defined as the induction of voltage in a conductor that moves across any magnetic field. (This induced voltage is also known as electromotive force, as was mentioned in the early part of our discussion on basic electricity.)

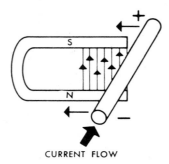

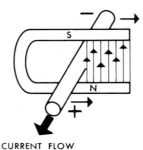

FIGURE 1-36 Inducing voltage flow in a wire. (*Courtesy of Delco Electronics Corporation, Subsidiary of GM Hughes Electronics*)

Figure 1-36 shows a simple horseshoe magnet with magnetic lines of force passing between the ends of the North and South Poles. If a length of copper wire were placed at the right-hand end of the horseshoe magnet and moved parallel to the magnet in order that the wire would be forced through the magnetic field, then a small voltage would be induced in the wire. This voltage could be measured by placing the ends of a voltmeter across the ends of the wire.

The wire must be moved so as to cut the magnetic lines of force. If the wire is moved up and down or parallel to the magnetic lines of force, we would not cut these lines of force, and no voltage would be induced in the wire.

From previous discussions, we indicated that the magnetic lines of force always originate from the North Pole to the South Pole of the magnet. For this reason, when the wire is moved from the right to the left in Fig. 1-36, the end of the wire closest to the North Pole will be the negative end, while the end of the wire closer to the South Pole will become the positive end. The positive and negative ends of the wire are reversed once we move the wire from the left-hand side of the magnet to the right-hand side.

Although we have shown the conductor (wire) as the moving object, there are instances whereby it may be easier to move the magnetic field rather than the wire, such as the spinning rotor design of an automotive alternator.

In summation, the factors that determine the magnitude or amount of induced voltage are:

- How strong the magnetic field is

- How quickly the magnetic lines of force are cutting across the conductor (wire)

- The total number of conductors (wires) that are cutting across these magnetic lines of force.

One other important point to consider is that when a straight wire is wound into a coil and moved across a magnetic field, all the loops of wire are in a series circuit arrangement, so that the induced voltage of all the loops will be added together to produce a higher voltage.

INDUCING VOLTAGE BY ELECTROMAGNETIC INDUCTION

Since the induction of voltage in a wire is necessary in any electrical circuit to produce current flow, how can we actually do this successfully? Three methods are commonly employed to induce voltage flow in a wire conductor.

One of the most widely used methods is that of using the magnetic field in a generator to produce current to keep the vehicle's battery in a permanent state of charge. This method is generated voltage. Figure 1-37 shows a simple line diagram of the basic components required to produce this voltage flow in the wire. This generator produces direct-current (d.c.) by moving a wire through a stationary magnetic field.

There is only one single loop of wire shown rotating through the magnetic field. In reality, a generator uses many loops of wire; however, the principle remains the same. These wires are wrapped around an iron core called an

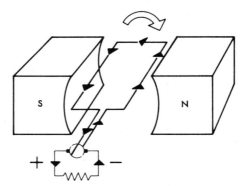

FIGURE 1-37 Basic generator principle. (*Courtesy of Delco Electronics Corporation, Subsidiary of GM Hughes Electronics*)

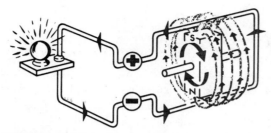

FIGURE 1-38 Basic alternator principle. (*Courtesy of Delco Electronics Corporation, Subsidiary of GM Hughes Electronics*)

armature, with the ends of the wires attached to individual segments of the armature. These segments are known as a commutator.

As the loop of wire in Fig. 1-37 rotates (driven by a belt drive from the engine to the armature pulley), the current flow in the wire loop is from the negative to the positive terminals. The voltage induced in the wire loop produces a coil voltage at the two commutator segments attached to the wire ends. Spring-loaded brushes which are in contact with the rotating commutator/armature pick up the current generated and feed this to the external circuit. The current flowing through the wire loop is established by applying the right-hand rule for induced voltage, as was shown in Fig. 1-34. This method establishes the direction of current flow.

A second method which is used to create generated voltage is that used in the alternator or alternating-current generator. The main difference between this unit and the d.c. generator just discussed is that, in the alternator, the magnetic field is rotated, while in the d.c. generator the magnetic field was stationary. The principle of voltage generation within a simplified alternator is shown in Fig. 1-38.

In Fig. 1-38, the magnetic field is rotated by a shaft connected to a pulley or gear drive on the engine. The wire or windings of wire are attached to the stationary alternator body or frame. Applying the right-hand rule, current will flow through the wire loop. We have demonstrated in Fig. 1-37 and Fig. 1-38 that voltage can be induced in a wire loop either by moving the wire through the stationary magnetic field, or by rotating the magnetic field past a stationary wire loop.

SELF-INDUCED VOLTAGE

Another way in which we can induce voltage in a conductor is by self-induction in which no separate magnetic field is used. Instead, by changing the current flowing through a wire which is wrapped around an iron core, the magnetic lines of force around the wire are caused to increase or

decrease. The changing current through the wire will induce a voltage in the wire; therefore, the voltage is self-induced.

A good example of self-induced voltage is the standard ignition system coil that produces the high voltage surge to fire the spark plugs. Basically, the coil consists of an iron core with two sets of wire coils wrapped tightly around the iron core. One set of these coils is of a larger heavy wire, while the other coil is made up from much smaller and finer wire. The large coil is known as the primary coil, while the smaller coil is known as the secondary coil.

An increase in current flow through one loop will cause an increase in the strength of the magnetic field around the wire of the coil. This magnetic field will cut across the neighboring loops of wire, thereby inducing a voltage in these loops.

Current flowing from the battery of the vehicle through the primary coil winding will set up a magnetic field which is absorbed by the secondary windings in the coil. When the distributor contacts open, the current will drop to zero, since the energy from the battery flowing through the primary winding of the coil can no longer return to the battery circuit.

Since the secondary winding of the coil has not only a smaller diameter of wire than the primary, but contains a much greater number of turns, the making and breaking of the contact breaker points transfers by mutual induction of the magnetic field within the coil an increase in voltage through the secondary winding. This voltage increase induced in the secondary winding of the coil will be proportional to the ratio of the number of turns between the primary and secondary coil windings.

For example, if the primary winding has ten turns, and the secondary winding has one hundred turns, then the voltage induced in the secondary windings will be one hundred times greater than that developed in the primary windings. The battery voltage of 12 volts flowing through the primary coil windings will create a magnetic field which induces a voltage of approximately 250 volts. This 250 volts of energy will be boosted to 25,000 volts in the secondary winding, forming the arc at the spark plug to fire the mixture in the cylinder.

MUTUAL INDUCTION

Another method of inducing voltage in a wire is mutual induction, whereby a voltage is induced in one coil due to the changing current in another coil. The changing magnetic flux created by the current flow in one coil links or cuts across the windings of the second coil, thereby inducing voltage in proportion to the number of turns in both coils. This mutual induction follows the same pattern as that of self-induction.

REVIEW QUESTIONS

The following questions are simple, but are designed to allow you to quickly ascertain to what degree you remember the material that was discussed.

1-1 Water flow through a pipe is measured in gallons per minute, or liters per minute. What is the electrical term for capacity or volume?

1-2 Electricity is made up of many small particles called _____?

1-3 The pressure or force that causes electrons to move is known as _____?

1-4 Electrical pressure or voltage is similar to water pressure in a pipe. This pressure or voltage causes what to flow through a wire?

1-5 The resistance in a wire is affected by its _____and its _____?

1-6 If two wires of equal length were placed in a circuit and one wire were smaller in diameter than the other, which wire would create the greater resistance to current flow?

1-7 Electrical resistance can be compared to the size of what item in a simple water system?

1-8 Write down the electrical term or measurement that expresses current, pressure and resistance?

1-9 The amount of electrons flowing past a fixed point in a given time period is actually a measurement of _____?

1-10 The load on any electrical circuit is established by the current draw of the _____?

1-11 Each accessory in an electrical circuit offers some resistance to current flow. How would you measure this resistance?

1-12 Current can only flow in a _____circuit?

1-13 Current will not flow in an _____circuit?

1-14 A pump in a water system produces the energy for the system to operate. What do we use in an electric circuit to provide the source of energy?

1-15 In order to have a complete electric circuit, we must allow current to flow from the battery through a wire, and allow it to return through another wire back to _____?

1-16 What are the names of the terminals on a battery?

1-17 Sketch the symbol commonly used to illustrate the terminal names in Question 1-16.

1-18 A break in the wiring of an electrical circuit creates an _____?

1-19 The word circuit is derived from the word _____?

1-20 State the two theories used to describe the direction of current flow in an electrical circuit.

1-21 What is a conductor?

1-22 What is a resistor?

1-23 What is the difference between a fixed and variable resistor?

1-24 Sketch the symbol used to show both a fixed and a variable resistor.

1-25 What is an insulator?

1-26 Which has the greatest resistance to current flow: a conductor, a resistor, or an insulator?

1-27 To increase the current flowing in a circuit, you must increase the _____?

1-28 To decrease the current flow in a circuit, we could decrease the voltage. What else could we do?

1-29 To increase current flowing in a circuit, you must decrease the _____?

1-30 Write the formula to show Ohm's Law.

1-31 Write the three combinations available from Ohm's Law, stating not only the transposed formula but also what each letter in the formula means.

1-32 What are the three types of circuits that we looked at in Chapter 1?

1-33 Briefly describe a series circuit.

1-34 Briefly describe a parallel circuit.

1-35 Briefly describe a series/parallel circuit.

1-36 Sketch a simple line diagram depicting a series circuit.

1-37 Sketch a simple line diagram depicting a parallel circuit.

1-38 Sketch a simple line diagram showing a series/parallel circuit.

1-39 To determine the value of the total resistance in a series circuit, (1) you add all resistances, (2) you multiply all resistances, (3) you subtract all resistances, or (4) you divide all resistances by the total number in the circuit?

1-40 What is voltage drop in an electrical circuit?

1-41 What is the total amount of voltage drop that can occur in a series circuit?

1-42 How would you establish the total resistance of a parallel circuit?

1-43 Is the total resistance in parallel circuit greater or less than that of any individual resistor?

1-44 With respect to magnets, like poles _____ and unlike poles _____?

1-45 Do the lines of magnetic force flow from the North Pole to the South Pole, or opposite?

1-46 What is the basic difference between a d.c. generator, and an alternating current (a.c.) generator?

1-47 What are the two basic methods of producing electron flow in a wire?

1-48 What is an electromagnet?

1-49 How would you determine the direction of the lines of force around a wire?

1-50 Why is an iron core used with a coil?

ANSWERS

A1-1 The term used is current.

A1-2 Electrons.

A1-3 Electromotive force or voltage.

A1-4 Current.

A1-5 Length and diameter.

A1-6 The smaller one.

A1-7 The size of the water pipe.

A1-8 Current is called amperes, pressure is called voltage, and resistance is called ohms.

A1-9 Current or ampere flow.

A1-10 Components or accessories.

A1-11 By the use of an ohmmeter.

A1-12 Closed circuit.

A1-13 Open circuit.

A1-14 The battery is the source of electrical energy.

A1-15 The source of supply, which is the battery.

A1-16 The positive terminal or post, and the negative terminal or post.

A1-17 Positive (+), and negative (−).

A1-18 Open circuit, therefore no current flow.

A1-19 Circle (circuit: to complete the path around the circle, or more commonly, the circuit).

A1-20 Theory 1 is the conventional theory in which the direction of current flow is assumed to be from the positive terminal of the voltage source, through the external circuit, and then back to the negative terminal of the source.

Theory 2 is the electron theory of current flow in which flow is from the negative terminal, through the external circuit, and then back to the positive terminal of the source.

A1-21 A conductor allows a flow of electricity with a minimum of resistance. Good conductors are those elements with less than four electrons in the outer ring of the atom.

A1-22 A resistor is an element containing four electrons in the outer ring of its atom; it is the resistance of a wire that slows down the current flow.

A1-23 A fixed resistor has a specific amount of resistance, therefore its value doesn't change; a variable resistor has a sliding contact that allows you to change the value of the resistance.

A1-24

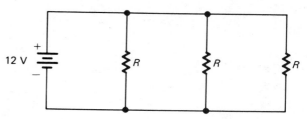

Fixed resistor

Variable resistor

A1-25 An insulator is any element that contains more than four electrons in the outer ring of its atom; insulators are used to prevent short circuits and loss of current through wires coming into contact with another conductor.

A1-26 An insulator.

A1-27 Voltage.

A1-28 Increase the resistance.

A1-29 Resistance.

A1-30 $I = E/R$, where I = amperes, E = voltage, R = resistance (ohms)

A1-31 (1) amperes = voltage/resistance, or $I = E/R$; (2) voltage = (amperes) × (ohms), or $E = I \times R$; (3) ohms = voltage/amperes or $R = E/I$.

A1-32 (1) The series circuit; (2) The parallel circuit; (3) The series/parallel circuit.

A1-33 A series circuit is one where the current leaves one battery terminal and returns to the other battery terminal by means of one direct path through the circuit.

A1-34 A parallel circuit provides more than one path for the current to flow; therefore, a break in one path or branch of a parallel circuit will not prevent current from flowing to and through other parts of the circuit. For this reason, each accessory or component in a parallel circuit can be turned on or off independently of the other accessories. This is the type of circuit most used in both automotive and heavy-duty equipment applications, as well as in house-wiring.

A1-35 A series/parallel circuit is a combination of both a series and a parallel circuit. Of the three types of circuits, the series/parallel circuit offers medium resistance, the series circuit offers higher resistance, and the parallel circuit offers the lowest resistance of all.

A1-36

A1-37

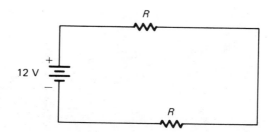

A1-38

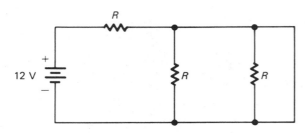

A1-39 You add all of the resistances.

A1-40 Voltage drop is the loss in voltage that occurs as the current flows through a resistor, accessory, or load.

A1-41 The total amount of voltage drop that can occur in a circuit is the same as the source voltage.

A1-42 To establish the total resistance in a parallel circuit, you would use the formula

$$R = \frac{R_1 \times R_2}{R_1 + R_2}$$

A1-43 The total resistance in a parallel circuit is less than that of any individual resistor.

A1-44 Like poles repel; unlike poles attract.

A1-45 Magnetic lines of force radiate from both ends of a bar magnet; however, in a horseshoe magnet arrangement, flow is from the north to south pole.

A1-46 In a d.c. generator, the conductors (wires of the armature) are rotated across a stationary magnetic field to produce both voltage and current; in the a.c. alternator/generator, the magnetic field is rotated and made to cut across stationary conductors (wires known as the stator) in order to produce voltage and current.

A1-47 By applying voltage to the wire, or by moving the wire through a magnetic field.

A1-48 An electromagnet is produced by passing a current through a wire would coil with an iron core.

A1-49 You can determine the direction of the lines of force around a wire by applying the right-hand rule; grasp the wire with the thumb extended in the direction of conventional current flow (positive to negative), and the fingers will then point in the direction in which the lines of force surround the conductor.

A1-50 An iron core is used with a coil to increase the field strength.

CHAPTER 2

◆

Introduction to Electronics

VARIOUS ELECTRONIC DEVICES APPLIED TO CARS AND TRUCKS

The word electronics is now used in all languages, and it immediately conjures up visions of hundreds of items that owe their success to this field: computers in automobiles, heavy-duty equipment, medical equipment, home entertainment devices, business and space research programs, hand-held computers, and numerous other devices that we come into contact with in our daily lives.

Vehicle and equipment electrical systems have improved tremendously as a direct result of the electronics explosion, with their use being particularly prominent in the application of gasoline and diesel fuel-injection systems, ignition systems, anti-skid braking systems, automatic airbag and seat belt tighteners, tone sequence control devices, car alarms, cruise control, overvoltage protection alternator controls, trip computers, transmission controls, power seat positioning systems, automatic in-car heater and climate control systems, driver guidance and data systems, car ride height controls, digital instrumentation systems, and on-board computerized logbooks for heavy-duty on-highway trucks. These are just a few of the more well-known applications that would not have been possible without the successful adaption of electronics to these systems.

The acceptability of electronic devices to passenger cars, however, has been a slow and steady transformation, especially when you consider that it was the mid-1950's before germanium-type power transistors started to replace the widely used vacuum tubes in car radios. Germanium has

several serious limitations that was to render its use obsolete in automotive applications. One of its limitations is that it has poor high temperature operating characteristics. In underhood environments, such as that found in passenger cars, the germanium transistor became essentially useless.

Moreover, germanium does not lend itself to what is known as the planer process, in which an insulating oxide is thermally (heat) grown onto the surface of a semiconductor. This oxide serves the dual purpose of becoming a dielectric insulator. A mask can then be selectively etched onto it to allow the subsequent doping of the underlying semiconductor material. Germanium does not form a thermal oxide with these properties. Silicon, on the other hand, does form an excellent thermal oxide, and so silicon transistors possess good high temperature operating characteristics.

The first successful application of integrated circuits (IC's) to automotive applications dates back to about 1959, but these were not the result of the mass-produced efforts that we know and accept today. Early efforts at employing silicon in passenger car electrical systems first saw the development of silicon rectifiers for alternators, which was followed by the use of power transistors in the early 1960's. The successful development of silicon, as the base material for producing automotive transistors and diodes, has led to an explosion of technological accessories for use in passenger cars and trucks.

Consider that in 1970, approximately $1.50 per vehicle went into electronic components, and that by the 1985 model year this amount had leaped to $350 per vehicle. Future projections suggest that by the early 1990's this cost will have climbed to somewhere around $1400 per vehicle. Typical electronic devices now being used extensively in current production passenger cars and trucks are illustrated in Figure 2-1.

Figure 2-2 illustrates where the various transistors, diodes, IC's (integrated circuits), capacitors, thryristers, and other electronic devices now in wide use on passenger cars are applied on a typical high performance mass-produced car. A description of each component shown can be found in the Glossary of Terms Section, located at the back of this book.

The use of the word *electronics* refers to the design and use of devices and components that are totally dependent upon the conduction of electricity, not through the conventional copper wire as in the typical wiring in a car or truck, but rather through a vacuum, a gas, or what has now become known as a *semiconductor*. These electronic devices consist of solid, nonmoving parts capable of transmitting an electrical signal without the use of bulky devices such as tubes, relays, or mechanical switches. In addition, these solid-state devices can be a fraction of the size and weight of devices used in the past, still perform the same job as well, and do it considerably faster. Also, electronic devices are much more compact, efficient, and reliable than their mechanical or semimechanical predecessors, and they have the capability as well to perform many more jobs within a single electrical/electronic system.

The term *solid-state* element was coined with the introduction of electrical systems that used devices such as transistors, diodes, conductors, and capacitors to form what is commonly called an integrated circuit, rather than the conventional copper-wire designed system.

Automotive integrated circuit use, although prevalent today, is not a recent development. As far back as the late 1950's, germanium transistor radios were being installed in passenger cars, while the mid 1970's saw the introduction of the on-board microprocessor or minicomputer, with the adoption of the early-stage gasoline fuel injection systems manufactured by Robert Bosch Corporation. Today, and on a worldwide basis, almost every manufacturer of gasoline engines in passenger cars employs a derivative fuel injection system produced by this corporation. In addition, the majority of domestic and foreign-built vehicles have microprocessor (computer-based) control systems that contain integrated circuits for their base of operation.

Integrated circuits or *IC*'s as they are commonly referred to can contain as little as two or three to as many as several thousand electrical circuits that incorporate diodes, transistors, capacitors, resistors, etc. These circuits are then assembled or built onto a silicon chip, an example of which

FIGURE 2-1 Typical electronic devices in use in passenger cars and trucks. (*Courtesy of NEC Corporation*)

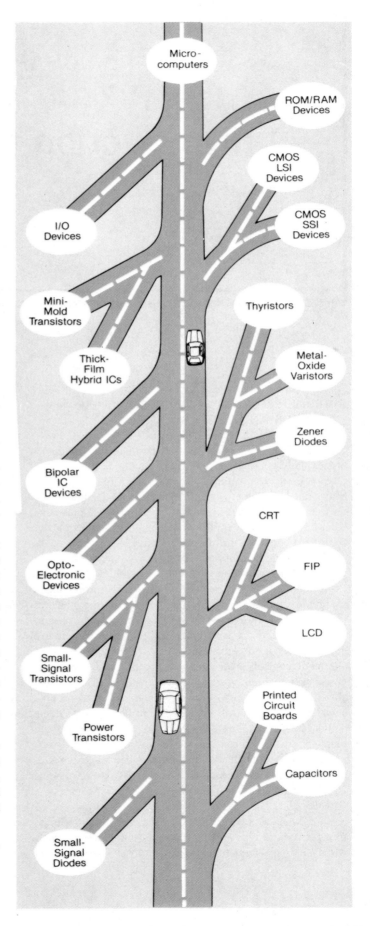

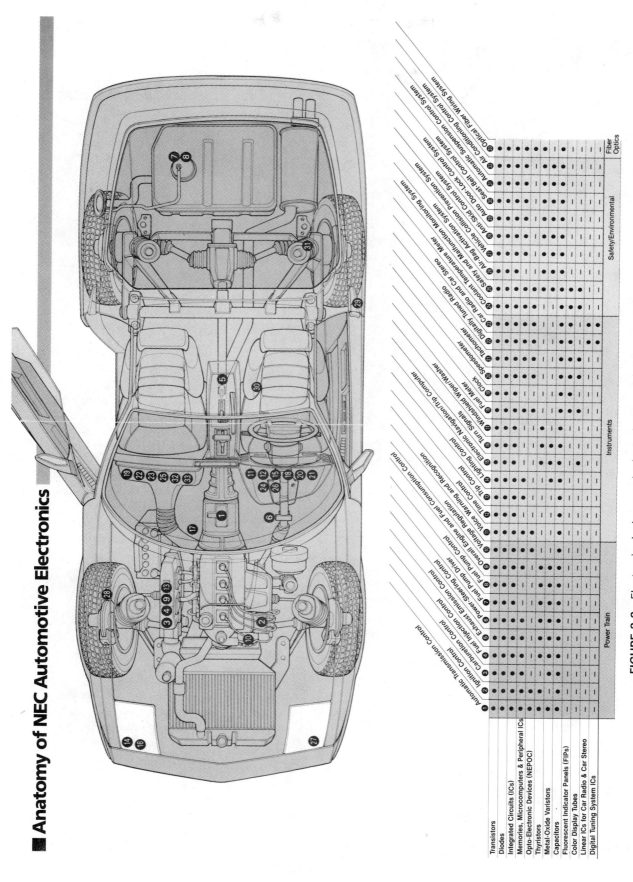

FIGURE 2-2 Electronic devices, and where they are used on a typical passenger car. *(Courtesy of NEC Corporation)*

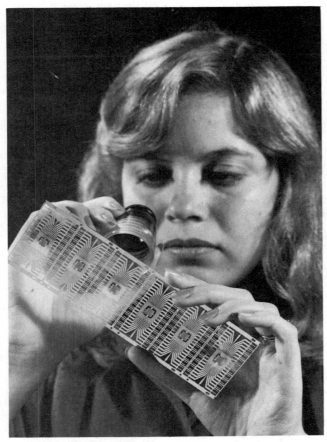

FIGURE 2-3 Inspecting a silicon chip less than a quarter inch square through a magnifying glass. The chip contains 10,000 elements and is used in GMC passenger car ECM's (Electronic Control Modules). (*Courtesy of Delco Electronics Corporation, Subsidiary of GM Hughes Electronics*)

Enclosures for integrated circuits
Left: Dual in line
Centre: Flat pack
Right: TO5 package

FIGURE 2-4 Examples of various IC's (Integrated Circuits). (*Courtesy of Robert Bosch Corporation*)

To highlight the physical size of a silicon chip, Figure 2-6 illustrates dramatically the term "as small as a pinhead." In this particular diagram, we see a magnified needle and thread being used to show the relative size of a Delco Electronics microprocessor chip in a General Motors electronic engine control system. The chip, which is 2/10″ × 2/10″ or 5 mm square, is the heart of the ECM (Electronic Control Module) that calls the signals for GM's CCC (Computer Command Control) exhaust emission control system. Delco Electronics engineers designed this chip to contain 10,000 elements, with the original layout covering an area of more than 10 feet (3 meters) square.

is shown in a magnified state in Fig. 2-3. Note in this diagram that the electrodes are generally connected through gold-wire-type connections. Each electrode serves a particular component of the chip. The silicon wafers shown being inspected in Fig. 2-3 contain a complete IC (integrated circuit), which consists of diodes, transistors, and various logic gates. A transistor built onto such a silicon wafer might have a thickness of half-a-millimeter (0.020″). All of the active parts of microelectronic devices are very near the surface of the wafer or chip, usually within the top 1 to 5 microns. A micron is a millionth of a meter, or as a decimal, by the numbers 0.00003937 inches.

Figure 2-4 illustrates a chip with its IC's assembled and encased in a ceramic coating, while Figure 2-5 shows this finished IC in its plastic or ceramic holder assembly. A chip can be as small as a pinhead, with current designs including chips of one centimeter square (0.3937 inches) and containing approximately 500,000 transistors. Future designs will provide up to one million transistors per chip.

FIGURE 2-5 Assembled IC unit in its enclosed casing. (*Courtesy of Delco Electronics Corporation, Subsidiary of GM Hughes Electronics*)

STEPS IN PRODUCING A MICROCHIP

Since the electronic circuits now in use in passenger cars, heavy-duty trucks, and other types of equipment could not exist without silicon chips, it is interesting and important that you have some basic knowledge of just how these chips

FIGURE 2-6 Microprocessor chip shown alongside a needle and thread for size comparison. (*Courtesy of Delco Electronics Corporation, Subsidiary of GM Hughes Electronics*)

are, in fact, manufactured. The microchip is so named because of its ability to shrink the basic building blocks of electronics, namely transistors, diodes, resistors and wiring, to microscopic proportions. In addition, microprocessors (small on-board vehicle computers) also require much less energy to perform the same functions that are carried out by nonsolid-state devices.

The foundation of producing an integrated circuit containing transistors, diodes, and resistors begins with a simple grain of sand which has been reduced and purified into the element silicon. Silicon crystals are grown molecularly inside special furnaces through the process of carefully controlled temperature. These silicon crystals are produced in the general shape of a large sausage, similar to one you might see hanging in a local delicatessen. The sausage of silicon crystal can be anywhere from 2 to 6 inches (50.8 to 152.4 mm) in diameter, and between 4 and 12 inches in length. It is then cut into thin round slices of nearly pure crystalline material, with the thickness of each slice generally being about 10 mils (0.01″) or 0.254 mm. Each slice is generally referred to as a wafer of silicon.

Each slice is then ground and polished so that one side is as smooth as a mirror, and then the individual circuits are formed on these chip slices through the use of laser technology, which imprints (cuts) a matrix of rows and columns to form literally thousands of circuits on a single slice, as is illustrated in Figure 2-7. All of the components of the IC are formed at the same time by using photolithography (photographic printing) and diffusion, which is the process of modifying one material by combining it with another through the use of technology.

Once the individual circuits have been formed on the slice, the individual chips are cut from the silicon slice with either a diamond scribe or laser. Each chip is then mounted to a metallized frame for support and, more importantly, to provide a means of connecting the chip with its circuitry to other IC's in a large interconnecting system. To appreciate the intricate manufacturing process involved in producing

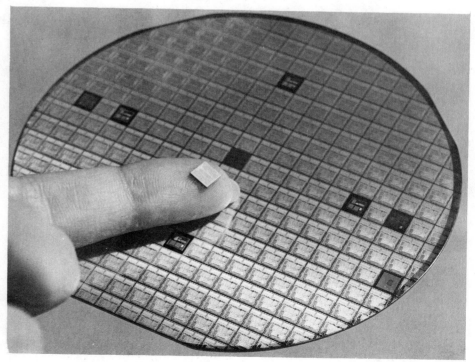

FIGURE 2-7 Microprocessor chip shown on a fingertip. (The chip was produced from a 3″ wafer of silicon. (*Courtesy of Delco Electronics Corporation, Subsidiary of GM Hughes Electronics*)

a silicon wafer chip, consider that only several years ago the connecting lines on most silicon chips averaged 4 to 6 microns in width. A micron is 1/1,000,000th of a meter or 0.00003937 of an inch.

A human hair is about 50 microns in diameter or approximately 0.002 inches. Current CMOS (complementary metal oxide semiconductor) chips are now in the 1.5 micron range (0.00006 inches). The smaller these junctions, the denser a chip can be and, therefore, the greater its operating efficiency. Current chips are made by either the MOS (metal oxide semiconductor) or CMOS process, although much research is under way to produce a chip from a gallium arsenide process, since this material is capable of operating at faster speeds than silicon chips.

The easiest way to picture this process is to list the steps required to actually produce the chip and integrate it into an electronic circuit. The following numerical listing systematically leads you through this manufacturing process.

1. The actual circuit that is desired on the chip must first of all be drawn by an engineer. Today, this is usually accomplished by creating a composite drawing of what is desired. This is done on a lighted- or transparent-type drafting table, which is also known as a flatbed digitizing device—35 mm slides are viewed on similar light tables.

2. A horizontal and vertical guide bar, which contains a cursor mechanism on the flatbed, can be slid up, down, and sideways by the individual who is electronically tracing the prepared circuit drawing. During what is known as the "digitizing" process, when the cursor is centered over an element in the drawing such as a transistor, diode, etc., a button is pressed that enters this information and transfers it to the computer storage system.

3. When the complete drawing has been electronically traced, the entire circuit can be called up on the face of a computer screen (CRT or cathode ray tube), where it can be modified if desired. This is done by use of an electronic light pen touched to the screen, or by typing in new commands to add, remove, or redirect the lines in the electronic circuit.

4. Prior to the actual manufacturing of the chip, the initial digitized circuit drawing is blownup (magnified) to as much as 500 or 600 times its original size on a backlighted transparent screen. Careful analysis is then made of the circuit to check for any possible problems or mistakes.

Another option that is used to check out the circuitry of a chip is shown in Figure 2-8, which illustrates a team of engineers working on a hugely magnified plot of a single computer chip. This large scale duplication of the very tiny chip makes the job of

FIGURE 2-8 More engineers fit onto microchip. IBM engineers in Tucson, Arizona work on hugely magnified plot of a single computer chip. Increased size makes job of designing chip easier.

designing much easier. This circuit reproduction or image can then be reduced or scaled down in size by a photographic process to the actual finished size of the desired chip. Once prepared, the circuit can then be duplicated several hundred times or more on the silicon wafer slice.

5. The chip is made from an ingot of silicon which is produced in a molten state, with the end result being a shape similar to a large sausage. Both the diameter and the length of this ingot can vary, depending upon the desired number of chips that are to be reproduced from a single slice.

6. Once the ingot has been produced, it is sliced into wafers, just as a delicatessen owner does, when you ask for a pound of a certain type of sausage in slice form. One side of the chip is ground and polished to a mirror-like image.

7. The wafers are then immersed in a photoresist bath of liquid-type honey or emulsion that will harden when exposed to ultraviolet light.

8. Chip manufacturing is carried out in extremely sterile rooms, even more sterile than operating rooms in hospitals, because the smallest particles of dust or dirt would cause a malfunction of the chip. Once this emulsion-type liquid has hardened, a stencil-type mask that represents the previously drawn circuit is laid over each wafer slice, and ultraviolet light is projected through this stencil. In this way, only the desired circuit receives this light and, because of the photoresist applied in Step 7, hardens to form the desired circuitry. Since each wafer can be anywhere from 3 to 6 inches in diameter, the chip design is repeated hundreds of times on the surface area of the wafer during this process, just as sheets of stamps are printed. Each chip must be identical.

9. The areas of the wafer that are not exposed to this ultraviolet light will not harden. Therefore, the chip must be washed/rinsed to remove this nonhardened photoresist material. Since each chip is constructed to represent more than one circuit in a layered fashion, it is necessary to repeat this stencil/mask process anywhere from 5 to 20 times.

10. The completed chip is then inspected under a microscope in an inspection room that has subdued lighting (often called a yellow room because of the type of lighting) to ensure that no outside ultraviolet rays can enter the room during this inspection time.

11. The individual chips are then cut from the wafer by a diamond-tipped die-cutting machine, although laser technology is now sometimes used for this procedure.

12. Robots then connect minute wires between the chip and its metal carrier to allow electrical current to pass into and out of the chip circuitry.

13. One or more chips can then be mounted to a circuit board to create the desired operating system.

14. Or the chip can be packaged as is for sale to the end user in a hermetically-sealed and damage-proof package.

Improvements in fabrication techniques and device design now allow hundreds of transistors to be included in areas of a square millimeter. Circuits with more than 100,000 transistors are now conventionally fabricated for use in numerous applications.

An integrated circuit is basically a silicon wafer or chip that has been doped, insulated, and etched many times so that an entire circuit can be contained within each tiny chip. The chips are then encased in insulated capsules for use in the electrical system of a vehicle or any other solid-state system. Figure 2-9 illustrates an IC for a passenger car hazard-warning and turn-signal flasher shown 400 times its actual size, with the numbers 1 through 10 simply indicating the number of terminals connected to this IC. In addition, Figure 2-10 depicts the schematic for this same IC.

The classification of IC's is generally based upon the number of its parts, elements, or logic gates included on the one chip. Its designation is classified as follows:

1. SSI (Small Scale Integration), containing about 100 elements.

2. MSI (Medium Scale Integration), containing between 100 to 1000 elements.

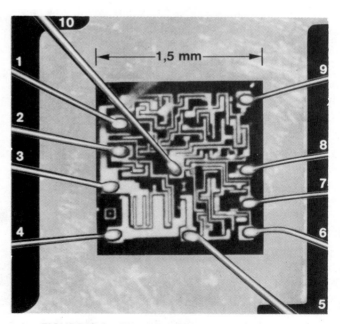

FIGURE 2-9 Magnification of an IC chip to 400 times actual size. (*Courtesy of Robert Bosch Corporation*)

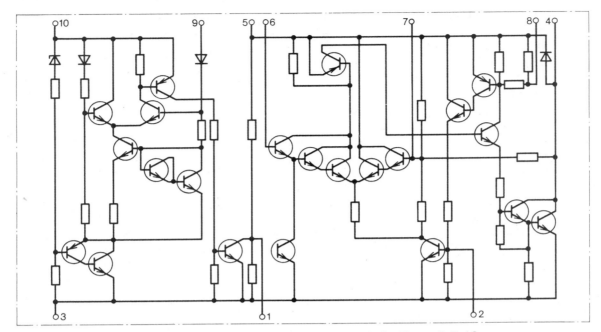

FIGURE 2-10 Schematic of the IC chip circuit for Figure 2-5. (*Courtesy of Robert Bosch Corporation*)

3. LSI (Large Scale Integration), containing between 10,000 to 100,00 elements.

4. VLSI or ELSI (Very Large Scale Integration or Extra Large), containing in excess of 100,000 elements.

Chips with 10,000 or more elements or logic gates, as they are known, translate into more than 32,000 bits of memory. Therefore any LSI, VLSI, or ELSI chip provides the power of a microcomputer on a single chip. Chips presently under test have shown that they take only 210 trillionths of a second to complete a calculation in a central processing unit (CPU). However, current chips operate at speeds of between 16 and 47 billionths of a second.

Integrated circuits are classified as being either of the "analog" or "digital" type. The analog-type IC is one that handles or processes a wave-like analog electrical signal, such as that produced by the human voice, and also similar to that shown on an ignition oscilloscope. An analog signal changes continuously and smoothly with time as shown in Figure 2-11. Its output signal is proportionate to its input signal.

Digital signals, on the other hand, show a wavelength that is more rectangular in shape, as shown in Figure 2-12. This is because these signals change intermittently with time, which means that, simply put, they are either ON or OFF. This, of course, is quite different from the analog operating mode. The general characteristic of operation of the digital circuit can best be explained by considering that when the input voltage signal rises to a predetermined level, the output signal is then triggered into action. For example,

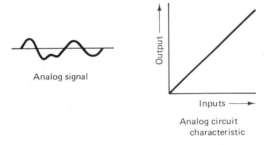

FIGURE 2-11 Analog wave signal shape.

assume that a sensor is feeding a varying 5 volt maximum reference signal to a source such as a diode. In this condition, the output signal remains at zero until the actual input signal has climbed to its maximum of 5 volts.

This is why digital signals are classified as being either ON or OFF. ON means that a signal is being sent, and OFF, that a signal is not being sent. For convenience sake,

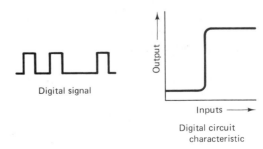

FIGURE 2-12 Digital wave signal shape.

FIGURE 2-13 Digital voltage signal in an ON and OFF mode; 5 volt reference or trigger value.

in electronics terminology, when a voltage signal is being sent (ON), the numeral 1 is used. When no voltage signal is being sent (OFF), it is indicated by the numeral 0. These numerals are used so that the computer can distinguish between an "ON" and "OFF" voltage signal.

Figures 2-13 and 2-14 show how this numerical system operates. Since most sensors in use today in automotive applications are designed to operate on a 5 volt reference signal, anything above this level is considered as being in an ON or numeral 1 condition, while any voltage below this value is considered as an OFF or 0 numeral, since the voltage signal is too low to trigger a diode response.

Digital systems consist of many numbers of identical "logic gates" and "flip-flops," both of which are discussed in Chapter 3 under the description of how a basic minicomputer operates.

There are few home appliances, entertainment devices, children's toys, cars, trucks and industrial machinery today, that do not use solid-state devices to perform one or more functions. When these solid-state devices are combined to operate in a system, they are generally referred to as *integrated circuits*, with each one doing a specific job in the overall successful performance of the designed unit, whether it be a microwave oven, a car or home stereo system, a wristwatch, an on-board vehicle computer, or a child's fancy toy.

Over the last five years, the greatest growth of the solid-state or integrated circuit (IC) in vehicles has been in the adoption of electronically-controlled gasoline fuel-injection and distributorless ignition systems for passenger cars. Few car manufacturers today, whether they be domestic or foreign, do not use some form of solid-state device (IC's) or minicomputer to achieve superior results from their automotive products. Heavy-duty on-highway trucks are now leaving the factory with minicomputers that perform a similar job for the diesel fuel-injection system, engine and road-speed governing, as they have done for their gasoline coun-

terparts. A perfect example of this is the DDEC (Detroit Diesel Electronic Controls) system on Detroit Diesel Allison Division (GMC) engines, as well as that employed by the same company on their Allison Automatic transmissions, namely the ATEC (Allison Transmission Electronic Controls) for both on- and off-highway equipment. Both Caterpillar with its PEEC (programmable electronic engine control), and Cummins diesel engines with its "Pace" system will soon join DDA with the release of a similar heavy-duty electronically-controlled fuel-injection system. Robert Bosch, Lucas C.A.V., Stanadyne Diesel Fuel Systems, and United Technologies are others who are committed to such technology.

Many later model passenger cars now on the market are leaving the factory with digital-type instrument clusters rather than the long-used and conventional analog type system which was used for decades. Many of the electronic circuits in a car interact with one another and provide feedback to engine control functions or to other systems based on signals received from other operating sensors.

BASIC ELECTRONIC CONTROL DEVICES

We will begin our discussion of basic electronic devices by considering the semiconductor. The fundamental operating principle of the semiconductor was first discovered in 1948, and from this basic discovery sprang the modern world of electronics. Semiconductors refer to devices that have no moving mechanical parts; however, electricity can flow through them. Although capable of conducting electricity, the semiconductor is a material that will not do so as readily as that of copper or iron—two materials that are used extensively in a conventional electrical system. The resistance of the semiconductor, although higher than that of copper (nonferrous metal) and iron (ferrous metal), is lower than that of such insulators as glass or rubber, which are poor conductors of electricity. Typical resistances of various components used in automobile electrical circuits are shown in Figure 2-15.

From our earlier discussion in Chapter 1 dealing with basic electricity, you will recall that a conductor allows electricity to flow through it with a minimum amount of resistance, while an insulator is designed to prevent the free flow of electrons (electricity) through it. A semiconductor has the following properties:

1. Its electrical resistance will change with an increase in temperature.
2. Its ability to conduct electricity will rise when it is mixed with certain other substances.
3. When struck by light, the semiconductor's resistance changes greatly, and it will give off or emit light when an electrical current is passed through it.

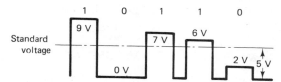

FIGURE 2-14 Example of digital wave signal when voltage values are either above or below the standard voltage reference.

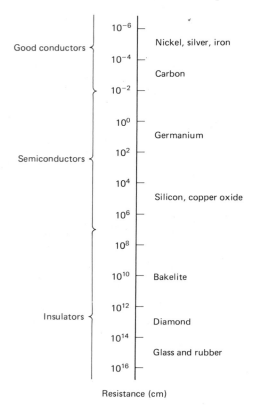

Good conductors {	10^{-6} — Nickel, silver, iron
	10^{-4} —
	Carbon
	10^{-2} —
	10^{0} —
	Germanium
Semiconductors {	10^{2} —
	10^{4} —
	Silicon, copper oxide
	10^{6} —
	10^{8} —
	10^{10} — Bakelite
	10^{12} —
Insulators {	Diamond
	10^{14} —
	Glass and rubber
	10^{16} —

Resistance (cm)

FIGURE 2-15 Typical resistances of various automotive electrical components.

You may remember from our discussion in Chapter 1 that all matter is composed of atoms. The atom is the smallest particle into which an element can be decomposed. Any element that has less than four electrons (negative charge of electricity) contained within its outer valence (ring) is a good conductor of electricity, while any element that contains more than four electrons in its outer ring is a poor conductor of electricity. In any element, the number of electrons in the valence ring is never greater than eight.

Two elements that have four valence ring electrons which are widely used in semiconductors are silicon and germanium. The electrons in the valence ring of one silicon atom join with the outer ring electrons of other silicon atoms when they are combined in crystalline form, so that the atoms will share electrons in the valence ring. With this combination, we have each atom effectively sharing eight electrons, which causes the material to be an excellent insulator since any element that contains more than four electrons in its outer ring is a poor conductor of electricity.

By adding a mixture of other materials to the silicon crystal, the end result is that the new material comes to possess different electrical properties. In fact, the material is no longer a good insulator, and is commonly said to have been doped. The elements that are used most widely to dope the silicon crystal are phosphorous and antimony, which both contain five electrons in their valence ring.

Combining the phosphorous element with silicon creates a condition known as covalent bonding. The one electron left over is commonly referred to as a free-electron, and it can be triggered into moving through the material quite easily.

NOTE: Any material that contains a free-electron or excess of electrons is referred to as a NEGATIVE type or N-type material doped with arsenic (As) or antimony (Sb).

In addition to the use of phosphorous and antimony to dope the silicon crystal, boron and indium can also be used, since these two additional elements contain only three electrons in their valence ring.

The addition of these various new materials to the silicon crystal in extremely small quantities can produce a wide variety of results in the finished product. Adding the material boron to the silicon will produce covalent bonding, which simply means that the final material will possess properties that neither one of the original materials possessed alone. This is similar to alloying metals to produce stainless steel, high carbon steel, etc.

The boron additive to the silicon results in a deficiency of one electron (negative charge) which creates a hole which can be considered to be a positive charge of electricity or a P-type of material, doped with gallium (Ga) or indium (In).

Doping material that is added to either the silicon or germanium semiconductor can be as little as one part doped material to ten million parts of silicon crystal. Another interesting feature is that the silicon or germanium crystal is refined to a state of purity that contains only a few parts of impure material to over one billion parts of pure crystal.

Electricity can be made to flow through semiconductors in the same basic way as electricity is made to flow through a copper wire. This action was described in Chapter 1 under the subheading, Electron Flow in a Copper Wire.

In summary, a semiconductor, such as germanium or silicon, falls between that of a good conductor or good insulator. The two most widely used materials from which semiconductors are manufactured are either germanium or silicon to which has been added such other materials as phosphorous, antimony, boron, and indium. When phosphorous is added, the doped material is commonly called an N-type substance; if doped with boron, it is called a P-type substance, with N denoting negative and P denoting positive. Both the N- and P-type substances have lower resistance than the associated pure substances.

CURRENT FLOW AND SEMICONDUCTORS

Applying battery voltage to an N or P semiconductor is commonly known as *biasing*. If the positive battery terminal is connected to the P-side (anode) of the semiconductor and the negative side to the N-type (cathode), this is known as *forward biasing*, with most diodes having a forward resistance of between 5 to 10 ohms.

If the positive battery terminal is connected to the N-side (cathode) of the semiconductor, and the negative side to the P-type (anode), this is known as *reverse biasing*. Diodes are excellent insulators when reverse biased, having a resistance of one million ohms or more. A more detailed description of this action is described in later sections of this chapter and is illustrated in Fig. 2-18 and 2-19.

Because of this feature of the semiconductor, too much forward or reverse voltage and current can completely destroy any diode. This is one of the reasons that diodes in an alternator can be severely damaged if a battery is hooked up backwards (reverse polarity), or if high voltage from a battery charger is applied to a battery without disconnecting it from the vehicle electrical system. Therefore, diodes operate as one way check valves in an electrical system by allowing flow in one direction, but not in the other.

NOTE: Although a solid-state diode is similar to a transistor in general makeup, the diode does not provide any gain (voltage greater than its input). Transistors, on the other hand, are active elements, since they can amplify or transform an input signal level.

DIODES

A diode is similar to a one-way resistor or current check valve in that it is a device that passes electric current in one direction, but blocks or restricts current flow in the other direction. The diode is used extensively in many fields of electronics; however, in automobiles, trucks, and heavy-duty equipment, it is used specifically to change alternating current to direct current. The classic example of the use of the diode is in the battery-charging alternator, in which six diodes (three positive and three negative) are used to handle the alternating current that is developed in the three-phase stator windings, so that current can only flow to the battery in the direction to charge it. Any reversal of battery current is blocked or prevented by the diodes.

The diode allows electrons to flow from its cathode to its anode terminal, such as is shown in Fig. 2-16.

Flow through a diode is always indicated by the arrowhead symbol. The diode is actually made up of two sections

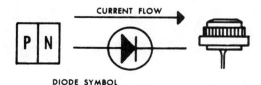

FIGURE 2-16 Typical semiconductor diode symbol.

of material, with one of the semiconductor materials formed into an N (negative) material, while the other part represents the P (positive) material. These two sections of material form a junction of P- and N-type substance that are structurally integral with one another, as shown in Fig. 2-16.

Diode Operation

If we consider the basic principle that unlike charges attract while like charges repel, then the structural components of the diode consisting of both N (negative) and P (positive) materials would be attracted to one another. Figure 2-17 shows what actually happens within the diode.

In Fig. 2-17, an attraction exists between the free electrons (negatively charged) and the holes (positively charged); however, as the electrons drift toward the junction area at the center of the diode, they leave behind charged particles called positive ions, which are atoms having a deficiency of electrons. Similarly the holes (positive) leave behind negative ions which exert an attractive force on the remaining holes to prevent them from crossing the junction, because the positive ions exert an attractive force on the remaining free electrons to prevent additional electrons from crossing the junction. The end result is that a stabilized condition with a deficiency of both electrons and holes occurs at the junction area.

The condition that would exist in the diode if a battery were connected to it is shown in Figs. 2-18 and 2-19.

In Fig. 2-18, the negative battery voltage tends to repel the electrons in the N material, while the positive battery voltage will repel the holes in the P material. This condition will therefore produce current flow from the negative to the positive battery terminal, and is known as a forward bias connection.

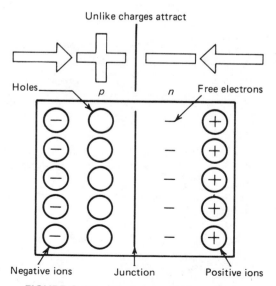

FIGURE 2-17 Electrons within a diode.

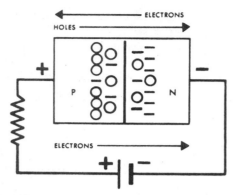

FIGURE 2-18 Diode condition when forward-biased.

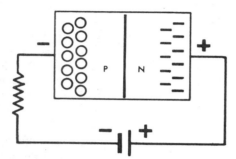

FIGURE 2-19 Diode condition when reverse-biased.

In Fig. 2-19, if the battery connections are reversed, the positive battery terminal will attract the electrons away from the junction area in the N-type material, while the negative battery terminal will attract the holes away from the junction area of the P material. This arrangement produces no current flow, since a very high resistance is created at the junction area. The diode is therefore blocking current

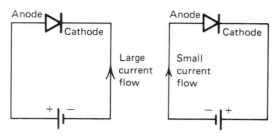

FIGURE 2-20 Battery connected to a diode junction.

flow, and this configuration is commonly called a reverse bias connection.

To clarify this arrangement, let's look at Fig. 2-20. When a battery is connected across the diode in forward polarity, a large amount of current will flow. Reversing the battery leads to the diode allows a very small or nearly zero amount of current flow.

If an ohmmeter is placed across a diode, the measured forward resistance value will be very much smaller than the reverse value. Should this not be the case, then the diode is defective. Silicon diodes have a higher forward resistance value than germanium diodes.

Diode Designs

Typical diodes which are used in automotive applications are shown in Fig. 2-21. Some diodes are designed for higher voltages and currents than are others. Therefore, when replacing a faulty diode, use the correct type. Excessive heat or mechanical stress can damage a diode.

An example of a diode's placement would be the ones pressed into the metal end-frame of the alternator housing

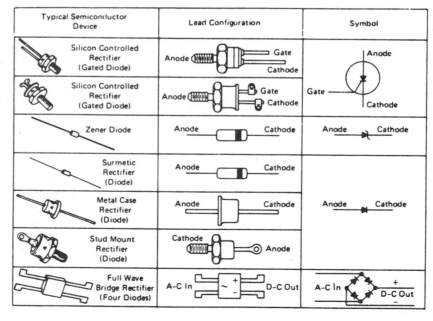

FIGURE 2-21 Typical semiconductor devices.

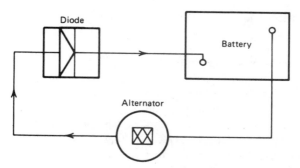

FIGURE 2-22 Diode placement to prevent a reversal of current flow.

in order to allow dissipation of heat from the diode. This area is called a heat-sink.

In any electrical conductor, moisture can create serious problems. Therefore, a dessicant material is used inside the diode housing to absorb any moisture. The glass seal aound the diode stem prevents the entry of any moisture.

Diodes can be damaged if reverse polarity connections are made to them.

A typical example of the placement of a diode in an oversimplified alternator charging system is shown in Fig. 2-22.

In Fig. 2-22, should the battery polarity be reversed, a small current can flow through the diode. However, this reverse current, if high enough, will break down the co-valent bond structure of the diode, and a sharp increase in the reverse current will occur, which will overheat the diode and burn it out. Normally, the diodes selected for operation in any given situation are capable of handling an adequate reverse voltage so that normally this condition will not occur during operation. Attempting to polarize an alternator or reversing the battery leads usually succeeds in burning out the diodes within the alternator.

ZENER DIODE

Another type of special diode that is widely used in electronic ignition systems as well as in many other areas of vehicle electric systems is the zener diode.

The main function of this type of diode is to provide protection for standard diodes in a circuit when reverse current and voltage exist. Although the zener diode can conduct current in a reverse direction, it will only do so when a predetermined reverse bias voltage is obtained. For example, the zener diode used in a particular electronic circuit may have a threshold as high as 100 volts in an electronic ignition system before it will actually allow this reverse bias voltage to conduct. When the contact breaker points open, the zener diode provides an escape route for the kickback energy that occurs so that the collector junction of the transistor used in the ignition system is not

damaged. At any voltage below a given value for the particular zener diode being used, no current can flow when the reverse bias voltage occurs.

Another common use for the zener diode is in the control of the electronic voltage regulator in most heavy-duty alternators. The zener diode activates transistors that shut off current to the field winding of the rotor to effectively reduce the alternator voltage output. As soon as the output voltage falls below the trigger value of the zener diode, it will no longer conduct the reverse current. This allows deactivation of alternator transistors, which will again let battery current flow through a brush to the slip ring and field-winding of the rotor, and as a result alternator ouput again rises. Figure 2-23 shows the symbol and action of a typical zener diode.

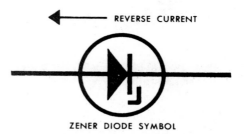

FIGURE 2-23 Zener diode symbol and operation.

Figure 2-23 illustrates that the diode will remain in the off position when the applied voltage is less than the conduction voltage of the diode, in this instance less than 10 volts. As the voltage increases to 10 volts, a very high resistance builds up until a critical voltage known as the zener, or operating, voltage is reached. When 10 volts is present in this particular example, the diode will conduct and act like a very low resistance or closed switch. At approximately 10.2 volts, the diode is in full conduction or turned on.

TRANSISTORS

The transistor is probably the most important semiconductor device in the electronic circuit, because current can be amplified and switched on and off through the transistor. The word transistor basically is a combination of two words, transfer and resist. It is used to control current flow in a circuit. It can be used to control a predetermined flow of current in the circuit and can also be used to resist this flow; in so doing, circuit current is controlled.

Transistors are used at junction points in the electrical system and therefore are often referred to as junction transistors. The transistor can be made from either germanium or silicon material with N and P substances sandwiched together, as shown in Fig. 2-24.

In the transistor symbol shown in Fig. 2-24, the *B* represents the base, which is normally identified by a thick or

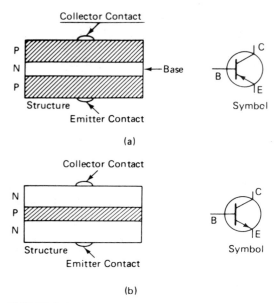

FIGURE 2-24 (a) PNP transistor structure; (b) NPN transistor structure.

heavy solid line; the *E* is the emitter, which is the line with the arrow; and the *C* is the collector, which is always shown as simply a straight line. The arrow (emitter) is shown as pointing in the direction of conventional current flow, which is accepted as being from positive (+) to negative (−) in the external circuitry.

Current flow in a PNP transistor is generally considered to be the movement of holes (positive charge), while in the NPN transistor, the current flow is considered to be a movement of electrons (negative charge). Based on this theory, the electrons move against the emitter arrow in the NPN transistor since it is easier to picture the flow of electrons as being sent out by the emitter into the transistor base and collector. This is explained below in the Transistor Operation section.

Figure 2-24 shows that two types of transistors are readily available for use in electronic systems, namely the PNP- or NPN-type. In automotive electronics, the PNP-type is more commonly used than the NPN-type. It is important that you remember this fact, because a PNP transistor cannot be replaced with an NPN transistor, for example, in an electronic ignition system.

As shown in Fig. 2-24, the transition regions between N-type and P-type substances are called the collector base junction, and the emitter base junction. When these two transistors are connected into a circuit, either an N-type or a P-type will operate as an amplifier or as an electronic switch.

Transistors used in automotive electrical systems are generally either classified as a signal-type or a power-type. The major difference is that the signal-type operates with an input voltage up to 10 millivolts, whereas the power

transistor functions with an input voltage greater than 10 millivolts.

Transistor Operation

As mentioned earlier in this chapter, the transistor can be operated as either an amplifier or as a switch. The actual construction of the transistor accounts for this unusual operating characteristic. By controlling the base current, a much greater collector current can also be controlled. The easiest way to follow what actually occurs within the transistor is to refer to Fig. 2-25.

In an NPN transistor, the emitter (*E*) conducts current flow to the collector (*C*) only when the base (*B*) and collector (*C*) are positive with respect to the emitter. The transistor, however, cannot conduct until the base voltage exceeds the emitter voltage by approximately 0.4 volt for germanium type transistors, and approximately 0.7 volts for silicon types.

In the PNP-type transistor shown in Fig. 2-25(b), the emmitter (*E*) current will flow to the collector (*C*) only when the base (*B*) and collector are negative with respect to the emitter.

For example, when the transistor is used in a voltage regulator, it functions as a switching device when the collector (*C*) current is allowed to flow. The transistor will then become saturated and its emitter-collector voltage drops to a very low value. In this condition, the transistor is operating similar to a closed switch (transistor is on) or in a low resistance state.

When collector current is cut off, the transistor appears as an open switch (transistor is off) due to the high resistance within it. See Fig. 2-25(b).

In Fig. 2-26, we have oversimplified a circuit with a transistor placed into it. With battery power connected to a PNP transistor, current will flow through the emitter-base of the transistor, because the switch connected to the transistor base is closed. Current will also flow through the collector circuit where it will meet or join with the current flow leaving the base circuit switch, where the current then returns to the battery to complete the path of flow or circuit path.

For simplicity, let's assume that the transistor in the example has an emitter-base current of 3 amperes. With both switches closed, you might assume, and rightly so, that the current flow through both switches would be the same. It is not!.

The reason for unequal current flow through both switches is due to the physical arrangement of the component parts of the transistor, which includes the emitter, the base-ring, and the collector. The emitter and the collector are closer together than the emitter and the base-ring. Because of this placement, the holes (positive charge) injected into the transistor base from the emitter will travel

+
C
B
LESS THAN
APPROX.
+0.7V
E
O
"OFF"
SW
OPEN
B = BASE
E = EMITTER
C = COLLECTOR
+
C
B
APPROX.
+0.7V
E
O
"ON"
SW
CLOSED
(a)
–
C
B
LESS THAN
APPROX – 0.7V
E
O
"OFF"
SW
OPEN
B = BASE
E = EMITTER
C = COLLECTOR
–
C
B
APPROX – 0.7V
E
O
"ON"
SW
CLOSED
(b)
UA-1250

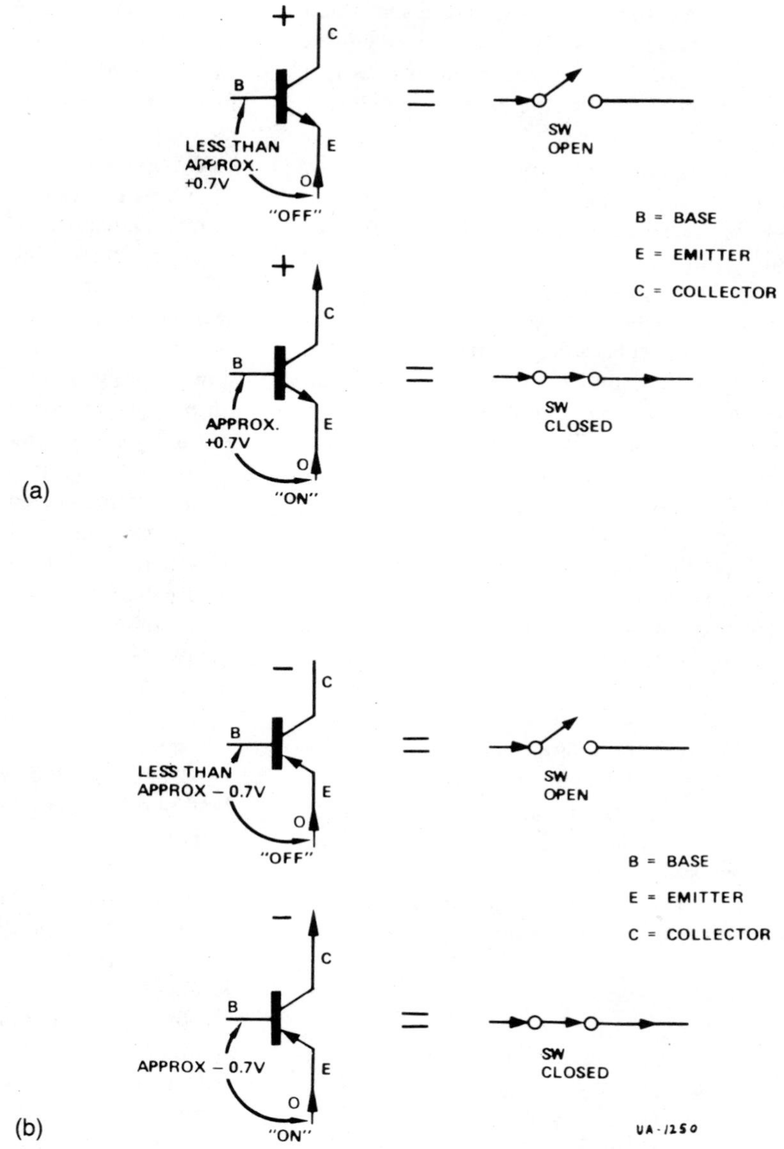

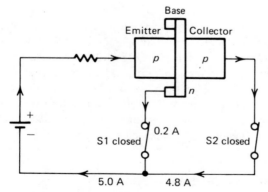

FIGURE 2-25 (a) NPN transistor action; (b) PNP transistor action.

Base
Emitter
Collector
p
p
n
+
–
0.2 A
S1 closed
S2 closed
5.0 A
4.8 A

FIGURE 2-26 Simplified transistor circuit flow. *(Courtesy of Delco Electronics Corporation, Subsidiary of GM Hughes Electronics)*

on into the collector because of their velocity (speed and direction).

This movement is further assisted by the negative potential at the right-hand side of the collector, which will attract the positive holes from the transistor base into the collector. The resultant action might produce a current flow of 2.8 amperes through the collector switch, with the remaining 0.2 amperes passing through the base switch. The exact values that will flow through any transistor will vary based upon the specific type and size of transistor used, as well as the circuit design. The collector current in this example would be 14 times that of the base current. This is one of the unusual operating characteristics of a transistor.

Another condition possible in this same circuit would be caused by opening the switch connected to the collector while leaving the switch to the base closed. The result would be that we would have a current of 3 amperes through this circuit only. One other phenomenon of the transistor would be to open the switch connected to the base, while closing the switch to the collector. Again, you would anticipate that the current flow through the closed switch should be that of the circuit, namely 3 amperes.

However, no appreciable current will flow under this condition because with the base circuit switch open, there are no holes (positive charged) being injected into the base from the emitter. Subsequently, the negative battery potential cannot attract nonexistent holes in the base into the collector. In addition, the junction at the base-collector undergoes a very high resistance condition due to the negative battery potential at the collector attracting the holes (positive charged) in the collector away from the base-collector junction, further preventing current flow.

The operation of an NPN transistor is the same as that for a PNP; however, the current flow consists of electron (negative charge) movement from the emitter to the base and collector. The examples given in Fig. 2-26 showed that the transistor can be operated in the amplifier condition, such as when both switches were closed. We were able to increase the bias current flow in the base-emitter circuit by stepping it up in the collector emitter circuit. Our example showed a base current of 0.2 amperes stepped up to 2.8 amperes in the collector circuit for a current gain or amplification of 14 times. When the collector switch was closed, and the base switch was opened, no flow was apparent in the circuit. The transistor acted as a switch to prevent a flow of current through the circuit.

Application of the Transistor

Let's see if we can put into practice the examples just discussed in Fig. 2-26 by applying the same transistor principle to a voltage regulator used with a generator or alternator arrangement as shown in Fig. 2-27.

The purpose of any voltage regulator is exactly what

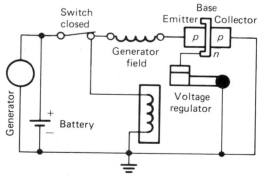

FIGURE 2-27 Basic transistor regulator action. (*Courtesy of Delco Electronics Corporation, Subsidiary of GM Hughes Electronics*)

the name implies—to regulate the maximum voltage output of the charging system. It accomplishes this by automatically opening and closing the current flow to the generator field windings so that the output decreases or stops until the battery or accessories require additional charging or electrical energy.

When the generator voltage reaches a preset level (adjustable), magnetism developed in the core of the voltage regulator shunt winding will pull the regulator points directly above it apart against light spring pressure. When the contact points separate (see Fig. 2-26), there will be no current at the transistor base. Therefore, no collector current can flow either. This action causes the transistor to cut off or stop any current flow to the generator field windings and automatically reduces the generator ouput.

Immediately after this occurs, the magnetic field of the shunt winding decreases, and spring pressure pulls the contact points together again. This action is similar to closing a switch, and field current will again flow to the generator field windings, allowing the generator to again produce its maximum value. This action of the points opening and closing can occcur ten times a second or several thousand times a second depending on actual conditions. With this type of transistorized regulator, minimal current exists at the contact points, which ensures much longer point life.

There are other voltage regulators that do not use vibrating contact points at all to control the generator output. This second type of regulator is similar in action to the one shown in Fig. 2-26. If the switch to the base circuit is opened, although we keep the switch to the collector closed, no current flows in the circuit because of the design of the transistor. Figure 2-28 shows this type of voltage regulator arrangement.

In Fig. 2-28, other diodes can be used to alternately impress both a forward or reverse bias across the emitter-base of the transistor shown (a PNP-type). Anytime that a forward-bias is present, the transistor will conduct current through the collector to the generator field windings to allow generation of voltage and current flow to the accessories and battery circuit.

When a reverse bias is impressed across the emitter base of the transistor (similar to opening the switch at the base circuit as was explained in Fig. 2-26), no current flows in the collector to the generator field winding. Therefore, the output of the generator drops off. When a minimum value is reached, the transistor is triggered to a forward-bias condition again, which allows the restoration of field current, and the generator produces current once more.

TRANSISTOR AMPLIFIERS

Electrical and electronic automotive solid-state systems, which now make extensive use of silicon diodes and transistors, require some means of multiplying or amplifying

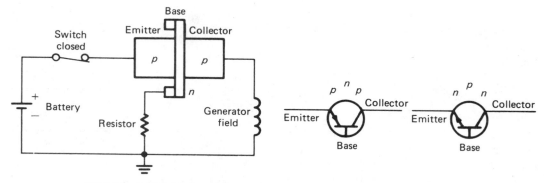

FIGURE 2-28 Noncontact point transistorized regulator arrangement. (*Courtesy of Delco Electronics Corporation, Subsidiary of GM Hughes Electronics*)

the low-current values produced in these devices. The widely-used silicon bipolar transistor is a semiconductor device with amplification caused by current gain. The maximum available gain (MAG) is theoretically the highest transducer power gain that the transistor can deliver at a given frequency.

Simple frequency can be considered as the number of complete cycles per second of an alternating current, such as the 60 cycles per second used in all electrical devices in homes in North America. In other countries of the world, the frequency for home electrical devices is often only 50 cycles (design factor only).

In a transistor, for example, it is the natural frequency of free oscillations of the sensing element of a fully-assembled transducer. The resonant frequency of the element is the measured frequency as a transducer responds with maximum output amplitude. The advantages that silicon bipolar transistors have over other transistor types are mature technology, low cost, and proven reliability.

In solid-state electronic circuits and because of the low current flow design of the diodes and transistors used in a circuit, it is often necessary to increase the output current signal in order to activate the end-accessory (load). This accessory can be any component requiring current to cause it to output its desired characteristic. One such example is an idle air-control valve that is incremented while the engine runs at idle speed so that a predetermined air/fuel ratio figure can be maintained.

The transistor or operational amplifier is designed to increase the power level of the input signal to a predetermined output that will successfully handle the necessary load on the circuit. An operational amplifier is a standard analog circuit that can have a vey high voltage gain of 10,000 or more. An example of how operational amplifiers are adapted to automotive solid-state circuits can be seen in Fig. 2-29.

In Figure 2-29(a), the operational amplifier is arranged so that it has two inputs and one output. Any signal applied to the inverting input (−) is therefore amplified and sub-

sequently inverted at the output. Any signal that is applied to the noninverting input (+) is amplified, but it is *not* inverted at the output.

The percentage of actual gain from any operational transistorized amplifier can be adjusted/controlled by the actual ratio of the two resistors. The amplifier is not normally

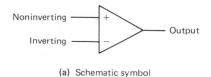

(a) Schematic symbol

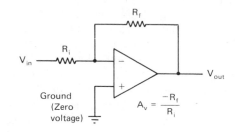

(b) Inverting amplifier

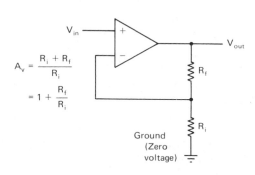

(c) Noninverting amplifier

FIGURE 2-29 Typical arrangement of automotive operational amplifiers.

operated at maximum gain, but is tailored for a specific systems circuit. This action can best be described by referring to Figure 2-29(b), where the percentage of gain can be calculated by the formula

$$Av = \frac{-Rf}{Ri} = \frac{V_{out}}{V_{in}}.$$

By applying the input signal to the $(-)$ terminal of the inverting amplifier, the minus sign in the formula indicates that the signal is inverted from the input to the output. In other words, if the input is positive, then the output will be negative. Since an operational amplifier increases (gains) the voltage difference between its two inputs, it is possible to select the op amp's capability as either a differential amplifier, or as a single-value output.

A third option open to us from an op amp is the capability of using it as a noninverting amplifier, such as that illustrated in Figure 2-29(c). In this option, the input signal is connected to the noninverting $(+)$ terminal, while the output is fed back through a "series" connection of resistors to the inverting $(-)$ terminal. This action results in gain Av through the op amp as shown by the formula

$$Av = \frac{V_{out}}{V_{in}} = 1 + \frac{Rf}{Ri}$$

In addition to adjusting output gain, this negative feedback signal can also assist in correcting the amplifier's tendency for nonlinear operation as well as the distortion of the signal. This distortion occurs as a result of the increased noise from a stronger signal which is added to the desired signal, as well as from the distortion of the input signal. The end result is that the amplified output waveform will appear slightly different than the input waveform. Depending upon the desired rate of signal amplification, the frequency of the input signal, and various other conditions such as heat effects, the output characteristics of the amplifier will change.

LIGHT-EMITTING DIODE (LED)

The light-emitting diode, or LED for short, is used extensively in vehicle electric systems for a variety of functions. The LED has a P-N junction diode that radiates both light and heat rays when it is subjected to an electric current in the forward direction. The typical symbol used for a LED is shown in Fig. 2-30(b).

LED's have three distinct advantages when used as a light bulb. These are:

1. Low power consumption.
2. Operate at lower voltages (about 3 volts) than a standard light bulb.

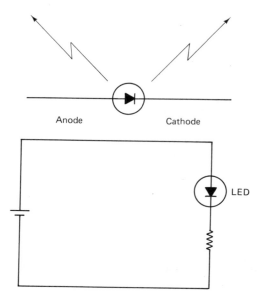

FIGURE 2-30 (a) LED (light emitting diode) graphical symbol; (b) typical placement of a LED in a basic electronic circuit.

3. Because of the operating characteristics listed in (1) and (2), LED's operate at a cooler temperature than an ordinary light bulb and therefore exhibit longer overall bulb life.

Illustrated in Fig. 2-30(a) is the graphical symbol used to represent a LED (light-emitting diode). LED's are available in a variety of colors, with the three common colors being high-efficiency red, yellow, and high-performance green. The red and yellow LED's use gallium arsenide phosphide on gallium phosphide light-emitting diodes, while the green devices use a gallium phosphide light-emitting diode.

These rugged solid-state lamps are designed for applications requiring a bright, compact source of light with uniform light output, wide viewing angle, and with a flat top which makes the lamp ideal for flush mounting on a front panel. Figure 2-30(b) illustrates in simplified form how a simple LED would appear in a circuit, while Figure 2-31 shows the basic makeup of a LED.

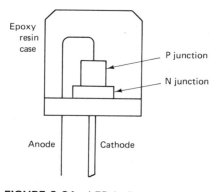

FIGURE 2-31 LED bulb arrangement.

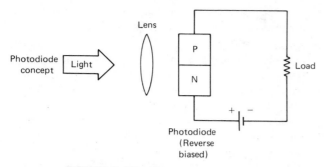

FIGURE 2-32 Photodiode concept.

PHOTODIODE

A typical junction-type photodiode is shown in Fig. 2-32. A photodiode functions as a switch when it is actuated by a light beam. If a predetermined reverse-bias voltage is applied to it, and a light is shone on the diode, then reverse current will indeed flow, with the amperage of the current being inversely proportional to the amount of light directed onto the diode.

The photodiode will not conduct electric current, however, in the reverse direction while the diode is in the dark. When exposed to light, the diode no longer blocks current flow. Therefore, the light triggers the diode and it operates as a switch. These types of diodes can be used as basic elements in breakerless (solid-state) ignition systems or to control the operation of an automatic air conditioner in direct response to the amount and intensity of the daylight.

PHOTOCONDUCTIVE CELL

Somewhat similar to the photodiode, the photoconductive cell, when exposed to light, will exhibit a resistance change. An example of such a device is illustrated in Fig. 2-33,

which consists of a cadmium sulfide (CdS) photocell designed to act as a variable resistor based upon the degree of light that it is exposed to. Because of such a feature, this device is commonly used to turn the vehicle headlights automatically on and off in response to the changing light patterns during the day or evening. By allowing light to strike the CdS element, voltage applied to its electrodes will cause the amperage requirement to change in response to the resistance that is controlled by the degree of light.

PHOTOTRANSISTOR

The phototransistor operates in proportion to the degree of light to which it is exposed, with this light being converted into an electrical current. This device is commonly used to monitor either vehicle or engine speed in conjunction with a LED (light emitting diode), as is shown in Fig. 2-34. When it is employed in this fashion, it is often referred to as a photocoupler, such as that shown in Fig. 2-33.

In Fig. 2-34, which illustrates the arrangement for an optical crank-shaft position sensor, the sensor is capable of sensing static position, and it can have constant output with speed. A disadvantage of these types of optical sensors in automotive applications is that, when used in an external environment such as an engine compartment, they are difficult to protect from dirt and possible engine oil accumulations. To operate they require a light source, a photodetector and a preamplifier integral to the sensor.

In Fig. 2-34, a fiber-optic light tube/pipe is used to reflect the light source to the phototransistor, thereby allowing remote mounting capability. Rotation of the crankshaft continually makes and breaks the beam of light passing between the LED and the phototransistor. The net effect is that the transistor will be alternately turned on and off by this action, with the speed of engine rotation controlling

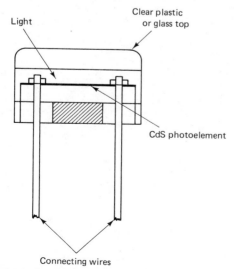

FIGURE 2-33 Photoconductive cell arrangement.

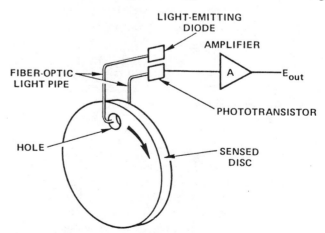

FIGURE 2-34 Arrangement of an optical crankshaft position Sensor. (*Courtesy of Society of Automotive Engineers Inc; Copyright 1987*)

this switching affect. Another location for the use of the optical sensor is in some ignition distributor assemblies, where it senses a number of slots that have been chemically etched onto a thin stainless steel plate. This arrangement allows a pulse signal to be generated for a given number of crankshaft degrees of rotation.

USING AN OHMMETER

Ohmmeters are used in electrical circuits to check resistance values between two points and also to check for continuity between two points. For example, by placing one end of the ohmmeter on a wire with the other lead on the opposite end of the wire, we can measure the resistance of the wire.

If, however, a break exists in the wire, then no reading signifying a problem will be registered on the ohmmeter faceplate.

CAUTION: An ohmmeter should only be used to test circuit continuity (no breaks in the wiring) and resistance with no power applied to the circuit from the battery. Therefore, disconnect the battery, or if the wire or component has been removed from the circuit, then the ohmmeter can be used. Failure to disconnect the circuit from the battery can result in damage to the ohmmeter unit.

The selector switch used on the ohmmeter can normally be placed at position R1, R10, R100, R1000, and R10,000, which controls the top range of resistance that can be measured accurately on the ohmmeter. For example, if the ohmmeter reads 8 on the scale with the selector at position R1, then 8 ohms is the resistance; similarly, if the scale selector switch were at position R10, then 80 ohms would be the measured resistance; at R100 it would be 800 ohms and so on, depending on the selector switch position.

Prior to using the ohmmeter, zero in the scale by plugging in both the red and black contact probes to the meter; touch them together with the range selector switch at the desired position for the test, and with the two contact probes held together at their contact ends, turn the adjustment knob on the meter until the scale needle indicates zero.

When using an ohmmeter, the following conditions may exist:

1. *Infinity*: With the test probes placed across a circuit, should the needle on the scale swing across and hit the stop peg, then you should switch to the next highest scale; however, if you are already on the highest scale, then the reading that you have obtained obviously has a much higher resistance than you can measure. Therefore, it is described as infinity, and the sign for infinity resembles a figure 8 lying on its side (∞).

2. *Open*: When checking a wire with an ohmmeter, a deflection of the meter needle is an indication that the

wire is good. Failure of the needle to register is an indication that the wire is defective or open.

3. *Grounded*: When using an ohmmeter on an insulated circuit, no reading should exist between the insulated terminal and ground. Otherwise, it indicates that there is a short circuit somewhere connecting both the insulated terminal and grounded connection to the same common location, such as the vehicle frame or body. Therefore, a short circuit is generally indicated by a low or zero ohms reading.

Diode Resistances

Obviously the resistance through various diodes and transistors varies depending on its particular location/circuit. However, a general consideration in a typical situation would indicate a forward resistance through a diode of 3,000 ohms and a reverse resistance value of possibly 4 million ohms. This is known as the front-to-back ratio; in this instance it is somewhat greater than 1,000 : 1. If a diode measures open-circuited (infinite ohms), then it is defective, while a zero ohms reading indicates that it is shortcircuited. Acceptable industry standards or a rule-of-thumb figure for an operational diode is a front-to-back ratio of at least 100 : 1.

TESTING DIODES AND TRANSISTORS

If it is necessary to check the operation of either a diode or a transistor, select an ohmmeter having a 1.5 volt cell across the diode or transistor. Refer to Fig. 2-35. To check the diode, select the lowest scale on the selector switch of the ohmmeter to start with. If the reading is too low, switch the selector to the next higher scale.

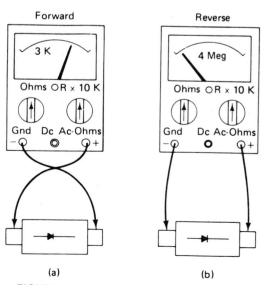

FIGURE 2-35 Checking diode condition.

When checking the diode, both the forward and the reverse resistance values must be checked. If a reading of zero is obtained with the ohmmeter leads placed both ways across the diode, then the diode is shorted out and should be replaced. If both readings are high, then the diode is open and should also be replaced. When checking a diode, it is important that the measured forward-resistance value is much smaller than the reverse-resistance value. If not, the diode is defective. A good diode will give one very low and one very high reading.

To check out the condition of a diode when no ohmmeter is readily available, select a 12 volt d.c. test light. When the leads of the light are connected across the diode both ways, failure to light in both checks indicates that the diode is open. If the light glows in both checks, the diode is shorted. Figure 2-36 shows the check required on the transistor to indicate its condition.

Several steps in using the ohmmeter to check the condition of the transistor are listed below:

1. With the ohmmeter connected as shown, note the reading. Then reverse the leads, the transistor is shorted if both readings register zero.

2. Connect the ohmmeter as shown, and if the reading is zero in both directions when the leads are reversed, the transistor is shorted. If both readings are high, the transistor is open.

3. For Step 3, basically follow the same procedure as for Step 2.

When checking the same diodes or transistors, different ohmmeters can show different readings because of battery condition or internal ohmmeter conditions, such as resistance, etc. Therefore, always use the same ohmmeter when checking the condition of diodes and transistors.

CAUTION: Many shops and service personnel today use a digital type of ohmmeter to check diodes and transistors. This can present a problem because some of these digital ohmmeters have an output current limitation of 0.001 amperes, while others may only have an output current of as little as 0.000001 microamperes. This low current is in-

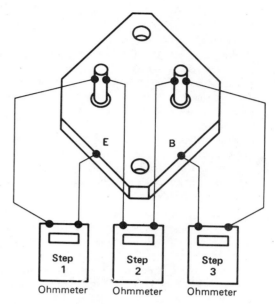

FIGURE 2-36 Transistor check. (*Courtesy of Delco-Remy, Div. of GMC*)

adequate to turn a PN junction on, even though it is forward-biased. The problem is that, when the ohmmeter is connected to a forward-bias condition, a very high resistance will be registered. This may lead you to believe that the diode or transistor is defective, when in fact it may be perfectly OK. Therefore, these types of digital ohmmeters should not be used for this purpose.

NOTE: Certain models and makes of digital ohmmeters may be used for checking both diodes and transistors, however. Such ohmmeters are designed to produce sufficient current flow and will therefore provide an accurate test of the diode's or transistor's condition. Always check the particular ohmmeter to be used to be sure that it does use at least one or two 1.5 volt cells.

NOTE: Chapter 14 (Special Tools) illustrates and discusses in greater detail the use of digital-type ohmmeters for electronic system-checking.

REVIEW QUESTIONS

2-1   What is a semiconductor?

2-2   What is a diode?

2-3   What is a zener diode?

2-4   What is a transistor?

2-5   What is a photodiode?

2-6   What is a light-emitting diode?

2-7   What is an integrated circuit?

2-8   How does an NPN transistor differ from a PNP transitor?

2-9   What would you use to check the condition of a diode?

2-10   What precaution must be exercised when using digital-type ohmmeters on a diode check?

ANSWERS

A2-1   A semiconductor is the term used to indicate that the electrical conductivity of these units lies between that of conductors and insulators. The two most commonly used materials that semiconductors are manufactured from are either germanium or silicon, to which has been added such other materials as phosphorous, antimony, boron and indium.

The material is known as an N-type substance when phosphorus is added to the substance, and it is a negative-conducting unit. It is a positive-conducting unit when doped with boron and is therefore known as a P unit.

A2-2   A diode is similar to a one-way check valve in that it is designed to pass electric current in only one direction, while blocking or restricting flow in the other direction. It is used, for example, in an alternator to change alternating current to direct current.

A2-3   The zener diode is designed to protect standard diodes when reverse current and voltage exist. It can conduct current in one direction (reverse only) and will only do so when a predetermined reverse bias voltage is reached. At any voltage below a given value, no current can flow when the reverse bias voltage occurs.

A2-4   A transistor is designed to amplify and switch current on and off. It can therefore be used to control a predetermined flow of current in the circuit, and can also be used to resist this flow. The transistor can be made from either germanium or silicon material with N and P substances sandwiched together as necessary.

A2-5   A photodiode functions as a switch when actuated by a light beam.

A2-6   The LED (light emitting diode) has a junction that radiates both light and heat rays when it is subjected to an electric current.

A2-7   An integrated circuit is an electronic circuit that consists of several or even thousands of semiconductors grouped together. The circuit is a solid-state grouping consisting of diodes, transistors, etc.

A2-8   An NPN transistor differs from a PNP transistor in that in the NPN unit, the emitter (E) conducts current flow to the collector (C) only when the base (B) and collector (C) are positive with respect to the emitter. The transistor, however, cannot conduct until the base voltage exceeds the emitter voltage by approximately 0.4 volt for germanium-type transistors, and approximately 0.7 volt for silicon-type transistors. In the PNP transistor, the emitter (E) current will flow to the collector (C) only when the base (B) and collector are negative with respect to the emitter.

A2-9   Select an ohmmeter having a 1.5 volt cells across the diode or transistor, and select the lowest scale on the selector switch to start with. A good diode should give one high and one low reading when the leads are reversed on the ohmmeter. If no ohmmeter is available, then select a 12 volt d.c. test light, and if the diode causes the test light to glow both ways, then it is defective.

A2-10   Some digital-type ohmmeters have an ouput current limitation of 0.001 ampere, while others may only have an output current of as little as 0.000001 ampere, which is too low a current to turn a PN junction, and thus a false reading can be interpreted. Always check the particular ohmmeter to make sure that it does use at least one or two 1.5 volt cells.

CHAPTER 3

♦

Introduction to Automotive Computers

BASIC HISTORY AND TERMINOLOGY OF MINICOMPUTERS

The adoption of "on-board" minicomputers not only to passenger cars but also to heavy-duty highway trucks since the 1980 model year in North America came about as a direct result of the necessity to comply with the United States EPA (Environmental Protection Agency) exhaust-emissions legislation and to meet the similarly legislated EPA CAFE (Corporate Average Fuel Economy) standards which have become more stringent over the years. Other countries have enacted similar legislation, with both the EEC (European Economic Community) and the Australian government following a similar stance against exhaust emissions and in favor of improved fuel economy in passenger cars, heavy-duty trucks, and buses.

The only way that these standards could have been met was through the application of electronics as a substitute for mechanical components. The carburetor, as we have known it, is to all intents and purposes a part of history, since both throttle body injection (TBI) and multiport fuel injection (MPFI) systems have both shown that they are not only technically superior to the carburetor but also absolutely necessary if the ever stringent exhaust emissions are to be met. The brains behind the success of these fuel injection systems is the solid-state minicomputer, or "on-board" black box.

Various vehicle manufacturers refer to this on-board computer as:

1. An ECU: electronic control unit
2. An ECM: electronic control module

3. A CPU: central processing unit, although the CPU is actually an operational part of the on-board computer. When the CPU is combined into an integrated circuit, it is commonly referred to as a microprocessor, because it is in this device that all of the arithmetic and logical decisions are carried out. The CPU is, in effect, the part of the computer that performs the necessary calculations.

Regardless of the terminology used by various manufacturers, the major purpose of this electronic control unit is to monitor all of the various engine and vehicle parameters through a number of sensor systems, to control the various systems, such as the ignition and fuel control systems, and to ensure that the exhaust emission and fuel economy standards are maintained. In addition, the on-board computer system ensures that vehicle driveability and satisfactory performance is maintained under all operating conditions.

The automotive computer is, of course, a direct result of development of computer applications that have been widely adapted for use in business and industry. There have been several main events that have led to the current technology now in use in our everyday dealings with on-board vehicle minicomputers, and these chief points are:

1. The development of first-generation computers which made use of a large number of vacuum tubes to operate. This development occurred during the years 1951–58.
2. The second-generation units which took advantage of the discovery of solid-state devices, such as the transistor, not only to downsize the computer but also to

increase its speed of operation. This phase took place between 1959 and 1964.

3. The third-generation models which adopted the technology of integrated circuit design. This happened in the years of 1965 to 1970.

4. The fourth-generation systems were downsized even more by advancements in technology, such as miniaturized integrated circuits. This application began in 1971.

5. The adoption of multiple miniaturized circuits and a further reduction of system size as well as an improvement in the materials used to produce silicon wafer chips in the late 1970's and early 1980's.

The next generation of computers due in the 1990's will be capable of artificial intelligence (AI). These machines hopefully will be able to deduce, infer, and learn on their own.

ANALOG- VERSUS DIGITAL-TYPE COMPUTERS

There are two basic types of computers in use today, with the choice being dependent upon the type of job that has to be done. One of these is the "analog computer," and the other is known as a "digital computer."

Analog computers are designed to accept continually varying signals, with the computer consisting of signal adders, multipliers, and other circuitry designed specifically for analog interpretation. The digital computer, on the other hand, is designed for use with digital circuitry comprised of logic gates, binary adders, multipliers, data latches, memory circuits, etc. The major advantage of the digital system over the analog type is that it overcomes the inherent problems of temperature drift and noise disturbance, which affect the analog systems.

An analog computer is designed to measure quantities, such as the amount of gasoline pumped into your car's tank at a local service station. Another example is the VSS (vehicle speed sensor), which employs an analog signal to measure drive shaft rotation. This signal is then converted into a speedometer reading.

A digital computer, on the other hand, is designed to count rather than measure. On a passenger car, for example, various counters are used by the digital system functioning in the computer. The exhaust gas oxygen sensor feeds information to the CPU many times a second to inform the computer how often the oxygen content in the engine exhaust system changes. In other words, the sensor counts the number of times that this air/fuel ratio changes in a given time period. This is known as a discrete phenomena, since this action is specific to the exhaust oxygen sensor circuit. Other sensors and systems that are monitored also feed information to the "on-board" computer system on a continuous basis.

The main problem with analog circuits and analog computers, however, is that their performance changes with an increase or decrease in temperature, supply voltage, signal levels, and noise levels. These problems can be eliminated when a digital circuit is used.

Digital computers used in automotive applications are fed analog signals from a variety of engine and vehicle sensors, and these signals are then sent through a signal processor commonly known as an analog-to-digital converter (ADC) so that the CPU (central processing unit) can process this information. The computer processes information very quickly, with some computers capable of performing this operation in milliseconds (thousandths of a second), while some can do it in microseconds (millionths of a second). In the latest industrial computers used in business and industry, a cycle of informational computation can be done in a nanosecond, which is billionths of a second. As an example, there is now a computer that can compute a cycle of information in 12.5 nanoseconds. Simply put, this means that it can complete 80 million cycles every second.

ELECTROSTATIC DISCHARGE

Since the mass introduction of on-board vehicle computer systems in the 1980–81 model year in North America, many mechanic/technicians have felt that these so called "black boxes," as they were initially referred to, were not robust enough to stand up to the rigors of automotive service. In many cases, computers and their associated circuitry failed, and this failure was blamed on the inadequacies of the so-called "black box." Further analysis, however, led to attributing many of these failures and difficulties not to the design characteristics of the microprocessor (computer) itself, but often to the improper installation of these "black boxes" into the vehicle, either at the factory or dealer level.

Many hours of research at Delco Electronics have disclosed that "electrostatic discharge," or ESD, has been directly responsible for the damage to electronic components, either at the production stage or when service is carried out by a mechanic/technician at a dealership. Both ESD and a related problem known as EOS (electrical over stress) account for 40 percent of the failures in on-board computers, and 44 percent of the failures in car radio systems. ESD failures can result in a radio switching from AM to FM without the driver or passenger touching the control panel, and with the radio drifting from station to station and unable to hold the selected station. Sometimes the radio becomes totally inoperative.

ESD can't be seen, heard, or felt, but it can destroy any electronic component made. ESD is the same electrical phenomenon that causes socks to cling to shirts in the dryer, and a spark to jump from your hand to a door knob when you walk on carpets in your home or office.

ESD in much larger doses is like a lightning bolt that can shatter a tree! The human body can only detect ESD when it reaches approximately 3500 volts, which by then is too late, since IC's (integrated circuits) can be damaged by voltages of as little as 100 volts. Approximately 40 percent of IC's used in automotive applications are capable of withstanding 2000 volts, which is still well below the level at which a human being can perceive this ESD.

This static electricity has been measured on the skin of employees working in plants that produce IC's, with values as high as 12,000 volts. Tests by Delco Electronics engineers found that employees carried a charge that averaged nearly 6000 volts under low-humidity conditions, while high-humidity conditions lowered this value to about 1500 volts. Both values are still well in excess of the 100 volts required to kill many electronic components.

Investigators have found that under high-humidity conditions, foam-padded chairs can give off 2000 volts of ESD, fiberglass tote-pans and conveyor belts up to 1500 volts, radio faceplates up to 1200 volts, and plastic-foam coffee cups up to 1000 volts. The value charge of static electricity depends upon four main elements. These are:

1. Material involved.
2. Closeness of their contact.
3. Speed of separation.
4. Moisture in the air.

Synthetic materials, mainly plastics, generate static charges easily. Therefore, to protect IC's from these possibly devastating ESD voltages, the following basic rules can help to control this invisible problem:

1. Sensitive parts and assemblies *must* be handled at an ESD-protected work station.
2. Parts *must* be transported and stored in conductive containers or static-shielded bags.
3. Where frequent movement of parts and assemblies is necessary and it is not practical for operators to wear wrist straps, conductive floors must be installed and maintained properly, and operators *must* wear heel straps.

IMPORTANT PRECAUTION: When performing any type of service on electronic circuits, you *must* discharge yourself of static electricity (ESD) by touching a good vehicle ground, such as the door post or vehicle shift lever. Failure to do so can result in damage to voltage sensitive electronic components. If for any reason you leave the vehicle during servicing, after re-entering to continue work, you *must* again ground yourself of ESD in order to drain any static electrical charge. Also, if you are performing control head/radio type checks on a new vehicle, remove the plastic seat covers, since they increase the possibility of creating a static charge.

COMPUTER LAYOUT AND ARRANGEMENT

The on-board computer used today in passenger cars and trucks is normally classified as a "minicomputer" because of its relatively small physical size. It does not perform as many and as varied a number of calculations as that of a large mainframe computer that you might find in a large business organization or factory.

An example of a minicomputer in its basic arrangement is that of a wristwatch with a built-in calculator. Figure 3-1 compares the well-known mechanical type of wristwatch alongside two electronic models. Note, in the description included with the figure, the "function" and basic details of the three time pieces.

Unlike a mainframe computer which would contain literally thousands of micro-chips, the digital wrist-watch shown in Fig. 3-1 would contain all of the necessary solid state componentry in a few tiny silicon chips, depending

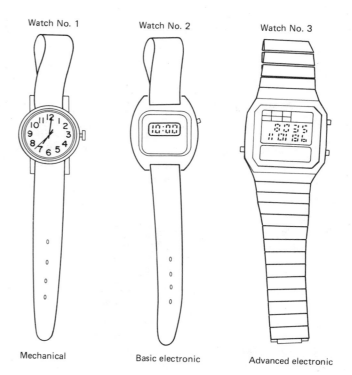

Watch No. 1   Watch No. 2   Watch No. 3

Mechanical   Basic electronic   Advanced electronic

Mechanical watch

Function is to tell time only. To operate, it employs all mechanical components that include a small and large hand, a gearing mechanism, an internal spring, and a small winding knob.

Solid-state electronic watch

Can function not only to tell time and date, but also the actual day of the week; acts as a wakeup alarm or reminder buzzer/beep, and a stop watch; used to enter coded messages; and also functions as a calculator. Small mercury batteries are required to power the IC's, which display their information in LCD (Liquid Crystal Display) mode.

FIGURE 3-1 Comparison of mechanical- and solid-state (electronic) Wristwatches.

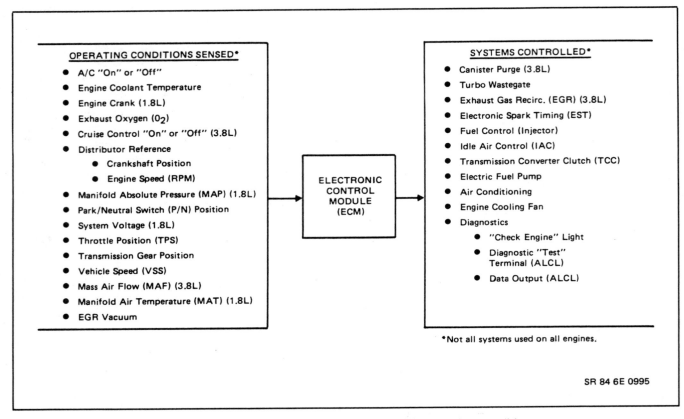

OPERATING CONDITIONS SENSED*

- A/C "On" or "Off"
- Engine Coolant Temperature
- Engine Crank (1.8L)
- Exhaust Oxygen (O₂)
- Cruise Control "On" or "Off" (3.8L)
- Distributor Reference
  - Crankshaft Position
  - Engine Speed (RPM)
- Manifold Absolute Pressure (MAP) (1.8L)
- Park/Neutral Switch (P/N) Position
- System Voltage (1.8L)
- Throttle Position (TPS)
- Transmission Gear Position
- Vehicle Speed (VSS)
- Mass Air Flow (MAF) (3.8L)
- Manifold Air Temperature (MAT) (1.8L)
- EGR Vacuum

ELECTRONIC CONTROL MODULE (ECM)

SYSTEMS CONTROLLED*

- Canister Purge (3.8L)
- Turbo Wastegate
- Exhaust Gas Recirc. (EGR) (3.8L)
- Electronic Spark Timing (EST)
- Fuel Control (Injector)
- Idle Air Control (IAC)
- Transmission Converter Clutch (TCC)
- Electric Fuel Pump
- Air Conditioning
- Engine Cooling Fan
- Diagnostics
  - "Check Engine" Light
  - Diagnostic "Test" Terminal (ALCL)
  - Data Output (ALCL)

*Not all systems used on all engines.

SR 84 6E 0995

FIGURE 3-2 ECM (electronic control module) operating conditions sensed and systems controlled (*Courtesy of Oldsmobile Div. of GMC*)

on the various options required in the watch other than to simply tell time.

Minicomputers now in use in passenger cars and heavy duty trucks would still only have a small number of chips containing the necessary circuits, and not the hundreds or thousands necessary for a mainframe computer to operate successfully.

Even though the minicomputer is smaller than its larger mainframe computer, it is designed to perform substantially the same tasks of receiving, computing, and sending out corrective controlling voltage signals that effectively maintain successful operation of all of the sensed "on-vehicle options," such as the ignition system, the fuel injection system, ride quality, automatic interior temperature control, anti-skid monitoring, trip computing, etc. Typical engine operating conditions sensed and fed into the computer or electronic control module and the resultant systems controlled by this action are illustrated in Fig. 3-2. A simplified arrangement of the main components within the computer appear in block form, as shown in Fig. 3-3. Prior to studying the various data-processing actions within the computer, it would be helpful for you to refer to Fig. 3-4, which illustrates the three major operating sections of an "on-board" minicomputer. These three sections are as follows:

1. The "input section" which consists of the various sensors used to constantly monitor numerous functions on the engine or vehicle. Typical input or operating con-

ditions sensed and the succeeding systems which are controlled by such action were shown earlier in Fig. 3-2.

2. The "control section" which incorporates the actual minicomputer and its componentry. Input signals are logically converted within the computer by the various logic gates into digital signals from analog signals. These digital signals are stored as strings of "0's" (OFF) and "1's" (ON). The computer then compares these sensor signals to pre-programmed levels, makes the necessary decisions of acceptance, and a corrected signal is then sent out of the computer to control each on-board electronic system.

3. The "output section," which is generally made up of "actuators" such as the fuel injectors on either a gasoline or diesel engine. These components receive a pulsed-voltage signal, the duration of which determines how much fuel will be delivered to the individual cylinders. In this case, the electrical signal is converted into mechanical energy through a small solenoid which acts to open the fuel injector valve. The longer the pulse-width signal, the longer the fuel-injection duration and, therefore, the speed and horsepower developed by the engine for a given throttle position. A shorter pulse-width signal will result in less fuel delivery and, therefore, a lower engine speed and horsepower setting. The ignition system would also have the timing advanced or retarded as necessary, which would

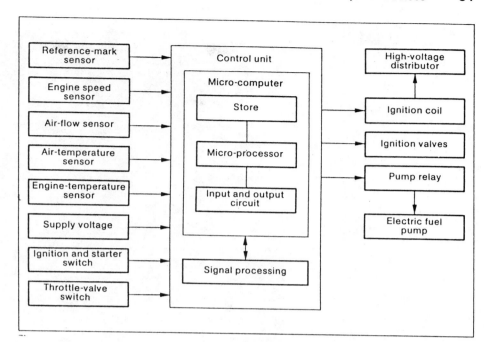

FIGURE 3-3 Operational block diagram of an ECU (electronic control unit) for a Motronic model fuel-injection and Ignition System. (*Courtesy of Robert Bosch Corporation*)

be based on the decision made by the computer from the sensor-input data that it has received.

An actual block diagam arrangement for a typical ECU (electronic control unit) "on-board" vehicle minicomputer is shown in Fig. 3.3

COMPUTER DEVICES

The on-board vehicle computer contains the following major operating devices:

1. A CPU or Central Processing Unit.
2. Temporary storage units.
3. Arithmetic and logical unit (ALU) or section.
4. Control unit.
5. Backup storage units.
6. Input devices or sensors.
7. Output devices or actuators.

Figure 3-5 illustrates a typical electronic control unit or minicomputer that is typical of that now in use in many passenger cars and trucks and manufactured by Robert Bosch Corporation. The function and operation of the computer components shown in Fig. 3-5 can best be understood

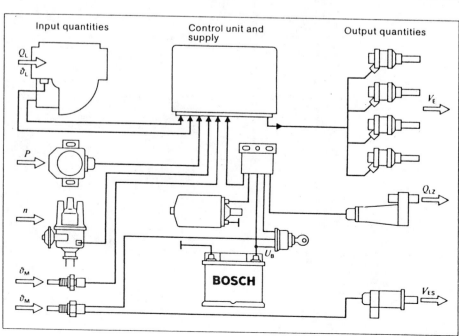

FIGURE 3-4 Input/control/output sections of a typical on-board vehicle computer system. (*Courtesy of Robert Bosch Corporation*)

Signals and control quantities fed into the control unit:

Q_L *air drawn in* φ_L *air temperature, n engine speed, P engine load-range, φ engine temperature, V_E fuel quantity injected, Q_{LZ} auxiliary air, V_{ES} excess fuel for starting, U_B vehicle-system voltage*

Control unit

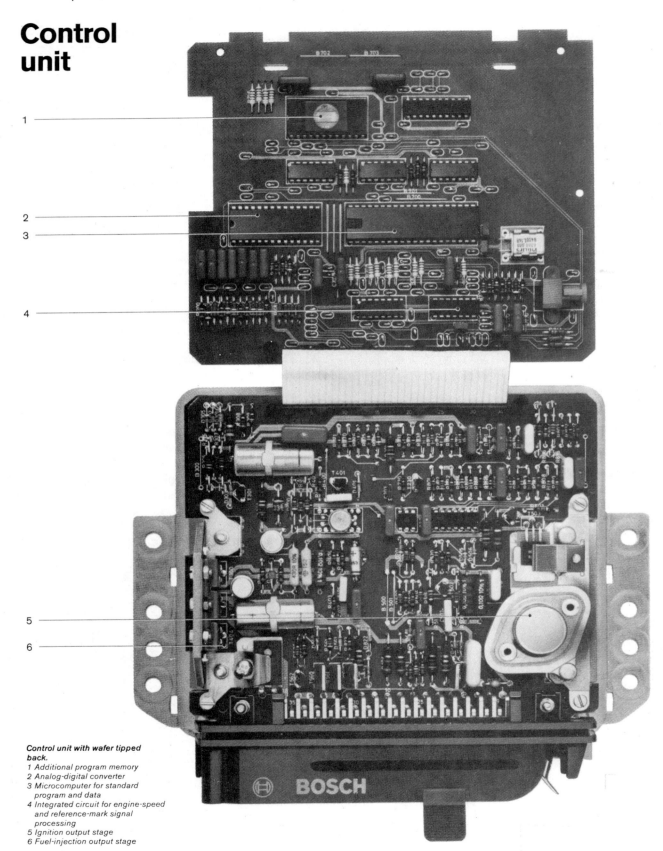

Control unit with wafer tipped back.

1 *Additional program memory*
2 *Analog-digital converter*
3 *Microcomputer for standard program and data*
4 *Integrated circuit for engine-speed and reference-mark signal processing*
5 *Ignition output stage*
6 *Fuel-injection output stage*

FIGURE 3-5 Actual view of a typical on-board vehicle computer or control unit. (*Courtesy of Robert Bosch Corporation*)

by referring to the simplified operational diagram shown in Fig. 3-6, while Figure 3-7 illustrates the actual data-processing function within the computer unit.

COMPUTER PROGRAMMING

Although each computer contains the same major basic components for successful operation, the system must be programmed with a set of instructions that, in effect, tell the computer what it must do.

With its diodes, transistors, and resistors, the computer cannot accept a program that has been written in the normal everyday form of letters and numbers. Therefore, one function of a computer program is to transform data into a recognizable computer language so that the computer's solid-state devices can react to various commands. This requires that the input analog-voltage signals from the various sensor devices be converted into "digital" form (1's for ON, and 0's for OFF).

Figure 3-8 illustrates, in simplified form, the wave sine for an analog signal, and the rectangular box shape of the digital sine wave. The operation of both of these sine waves was discussed earlier and was shown in Figures 2-11 and 2-12.

Although we could take the regular digital numbers of 1 and 0 and program the computer, it would be very difficult to understand and use strings of 1's and 0's, particularly when we would need to use thousands of numbers. Therefore, to simplify this bulky system into a more manageable state, special programming language has been developed.

Minicomputers in use in automobiles and trucks perform a limited number of calculations when compared to that of a large mainframe computer in an office or factory. Therefore, their programs are fairly simple to construct. A fixed program is built directly into the computer at the factory and is commonly referred to as "hardwiring," because it is burned into the PROM (Programmable Read Only Memory) or ROM (Read Only Memory) unit integrated chip by a laser beam in the latest systems. These cannot be

FIGURE 3-6 Operational block diagram of an on-board vehicle electronic control unit. (*Courtesy of Robert Bosch Corporation*)

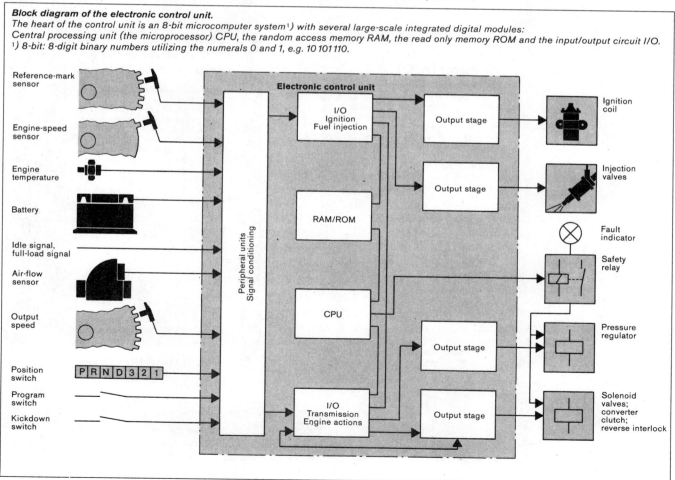

Block diagram of the electronic control unit.
The heart of the control unit is an 8-bit microcomputer system[1]) with several large-scale integrated digital modules:
Central processing unit (the microprocessor) CPU, the random access memory RAM, the read only memory ROM and the input/output circuit I/O.
[1]) 8-bit: 8-digit binary numbers utilizing the numerals 0 and 1, e.g. 10 101 110.

Data processing in the microcomputer

This schematic and the operational principles described here apply to microcomputers and microprocessors in general. Differences lie mainly in the memory capacities of the ICs used, the necessary programs and the data quantities to be processed.

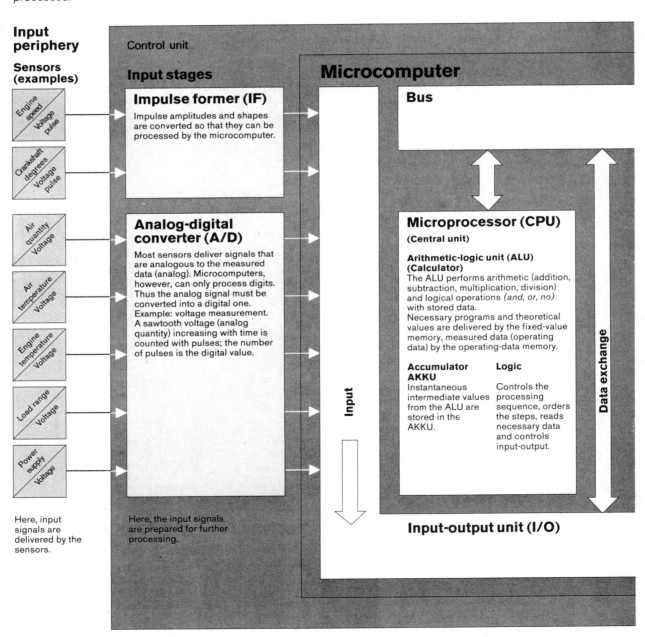

Input periphery

Sensors (examples)

Engine speed / Voltage pulse

Crankshaft degrees / Voltage pulse

Air quantity / Voltage

Air temperature / Voltage

Engine temperature / Voltage

Load range / Voltage

Power supply / Voltage

Here, input signals are delivered by the sensors.

Control unit

Input stages

Impulse former (IF)

Impulse amplitudes and shapes are converted so that they can be processed by the microcomputer.

Analog-digital converter (A/D)

Most sensors deliver signals that are analogous to the measured data (analog). Microcomputers, however, can only process digits. Thus the analog signal must be converted into a digital one. Example: voltage measurement. A sawtooth voltage (analog quantity) increasing with time is counted with pulses; the number of pulses is the digital value.

Here, the input signals are prepared for further processing.

Microcomputer

Bus

Microprocessor (CPU)

(Central unit)

Arithmetic-logic unit (ALU) (Calculator)
The ALU performs arithmetic (addition, subtraction, multiplication, division) and logical operations *(and, or, no)* with stored data.
Necessary programs and theoretical values are delivered by the fixed-value memory, measured data (operating data) by the operating-data memory.

Accumulator AKKU
Instantaneous intermediate values from the ALU are stored in the AKKU.

Logic
Controls the processing sequence, orders the steps, reads necessary data and controls input-output.

Input

Data exchange

Input-output unit (I/O)

FIGURE 3-7 Data-processing path within the vehicle computer. (*Courtesy of Robert Bosch Corporation*)

IF: Impulse former
A/D: Analog-digital converter
CPU: Central processor unit
ALU: Arithmetic-logic unit
I/O: Input-output
ROM: Read-only memory
RAM: Random-access memory

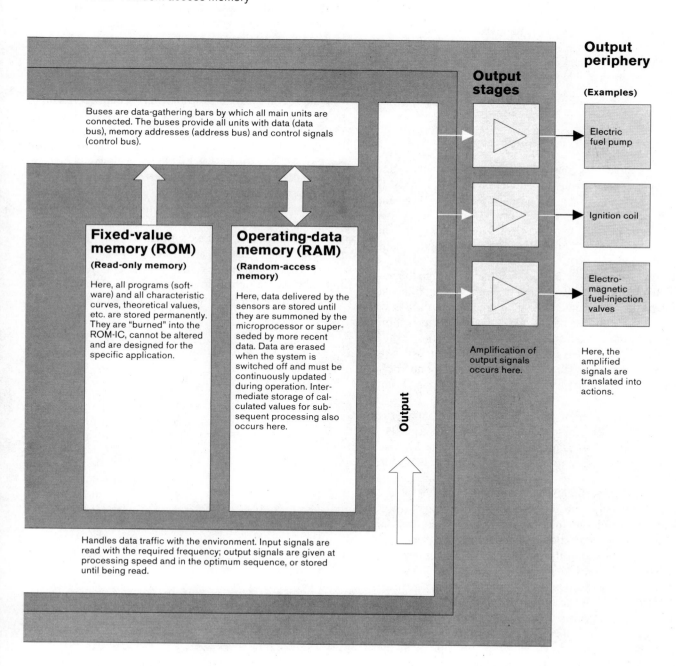

Output periphery

Output stages

(Examples)

Buses are data-gathering bars by which all main units are connected. The buses provide all units with data (data bus), memory addresses (address bus) and control signals (control bus).

Electric fuel pump

Ignition coil

Electro-magnetic fuel-injection valves

Fixed-value memory (ROM)

(Read-only memory)

Here, all programs (software) and all characteristic curves, theoretical values, etc. are stored permanently. They are "burned" into the ROM-IC, cannot be altered and are designed for the specific application.

Operating-data memory (RAM)

(Random-access memory)

Here, data delivered by the sensors are stored until they are summoned by the microprocessor or superseded by more recent data. Data are erased when the system is switched off and must be continuously updated during operation. Intermediate storage of calculated values for subsequent processing also occurs here.

Amplification of output signals occurs here.

Here, the amplified signals are translated into actions.

Output

Handles data traffic with the environment. Input signals are read with the required frequency; output signals are given at processing speed and in the optimum sequence, or stored until being read.

FIGURE 3-8 Computer accepts (eats) only digital signals in order to operate.

altered unless the PROM unit is removed and replaced with another memory chip. Since each PROM chip is designed for a particular application, these chips should *never* be intermixed between vehicles. We will discuss this later in the book.

BINARY NOTATION

Since the computer is constructed to understand only "digital" voltage signals, which are either in the ON (1) or OFF (0) mode, the many combinations of these numbers are represented in what is called "binary form." What this means is that only the numerals 1 or 0 are used rather than the numbers from 0 through 9, which would represent 10 possible numbers.

In order to convert the decimal numbers into binary notation or form, a device within the minicomputer known as an "encoder" is required. In addition, in order to convert "digital" data (that is, binary numbers) into decimal form at any time, the computer also contains a "decoder." Figure 3-9 illustrates the system of numbers used with the "binary system" of notation. This is the system of numbers that are used to tell the computer what is going on at any time.

The binary system of numbers used with a computer is commonly called a "base 2 system," while the conventional decimal system using 10 digits, is known as a "base 10 system." The word *decimal* is derived from the Latin word for ten.

The computer can only interpret numbers in the base 2 system. Since only zeros or ones (0's = OFF, and 1's = ON) are continually produced by the various input sensors (analog to digital conversion done through an analog to digital converter within the computer unit), some form of equitable conversion system must be employed. Figure 3-9 illustrates a comparison between a "base 2" and a "base 10" system. Note, for example, that the "binary" number 0011 is read and interpreted as the number, "zero, zero, one, one," and not as the number eleven.

Your initial reaction to viewing Fig. 3-9 is probably the same as that for most people when they are initially confronted with such a comparison. It just doesn't make any

sense, does it? Therefore, let's see if we can simplify this concept, so that you will have a solid foundation on which to base your interpretation of just how the computer is able to understand all these strings of 1's and 0's and make sense out of them.

The position of each individual digit in the decimal system, when read from right to left, represents the base number to the power 10. For example, the number 1, which would be the first number on the right, would simply be represented by 10 to the power zero, or 10^0. Note the small zero above and to the right of 10.

The second position from the right would be representative of 10 to the power one, or 10^1, with a small 1 above it. Therefore, 10 times 1 = 10! The third position from the right would represent 10 to the power 2 or 100, commonly stated as 10^2, with a small 2 above the ten. Therefore, 10 times 10 = 100!

The fourth position from the right would represent 10 to the power 3, or 1000, which is calculated simply by multiplying 10 times 10 times 10. Therefore, the 10 would be commonly represented by the number 10^3, with a small 3 above it! Each successive digit to the right would increase the number ten's power by another number up the line— namely, to the power 4, 5, 6, and so on.

In the "binary" system of numbers used within the computer, the numbers are also grouped from right to left, with each additional digit increasing the power of the number from 0 to 1, 2, 3, 4, and so on.

As with the decimal system, in the binary system the first digit on the right is in the one's place. Therefore, it is represented by 2 to the power zero, or 2^0 with a small "0"

Decimal Base 10 System	Binary Base 2 System
0	0 0 0 0
1	0 0 0 1
2	0 0 1 0
3	0 0 1 1
4	0 1 0 0
5	0 1 0 1
6	0 1 1 0
7	0 1 1 1
8	1 0 0 0
9	1 0 0 1
10	1 0 1 0
11	1 0 1 1
12	1 1 0 0
13	1 1 0 1
14	1 1 1 0
15	1 1 1 1
16	1 0 0 0 0
255	1 1 1 1 1 1 1 1
256	1 0 0 0 0 0 0 0 0

FIGURE 3-9 Minicomputer binary notation base 2 system of numbering versus decimal 10 system.

	Decimal—Base 10				Binary—Base 2				
Place	4	3	2	1	5	4	3	2	1
Value	1000	100	10	1	16	8	4	2	1
Power of base	3	2	1	0	4	2	2	1	0

FIGURE 3-10 Decimal base 10 binary comparison. Value and power of base versus computer base 2 number system.

above it. Since the computer is programmed to accept only 0's and 1's, this second digit must be the two's place, with 2^1 being raised now to the power "1." Moving left, the third digit would represent the four's place or 2 to the power 2—2^2, with a small 2 above it.

Moving left, the fourth digit would represent the eight's position or place, or 2 to the power three (2^3, with a small 3 above it). Each successive digit to the left would represent another power added to the base figure of 2. If you compare this system of decimal and binary notation, which is shown in Fig. 3-10, the above-listed information may be easier to understand.

From the information presented, we can now readily understand that a number such as 6524 in the decimal system can be presented by the following notational system:

6×10^3 (to the power 3) plus

5×10^2 (to the power 2) plus

2×10^1 (to the power 1) plus

4×10^0 (to the power 0)

The number 6524 can also be shown as follows:

10^3	10^2	10^1	10^0	Ten taken to different powers
(1000)	(100)	(10)	(1)	
6	5	2	4	

4 → Means 4×1 = 4

2 → Means 2×10 = 20

5 → Means 5×100 = 500

6 → Means 6×1000 = 6000

6524

To convert from decimal to binary, let's use the number 49 as an example, and transpose it into its equivalent binary number. What we have to do here is to consider that we are going from a base 10 system to a base 2 system.

Therefore, we have to start by determining the largest number that is a power of 2 (divisor) and which will actually divide into the decimal number (49 in this case), with a 1 as a quotient. The largest number that is a power of two and which will divide into 49, with a quotient of 1, is 32 (2 to the power 5). This conversion is calculated as follows:

$$(2^5) \; \frac{49}{32} = 1 \qquad 49 - 32 = 17$$

$$(2^4) \; \frac{17}{16} = 1 \qquad 17 - 16 = 1$$

$$(2^3) \; \frac{1}{8} = 0$$

$$(2^2) \; \frac{1}{4} = 0$$

$$(2^1) \; \frac{1}{2} = 0$$

$$(2^0) \; \frac{1}{1} = 1 \qquad 1 - 1 = 0$$

Therefore, the decimal number 49 in binary form appears as 110001, and is known as "one-one-zero-zero-zero-one" and not as one hundred and ten thousand and one.

Conversely, we could take a known binary number, such as 110001 for 49, and find its decimal equivalent, remembering, of course, that the binary system operates on a base 2 rather than a base 10 system.

We start with the decimal number to the power of 5 on the left-hand side of the power number shown below. If we multiply each binary number (1 or 0) by its power base of 2, we get the following results:

Power number	5	4	3	2	1	0
Binary number	1	1	0	0	0	1
Multiplied	1×2^5 +	1×2^4 +	0×2^3 +	0×2^2 +	0×2^1 +	1×2^0
Result	32 +	16 +	0 +	0 +	0 +	1 = 49

Therefore, we have proved that the decimal number 49 is shown in its binary equivalent number as 110001! Another way to show this and perhaps easier for you to see is to present the data in tabular form:

$2^6 = 64$	$2^5 = 32$	$2^4 = 16$	$2^3 = 8$	$2^2 = 4$	$2^1 = 2$	$2^0 = 1$
. . .	1	1	0	0	0	1

$$1 \times 1 = 1$$
$$0 \times 2 = 0$$
$$0 \times 4 = 0$$
$$0 \times 8 = 0$$
$$1 \times 16 = 16$$
$$1 \times 32 = 32$$

$$\text{TOTAL} = 49$$

BASE 8, OR OCTAL SYSTEM

Although we have discussed the decimal system (base 10) and compared it to that of the binary system (base 2), any base to power number can be used. Computers often employ a "base 8" system, which is referred to as an *octal* system since it uses the numbers 0 through 7. Instead of using numbers 0 through 9 as in the decimal system (base 10 system), each digit 0-1-2-3-4-5-6-7 represents the base number 8 raised to an exponent related or based upon that position.

Since digital signals are either ON or OFF and are represented by a 1 or 0, the binary system is based upon a base 2 system, with the position of each digit representing the number 2, which is the base number raised to an exponent based upon that particular position. One other numbering system used with computers is the "hexadecimal" or what is more commonly known as a "base 16" system.

Earlier we considered how to convert the decimal number 49 into binary form and vice-versa. However, as decimal numbers increase in relative size, for example into the thousands, then the equivalent binary length of 1's and 0's also increases and can, in effect, become quite cumbersome. In addition, true binary numbers can only represent numeric data, such as the counting of digital pulses that have been produced in analog form from a sensor and then converted through an analog/digital converter within the computer.

True binary representation cannot, however, handle items or bits of data such as letters of the alphabet, or special characters such as periods, commas, exclamation marks, question marks, + signs, dollar signs and various other special symbols that we often use.

Because of the change in length of the binary number when a decimal number such as 49 versus 6524 is represented, the computer would have some trouble when receiving or transmitting data in pure binary form, since it wouldn't quite know when one string of bits ended, and the other began. Therefore, fixed-length codes allow the computer to determine when one character ends and another begins.

EBCDIC AND ASCII CODES

The two most widely used codes that are employed to allow the computer to determine between decimal numbers, letters of the alphabet, and special lettering are known as:

1. EBCDIC: Extended Binary-Coded Decimal Interchange Code
2. ASCII: American Standard Code for Information Interchange

The EBCDIC system was developed by IBM (International Business Machines) and is used extensively in their line of computers, while the ASCII system is widely used on other makes of CPU's (Central Processing Units). The EBCDIC system uses 8 bits (a bit is a unit of information, either a 0 or a 1) to represent a character, and since the binary system is known as a base 2 system, a group of 8 bits has 256 (2 to the power 8) different combinations that can represent 256 characters. This number of 256 is sufficient to allow for all the letters of the alphabet (both upper and lower case), the ten decimal digits, and for a number of special characters as well.

ASCII, on the other hand, was developed as a 7-bit code and can represent only 128 characters (2 to the power 7 obtained from the base 2 system of 1's and 0's). Whether a 7-bit or 8-bit code system of word length is used to represent information characters, each one is referred to as a "byte." Figure 3-11 illustrates the sequence of characters and its equivalent EBCDIC and ASCII binary bit number.

BITS AND BYTES

The digital signals created and interpreted in the computer are, as we now know, identified by binary numbers of 1 or 0, with 1 being an ON signal, and with 0 representing an OFF signal. These 1's or 0's are commonly referred to as "bits," which is a word combination form contrived from the two words, binary digits. A bit is the term used to indicate one unit of data or information and is indicated to the computer by the numeral 1 or 0. Each one of these digital numbers contains a very small unit of information. Therefore, in order to handle large amounts of useable information, the computer is designed to combine and handle these separate bits into words of different lengths. Various computers are designed to handle informational data in word lengths of 4, 8, 16, 32 or 64 bit sizes.

The commonly used term in computer language for a word length of 8 bits is the "byte," which is used to indicate the storage capacity of the computer memory devices. A group of 4 bits is often referred to as a "nibble." The computing power of the computer is dependent upon its memory storage capacity, which in turn is based upon how many "bytes" of information it can retain. One byte represents a single addressable storage location.

If you have purchased a home computer of your own, or have ever read the advertising brochures for this type of equipment, reference is always made to the computer's memory capacity. For example, a 128K system versus a 64K system means that the 128K system has the capability to hold and store 128,000 characters of data or information, while the 64K unit can only hold and store 64,000 characters of information.

Character	EBCDIC Bit Representation	ASCII Bit Representation	Character	EBCDIC Bit Representation	ASCII Bit Representation
0	1 1 1 1 0 0 0 0	0 1 1 0 0 0 0	I	1 1 0 0 1 0 0 1	1 0 0 1 0 0 1
1	1 1 1 1 0 0 0 1	0 1 1 0 0 0 1	J	1 1 0 1 0 0 0 1	1 0 0 1 0 1 0
2	1 1 1 1 0 0 1 0	0 1 1 0 0 1 0	K	1 1 0 1 0 0 1 0	1 0 0 1 0 1 1
3	1 1 1 1 0 0 1 1	0 1 1 0 0 1 1	L	1 1 0 1 0 0 1 1	1 0 0 1 1 0 0
4	1 1 1 1 0 1 0 0	0 1 1 0 1 0 0	M	1 1 0 1 0 1 0 0	1 0 0 1 1 0 1
5	1 1 1 1 0 1 0 1	0 1 1 0 1 0 1	N	1 1 0 1 0 1 0 1	1 0 0 1 1 1 0
6	1 1 1 1 0 1 1 0	0 1 1 0 1 1 0	O	1 1 0 1 0 1 1 0	1 0 0 1 1 1 1
7	1 1 1 1 0 1 1 1	0 1 1 0 1 1 1	P	1 1 0 1 0 1 1 1	1 0 1 0 0 0 0
8	1 1 1 1 1 0 0 0	0 1 1 1 0 0 0	Q	1 1 0 1 1 0 0 0	1 0 1 0 0 0 1
9	1 1 1 1 1 0 0 1	0 1 1 1 0 0 1	R	1 1 0 1 1 0 0 1	1 0 1 0 0 1 0
A	1 1 0 0 0 0 0 1	1 0 0 0 0 0 1	S	1 1 1 0 0 0 1 0	1 0 1 0 0 1 1
B	1 1 0 0 0 0 1 0	1 0 0 0 0 1 0	T	1 1 1 0 0 0 1 1	1 0 1 0 1 0 0
C	1 1 0 0 0 0 1 1	1 0 0 0 0 1 1	U	1 1 1 0 0 1 0 0	1 0 1 0 1 0 1
D	1 1 0 0 0 1 0 0	1 0 0 0 1 0 0	V	1 1 1 0 0 1 0 1	1 0 1 0 1 1 0
E	1 1 0 0 0 1 0 1	1 0 0 0 1 0 1	W	1 1 1 0 0 1 1 0	1 0 1 0 1 1 1
F	1 1 0 0 0 1 1 0	1 0 0 0 1 1 0	X	1 1 1 0 0 1 1 1	1 0 1 1 0 0 0
G	1 1 0 0 0 1 1 1	1 0 0 0 1 1 1	Y	1 1 1 0 1 0 0 0	1 0 1 1 0 0 1
H	1 1 0 0 1 0 0 0	1 0 0 1 0 0 0	Z	1 1 1 0 1 0 0 1	1 0 1 1 0 1 0

FIGURE 3-11 EBCDIC and ASCII character and bit number representation.

The term kilobyte or the letter "K" indicates that the memory storage unit of the CPU can hold 1000 bytes (1 byte being equal to a word length of 8 bits for example). Actually, 1K represents 1024 bytes, which is arrived at by taking the digital "base 2" system and elevating it to the power of 10—namely, 2 to the power 10. (The base 2 system was discussed under binary notation.) A greater unit of measurement is a megabyte (MB), which represents 1 million bytes.

In order for the computer to handle as much information as possible in as small a space as possible, it is advantageous to use longer words rather than shorter ones, since this will allow a greater amount of data to be handled at any given time, and by doing so, the computer will have greater information-processing capability. The word size that the computer can handle is indicated by its capacity number such as 8 bit, 16 bit, 32 bit, 64 bit, etc.

Most home computers and main frames can handle substantially greater information than that used in a passenger car microprocessor. The information and computations that the automotive microprocessor is required to handle can be adequately accommodated by using an 8 bit word length system, although some of the newer models are now up to a 16 bit system to accommodate the greater number of systems that are now electronically controlled.

By using an 8 word bit system, 2 to the power 8 or 256 combinations are possible, while a 16 bit system can handle 512 combinations for a total of 65,536 memory locations (2 to the power 16). Therefore, the greater the word bit capacity of the computer, then the larger its memory ca-

pacity as well as its speed of computation will be. Typically, on a 16 bit machine, the first 6 bits are reserved for instructions, which permits 2 to the power 6(2), or 64 different instructions.

LOGIC CIRCUITS

In Chapter 2 we discussed briefly the makeup of an integrated circuit or IC. Several examples of the use of diodes, transistors, and resistors were discussed and how they would function in the typical alternator used in a car or truck. The overall purpose of each solid-state device and its importance to the successful operation and control of the charging rate were shown and discussed in various diagrams. Let's build on that knowledge now, and move one step further towards understanding the function and operation of the on-board minicomputer that is now in use on many passenger cars and trucks.

We also talked earlier about the difference between "analog" versus "digital" voltage signals. You may recollect that "analog" signals resemble the sound made by the human voice in that the voltage signal is undulating or wavy, whereas the "digital" signal is either ON or OFF and is reflected by rectangular box shapes rather than by a wavy sine line. If you wish, refer to Figs. 2-11 and 2-12 to refresh your memory before proceeding.

Since microprocessors operate on digital signals, any analog signal must be converted to a digital signal so that the feedback information from any sensor can be readily

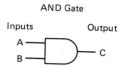

FIGURE 3-12 Typical logic symbol for an AND gate system.

understood and acted upon. Components within the computer are designed and programmed to recognize voltage signals by a number assigned to a specific input signal. Because of the many functions that the computer is asked to do, the various input signals are converted to a specific number through the use of "logic gates," which are discussed below. Fig. 3-2 illustrates typical operating conditions that are sensed by specific sensors attached to the engine/vehicle. These voltage signals are then fed into the on-board electronic control module (minicomputer), where the various solid-state devices, assisted by the different "logic gates," are able to interpret this input data. The electronic control module then outputs a voltage signal to the gas or diesel fuel injectors, for example, to control how long they operate. In this way, the amount of fuel delivered to the engine cylinders becomes proportional to the throttle position. Similarly, an output voltage signal from the computer controls the ignition timing and any other sensed components.

Paramount to the importance of IC's is the operation of the transistors. The converted digital voltage signals or circuits are known as "logic circuits," and they consist of a series or combinations of varying types of systems that are commonly referred to as "gates."

These "gates" are designed to accept voltage signals and logically make sense of them. In effect, they process two or more voltage signals. This is why they are called "logic gates." They have the ability to make some sense out of all of the various voltage feedback signals that are fed to the computer from the numerous sensors on the vehicle.

There are five basic types of "logic gates" in use on microprocessor-equipped vehicles, which are the following ones:

1. AND gates
2. OR gates
3. NOT gates
4. NAND gates
5. NOR gates

Each "logic gate" listed above is designed to perform a specific function within the computer. Funny as these terms may sound, once they are described in more detail, you will realize just how important these gate types are to the successful operation of the logic section of the on-board computer.

AND GATE CIRCUIT

The logic symbol that is commonly used to identify an AND gate in a schematic diagram of an electronic circuit is shown in Fig. 3-12. The logic symbol for an AND gate

actually contains 2 diodes, 3 transistors, 3 variable resistors, and 4 fixed resistors as shown in Figs. 3-12 and 3-13. In these schematics, *A* and *B* represent the two voltage input terminals, and *C* represents the output. You may find that the letter *X* is also often used to signify the output terminal.

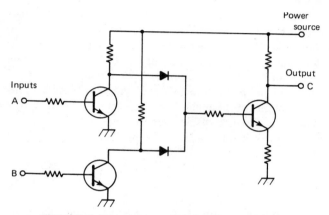

FIGURE 3-13 Equivalent electronic circuit arrangement for an AND gate logic circuit.

Compare Fig. 3-13 with Fig. 3-14, and consider the parallels that exist between a typical mechanical-switch electrical circuit and that of a solid-state circuit (Fig. 3-13). The mechanical switches *A* and *B* function the same as the voltage input terminals *A* and *B* in the solid-state AND gate circuit, while the small light bulb in the mechanical circuit is the same as the output terminal *C* in the AND gate system. The term AND gate is used in this context because power can only flow to the light bulb when both switch *A* and *B* are closed or both inputs are high (1). Should one or both switches be open (low or zero), then obviously the light bulb would not come on, because the output would also be low or zero (0). If we therefore compare this arrangement of the mechanical circuit with that of the solid-state AND gate system, the same thing holds true. Voltage

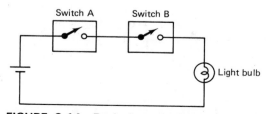

FIGURE 3-14 Equivalent mechanical circuit for an AND gate logic circuit.

AND Gate

Inputs A B	Output C
0 0	0
0 1	0
1 0	0
1 1	1

FIGURE 3-15 Truth table for *A* and *B* Inputs, with a *C* output for an AND gate logic circuit.

at the output terminal *C* only exists if a voltage is evident at terminals *A* and *B*.

Earlier when we discussed the fact that the computer requires analog voltage signals to be converted to a digital format so that the computer can make sense out of data, the numeral 1 was used to signify an ON condition with a voltage present, while the numeral 0 was defined as an OFF condition, with no voltage signal present. Since various combinations of these numbers can occur at any time, it is industry practice to display such combinations in what is known as a "Truth Table." See Fig. 3-15.

OR GATE CIRCUIT

Illustrated in Figs. 3-16, 3-17 and 3-18 are the logic symbol, the solid-state element arrangement, and the equivalent mechanical circuit for an OR gate system. Solid-state components used in the OR gate circuit are made up of 2 transistors, 2 diodes, 3 fixed, and 3 variable resistors. The OR gate circuit differs from the AND circuit in that the

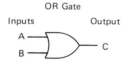

OR Gate

FIGURE 3-16 Typical logic symbol for an OR gate logic circuit.

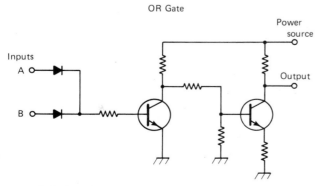

OR Gate

FIGURE 3-17 Equivalent OR gate system electronic circuit.

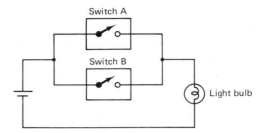

FIGURE 3-18 Equivalent mechanical OR circuit.

OR Gate

Inputs A B	Output C
0 0	0
0 1	1
1 0	1
1 1	1

FIGURE 3-19 Truth table for *A* or *B* (voltage at both input terminals, or voltage at only one) and resultant output for an OR gate logic circuit.

light bulb will be illuminated whenever one or both inputs are high (1). For the bulb to have been illuminated in the AND gate circuit, both switches had to be closed. (Both inputs have to be high or 1.)

In Fig. 3-16, a voltage signal at either *A* or *B* or both reflects an output voltage signal at *C*. Possible combinations for this OR circuit are shown in the Truth Table in Fig. 3-19.

NOT GATE CIRCUIT

The logic symbol for a NOT gate circuit is similar to that for a diode, and it is illustrated in Fig. 3-20. The actual solid-state arrangement and equivalent mechanical circuits are shown in Figs. 3-21 and 3-22. The NOT gate system has 1 transistor, no diodes, 2 fixed resistors, as well as 1 variable resistor.

In the OR gate circuit, the light bulb is illuminated when either one or both switches are closed. [Inputs are high (1).] However, in the NOT gate circuit, when the switch *A* is closed (input is high or 1), the relay shown in Fig. 3-22 is opened. There is no power flow to the bulb, and it will *not* light. When switch *A* is opened (input is low or zero), the relay will close, and the light bulb will illuminate.

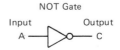

NOT Gate

FIGURE 3-20 Typical logic symbol for a NOT gate circuit.

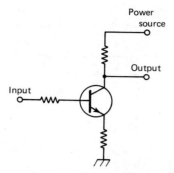

FIGURE 3-21 Equivalent NOT gate logic system electronic circuit layout.

NOT Gate

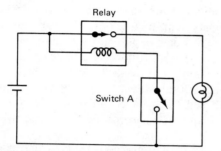

FIGURE 3-22 Typical equivalent mechanical system for a NOT gate logic circuit.

NOT Gate

Input A	Output C
1	0
0	1

FIGURE 3-23 Truth table for a NOT gate logic circuit. (Output is always opposite the input.)

Therefore, in the solid-state circuit shown in Fig. 3-21, a voltage signal at the input terminal *a* will result in no output signal *c*, and vice-versa. In other words, the output signal is always the opposite of the input signal, or inverted. The Truth Table in Fig. 3-23 illustrates the various combinations in numeric form, with 1 representing an ON condition, and with 0 signifying an OFF condition.

NAND GATE CIRCUIT

The term NAND gate is a combination of both the AND and NOT gate circuits discussed earlier (NAND = NOT AND for the reduced term NAND). The logic symbol for a NAND gate circuit is illustrated in Fig. 3-24, while its "truth table" depicting the various input/output combinations possible from such an arrangement is shown in Fig. 3-25.

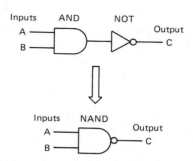

FIGURE 3-24 Typical logic gate symbol for a NAND circuit.

NAND Gate

Inputs A	B	Output C
0	0	1
0	1	1
1	0	1
1	1	0

FIGURE 3-25 Truth table for a NAND gate logic circuit composed of a combination NOT and an AND gate system.

Because of the combination of an AND and NOT gate in this system, zero voltage will appear at the output terminal *C* only if a voltage signal 1 is apparent at both input terminals *A* and *B*. Conversely, if there is a 0 or no input voltage signal at either input terminal *A* or *B*, then an output voltage signal 1 will appear at terminal *C*.

NOR GATE CIRCUIT

The last type of logic circuit that we will look at is known as the NOR gate circuit. Its symbol is shown in Fig. 3-26, while its "truth table" is illustrated in Fig. 3-27. This particular circuit consists of a combination OR gate and NOT gate arrangement (NOR = NOT OR); hence the term NOR.

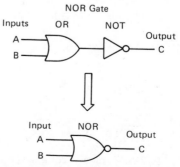

FIGURE 3-26 Typical logic symbol for a NOR gate circuit.

NOR Gate

Inputs A B	Output C
0 0	1
0 1	0
1 0	0
1 1	0

FIGURE 3-27 Truth table for a NOR gate logic system composed of a combination OR and NOT gate circuit.

Logic Circuit

Inputs A B	Output C
0 0	1
0 1	0
1 0	0
1 1	1

FIGURE 3-29 Truth table for a combination logic circuit for an OR, AND, and NOR gate system.

In this circuit, when a 0 or no input voltage is apparent at terminals *A* and *B*, an output voltage 1 will appear at the terminal *C*. If on the other hand, there is a 1 (voltage signal) at either input terminal *A* or *B*; or both, then the output terminal *C* will be 0.

APPLICATION OF LOGIC GATES TO A COMPUTER SYSTEM

In order for an on-board minicomputer to receive an assortment of voltage signals, analyze their meaning and send out a controlling or corrected signal to the ignition or fuel injection system, for example, it is necessary that all of the logic circuits discussed above be used within the electronic control system. Some logic circuits will supply the required function under certain conditions, while others alone or in combination with another must perform the necessary output information that engine systems need to operate under all types of conditions. Consequently, both NAND and NOR gates, which are combinations of the single circuit AND, OR and NOT gates, are used extensively within the computer circuitry.

A circuit that is designed to output a voltage 1, when both inputs (*A* and *B*) have the same value, is not available to-date from one single logic circuit alone. Therefore, a combination of several of the logic circuits illustrated above must be used to operate in such a mode. Such a circuit is illustrated in Fig. 3-28, while Fig. 3-29 shows the truth table that proves the facts of such a system.

XOR, ADDER CIRCUITS

Another logic gate which is commonly used for comparison of two binary numbers (used to add binary numbers) is the XOR gate. If both inputs are the same (1 + 1), then the output is zero. A 1, now called a carry, is placed in the next place value to be added with any bits in that place value. Fig. 3-30(a) illustrates an XOR gate schematic symbol, truth table, and logic symbol. In the XOR gate, the output is high only when one input or the other is high, but not both.

A typical digital automotive circuit that performs the addition of two binary bits is illustrated in Fig. 3-30(b) and is commonly known as a half-adder, because it produces the sum and any necessary carry as shown in the accompanying truth table.

Since a half-adder is not provided with an input to accept a carry from a previous place value, a circuit known as a 'full-adder' is used when required [Fig. 3-30(c)]. Cou-

Truth table

Inputs A B	Output C
0 0	0
0 1	1
1 0	1
1 1	0

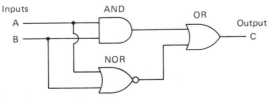

FIGURE 3-28 Typical combination AND, NOR, and OR gate logic circuit arrangement.

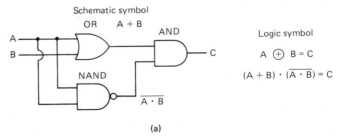

(a)

FIGURE 3-30(a) An XOR gate schematic symbol, truth table, and logic symbol.

Schematic symbol

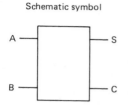

Truth table

A	B	C	S
0	0	0	0
0	1	0	1
1	0	0	1
1	1	1	0

Schematic symbol

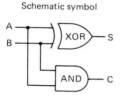

Logic symbol

$$S = A\overline{B} + \overline{A}B$$
$$C = AB$$

FIGURE 3-30(b) Half-adder circuit schematic symbol and truth table.

Schematic symbol

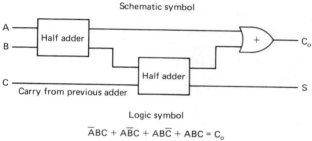

Carry from previous adder

Logic symbol

$$\overline{A}BC + A\overline{B}C + AB\overline{C} + ABC = C_o$$
$$A\overline{B}\,\overline{C} + \overline{A}B\overline{C} + ABC + \overline{A}\,\overline{B}C = S$$

(c)

FIGURE 3-30(c) Full-adder circuit schematic and logic symbol.

pling a number of full-adder circuits together in series allows the addition of binary numbers with as many digits as necessary to handle the information being generated.

A good example of where full-adder circuits are used is in a typical hand-held calculator. It performs all of the arithmetic operations, together with several other logic circuits. This configuration is required because for computations to be made subtraction is changed to addition, multiplication becomes repeated addition, and division becomes repeated subtraction.

SEQUENTIAL MEMORY LOGIC CIRCUITS

The various combinations of logic circuits discussed so far have mainly involved the use of the AND, OR and NOT gates, with the output of each system being controlled by the actual input signals. Consequently, these circuits are known as combinational logic circuits. The basis of semiconductor computer memories rely on these sequential logic circuits, since they hold or retain information even after the input signal has been removed.

It is desirable in certain circumstances to employ a logic circuit which is capable of retaining previous input signals or past logic states. This circuit is called a sequential logic system, because the actual sequence of past input signals/values and the logic state at the time determines the present output state or mode. Such a circuit can be put together by interconnecting two NAND gates, as is shown in Fig. 3-31(a). This type of sequential logic circuit is commonly referred to as an *R-S* (Reset-Set) Flip-Flop, since it describes the action of the logic level changes.

For example, in Fig. 3-31(a), note that, when *S* is high (a 1 signal) and *R* is low (a 0 signal), the output *Q* is set to a high (1), where it will stay regardless of whether *S* is high (1) or low (0). In other words, the high (1) state of *S* is latched into the state of *Q*, and the only way *Q* can become unlatched (to a 0 signal) is to allow *R* to go high (1) and *S* to go low (a 0 signal). This action will reset the latch. Also notice from the truth table that *R* and *S* must not be high (1) at the same time; otherwise the two gates would be opposing or bucking one another, and this action would create an output in a flip-flop condition or an uncertain state.

Schematic symbol

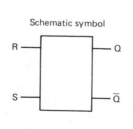

Logic diagram

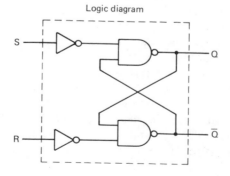

Truth table

Inputs		Outputs	
S	R	Q_1	$\overline{Q}_1$
0	0	Q_0	$\overline{Q}_0$
0	1	0	1
1	0	1	0
1	1	·	·

· State is uncertain subscripts

0 before inputs
1 after inputs

FIGURE 3-31(a) Sequential memory R-S (Reset-Set) flip-flop logic circuit.

(a)

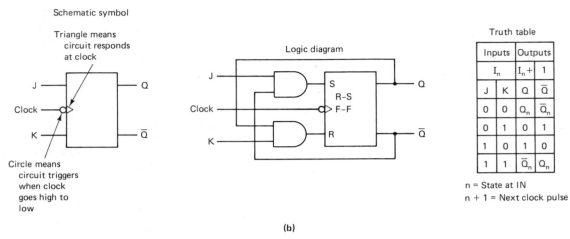

Schematic symbol

Triangle means
circuit responds
at clock

Logic diagram

Truth table

Circle means
circuit triggers
when clock
goes high to
low

n = State at IN
n + 1 = Next clock pulse

(b)

FIGURE 3-31(b) Sequential memory J-K (uncertain state) flip-flop logic circuit.

This uncertain state could be solved by using what is known as a *J-K* flip-flop, which is illustrated in Figure 3-31(b). This arrangement can be obtained from the use of an *R-S* flip-flop arrangement (a synchronized one) with an additional logic gate, as shown in the figure. When the input signal of both *J* and *K* are high (1), then the flip-flop will change to a different state at a particular time that is determined by a timing pulse called a "clock applied," which is shown in the circuit illustration at the terminal by a triangle symbol. The small circle at the clock terminal indicates that the circuit responds only when the clock switches from a high (1) level to a low level (0). If no circle were present in a clock circuit diagram, then the circuit would respond only when the clock switched from a low (0) level to a high (1) level.

SYNCHRONOUS CLOCK COUNTER

Synchronous counters are the basis of digital clocks and are employed extensively in circuits that convert binary values (base 2 system) to decimal numbers (base 10 system), as was discussed earlier in this chapter. These synchronous counters are made up from a succession of *J-K* flip-flops. Figure 3-32 illustrates a four-stage synchronous counter, so named because all stages are triggered at the same time by the same clock pulse signal. Since the clock has a 4 stage unit, it counts 2 (2 to the power 4), which equals 16 clock pulses, before it returns to a starting position. Since the system is digital in nature (ON = 1 or OFF = 0), these waveforms are also shown in Fig. 3-32 as they would appear at each *Q* output.

Because of this waveform, it becomes an easy matter to employ this type of circuitry for any circuit that requires a count to be monitored in order to activate/deactivate a

signal. It could also be used for generating other timing pulses and is particularly helpful for establishing any engine timing sequence or other circuit requiring timed responses. Various engine-monitored systems can be accessed during trouble-shooting by withdrawing stored trouble codes from the computer memory system. See each manufacturer's ECM system description for the correct procedure. Typical systems that employ "counters" for their monitoring system are such items as:

1. Detonation sensor, with the counter increasing from 0 to 255 and repeating.

2. Oxygen sensor counter, which also ranges from 0 to 255 before it is automatically reset.

3. Fuel integrator (makes temporary changes in the amount of fuel delivered to the engine during closed loop operation); the counter operates with a nominal value of 128 and which varies slightly based upon a rich or lean condition. This value can vary between engine manufacturer and from engine to engine.

4. Block-learn memory, which operates similar to the fuel integrator during closed loop operation, with 128 being the nominal value.

5. Idle air-control motor, which is used to control engine rpm during closed throttle conditions to prevent stalling when loads are applied at idle. Counter operates from 0 to 255 counts.

6. Engine load counter, which is based upon the amount of air entering each cylinder in grams per second. Arrived at by taking the intake airflow divided by the engine rpm. Counter operates between 0 and 255 counts.

7. The ignition cycle counter counts the number of ON/CRANK/OFF cycles of the ignition switch since a trou-

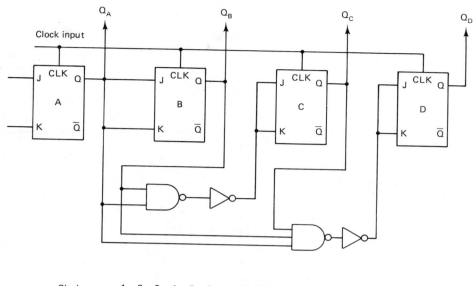

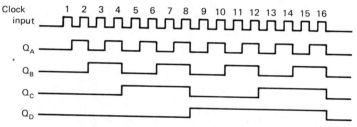

FIGURE 3-32 Four-stage synchronous counter with clock input circuit.

QA, B, C and D are the clock counter outputs

ble code was stored. Operates on a 0 to 50 cycle display, then resets to zero, and erases from memory the stored trouble code.

More detailed examples of the operation of these counters can be found in Chapter 7, which discusses General Motors ECM's. Employing a series of clock stages allows storing the digits of a binary number. If the storage is temporary, the combination of the various clock stages is known as a *register*, while if the storage is permanent, then it is referred to as *memory*.

NOTE: All of the logic gates discussed herein are so small that literally hundreds of them can actually be placed in the area of a . (dot). The number of gates that can actually be placed on a single integrated chip has mushroomed over the years with the advancement in technology of producing silicon chips. For example, consider the following advancements:

- 1960: (SSI = small scale integration), 10–12 gates per chip.
- 1969: (MSI = medium scale integration), 1000 gates per chip.

- Early 1970's: (LSI = large scale integration) to VLSI (very large scale integration), 50,000+ gates per chip.

ANALOG TO DIGITAL CONVERTER

So far we have discussed the basic operation of the various logic gates used within the CPU (central processing unit) to perform a number of different tasks related to its successful operation. You may recollect that the engine and vehicle sensors that are employed to monitor the various systems (see Fig. 3-2) produce an analog voltage signal, while the computer is designed to operate only on *digital* signals.

Therefore, in order to supply a continuous input to the computer of the constantly changing conditions of both the engine and vehicle in digital form, we must employ what is commonly called an ADC (analog to digital converter). The type of computer and bit size employed determines just how fast this ADC must operate. This can be as quick as a few millionths of a second to as long as a second.

The analog signals from the sensors produce an output sine much like a wave (Fig. 2-11), while the computer requires an input signal which is digital (either ON or OFF), (Fig. 2-12), with ON represented by a binary number 1 and

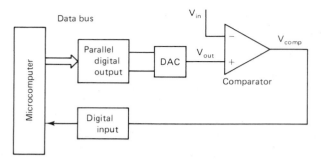

FIGURE 3-33 ADC (analog to digital converter) system circuitry.

with OFF by 0. Figure 3-33 illustrates in line diagram form one method that is employed to produce this conversion.

In Fig. 3-33, a DAC (digital to analog) converter and a voltage comparator are used, with the input signal to the DAC being in binary form. This signal is generated at the parallel output of the computer, beginning with a minimum value and increasing to its maximum. The output from the DAC or V_{out} is only one of the inputs fed to the comparator, while the other input signal originates at V_{in}, which is the actual sensor analog input voltage. If the analog voltage value at V_{in} is greater than V_{out} from the DAC, then the voltage output signal from the comparator V_{comp} would be a low logic level. On the other hand, if the V_{in} analog signal is lower than the V_{out} signal from the DAC, then the output voltage signal from the comparator would be a high logic level.

The voltage output signal (binary number of 1) from the computer immediately causes the DAC output to be higher than the analog V_{in} signal. This will cause the comparator output to be high, which will halt the computer and prevent it from altering the binary number input any further. Since the computer can only recognize a binary number, it is this number that indicates to the computer the value of the analog input voltage signal V_{in}. Continuous sampling of the analog input voltage signal is carried out by the computer so that it can determine when to reset and start the binary number generation all over again. In this way, a binary number which is equivalent to the changing analog input voltage signal is being output from the computer on a continuing basis. The output voltage signal from the comparator is always fed back to the computer through its digital input.

Figure 3-33 illustrates the analog to digital conversion signal in its simplified form. Let's look now at just what actually transpires within the CPU to switch this analog input signal to an actual digital signal that it can interpret. To consider an application, let's look at how the coolant temperature sensor used on the engine transfers its changing analog signal and converts it into a digital signal for various temperature readings.

The coolant temperature sensor is mounted on the en-

gine and relays temperature information to the ECM (electronic control module). The ECM monitors a 5 volt reference signal, which it applied to the coolant temperature sensor signal circuit through a resistor in the ECM. Note that the coolant sensor is in reality a thermistor, which means that it changes its internal resistance as its temperature changes. These concepts are treated in Chapter 4. Specifically, when the sensor is cold, such as when starting up an engine which has been sitting for some time, the sensor resistance is high, and the ECM monitors a high signal voltage. As the engine coolant warms up however, the internal resistance of the sensor will decrease and cause a similar decrease in the reference voltage signal. Therefore, the ECM will then interpret this reduced voltage signal as signifying a warm engine. The coolant temperature sensor range will vary slightly between various engine/vehicle manufacturers, but normally this is between −40°F to 306°F (−40°C to 152°C). At the low temperature end of the scale, namely −40° F/C, the resistance of the sensor would be 100,000 ohms, while at 266°F (130°C), its internal resistance would have dropped to only 70 ohms. Figure 3-34 illustrates how a temperature of 150°F (65.5°C), which is an analog signal, is converted from analog to digital within the A/D converter. In Fig. 3-34 we see a typical upward moving sine wave which is representative of the changing voltage output signal from the coolant sensor as the engine coolant temperature increases because of the decreasing resistance value of the sensor. At a temperature of 150°F, the sensor analog output voltage is sampled by the A/D converter which converts values into a *binary number value* or code.

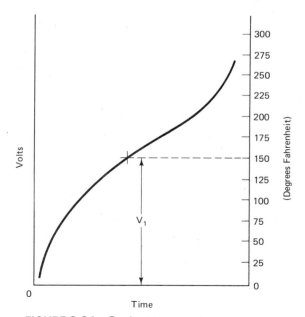

FIGURE 3-34 Coolant temperature versus analog output voltage signal.

The A/D controller uses the binary code and refers to a *look-up* table that is stored within the computer memory to determine the equivalent temperature in degrees F or C from this series of binary numbers. The 150°F voltage reading from the sensor is placed in a temporary storage register such as R2. (See Fig. 3-35.) The CPU controller then goes through a comparison check of the stored binary code numbers equivalent to 150°F on a bit by bit basis using an OR logic gate (see logic gate information in this chapter) and then stores the comparisons in another register—R1, in this example. Basically, an OR logic gate has the capability to output a binary number of 1 if either of the inputs to the OR gate is 1. If, however, both inputs are 1 or 0, then the output will be the binary number 0! When the binary codes are the same, each comparison, bit by bit, will produce an output code from the OR gate that has a 0 in each bit position in register R1.

When this occurs, the controller is alerted that the correct temperature code has been located in the stored *lookup* table. Once matched, the controller uses the warm-up time code in the look-up table that corresponds to the 150°F code. For 150°F, the digital code is 10010110, which in this example represents a warm-up time of 4 minutes.

Since the engine coolant temperature sensor is used to calculate the control parameters for most of the other ECM-controlled systems, this digital produced number through the A/D converter becomes critical to the successful operation of the engine. In Fig. 3-35, we have only shown temperature changes of 10°F. In reality, the computer look-up table would be constructed in multiples of 1°F changes, so that very close control of the engine fuel and ignition systems can be maintained under all conditions of operation. Figure 3-36 illustrates just how the analog to digital (A/D) converter would output the temperature reading based upon the analog signal which has been converted to binary number codes that are equivalent to the 150°F engine coolant temperature. This example is similar to the way that many of the other sensor signals would be received and converted to a digital signal for control of the engine systems.

DIGITAL TO ANALOG CONVERTER

It is often necessary to employ a DAC (digital to analog converter) in the computer system to convert binary signals (numbers) from the computer into analog output voltages that are proportional to the binary number that has been encoded in the actual input signals. These DAC's are available in a wide variety of versions. However, one of the most widely used types of DAC's is one that has 8 bit inputs and a 0 to 5 volt output range to match the sensors used on

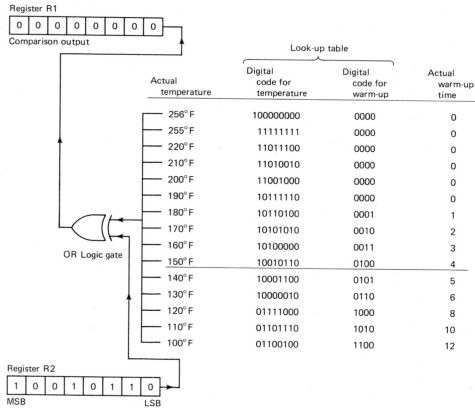

Register R1

| 0 | 0 | 0 | 0 | 0 | 0 | 0 | 0 |

Comparison output

Look-up table

Actual temperature	Digital code for temperature	Digital code for warm-up	Actual warm-up time
256°F	100000000	0000	0
255°F	11111111	0000	0
220°F	11011100	0000	0
210°F	11010010	0000	0
200°F	11001000	0000	0
190°F	10111110	0000	0
180°F	10110100	0001	1
170°F	10101010	0010	2
160°F	10100000	0011	3
150°F	10010110	0100	4
140°F	10001100	0101	5
130°F	10000010	0110	6
120°F	01111000	1000	8
110°F	01101110	1010	10
100°F	01100100	1100	12

OR Logic gate

Register R2

| 1 | 0 | 0 | 1 | 0 | 1 | 1 | 0 |

MSB   LSB

Input from sensor

FIGURE 3-35 Temperature look-up table, OR logic gate, and registers.

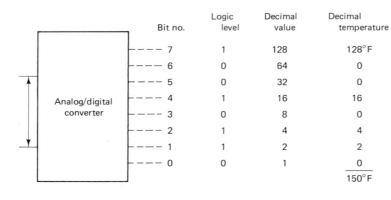

Bit no.	Logic level	Decimal value	Decimal temperature
7	1	128	128°F
6	0	64	0
5	0	32	0
4	1	16	16
3	0	8	0
2	1	4	4
1	1	2	2
0	0	1	0
			150°F

FIGURE 3-36 Analog/digital converter binary to Decimal number 8 bit temperature scale.

the engine and vehicle. The 0 output represents an OFF signal, and the 5 represents an ON signal.

Figure 3-37 illustrates a typical DAC using a parallel input interface to examine and control an 8-bit DAC, together with two operational amplifiers, which are also discussed in this chapter. The 8 bits are written into the parallel interface and stored in what are commonly called data latches. The digital output from each latch is always zero if the bit is low, and 5 volts if the bit is high (1).

The first op amp in this simplified system is what is known as a summing amp with a gain (output) of $-Rf/Ri$. The second op-amp is designed for a gain of -1, which indicates that it is, in fact, only an inverter. The net result of using these two op-amps is to scale each individual bit of the parallel interface by a predetermined factor, and then to add the resultant voltages together. The easiest way to

understand this DAC is to give an actual example and calculate it to its conclusion.

Familiarize yourself first with the diagram shown in Fig. 3-37. Then consider the following situation. Suppose that for instructional purposes we assume that only bit 0 is high, and the other 7 bits are low. Then what kind of an analog output might we have at the V_{out} terminal.

EXAMPLE 1

Bit 0 is high, and all others are low. Therefore,

$$V_{out} = 5 \text{ volts}$$

$$1 \frac{(1)}{256} + 0 \frac{(1)}{128} + \frac{(1)}{64} + \ldots + 0 \frac{(1)}{2}$$

Therefore, V_{out} now equals (5/256) carried to $V_{out} = 0.0195$ volts

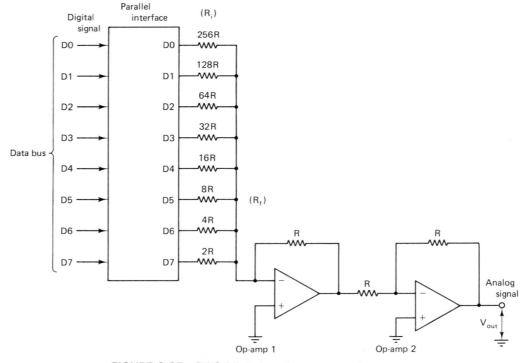

FIGURE 3-37 DAC (digital analog converter) system.

EXAMPLE 2

Bits 0 and 7 are high, all others are low. Therefore,

$$V_{out} = 5 \text{ volts}$$

$$1\frac{(1)}{256} + 0\frac{(1)}{128} + 0\frac{(1)}{64} \ldots + 1\frac{(1)}{2}$$

carried to $V_{out} = (645/256)$. Therefore, $V_{out} = 2.5195$ volts.

Although you would expect the output voltage from the DAC system to be in analog form (wavy sine), because the voltage levels would be output at constantly changing discrete signals of the high and low values (ON and OFF) reaction within the DAC, the actual output would still be a digital signal similar to that shown in Fig. 3-38. This results from the binary number at the input increasing in graduations of one bit at a time from its minimum to its maximum value so that it provides a total possible combination of 256 different voltage levels. With this many levels and although the output appears in step form, if we were to draw an average value line through all of these stepped signals, then the result would closely resemble an "analog voltage signal output." If the sampling rate were less than 256 different levels, then the analog voltage output would not be as smooth as that shown in Fig. 3-38.

DATA AND ADDRESS BUSES

Figure 3-3 represented the computer unit in its simplest form, namely that of a block diagram representing the input and output devices, the computer memory, the CPU (central processing unit), and the input/output interface. Within

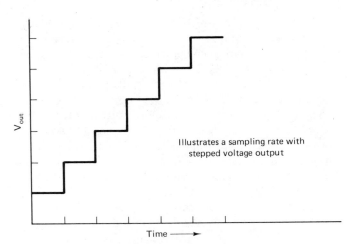

FIGURE 3-38 Typical stepped output voltage from a DAC (digital analog converter) system to form a near analog voltage signal.

the various sections of the computer, these devices are all interconnected by signal lines commonly known either as *address buses* or *data buses* and which are similar to the copper wires used in a typical automotive electrical system. The difference is that the buses are etched or burned onto a chip by the use of laser technology and assembled into a circuit board to form a complete system.

These buses can be as thin as 1.5 microns (0.00006 inches) in size. Figure 3-39 illustrates both the address and data buses in a typical microcomputer and shows how they interconnect the CPU with the memory and input/output interface components.

When the CPU requests information from memory, it does so by calling up this data from its allocated memory address. This information is drawn from either the PROM

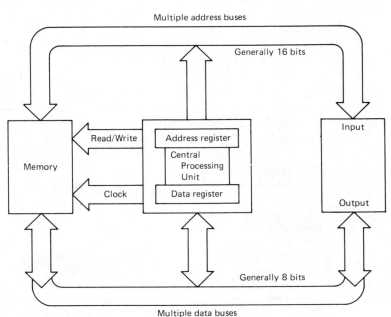

FIGURE 3-39 Data and address buses within a typical on-board ECM (electronic control module) circuit.

or ROM unit, which are both hardwired (memory is non-changeable), or from the RAM memory that is continually being updated during computer operation as the various sensors relay changing data to the system.

PROM, ROM and RAM are described in greater detail later in this section. PROM means (programmable read only memory); ROM, (read only memory); and RAM, (random access memory). Each address in ROM and PROM memory stores fixed data, while accessing an address in RAM results in the latest up-to-date information being received from the various sensor systems while the engine/vehicle is running. The address of each location in memory never changes, but can be likened to that of a mailbox.

Keep in mind, however that although the address may not change, the contents will change when retained data (picking up mail) is removed and when new data (new mail) is inserted. Each address with its character bits of information is stored in the CPU as a binary number in a temporary data latch type memory called a register. The size of the register depends upon the computer design, but it can be either an 8, 16, 32 or 64 bit system. For example, if the address register contains a 16 bit system, then the CPU has direct access, when required, to 65,536 memory locations or addresses, which total is arrived at by taking the binary base 2 system to a power of 16.

Informational data is sent *to* the CPU via the various data buses, while information signals on the address buses come *from* the CPU and are sent to the various devices attached to the bus. Therefore, information signals on the data bus can be sent or received at the CPU by the data register, which in effect makes the data bus capable of two-way informational flow. The address bus is only capable of single direction flow.

Keep in mind, however, that although the data-bus is capable of transmitting information signals in both directions, it can only do this in one direction at a time. In order for the memory storage system to know in what direction the information data signals are flowing, the CPU is designed to provide a control signal that indicates whether the information is to be read from or written into memory.

This control signal goes through a timing system that appears as shown in Fig. 3-40. Anytime that the read/write signal is high (1), then the CPU is requesting or reading information from a specifically accessed memory location. If, on the other hand, the read/write signal is low (0), then the CPU is trying to insert (write) information into a particular memory address location. The action illustrated in Fig. 3-40 can be listed as follows:

1. The computer is commanded to fetch (read) data from a specific memory address. For example, location number 9.

2. The CPU activates the read/write signal to the high (1) level in order to alert the memory for a read rather than a write cycle of operation, as shown in the second line in the figure.

3. The specific address, for example, location 9 (binary number 1001) is placed on the address bus, or on the third line down in the figure.

4. When memory location 9 recognizes that its address has been signalled, its then places a copy of its mail (data or instruction) on the data bus as shown on the bottom line.

5. Although this information is extracted very quickly, to ensure that the information/data does have time to receive and relay this signal, the CPU will momentarily delay its action. Then the CPU will open the necessary logic gate circuitry between the data bus and the CPU data register to lock address 9 data into the CPU. The CPU clock (timing signal) tells the memory when it can take and release control of the data bus. This read cycle is terminated when the clock signal switches from high (1) to low (0) within the time frame that the read signal is valid.

MICROCOMPUTER CONTROL

Voltage signals generated by the system control section allows the computer to perform its designed task related to the CPU (central processing unit) and memory and input-output (I/O) interface (Fig. 3-39). The control section therefore becomes the coordinating device within the system. It does this by generating a signal through its *clock signal generators circuitry* shown in Fig. 3-41, which synchro-

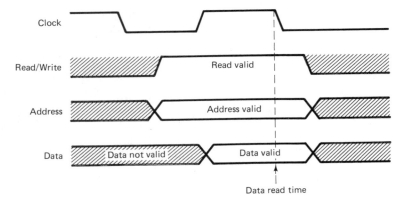

FIGURE 3-40 Typical timing diagram for CPU (central processing unit) memory read and write functions. (The clock provides the synchronization for the system).

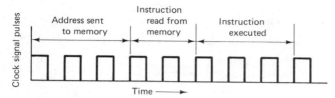

FIGURE 3-41 Microcomputer clock signal generator circuitry.

nizes all of the on-going computer devices to ensure that they output their voltage signals in an order and sequence which will not interfere with one another.

System Layout

Figure 3-42 illustrates a typical system layout for a minicomputer in line form, while Figure 3-43 shows the same componentry but in an acceptable block form, similar to how it would appear inside an assembled minicomputer on a vehicle.

CPU (CENTRAL PROCESSING UNIT)

The brain or heart of the minicomputer is the CPU, which contains the following devices:

1. Control section

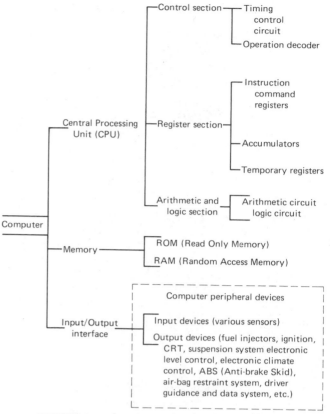

FIGURE 3-42 General arrangement of the on-board electronic control unit system.

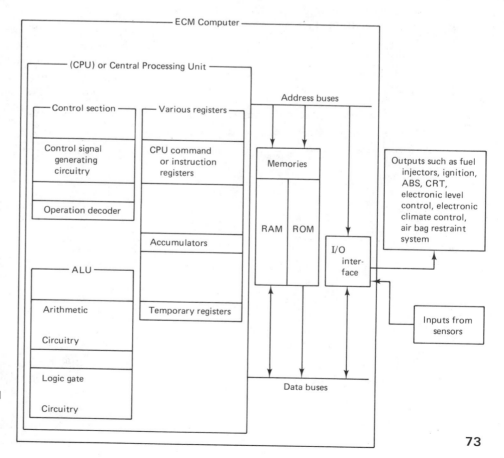

FIGURE 3-43 Typical layout and arrangement of operating components within the on-board computer system.

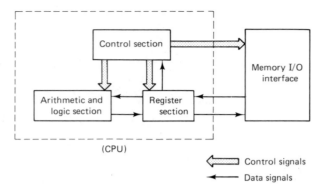

FIGURE 3-44 CPU (central processing unit) control and data signal flow.

2. Arithmetic and logic section
3. Register section

Figure 3-44 shows how these devices are interconnected within the CPU.

CONTROL SECTIONS

Within the control section (Fig. 3-45) of the CPU are the control signal generating circuitry and a command decoder. Program instructions from the computer memory are accessed by the control section as needed and are temporarily stored in the command register where they are then decoded by the operation decoder. From here, signals are sent via the buses to the relevant parts of the microcomputer to carry out the necessary action. These signals are timed by the control circuit generator, with the control signals performing the following operations:

1. Arithmetic calculations,
2. Relaying data from one area of the computer to another,
3. If necessary, jumping to (accessing) another instruction during running of a program,

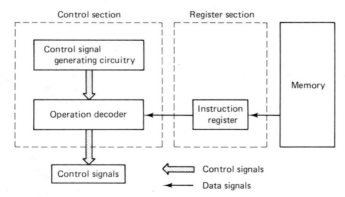

FIGURE 3-45 On-board computer control section data and control signal flow arrangement.

4. Inputting or outputting data to or from the microcomputer,
5. Stopping computer operations at any time.

In summation, the control section or unit of the CPU is designed to direct the flow of information between the memory and the arithmetic/logic unit, as well as between the CPU and the input/output devices. Therefore we can safely say that it coordinates the computer operation.

ARITHMETIC AND LOGIC SECTION

This section of the computer actually carries out the processing of informational data under the guidance of the control section, as was discussed above. Within the solid-state devices of the arithmetic and logic section are the various logic gates such as the AND, OR, NOT, NAND, and NOR systems. All of the addition, multiplication, square root extraction and any other necessary calculations are performed here.

The sequence of events involved in doing these calculations is that the information from the memory or input/output interface is temporarily stored within the register section. When this information is required, the logic section withdraws the data from these temporary registers or accumulators, where it then sends the data to either the arithmetic or logic circuitry. Any additional calculations are then carried out, and the results of these are sent to the relevant accumulators: to the memory (RAM), or to the input/output interfaces.

Logical operations involve the comparison of two items of data to determine if they are equal or not. If not, then the computer (CPU) determines which one is larger. This action is shown in schematic form in Fig. 3-46.

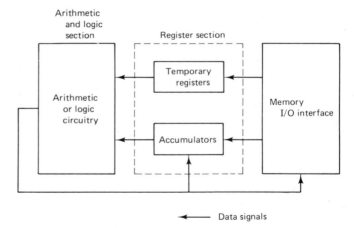

FIGURE 3-46 On-board computer data signal flow paths within the arithmetic and logic sections of the CPU.

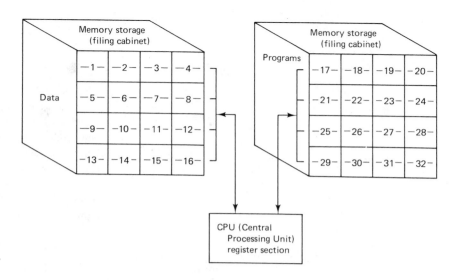

FIGURE 3-47 The CPU (central processing unit) register section can access memory (filing cabinet), and data can be read from or written into a specific memory location by calling up a specific address (drawer number).

REGISTER SECTION

This section is designed to store data or programs temporarily until they are required for use by the arithmetic or logic sections or by the control section (Fig. 3-47).

Several basic types of registers are used, which are the *instruction registers*, address register, storage register, and *temporary registers* (accumulators), which store data.

Before the CPU can process a command, it must first break the command information into two distinct parts. First, it must advise the system to add, multiply, or compare within the instruction register, and then it must give the address of the data to be accessed to the address register.

The storage register temporarily stores data that has been taken from memory immediately prior to processing. The accumulators or temporary registers also temporarily store the results of ongoing arithmetic calculations. Therefore, when each operation or addition, subtraction, etc. are completed, the answers are accumulated into this particular register.

The three main parts of the computer—namely, the memory, the arithmetic/logic section, and the registers—all work together to process a desired request of information data effectively.

DATA/INSTRUCTION PROCESSING

When the computer is asked for information, the control unit initiates the necessary activity within the computer. This is often referred to as a *machine cycle*, and it involves two major operations. These are:

1. An *I* or instruction cycle—
   (a) Withdrawn or pulled from memory by the control unit is the next instruction to be performed.
   (b) Decoding of this instruction/data by the control unit.
   (c) Directing and inserting the necessary action into the instruction register by the control unit.

   (d) Inserting the necessary instruction into the address register to indicate where the desired data is located by the control unit.

2. An *E* or execution cycle—
   (e) Information stored in the address register is used by the control unit to retrieve data from main memory and insert it into the storage register within the arithmetic logic unit (ALU).
   (f) The control unit directs the ALU to perform the required operation based upon the information withdrawn from the instruction register.
   (g) The ALU carries out the desired command.
   (h) The result of this action computed within the ALU is then transferred to the accumulator by the control unit.

Figure 3-48 illustrates graphically just what the sequence of events is in the two main steps of the machine cycle that were explained in Steps 1 and 2 above (a through h). Note that the upper half of the circle represents the *I* (instruction) part of the process or Steps a through d, while the lower

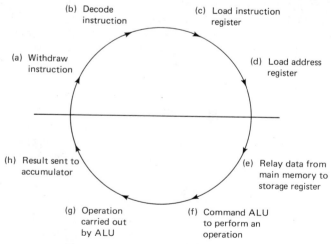

FIGURE 3-48 Sequence of events involved in a computer machine cycle.

half represents the *E* (execution) part of the cycle from Steps e through h.

COMPUTER MEMORY

Three types of *memory* contained within the microcomputer are the following ones:

1. ROM (read only memory), allows the computer to read a predetermined pattern of zeros and ones (binary notation). See Fig. 3-9. This predetermined information is permanently stored in ROM at the time of manufacture. A ROM is similar to a dictionary in that a certain address which is accessed in ROM will result in a predetermined output of information.

   The ROM is hardwired or soldered into the printed circuit boards at the time of manufacture and therefore cannot be changed. This programmed information can only be read by the ECM. Therefore, the ROM contains the overall fuel injection system control algorithms. Since the ROM is hardwired into the system at the time of manufacture, the ROM will be retained if the battery voltage is disconnected. Therefore, the ROM unit is said to be nonvolatile. Some systems may employ an EEROM (electrical erasable read only memory), in which the memory can be erased and new information programmed into the device.

2. The PROM system (programmable read only memory) also consists of stored programs and data that have been hardwired. This means that a circuit board has been constructed and arranged so that specific information is retained and generally cannot be erased or changed even when the battery is disconnected.

   In some systems, the PROM is an electronic memory which may be permanent (nonvolatile) or semipermanent (erasable electronically or with ultraviolet light), and therefore can be programmed one or more times. This type of PROM is generally referred to as EE-PROM (electrical erasable programmable read only memory).

   PROM chips are designed for use in particular vehicles and include information on engine calibration data, transmission, vehicle weight, and rear-axle ratio. Therefore, the PROM should never be intermixed between computers in different vehicles, even though they may be of the same manufacture.

   PROM IC's (integrated circuits) can be removed if faulty and replaced with a new unit of the same design and program. There will be more on this topic in the troubleshooting and service section. The PROM is a nonvolatile memory—doesn't need battery power to be retained—that is only read by the ECM. Some vehicles have been manufactured using two PROM's. However, most use only one. The ECM is able to tell what specific PROM unit has been installed in the system, and it will indicate the actual PROM either by model or part number when the mechanic/technician accesses the diagnostic system of the ECM during a troubleshooting sequence. If, however, the wrong PROM is installed into an ECM, then the PROM may become unreadable to the ECM. Should this ever happen, then the ECM is programmed to run the engine on a *backup fuel mode* that is retained in ROM.

   When this occurs, however, a trouble code will be set in memory, and the *Check Engine*, or *Service Engine Soon or Now* light will illuminate on the vehicle instrument panel to warn the driver of a problem.

3. RAM or random access memory is data that can be erased or changed after it has been read. It is sometimes called primary memory. The stored information in RAM is immediately available when addressed regardless of the previous memory address location. Since the memory words can be selected in any order, there is equal access time to all. This unit is the decision-making center for the central processing unit (CPU). It, in effect, becomes the microprocessor's *scratch pad*, and the processor can write into or read from this memory as needed. This memory is *volatile*, meaning that it requires a constant battery voltage in order to be retained. Therefore, a loss of voltage quite simply means a loss of stored memory in the system.

   The volatile memory in RAM contains the following information:

   (a) Block learn and fuel integrator values (pulse counts).
   (b) Malfunction codes—pending flags.
   (c) Ignition counter (counts the number of ON/OFF cycles of the ignition switch since a trouble code was stored. Usually 50 cycles, after which time the system will reset to 0 and the trouble code is erased from memory.
   (d) FDP (Fuel Data Panel) information if used and OAT (outside air temperature)
   (e) Check sums

   Unlike the PROM unit, however, the information stored in the RAM unit can be lost if the battery power is disconnected from the system. The major function of the RAM unit is simply to store informational data that is to be erased or changed. Data delivered by the sensors is stored in the RAM unit until summoned by the microprocessor, or superseded by more recent input data. Informational data is erased when the ignition system is switched off. Therefore, it must be continuously updated during engine operation. Intermediate storage of calculated values for subsequent processing also occurs in this unit.

4. CALPAC or CALPAK (both terms are used), is a de-

vice on General Motors Corporation vehicles that controls continued fuel delivery if other parts of the ECM are damaged. It is basically a vehicle *limp home* system.

This back-up mode is a rough fuel-spark calibration system built into ROM. Therefore the ECM will operate in back-up when the PROM is not readable for any reason.

When the vehicle is in the back-up mode, it is characterized by the following symptoms:

(a) Poor driveability and performance,
(b) Erratic or no ECM serial data,
(c) *Check, Service Soon* or *Service Now* engine warning light ON
(d) ISC (idle speed control) motor is inoperative
(e) ECM diagnostics may not be accessible
(f) FDP (fuel data panel) and OAT (outside air temperature), if so equipped, reads zero or becomes blank

The CALPAK module can be removed through an access door in the ECM. It must be removed from a faulty ECM and installed in a new service replacement unit along with the PROM module, since the service replacement ECM does not contain either the PROM or the CALPAK units. If, however, either the CALPAK or the PROM are damaged, then new units must be ordered and installed.

These four types of memory should not be confused with the various registers also used within the computer. These registers store information data temporarily for immediate use only. For this reason, the memory circuit is often referred to as *main memory* in order to distinguish it from the registers or accumulators. Figure 3-47 (cited previously) illustrates how main memory differs from that stored in the registers for immediate use. Informational data that is to be read from or written into a specific memory location or filing drawer cabinet is first of all identified via an address bus similar to that shown earlier in Fig. 3-39. Since large amounts of data are constantly being entered (written) into and removed (read) from memory, all of the various loca-

tions for information storage must be identified by their own address. Therefore, each location has a number assigned to it in digital form, as shown in Fig. 3-47.

INPUT/OUTPUT INTERFACE SYSTEM

The ECM contains power supplies, input/output (I/O) devices, memory, and the processing unit, with the power supplies regulating the batteries 12 volt input to 5 volts for the various sensors, and with certain switches, etc. being regulated to 8 volts.

The I/O devices include analog to digital converters, signal buffers, counters, and special drivers to handle larger loads such as the fuel injectors and solenoids.

Sensors used in automobiles and trucks because of their design relay an analog type of voltage signal to the computer. In order for the computer to make sense out of these input analog signals, they must be converted into digital signals before being sent to the CPU (central processing unit). The actual process for converting analog signals into digital signals was explained in a previous section of this chapter. The input/output (I/O) interface is the device that allows data to be transferred between input and output devices, CPU and memory. Output voltage signals are amplified in order to operate electrical loads, such as the fuel injector solenoids. Figure 3-49 illustrates in simplified form the sequence of events between an input/output interface.

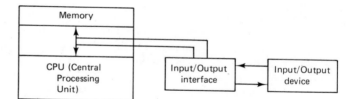

FIGURE 3-49 Computer input/output interface allows sensor input data to be understood by the CPU and storable by memory. In addition, the I/O interface reconverts output data into a language that the output device can understand and comprehend.

CHAPTER 4

Engine/Vehicle Sensors

Although the heart of the 'on-board' computer system is the electronic control unit (ECU) or electronic/engine control module (ECM), depending on the term used by each particular vehicle manufacturer, these solid-state computer devices are connected to the vehicle electric system by a conventional wiring harness fitted with a multi-pin adapter. Many passenger cars now on the market employ more than one on-board computer, with an ECM (engine control module) coordinating all engine functions such as the fuel-injection and ignition system. In addition, a BCM (body control or body computer module) handles the functions of controlling such items as the ECC (electronic comfort control) system, which incorporates the heating and air conditioning systems. The BCM also handles other optional accessories, such as the instrument panel cluster, the voice/chime module, vehicle level control, etc. The BCM is the central processor for the vehicle functions, and it therefore communicates through a data link with the ECM and the Programmer. All vehicles equipped with electronic engine and body control modules receive input information from a variety of sensors designed to monitor a specific condition on the engine or vehicle.

Most sensors are similar to simple sending units, such as an oil pressure switch or a fuel level gauge. Therefore, they are usually in an ON or an OFF condition. While the engine is running at normal operating temperature and the vehicle is moving however, the sensors are continuously feeding voltage signals back to the ECM or BCM to alter the operating parameters of the vehicle constantly for optimum efficiency. Each sensor is designed to operate either on a changing temperature or pressure condition which causes its internal resistance to change with a resultant variation in its output voltage signal.

The ECM (Electronic Control Module) generally applies and monitors a 5 volt reference signal to the sensor at all times, although some automobile sensors may operate on a voltage signal as high as 8 volts. As each sensor is subjected to either a changing temperature or pressure condition, the ECM or BCM checks each sensor input continuously and makes a decision based upon preprogrammed inputs to alter one or more operating conditions on either the engine or vehicle systems.

Once the ECM or BCM receives these sensor voltage signals, computer commands are carried out by various solenoids, small motors, and other control devices. For example, solenoids are used to control the fuel injectors and, therefore, also control the fuel flow, air bleed valves, vacuum controls, EGR, etc. Small motors are used for idle-speed control and mixture adjustment on feedback carburetor models.

If, for example, a detonation sensor interprets a "knocking" condition, the computer will retard ignition timing either directly or, on some systems, the ECM will activate a solenoid to cut off distributor vacuum advance if so used. Various methods are in use on different makes of vehicles. However, the end result is the same.

SENSORS AND SWITCHES

The number and types of sensors and switches used on any vehicle will depend upon the type of fuel-injection system used, the ignition system employed, and also on the optional accessories employed in that particular vehicle. In addition, the actual year of vehicle manufacture will also determine to a great extent just what and how many sensors/ switches are used.

Information contained within this chapter will illustrate and describe all of the various sensors/switches that may be found on vehicles. Keep in mind, however, that some or all may be found on certain vehicles. Vehicles equipped with FBC (feedback carburetors), TBI (throttle body injection), and PFI (port fuel injection) will employ many of the same sensors, but will have specific sensors/switches common to the fuel and ignition system in use for that year and make of vehicle. Regardless of the system employed, the sensor/switch function is similar in its basic operation.

An example of the number of various electrical sensors and switches available for use in a typical 1986 model GMC vehicle is illustrated in Fig. 4-1. (Refer to Fig. 3-2 to see the various ''inputs'' and ''outputs'' for a typical passenger car.

BASIC SENSOR ARRANGEMENT

All sensors are devices that are designed to convert energy from one medium to another. Sensors are activated either through heat being applied to them or by heat being reduced, while others are designed to respond to a change in pressure. Current vehicle sensors are designed to operate on an input voltage signal from the 12 volt battery system. However, because of each sensor's individual operating characteristics, a sensor's output voltage signal is designed to operate in a range of from 0 to 5 volts.

Some of the more common signals that need to be monitored on an automotive application are such items as the following: throttle position, exhaust oxygen content (air-fuel ratio), air inlet temperature, air inlet pressure, coolant temperature, oil temperature, oil pressure, etc. Sensors convert a portion of these various energies into a form that can be used by a signal processor. Because of changing engine/ vehicle operating conditions and the corresponding changing output of the sensor, a signal processor is required to monitor this change on a continuous basis. The ideal is for a stoichiometric air/fuel ratio of 14.7: 1 to be maintained under all operating conditions of ''closed-loop'' control.

NOTE: Closed-loop control is the condition that exists when the engine is at operating temperature and the on-board computer is controlling the air-fuel ratio as close to stoichiometric as possible, based upon the various feedback

signals that it receives from the different sensors. Closed-loop control is discussed in greater detail in several sections of this textbook.

Figure 4-2 illustrates a simplified diagram of the basic sensor measurement system, where the sensor itself absorbs either a heat or pressure signal from a monitored engine condition. The sensor then converts this signal into an electrical output and relays it to the signal processor. Within the signal processor, the sensor signal is amplified so that it can be sent to an analog or digital display, or alternately, it may be used to activate a specific actuator on the engine or vehicle.

Signal processing can be accomplished with either analog devices or digital devices, both of which were discussed earlier in Chapters 2 and 3. (See Figs 2-11 and 2-12.) Analog signals resemble the human voice and have a continuous waveform type signal, while a digital signal forms a series of boxes to indicate either an ON or OFF voltage condition.

Analog signal processing employs the use of amplifiers, filters, adders, multipliers, and other components, while digital signal processing employs the use of logic gates. (See Figs. 3-12 through 3-32.) In addition, digital processing requires the use of counters, binary adders, and micro-computers.

A simplified example of an analog signal is that generated from a speedometer sensor that changes continuously as the vehicle speed increases or decreases. An example of an applied digital signal that is either ON or OFF can be related to the opening and closing of a car door. When open, the interior light comes on; therefore, the signal is at its maximum of 12 volts. If, on the other hand, the door is closed, then the signal is at zero volts.

TYPES OF SENSORS

All of the various engine/vehicle sensors are described individually within this chapter. However, the physical operating characteristics of each unit depends upon the following design types:

1. Two-wire design,
2. Three-wire design,
3. Pulse-counter-type design.

Each one of these operating types is illustrated and explained below so that an understanding of just how various sensors operate can be more clearly understood.

1. *Two-wire design:* Figure 4-3 illustrates the two-wire design type of sensor, which is basically a variable resistor in series with a known-fixed resistor contained within the ECM. Three such sensors that use the two-

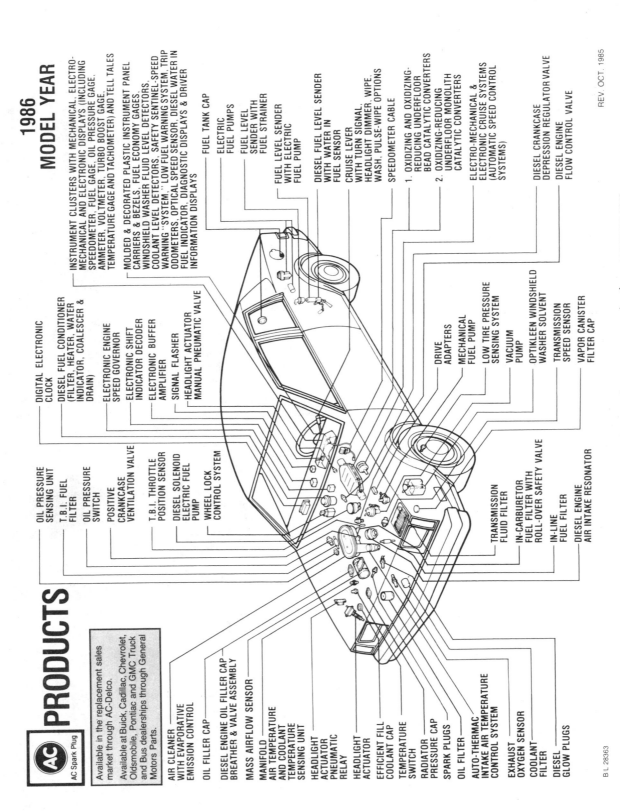

FIGURE 4-1 Typical sensors and switches used on current production passenger cars. *(Courtesy of AC Spark Plug Div. of GMC)*

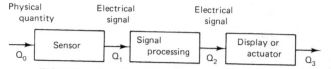

FIGURE 4-2 Simplified sensor measurement operational system.

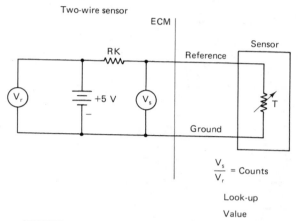

FIGURE 4-3 Basic arrangement of a two-wire design sensor unit. (*Courtesy of Cadillac Motor Car Div. of GMC*)

wire type of design are the CTS (coolant temperature sensor), MAT (manifold air temperature), and OAT (outside air temperature) units. All of these sensors operate on a varying resistance, since their resistance varies inversely with temperature (thermistor principle). Each one of these sensors is described more fully in later sections of this Chapter.

Since most sensors in use in automotive applications use a base voltage input of 5 volts (some use 8 volts), the value of the variable resistor can be determined from the base voltage along with the known voltage drop across the fixed resistor.

When checking a two-wire type of sensor for possible problems, refer to Fig. 4-4, which illustrates and describes the types of voltage readings (high or low) that might be achieved, and where to check for system opens or shorts in the microprocessor, the harness, and the sensor. The reference in the figure to 50 and 60 series codes are a direct indication to the code numbering system used by Ford Motor Company for their vehicles. However, the symptom of an intermittently high or low value when checking the sensor applies to all two-wire type sensors.

2. *Three-wire design:* Figure 4-5 illustrates the three-wire design type of sensor arrangement, which is commonly in use in TPS (throttle position sensors), MAP (manifold absolute pressure), and BARO (barometric pressure sensors). These types of sensors have a reference voltage, a ground, and a variable wiper, with the lead coming off of the wiper being the actual signal feed to the ECM. A change in the wiper's position will automatically change the signal voltage being sent back to the ECM.

Figure 4-6 illustrates how to check the sensor for possible faults, such as opens or shorts when an intermittent high or low value is achieved. As with the two-wire sensor system, the numbers 50 and 60 in the figure refer to trouble codes used in Ford Motor Company vehicles. However, the sequence can be equally applied to any three-wire sensor.

3. *Pulse counters:* Figure 4-7 illustrates the basic operation of a pulse counter. Sensors relying on this type of counting system are typically the VSS (vehicle speed sensor), the RPM or engine speed sensor, which could be a crankshaft or camshaft sensed Hall-effect type on various makes of vehicles, and also the distributor reference sensor on those vehicles employing this style of ignition system.

NOTE: Many vehicles today, particularly many General Motors manufactured units, employ a distributorless ignition system, as do some SAAB vehicles. These systems rely on either a crankshaft or camshaft type of sensor to trigger the ignition pulse. Refer to the ignition system types section in this book for further information on these types of designs.

These types of sensors are designed to create or produce a given number of pulses per engine revolution or per mile of the VSS. The ECM monitors and determines from the time between pulses just how fast the engine or vehicle is moving. As you can see from the illustration in Fig. 4-7, these timed pulses are similar in nature to the digital signals produced within the computer. This topic was discussed in Chapter 2. Also refer to Fig. 2-12.

OXYGEN SENSOR

All engines today used in gasoline engines that comply with the United States EPA (Environmental Protection Agency) and ECE (Economic Commission for Europe) exhaust emissions standards employ what is commonly known as an "oxygen" sensor, which is located in either the engine exhaust manifold or piping. See Fig. 4-8. The oxygen sensor is one of the most important sensors on the engine, since it controls the air/fuel mixture or ratio under all operating conditions of speed and load.

Stoichiometric Ratio

The purpose of the oxygen sensor is to monitor the percentage of oxygen contained within the engine exhaust gases at all times when the engine is running, so that the ECM

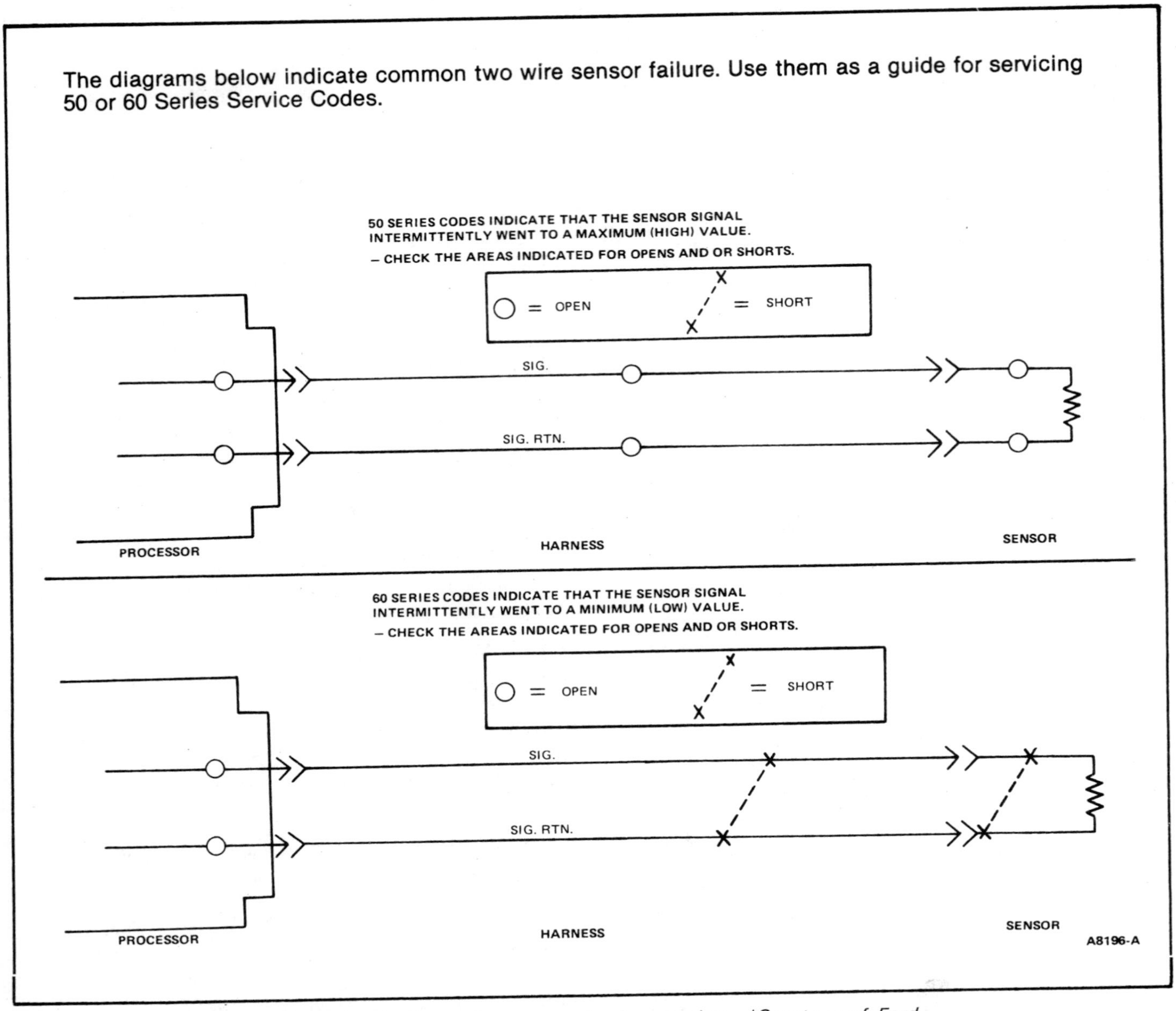

The diagrams below indicate common two wire sensor failure. Use them as a guide for servicing 50 or 60 Series Service Codes.

50 SERIES CODES INDICATE THAT THE SENSOR SIGNAL INTERMITTENTLY WENT TO A MAXIMUM (HIGH) VALUE.
— CHECK THE AREAS INDICATED FOR OPENS AND OR SHORTS.

◯ = OPEN   ╱ = SHORT

SIG.

SIG. RTN.

PROCESSOR   HARNESS   SENSOR

60 SERIES CODES INDICATE THAT THE SENSOR SIGNAL INTERMITTENTLY WENT TO A MINIMUM (LOW) VALUE.
— CHECK THE AREAS INDICATED FOR OPENS AND OR SHORTS.

◯ = OPEN   ╱ = SHORT

SIG.

SIG. RTN.

PROCESSOR   HARNESS   SENSOR   A8196-A

FIGURE 4-4 Two-wire sensor check procedure. (*Courtesy of Ford Motor Company, Dearborn, MI.*)

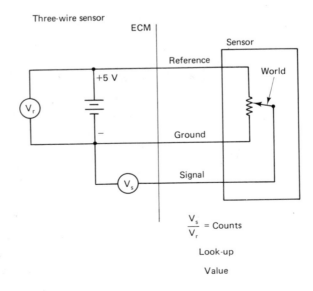

Three-wire sensor

ECM

Sensor

Reference

World

V_r +5 V

Ground

Signal

V_s

$$\frac{V_s}{V_r} = \text{Counts}$$

Look-up

Value

FIGURE 4-5 Basic arrangement of a three-wire design sensor unit. (*Courtesy of Cadillac Motor Car Div. of GMC*)

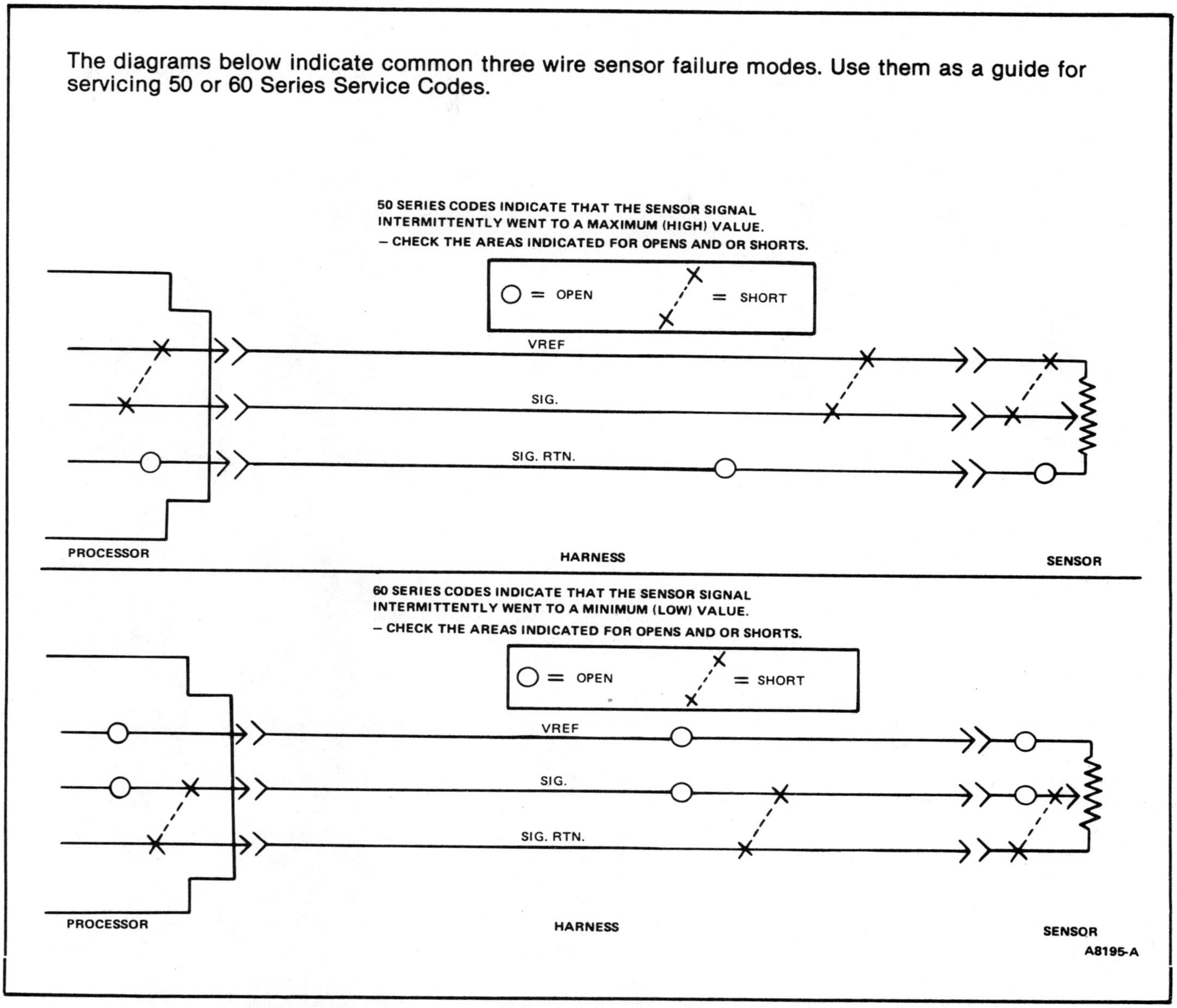

The diagrams below indicate common three wire sensor failure modes. Use them as a guide for servicing 50 or 60 Series Service Codes.

50 SERIES CODES INDICATE THAT THE SENSOR SIGNAL INTERMITTENTLY WENT TO A MAXIMUM (HIGH) VALUE.
— CHECK THE AREAS INDICATED FOR OPENS AND OR SHORTS.

◯ = OPEN   ✕ = SHORT

VREF

SIG.

SIG. RTN.

PROCESSOR   HARNESS   SENSOR

60 SERIES CODES INDICATE THAT THE SENSOR SIGNAL INTERMITTENTLY WENT TO A MINIMUM (LOW) VALUE.
— CHECK THE AREAS INDICATED FOR OPENS AND OR SHORTS.

◯ = OPEN   ✕ = SHORT

VREF

SIG.

SIG. RTN.

PROCESSOR   HARNESS   SENSOR

A8195-A

FIGURE 4-6   Three-wire sensor check procedure. (*Courtesy of Ford Motor Company, Dearborn, MI.*)

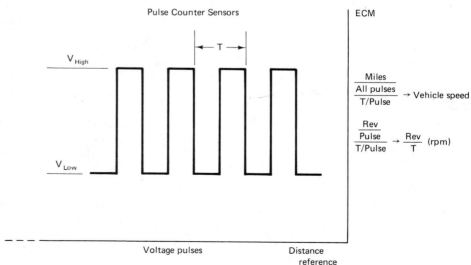

Pulse Counter Sensors

ECM

V_{High}

V_{Low}

$\dfrac{\dfrac{\text{Miles}}{\text{All pulses}}}{\text{T/Pulse}} \rightarrow$ Vehicle speed

$\dfrac{\dfrac{\text{Rev}}{\text{Pulse}}}{\text{T/Pulse}} \rightarrow \dfrac{\text{Rev}}{\text{T}}$ (rpm)

Voltage pulses

Distance reference
— or —
$\dfrac{V_{SS}}{\text{Input}}$

FIGURE 4-7   Pulse counter mode of operation. (*Courtesy of Cadillac Motor Car Div. of GMC*)

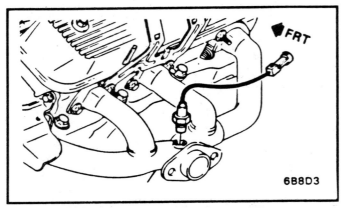

FIGURE 4-8 Location of a typical exhaust oxygen sensor. (*Courtesy of Oldsmobile Division of GMC*)

can maintain the air/fuel ratio at as close to stoichiometric as possible for complete fuel combustion and minimum exhaust emissions.

In gasoline engines, minimum fuel consumption occurs at an air-fuel mixture between approximately 14 to 18 kg (31 to 40 lbs) of air to 1 kg (2.2 lbs) of fuel. Simply put, it requires between 10,000 to 11,500 liters of air to burn 1 liter of gasoline. The chemical minimum for complete combustion is called the *stoichiometric ratio,* which is 14.7:1. To indicate how far the actual air-fuel ratio deviates from the theoretical (14.7:1), this air ratio is denoted by the Greek letter λ (lambda). When the input air supply is less than lambda, a rich air/fuel mixture results. With an excess of air, a lean mixture and reduced fuel consumption results.

The ECM receives a low voltage signal from the oxygen sensor for all operating conditions. The signal received at the ECM is a measure of the unburned oxygen in the exhaust gases. Therefore, if the amount of oxygen in the exhaust gas is low, this is an indication that the mixture is rich (too much fuel), and that the oxygen sensor voltage signal will be high. On the other hand, if the oxygen in the exhaust gases is lean (excess air), then the oxygen sensor will generate a low voltage signal to the ECM.

Three-way catalytic converters are designed to control HC (hydrocarbons), CO (carbon monoxide) and NO_x (oxides of nitrogen), but for the converters to be effective, the exhaust chemistry must be maintained near the stoichiometric ratio of 14.7:1 as these gases enter the converter.

Types of Oxygen Sensors

Two types of exhaust oxygen sensors are in wide use on today's passenger cars. These are:

1. The unheated type illustrated in Fig. 4-9, which will not output a voltage signal to the on-board ECU until the sensing element has reached a temperature of be-

FIGURE 4-9 Unheated zirconia exhaust oxygen sensor. (*Courtesy of Autolite Division of Allied Automotive*)

tween 300 to 350°C (572° to 662°F). Therefore, when the engine is first started, the engine operates in what is known as an "open-loop" condition, since the ECM ignores any voltage signals generated from the oxygen sensor, and the engine operates on a preprogrammed ECU sequence.

2. The heated type of sensor illustrated in Fig. 4-10 which operates on a voltage of approximately 14 volts and is, therefore, self-heating. This type of sensor is fully operational within 10 seconds of engine startup regardless of the exhaust gas temperatures. Since it operates almost immediately, the engine can enter what is known as the "closed-loop" mode quickly, allowing the ECM

SENSOR MATERIAL AND CONSTRUCTION

Two types of material are commonly used for oxygen sensor construction: the resistive-type titania semiconductor ceramics; or the potentiometer-type zirconia ceramic electrolyte. Both are available as either a heated- or unheated-type sensor.

In the development years of oxygen sensors, the zirconia-based sensor reached acceptability factors earlier than did the titania-based sensor, and it therefore captured the market first. However, tests have shown that titania sensors have demonstrated superior durability against the use of gasolines containing lead.

The widely used unheated zirconia sensor is generally limited to operation under conditions which keep its inside tip temperature above 350°C (662°F). In other words, an unheated sensor takes longer to come on line and relay a voltage signal to the ECU or ECM. Moreover, it will be nonoperational anytime the engine exhaust temperatures fall below approximately 350°C (662°F), a condition that exists at initial engine startup as well as when the engine is idling for extended periods of time. An exhaust oxygen sensor which reaches operating temperature within seconds after the ignition is turned on permits early closed-loop control (ECM or ECU controlling air/fuel ratio). Therefore, this condition can result in emission improvements on a cold engine or at idle conditions when the exhaust temperatures can drop lower than 350°C (662°F), since it causes the engine to switch back into an open-loop mode. Because of this advantage, the industry trend shows a greater number of heated oxygen sensors being installed on newer vehicles, whether they be the titanium- or zirconium-type. Figure 4-11 illustrates a cutaway/section view of an unheated zirconia oxygen sensor, while Fig. 4-12 shows a cutaway/sectional view of a heated titania oxygen sensor.

FIGURE 4-10 Heated-type of titania exhaust oxygen sensor. (*Courtesy of Autolite Division of Allied Automotive*)

to maintain the engine air/fuel ratio at stoichiometric almost as soon as it is started. Since this type of sensor generates its own heat, it can be mounted downstream in the exhaust system rather than having to be mounted on the exhaust manifold itself. The heated type of sensor is a resistive type sensor and does not require reference air as does the traditional nonheated type. Therefore, it is capable of responding to changes in exhaust oxygen content faster than the nonheated type, plus it is unaffected by road splash and grime—conditions that can affect the nonheated type. When this type of sensor is used in conjunction with a fuel-injected engine, an oxidation catalyst can often be eliminated from the system.

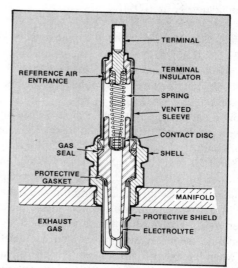

FIGURE 4-11 Sectional view of an unheated zirconia exhaust oxygen sensor. (*Courtesy of Autolite Division of Allied Automotive*)

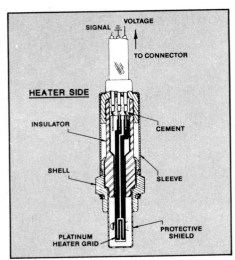

FIGURE 4-12 Sectional view of a heated titania exhaust oxygen sensor. (*Courtesy of Autolite Division of Allied Automotive*)

FUNCTION AND OPERATION

Oxygen sensors are often referred to as Lambda sensors for the reason that their main function is to feed a voltage signal to the ECM in order to maintain an air/fuel ratio as close to stoichiometric (14.7:1) as possible. The oxygen or Lambda sensor allows accurate adjustment of the air/fuel ratio to a tolerance of 0.02% of the stoichiometric value in a fuel-injected engine system, up to 120 times a minute. With this stoichiometric air/fuel ratio, the excess air factor (greater than stoichiometric) is:

$$\text{Lambda} = \frac{\text{Quantity of air supplied}}{\text{Theoretical requirement}},$$

where lambda = 1, or 100%.

The air/fuel ratio in a spark-ignited engine must be between 0.7 and 1.25 (Lambda), whether the engine uses a carburetor or a fuel-injection system. With an air/fuel ratio of 1.25, the air/fuel mixture is no longer ignitable; this is known as the *lean misfire limit.*

Gasoline engines tend to obtain their maximum power output with a rich mixture (less air) of between 0 and 10%, while minimum fuel consumption is obtained with an excess of air (10% and above). Satisfactory idling and good transition occurs with an air deficiency of between 30 and 40%. The most efficient mixture to minimize exhaust emissions is 14.7:1 (stoichiometric), which allows the catalytic converter to operate most efficiently. Carbon monoxide (CO) tends to decrease, and the oxygen content (O_2) increases when the exhaust gases move from a rich to a lean mixture. The outer surface of the sensor is continually exposed to the hot exhaust gases that swirl around the flutes at the sensor base, which is constructed of stainless steel. The inner surface is subjected to ambient air which enters the sensor through the reference air holes at the top of the nonheated sensor. (See Fig. 4-11.) The difference in the amount of oxygen actually contacting these two surfaces of the sensor creates a pressure which will result in a generated voltage signal to the ECM.

Materials used in the construction of the oxygen sensor can vary, with both zirconia and titanium being two of the more widely employed substrates. In addition, platinum-coated outer and inner surfaces are also used for these types of sensors.

Titanium dioxide film type exhaust gas sensors have improved transient response and can apparently respond faster than the titanium dioxide ceramic type sensor and the zirconium dioxide sensor. The two basic designs of oxygen sensors in use are as follows:

1. The titanium dioxide film is deposited on an insulating substrate and is contacted with platinum electrodes. This design permits the simple incorporation of a film-type heater and/or a compensating thermistor.

2. The titanium dioxide film is deposited on a precious metal electrode and contacted with a second electrode.

The ceramic material used becomes conductive for oxygen ions at temperatures of about 572°F (300°C) and higher. Therefore, if the concentration of oxygen at the probe differs from that of the oxygen outside the probe, an electrical voltage is generated between the two surfaces, which is then sent to an ECU (electronic control unit) or its equivalent to interpret and analyze. The ECU will then send out a corrective signal to the engine fuel injection and ignition timing controls to rectify the situation and to reduce the concentration of oxides of nitrogen emanating from the engine as a by-product of combustion.

Figure 4-13 illustrates the typical construction of a zirconia unheated oxygen sensor, while Fig. 4-14 shows the construction of a heated titanium thick film oxygen sensor in a cross-sectional view.

Electricity is produced in an oxygen sensor when oxygen ions from the surrounding ambient air move from the positive electrode (the platinum coating inside the thimble in Fig. 4-13), through the electrolyte which is the thimble itself, and to the negative electrode, which is the platinum on the outside of the thimble. As with a battery, the ion movement only occurs to produce electricity when there is a difference in potential between one electrode and the other. This is the case that exists when the engine is running and there is a rich air/fuel ratio, since a rich mixture contains less oxygen and allows ions to move from the inside to the outside of the thimble, thereby producing as much as 1 volt

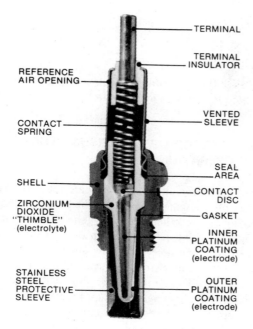

- TERMINAL
- TERMINAL INSULATOR
- REFERENCE AIR OPENING
- VENTED SLEEVE
- CONTACT SPRING
- SEAL AREA
- SHELL
- CONTACT DISC
- ZIRCONIUM DIOXIDE "THIMBLE" (electrolyte)
- GASKET
- INNER PLATINUM COATING (electrode)
- STAINLESS STEEL PROTECTIVE SLEEVE
- OUTER PLATINUM COATING (electrode)

Cutaway view of Autolite oxygen sensor

FIGURE 4-13 Cutaway view of an Autolite zirconia nonheated exhaust oxygen sensor. (*Courtesy of Autolite Division of Allied Automotive*)

of electricity. With a lean mixture (excess air), ion movement produces very little or no ion movement. Therefore, little electricity is created. Figure 4-15 illustrates the CO, HC and NO_x percentages in relation to the catalytic converter efficiency, and the air/fuel ratio above and below the Lambda point (14.7:1).

The heated titania sensor shown in Fig. 4-14 consists of a thick-film platinum heater pattern printed and fired onto one side of a flat alumina substrate. A fine particle titania ink is printed and sintered onto an electrode on the opposite

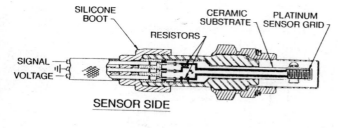

- SILICONE BOOT
- CERAMIC SUBSTRATE
- PLATINUM SENSOR GRID
- RESISTORS
- SIGNAL
- VOLTAGE

SENSOR SIDE

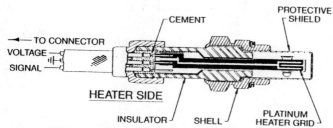

- TO CONNECTOR
- VOLTAGE
- SIGNAL
- CEMENT
- PROTECTIVE SHIELD
- INSULATOR
- SHELL
- PLATINUM HEATER GRID

HEATER SIDE

FIGURE 4-14 Sectional view of a heated titania exhaust oxygen sensor. (*Courtesy of Autolite Division of Allied Automotive*)

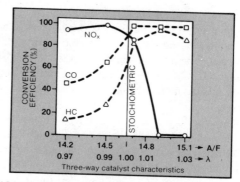

FIGURE 4-15 Typical exhaust emissions as the air/fuel ratio changes. (*Courtesy of Autolite Division of Allied Automotive*)

side of the substrate to form a porous, but adherent, sensing film.

OXYGEN SENSOR VOLTAGE

The oxygen content in the exhaust reacts with the oxygen sensor to produce a voltage output. This voltage can range from approximately 0.1 volts (high oxygen = lean mixture) to 0.9 volts (low oxygen = rich mixture). The voltage signal generated from the oxygen sensor which is sent to the ECM causes the ECM to send out a command signal to the injector (s) to vary its pulse-width time (how long the injector is energized = fuel delivery). For example, a lean mixture (high oxygen in exhaust) will generate a low voltage signal at the sensor, causing the ECM to send out an enrichment command to the engine fuel system. On the other hand, a rich mixture (low oxygen content in the exhaust) will cause the sensor voltage signal to be high, and the ECM will send out a lean command to the engine fuel system controls. Figure 4-16 illustrates a typical characteristic curve for an oxygen sensor for a rich, lean, and correct air/fuel ratio mixture.

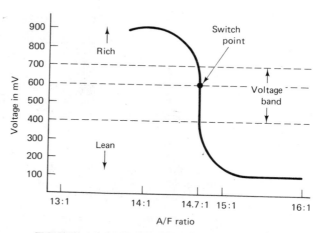

FIGURE 4-16 Oxygen sensor characteristic curve. (*Courtesy of Cadillac Motor Car Div. of GMC*)

As shown in Fig. 4-16, when the air/fuel ratio is correct (stoichiometric = 14.7:1), the ECM will receive a voltage of 0.45 volts. If, however, the engine is in a rich mode (less oxygen), the oxygen sensor voltage will rise above its bias voltage of 0.45 volts. Should the engine enter a lean condition (excess oxygen), then the voltage will drop below 0.45 volts.

Voltage produced, for example, in oxygen sensors of GM vehicles will generally be in the region of 200 mV to the ECM when the exhaust gases show a lean mixture (high oxygen content), while a high voltage (over 500 mV) will be transmitted to the ECM anytime that there is a low oxygen content in the exhaust (rich air/fuel ratio mixture). The ECM continually sends a 450 mV reference signal to the oxygen sensor. Therefore, a lean exhaust mixture lowers this 450 mV signal. A rich exhaust mixture, on the other hand, will increase the 450 mV signal. When the engine is running at its normal idle rpm, the voltage signal will alternate between a low range of 200 and a high range

as high as 900 mV in order to maintain as close to a stoichiometric air/fuel ratio as possible.

OXYGEN SENSOR OPEN- VERSUS CLOSED-LOOP OPERATION

The term *open loop* and *closed loop* are regularly used on current gasoline engines to indicate whether or not the ECM is receiving and reacting to the oxygen sensor voltage signal. Whether or not the oxygen sensor is of the heated or nonheated type will determine how quickly the ECM will receive a voltage signal from the sensor, and therefore just how quickly it will enter the closed-loop mode (under ECU or ECM control) after engine startup. Figure 4-17 illustrates a typical open- and closed-loop engine operating mode.

When the engine is started from cold (open loop), the ECM will ignore the generated voltage signal from the unheated oxygen sensor until the exhaust temperature has risen

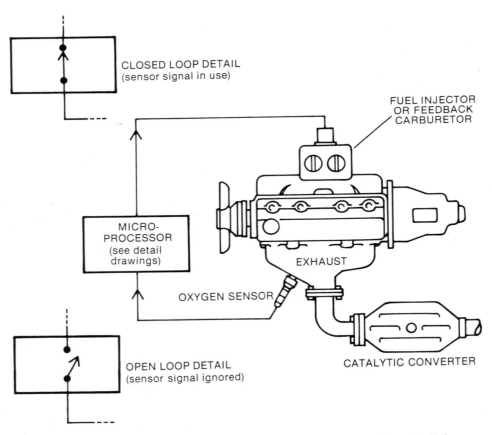

Illustration of open and closed loop modes of engine operation. The detail drawings show the difference: In closed loop the microprocessor accepts signals from the oxygen sensor; in open loop, the signals from the sensor are ignored.

FIGURE 4-17   Oxygen sensor, catalytic converter, and microprocessor unit in open-versus closed-loop mode. (*Courtesy of Autolite Division of Allied Automotive*)

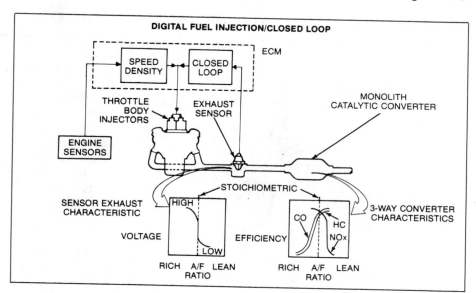

FIGURE 4-18 Closed-loop DFI (digital fuel injection) Operation. (*Courtesy of Cadillac Motor Car Div. of GMC*)

to between 300° and 360°C (572° to 680°F). Within 8 to 10 seconds of starting the engine from cold with the heated type of sensor, the ECU or ECM will place the engine ignition and fuel systems under its control, since the oxygen sensor will have reached its operating range of approximately 700°C (1292°F) and will have placed the engine into the closed-loop mode of operation. The engine will operate on a preprogrammed reference signal from the ECM during the open-loop mode.

When the exhaust gases are hot enough to activate a voltage signal from the unheated type oxygen sensor, the ECM will enter the control function and alter the air/fuel ratio to maintain stoichiometric operation. This is known as closed-loop operation and is illustrated in Fig. 4-18.

On a normal operating engine, the dwell meter needle at both idle and part throttle will be between 10° and 50° dwell and varying, which is termed the closed-loop cycle. In the open-loop cycle, the dwell reading will not vary with the engine cold, and with the oxygen sensor below approximately 360°C (680°F) or at wide open throttle on the nonheated type.

After an engine has been idling for a few minutes, a nonheated oxygen sensor tends to cool off, placing the ECM system into an open-loop condition. For testing purposes when diagnosing the system at any time, the engine has to be run at part throttle to initiate enough exhaust gas flow in order to restore the system back into the closed-loop mode, such as is shown in Fig. 4-17 or 4-18. The ECU or ECM will automatically shift the system into an open-loop mode during wide open throttle or deceleration conditions, because when the engine is being accelerated, a rich air/fuel ratio is needed. On a deceleration condition, a lean mixture is required because of the high vacuum created with a closed throttle.

OXYGEN SENSOR TROUBLESHOOTING

Since the oxygen sensor plays a major role in maintaining the engine air/fuel ratio at stoichiometric (14.7:1) under all operating conditions, a fault in the sensor will result in the following general conditions:

1. Poor engine performance,
2. Increased fuel consumption,
3. Inefficient operation of the catalytic converter.

When a malfunction occurs in the oxygen sensor system, usually a flashing *check engine* or *service engine soon* light will appear on the instrument panel to warn the driver of a problem condition. Similarly, any fault in other sensed systems will trigger a similar response by the warning lamp.

Maintenance intervals for oxygen sensors tend to vary between makes of engines/vehicles, and this is because of the type of sensor that is employed—namely, heated or nonheated types, and titanium- or zirconia-type elements. However, mileage ratings of between 30 (48279 km) and 50,000 miles (80465 km) are common, with the latest type sensors being on the high end of this scale before they require replacement. Oxygen sensor condition should be checked when the engine surges or chuggs, runs rough, becomes unstable, runs at incorrect idle, or stalls frequently. However, before condemning the oxygen sensor, access the diagnostic codes stored in the on-board computer as per the manufacturer's recommendations for the particular vehicle.

If the flashing trouble code indicates that the fault is in the oxygen sensor circuit, visually inspect the sensor at its manifold or exhaust pipe location for any signs of plugged reference (ambient) air holes and any possible wiring damage. If none of these conditions are evident, then it is possible that the following sensor problems exist:

1. The sensor is worn, clogged, or malfunctioning.
2. The voltage signals from the sensor terminal are not reaching the ECM (computer) terminal because of high circuit resistance, or loose or faulty wiring.
3. Other areas of the engine which are ECM-sensed and controlled may be malfunctioning. These include a loose or leaking air duct between the air flow sensor and throttle body; a faulty alternator output voltage (less than 9 volts or more than 16 volts); a faulty vehicle speed sensor; an EGR problem; an ignition timing control problem; plugged fuel filters; low fuel pressure; faulty spark plugs or wires; faulty throttle position switch; sticking or binding throttle linkage; an IAC system problem; PCV valve problem; a fault in the evaporative emission control system; low engine compression; or a faulty gear selector switch. Therefore, always check these areas if the oxygen sensor appears to be operational.

One of the most common symptoms of a faulty oxygen sensor is exhibited when the driver attempts to cruise at a steady speed, but the engine continues to surge and slow down. This is caused by the fact that the sensor pores have generally become contaminated, and therefore oxygen cannot pass through the sensor readily.

It is also possible that the ambient air that flows into the sensor at all times through the reference air entrance (see Fig. 4-13) is clogged with substances such as rustproofing, road tar, or even motor oil that has leaked underneath the vehicle and has run down the exhaust piping. Inspection of the oxygen sensor will usually reveal that silicon is present as a result of:

1. Contaminated fuel containing silica.
2. Leaded gasoline which will poison both the oxygen sensor and the catalytic converter and create the same engine operating problems/conditions.
3. A leaky cylinder head gasket, which can allow antifreeze to enter the exhaust system. The silica in the antifreeze can damage the sensor.
4. Coating of the sensor surface by excessive use of RTV sealant either on the threads of the sensor or when an engine was assembled. Don't use a RTV sealant on exhaust manifolds, where it can burn and give off fumes that can be deposited on the sensor. Also avoid its use on the intake manifold unless the engine manufacturer specifically states that it should so be used. If so, apply it sparingly! Similarly, when using RTV sealant on oil pan and rocker covers, don't spread it on so that blobs of sealant can be washed into the engine oil. The RTV

sealant can carry silcates into the combustion chamber, and the by-products can damage the sensor surfaces.

Contamination of the sensor is confirmed by the evidence of a white powdery coating. This will result in a high but false signal voltage (rich exhaust indication), and the ECM will automatically reduce the quantity of fuel delivered to the engine. This condition will create a severe driveability problem. Figure 4-19 illustrates a contaminated sensor on the left-hand side, while the right-hand side shows a carbon-coated sensor that is still functional.

When the pores in the oxygen sensor are clogged by contamination, the voltage signals emanating from the sensor to the on-board computer (ECU or ECM) are slowed down. The ECM, however, continues to operate at its normal lightning speed. Therefore, the ECM will respond to the last signal that it received from the sensor. If, for example, this signal had indicated a rich air/fuel ratio condition, then the ECM would have responded by sending a signal to the feedback carburetor or fuel injector(s) to lean out the mixture. With an operating sensor slowed down because of contamination, the engine air/fuel ratio will have been leaned out too much, and the engine will start to lose power before the slow operating sensor finally starts responding to this overlean air/fuel ratio.

The ECM signal from the sensor will now attempt to richen the air/fuel ratio, but as it does so, again the slow

YOU CAN'T DIAGNOSE A SENSOR BY LOOKING AT IT:

The oxygen sensor in the photos at left may look fine, but it has been poisoned by lead or silicates. The carbon coating on the sensor in the right photos may look bad, but the sensor is still functional.

(Upper photos show complete sensors. Protective covers have been cut away in lower photos, exposing sensor "thimbles.")

FIGURE 4-19 Comparison of a nonoperational and operational exhaust gas oxygen sensor. (*Courtesy of Autolite Division of Allied Automotive*)

responding oxygen sensor will fail to react quickly enough to hold the air/fuel ratio at stoichiometric (14.7:1). By the time the sensor realizes that the mixture is too rich, the engine will have entered a high-speed surge condition, as the ECM regulates the air/fuel ratio from rich-to-lean to rich-and-back. The driver will feel this reaction as an engine surge condition.

Oxygen Sensor Test Procedure

Because of the different types of oxygen sensors in use—namely, the nonheated versus the heated type, and also the different material types—there is no one single procedure that can be used to clarify whether or not the oxygen sensor is the culprit. Different makes of vehicles, as well as those manufactured by the same company, can have optional equipment fitted to them that will cause them to resort to an open-loop condition at different times and with different engine operating conditions. Therefore, always refer to the specific manufacturers shop-service manual and the make and model of vehicle that you are working on for the step-by-step procedure to follow. Refer to the VIN (vehicle identification number) as well as the EPA emissions label sticker so that you are sure to use the correct service manual information.

You should also remember that the engine is equipped with a coolant temperature sensor that tells the computer what the engine temperature is. If this sensor is faulty, it could lead the computer to think that the engine has not yet reached operating temperature, when in fact it has. This causes the ECM to place the engine into an open-loop mode, which may lead you to suspect that the problem lies only with the oxygen sensor.

A typical oxygen sensor test, however, usually follows the procedures stated below. These procedures should not be followed for all engines. However, in the absence of a specific test procedure in a service manual, following these procedures will give you a pretty good idea regarding the condition of the oxygen sensor.

Procedure

1. Obtain a *digital* volt/ohmmeter, a small cotter pin, and an alligator clip lead.
2. Warm up the engine and unplug the oxygen sensor signal wire.
3. Reconnect the wire by inserting the cotter pin inside the insulation shielded half of the connector. Then attach the clip lead between the cotter pin and the other connector from the signal wire.
4. Attach the red lead of the DVOM to this jumper wire, and place the black lead to ground.
5. Run the engine between 1500 and 2000 rpm for at least three minutes to stabilize the exhaust temperature and

to ensure that the oxygen sensor is at operating temperature (nonheated type).

6. With the engine running between 1500 and 2000 rpm, pull off a large vacuum hose from the engine, such as the brake booster hose, and carefully watch the DVOM needle. It should change rapidly and also be below 500 mV (millivolts), which indicates the oxygen sensor is operating correctly at a lean mixture. Replace the vacuum hose.
7. Partially close the choke on a feedback carburetor engine, or activate the cold start valve on a fuel injected engine to simulate a rich air/fuel ratio condition. The DVOM needle readings should again fluctuate rapidly. However, they should remain above 500 mV.
8. If the readings in Steps 6, and 7 are as stated, the oxygen sensor is more than likely operational.

Another quick test to confirm if the oxygen sensor is operational is to connect up a test lead as was done in the above procedure. However, instead of using a short lead, attach a long enough lead to allow you to connect it to the red lead of the DVOM inside the passenger compartment of the vehicle, with the black lead connected to ground. With the engine fully warmed up, drive the vehicle at 50–55 mph on a level road, and monitor the needle on the DVOM meter. It should show constantly changing voltage signals if the oxygen sensor is operational, since with the engine running under such a condition, the sensor continually sends signals to the ECM to maintain a stoichiometric (14.7:1) air/fuel ratio condition.

If the DVOM needle doesn't change regularly, then it is possible that the oxygen sensor is at fault. Also check, however, that the coolant temperature sensor is fully operational before putting a new oxygen sensor in place. For specific information on a vehicle oxygen sensor, refer to the chapter dealing with a particular make of car in this book.

EXHAUST SYSTEM BACK-PRESSURE CHECK

Many times when the engine performance is poor, particularly when a low power complaint occurs, technicians often concentrate their efforts on troubleshooting either the fuel system and injectors, or the ignition system as being the source of the low-power complaint. In a number of cases, the main problem is a restricted exhaust system, which can be caused by a restricted catalytic converter, a collapsed exhaust pipe, heat distress, or internal muffler failure. Therefore, before replacing the exhaust oxygen sensor or any other components which you think might be the reason for the low power complaint, perform an exhaust back-pressure check on the system with the use of a slack or

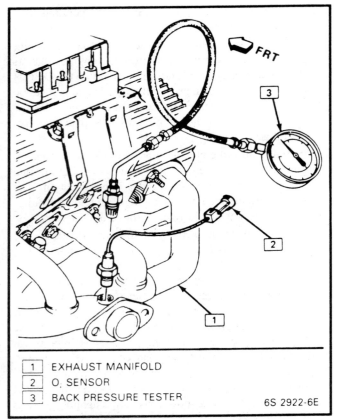

1	EXHAUST MANIFOLD
2	O₂ SENSOR
3	BACK PRESSURE TESTER

6S 2922-6E

FIGURE 4-20 Checking exhaust back pressure value. (*Courtesy of Oldsmobile Div. of GMC*)

solid tube Mercury (Hg) manometer or Borroughs-type gauge, such as the one illustrated in Fig. 4-20.

The procedure given below is typical of that required on most GM cars, and the specification of 1.25 psi maximum exhaust back pressure is that for the 3.8L V6 fuel-injected engine used by Oldsmobile in their Toronado model passenger car. This same basic specification also applies to other GMC division cars using the 3.8L V6 engine.

Procedure

1. Remove the exhaust oxygen sensor from the exhaust system.

2. Install the Borroughs-type gauge or a coupling for the mercury manometer into the oxygen sensor hole.

   NOTE: This fitting should be a brass fitting. Never use steel, since steel fittings, if left in place until the engine cools, will tend to freeze in place, and thereby become difficult to remove.

3. Bring the engine up to normal operating temperature.
4. Accelerate the engine speed to 2500 rpm.
5. Observe the reading on the Borroughs gauge, which

should not be higher than 1.25 psi (8.62 kPa). If higher, a restricted exhaust is indicated.

NOTE: If using a mercury manometer, the fluid will be displaced 2.036″ (52 mm) for every psi (6.895 kPa) applied to the manometer. Therefore, the maximum reading on the manometer should not exceed 2.54″ (64.6 mm).

6. Once the problem has been solved, be sure to lightly coat the threads of the oxygen (O₂) sensor with an antisieze compound prior to installation, taking extreme care not to get any on the electrode part of the sensor. Otherwise, the compound will bake itself onto the surface, and the sensor will not operate correctly and so fail.

7. Torque the sensor to the manufacturer's recommended torque, using a special deep socket which is cut-away on one side, to allow clearance for the sensor wire harness attachment.

THROTTLE POSITION SENSOR

One of the most important engine sensors is, of course, the TPS or throttle position sensor, since it tells the ECU or ECM exactly how much fuel should be delivered (injector pulse-width time) in relation to the throttle opening for all loads and speeds. The TPS functions to control the following engine operating characteristics:

1. Idle speed control (through the ISC or idle speed control motor) for both prestart throttle setting and a coast-down air setting,

2. Clear flood mode during starting if the driver pumps the pedal or holds it in an open position,

3. Acceleration and power enrichment reaction,

4. Emissions control.

The TPS in its simplest (3-wire sensor) form is basically one of a variable resistor (potentiometer) connected to the throttle linkage, so that when the throttle pedal is depressed by the vehicle driver, a variable resistance voltage signal is sensed at the ECU or ECM. The TPS is generally located on the throttle body and connected to the throttle shaft, an example of which can be seen in Fig. 4-21, and also in various figures throughout this book. (Refer, in particular, to the various diagrams of Robert Bosch Corporation's types of fuel-injected systems.)

In the three-wire type of sensor (Fig. 4-5), the signal wiper is spring-loaded to force it to the closed throttle position. Therefore, at an idle rpm, the voltage signal from the TPS will be low, and as the throttle angle is increased (open), the voltage signal will increase.

The TPS mounted in the throttle body supplies the ECM with a voltage reading that corresponds directly with the degree of throttle opening. This voltage reading at the ECM is in the range of 240 to 500 mV at a closed throttle or idle position, and it increases to its highest voltage of about 5100 mV at wide-open throttle. One end of the TPS or potentiometer is connected to a 5 volt reference voltage signal from the ECM, while the other end is connected to ground.

A third wire connected between the TPS and ECM allows the varying mV signal to be continually sensed for all conditions of throttle opening. The TPS can usually be adjusted on the engine to ensure that it will be within the correct range of voltage at both idle and WOT (wide open throttle). This adjustment simply ensures that the varying voltage will be proportionate to the throttle position opening; it does not actually allow you to change the internal resistance manufactured into the TPS. If the TPS is out of adjustment, it will generally reflect a condition of poor idle control and/or poor performance at WOT (wide open throttle). For example, if the TPS is open, then the on-board ECM will assume that the throttle is in a closed position. Therefore, the voltage signal sent to the ECM will reflect a low mV reading. Consequently, the pulse-width injector signal (time that the injector is open) will be too short, and the amount of fuel delivered to the engine will be insufficient for a given throttle opening. The result will be a low power complaint. With such a condition, however, a trouble code is stored in the memory bank of the on-board computer or ECM. The mechanic/technician can access this trouble code when the engine check procedure is activated.

On the other hand, if the TPS was shorted to voltage, then the ECM would assume that the throttle was in a wide open position and the injector pulse width signal would be long, meaning that too much fuel would be delivered to the engine. Again, a trouble code would be stored in the memory system of the ECM or ECU.

Should the TPS be loose on its mounting bracket, then the ECM would receive erratic voltage signals that were not a true reflection of actual throttle position. Therefore, the fuel injector(s) would fluctuate between short and long pulse widths, causing conditions such as unstable or erratic idle speeds.

When any of the above conditions of faulty TPS operation exist, a trouble code is stored in the ECM for access by the mechanic/technician. Once this trouble code is set, the ECM is programmed to resort to an artificial value for throttle position. Therefore, the vehicle can generally be driven (limp home capability), but the *service engine soon* light will be activated on the vehicle instrument panel.

Figure 4-22 illustrates a number of various position sensors which are in wide use on many different makes of cars and trucks. These various position sensors are available in either rotary or linear motion types and are manufactured

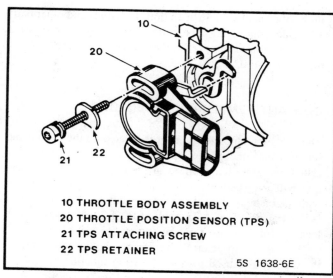

10 THROTTLE BODY ASSEMBLY
20 THROTTLE POSITION SENSOR (TPS)
21 TPS ATTACHING SCREW
22 TPS RETAINER

5S 1638-6E

FIGURE 4-21 Typical location of a throttle position sensor (TPS). (*Courtesy of Oldsmobile Div. of GMC*)

with proprietary resistor materials on either ceramic or polyimide substrates. High-quality noble metal alloy contacts are used in order to allow at least one million full duty cycles and many millions of dither cycles (partially open and closed operation), which is a minimum of 100,000

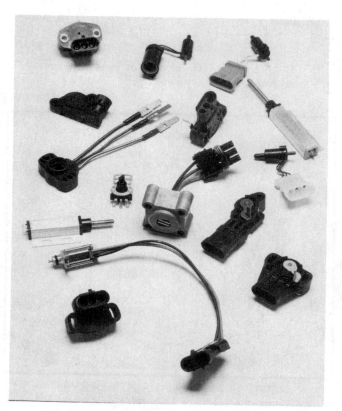

FIGURE 4-22 Various types and styles of position sensors. (*Courtesy of CTS of Canada Limited*)

miles of normal vehicle operation. Housings and other parts are made from high temperature thermoplastics or die castings to meet typical operating temperatures of from $-40°C$ to $+150°C$ ($302°F$).

COOLANT TEMPERATURE SENSOR

The coolant temperature sensor is located on the engine and screwed into one of the top coolant passages to sense the actual operating temperature of the engine. Its exact location will vary between different sizes of engines and also with the make of the vehicle. One example of such a sensor is illustrated in Fig. 4-23, while Fig. 4-24 shows one such location for the sensor on the engine block itself.

In addition to determining engine coolant temperature, the CTS is also used for the following functions:

1. For prime pulses,
2. Cold engine enrichment/idle,

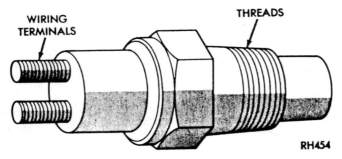

FIGURE 4-23 Typical coolant sensor. (*Courtesy of Chrysler Corporation*)

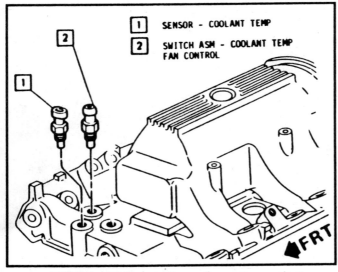

FIGURE 4-24 Location of engine-coolant temperature sensor. (*Courtesy of Oldsmobile Division of GMC*)

3. Closed-loop operation,
4. Exhaust emissions control,
5. Climate control.

The on-board ECU or ECM supplies a 5 volt reference voltage signal to the coolant sensor at all times through a resistor located in the ECM. The ECM monitors the voltage signal generated from the coolant temperature sensor, which is, in effect, a thermistor unit. This means that the voltage from the sensor will be high when the engine is cold, and low when the engine is hot. A thermistor is a device that is made of oxidized nickel, cobalt, manganese, iron, and copper that have been fused together. This combination of metals causes the electrical resistance of the sensor to vary with a change in temperature. Two types of thermistors are in common use. These are:

1. The negative temperature coefficient type, in which the resistance decreases as the temperature increases. This type is most commonly used in automobiles.
2. The positive temperature coefficient type, in which the resistance increases with a temperature rise.

Figure 4-25 illustrates the temperature characteristic of a negative type of thermistor, while Fig. 4-26 shows a typical internal view of such a device.

Low-coolant temperature will generally produce a high circuit resistance in the range of 100,000 ohms at coolant temperatures of $-40°C/40°F$, while high coolant temperatures of $130°C/266°F$ will exhibit very low circuit resistance in the region of about 70 ohms. Information from the coolant temperature sensor is used as follows:

1. Advances the ignition timing when the engine is cold,
2. Retards the ignition timing when the engine is hot.

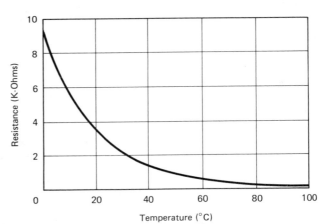

FIGURE 4-25 Negative temperature thermistor characteristic curve. (*Courtesy of Cadillac Motor Car Division of GMC*)

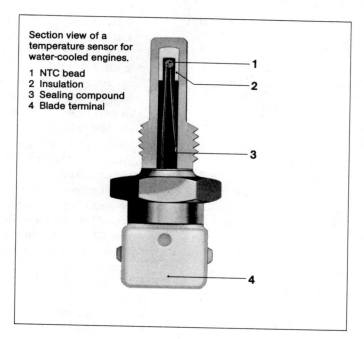

FIGURE 4-26 Sectional view of a water temperature sensor assembly. (*Courtesy of Robert Bosch Corporation*)

Failure of a coolant temperature sensor or circuit will result in a trouble code being set in the memory bank of the on-board computer which will flash when the system is accessed.

MANIFOLD AIR TEMPERATURE SENSOR (MAT)

The MAT sensor or ACT (air charge temperature) is very similar in design to the coolant temperature sensor, since it monitors and reacts to the air temperature within the engine intake manifold or air cleaner assembly. It exhibits the same

basic resistance values as those stated for the coolant temperature sensor. This sensor also receives a 5 volt reference voltage signal from the ECM. Figure 4-27 illustrates the location of the ACT sensor on a V8 engine.

MANIFOLD ABSOLUTE PRESSURE SENSOR (MAP)

The MAP (manifold absolute pressure) sensor measures intake manifold pressure and under certain conditions will also measure barometric conditions. However, many vehicles are equipped with both a MAP and BARO sensor.

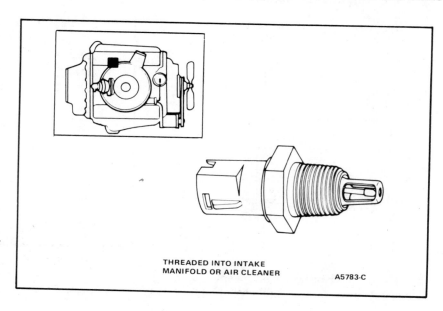

FIGURE 4-27 MAT (manifold air temperature) sensor location. (*Courtesy of Ford Motor Company, Dearborn, MI.*)

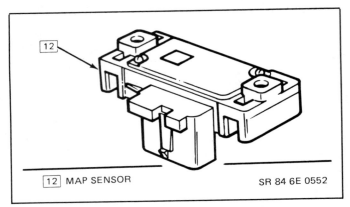

FIGURE 4-28a MAP (manifold absolute pressure) sensor unit. (*Courtesy of GMC Service Research*)

Its voltage signal, along with that from the MAT sensor, is relayed to the ECU or ECM to determine how long the fuel injector(s) will be energized (held open). The ECU or ECM also uses the MAP sensor signal on some engines to establish both the fuel delivery and ignition timing characteristics. Figure 4-28(a) illustrates one such MAP sensor, which is connected electrically to the ECM. If not threaded directly into the intake manifold, it may have a hose running from the throttle body, which provides a pressure signal to the sensor.

With an opening throttle, the intake manifold pressure will increase. Consequently, more fuel is required. Along with the TPS, the MAP sensor sends a voltage signal to the ECM to increase the fuel injector pulse width in order to deliver more fuel. With a closing throttle condition, the exact opposite happens, and the injector pulse width is shortened to decrease fuel delivery.

Figure 4-28(b) illustrates the basic design concept used in the MAP sensor, which is constructed using a silicon wafer diaphragm. The majority of passenger car MAP sensors use this type of design, with others using an alumina ceramic capacitor design. The silicon wafer diaphragm type is often referred to as a silicon capacitor absolute pressure sensor, or SCAP for short. Very simply, within the assembled MAP sensor housing, one side of the silicon wafer diaphragm is exposed to intake manifold pressure, while the other side is acted upon by a vacuum. Consequently, a changing throttle position will create a deflection of the silicon wafer diaphragm, and therefore a change to the resistance value of the chip based upon this deformation. Within the sensor is a small IC (integrated circuit) which converts this resistance value into a voltage. This signal is relayed to the on-board computer, which uses this signal and others to help determine both the air/fuel ratio (injector pulse width) and ignition advance characteristics for the engine.

Figure 4-29 will help you more fully understand this widely-used conceptual term—namely MAP (manifold absolute pressure). The figure illustrates the relationship between manifold vacuum in inches of mercury (Hg) versus pressure indicated in psi. In addition, the third column of the figure shows absolute pressure measured in the metric scale. Measurements are given in kPa, which stands for kilopascals.

$$1 \text{ psi} = 6.895 \text{ kPa}$$

$$1 \text{ psi} = 2.036'' \text{ of mercury (Hg)}$$

Vacuum Reading (In.-Hg.)	Pressure Indicated (psi)	Absolute Pressure (kPa)
0	15	103
2	14	97
4	13	90
6	12	83
8	11	76
10	10	69
12	9	62
14	8	55
16	7	46
18	6	41
20	5	34
22	4	28
24	3	21
26	2	14
28	1	7
30	0	0

FIGURE 4-29 Relationship of intake manifold vacuum versus pressure. (*Courtesy of Cadillac Motor Car Div. of GMC*)

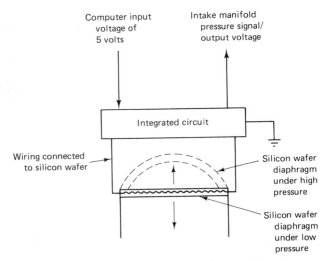

FIGURE 4-28b Basic operational concept of a MAP (manifold absolute pressure) sensor.

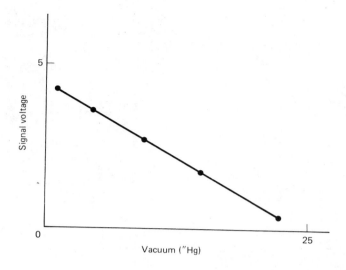

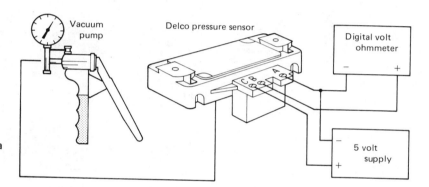

FIGURE 4-30 Test hookup for a MAP or BARO pressure sensor check.

In the chart of Fig. 4-29, note that a high manifold vacuum in inches of Hg caused by a closed throttle is indicative of a low pressure and vice versa.

Should either a MAP or BARO pressure sensor be suspected of being faulty, a quick check can be made. See Fig. 4-30, which illustrates a simple hand-operated vacuum pump along with a DVOM (digital volt/ohm meter). By supplying a 5 volt reference voltage to the MAP or BARO unit, the voltage signal can be easily plotted for any given position. Since these sensors are designed to have a linear voltage-pressure curve between 20 and 110 kPa (2.9 and 16 psi), failure to have such a progressive voltage reading indicates a faulty sensor.

AIR FLOW SENSOR

Several types of air flow sensors are in use and are illustrated and described below. These air flow sensors are designed to measure the actual volume of air flowing into the engine cylinders. Three main types in use are:

1. The moveable (pendulant) flap or vane-type system,

which is connected to a potentiometer to relay a voltage signal to the ECU or ECM.

2. The hot-wire MAF (mass air flow) sensor type, which relies on air flow to keep a thin platinum wire at a fixed temperature.

3. The Karman Vortex air flow meter.

Type 1: Vane Air Flow Meter

This type of air flow meter is commonly referred to as a vane-type because a moveable flap or vane rotates inside an air inlet housing to the engine cylinders. The function of the air flow meter (air-valve) sensor is to generate a voltage signal proportional to the amount of air drawn into the engine. Contained within the air flow meter housing is an air temperature sensor which also sends a voltage signal to the ECU or ECM. Figure 4-31 illustrates a typical air-flow sensor unit manufactured by Robert Bosch Corporation, which is now in wide use on many of the world's passenger cars.

The vane air flow meter operates on the principle of a potentiometer connected to the rotating flap inside the hous-

Fuel metering

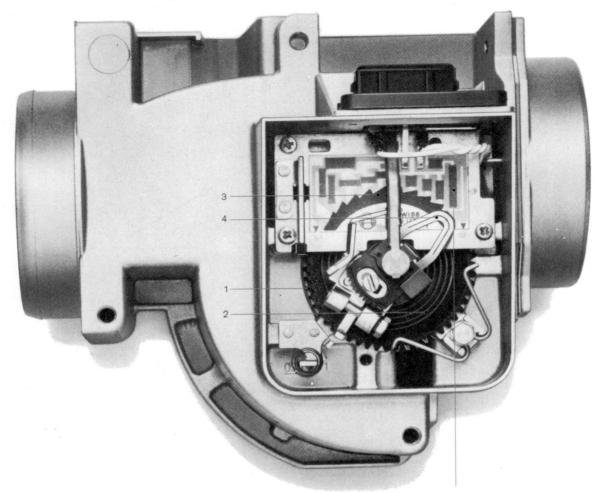

34) Air-flow sensor (above).
1 Ring gear for spring preload
2 Return spring
3 Potentiometer
4 Sliding contact

Thick-film potentiometer of the air-flow sensor.
The resistances can be identified as dark rectangular surfaces in the upper half of the Figure. The resistive material is a ceramic-metal mixture which is burnt into the ceramic plate at a high temperature.

FIGURE 4-31 Bosch vane-type air flow sensor. (*Courtesy of Robert Bosch Corporation*)

ing, as is shown in Fig. 4-32. Therefore, the angular position of the sensor flap is transformed by the potentiometer position into a voltage signal at the ECU or ECM. The throttle valve is not connected directly to this flap, but is downstream, as is shown in Fig. 4-33.

The force of the return spring (Item 2 in Fig. 4-31) exerts a counterforce on the air sensor flap, which is drawn open by the flow of air into the engine cylinders. The further the flap rotates around its support shaft, the greater the change in the voltage signal that will be sent to the ECU or ECM. Because of the position of the throttle valve, the quantity of air drawn into the engine must first of all pass through the air flow sensor prior to entering the engine. (See Fig. 4-34.) Therefore, during an accelerating condition, the voltage signal will pass to the ECU or ECM before the air has actually entered the engine cylinders. This allows the ECU or ECM to increase the fuel delivery to the

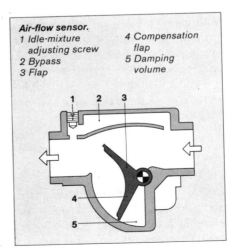

Air-flow sensor.
1 Idle-mixture adjusting screw
2 Bypass
3 Flap
4 Compensation flap
5 Damping volume

FIGURE 4-32 Bosch vane air-flow meter components. (*Courtesy of Robert Bosch Corporation*)

FIGURE 4-33 Air flow sensor location in intake system. (*Courtesy of Robert Bosch Corporation*)

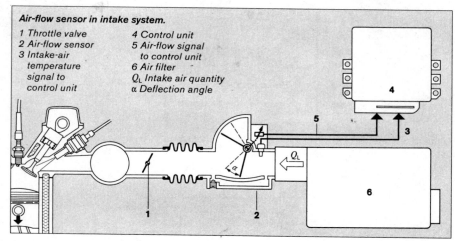

Air-flow sensor in intake system.

1 Throttle valve
2 Air-flow sensor
3 Intake-air temperature signal to control unit
4 Control unit
5 Air-flow signal to control unit
6 Air filter
Q_L Intake air quantity
α Deflection angle

FIGURE 4-34 Air flow meter and electrical contacts. (*Courtesy of Ford Motor Company, Dearborn, MI.*)

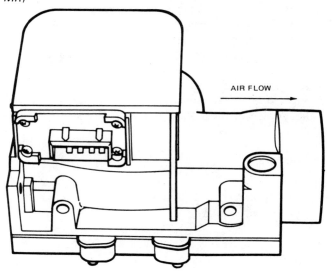

AIR FLOW

engine for rapid throttle response. In order to set the air/fuel ratio at an idle rpm, an adjustable bypass duct, shown as item 2 in Fig. 4-32, is employed along with an adjustment screw—Item 1 in the same figure. The relationship among the actual air quantity, the angle of the sensor flap, the potentiometer voltage, and the quantity of injected fuel is shown in Fig. 4-35.

Type 2: Hot-Wire Mass Air Flow Sensor

Figure 4-36 illustrates the components of the hot-wire air flow sensor assembly, while Fig. 4-37 illustrates its location in a typical Robert Bosch LH Jetronic type gasoline F.I. engine. This system employs a thin platinum wire strung within the housing and shown as Item 5 in Fig. 4-36, while Fig. 4-38 shows this same wire strung inside the housing when viewed end on. The hot-wire arrangement used in this system employs a very thin platinum wire (70 um thick).

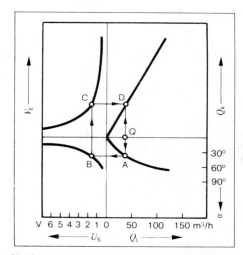

The relationships between air quantity, sensor-flap angle, voltage at the potentiometer and fuel quantity injected.
Starting with a certain volume of air Q_L flowing through the air-flow sensor (point Q), we can derive the theoretically required amount of fuel Q_K (point D). In addition, the sensor flap is deflected to a certain flap angle α (point A) depending on the amount of air. The potentiometer activated by the air-flow sensor flap sends a voltage signal U_S to the control unit (point B). The control unit controls the injection valves, whereby point C represents the amount of fuel injected V_E. It can be seen that the amount of fuel theoretically required and the amount of fuel injected are the same (line C-D).

FIGURE 4-35 Vane-type air flow meter sensor flap voltage and fuel delivery rate. (*Courtesy of Robert Bosch Corporation*)

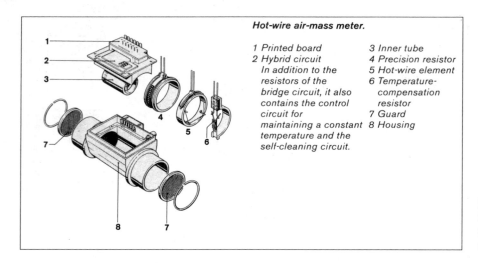

Hot-wire air-mass meter.

1 Printed board
2 Hybrid circuit
  In addition to the
  resistors of the
  bridge circuit, it also
  contains the control
  circuit for
  maintaining a constant
  temperature and the
  self-cleaning circuit.

3 Inner tube
4 Precision resistor
5 Hot-wire element
6 Temperature-
  compensation
  resistor
7 Guard
8 Housing

FIGURE 4-36   Hot-wire mass air flow sensor components. (*Courtesy of Robert Bosch Corporation*)

Air flowing over the wire draws heat from it so that the wire's electrical resistance changes with temperature. An electronic amplifier in the system responds instantly to any electrical resistance change and regulates the current flow of from 500 to 1200 mA (depending upon the air flow rate) to the hot wire in order to maintain it at a virtually constant temperature. The current flow required to maintain a stable temperature of 75°F at the platinum wire becomes, in effect, a measure of the air mass flowing over the wire, with the output signal being a voltage.

The air flow is determined much more accurately in this system than in the moveable-flap type by applying a current to the wire grid inside the MAF unit housing to maintain a constant grid temperature of 75°F. (See Fig. 4-39.) The ECM can then determine the temperature and volume of air in grams per second actually entering the engine. Therefore, the air flow is calculated electronically by determining the energy required to keep the heated wire grid at a steady temperature of 75°F regardless of the intake air temperature. A resistor is used to measure the intake air tempera-

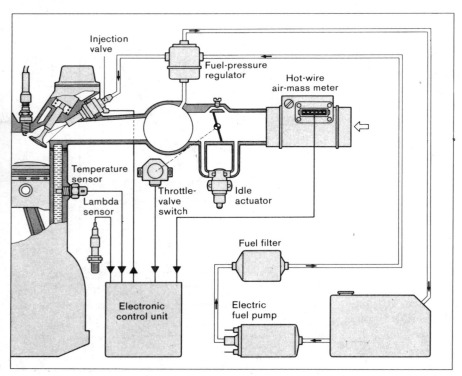

The idle potentiometer which is also accommodated in the hot-wire airmass meter is used for setting the idle mixture.

The basic design of the LH-Jetronic is the same as that of the L-Jetronic. However, the hotwire airmass meter is used in place of the mechanical airflow sensor. It supplies the airflow signal.
The idle actuator is a controlled bypass of the throttle valve. It supplies a specific quantity of air to the engine during idling. This quantity of air is specified by a microcomputer in the control unit in accordance with the input signals.

FIGURE 4-37   Hot-wire mass air flow meter location on an engine equipped with a Bosch model LH-Jetronic fuel-injection system. (*Courtesy of Robert Bosch Corporation*)

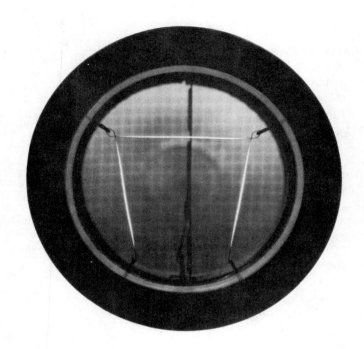

FIGURE 4-38 Actual close-up view of a hot-wire mass air-flow sensor. (*Courtesy of Robert Bosch Corporation*)

ture. The warmer the incoming air, the lower the energy requirements to keep the wire (heated film) at the predetermined temperature. This lowering of the air mass—air expands when it is heated—will cause a resistance change in the sensor wire. A voltage signal corresponding to this air temperature increase (air mass decrease) will be fed to

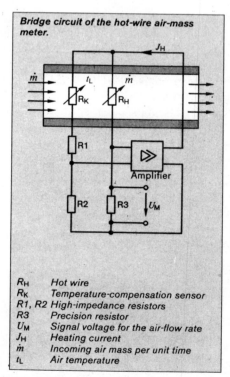

FIGURE 4-39 Electrical bridge-circuit for a hot-wire mass air flow sensor system. (*Courtesy of Robert Bosch Corporation*)

the ECM, which will send out a signal to the injectors to alter the time period at which they remain open. In this way, the air/fuel ratio is maintained as close as possible to ideal (stoichiometric = 14.7:1) under varying throttle, engine load, and speed conditions.

As the amount of air passing the wire grid increases, it has a cooling effect on the wire, and more current must be applied to maintain the constant wire temperature. The ECM is able to measure this change in current flow. Therefore, the ECM monitors the air temperature and volume entering the engine in grams per second and responds immediately. Major advantages of the hot-wire system of air flow measurement are its very small dimensions and the complete lack of any moving parts. It has another unique feature. Because impurities may accumulate on the heated wire's surface, the voltage output signal may change. Therefore, the system includes a provision for automatically increasing the wire's temperature for one second each time the engine is switched off to allow the wire to burn off impurities or corrosion. The burn-off command comes from the ECU or ECM. Due to the sensitivity of this hot-wire air flow system, removal of the engine oil filler cap will cause it to react.

Normal air flow will, of course, vary between engine sizes and makes. As an example, however, the 3.8 liter V6 engine employed by GM in many of their cars consumes between 4–12 grams per second at an idle rpm.

Information from the MAF (mass air flow) sensor is used by the ECM and ignition module as follows:

1. Advances the ignition timing (spark) when the engine load is light.

2. Retards the spark when the engine load is heavy.

Type 3: Karman Vortex Air Flow Sensor

A number of Japanese automobiles employ the Karman-Vortex-type air flow sensor manufactured by Mitsubishi Electric, which claims that this type of air measurement system is superior to the ubiquitous Bosch-type pendulant flap or moveable vane type system, discussed as Type 1. Two examples of vehicles employing the Karman air flow meter are the turbocharged Dodge Colt, and the Mitsubishi Galant and Sigma fuel-injected 1.8 and 2.0 liter capacity engines. Figures 4-40 and 4-41 illustrate the concept of operation of the Karman air flow sensor assembly.

The air-flow sensor shown in Figure 4-40 and 4-41 operates on the basis of what is called the Karman Vortex phenomenon in the form of electric pulses that are converted by the modulator. Air entering the throat of the air-flow sensor is deflected around a small triangular casting that causes a velocity increase to occur. This action induces an air flow that creates a pulse condition in the form of ultrasonic waves, with a constant frequency through the throat vortex in proportion to the air flow from the turbocharger.

The receiver detects these modulated waves (pressure and flow), and the modulator converts them into electric pulses that are relayed to the ECU. The ECU monitors these voltage signals and alters the pulse time of both fuel injectors as well as controlling secondary air management. An air temperature sensor is generally located on the modulator within the air cleaner assembly and functions to measure the temperature of the air flowing through the air cleaner.

A change in air temperature affects its density; therefore, the engine's volumetric efficiency will change. The generated sensor voltage signal is monitored by the ECU, which will then alter the fuel delivery characteristics by

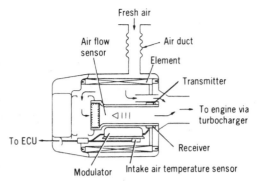

FIGURE 4-40 Karman air-flow sensor, air cleaner/sensor location. (*Courtesy of Chrysler Corporation*)

changing the pulse-width (opening) time of the fuel injectors. An air pressure sensor used with this system is generally located in the engine compartment area and senses both ambient barometric pressure and absolute pressure within the engine intake manifold. An example of this sensor and its arrangement to the engine and ECU is shown in Fig. 4-42. Voltage signals generated at the air pressure sensor, and which are based upon the weather and altitude conditions, are fed to the ECU. Immediately after engine startup, the ambient barometric pressure is sensed by this air pressure sensor, which energizes the solenoid valve, as is shown in Fig. 4-42, via the ECU. After engine startup, the solenoid valve is de-energized, and the sensor detects absolute pressure in the manifold from the turbocharger and feeds a voltage signal to the ECU, which will control the air/fuel mixture and idle speed.

In the Toyota engine, it is claimed that the air-flow metering device, known as a Karman-Vortex street principle, provides precision metering, smaller intake resistance,

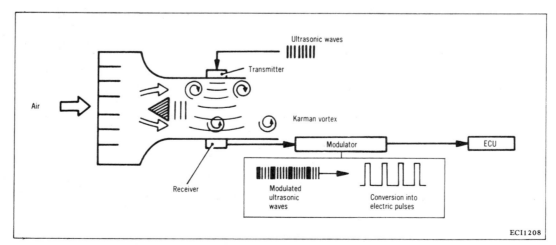

FIGURE 4-41 Karman air-flow sensor operational schematic. (*Courtesy of Chrysler Corporation*)

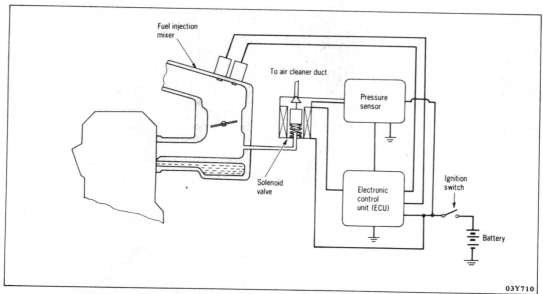

FIGURE 4-42 Air pressure/sensor ECU arrangement. (*Courtesy of Chrysler Corporation*)

more compact size, and lighter weight. Toyota's system differs from that used by Mitsubishi in that the vortex is optically measured. See Fig. 4-43.

In Figure 4-43, the pressure created by the vortex effect is led to a thin metal mirror, and the mirror's vibrations are optically measured by a LED (light-emitting diode) and a phototransistor.

VEHICLE SPEED SENSOR (VSS)

The vehicle speed sensor (VSS) tells the ECM that the vehicle is, in fact, moving, as well as its rate of forward or reverse motion. This sensor operates on a pulse-counter principle, described and shown in Fig. 4-7. The VSS location will vary between different makes and models of passenger cars. However, it is generally located at either

the transmission or transaxle (front-wheel drive vehicles) to monitor the output shaft speed to the road wheels. This speed is relayed as a pulsing voltage signal to the BCM (body computer module) on some vehicles, which converts this signal to miles per hour or kilometers per hour. The main function of the VSS is to control the operation of the torque converter or TCC (transaxle converter clutch), which provides lockup between the pump and turbine elements of the torque converter. This action provides direct drive through the converter to improve fuel economy (no slippage).

In addition, on some vehicles the VSS sensor signal sent to the ECM is used for cruise-control functions and fuel data calculations (mpg sentinel). An example of a VSS wiring system is shown in Fig. 4-44. This system employs a *photo chopper* assembled into the back of the speedometer head. As the speedo cable is rotated, the sensor creates a

FIGURE 4-43 Optical Karman-Vortex air flow metering principle. (*Courtesy of Society of Automotive Engineers; Copyright 1986*)

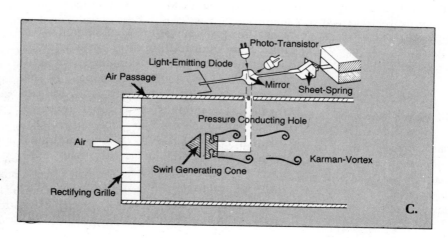

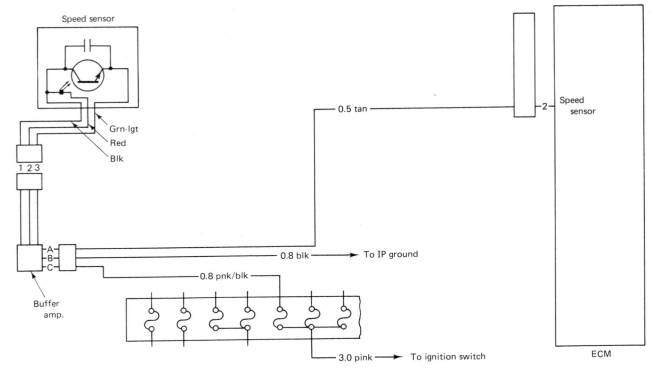

FIGURE 4-44 Typical wiring circuit for a photochopper longitudinal type VSS (vehicle speed sensor). (*Courtesy of Cadillac Motor Car Div. of GMC*)

string of pulses on the green wire to the buffer amplifier, which when it senses these pulsing signals, pulls the circuit (961) to ground to create a series of pulses to the ECM, and thereby indicating vehicle speed.

Some vehicles employ a transmission output-shaft type of permanent magnet generator to produce an ac voltage at a frequency proportional to the rotation of the vehicle drive wheels. See Fig. 4-45. In this system, the generated voltage signal is relayed to the buffer amplifier on circuits 400 and 401. This signal grounds the circuit from the speedo head and the ECM at the same frequency as the output shaft generators ac signal. It thereby creates a series of pulses which are used equally by both the speedo and the ECM to determine the vehicle speed. The information is then sent to the ECM or BCM (on vehicles so equipped) via the ECM to the BCM. An example of the location of a transverse engine VSS is illustrated in Fig. 4-46.

CRANKSHAFT SENSOR

The main purpose of this sensor is to inform the ECM of the engine speed, as well as the relative position of the crankshaft. Various types of crank sensors are in use. However, they operate on the *Hall-effect* switch principle, which is discussed in detail under electronic ignition systems. Briefly, a Hall-effect switch consists of a semiconductor

chip and a magnet. When the magnet is brought close to the chip, the resulting magnetic field creates a small voltage in the chip. When the voltage is induced in the chip, it is said to be ON. The location of one such sensor in wide use on GM vehicles is illustrated in Fig. 4-47, which also shows the camshaft position sensor. Figures 4-48 and 4-49 show the crankshaft harmonic balancer and close-up view of the crankshaft position sensor, respectively.

The function of the crankshaft position sensor is to maintain the ignition spark timing sequence. When the crankshaft sensor is bolted to the engine front cover, it is mounted so that the rotating harmonic balancer will rotate between the magnet and semiconductor. The interrupter ring (solid vanes on the rear of the balancer) has a clearance of approximately 0.030 inch (0.762 mm) on each side, as it rotates between the crankshaft position sensor containing the magnet and the semiconductor chip. The rotation of the interrupter ring within the magnetic field will turn the chip ON and OFF, as per the Hall-effect principle. A malfunctioning crank position sensor can create problems of engine stumble, hesitation, sag, or even dieseling.

If a problem exists between the crank position sensor and the engine ignition module, the engine will not start, because the ignition module cannot determine or establish the position of the No. 1 piston. A faulty crank sensor will cause a trouble code to be stored in the memory of the ECM, which can be accessed by the mechanic/technician.

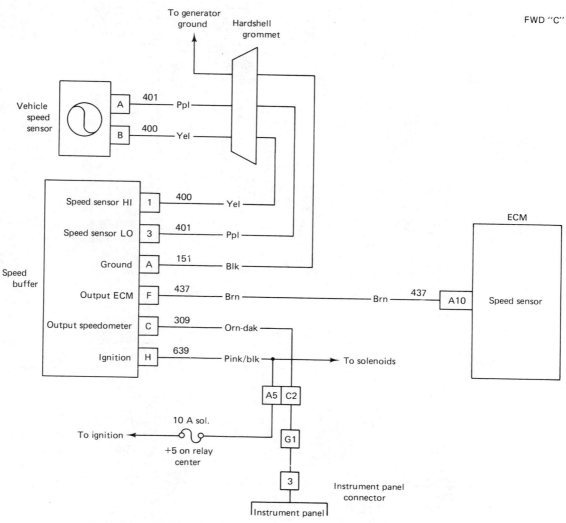

FIGURE 4-45 Typical wiring circuit for an output shaft type of transverse VSS. (*Courtesy of Cadillac Motor Car Div. of GMC*)

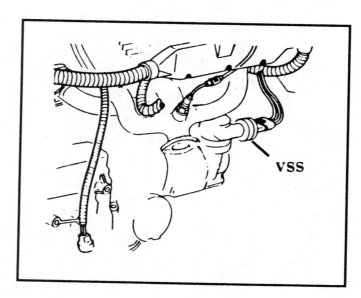

FIGURE 4-46 Transverse egine VSS (vehicle speed sensor) location. (*Courtesy of Oldsmobile Div. of GMC*)

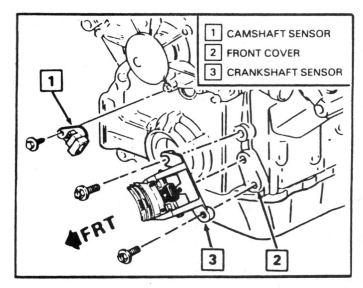

FIGURE 4-47 Crankshaft and camshaft position sensor location. (*Courtesy of Oldsmobile Div. of GMC*)

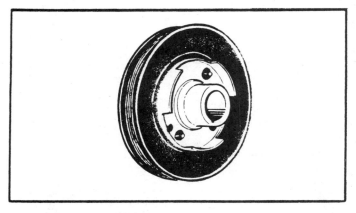

FIGURE 4-48 Harmonic balancer showing three-blade interrupter ring on the rear for a V6 engine configuration. (*Courtesy of Oldsmobile Div. of GMC*)

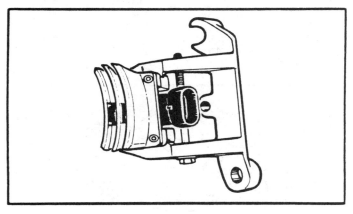

FIGURE 4-49 Close-up of a crankshaft position sensor. (*Courtesy of Oldsmobile Div. of GMC*)

CAMSHAFT POSITION SENSOR

The camshaft sensor also operates on the Hall-effect principle, similar to that for the crankshaft position sensor. The location for the cam sensor was shown in Fig. 4-47. One such cam sensor and its magnet is shown in Figs. 4-50 and 4-51.

Unlike the crankshaft position sensor which turns the chip ON and OFF three times in each revolution in a V6 engine, the camshaft sensor will only turn the chip ON and OFF once for each rotation of the camshaft, because of the Hall-effect principle described earlier. The camshaft sensor signal is relayed to the ECM, which then determines just when the No. 1 piston is on the compression stroke and initializes the correct ignition timing sequence as per the engine firing order, as well as the fuel-injection timing. Although the ignition module is able to determine where No. 1 piston is from the first camshaft sensor signal. This is used as a reference only. For example, on a V6 engine configuration, the first cylinder that fires is the No. 6. The reason for this is that the signal from the No. 1 piston will reach the ignition module when the piston is ATDC (after top dead center). Since the spark plug fires BTDC (before top dead center), the next cylinder in the firing order sequence is the first one to fire. At speeds below 400 rpm, the ignition module will control spark-timing on GMC vehicles, as well as firing the fuel injectors in simultaneous injection. With the engine speed beyond 400 rpm, the ECM will control spark-timing, and the injectors are pulsed in a sequential injection mode rather than simultaneously.

As long as the engine is running, the cam sensor signal voltage is employed to maintain fuel-injector timing. If, however, this cam signal is lost during engine operation, the ECM will take over operation of the fuel injector(s) in a simultaneous rather than a sequential fuel injection firing sequence. It does so on all GMC vehicles employing such a system. Should the ignition module not receive a cam sensor voltage signal during engine cranking, then the engine will not start. Cam sensor problems will cause a trouble code to be stored in the ECM.

DISTRIBUTOR REFERENCE SIGNAL

When an engine is not equipped with a distributorless ignition system, the distributor reference signal (engine speed signal) can be used in lieu of a crankshaft or camshaft-generated Hall-effect-type signal. This signal is used for:

1. EST (electronic spark timing) control,
2. Fuel injector timing,
3. Idle speed control through the ISC motor,
4. TCC (transaxle converter clutch) or VCC (vehicle converter clutch) engagement testing,
5. Exhaust emissions control.

This signal is supplied to the ECM via a "distributor reference" line from the distributor, and its input creates the "timing" signal for the necessary pulsing of the fuel injectors, as well as for EST (electronic spark timing) functions.

DETONATION SENSOR

The purpose of a detonation sensor is to sense cylinder ignition knock and retard the ignition timing to prevent piston damage. The active element of the sensor is a pieso-

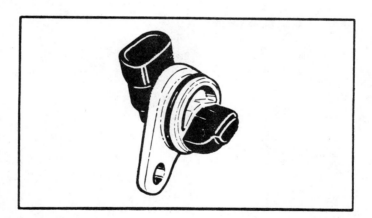

FIGURE 4-50 Camshaft sensor unit containing semiconductor chip. (*Courtesy of Oldsmobile Div. of GMC*)

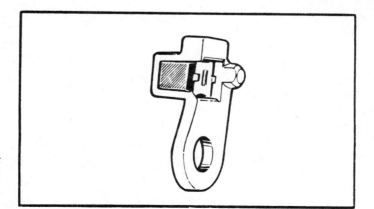

FIGURE 4-51 Camshaft sensor magnet bolted to the cam gear. (*Courtesy of Oldsmobile Div. of GMC*)

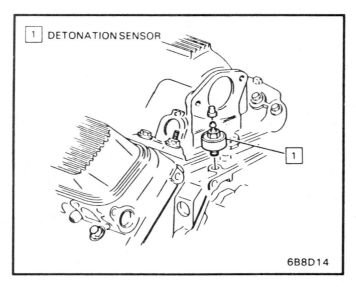

1 DETONATION SENSOR

6B8D14

FIGURE 4-52 Rear-mounted engine detonation sensor. (*Courtesy of Oldsmobile Div. of GMC*)

ceramic material that is mounted on the engine, with its location being either in the engine intake manifold vicinity, or even screwed into the coolant jacket on some engines. One such detonation sensor is shown in Fig. 4-52, where it is located at the rear of the engine. Other locations may be at the front end of the engine block, or even along the side. Locations vary among vehicle/engine manufacturers.

Another example of the detonation sensor location is shown in Figure 4-53, where the unit is screwed into the cylinder block of an in-line engine in the vicinity of the cylinder.

With the reduction in the octane level (rating) of gasoline in North America, partly due to the extraction of lead from the fuel, and with concerns about meeting the stringent EPA exhaust emissions levels, car manufacturers were forced into redesigning their engines. Not only was the trend away from large displacement V8 engines, but also the emissions regulations caused a reduction in the overall compression ratio.

The smaller high-speed engines, of course, offered substantial fuel economy improvements, but they lacked the power of their older V8 rivals. Consequently, engine manufacturers turned to turbocharging as one method of providing boosted power on demand for acceleration, with the latest technology engines employing four-valve cylinder heads in either the turbocharged or nonturbocharged models. Compression ratios have slowly begun to climb again with the adoption of electronic controls, which are capable of handling both the fuel and ignition management systems on the engine.

An increase in compression ratio, however, produces a condition in high-speed, high-performance engines that is conducive to violent and dangerous combustion chamber knocking, which is caused by the gas vibrations of uncontrolled burning. A knocking condition creates higher thermal and mechanical stresses on internal engine components.

The employment of a knock sensor allows very precise control of spark advance within the designed ignition timing

Knock sensor: a wide-band acceleration sensor with natural frequency of more than 25 kHz.
The active element is of piezo-ceramic material. For thermal decoupling, the sensor is coated with plastic. Allowable operating temperature: 130°C

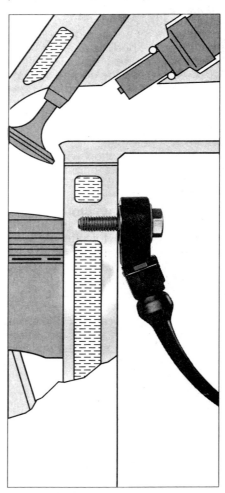

FIGURE 4-53 Side-mounted engine detonation sensor. (*Courtesy of Robert Bosch Corporation*)

108

map for a specific model of engine. Therefore, the ignition system can be calibrated for normal operating conditions, and the dangers associated with detonation or ignition knock can be eliminated by means of the closed-loop knock control.

Dangerous vibrations which are caused by an ignition knocking condition are registered in what is known as a recognition circuit. The amplitude and acceleration of these serious vibrations are converted into electrical signals with the aid of the piezo-electric sensor element.

The sensor is designed to resonate at approximately the same frequency as the engine knock frequency, which is normally within a range of 5–6 kilohertz (kHz). Note, however, that different engines will emit higher or lower sounds of anywhere between 5 and 10 kHz.

The sensor employs the resonant frequency to amplify mechanically the variations in the 5–6 kHz range, thereby allowing relatively large signals to be achieved without electrical amplification and also within a small package size. The sensor is usually made from a thin circular piezo-electric ceramic disc that is bonded to a metal diaphragm, with electrical connections made through a two-pin integral connector. Alternately, it consists of a poled material, such as barium titanate, that generates a voltage across the sensor during a combustion chamber knock condition, such as the sensor shown in Fig. 4-54. The sensor is designed to vibrate when a given level of resonance is attained; therefore, when combustion knock occurs in the engine, the metal diaphragm will vibrate (or resonate), which causes an electrical connection to occur between the disc and the integral pin connectors. This action completes the electrical circuit back to the ECM ignition module, which will retard ignition spark-timing until the combustion knock disappears. A buffer sorts these signals and eliminates everything except for those in the predetermined range of detonation for that engine.

The ECM contains a counter that increments every time that detonation is detected. The degree of the increment will depend upon how long detonation is detected. Therefore, this signal is used by the ESC (electronic spark con-

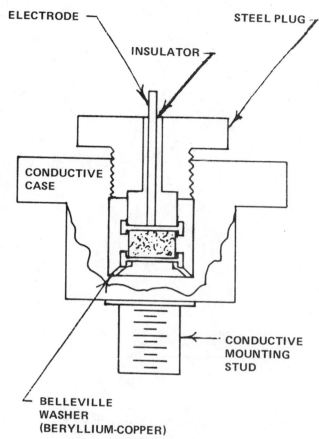

FIGURE 4-54 Example of a piezo-electric knock sensor unit. (*Courtesy of Society of Automotive Engineers Inc., Copyright 1987*)

trol) module in determining the degrees of ignition-retard required. Figure 4-55 illustrates the generated sensor signal both in a "no-detonation" versus a "detonation" condition. Ignition-timing retardation in a turbocharged engine, however, would create a condition that would add to the high exhaust gas temperatures. If the turbocharger boost alone was reduced, then unsatisfactory engine performance would result. Therefore, when ignition knock is detected

FIGURE 4-55 Typical knock sensor signals generated in a spark ignition engine. (*Courtesy of Robert Bosch Corporation*)

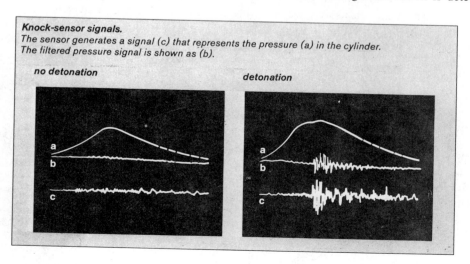

Knock-sensor signals.
The sensor generates a signal (c) that represents the pressure (a) in the cylinder. The filtered pressure signal is shown as (b).

no detonation

detonation

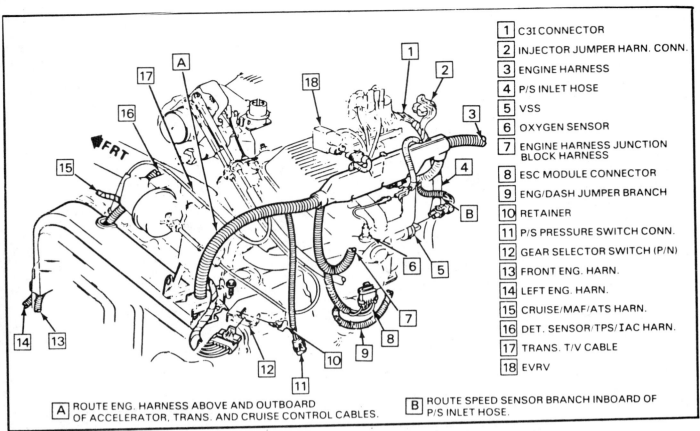

1	C3I CONNECTOR
2	INJECTOR JUMPER HARN. CONN.
3	ENGINE HARNESS
4	P/S INLET HOSE
5	VSS
6	OXYGEN SENSOR
7	ENGINE HARNESS JUNCTION BLOCK HARNESS
8	ESC MODULE CONNECTOR
9	ENG/DASH JUMPER BRANCH
10	RETAINER
11	P/S PRESSURE SWITCH CONN.
12	GEAR SELECTOR SWITCH (P/N)
13	FRONT ENG. HARN.
14	LEFT ENG. HARN.
15	CRUISE/MAF/ATS HARN.
16	DET. SENSOR/TPS/IAC HARN.
17	TRANS. T/V CABLE
18	EVRV

A ROUTE ENG. HARNESS ABOVE AND OUTBOARD OF ACCELERATOR, TRANS. AND CRUISE CONTROL CABLES.

B ROUTE SPEED SENSOR BRANCH INBOARD OF P/S INLET HOSE.

FIGURE 4-56 EVRV (electronic vacuum regulator valve) location on a 3.8L V6 GMC engine. (*Courtesy of Oldsmobile Div. of GMC*)

in a turbocharged engine, the ignition-timing is retarded in concert with a reduction in boost pressure, thereby providing acceptable performance.

ELECTRONIC VACUUM REGULATOR VALVE (EVRV)

The EVRV generally contains a N.C. (normally closed) vacuum solenoid that is controlled by the ECM. It also contains a N.O. (normally open) vacuum switch that monitors the vacuum to the EGR (exhaust gas recirculation) valve and also signals the ECM when actual vacuum is present. The EVRV signal is very important, since EGR at the wrong time creates idle as well as driveability problems. The location of the EVRV will vary between makes of vehicles. However, one such example is shown in Figure 4-56, in Item 18 for a 3.8L V6 ported fuel-injected engine manufactured by GMC's Oldsmobile Division.

PARK/NEUTRAL GEAR SELECTOR SWITCH

The voltage signal from this switch is used to maintain a constant idle speed, as well as being a controlling factor for the VSS, EGR, and TCC units. To determine if the transmission or transaxle is in park/neutral or in gear, the ECM monitors and sees a low voltage at the N.C. (normally

closed) gear selector switch (closed in park/neutral). When the transaxle is placed in gear, this switch opens, causing the ECM to sense a high voltage. The switch is located on the transmission with its exact location varying depending upon the make and model of vehicle.

POWER STEERING SWITCH

This normally closed (N.C.) switch is used to signal the ECM when higher than normal power steering loads are encountered, such as when parking a vehicle in a tight location. Figure 4-57 illustrates a typical power-steering pressure switch. These higher than normal pressures will cause the switch to open, and the ECM will sense a higher than normal voltage and will therefore increase the idle speed by backing out the IACV pintle. In some vehicles, the A/C compressor clutch relay is also on this same circuit. Therefore, the A/C compressor shuts off anytime that the power-steering pressure switch is open.

FOURTH-GEAR SWITCH

Most automatic transmission equipped passenger cars today employ a torque converter lockup clutch to mechanically couple the turbine to the pump section. This allows direct drive through the torque converter assembly (no slippage)

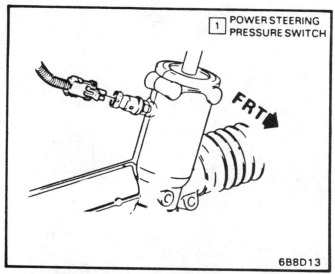

FIGURE 4-57 Power-steering pressure switch location. (*Courtesy of Oldsmobile Div. of GMC*)

and therefore provides improved fuel economy. When the vehicle road speed is high enough to cause a shift into fourth gear, the normally closed (N.C.) fourth-gear switch provides the ECM with a high voltage signal, since the switch opens at this elevated road speed. This information from the ECM is then used to engage the TCC (transaxle converter clutch) on front-wheel-drive vehicles, or the transmission converter clutch on rear-wheel-drive vehicles. In addition, the fourth gear switch, when opened, will also allow the ECM to determine the EGR duty cycle.

CANISTER PURGE SOLENOID

All EPA certified vehicles employ an evaporative emission control system (EECS) to transfer fuel vapors from the fuel tank to an activated carbon (charcoal) canister, which holds the vapors when the vehicle is not in an operating mode.

Anytime that the engine is running, these trapped fuel vapors will be drawn from the carbon element canister by the normal air intake flow and will be recirculated into the engine, where they will be burned in the combustion chamber. Figure 4-58 illustrates a typical carbon charcoal canister and its solenoid, which is normally located on the inner fender under the hood.

The ECM controls a solenoid valve shown as Item 2 in the figure, which in turn controls the engine vacuum to the purge valve in the charcoal canister. When the engine is cold or at an idle, the solenoid is turned on by the ECM, which closes the valve and therefore blocks any engine vacuum to the canister purge valve. The ECM will turn off the solenoid valve and allow canister purge when the following conditions are met:

1. The engine coolant operating temperature is generally over 145°F (63°C).

2. The engine is operating in the closed-loop mode. (The ECM is reacting to the oxygen sensor signal, but it is not in the fuel shutoff mode—decelerating.) When rapid deceleration occurs, the ECM can cut off fuel completely for short periods of time.

3. The TPS (throttle position sensor) is opened greater than 6% and provides a voltage of 0.73 volts.

4. The vehicle is actually travelling at a road speed in excess of 7 mph.

5. The engine has been running for longer than 30 seconds.

Should the solenoid valve be open or not be receiving power, the canister can purge vapors/fumes to the intake manifold continuously. The only problem with this situation is that this can allow extra fuel when idling or while the engine is warming up, with a resultant rough or unstable idle or with too rich a mixture during warmup.

MULTIPLEXING

The term multiplexing simply means that more than one electrical/electronic component shares the same signal wire. I'm sure that you have often looked at a typical automotive

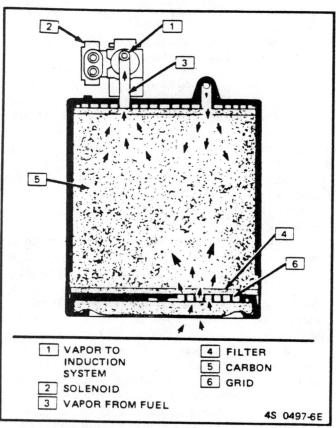

	VAPOR TO		FILTER
1	INDUCTION	4	
	SYSTEM	5	CARBON
2	SOLENOID	6	GRID
3	VAPOR FROM FUEL		

4S 0497-6E

FIGURE 4-58 Typical charcoal canister vapor canister. (*Courtesy of Oldsmobile Div. of GMC*)

or heavy-duty truck wiring harness when you were faced with pinpointing an electrical problem and didn't quite know where to begin.

One of the most cumbersome, bulky, and expensive items on a car or truck today is the actual wiring harness required to tie all of the various electrical components together. The greater the number of wires and connections, then the greater the possibility and probability of a problem occurring at some time or another. With the greater number of electrical options now used, particularly on upscale passenger cars, the size and number of wires have risen steadily over the last five years.

Much research has gone into trying to simplify the physical size and complexity of the wiring harness used in today's cars and trucks. The wide-scale use of on-board computers offers an opportunity for designers and engineers to drastically reduce the number of wires used in a typical harness assembly. The use of computers requires that various engine sensors be employed to feed an analog signal back to the computer or ECM for both fuel- and ignition-setting characteristics.

Each individual sensor continually monitors its system, and unless there is a major change in the system operation, this signal remains relatively constant at a given engine speed. Since sensors react many times a second to their monitored system, the computer can logically access these signals as required. All sensors can be routinely sampled a number of times every minute, or more often if desired.

Although multiplexing is not as yet widely in use, engineers feel that it will only be a matter of time before this happens. One example of a multiplexed system is illustrated in Fig. 4-59, where a single wire with a ground return can be connected between all of the sensors and the ECM (electronic control module) or microprocessor. Since all sensors would access the same wire, it would be known as a data bus.

When the ECM or central processing unit wanted to access a sensor to monitor a system, it would do so by signalling each sensor through a small transmitter/receiver or T/R unit, as is shown in Fig. 4-59. The CPU would send out a coded signal on the data bus and through the connecting address bus to every T/R in the system. To prevent any confusion at the T/R units, each one would be assigned a coded address made up of a series of binary numbers (ON/OFF voltage pulses). Each would only respond to its code, and to no other. When a particular T/R unit recognized its code number (address), it would activate an analog/digital converter. The sensors analog voltage signal would then be immediately converted into digital form so that the CPU could understand its information. The digital sensor signal would leave the T/R unit and move out along the *data* rather than the *address* line towards the common data bus and back to the CPU within the ECM.

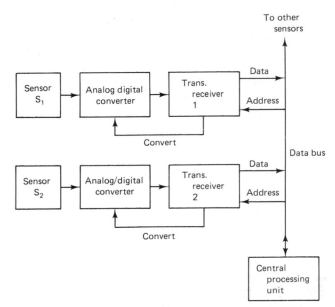

FIGURE 4-59 Simplified sensor multiplexing system.

Each specific sensor voltage signal (binary numbers), as well as the T/R address, would be fed into the CPU (central processing unit), which would read and interpret this data. The information would be used by the ECM to control the operation of the monitored systems, such as the fuel-injection and ignition system. The CPU would then proceed through a systematic analysis of the remaining sensors in a similar fashion. As mentioned, the rate of sensor sampling can be designed to suit each particular type of ECM being used, although major similarities exist between them all.

Another multiplexing system under development involves the use of a two-bus setup rather than one, as in the sensor/CPU system. The two-bus arrangement would be necessary to control the actual switching of electrical power to the various accessory circuits on the vehicle. These would include the headlights, power solenoids, power windows, power seats, heater fan, etc.

Figure 4-60 illustrates the two-bus system which is required for power switching, because one bus would be needed for carrying battery power, and the other for carrying the control signal from the particular accessory switch that we want to activate. Each switch for the accessory is indicated by an S in Fig. 4-60 with a receiver module M actually used to activate the switch. The receiver module is itself controlled by a command signal originating at the CPU, and which travels along the signal bus rather than on the bus that carries the battery power. When the operator activates a particular accessory switch, the CPU sends out a coded binary address along the signal bus that would only be recognized by a certain receiver module (M). When the

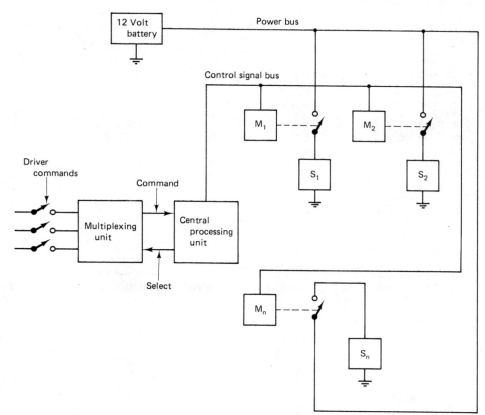

FIGURE 4-60 Control signal MUX (Multiplexing) system arrangement.

module recognizes its code, it activates its accessory switch (S) to either an OFF or ON mode, depending on the CPU command signal.

FIBER OPTICS

Another system that is now in use in automotive applications is the use of an optical fiber as a signal bus, rather than a stranded 14 gauge copper wire. When the CPU sends out a coded address signal (binary pulses), these signals are converted into light signals rather than voltage. The fiber tube is actually a very thin hollow pipe, often of the thickness of human hair.

The generated light impulses (signals) continue through the tube regardless of bends until they reach their intended goal, usually a receiver module with an optical disc connected to it. The receiver module then switches a system ON or OFF, based upon the code from the CPU. Major advantages of the fiber optic system is that it is not affected by external electrical noise. Therefore, the electrical signal is not distorted.

CHAPTER 5

Electronic Fuel-Injection Systems

Since this textbook's emphasis is on-board computers and the electronics component of the various systems in passenger cars and trucks, the detailed purpose, function, operation and troubleshooting of fuel-injection systems will not be covered in great detail. For a comprehensive treatment of this topic, you may wish to refer to my textbook entitled, *Automotive and Small-Truck Fuel-Injection Systems: Gas and Diesel,* which is published by Prentice Hall, Englewood Cliffs, New Jersey, U.S. 07632.

This chapter will introduce various gasoline-injection systems now in use by a number of major vehicle manufacturers, and cover, as well, the systems manufactured by Robert Bosch Corporation, which are used extensively by almost every passenger car manufacturer in the world today. An overview of system operation will be given, so that you may more fully understand just how important the on-board computer is to the successful operation of each of these systems.

FEEDBACK CARBURETOR SYSTEMS (FBC)

Engines equipped with FBC (feedback carburetors) are also monitored by various engine sensors which relay informational signals to the on-board ECM (electronic control module) in the same way that fuel-injected engines do. The ECM controls fuel delivery with information received from the following sensors:

1. Coolant temperature,
2. Crankshaft rpm,
3. Exhaust oxygen content,
4. Throttle position,
5. Intake manifold pressure.

Fuel delivery to the carburetor is controlled by an electrically-operated M/C (mixture control solenoid) mounted in the float bowl. See Figs. 5-1 and 5-2 for GM model E2SE and E2ME carburetors, both of which are widely used on nonfuel-injected engines.

In Fig. 5-2 the main metering rod position (Item 1) determines the amount of fuel flow needed to control the fuel/air ratio. In a fuel-injected system, the amount of fuel delivered to the cylinders is controlled by the pulse-width time, which is the actual duration that the injector valve remains open. The longer it is open, then the greater will be the fuel flow, since the injector valve opens the same distance each time it is energized. After receiving the various sensor signals, the ECM determines the position of the carburetor main metering rod. When the M/C solenoid is energized, there is less fuel flowing to mix with the air entering the carburetor, and a leaner fuel/air ratio will result. De-energizing the M/C solenoid allows more fuel to flow, thereby providing a richer fuel/air ratio. The ECM monitoring the various sensor signals turns (pulses) the M/C solenoid ON and OFF at a rate of 10 times per second in order to try and maintain the air/fuel mixture ratio as close to stoichiometric (14.7:1) as possible.

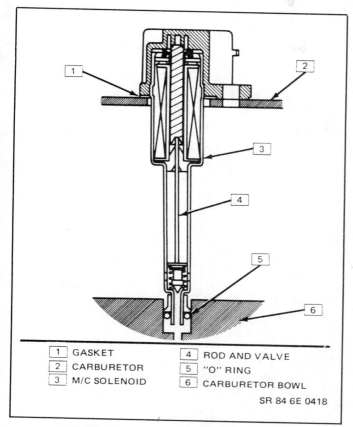

1	GASKET	4	ROD AND VALVE
2	CARBURETOR	5	"O" RING
3	M/C SOLENOID	6	CARBURETOR BOWL

SR 84 6E 0418

FIGURE 5-1 E2SE FBC mixture control solenoid. (*Courtesy of Oldsmobile Div. of GMC*)

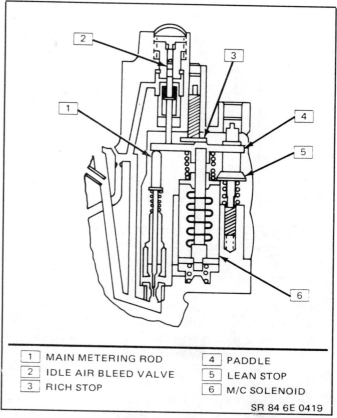

1	MAIN METERING ROD	4	PADDLE
2	IDLE AIR BLEED VALVE	5	LEAN STOP
3	RICH STOP	6	M/C SOLENOID

SR 84 6E 0419

FIGURE 5-2 E2ME FBC mixture control solenoid. (*Courtesy of Oldsmobile Div. of GMC*)

As with a fuel-injected system, the FBC system can operate in either open- or closed-loop. In an open-loop condition, the ECM will ignore the exhaust oxygen sensor feedback signal; in a closed loop, it will control the air/fuel ratio directly since the ECM continually receives and uses oxygen sensor feedback signals. The dwell meter will not vary during open-loop if it is connected as shown in the figure and connected to the M/C solenoid dwell connector (green), which is located in the harness near the solenoid, and if it is set on the 6-cylinder scale. When in a closed-loop operating mode however, the dwell meter will be between 10 and 50° dwell and varying. (See Fig. 5-3.)

Ford FBC

The system used by Ford Motor Company on its nonfuel-injected engines is similar to that employed by General Motors. Figure 5-4 illustrates the FBC actuator motor which is installed into the carburetor body. The on-board computer, namely the EEC (electronic engine control) or MCU (microprocessor control unit) system, continually receives voltage signals from the various engine sensors, and in turn energizes the actuator motor shaft to move it "in" or "out."

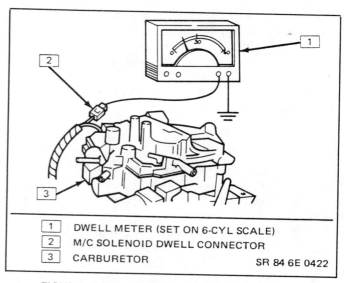

1	DWELL METER (SET ON 6-CYL SCALE)	
2	M/C SOLENOID DWELL CONNECTOR	
3	CARBURETOR	SR 84 6E 0422

FIGURE 5-3 FBC dwell meter connection. (*Courtesy of Oldsmobile Div. of GMC*)

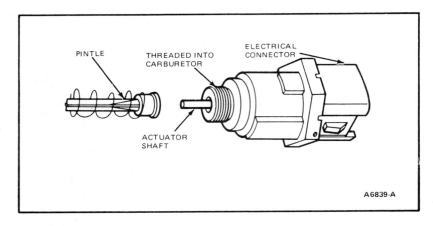

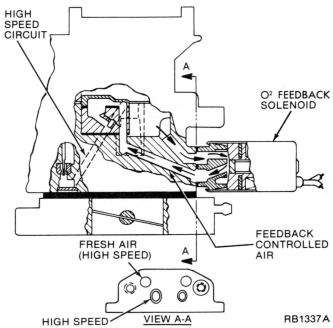

FIGURE 5-4 Feedback carburetor actuator motor. (*Courtesy of Ford Motor Company, Dearborn, MI.*)

This action causes the fuel metering pintle valve to produce a richer or leaner air/fuel mixture at the carburetor.

Chrysler FBC

In the Chrysler EFC (electronic feedback carburetor) system, an oxygen feedback solenoid mounted on the side of the carburetor body is essentially an emissions control system which utilizes an electrical signal from the spark control computer. It provides limited regulation of the air/fuel ratio. It performs this task by metering air flow only, but operates in parallel with a conventional fixed main-metering jet in the carburetor body. The exhaust oxygen sensor is the catalyst for the operation of the EFC system, since it continually feeds a voltage signal back to the computer system. In open loop, there is no effect from the oxygen sensor signal, while in closed loop, there is an electrical signal sent to the oxygen feedback solenoid.

Figure 5-5 illustrates the typical air flow control in the high speed mode that the oxygen feedback solenoid has on the carburetor system. The oxygen feedback solenoid also reacts to the air flow during the low speed engine operation as long as the system is in closed loop.

OPEN-LOOP VERSUS CLOSED-LOOP OPERATION

Two terms that you will come across when working with both electronic feedback carburetors and electronic fuel-injected systems are "open loop" and "closed loop." These terms refer to the situation in the engine when the air/fuel mixture is, or is not, being controlled by the ECM sensor inputs.

When the engine is cold and the exhaust temperature is below 360°C (680°F), the oxygen sensor located in the exhaust gas stream will not affect the system's operation, and therefore the ECM ignores this sensor. Under this condition, the engine is considered to be in an open-loop control operating mode.

FIGURE 5-5 Feedback carburetor system high-speed operation with oxygen sensor feedback signal to provide closed-loop operation. (*Courtesy of Chrysler Corporation*)

NOTE: The condition of "open" versus "closed" loop was discussed in detail in Chapter 4.

When the exhaust gases are hot enough to activate a voltage signal from the oxygen sensor, the ECM will enter the control function and alter the air/fuel ratio control to maintain efficient operation. This is the closed-loop operation, shown in Fig. 5-6.

The term "stoichiometric" is often used when discussing internal combustion engines. It refers to the theoretical ratio of the mass of air required for complete combustion of a given mass of fuel. For gasoline, this is an average of 14:1 (14 pounds of air to one pound of gasoline). With this

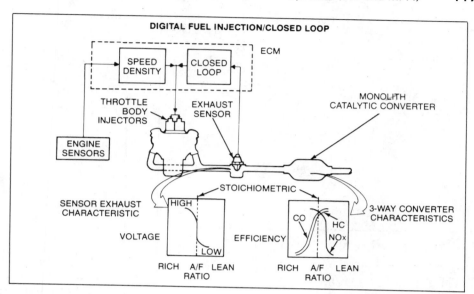

FIGURE 5-6 Closed-loop DFI (Digital Fuel Injection) schematic. (*Courtesy of Cadillac Motor Car Div. of GMC*)

stoichiometric air/fuel ratio, the excess air factor (greater than stoichiometric) is:

$$\text{Lambda} = \frac{\text{Quantity of air supplied}}{\text{Theoretical requirement}}$$

(where Lambda = 1, or 100%)

A lean mixture contains more air; a rich mixture contains less air. The air/fuel ratio in a spark-ignited engine must be between 0.7 and 1.25 (Lamba) whether it is using a carburetor or fuel-injected system. With an air/fuel ratio of 1.25, the air/fuel mixture is no longer ignitable; this is known as the lean misfire limit.

Gasoline engines tend to obtain their maximum power output with a rich mixture (less air) of between 0 and 10%, while minimum fuel consumption is obtained with an excess of air (10%). Satisfactory idling and good transition occur with an air deficiency of between 30–40%. The most efficient mixture to minimize exhaust emissions is 14.7 to 1, which allows the catalytic converter to operate most efficiently.

TYPES OF GASOLINE FUEL-INJECTION SYSTEMS (TBI AND MPFI)

Gasoline fuel injection first started to gain prominence in the early 1970's as a means not only to meet EPA (Environmental Protection Agency) exhaust emissions regulations but also to improve and meet the projected CAFE (Corporate Average Fuel Economy) standards. In addition, gasoline fuel injection provides superior overall performance to that of a carbureted system.

The major leader in the production, design, and application of gasoline fuel-injection systems has been and continues to be Robert Bosch Corporation. Every major passenger car manufacturer in the world today uses a system of Robert Bosch design, with minor design changes made to suit particular engine and vehicle models. Gasoline fuel-injection systems now in use by vehicle manufacturers fall into one of two categories. These are:

1. TBI, or Throttle Body Injection,
2. MPFI, Multi-Port, or Point Fuel Injection.

In TBI systems, a throttle body similar in appearance to a typical carburetor is mounted on the engine intake manifold. An example of a typical TBI unit is shown in Fig. 5-7, while Fig. 5-8 illustrates the location of the fuel injector for a ported type of injection system. Figure 5-9 shows the typical components that are used on a multi-port four-cylinder gasoline engine.

In the throttle body system, either one or two electronically-controlled fuel injectors are located within the throttle body unit, while in the ported fuel-injection system, an individual fuel injector is used for each engine cylinder. In both cases, the amount of fuel delivered to the cylinder depends upon how long the fuel injector is actually held open or energized electrically. The distance that the fuel injector valve lifts or opens is constant, regardless of the throttle pedal position. Therefore, in order to vary the amount of fuel delivered for a given throttle position, the more "time" that the fuel injector remains in the open (flowing) position, the greater the volume of fuel delivered to the engine cylinders will be. Figure 5-10 illustrates a typical electronically-controlled fuel injector, with a small solenoid consisting of a coil and armature built within the body.

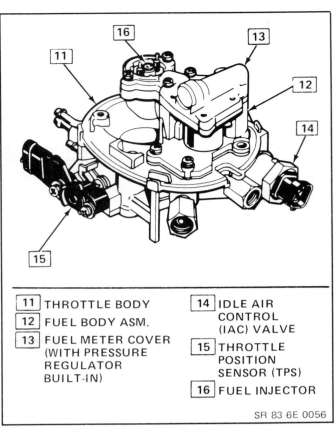

11	THROTTLE BODY	14	IDLE AIR CONTROL (IAC) VALVE
12	FUEL BODY ASM.		
13	FUEL METER COVER (WITH PRESSURE REGULATOR BUILT-IN)	15	THROTTLE POSITION SENSOR (TPS)
		16	FUEL INJECTOR

SR 83 6E 0056

FIGURE 5-7 TBI (throttle body injection) injection unit. (*Courtesy of Oldsmobile Division of GMC*)

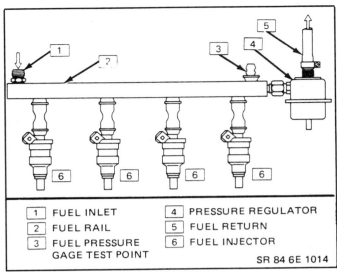

1	FUEL INLET	4	PRESSURE REGULATOR
2	FUEL RAIL	5	FUEL RETURN
3	FUEL PRESSURE GAGE TEST POINT	6	FUEL INJECTOR

SR 84 6E 1014

FIGURE 5-9 Multi-port injection fuel rail assembly. (*Courtesy of Oldsmobile Division of GMC*)

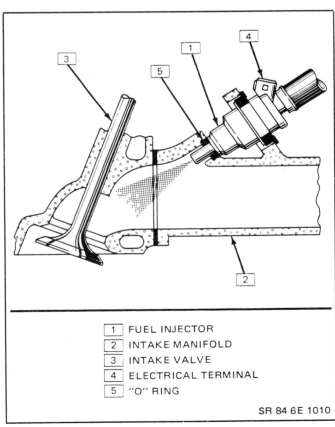

1	FUEL INJECTOR
2	INTAKE MANIFOLD
3	INTAKE VALVE
4	ELECTRICAL TERMINAL
5	"O" RING

SR 84 6E 1010

FIGURE 5-8 Fuel-injector location on a ported fuel-injection system. (*Courtesy of Oldsmobile Division of GMC*)

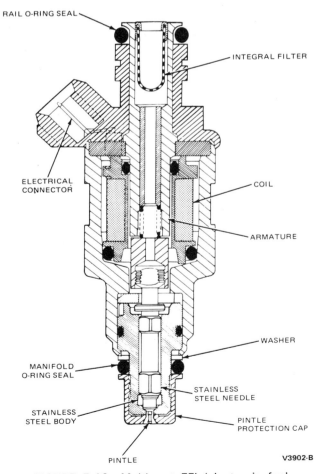

FIGURE 5-10 Multi-port EFI (electronic fuel injection) system fuel injector. (*Courtesy of Ford Motor Company, Dearborn, MI.*)

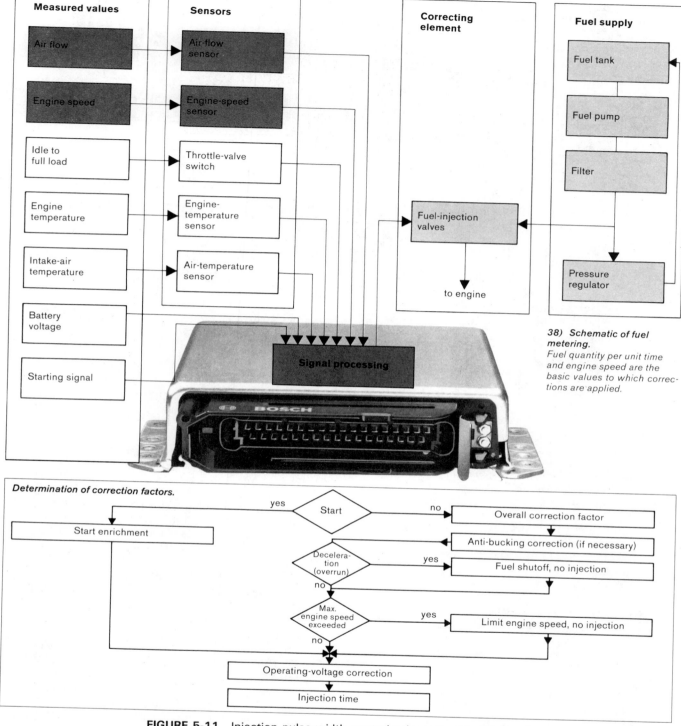

Measured values

- Air flow
- Engine speed
- Idle to full load
- Engine temperature
- Intake-air temperature
- Battery voltage
- Starting signal

Sensors

- Air-flow sensor
- Engine-speed sensor
- Throttle-valve switch
- Engine-temperature sensor
- Air-temperature sensor

Signal processing

Correcting element

Fuel-injection valves

to engine

Fuel supply

- Fuel tank
- Fuel pump
- Filter
- Pressure regulator

38) Schematic of fuel metering.
Fuel quantity per unit time and engine speed are the basic values to which corrections are applied.

BOSCH

Determination of correction factors.

Start
→ yes → Start enrichment
→ no → Overall correction factor
→ Anti-bucking correction (if necessary)

Deceleration (overrun)
→ yes → Fuel shutoff, no injection
→ no

Max. engine speed exceeded
→ yes → Limit engine speed, no injection
→ no

Operating-voltage correction

Injection time

FIGURE 5-11 Injection pulse-width control schematic. (*Courtesy of Robert Bosch Corporation*)

The fuel injector illustrated in Fig. 5-10 is similar in both design and operation, whether or not the system is of TBI or MPFI design. Each fuel injector receives a voltage signal from the on-board vehicle computer to control its operation. This voltage signal is commonly referred to as a pulse-width signal, meaning that the longer the pulse width, then the longer the fuel injector will remain open. Simply put, this means that more fuel will be delivered,

and greater speed and horsepower will be the result. Similarly, the shorter the pulse-width signal, the less fuel will be delivered, and this will result in lower speed and horsepower. Figure 5-11 schematically illustrates how this pulse-width voltage signal is determined and controlled by the on-board vehicle computer. The injector pulse-width or duration calculation is based upon air flow into the engine, as well as the engine speed sensor and various correction

119

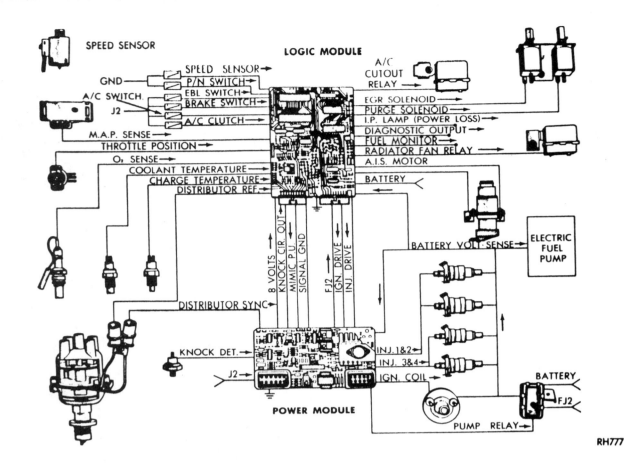

FIGURE 5-12 Electronic control system arrangement for the Chrysler 2.2L turbocharged engine with multi-point fuel injection. (*Courtesy of Chrysler Corporation*)

(1) Charge Temperature Sensor
(2) Coolant Temperature Sensor
(3) Throttle Position Sensor
(4) MAP Sensor
(5) Distributor pick ups
(E) Automatic Idle Speed Motor activated by FJ2 from Logic Module
(F) Logic sends information to Power Module:
  (1) Ignition timing (anti-dwell)
  (2) Injector turn on
  (3) Injector turn off
(G) Power Module requires:
  (1) Distributor signal within 1/2 second of cranking
  (2) Distributor and injector pulses greater than 60 RPM
(H) Power Module then:
  (1) Commands injector to supply fuel
  (2) Triggers the ignition coil (−)

With the ignition key in the RUN position, the following information must be available to the Power Module and Logic Module or the engine will stop.

(A) Logic Module 21 way red connector		OUTPUT
(1) Number 2 pin—sensor ground		INPUT
(2) Number 3 pin—8 volts		OUTPUT
(3) Number 4 pin—5 volts		OUTPUT
(4) Number 5 pin—injector off		OUTPUT
(5) Number 7 pin—anti-dwell		OUTPUT
(6) Number 8 pin—injector on		OUTPUT
(7) Number 11 pin—distributor reference signal		INPUT
(8) Number 19 pin—distributor synchronization signal		OUTPUT
(B) Power Module 10 way black connector		
(1) Number 1 pin—coil (−)		OUTPUT
(2) Number 2 pin—J2		INPUT
(3) Number 3 pin—fused J2		OUTPUT
(4) Number 4 pin—injector driver number 2		OUTPUT
(5) Number 5 pin—injector driver number 1		OUTPUT
(6) Number 6 pin—ASD relay ground		OUTPUT
(7) Number 8 pin—battery supply		INPUT

factors. These include the temperature of the engine on startup, and the actual temperature of the ambient air flowing into the engine.

Another popular system is shown in Fig. 5-12, which illustrates the electronic control system used by Chrysler in its 2.2L turbocharged multi-point fuel-injection system found in the Laser and Daytona front wheel drive vehicles.

Information from the various input sensors on the engine is fed into the ECU (electronic control unit). The logic module determines from computer computation what, when, and how much fuel should be injected. Therefore, it outputs a signal to the power module, which increases the strength of the signal so that it will be strong enough to activate the fuel injector solenoid. The duration of injection is controlled by the pulse-width signal, as was mentioned earlier.

INJECTION SYSTEM CONTROLS

Regardless of the type of gasoline fuel-injection system in use, all systems use fuel injectors that are pulsed open and closed by an electrical signal. The length of time that the injector is energized (open) determines the volume of fuel that will be injected into the engine. The fuel injector is either open or closed. It opens the same distance each time that it is energized to allow fuel to flow.

These electrical signals are determined by an electronic control module with memory capability. The electronic control module (or ECM) is located in various positions on different vehicles, but it is usually found inside the passenger compartment area of the vehicle so that it is well protected against the elements.

Vehicle manufacturers refer to the ECM by various terms, as they do with their terminology for their fuel systems. General Motors refers to its system as an ECM, while Ford refers to its electronic control system as an EEC/MCU, or electronic engine control microprocessor control unit. Chrysler calls its system a CCC (computer controlled combustion) when used with its port fuel-injection system and an ECU (electronic control unit) when used with its TBI system.

Each electronic control module is designed to operate with a number of engine and vehicle sensors that are fed a 5-volt reference signal from the ECM. Typical sensors used and the systems that are monitored can be seen in Figure 5-13. Each sensor is designed to operate on the principle of resistance either through a change in temperature or a change in pressure. Each sensor, in effect, becomes a potentiometer, or variable resistor. A reference voltage of about 5 volts from the ECM is fed to each sensor, and a signal voltage is returned to the ECM from the sensor unit. When the ECM receives these various voltage signals from each individual engine/vehicle sensor, it compares and computes these signals with a preprogrammed memory system. Based on a reference mode, the ECM then sends out voltage signals to alter the air/fuel ratio under various speeds, loads, and operating conditions. In this way, the engine's performance, fuel consumption, and exhaust emissions are held at the maximum efficiency level.

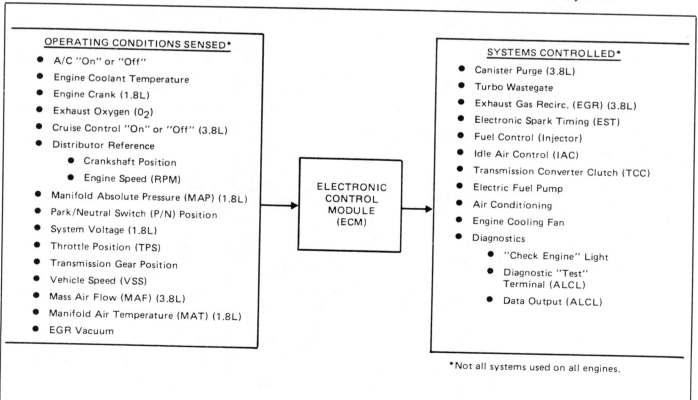

FIGURE 5-13 Electronic control module (ECM) operating conditions sensed and systems controlled chart. (*Courtesy of Oldsmobile Division of GMC*)

If any condition arises whereby a sensor fails or an abnormal condition exists with the engine or vehicle monitored systems, then a voltage signal from the ECM will sense the problem and will flash a *Check Engine* light on the instrument panel.

The mechanic/technician, by using a simple jumper wire arrangement, can then access the memory bank of the ECM by an ALCL (assembly line communication link) or similar arrangement, which is located under the dashboard/instrument panel of the vehicle inside the passenger compartment. This initiates a sequence that will cause a series of flashing numbers to show on the instrument panel. The mechanic/technician then follows the vehicle/engine service manual diagnostic routine to isolate the given problem.

Each service manual contains a troubleshooting chart and a list that indicates where and what the problem might be for a particular flashing number. These code numbers, as they are commonly referred to, can be found in sections of this book dealing with General Motors, Ford, Chrysler, AMC, Toyota, and Nissan vehicles.

Effective troubleshooting with gasoline fuel-injected vehicles is no more difficult than it is for a carbureted engine. The basic rules of troubleshooting apply equally well to both types of fuel systems. Information contained in each chapter for a specific fuel system can in many cases be applied to general service/repair work for other types of fuel systems; therefore, store this information in your head just like an ECM system, and use it to advantage when troubleshooting and servicing any type of fuel-injection system.

ROBERT BOSCH GASOLINE FUEL-INJECTION SYSTEMS

Robert Bosch Corporation is the major producer of gasoline fuel-injection systems worldwide. Systems manufactured by Bosch are all multi-port design with the exception of the Mono-Jetronic system, which is a throttle body injection system. Major systems are the D, K, KE, L, LE, LH, LU, the Motronic, and the Mono-Jetronic models.

Basic differences among these systems are as follows:

1. D-Jetronic was the first electronically produced system, and it first appeared in the early 70's. The "D" comes from the German word "druck," which means "pressure." The word Jetronic, meaning injection, was coined by the Robert Bosch Corporation.

2. K-Jetronic is a continuous mechanical injection system, with the letter "K" standing for the word continuous in German. This system has also been called a CIS (continuous injection system).

3. The KE system is a later version of the straight K system. This system uses the designation "E" to indicate that the system is electronically- rather than mechanically-controlled.

4. The L system derives its name from the German word for air (luft). An air flow sensor is contained within the intake manifold to determine through a potentiometer (variable resistance) where the throttle is at any given time.

5. The LE system is a further improvement to the L system. Its major improvement includes an expanded scope of functions for precise adaptation of fuel delivery.

6. The LH system uses a hot-wire mass air flow sensor in the intake manifold rather than a swinging plate and potentiometer system.

7. The LU system is designed specifically for use with unleaded gasoline.

8. The Motronic system is an integrated system for the dual control of both the gasoline fuel-injection, as well as for the electronic ignition system.

9. The Mono-Jetronic system is a throttle body injection system employing a single injection valve mounted centrally in the body.

KE-Jetronic System

Components used with the KE-Jetronic system are illustrated in Fig. 5-14, while Figs. 5-15 and 5-16 illustrate the basic difference between the K and KE systems.

In Figs. 5-15 and 5-16, gasoline is drawn from the tank by the electrically-operated roller-cell pump, which in some vehicle applications can be mounted inside the fuel tank. The fuel under pressure from the roller-cell unit passes to an accumulator which maintains pressure in the system even when the engine is shut off. Fuel then passes to a filter assembly and onto a fuel distributor unit mounted on the engine intake manifold. In the K system, the position of an air-flow sensor plate within the intake manifold controlled by throttle pedal position determines the position of a fuel plunger within the fuel distributor unit, and therefore the fuel flow to the injectors. In the KE system, various sensors feed a voltage signal to the on-board vehicle computer which in turn determines the amount of fuel to the injectors. Figure 5-17 shows a block diagram of the KE system inputs and outputs from the ECU (electronic control unit), while Fig. 5-18 is a schematic of the ECU.

D-Jetronic System

The D system has been superseded by the L systems and the Motronic model.

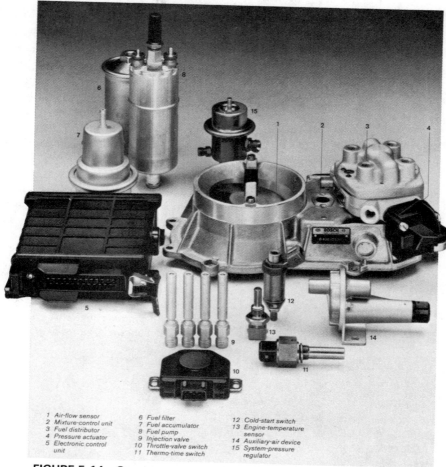

1 Air-flow sensor	6 Fuel filter	12 Cold-start switch
2 Mixture-control unit	7 Fuel accumulator	13 Engine-temperature
3 Fuel distributor	8 Fuel pump	sensor
4 Pressure actuator	9 Injection valve	14 Auxiliary-air device
5 Electronic control	10 Throttle-valve switch	15 System-pressure
unit	11 Thermo-time switch	regulator

FIGURE 5-14 Component parts of a model KE-Jetronic Fuel Injection System. (*Courtesy of Robert Bosch Corporation*)

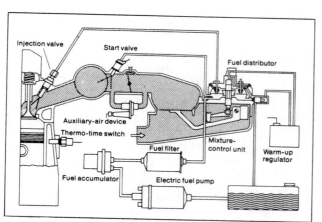

FIGURE 5-15 K-Jetronic system operational diagram. (*Courtesy of Robert Bosch Corporation*)

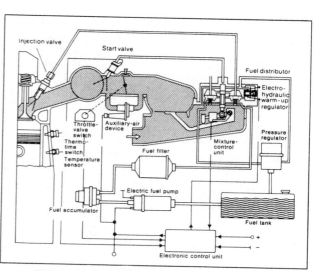

FIGURE 5-16 KE-jetronic system operational diagram. (*Courtesy of Robert Bosch Corporation*)

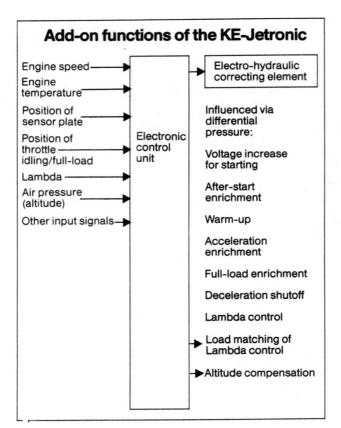

Add-on functions of the KE-Jetronic

Engine speed →
Engine temperature →
Position of sensor plate →
Position of throttle idling/full-load →
Lambda →
Air pressure (altitude) →
Other input signals →

Electronic control unit

→ Electro-hydraulic correcting element

Influenced via differential pressure:

Voltage increase for starting

After-start enrichment

Warm-up

Acceleration enrichment

Full-load enrichment

Deceleration shutoff

Lambda control

→ Load matching of Lambda control

→ Altitude compensation

L-Jetronic System Operation

The L system derives its name from the fact that the German word for air is *luft;* therefore the letter L. The system relies on an air-flow sensor that generates a voltage signal proportional to the volume of air actually drawn into the engine intake manifold. The EFI L-Jetronic system is a more advanced system than the D series, and it therefore provides a more effective system to meet exhaust emissions regulations. The air-flow sensor on the L-Jetronic system is different from that on the K. Refer to Figs. 5-19 and 5-20 for a more detailed view of its operation.

The main difference between the L/LE and the LH fuel-injection systems is in the type of air-flow sensor that each one employs. The LE system (see Fig. 5-21) differs from the straight L system in that the LE system has an expanded scope of functions for precise adaptation of fuel delivery. In addition, Lambda closed-loop control is possible as an

FIGURE 5-17 K-Jetronic CIS (continuous injection system) with Lambda (exhaust oxygen sensor) control—operational diagram. (*Courtesy of Robert Bosch Corporation*)

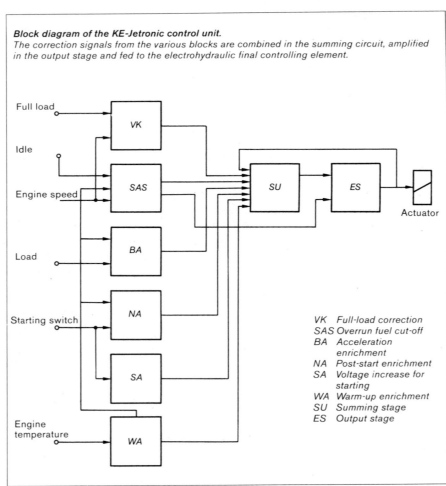

Block diagram of the KE-Jetronic control unit.
The correction signals from the various blocks are combined in the summing circuit, amplified in the output stage and fed to the electrohydraulic final controlling element.

Full load
Idle
Engine speed
Load
Starting switch
Engine temperature

VK
SAS
BA
NA
SA
WA
SU
ES

Actuator

VK   Full-load correction
SAS Overrun fuel cut-off
BA   Acceleration enrichment
NA   Post-start enrichment
SA   Voltage increase for starting
WA   Warm-up enrichment
SU   Summing stage
ES   Output stage

FIGURE 5-18 Block diagram of the model KE-Jetronic electronic control unit. (*Courtesy of Robert Bosch Corporation*)

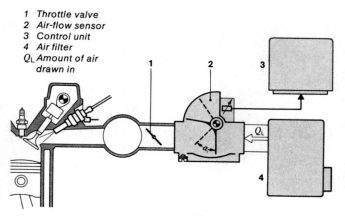

1 Throttle valve
2 Air-flow sensor
3 Control unit
4 Air filter
Q_L Amount of air
  drawn in

FIGURE 5-19 L-Jetronic air flow sensor. (*Courtesy of Robert Bosch Corporation*)

additional function if unleaded gasoline is used. The system is then known as an LU, with "U" standing for unleaded fuel.

Specific differences lie mainly in the improvements over the original L model system. These include the following:

1. Improved functions, reduced costs, and optimized circuitry of the electronic control unit for a reduced power loss.

2. Injectors with a high internal resistance (without series resistor).

3. An air-flow sensor with an integrated intake-air temperature compensation.

4. A reduced number of connectors.

5. Expanded scope of functions for increased economy in

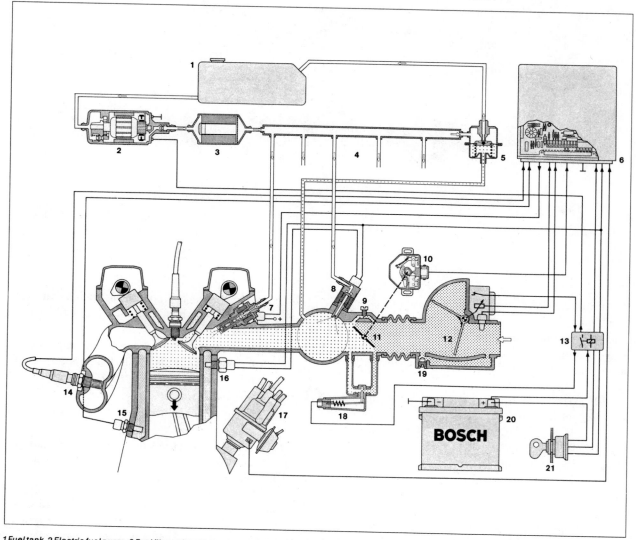

1 Fuel tank, 2 Electric fuel pump, 3 Fuel filter, 4 Distributor pipe, 5 Pressure regulator, 6 Control unit, 7 Injection valve, 8 Start valve, 9 Idle-speed adjusting screw, 10 Throttle-valve switch, 11 Throttle valve, 12 Air-flow sensor, 13 Relay combination, 14 Lambda sensor (only for certain countries), 15 Engine temperature sensor, 16 Thermo-time switch, 17 Ignition distributor, 18 Auxiliary-air device, 19 Idle-mixture adjusting screw, 20 Battery, 21 Ignition-starter switch

FIGURE 5-20 L-Jetronic fuel system component layout. (*Courtesy of Robert Bosch Corporation*)

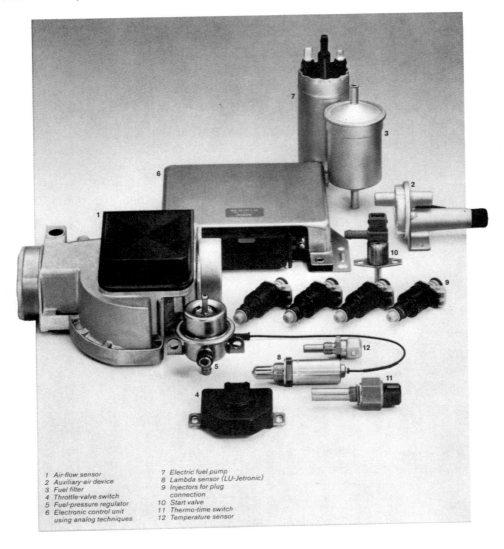

1 Air-flow sensor
2 Auxiliary-air device
3 Fuel filter
4 Throttle-valve switch
5 Fuel-pressure regulator
6 Electronic control unit
  using analog techniques
7 Electric fuel pump
8 Lambda sensor (LU-Jetronic)
9 Injectors for plug
  connection
10 Start valve
11 Thermo-time switch
12 Temperature sensor

FIGURE 5-21   Components of the LE-jetronic fuel injection system. (*Courtesy of Robert Bosch Corporation*)

the metering of fuel to suit the respective operating condition.

6. Control of the fuel pump through an electronic control relay; therefore, elimination of the pump contact in the air-flow sensor.

The LE system can be divided into three main functional areas, which are as follows:

1. Fuel supply.
2. Measurement of operating data.
3. Fuel metering.

The LH system (see Fig. 5-22), on the other hand, can be divided into five main functional areas, and these are:

1. Fuel supply.

2. Measurement of operating data, such as air mass, engine speed, load condition (idle/full load), and engine temperature.
3. Metering of basic fuel quantity and adaptation to cold starting, warmup, idle, full load, acceleration, and overrun.
4. Idle speed control.
5. Emission control, with Lambda closed-loop control.

NOTE: Closed loop means that the engine exhaust oxygen sensor is hot enough to create a reaction. As a result, a voltage signal is sent from this sensor to the ECU, which will influence the duration (pulse width) of the fuel injectors and therefore the quantity of fuel injected. By this method, the air/fuel ratio control can be maintained at nearly stoichiometric, or ideal, conditions of 14:1 under all operating conditions.

In an open-loop mode, the exhaust oxygen sensor does not influence the signal from the ECU, and the engine runs in a preset mode.

The LH system employs a hot-wire mass air-flow meter that measures the air mass being drawn into the engine rather than the vane-type air-flow meter used with the L and LE models. This hot-wire air-flow meter takes into account the possibility of temperature and altitude variations. This hot-wire mass air-flow sensor is shown in Chapter 4 in Figs. 4-36 through 4-39 and is used by General Motors on the Buick 3.8L V6 and the Chevrolet Corvette engines, just to name two commonly known North American passenger performance cars.

Of Robert Bosch design and manufacture, this system of air-flow measurement is a first of its kind. Rather than using an air-flow sensor flap (vane-type), which is used in the L/LE systems, the hot-wire arrangement used in the LH system employs a very thin platinum wire (70 μm thick)

set into the air intake system and contained within the bore area of Item 5 in Fig. 4-36 and shown in heated form in Fig. 4-38.

Air flowing over the wire draws heat from it so that the wire's electrical resistance changes with temperature. An electronic amplifier in the system responds instantly to any electrical resistance change and regulates the current flow of from 500 to 1200 mA (depending upon the air-flow rate) to the hot wire in order to maintain it at a virtually constant temperature. The current flow required to maintain a stable temperature at the wire becomes, in effect, a measure of the air mass flowing over the wire with the output signal being a voltage. Major advantages of the hot-wire system of measurement are its very small dimensions and the complete lack of any moving parts.

Another unique feature of the hot-wire system of air-flow measurement is that because impurities may accumulate on the heated wire's surface, the voltage output

FIGURE 5-22 Components of the LH-Jetronic fuel injection system. (*Courtesy of Robert Bosch Corporation*)

1 Hot-wire air-mass sensor	5 Fuel-pressure regulator	8 Injectors
2 Idle controller	6 Digital electronic	9 Temperature sensor
3 Fuel filter	control unit	10 Lambda sensor (only with
4 Throttle-valve switch	7 Electric fuel pump	lambda closed-loop control)

signal could change. Therefore, the system includes a provision for automatically increasing the wire's temperature for one second each time the engine is switched off to allow the wire to burn off impurities or corrosion. The "burn-off" command comes from the electronic control unit of the LH system.

Another difference between the L and the LH systems is that the L control unit is available in either analog or digital versions, while the LH control unit is digital with a microcomputer governing its adaptation to engine parameters. In addition, both the LE/U and the LH can be adapted for deceleration fuel shutoff, such as when in overrun (going down a hill) or in city traffic, as well as for engine speed limitation when the maximum allowable engine speed is reached. In the latter situation, the electronic control unit suppresses the injection pulses and protects the engine from over-revving.

Figure 5-21 illustrates the actual component parts of the LE-Jetronic system as they would appear on the vehicle, while Fig. 5-22 illustrates the newer LH system components. This visual identification will help you to associate the numbered items shown in the operating diagram in Fig. 5-20 and to readily locate parts on the vehicle when tracing the system. The air-flow sensor flap (2) in Fig. 5-19 is moved in relation to the volume of air flow being taken into the engine. An opposing restoring spring force maintains the sensor flap in a fixed position, i.e., for any preselected throttle position. A potentiometer is connected to the flap position and sends a voltage signal back to the ECU (electronic control unit). The compensation flap used with the air-flow sensor prevents oscillations of the sensor flap because it has the same effective area.

Unlike the D-Jetronic system, the L system does not require trigger contacts in the ignition distributor because all injection valves are connected electrically in parallel and will simultaneously inject half of the required amount of fuel twice during each camshaft rotation; therefore, a fixed relationship between the cam angle and the start of ignition is no longer necessary. The injection pulses are controlled from the ignition distributor contact points or reluctor pickup coil in electronic ignition systems.

In a 6-cylinder engine, the distributor must relay/time a high-tension spark six times in one operating cycle of the engine—namely, intake, compression, power, and exhaust (720° or two complete revolutions). Therefore, the frequency of injection must be divided in half in the control unit (ECU) for each engine revolution, which, for the 6-cylinder engine, would be divided by a factor of 3. In a 4-cylinder, the distributor delivers a high-tension spark four times during each operating cycle or 720°, and since fuel is injected only twice for each engine operating cycle, the frequency has to be divided in half at the ECU.

With no trigger contacts in the L system, as there were

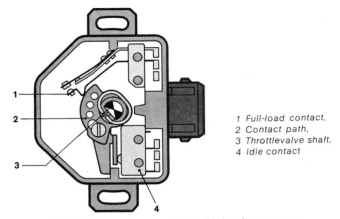

1 Full-load contact,
2 Contact path,
3 Throttlevalve shaft,
4 Idle contact

FIGURE 5-23   L-jetronic fuel injection system throttle valve switch. (*Courtesy of Robert Bosch Corporation*)

with the D system, the pulses from the ignition distributor are converted to rectangular pulses in a pulse shaper, such as shown in Fig. 5-23, within the throttle valve switch. An example of how the pulse shaper controls the injection system is best explained by reference to Fig. 5-24.

NOTE: In the breakerless (solid-state), high-energy-type ignition distributor, pulses of the ignition voltage would cause the same basic action to occur (Fig. 5-24).

Because fuel injection will take place twice for every camshaft rotation related to four ignition distributor pulses, the frequency of the system must be divided in half by the frequency divider shown in the block diagram in Fig. 5-25. A capacitor is charged by these rectangular pulses; therefore, each injection pulse is initiated by the discharge of the capacitor. Air flap position determines the duration of injection (wider throttle position, longer fuel injection period, and vice versa). The other input signals shown in Fig. 5-25 also contribute to the actual length of the injection period.

An example of an L-Jetronic fuel-injection system wiring arrangement for a 6-cylinder BMW is shown in Figs. 5-26 and 5-27.

In Figure 5-26, when the ignition is switched on, battery voltage is relayed through the relay set (9) and (10) to the ECU (1) and injection valves (5). When the engine starts, the relay set switches on the electric fuel pump, the start valve, the thermo-time switch (8), and the auxiliary air device. If the engine fires and runs, the power supply for the pump and the auxiliary air device is maintained through a contact in the air-flow sensor. If the engine fails to start, the relay set (9) and (10) interrupt the electric circuit to the fuel pump to prevent a flooding condition through continued pump operation with the engine being cranked continually.

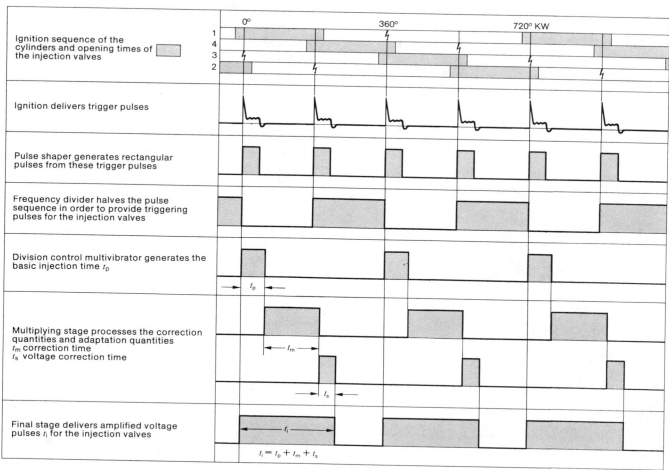

		0°		360°		720° KW

Ignition sequence of the cylinders and opening times of the injection valves

1
4
3
2

Ignition delivers trigger pulses

Pulse shaper generates rectangular pulses from these trigger pulses

Frequency divider halves the pulse sequence in order to provide triggering pulses for the injection valves

Division control multivibrator generates the basic injection time t_p

Multiplying stage processes the correction quantities and adaptation quantities
t_m correction time
t_s voltage correction time

Final stage delivers amplified voltage pulses t_i for the injection valves

$$t_i = t_p + t_m + t_s$$

FIGURE 5-24 Generation of the fuel injector pulses for a 4 cylinder L-Jetronic model system. (*Courtesy of Robert Bosch Corporation*)

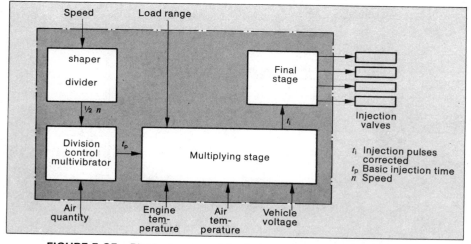

FIGURE 5-25 Block diagram of the L-Jetronic system electronic control unit. (*Courtesy of Robert Bosch Corporation*)

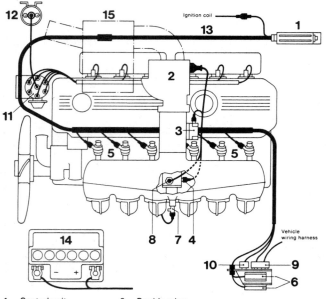

1 – Control unit
2 – Air-flow meter
3 – Throttle valve
4 – Temperature sensor
5 – Fuel injection valve
6 – Series resistor
7 – Start valve
8 – Thermo-time switch
9 – Double relay
10 – Start-valve relay
11 – Ignition distributor
12 – Ignition coil
13 – Wiring harness
14 – Battery
15 – Air filter

Fuel-injection pressure in the L system is controlled by the fuel pressure regulator to approximately 36 psi (2.5 bar). A relief valve in the pump is designed to open any time that fuel line pressure exceeds 43–64 psi (2.96–4.41 bar).

Motronic Fuel-Injection System

The Robert Bosch Motronic gasoline fuel-injection system uses an L-Jetronic system coupled with an electronic ignition system, with both systems being controlled by a common digital microcomputer. The same sensors can be used for both the fuel injection and the ignition. Thus more is achieved at a lower cost than with two separate systems. The operation of the sensors depends upon a reference voltage that is generated from the vehicle battery and fed through the ECU circuit at about 5 volts to each sensor.

FIGURE 5-26 L-Jetronic BMW wiring harness description. (*Courtesy of Robert Bosch Corporation*)

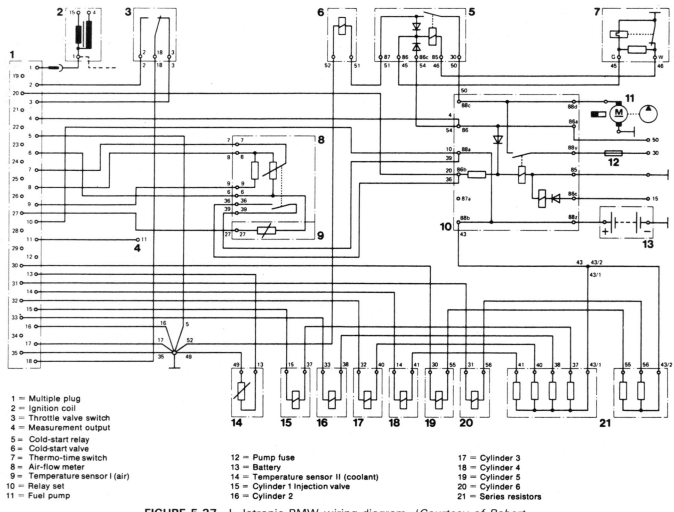

1 = Multiple plug
2 = Ignition coil
3 = Throttle valve switch
4 = Measurement output
5 = Cold-start relay
6 = Cold-start valve
7 = Thermo-time switch
8 = Air-flow meter
9 = Temperature sensor I (air)
10 = Relay set
11 = Fuel pump

12 = Pump fuse
13 = Battery
14 = Temperature sensor II (coolant)
15 = Cylinder 1 Injection valve
16 = Cylinder 2

17 = Cylinder 3
18 = Cylinder 4
19 = Cylinder 5
20 = Cylinder 6
21 = Series resistors

FIGURE 5-27 L-Jetronic BMW wiring diagram. (*Courtesy of Robert Bosch Corporation*)

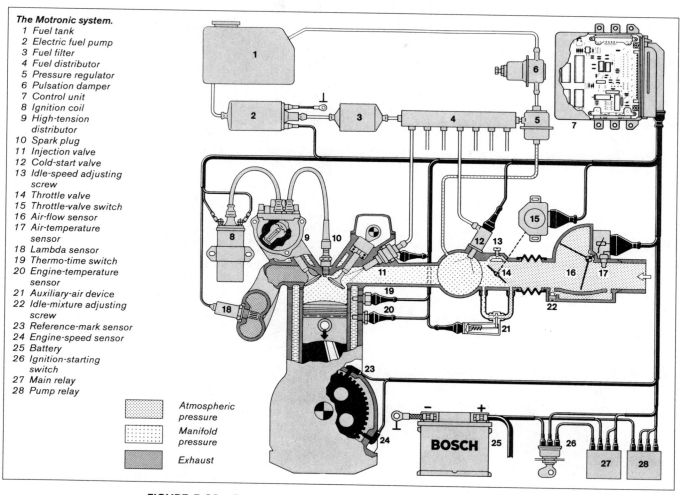

The Motronic system.

1 Fuel tank
2 Electric fuel pump
3 Fuel filter
4 Fuel distributor
5 Pressure regulator
6 Pulsation damper
7 Control unit
8 Ignition coil
9 High-tension distributor
10 Spark plug
11 Injection valve
12 Cold-start valve
13 Idle-speed adjusting screw
14 Throttle valve
15 Throttle-valve switch
16 Air-flow sensor
17 Air-temperature sensor
18 Lambda sensor
19 Thermo-time switch
20 Engine-temperature sensor
21 Auxiliary-air device
22 Idle-mixture adjusting screw
23 Reference-mark sensor
24 Engine-speed sensor
25 Battery
26 Ignition-starting switch
27 Main relay
28 Pump relay

Atmospheric pressure

Manifold pressure

Exhaust

FIGURE 5-28 Operational diagram—Motronic fuel-injection system. (*Courtesy of Robert Bosch Corporation*)

The various sensors are constructed in such a way that they generate a voltage based upon either a temperature rise/fall or a pressure change. A preprogrammed system is contained within the microcomputer and is used as a base reference for engine operation. Voltage signals received at the microcomputer from the sensors are compared with the actual values stored in the computer. Any deviation from the base reference voltage or optimum operating conditions causes the microprocessor to send out corrected voltage signals to both the injection and ignition control circuits.

The Motronic system therefore offers all of the advantages of the L-type systems plus increased fuel savings by adapting the fuel quantity and ignition advance to all operating conditions by means of the Lambda sensor map and the ignition-advance map.

The ignition angle can be modified according to engine coolant and intake air temperature, as well as by throttle position and other parameters. Rather than using the conventional mechanically-operated centrifugal and vacuum advance mechanisms within the distributor, Motronic has a spark-advance characteristic map stored in its control unit.

The microcomputer calculates the ignition angle between every two spark impulses from the information it receives about engine load and speed, as well as temperature and throttle position; thus it is able to adjust quickly to every operating condition and give optimum performance, fuel consumption, and emissions control.

The intermittent, electronically controlled fuel injection is based upon the L system with the important difference being found in the signal processing—which is digital with the Motronic. The Motronic fuel system is shown in Fig. 5-28 with its various sensors and engine controls, both for the ignition and the fuel-injection systems.

Since the fuel-injection portion of the Motronic system operates on the L-Jetronic principle, we will not repeat this information here. (Refer to the explanation earlier for the L operation.) The important difference is that the single ECU (electronic control unit) with digital microcomputer,

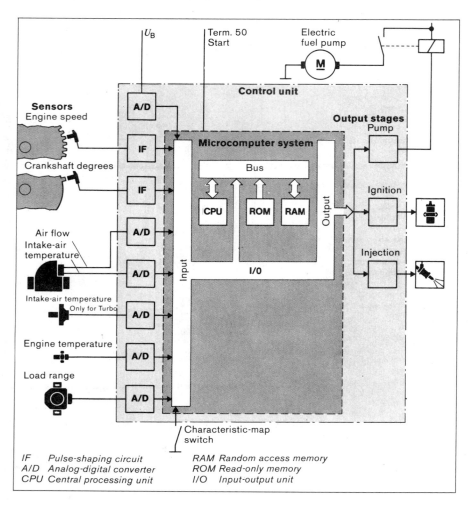

FIGURE 5-29 Motronic fuel system operational block diagram. (*Courtesy of Robert Bosch Corporation*)

on the basis of the characteristic map stored in it, determines both the ignition and fuel settings once the vehicle ignition key is turned on and the engine is cranked. Figure 5-29 illustrates a block diagram of the Motronic system that shows the microcomputer system contained within the ECU. A 35-pin connector is used to connect the ECU to the battery, the sensors, and the controlling elements.

Motronic Operation. When the ignition is turned on and the engine is stationary, no fuel is delivered. A power transistor in the ECU controls an external pump relay shown as Item 28 in Figure 5-28. When the ignition key is rotated to the start position, relay 50 shown in Fig. 5-29 is connected to the battery positive, the electric fuel pump is energized, and the system is primed and ready to run at a fuel pressure of about 2.5 bar (36 psi). The ignition system is energized, and it is ready to operate. During the primary current flow time, the coil is connected to ground through an output transistor in the ECU.

As the engine is cranked, fuel will be delivered via cold start valve and from the individual injectors, and the engine fires and runs at an idle speed. For a detailed de-

scription, see the L system explanation. With the engine running, the ECU processes the sensor's input signals and calculates from them the fuel injection duration (quantity) and the optimum dwell and ignition angles. The microcomputer's output signals are too weak for the system's correcting elements and must therefore be amplified at their output stages before they are suitable for controlling an ignition coil or fuel-injection valve.

The time for current to flow in the ignition coil is specified by the microcomputer as a function of the battery voltage and the engine speed. This stage also contains a control circuit for limiting the primary current of the ignition coil.

The engine speed is sensed by Item 24 in Fig. 5-28, which is an induction-type pulse generator (magnetic pickup) located over the rotating flywheel ring gear teeth. This unit provides pulses for the ECU. The engine crankshaft angle is determined by Item 23 in Fig. 5-28, which is an induction-type reference mark pulse generator on the flywheel ring gear. Pulses picked up from the rotating reference mark are sent to the ECU.

The air quantity flowing into the engine through the air-flow sensor is determined via the potentiometer mounted on the air flap as its angle of opening/closing is established by the throttle pedal. A voltage signal from here is also sent to the ECU.

The air-flow sensor flap measures the entire air quantity inducted by the engine, thereby serving, in addition to engine speed, as the main control quantity for determining the load signal and basic injection quantity. Current to the injection valves is regulated or pulsed on and off, thereby energizing and de-energizing the solenoid contained within the fuel injector body. The longer the solenoid is energized, the greater the flow of fuel (quantity) into the cylinder.

The ECU controls this pulse-width time at the injectors based on the input signals from the sensors. Maximum switch-on current to the individual injectors is approximately 7.5 A in a 6-cylinder engine and falls back at the end of injection to a low holding current of about 3 A. The injectors when energized only remain open from between 1 and 1.5 milliseconds. Continuous monitoring of the engine sensors up to 400 times a second allows rapid correction to both ignition dwell and fuel-injection pulse width.

Limiting Engine Speed. The maximum speed of the engine is controlled by suppressing the voltage signal to energize the injectors when the engine speed sensor relays a signal to the ECU. This is set to occur at 80 rpm ± the maximum speed that has been programmed into the ECU.

Stop/Start Operation. The Motronic system can be programmed to save fuel by stopping and starting the engine. If the vehicle is stationary at traffic lights or in heavy traffic jams, the ECU will interrupt the fuel-injection signal if the ECU has determined that fuel will be saved, since additional fuel is required to restart the engine.

The engine will be shut off if the clutch pedal is de- pressed and the vehicle speed is less than 1 mph(2 km/hr). To restart the engine, the driver must keep the clutch pedal depressed and simply step on the accelerator within the first one third of its travel.

Cylinder Cutout. Another feature of the Motronic system, which is still in the experimental stage, is the option of having several cylinders cut off during heavy city traffic so that the others will work more efficiently because of poor thermal efficiency at low loads and speed.

The Motronic cylinder cutout system allows only the working cylinders to be filled with air/fuel mixture and a minimum amount of throttling. Hot exhaust gases circulate through the inactive cylinders to maintain them at operating temperature.

The electronic circuitry in the ECU recognizes from the air-flow sensor's signal when cylinders can be switched.

Although this system is not yet in full production, Cadillac employed a similar system on their V8 engine in 1980– 81, whereby the engine would run on either 4, 6, or 8 cylinders, depending on engine/vehicle load demands.

GMC FUEL-INJECTION SYSTEMS

GMC employs both TBI and MPFI in its wide range of divisional vehicles, with system operation being very similar to that used by other manufacturers. Figures 5-7 and 5-8 illustrate the operational concept of both systems. Input sensors feed a voltage reference signal to the ECM (electronic control module), which in turn controls the pulse-width signal to the various fuel injectors.

Figure 5-30 illustrates the basic arrangement used with GMC TBI systems, while Fig. 5-31 shows the typical ar-

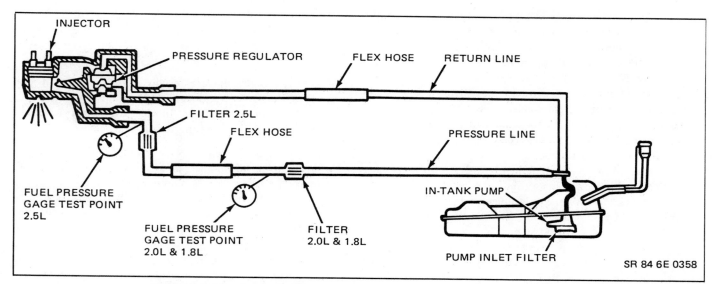

FIGURE 5-30   Basic TBI fuel system flow—2.0L engine. (*Courtesy of Oldsmobile Division of GMC*)

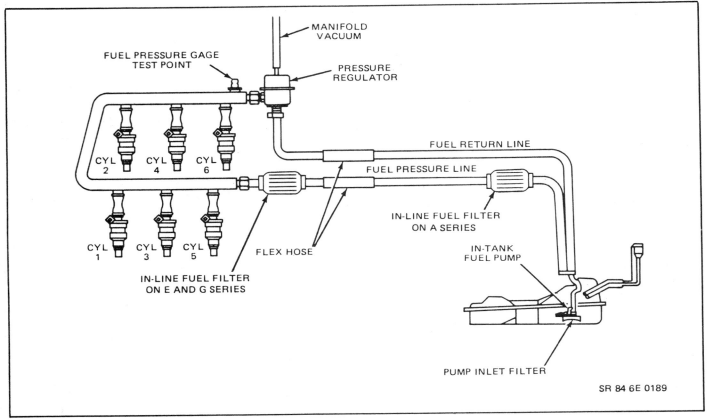

FIGURE 5-31 Port fuel-injection system layout—3.8L V6 engine. (*Courtesy of Oldsmobile Division of GMC*)

rangement that is found on a V6 ported fuel-injection system.

FUEL INTEGRATOR

A unit known as a fuel integrator is contained within the GMC ECM and is designed to make a temporary change in the amount of fuel delivered during closed-loop operation. This operation is the condition that exists when the ECM receives input voltage signals from the exhaust oxygen sensor (Fig. 4-17). Closed-loop operation only occurs once the temperature of an unheated oxygen sensor reaches approximately 600°F. This temperature can be obtained electrically when a "heated-type oxygen sensor" is used, usually within ten seconds after engine startup, or on an unheated sensor, only when the exhaust gas temperature is high enough. The oxygen sensor sends out a corrected voltage signal up to 120 times a minute during engine operation to the ECM in order to maintain an air/fuel ratio as close to stoichiometric (14.7:1) as possible.

In most engines, a counter monitors the changing voltage signal from the oxygen sensor (depending on air/fuel ratio—rich or lean), with a target figure of 128 being normal (neutral). At a figure of 128 counts, the injector pulse-width signal is *not* being affected by the fuel integrator. If the fuel integrator value climbs above 128 counts, then the fuel injector pulse-width will be lengthened to increase fuel. Similarly, should the value fall below 128 counts, the injector pulse-width time is reduced, thereby reducing the fuel delivery. The integrator value reflects the oxygen sensor's lean or rich trend and attempts to make the oxygen sensor "swing," with a mean average voltage output of 0.45 volts, to the ECM.

NOTE: The fuel integrator only corrects for short-term mixture trends. The correction of long-term mixture trends is the function of the BLM (block learn memory) system. (BLM will be discussed in greater detail below.)

On a full-throttle (wide-open) condition, the fuel integrator is reset to the neutral value of 128 counts by the ECM, since no fuel correction is required under such an operating mode. The "count" value can vary between 0 and 255, and the further the number is from 128, the greater the correction to the air-fuel ratio that the fuel integrator will make. By using the oxygen sensor voltage readings, the integrator knows whether the mixture is rich or lean and will increment accordingly. Values above 128 show that the integrator is attempting to enrich the air/fuel mixture ratio, while values below 128 indicate that the fuel integrator is attempting to lean out the air/fuel ratio mixture. What the fuel integrator does in reality is to indicate the amount of fuel injector pulse-width (time energized or open) correction that is needed to achieve an ideal fuel mixture. Although the target value shown above is 128 counts, this figure can vary from engine to engine and, of course, among vehicles of different manufacturers.

The actual injection pulse-width is determined by various other sensor inputs to the on-board computer or ECM (Figs. 3-2 and 5-13). If the injector pulse-width varies from the published expected values, then other parameters such as fuel pressure and the injector circuits have to be checked as per the detailed description in the engine/chassis service manuals.

Under engine operating conditions of ''power enrichment,'' the ECM sets the fuel integrator to a neutral value of 128 counts and freezes it there until power enrichment is no longer in effect. This is done to ensure that during a closed-loop factor the block learn memory will not attempt to correct for the ECM-commanded power enrichment. However, a typical example of how many fuel integrator and oxygen cross-counts would occur during typical engine/vehicle operating conditions is shown below, along with the changing voltage value of the oxygen sensor.

Oxygen Sensor, Fuel Integrator, and Oxygen Sensor Cross-Counts

Expected:

1. Hot closed-loop idle (A/C OFF)
   (a) Oxygen sensor, teens to eighties (voltage)
   (b) Fuel integrator, 89 to 159 counts
   (c) Oxygen cross-counts, 0 to 50 counts
2. Wide-open throttle acceleration
   (a) Oxygen sensor, above 0.75 volts
   (b) Fuel integrator, 128 (neutral count position)
   (c) Oxygen cross-counts, 0
3. Closed throttle and vehicle coasting
   (a) Oxygen sensor, below 0.45 volts
   (b) Fuel integrator, 128 (neutral count position)
   (c) Oxygen cross-counts, 0
4. Steady throttle cruise condition
   (a) Oxygen sensor, teens to eighties (voltage)
   (b) Fuel integrator, 89 to 159 counts
   (c) Oxygen cross-counts, 0 to 50

BLOCK LEARN MEMORY (BLM)

The block learn memory within the ECM operates similarly to the fuel integrator described above, and although it cannot make as large a correction as the fuel integrator, it will

do it for a longer time period. After a certain range of fuel integrator changes to the air/fuel ratio mixture, the BLM will react to compensate for a given set of operating conditions, and the fuel integrator will return to its target value of 128 counts (neutral setting) for stoichiometric setting (14.7:1).

It is possible under extreme conditions for both the BLM and fuel integrator systems to go to the same respective extremes, which is an indication that a problem is present in the fuel-ratio sensing system. This condition shows up in an open-loop driveability situation, in which state the ECM ignores the voltage signal from the oxygen sensor.

On most vehicles, the BLM (block learn memory) is a matrix of cells, usually numbering about 25 in all. These cells are arranged by a combination of RPM and MAP (manifold absolute pressure), with each cell of the BLM being an individual register similar to that in the fuel integrator system. Changing engine operating conditions cause the ECM to switch from cell-to-cell in order to determine what BLM factor to use in the fuel-injector base pulse-width equation.

The ECM simultaneously monitors both the BLM and the fuel integrator, and if the fuel integrator is far enough away from the neutral value of 128 counts, then the ECM will change the block learn value in an attempt to force the fuel integrator back to 128 counts (neutral). Should the oxygen sensor determine that the fuel/air mixture is still not correct, then the block learn value continues to change until a neutral value of 128 counts is achieved.

The PROM unit installed in the ECM establishes the values for both the BLM and the fuel integrator (see PROM information) for each vehicle. Should the fuel/air ratio mixture be beyond the neutral value of 128 counts, and should the block learn system reach the limit of its control value, then the fuel integrator will be forced to its maximum value in the same direction. With both units at their extreme values and the fuel/air mixture still outside of the stoichiometric value (14.7:1), either a lean or rich exhaust code will be set into the memory bank of the ECM, and a *Check Engine* or *Service Engine Soon or Now* warning light will become illuminated on the instrument panel to warn the driver of a problem condition.

INJECTOR PULSE-WIDTH

This term refers to the length of time that the injector solenoid in each injector assembly is energized. When the solenoid is energized, the fuel valve is open, and fuel will be delivered to the engine cylinders. On throttle body injection (TBI) or central fuel injection (CFI), one or two electronically-operated fuel injectors are located in the throttle body, which is similar in appearance to a carburetor body.

Multi-port fuel injection (MPFI), on the other hand, employs one fuel injector for each cylinder. (Figs. 5-8 and 5-9.) Since fuel injector valves open the same distance regardless of the throttle position, then the only way in which the quantity of fuel delivered can be altered is to lengthen or shorten the time in which the fuel valve at the tip of the injector remains open. This time duration is generally in ms (milliseconds), and the ECM makes this determination based upon the input voltage signals it receives from all of the various engine sensors. This value is directly controlled by the fuel integrator and block learn memory units, which rely on continuous inputs from the exhaust oxygen sensor.

A lean condition (excess oxygen flowing in the exhaust system) results in a longer injector pulse-width time in milliseconds to allow more fuel to be supplied, while a rich condition (low oxygen in the exhaust) results in a shorter millisecond injector pulse-width time. When two fuel injectors are used in a TBI system (mounted in the throttle body bore on top), or when multi-port fuel injection is employed, the sequence in which the injectors fire is not always one that follows the firing order. For example, the terms cross-fire injection, sequential port fuel injection, synchronous injection, and asynchronous injection are often used to describe these individual systems.

In a MFI system used on GMC Division Code 3 vehicles, the fuel injectors are energized every crankshaft revolution. Therefore, the term "simultaneously double-fire" is used to indicate that since all injectors fire once in each crankshaft revolution, this action results in two injections of fuel (four stroke cycle engine principle).

On GMC Division Code 9 vehicles (turbocharged), the SFI fuel injectors turn "on" independently of each other, or once every two crankshaft revolutions. This provides longer fuel injector pulse-width signals at low engine speeds. Better idle stability as well as low speed operation will be provided when a car is driven in heavy city traffic, for example. A more detailed explanation of "synchronous" versus "asynchronous" fuel injection is described below.

SYNCHRONOUS INJECTION

With the synchronous injection system, timing of the injector opening is triggered by an incoming distributor reference pulse. Therefore, on a two-injector TBI (throttle body injection) system, one injector will open every time there is a distributor reference voltage pulse. Figure 5-32 illustrates how this system operates on an engine, namely with one injector firing every 90 degrees of crankshaft rotation, or each time a spark plug fires. The ECM calculates the injector pulse-width time based upon the various signals that it receives from the various engine sensors. These include:

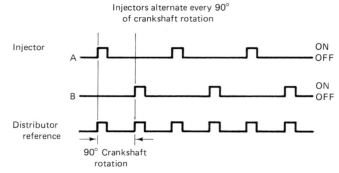

FIGURE 5-32 Synchronous fuel-injection operation. (*Courtesy of Cadillac Motor Car Div. of GMC*)

1. MAP (manifold absolute pressure) sensor
2. MAT (manifold air temperature) sensor
3. BARO (barometric pressure)
4. Volumetric efficiency
5. Commanded air/fuel ratio
6. Number of cylinders
7. EGR (exhaust gas recirculation) correction
8. Fuel pump voltage signal
9. Closed-loop control (oxygen sensor) signal

Of all the sensor inputs to the ECM which are listed above, both the MAT and MAP factors are measures of the air density within the engine intake manifold. They therefore play a very important part in the ECM determining the injector pulse-width. The MAP sensor has the greatest overall impact in making this calculation. An example of how the injector pulse-width varies with a change to both the MAT and MAP sensor outputs is illustrated in Figs. 5-33 and 5-34. Both MAT and MAP sensor signals are, in reality, a measure of the engine's Volumetric Efficiency or "VE."

The VE is the difference in the weight of air contained in the engine cylinder with the engine stopped and the piston at BDC (bottom dead center) versus the weight of air

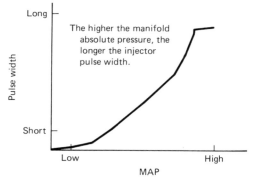

FIGURE 5-33 MAP Effect on fuel-injector pulse-width. (*Courtesy of Cadillac Motor Car Div. of GMC*)

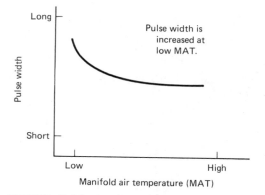

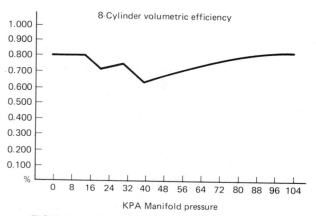

FIGURE 5-34 MAT effect on fuel-injector pulse-width. (*Courtesy of Cadillac Motor Car Div. of GMC*)

8-Cylinder volumetric efficiency

FIGURE 5-35 Typical relationship of volumetric efficiency versus intake manifold pressure. (*Courtesy of Cadillac Motor Car Div. of GMC*)

contained in the same cylinder with the piston at BDC, but with the engine running. A VE of 100% in effect indicates that the cylinder is filled with a maximum amount of air, which results in a pressure equal to atmospheric on a non-turbocharged engine. The VE will always be less than 100% or atmospheric when the engine is running, because of the restriction to air flow through the air filter assembly, the intake manifold, cylinder head shape, and valve porting, as well as because of the design of the exhaust manifold. On a turbocharged engine however, where the exhaust gases drive the turbine or hot end of the T/C, the VE will be greater than 100% or atmospheric. VE varies between 80 and 85% of atmospheric on a nonturbocharged engine, as is shown in Fig. 5-35. Therefore, the higher the engine's VE, the greater the amount of fuel that can be injected, and therefore the higher the horsepower produced from the engine.

FUEL/AIR RATIO

The ideal fuel/air ratio to minimize exhaust pollutants is 14.7:1, which is known as the "stoichiometric ratio."

When the engine is running, the various sensors, through their respective voltage signals to the ECM, attempt to achieve this ideal condition under all operating conditions.

However, there are periods whereby this ideal mixture will be changed in the following ways:

1. *Closed Loop*: Under this condition, the exhaust oxygen sensor is monitoring the percentage of air in the exhaust gases and sending a corrective signal to the ECM, which then alters the fuel/air ratio in order to maintain a stoichiometric value (14.7:1). In this state, the fuel integrator is registering 128 counts (neutral).

2. *Open Loop*: The ECM ignores oxygen sensor voltage signals when the engine is cold and the temperature of the unheated oxygen sensor is below 600°F. During open loop, the ECM varies the fuel/air ratio based upon the voltage inputs from the engine (CTS) coolant temperature sensor, the MAP sensor, and the time and change of the load conditions on the engine.

3. *Crank Enrichment*: When starting the engine from cold, the CTS tells the ECM to deliver additional fuel to the engine for ease of starting, in a way similar to what a choke system does on a carburetor-type engine. This is done through a separate "cold start valve" on some engines (Robert Bosch systems), or through a longer injector pulse-width time on others.

   The length of time that this extra fuel (pulse-width) exists depends, of course, upon the coolant temperature of the engine, from where the "commanded air/fuel ratio" signal emanates.

4. *Clear Flood Mode*: It is not necessary on fuel-injected engines to hold the throttle open or pump it several times prior to engine startup, because the various sensors tell the ECM just how much fuel is required. The ECM fixes the correct injector pulse-width time or cold-start valve activation time (Robert Bosch systems). If the driver depresses the throttle pedal, the TPS will tell the ECM of this condition, and the ECM will lean-out the mixture to approximately 1:25.5 fuel/air ratio on startup.

5. *Power Enrichment*: When the driver forces the throttle pedal wide open, the accelerator pump system in a carbureted engine ensures that sufficient fuel is delivered for rapid acceleration. On a fuel-injected system, however, the first thing that occurs is that the ECM receives a voltage signal from the TPS (throttle position sensor), which indicates that increased power is desired, and for which a longer injector pulse-width time is required.

   The ECM monitors the CTS (coolant temperature sensor) and TPS signals and overrides a closed-loop fuel/air ratio, if it is present. The ECM also diverts air flow from the AIR (air injection reactor) system to avoid overheating of the catalytic converter caused by the richening fuel/air ratio setting. During WOT (wide open throttle) power enrichment, the fuel integrator system

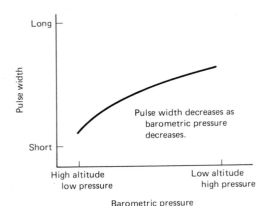

FIGURE 5-36 Injector pulse-width signal versus BARO pressure. (*Courtesy of Cadillac Motor Car Div. of GMC*)

is reset to neutral (128 counts) and frozen there until the throttle has stopped moving.

6. The BARO (barometric pressure sensor) makes small adjustments to the injector pulse-width with a respective increase or decrease in operation at various altitudes.

7. The EGR system also adjusts the injector pulse-width as a function of the commanded EGR by the ECM. When EGR is being diverted into the engine, this displaces a given amount of fresh air in order to reduce the production of "oxides of nitrogen" (smog-producing) at the exhaust system. When EGR is evident, the oxygen sensor monitoring the exhaust gases thinks that there is a rich mixture (lack of air). Therefore, to prevent this reaction and to allow a neutral count of 128 at the fuel integrator, fuel is cut back during EGR addition, and the injector pulse-width time is shortened.

Figures 5-36 and 5-37 illustrate how the injector pulse-width changes as BARO and EGR systems vary.

8. *Deceleration Enleanment*: When the throttle is being pulled closed during engine deceleration on a carbureted engine, less fuel enters the engine cylinders because of the decrease in air flow through the venturi.

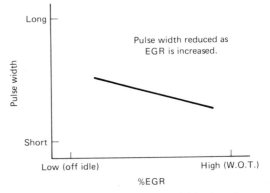

FIGURE 5-37 Injector pulse-width signal versus EGR. (*Courtesy of Cadillac Motor Car Div. of GMC*)

A lot of unburnt fuel vapors pass through the exhaust system during this action, which results in a high level of exhaust pollutants escaping into the atmosphere.

As soon as the throttle is moved towards a decreased position (closed throttle) on a fuel-injected engine, the ECM immediately senses this action from the TPS voltage, the MAP sensor, and the VSS (vehicle speed sensor) signals it receives.

Normally what happens in a dual-injector TBI system is that when a closed-throttle "coast-down" mode is sensed at the ECM, with the vehicle road speed above a threshold value, the ECM quickly reduces the injector pulse-width time. This action of a rapidly closed throttle and decrease in MAP (increase in manifold vacuum) causes the fuel in the intake manifold to condense and form droplets, leading to a rich mixture and a tendency for the engine to want to stall. Such a condition leads not only to poor driveability, but also to high hydrocarbon emissions at the exhaust system.

To prevent such an undesirable situation, the ISC (idle speed control) plunger is extended as the throttle switch is closed. The TPS voltage signal to the ECM allows it to determine just where to place the ISC plunger during such a closed-throttle coast-down mode. By monitoring the VSS, the ECM can determine when the coast mode is almost over. The ECM then sets the throttle angle based upon the signals it receives from the VSS, the TPS, and BARO sensors, as long as these signals indicate that the vehicle speed is above a "threshold value." Once the vehicle speed drops below this value of about 5 to 15 mph (8 to 24 km/hr) and depending on the vehicle PROM installed, an engine RPM signal is used by the ECM to determine throttle angle position. On some manufacturers' vehicles, if the throttle remains in a closed position for an extended period of time, it is possible for the ECM to completely shut off the injector pulse-width time cycle.

9. *Fuel Pump Voltage Correction*: Should the electric fuel pump voltage signal reduce, then the fuel pressure from the pump would decrease. Therefore, the ECM would react to this condition by increasing the injector pulse-width signal and would insert a trouble code into the ECM memory, which would signify that there was a problem in the fuel pump circuit. This occurs when the voltage drops below 10 volts, because the pump pressure and therefore the quantity of fuel that would flow past the injector valve would be less in this condition.

ASYNCHRONOUS INJECTION

On asynchronous injection, fuel delivery from the injectors takes place on a time interval and without regard to engine piston position. This mode of injection is designed to assist

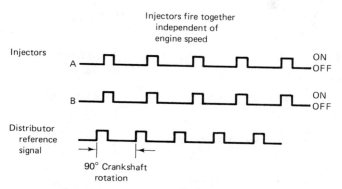

FIGURE 5-38 Asynchronous fuel-injector operating mode. (*Courtesy of Cadillac Motor Car Div. of GMC*)

the engine when it operates under transient or changing conditions. Figure 5-38 illustrates asynchronous injector operation. The firing of both injectors occurs every 10–12.5 milliseconds during transient operating conditions. These conditions are as follows:

1. When the engine is being cranked and in order to aid the fireup sequence, the ECM receives a cranking signal from the crankshaft sensor or distributor reference signal. This signal initiates what is known as "prime pulses" to the fuel injectors in the throttle body to ensure a rich mixture for starting. The action is similar to how a choke functions on a carbureted engine. The temperature of the engine coolant affects the number of pulses to both injectors during this cranking and starting period.

2. On a TBI system with two injectors in the throttle body housing, as the throttle is gradually opened to a set position, we require a system similar to that found in a carburetor system, namely the accelerator pump, to ensure smooth transition (acceleration). This is necessary because as the throttle is opened, manifold pressure suddenly increases and causes the fuel to condense on the manifold walls instead of vaporizing with the additional air. This reaction results in a lean mixture, and the engine hesitates/stumbles, instead of accelerating smoothly.

   To prevent such a condition on the TBI system, when the ECM senses the TPS increased opening, it moves to what is commonly called a "tip-in-enrichment phase." In other words, the fuel-injector pulse-width time (open) is increased and determined by the MAT (manifold air temperature), while the number of actual pulses is controlled by the signal from the CTS (coolant temperature sensor) to the ECM. With a lower MAT, there will be more pulses delivered in order to compensate for the extra fuel condensation at these lower temperatures.

3. Acceleration enrichment is required as soon as the driver moves into an opening throttle mode. Similar to a carburetor pump, the TBI system needs additional fuel immediately. Therefore, when the ECM senses the TPS voltage change as well as the increase in MAP, the ECM allows the two TBI injectors to operate in the "asynchronous mode" as long as the throttle is being pushed open.

   The injector pulse width is determined by how fast the throttle is opened, while the number of pulses is established by just how far the throttle is opened. If the throttle is placed into a WOT position, the ECM "time out's" the acceleration enrichment and places the fuel injector pulse width into a "power enrichment mode," as was described previously.

IDLE AIR CONTROL MOTOR

The idle air control valve (IACV) is shown as Item 2 in Fig. 5-39. The figure also illustrates the TPS (throttle position sensor), the detonation sensor, and the throttle body assembly. Fig. 5-40 illustrates the basic principle of operation of the IACV.

Figure 5-41 illustrates the ISC control actuator and its relationship to the TPS (throttle position switch). The ISC consists of a permanent magnet (PM) DC motor which can be driven either clockwise or counterclockwise by changing the polarity of the d.c. contacts at the motor. In effect, the actuator becomes a closed throttle stop, which allows the ECM to control both fuel and air depending upon the setting, since the TPS is either connected directly to the nose of the ISC motor or is in the immediate vicinity.

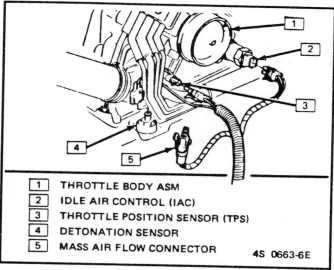

1	**THROTTLE BODY ASM**
2	**IDLE AIR CONTROL (IAC)**
3	**THROTTLE POSITION SENSOR (TPS)**
4	**DETONATION SENSOR**
5	**MASS AIR FLOW CONNECTOR**

4S 0663-6E

FIGURE 5-39 Location of a typical IACV. (*Courtesy of Oldsmobile Div. of GMC*)

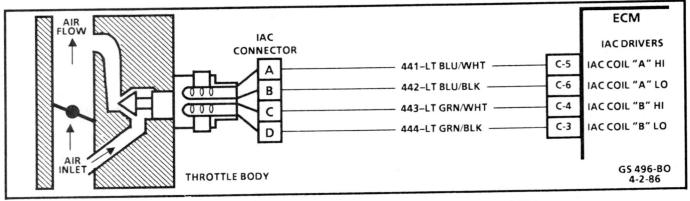

FIGURE 5-40 Basic principle of operation IACV. (*Courtesy of Oldsmobile Div. of GMC*)

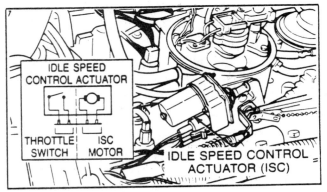

FIGURE 5-41 Idle speed control actuator on throttle body. (*Courtesy of Cadillac Motor Car Div. of GMC*)

Major functions of the idle speed control motor are the following:

1. Acts as a prestart throttle setting,
2. Controls idle rpm under all operating conditions,
3. Corrects for load on/off modes at idle (A/C, power steering, etc.),
4. Supplies coast down air when decelerating,
5. Prevents engine stall.

The IACV is available in different shapes and sizes for various models and makes of engines. One example of two such IACV's is shown in Fig. 5-42 for two GMC engines, while Fig. 5-43 illustrates the IACV placement on a TBI (throttle body injection) assembly also used on GMC engines. Dimension A must not be greater than 1.125″ (28 mm).

The purpose of the IACV is to control bypass air around the throttle plate when the engine is running at an idle speed (closed throttle) and prevent stalls due to increased engine load at idle. A small motor positions the IACV within its bore to control the amount of air which is directed around

the throttle slot. Should the ECM sense a low rpm (rpm sensor), then to prevent an engine stall condition, it compensates by increasing the injector pulse-width time (opening), while similarly retracting the IACV pintle to allow a greater air flow to pass by the throttle plate. When the engine is cold, the pintle valve will remain open to allow air to bypass the throttle plate so that a fast idle speed can be maintained. During idle, the proper position of the valve is determined by the ECM based upon battery voltage, coolant temperature, mass air flow, throttle position sensor, engine speed, A/C clutch signal, power steering pressure switch, and engine intake air temperature. These valves are designed to be used with a specific model of engine, and if they are intermixed in different engines, poor performance and a rough idle will result.

The dimensional check required of the IACV during service is supplied by the engine manufacturer and is nor-

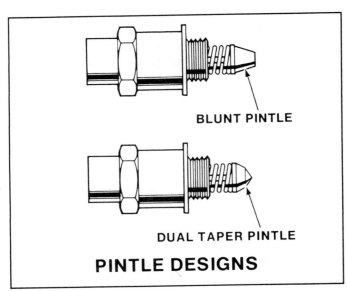

FIGURE 5-42 IACV (idle air control valve) designs. (*Courtesy of Oldsmobile Div. of GMC*)

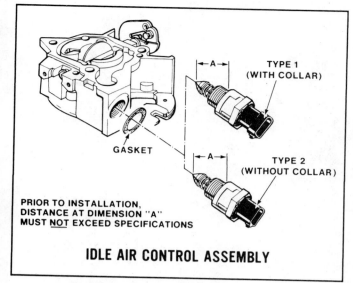

PRIOR TO INSTALLATION, DISTANCE AT DIMENSION "A" MUST NOT EXCEED SPECIFICATIONS

IDLE AIR CONTROL ASSEMBLY

FIGURE 5-43 TBI IACV location. (*Courtesy of Oldsmobile Div. of GMC*)

mally adjustable to the quoted manufacturer's specifications, as shown for example in Fig. 5-43. The IACV will only affect the idle characteristics of the engine. Therefore, if it is open fully, it will allow too much air to pass by the throttle plate, and the idle speed will therefore be high. On the other hand, if the IACV was stuck in the closed position, insufficient air would flow around the throttle plate at idle, resulting in a low idle speed. Should the IACV be stuck partway open, then a rough idle and a lack of response to engine load changes at idle would result.

Each time the engine is started and then the ignition key is turned off, the ECM will reset the IACV by sending enough counts to seat the valve. The fully seated valve is the ECM reference zero. A given number of counts is then issued to open the valve, and normal ECM control of the IACV will begin from this point. This is how the ECM knows what the IACV motor position is for a given idle speed.

FORD ELECTRONIC GASOLINE FUEL-INJECTION SYSTEMS

As of September 1988, Ford has decided to utilize multiport fuel injection on every gasoline-powered Ford, Lincoln, and Mercury automobile with the exception of the Ford Festiva. This is also true for all light trucks with the exception of the 2.0 liter engine offered on the Ranger S.

Ford offers either the throttle body injection system, commonly referred to as CFI (central fuel injection), or for higher performance engines, a multi-point electronic fuel injection (MPEFI) system, which is a port-type system similar to that used by other major manufacturers. The fuel injection systems used by Ford are a joint development with Robert Bosch Corporation, which, of course, supplies every major car manufacturer in the world with these fuel sys-

tems. The systems used on Ford vehicles are a derivative of the Bosch "L-Jetronic" system, described within this chapter.

Both the CFI and MPEFI systems employ Ford's own EEC-1V (electronic engine control) computer on latest model year vehicles. The various sensors feeding information to the computer and their respective locations on the engine can be seen in Fig. 5-44 for a 2.3L turbocharged engine. Figure 5-45 illustrates the actual sensors that input a voltage signal to the computer, as well as the respective voltage outputs to the system.

DODGE COLT 1.6L TURBOCHARGED ENGINE FUEL SYSTEM

The Dodge Colt 1.6L (97.4 cu.in.) in-line 4-cylinder engine is designated the G32B with a turbocharger (T/C). It has a compression ratio of 7.6:1 versus the nonturbocharged engine's 8.5:1. The engine firing order is 1–3–4–2, and initial ignition timing is 8 degrees BTDC versus the non T/C engine's 5 degrees BTDC.

The fuel system used with the turbocharged engine is of the throttle body design; however, this engine uses two single-point electronically-controlled fuel injectors rather than the one such as is found on the 2.2L design.

The throttle body is located downstream of the turbocharger compressor outlet as can be seen in Fig. 5-46, which is a schematic of the air/fuel system used with the 1.6L T/C engine.

ECI (Electronically-Controlled Injection) Control System

The 1.6L T/C engine fuel control system employs an ECU (electronic control unit) that receives various sensor inputs similar to that found on the 2.2L engines. The sensor inputs (parameters sensed) and output signals (parameters controlled) to and from the ECU are shown in Fig. 5-47, where there are 13 input signals and 8 output signals. Table 5-1 shows the diagnostic items and their code numbers. The following system components are discussed in detail individually as to their function and operation in the overall system.

Table 5-1.

1.6L Engine code numbers and diagnosis items

Code no.	Diagnosis item
1	Oxygen sensor and computer
2	Ignition pulse
3	Air-flow sensor
4	Pressure sensor
5	Throttle position sensor
6	ISC motor position switch
7	Coolant temperature sensor
8	Car speed

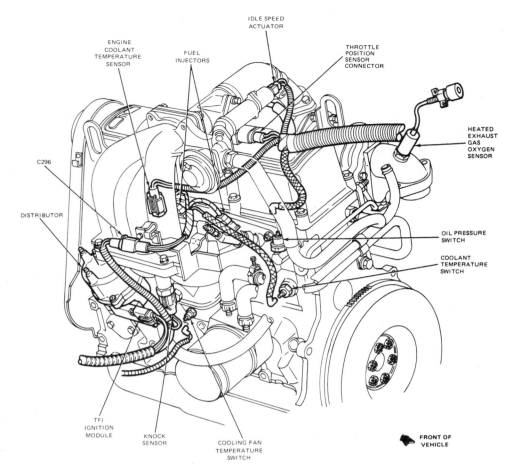

FIGURE 5-44 Bosch/Ford multi-point EFI system illustration— 2.3L T/C engine. (*Courtesy of Ford Motor Company, Dearborn, MI*).

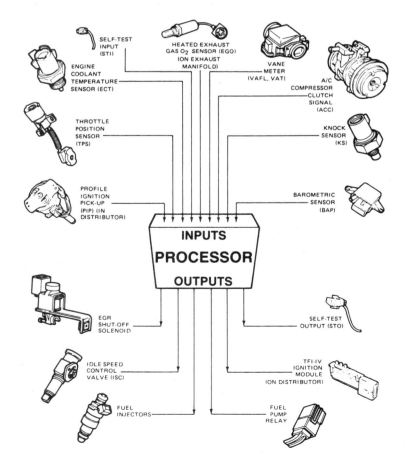

FIGURE 5-45 2.3L engine EFI sensor circuit components. (*Courtesy of Ford Motor Company, Dearborn, MI*).

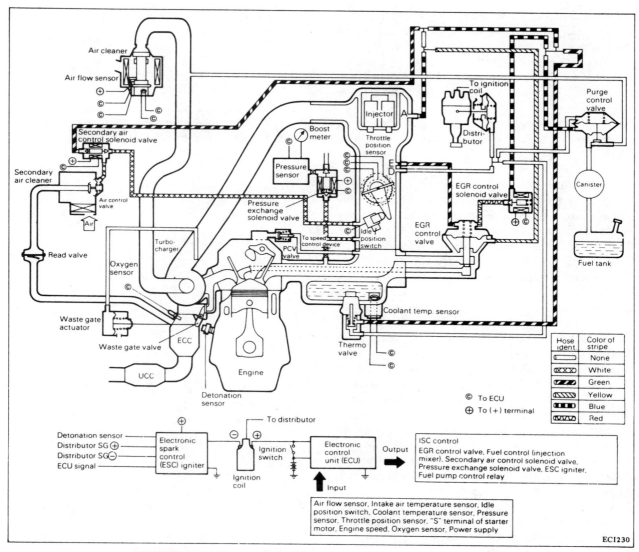

FIGURE 5-46 Dodge Colt 1.61 T/C engine fuel system schematic. (*Courtesy of Chrysler Corporation*)

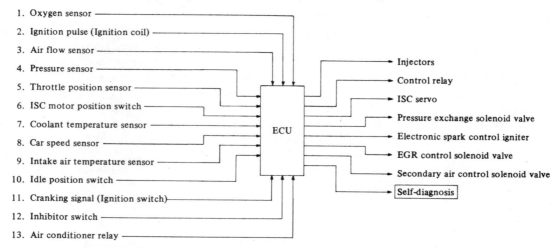

FIGURE 5-47 1.6L engine ECI/ECU sensor inputs and outputs. (*Courtesy of Chrysler Corporation*)

Air-Flow Sensor.   The amount of fuel delivered to the engine under all operating conditions is a function of the volume/weight of air delivered to the engine cylinders. The air-flow sensor used with the 1.6L T/C engine is installed within the air cleaner assembly (Fig. 4-40) and consists of a device known as a Karman Vortex unit (Fig. 4-41).

The longer the injectors are pulsed open (energized), the greater will be the rate of fuel delivery to the engine cylinders.

Air Temperature Sensor.   An air temperature sensor is located on the modulator within the air cleaner assembly and functions to measure the temperature of the air flowing through the air cleaner.

A change in air temperature affects its density; therefore, the engine's volumetric efficiency will change. The generated sensor voltage signal is monitored by the ECU, which will then alter the fuel delivery characteristics by changing the pulse (opening) time of the two injectors.

Air Pressure Sensor.   The air pressure sensor is located on the engine compartment bulkhead, or toe board area, and senses both ambient barometric pressure and absolute pressure within the intake manifold. Figure 4-41 illustrates the pressure sensor location and its connection to the ECU.

Voltage signals generated at the air pressure sensor are fed to the ECU based upon the weather and altitude conditions. Immediately after engine startup, the ambient barometric pressure is sensed by the air pressure sensor, which energizes the solenoid valve shown in Fig. 4-42 via the ECU. After engine startup, the solenoid valve is de-energized, and the sensor detects absolute pressure in the manifold from the turbocharger and feeds a voltage signal to the ECU, which will control air/fuel mixture and idle speed.

Temperature Sensor.   This sensor is installed into the water-cooled intake manifold and operates on the thermistor principle (Fig. 5-48). The generated voltage signal is fed to the ECU to vary fuel delivery time, EGR, secondary air management, and idle speed.

Exhaust Oxygen Sensor.   The exhaust oxygen sensor is located between the turbocharger and the three-way catalyst. The voltage signal is sent to the ECU to control closed-loop operation of the fuel delivery time. Closed loop is the operation of the engine air/fuel ratio based upon the voltage signals from the ECI system and the oxygen sensor.

Open loop is the condition whereby the air/fuel ratio is determined by the ECU without the voltage signal from the oxygen sensor, which does not emit a signal until approximately 300°C (572°F).

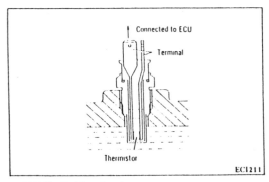

FIGURE 5-48 Coolant temperature sensor. (*Courtesy of Chrysler Corporation*)

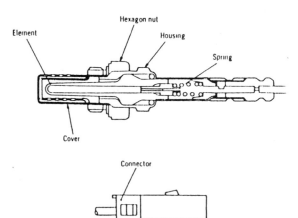

FIGURE 5-49 Exhaust oxygen sensor. (*Courtesy of Chrysler Corporation*)

A detailed explanation of the makeup and operation of an exhaust oxygen sensor can be found in Chapter 4. Figure 5-49 illustrates a cutaway view of the oxygen sensor.

Idle Position Switch.   Figure 5-50 illustrates the idle speed control motor and switch assembly that is installed on the fuel-injection mixer assembly (throttle body). The switch is only energized (on) when the throttle is at the closed, or idling, position. The position of this switch provides a voltage signal to the ECU to control fuel delivery pulse time of the injectors—especially during vehicle deceleration, idle speed, and secondary air management.

A throttle position sensor is also located on the throttle body shaft connected to the throttle blades so that when these are opened or closed, a rotary potentiometer (variable resistor) feeds a voltage signal to the ECU to control fuel injector pulse time (opening time). The electronic components for the ISC system are integral with the ECU.

EGR Control.   The EGR control valve is activated by an electric solenoid that is ECU (electronic control unit) monitored, based upon engine coolant temperature and speed.

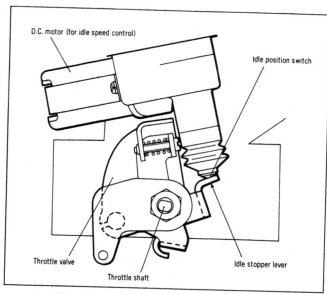

FIGURE 5-50 Idle speed control system. (*Courtesy of Chrysler Corporation*)

Secondary Air Control. Pressure applied to the secondary air control valve is switched by the solenoid valve from the intake manifold pressure to the turbocharger pressure or vice versa. Figure 5-51 illustrates the secondary air system used with the 1.6L turbocharged engine.

The reed valve in the system is actuated by exhaust vacuum being generated from pulsation in the exhaust man-

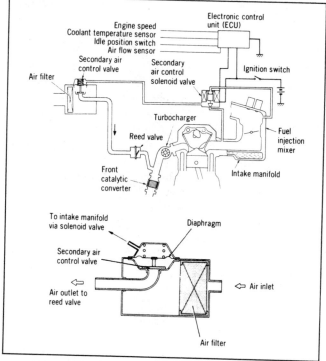

FIGURE 5-51 1.6L turbocharged engine secondary air supply. (*Courtesy of Chrysler Corporation*)

ifold. Extra air is supplied into the exhaust manifold through the secondary air control valve, which is opened by intake manifold pressure when the solenoid valve is energized by an ECU voltage signal. The reed valve supplies secondary air into the front catalytic converter to promote oxidation of exhaust gases during engine warm-up, engine hot start, and vehicle deceleration.

Vehicle Speed Sensor. A vehicle speed sensor employs a reed switch to pick up speedometer cable rpm and send these pulses to the ECU to control idle speed.

1.6L Turbocharged Engine Fuel System Operation

An electric motor driven roller vane-type fuel pump is located underneath the vehicle rear floor area as shown in Fig. 5-52. The fuel pump is capable of delivering fuel to the system at between 64 and 85 psi (441–588 kPa) at zero discharge flow rate. This pressure can be checked at the location shown in Fig. 5-53.

The pump can deliver between 90–120 liters (24–32 US gallons) or 20–26.5 Imperial gallons an hour at a delivery

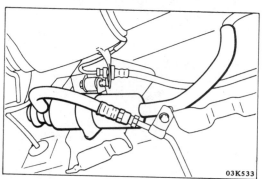

FIGURE 5-52 Electric fuel pump location. (*Courtesy of Chrysler Corp.*)

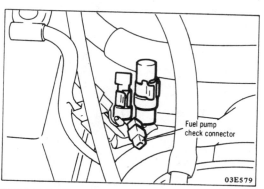

FIGURE 5-53 Fuel pump connector check location. (*Courtesy of Chrysler Corporation*)

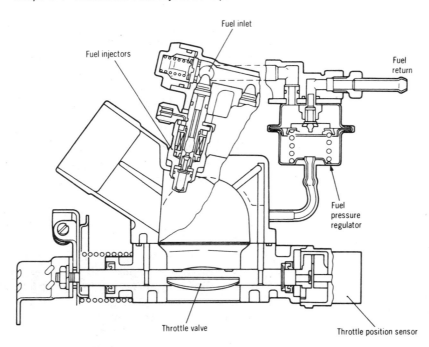

FIGURE 5-54 Fuel injection mixer assembly/throttle body unit for the 1.6L turbocharged Dodge Colt engine. (*Courtesy of Chrysler Corporation*)

pressure of 35–47 psi (245–324 kPa). Fuel drawn from the fuel tank leaves the fuel pump and is passed through a fuel filter prior to entering the throttle body unit, shown in Fig. 5-54, where it feeds both injectors and also the fuel pressure regulator unit. The fuel pressure regulator unit operates in the same manner as that described earlier for other engines. The regulator maintains a steady system pressure of 35.6 psi (245 kPa) by returning excess fuel/pressure back to the fuel tank.

The fuel injectors are alternately energized by a voltage signal from the ECU. The longer the pulse time signal from the ECU to the injectors, the greater the volume of fuel delivered to the engine. The injectors spray fuel above the throttle valve in an atomized state in the same operating mode as that explained earlier for other single point injector systems.

On engine startup (ignition key in the *start* position), fuel enrichment is assured by the ECU monitoring engine coolant temperature and other sensors but not air flow because of the unstable pulses created by the turbocharger lag.

A longer injector pulse time (open) ensures a rich air/ fuel mixture for successful startup under all ambient temperature conditions. When the engine fires and runs, this starting enrichment voltage signal to the injectors from the ECU will be changed by a monitored signal from the ECU based upon sensor inputs. During this time, if the exhaust oxygen sensor has not attained approximately 300°C (572°F), the engine will operate in the open-loop mode (no voltage signal from the oxygen sensor).

During engine warm-up, the ECU processes information from the coolant sensor to provide fuel enrichment during the open-loop operation and part of the closed-loop operation (voltage signal from the oxygen sensor). This continues until the coolant temperature sensor reaches its preset cutoff temperature when the ECU will then switch (pulse) the injectors to a normal air/fuel ratio level based upon the voltage signals from the other input sensors. The engine will now be in a closed-loop condition.

When the vehicle is accelerated in either the open-loop (cold) or closed-loop (warm) condition, smooth driveability is ensured by a signal from the ECU, which processes information based upon the throttle position sensor (a rotary potentiometer variable resistance).

CHAPTER 6

◆

Electronic Ignition System— Computer-Controlled

ADVANTAGES OF ELECTRONIC IGNITION SYSTEMS

Many ignition systems in use on gasoline engines today are designed and mapped out with the aid of a computer before the engine actually becomes a reality. Few engines today continue to use CB or "contact breaker" point ignition systems, because of the necessity to change the worn or pitted points on a regular basis. Also, they cannot deliver as high a voltage to the spark plugs as a solid-state ignition distributor unit. Conventional systems provide voltages as high as 22 to 25,000 volts, while a solid-state ignition system can approach 40,000 volts or higher. Moreover, the conventional distributor with CB points can only achieve simple spark advance characteristics, and these are incapable of meeting the higher demands of current engines equipped with gasoline fuel-injection systems.

Mechanical and vacuum spark advance is no longer used in many systems. Many manufacturers choose instead to employ the pulse-generator signal from within the computer for ignition triggering purposes. Based upon the various sensor input voltage signals, the computer is capable of determining the optimum ignition advance for all conditions of engine operation.

Additional advantages to using the pulse-generator signal from within the computer are those of improved engine starting, better idle speed control, and reduction of overall fuel consumption. On naturally aspirated as well as turbocharged engines, knock control is another feature that can be incorporated from the computer system.

One such system that employs not only the computer for control of the fuel-injection system but the ignition system as well is the Robert Bosch Motronic system described in Chapter 5.

Other manufacturers use ESC (electronic spark control), ESA (electronic spark advance), or EST (electronic spark timing) in their high-energy ignition (solid-state) systems, which are similarly controlled from a suitable on-board vehicle microcomputer. Manufacturers have coined different phrases for their electronic ignition systems, but in all cases they are breakerless (no points). Since a much higher voltage is possible from a breakerless type of ignition system, the term, *high-energy ignition system*, is one that is widely used, for example, on GM vehicles.

TYPES OF SOLID-STATE IGNITION SYSTEMS

Two basic types of electronic ignition systems are widely used by the majority of engine/vehicle manufacturers, and these are:

1. Induction-type pulse generator,
2. Hall-effect generator.

In both cases, the contact breaker points are replaced by either of the two items listed above. Figure 6-1 illustrates the types of rotors used with these two types of electronic ignition systems.

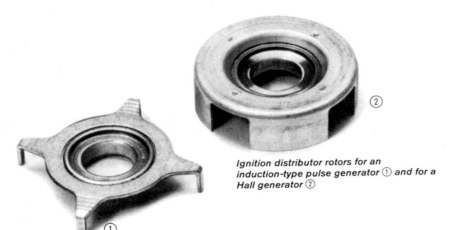

Ignition distributor rotors for an induction-type pulse generator ① and for a Hall generator ②

FIGURE 6-1 Two types of electronic ignition system distributor rotors. (*Courtesy of Robert Bosch Corporation*)

The induction-type pulse generator system is widely used by such vehicle manufacturers as GM and Ford, while the Hall-effect system is in wide use on Chrysler's manufactured vehicles. In order for either system to operate successfully, both an inductive speed sensor and an inductive reference-mark sensor are required.

Both of these sensors are generally mounted on the engine so that they can monitor the rpm and position of the Number 1 piston. Therefore, they are generally mounted on the engine at the front, although the flywheel ring gear can also be used. Both of these sensors can be either of the induction- or Hall-effect-type, in which the teeth of the flywheel ring gear or the teeth on the engine gear train can be used to make and break the magnetic flux field. Figures 6-2 and 6-3 illustrate the typical location of the sensor on the engine as well as the basic principle of its operation.

Principle of Operation—Type 1

In the induction-type pulse generator ignition system illustrated in Figs. 6-4, 6-5, and 6-6, rather than using contact breaker points, a toothed reluctor wheel—or what is sometimes referred to as the timer core—is used to initiate the high tension spark by making and breaking the primary voltage system.

In Fig. 6-5, the reluctor wheel or timer core (4) is mounted onto the distributor shaft. As it rotates past the permanent magnet (1) and the induction winding (2), its protruding teeth (same number as there are engine cylinders) reduce the "air gap" between the stator and rotor teeth. This air gap will be at its minimum when the teeth are directly opposite the individual stators. Because of the changing air gap resulting from the spinning toothed reluctor wheel or timer core, a magnetic flux (field) is generated, and this field produces an alternating voltage in the induction winding (2).

Maximum voltage is generated just before the individual teeth are directly opposite their respective induction windings (2). As the teeth move away from the induction

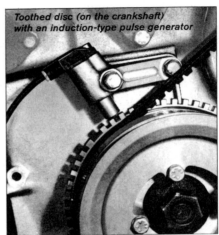

Toothed disc (on the crankshaft) with an induction-type pulse generator

FIGURE 6-2 Location of rpm or No. 1 piston reference sensor on the engine. (*Courtesy of Robert Bosch Corporation*)

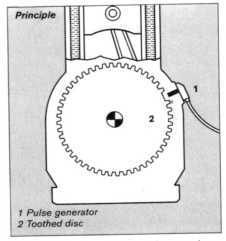

Principle

1 Pulse generator
2 Toothed disc

FIGURE 6-3 Basic principle of operation of a pulse-generator-type of speed or position sensor on the engine. (*Courtesy of Robert Bosch Corporation*)

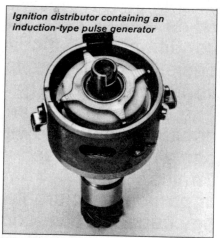

FIGURE 6-4 Typical 4 cylinder engine induction-type ignition distributor. (*Courtesy of Robert Bosch Corporation*)

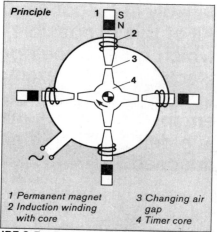

1 Permanent magnet
2 Induction winding with core
3 Changing air gap
4 Timer core

FIGURE 6-5 Basic layout of components in an induction-type ignition distributor. (*Courtesy of Robert Bosch Corporation*)

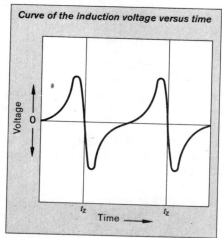

FIGURE 6-6 Typical voltage/time curve for an induction-type ignition distributor. (*Courtesy of Robert Bosch Corporation*)

winding, the air gap and hence the magnetic flux decrease, and the pulse generator changes its sense. With this continuous magnetic flux, we therefore produce an analog a.c. voltage signal such as that shown in Fig. 6-6.

Principle of Operation—Type 2

In the Hall-effect-type of electronic ignition system, a similar principle to that used in the induction-type system just described is employed. Figures 6-7, 6-8, 6-9 illustrate a typical Hall-effect distributor assembly, its principle of operation, and the digital-type voltage curve produced by this type of a system.

Note that in the illustration (Fig. 6-8) the four black marks on the circumference of the circle represent the four solid metal parts of the Hall-effect rotor assembly, which was shown earlier in Fig. 6-1. These solid parts are often

FIGURE 6-7 Hall-effect ignition distributor. (*Courtesy of Robert Bosch Corporation*)

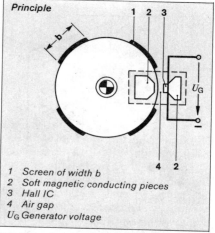

1 Screen of width b
2 Soft magnetic conducting pieces
3 Hall IC
4 Air gap
U_G Generator voltage

FIGURE 6-8 Principle of operation of a Hall-effect ignition distributor. (*Courtesy of Robert Bosch Corporation*)

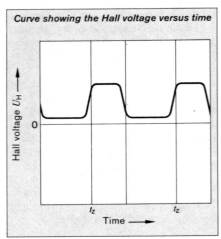

FIGURE 6-9 Voltage curve produced by a Hall-effect ignition distributor. (*Courtesy of Robert Bosch Corporation*)

referred to as "screens," because when they are directly opposite the conducting piece (2) and the Hall IC (3), the magnetic field is absorbed by the solid portion of the rotor. Therefore, the magnetic field does not reach the IC (3). When the solid part of the rotor passes out of the air gap area (4), both the IC and with it the Hall layer are subjected to the full strength of the magnetic field, and the voltage generated reaches its maximum.

Figure 6-10 illustrates the effect of the magnetic field in this type of a system whereby an excess of electrons will occur at point A1 in the diagram. Since at point A2 few electrons are visible, what is known as the "Hall Voltage" effect exists between points A1 and A2. The reason for this is that the electrons between the north and south poles are deflected perpendicularly (directly up and down) to the direction of the magnetic field, which flows horizontally between the two magnets.

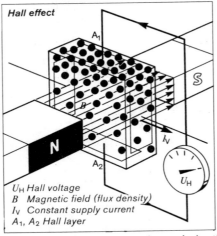

FIGURE 6-10 Hall-effect voltage induction. (*Courtesy of Robert Bosch Corporation*)

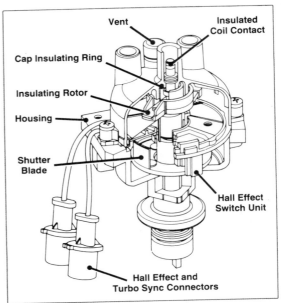

FIGURE 6-11 Chrysler labyrinth distributor assembly unit. (*Courtesy of Society of Automotive Engineers, Copyright 1985*)

Latest vehicles produced by Chrysler Corporation employ the Hall-effect distributor. However, it is commonly referred to as a "labyrinth distributor" because three concentric rings inside the distributor create a labyrinth that insulates the coil contact tower from the spark plug terminals (Fig. 6-11). Other advantages of this distributor assembly are that it is smaller than its predecessors, has fewer moving parts, and has a higher electrical power tolerance. This new design also allows for the addition of fuel synchronization for use on turbocharged engines.

HEI OR HIGH-ENERGY IGNITION DISTRIBUTORS (GMC)

High-energy and breakerless ignition systems are basically one and the same. No contact breaker points are employed, but instead a magnetic pulse generator is used to establish the primary coil circuit. The coil itself can be located under the top half of the distributor cap.

In addition, some HEI (high-energy ignition) systems employ the conventional vacuum and centrifugal advance mechanisms. Others do not have these features, but are controlled by an electronic computer on the vehicle that is connected to a variety of engine mounted sensor units. Figure 6-12 shows a typical HEI type distributor assembly.

The HEI distributor is an extremely compact unit in that it combines all of the necessary ignition components in one single assembly. External electrical connections are generally the ignition switch feed wire, a tachometer pickup,

(EST) HEI DISTRIBUTOR

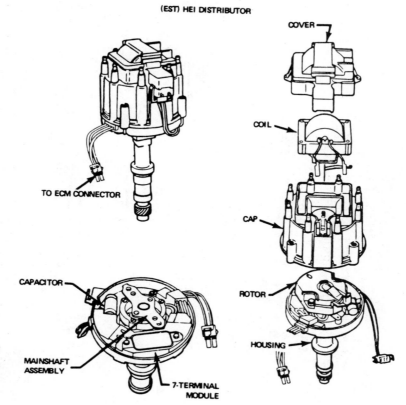

FIGURE 6-12 HEI (high energy ignition) system distributor assembly. (*Courtesy of Oldsmobile Div. of GMC*)

and a number of spark plug leads equal to the number of engine cylinders. When the ignition switch is turned to both the run and start positions, full battery voltage flows to the distributor. In the majority of HEI systems, there is no resistor wire connected from the actual ignition key switch to the distributor.

You will notice in Fig. 6-12 that the ignition coil is contained within the top half of the distributor cap and is connected through a resistance brush to the rotor. The major differences between the HEI distributor and the conventional breaker-point unit is that a module and pickup coil replace the contact breaker points. Figure 6-13 shows the location of both the module and pickup coil on the distributor assembly.

PICKUP COIL REMOVED AND DISASSEMBLED

ALUMINUM NON-MAGNETIC SHIELD REMOVED

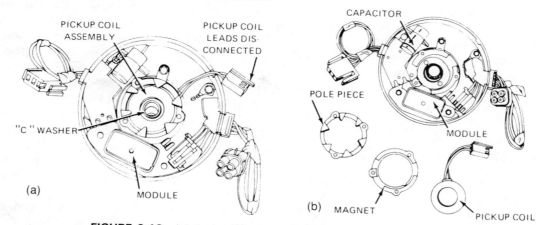

FIGURE 6-13 (a) Assembled view of module and pickup; (b) Disassembled view of module and pickup. (*Courtesy of Oldsmobile Div. of GMC*)

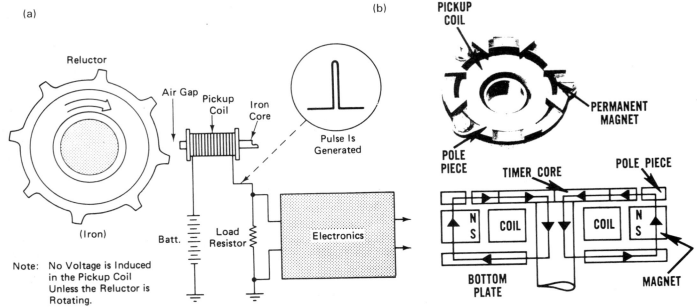

FIGURE 6-14   (a) Basic HEI system arrangement; (b) Side view of basic HEI system. (*Courtesy of Delco Electronics Corporation, Subsidiary of GM Hughes Electronics*)

HEI DISTRIBUTOR OPERATION

Figure 6-14(a) shows a simplified arrangement of the two major components of the HEI system. A toothed wheel known as either a reluctor or armature is driven directly from the distributor shaft. The speed of this reluctor will establish the timing of the spark generated and sent to the plug. Because reluctor speed varies the timing, some manufacturers refer to it as a timer core, as is shown in Fig. 6-14(b).

In Fig. 6-14(a) and (b), as the toothed reluctor wheel rotates with the distributor shaft, its teeth will approach a point where they are in direct alignment with the center of the pickup coil which is an electromagnet. When this occurs, a small air gap exists between the toothed wheel and the pickup coil. Battery power is continuously flowing through the pickup coil to produce a magnetic field in both the coil and the core. As each tooth of the rotating reluctor approaches the pickup coil core or center, the reluctance of the magnetic circuit will rapidly decrease, but the magnetic field strength will increase. This strong magnetic field is established through the center of the pickup coil and induces a voltage in the pickup coil which is then directed to an electronic module. As the tooth moves away from the core, the reluctance of the magnetic circuit will increase rapidly, while the magnetic field strength decreases. Therefore, the induced voltage disappears with no voltage signal going to the electronic module. The net result is that the changing field strength induces a positive voltage followed by a negative voltage in the coil winding. This pulse voltage is sent to the electronic module.

When the module receives the voltage signal from the pickup coil, primary winding coil flow is initiated. When the tooth of the reluctor wheel or timer core moves away from the pole piece teeth (center of pickup coil), the voltage signal is lost and the module turns the coil primary current off, which induces the high voltage flow in the secondary winding of the coil to fire the spark plug.

Figures 6-15 and 6-16 show a typical circuit layout for an HEI system along with an actual explanation of its operation.

Since the ignition module located in the distributor assembly contains a microminiature electronic circuit with components so small that they cannot be seen even with a magnifying glass, the module is strictly a replacement item and is therefore nonrepairable. Since we are concerned with how the module actually turns the ignition coil primary current on and off, only those components related to this action are shown in Figs. 6-15 and 6-16.

In Fig. 6-15, current is flowing through all areas shown by the bolder lines. To avoid any charge that could accumulate on the coil frame, it is grounded. The purpose of the capacitor in this circuit is simply to prevent radio noise interference. Battery power supplies the current when the engine is running.

Anytime that the teeth of the timer core or reluctor wheel are not in alignment with the pickup coil core or pole piece teeth, no ignition coil primary current will flow since

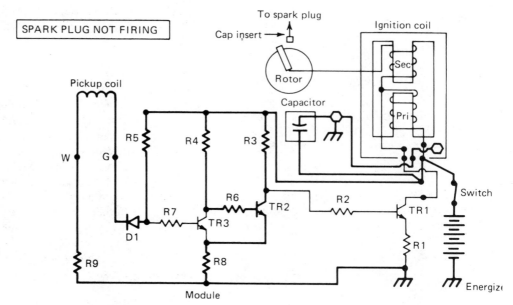

FIGURE 6-15 HEI system, spark-plug not firing. (*Courtesy of Delco Electronics Corporation, Subsidiary of GM Hughes Electronics*)

the current flow through R5, D1, the pickup coil and resistor R9 to ground reduces the voltage potential between R2 and R3 to such a low value that TR1 will not turn on. The basic flow is therefore from the battery or energizer through the switch, the ignition coil primary, TR1 and R1 to ground.

In Fig. 6-16, spark plug firing is initiated when the reluctor teeth approach alignment since a voltage is induced in the pickup coil as explained in detail earlier. Positive potential at terminal G stops current flow through the pickup coil, and the circuit current flow is as shown by the bolder lines in Fig. 6-15. This action turns transistor TR3 on,

which subsequently lowers the voltage potential between R4 and R6 so that TR2 is turned off. This combined action will turn TR1 on which initiates current flow through the ignition coil primary winding.

As mentioned earlier, when the reluctor tooth starts to turn past the pickup core, the pickup coil voltage is reversed and the system returns to the current flow shown in Fig. 6-15, with the spark plug not firing. Prior to this action occurring, however, the primary current must first of all decrease, which induces the voltage in the ignition coil secondary to fire the spark plug.

As a summation of the sequence of events that actually

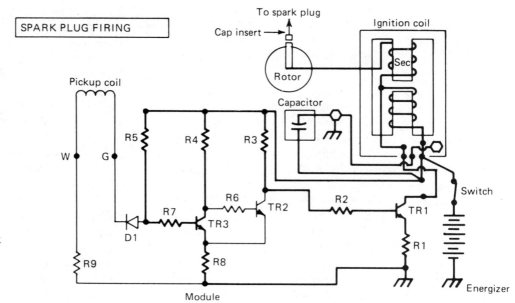

FIGURE 6-16 HEI system, spark plug firing. (*Courtesy of Delco Electronics Corporation, Subsidiary of GM Hughes Electronics*)

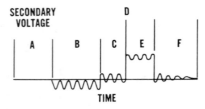

FIGURE 6-17 Typical HEI system oscilloscope pattern. (*Courtesy of Delco Electronics Corporation, Subsidiary of GM Hughes Electronics*)

occurs in firing the spark plug, Fig. 6-17 shows a simple line type diagram of a typical oscilloscope pattern. The sequence of events shown in Fig. 6-17 is as follows.

Period A.   No current flows through the ignition coil at this time since the timer core teeth are not in alignment with the pickup coil.

Period B.   As the teeth of the reluctor wheel or timer core approach alignment with the pickup coil, the primary current increases, which is reflected as a small secondary voltage.

Period C.   Primary current reaches its maximum value.

Period D.   Spark plug firing occurs as the timer core teeth start to separate with a decrease in primary winding current.

Period E.   The induced secondary winding voltage is lower but is sustained throughout period E to maintain the spark.

Period F.   Plug firing ceases, and the remaining energy in the ignition coil is dissipated in the form of damped oscillations. The cycle would then repeat again at period A.

Figure 6-18 illustrates a typical arrangement used with General Motors vehicles employing a high-energy ignition type breakerless ignition distributor and the resultant oscilloscope patterns found with this type of a system. The electronic control module used with this system is shown at the top right quarter of the diagram, with the various transistors and resistors illustrated.

All spark timing changes in the HEI-EST (high-energy ignition — electronic spark timing) distributor are done electronically by an ECM (electronic control module) which monitors information from various engine sensors, computes the desired spark timing, and signals the distributor to change the ignition timing as required. A backup spark advance system is incorporated to signal the ignition mod-

ule in case of ECM failure. No vacuum or mechanical advance is used with this particular system.

VARIATIONS IN HEI SYSTEMS (GMC)

General Motors Corporation uses two types of HEI distributors. One type employs the conventional style of spark advance with a set of weights to alter the spark advance as a result of increasing engine speed. The other system employs the usual vacuum advance concept described earlier in this chapter. In some applications, additional electronic controls are added to the basic mechanical HEI system to further control spark timing at certain engine operating levels to improve both fuel economy and engine performance characteristics.

The electronic systems employed with some HEI systems on GMC vehicles can take one of three forms.

1.   EST or electronic spark timing is a system in which no direct mechanical control is used for spark timing. Instead, engine parameters are monitored and these inputs are electronically processed to obtain optimum spark timing. This system is shown in Fig. 6-19.

2.   ESC or electronic spark control system is a closed-loop system that controls engine detonation by adjusting spark timing in the retarded mode as a function of how much detonation exists in the engine. This detonation is sensed by an engine located sensor as shown in Fig. 6-20.

For example, the electronic spark control on VIN-4 GMC engines modifies (retards) the spark advance when detonation occurs and holds this retard mode for 20 seconds, after which the spark control will again return to EST (electronic spark timing). The detonation monitoring process is continuous so that timing is automatically variable. The ESC controller is a hard-wired signal processor/amplifier which operates from 6 to 16 volts. There is no memory capability, however, in the controller.

The ESC sensor is a magnetorestrictive device mounted in the engine block as shown in Fig. 6-20 to detect the presence or absence as well as intensity of the detonation existing in the engine throughout all operating conditions. This output sends an electrical signal to the controller. Should the sensor unit fail, no ignition/spark timing retard would occur.

3.   EMR or electronic module retard is a spark control system employed with an HEI system with a timing retard feature. When the timing retard circuit is grounded the firing of the spark plugs is delayed for a calibrated number of crank degrees. Control of the grounding circuit is via a vacuum operated electrical

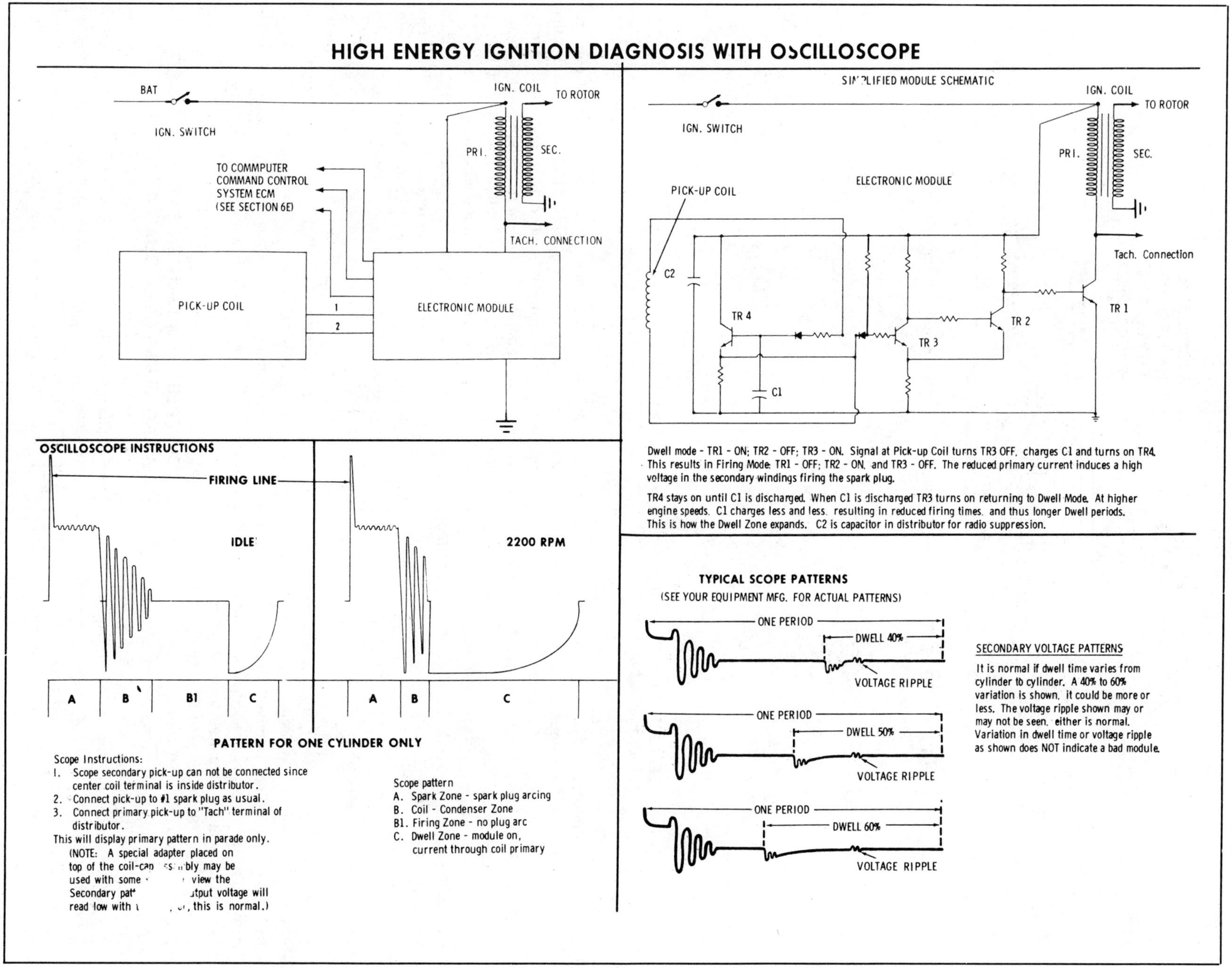

HIGH ENERGY IGNITION DIAGNOSIS WITH OSCILLOSCOPE

SIMPLIFIED MODULE SCHEMATIC

IGN. COIL
TO ROTOR
SEC.
PRI.
Tach. Connection
TR 1
TR 2
TR 3
TR 4
C1
C2
IGN. SWITCH
ELECTRONIC MODULE
PICK-UP COIL

Dwell mode - TR1 - ON; TR2 - OFF; TR3 - ON. Signal at Pick-up Coil turns TR3 OFF, charges C1 and turns on TR4. This results in Firing Mode. TR1 - OFF; TR2 - ON, and TR3 - OFF. The reduced primary current induces a high voltage in the secondary windings firing the spark plug.

TR4 stays on until C1 is discharged. When C1 is discharged TR3 turns on returning to Dwell Mode. At higher engine speeds, C1 charges less and less, resulting in reduced firing times, and thus longer Dwell periods. This is how the Dwell Zone expands. C2 is capacitor in distributor for radio suppression.

TYPICAL SCOPE PATTERNS
(SEE YOUR EQUIPMENT MFG. FOR ACTUAL PATTERNS)

ONE PERIOD — DWELL 40% — VOLTAGE RIPPLE
ONE PERIOD — DWELL 50% — VOLTAGE RIPPLE
ONE PERIOD — DWELL 60% — VOLTAGE RIPPLE

SECONDARY VOLTAGE PATTERNS

It is normal if dwell time varies from cylinder to cylinder. A 40% to 60% variation is shown. it could be more or less. The voltage ripple shown may or may not be seen. either is normal. Variation in dwell time or voltage ripple as shown does NOT indicate a bad module.

BAT
IGN. SWITCH
TO COMPUTER COMMAND CONTROL SYSTEM ECM (SEE SECTION 6E)
ELECTRONIC MODULE
PICK-UP COIL
IGN. COIL
TO ROTOR
SEC.
PRI.
TACH. CONNECTION
1
2

OSCILLOSCOPE INSTRUCTIONS

FIRING LINE
IDLE
2200 RPM

PATTERN FOR ONE CYLINDER ONLY

Scope Instructions:
1. Scope secondary pick-up can not be connected since center coil terminal is inside distributor.
2. Connect pick-up to #1 spark plug as usual.
3. Connect primary pick-up to "Tach" terminal of distributor.

This will display primary pattern in parade only.

(NOTE: A special adapter placed on top of the coil-cap assembly may be used with some _____ view the _____ Secondary patt_____ tput voltage will read low with t_____ , this is normal.)

Scope pattern
A. Spark Zone - spark plug arcing
B. Coil - Condenser Zone
B1. Firing Zone - no plug arc
C. Dwell Zone - module on, current through coil primary

A B B1 C
A B C
A B C

FIGURE 6-18 HEI system oscilloscope diagnosis. *(Courtesy of Oldsmobile Div. of GMC)*

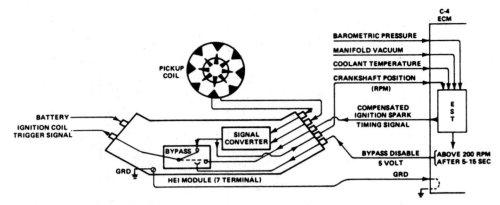

FIGURE 6-19   EST (electronic spark timing) control circuit. (*Courtesy of Oldsmobile Div. of GMC*)

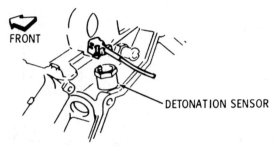

FIGURE 6-20   Example of a detonation sensor location. (*Courtesy of Oldsmobile Div. of GMC*)

switch. When the retard circuit is open, there is no delay and the distributor fires the spark plugs as controlled by engine speed and vacuum.

Figure 6-21 shows a typical EMR check chart and module connections. Should it become necessary to remove and/or replace the EMR-HEI module, the ignition timing must be rechecked and set to the manufacturer's specification.

ENGINE IGNITION SIGNAL

It is important for the computer to know when an ignition signal has been generated in order that the computer can calculate the predetermined injection quantity and also for fuel cutoff. This is generally done, as shown in Fig. 6-22, from a primary voltage signal as soon as the ignition key is turned on, when the voltage at the negative terminal of the ignition coil exceeds 150 volts.

Figure 6-23 illustrates the signal that is picked up by the computer when the engine is being cranked over (starter motor is turning) and is required to allow the computer to activate (energize) the "cold start valve," so that initial fuel/air enrichment can occur. This action avoids stumble when starting with a cold engine. The cold start valve fuel-

injection duration depends on the engine coolant temperature. This is monitored by a coolant temperature sensor that operates as a "thermistor," whereby its resistance changes as a result of variations in coolant temperature. This changing coolant temperature is therefore transformed into an electrical signal and relayed to the computer.

Figure 6-24 illustrates the basic electrical circuit for the "cold start valve/injector" system. Engine coolant temperature determines how long the cold start valve/injector will spray fuel. Once the engine starts, the voltage signal to the cold start valve is cut off.

When the engine is being cranked, and the negative voltage at the ignition coil rises to 150 volts or higher, the computer detects this as an ignition primary signal and converts this message into an engine rpm signal in order to establish the fuel-injection timing.

COIL PER PLUG IGNITION SYSTEM (SAAB AND OLDSMOBILE QUAD 4 ENGINE)

Another unique and recently developed ignition system is the design of using one ignition coil per spark plug. Such a system was developed in Sweden by Mecel AB, which is a research company within the Saab-Scania Group. Fig-

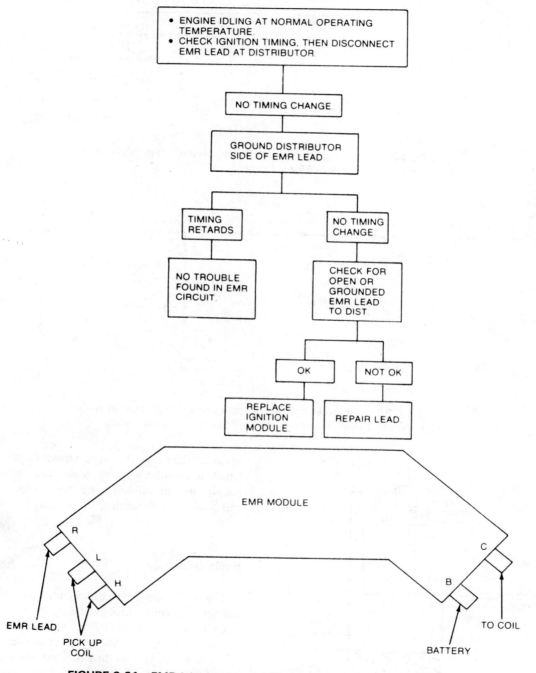

FIGURE 6-21   EMR (electronic module retard) check chart. *(Courtesy of Oldsmobile Div. of GMC)*

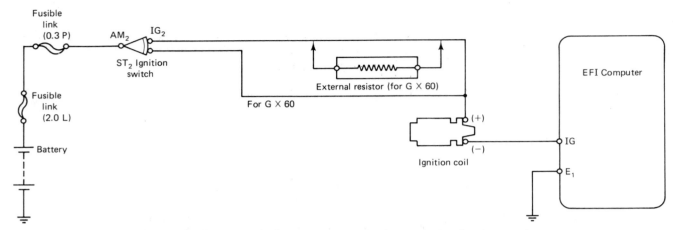

FIGURE 6-22   Engine ignition switch voltage signal when key is turned ON. (*Courtesy of Toyota Motor Corporation*)

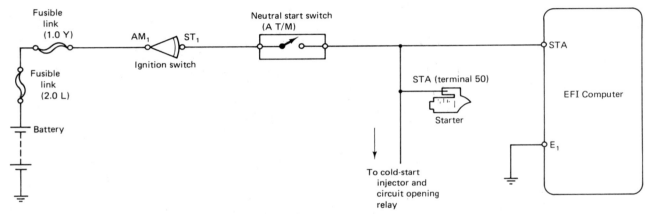

FIGURE 6-23   Computer cold-start valve voltage signal when engine is first cranked over. (*Courtesy of Toyota Motor Corporation*)

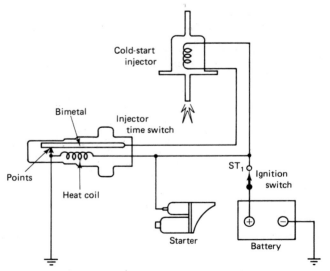

FIGURE 6-24   Cold-start valve/injector electrical system. (*Courtesy of Toyota Motor Corporation*)

ure 6-25 illustrates the basic arrangement of this system, which is commonly called SDI (Saab Direct Ignition). It has no conventional distributor, but employs individual coils and condensors for each spark plug, as is illustrated in Fig. 6-26.

Basic Operation

In Fig. 6-25, the high-tension cartridge (1), is fed battery voltage (12 volts) through the ignition key and the SDI (ECU) unit (2). The Hall-effect-type sensor (3) continually registers the angle of the engine crankshaft as well as the speed of the engine via the small toothed wheel at the front end of the engine. The crankshaft nose-mounted sensor and toothed wheel, in effect, function as an ignition distributor for timing purposes. These ignition pulses created through the Hall-effect sensor are sent to the SDI/ECU (Saab Direct Ignition/Electronic Control Unit) along with information regarding engine speed.

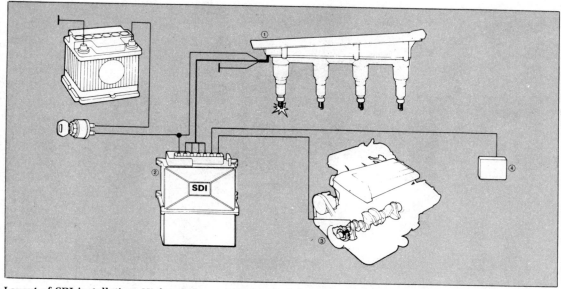

Layout of SDI installation. High-tension cartridge (1) is fed with 12 V from battery and electronic control unit (2). Hall-type sensor (3) registers crankshaft angle and rotational speed from toothed wheel, serves as distributor for timing reference. It triggers basic ignition pulses sent to ECU, together with speed information, while pressure sensor (4) inputs engine load data. Microprocessor then regulates timing according to its performance map program.

FIGURE 6-25 General layout of SDI (SAAB Direct Ignition) system. (*Courtesy of Society of Automotive Engineers, Copyright 1985*)

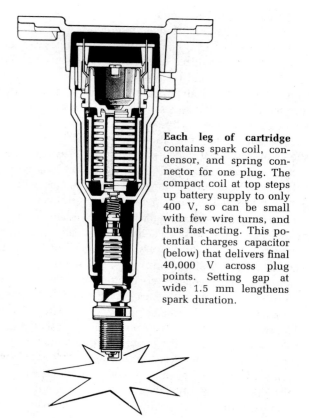

Each leg of cartridge contains spark coil, condensor, and spring connector for one plug. The compact coil at top steps up battery supply to only 400 V, so can be small with few wire turns, and thus fast-acting. This potential charges capacitor (below) that delivers final 40,000 V across plug points. Setting gap at wide 1.5 mm lengthens spark duration.

FIGURE 6-26 Closeup view of SDI coil/condensor on top of individual spark plugs. (*Courtesy of Society of Automotive Engineers, Copyright 1985*)

In addition, the intake manifold depression pressure sensor (4) constantly feeds a sensor voltage to the ECU, based upon throttle position and engine load factors. All of this information is computed within the ECU, and ignition timing as well as fuel injector pulse width is automatically controlled for all situations.

The mini-coil above each spark plug boosts the 12 volt battery supply up to approximately 400 volts, and the condensor boosts this to the final high-tension voltage required to jump across the spark plug gap, which in this system can be set to as wide as 0.060 inch (1.5 mm).

This system is capable of attaining its maximum plug firing voltage in only 1 microsecond, which is about 1/20th of the time required in a conventional ignition system. To circumvent the difficulties inherent with such a fast acting system, such as short spark duration, unacceptable firing and exhaust emissions problems particularly at low speed and part open throttle settings, SDI handles the spark distribution on the low voltage side of the circuit, thereby separating the high-voltage elements.

Figure 6-27 illustrates a four-cylinder ignition cartridge similar to that shown in Fig. 6-25 (basic layout). All high-tension components and connectors are sealed inside a metal casing to ensure exclusion of all dirt and moisture as well as suppressing radio noise (interference) and preventing possible electric shock to the service technician from the 40,000 volt discharge capability.

SDI four-plug ignition cartridge incorporates all high-tension parts and connectors in sealed metal casing that excludes dirt and moisture, suppresses radio interference, and prevents electrical shock injury from the exceptional 40,000 V.

FIGURE 6-27   SDI four-plug ignition module. (*Courtesy of Society of Automotive Engineers, Copyright 1985*)

System Operation

The SDI ignition system is a capacitive- rather than an inductive-type of design. The system employs a Hall-effect-type sensor and toothed wheel pickup on the front of the engine crankshaft nose to act as a distributor. Since the crankshaft is free from gear backlash, timing is kept within 0.5 degrees during the life of the engine versus the usual 3 degrees when employing a typical camshaft driven distributor.

An on-board ECU microprocessor receives continuous informational data on crank position and engine speed. The ECU, in turn, triggers a low-voltage ignition pulse for each individual spark plug coil.

Ignition timing is controlled by the ECU (electronic control unit) which has been programmed (hard-wired) with an optimized performance map for the specific engine for which it has been designed. A second input from a manifold depression sensor also feeds a signal to the ECU when the engine is running. This signal will vary with the position of the throttle pedal.

The metal cartridge coil/ignition module hollow legs fit directly over the spark plugs, with internal rubber sleeves ensuring a tight fit and a seal around the individual insulators. This arrangement requires only one multi-core 12 volt cable which is wired to the battery and the ECU module.

Figure 6-28 illustrates the assembled ignition module in place on the Saab 9000 2 liter, four-cylinder 16 valve engine. The electronic system is "fail safe" since the individual coils are energized directly from the crankshaft sensor should a fault exist anywhere else. Such a situation would occur, for example, during initial engine startup, thereby avoiding the possibility of ECU (microprocessor) malfunction because of low battery voltage.

A similar type of ignition system to the SDI design shown above is that which is now in use (1988) on Oldsmobile's Quad 4 high-performance engine. This is a 16 valve, double overhead camshaft design engine with hydraulic lifters and 9.5:1 compression ratio pistons.

An Integrated Direct Ignition (IDI) system similar to the Saab system will be located under the cam cover in the valley between the cam towers, as is shown in Fig. 6-29. The IDI system will comprise the ECU module, dual ignition coils and secondary conductors, and the necessary printed circuits required to carry the high-tension spark to each plug in order to eliminate all spark plug wires. A Hall-effect sensor mounted on the front of the crankshaft similar to the Saab system will be used, thereby eliminating the need for a distributor. In its present form, this engine will develop 150 bhp, with future versions employing balance shafts and turbocharging being rated at 180 bhp in nonturbocharged form, while a turbocharged version will put out in the region of 250 bhp.

Cutaway section of 16-valve cylinder head shows how SDI cartridge slots between two camshaft covers. Single six-core cable at right carries only battery voltage, so there is no flash-over or shock risk.

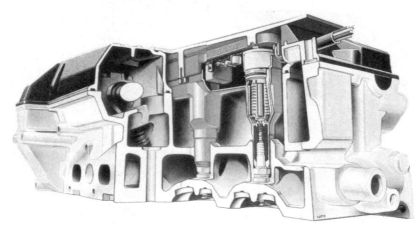

FIGURE 6-28 SDI four-plug ignition module cutaway view. (*Courtesy of Society of Automotive Engineers, Copyright 1985*)

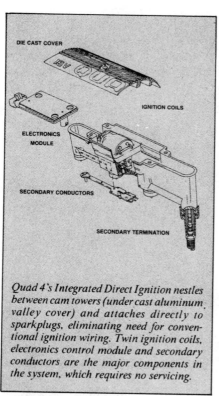

Quad 4's Integrated Direct Ignition nestles between cam towers (under cast aluminum valley cover) and attaches directly to sparkplugs, eliminating need for conventional ignition wiring. Twin ignition coils, electronics control module and secondary conductors are the major components in the system, which requires no servicing.

FIGURE 6-29 Oldsmobile 2260cc Quad 4 DOHC 16 valve engine integrated direct ignition system arrangement. (*Courtesy of Oldsmobile Division of GMC*)

GENERAL MOTORS C3I SYSTEM

Several General Motors Corporation passenger car divisions use what is commonly referred to as C3I or "computer-controlled coil ignition" on their engines, such as the 3.8L fuel-injected V6 engine from Buick and Oldsmobile, as well as Chevrolet in its Corvette and 2.8L fuel-injected V6 in its 1988 model Beretta.

These are known as "distributorless" ignition systems because they do not use the conventional distributor with a rotor and cap, but rather the coil and distributor of the ignition system is replaced by an electronic coil module that incorporates three separate ignition coils, each of which fires two spark plugs simultaneously (one from the positive end and one from the negative end of the coil). This ignition system is also referred to as a "waste spark" system because while firing one spark plug in the cylinder on compression, it also fires the mated cylinder which is moving up towards the end of its exhaust stroke.

Because of the low cylinder pressure, the cylinder on its exhaust stroke requires only a small voltage to create an arc at the spark plug—hence the term "waste spark."

The cylinders on the 3.8L V6 engine are arranged in pairs so that 1–4, 5–2, and 6–3 are fired in pairs from the firing order of 1–6–5–4–3–2, which provides for an even firing crankshaft and 120 degrees between ignition for each of the cylinders. Starting at the front of the engine, cylinders in the left bank are numbered 1–3–5; and in the right bank, they are numbered 2–4–6. Figure 6-30 illustrates the basic layout of the C3I system, while Fig. 6-31 shows the C3I ignition module assembly location on a typical 3.8L V6 port fuel-injected engine.

The ignition system consists of a "coil pack module assembly," the ECM, the camshaft, and crankshaft position sensors and connecting wires. Both the camshaft and crankshaft sensors operation was discussed in detail in Chapter 4, in which both sensors and switches operated on the Hall-effect principle employing a magnet and a microcomputer chip assembly. Review by referring to Fig. 4-47.

Engines in the 1984 model year used a coil arrangement

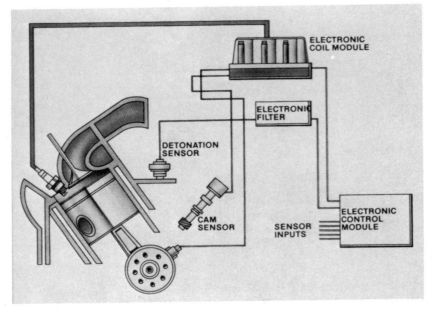

FIGURE 6-30 Basic layout of C3I GMC System. (*Courtesy of Society of Automotive Engineers*)

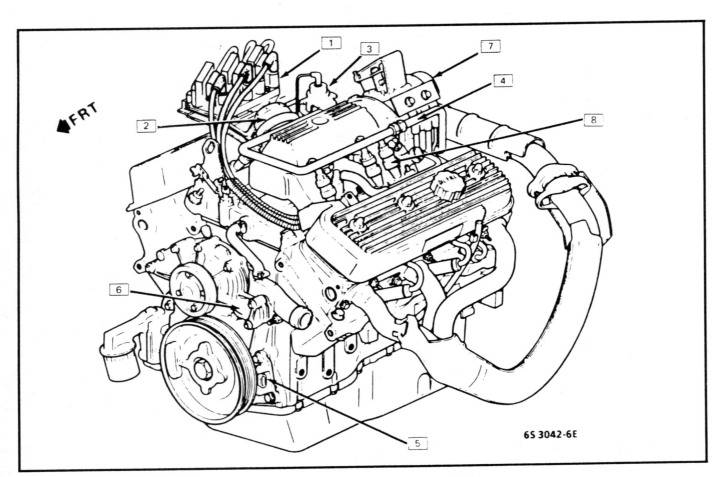

6S 3042-6E

1. C3I Assembly
2. EGR Valve
3. Pressure Regulator
4. Fuel Rail
5. Crankshaft Sensor
6. Cam Sensor
7. Throttle Body
8. Injectors

FIGURE 6-31 3.8L Engine C3I module/engine composite view. (*Courtesy of Oldsmobile Div. of GMC*)

that was enclosed in a one-piece housing; however, later engines employ three separate coils mounted onto an ignition module base. This is known as a Type 11 system. The Type 1 and 2 C3I systems are illustrated in Fig. 6-32, while Fig. 6-33 shows the coil pack and module assembly.

On the latest GMC vehicles, the coil pack assembly consists of three coils mounted as shown in Fig. 6-33, with each coil providing the spark for two plugs simultaneously, as described previously. The ignition module monitors both the crank and cam sensors where this information is passed on to the ECM to ensure that correct spark and fuel injector timing can be maintained during all driving conditions. During cranking, the ignition module must receive a camshaft and crankshaft sensor voltage signal from the Hall-effect magnet and semiconductor arrangement which encompasses the sensor unit in order to initiate ignition and fuel delivery.

The camshaft sensor signal is used by the ECM to determine when the Number 1 piston is on its compression stroke. When it receives this signal, number 6 cylinder will fire first as it comes up on compression, since Number 1 piston will already be past TDC when the signal is received during cranking, and the spark plug fires BTDC.

Below 400 rpm, the ignition module maintains spark timing by triggering each of the three coils at the correct time, and the ECM will start injector timing (simultaneous) as soon as the module gets a cam signal to initialize both spark and fuel timing sequence. At speeds above 400 rpm, the ignition module relays the crank voltage signal on the "bypass line" to indicate that the timing will now be ECM-controlled, which then maintains the spark and fuel injector timing sequence. The "bypass signal" circuit receives a 5 volt signal from the ECM to switch spark timing control from the ignition module to the ECM when the engine speed is above 400 rpm. Should the "bypass circuit" be open or grounded, then a trouble code will be set into the ECM memory, and the engine will run in a backup mode at a predetermined timing value. If a problem exists between the crankshaft sensor and ignition module, then the engine will not start, since the module cannot determine the position of the Number 1 piston. Similarly, if the camshaft sensor circuit is open, the engine will not start.

The high voltage produced from the individual coils operates on the same basic principle as a conventional high-energy GM ignition system. The difference is that instead of having a separate distributor unit with the coil in cap arrangement to produce and distribute the spark, the concentric Hall-effect harmonic balancer (Fig. 4-48), together with the crankshaft and camshaft sensors (Fig. 4-47), triggers a voltage signal from the ECM to the individual three coils. This action produces a high-tension voltage that fires the spark plug in firing order sequence.

The base ignition timing on the 3.8L V6 engines with C3I is preset at the time of factory assembly and *no* ad-

justment is possible or provided. Both timing advance and retard are accomplished through the ECM (engine control module) with EST (electronic spark timing) and ESC (electronic spark control). The distributorless ignition system consists of the following serviceable components:

1. Coil Pack – Type 1, where the coil which is contained inside a single housing must be serviced as a complete unit.

2. Type 11 – such as that shown in Fig. 6-33. Individual coils are available.

3. The ignition module, which must be replaced as a complete unit.

4. Both the crankshaft and camshaft sensors, which are serviced as complete units.

NOTE: The ignition module is not serviceable; therefore, when a module is replaced, the three coils must be transferred to the new module.

C3I Simplified Operating Description

Now that you are familiar with the layout and arrangement of the General Motors C3I distributorless ignition system, let's look at just how this "no distributor" system manages to generate and time the high-tension spark of 25,000 volts to each spark plug in firing order sequence. Figure 6-34 illustrates a wiring diagram of the ECM and the C3I Type-11 ignition module. Note that there are, in fact, three separate coils contained in the ignition module. They are arranged so that spark plugs for cylinders 1 and 4, 5 and 2, and 3 and 6 are interconnected on the 3.8L V6 engine. The 3.8L V6 engine firing order is 1–6–5–4–3–2 with 120 degrees between firing impulses.

From previous information in this chapter, you may recall that the timing of the spark plug firing is accomplished by a Hall-effect camshaft sensor switch. This cam sensor sends a signal (synchronous pulse) to the ignition module when cylinder No. 1 is 25 degrees ATDC on the power stroke. The No. 4 piston is also 25 degrees ATDC, but it would be finishing its exhaust stroke and is actually on its intake.

This cam sensor signal from cylinder No. 1 is then used to start the correct sequence of coil firing as well as to enable sequential fuel injection. The C3I ignition module employs this cam sensor signal to begin the coil firing sequence starting with the No. 3 and 6 coil, with No. 6 plug actually receiving the major spark, since its piston is approaching TDC on compression, while cylinder No. 3 would be on exhaust and would be receiving the "waste spark." Therefore, since there are only exhaust gases and no actual fuel/air charge in cylinder No. 3, very little energy is required to fire the No. 3 spark plug, and this action ensures that No. 6 spark plug receives maximum voltage.

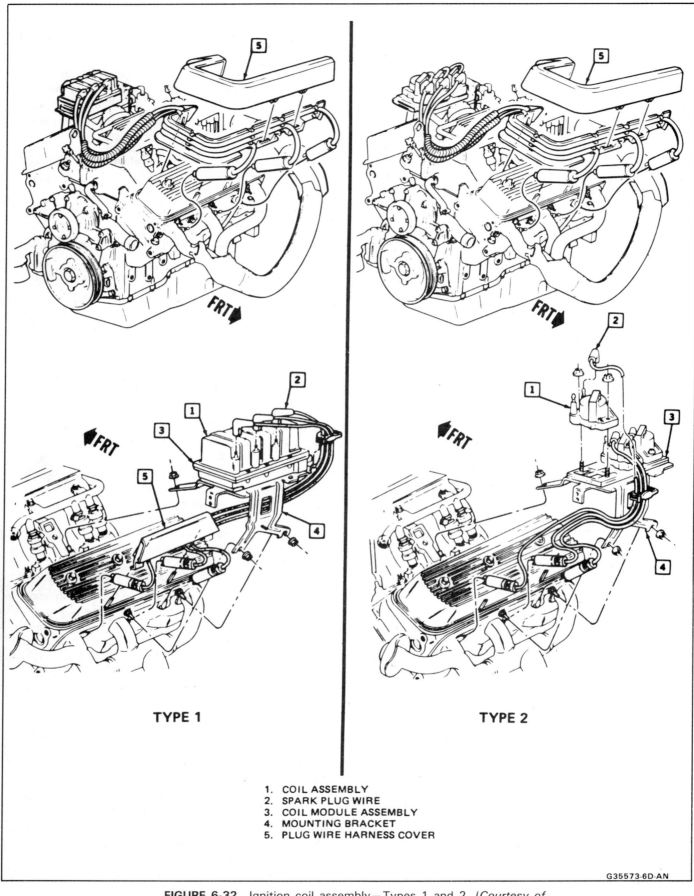

TYPE 1

TYPE 2

1. COIL ASSEMBLY
2. SPARK PLUG WIRE
3. COIL MODULE ASSEMBLY
4. MOUNTING BRACKET
5. PLUG WIRE HARNESS COVER

G35573-6D-AN

FIGURE 6-32 Ignition coil assembly—Types 1 and 2. (*Courtesy of Oldsmobile Div. of GMC*)

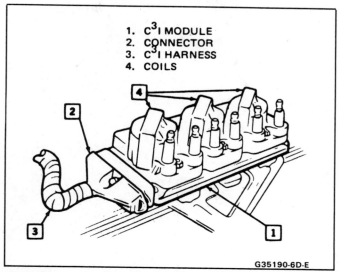

FIGURE 6-33 Coil pack and module—Type 11 (*Courtesy of Oldsmobile Div. of GMC*)

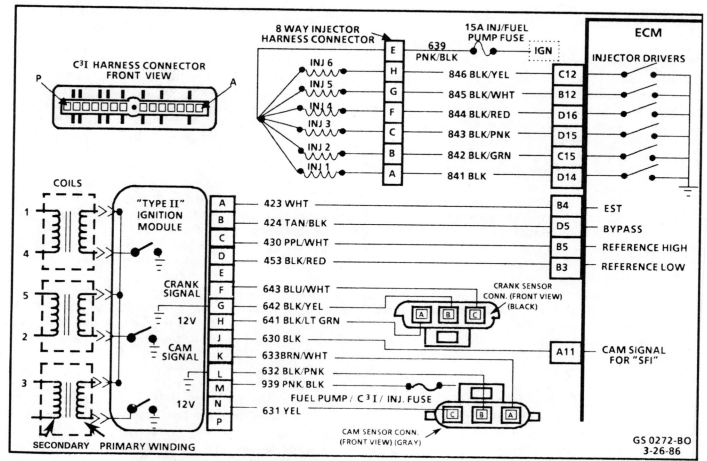

FIGURE 6-34 C3I distributorless ignition/ECM system wiring diagram. (*Courtesy of Oldsmobile Div. of GMC*)

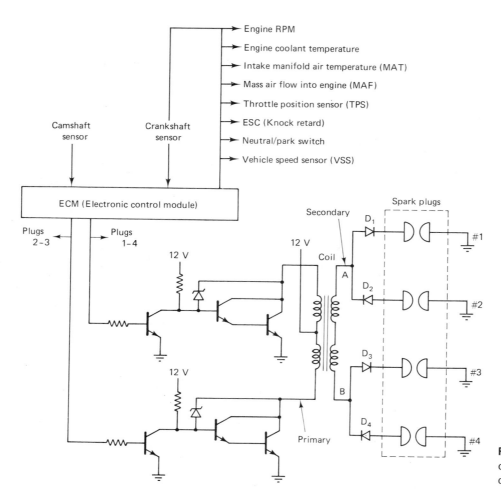

FIGURE 6-35 Simplified operational diagram for a distributorless ignition system.

If the cam signal is lost while the engine is running, it will continue to run; however once it has been stopped, it will not restart. In addition to the camshaft sensor, you probably recall that a crankshaft sensor is also employed. This sensor sends a signal to the ignition module and then to the ECM for reference rpm as well as actual crankshaft position.

Mounted to the harmonic balancer at the front of the engine are three slots or windows in the disc arranged so that as each slot/window passes the sensor, the next one of the ignition coils in firing order sequence will be triggered.

Figure 6-35 illustrates the basic concept of operation for a distributorless ignition system, similar to that now in use on the 2.0 liter 4 cylinder Generation 11 engine offered by General Motors Corporation in many of its passenger cars. The Generation 11 engines employ a magnetic sensor mounted through the engine block crankcase wall, which reads indexing notches in a disc that is actually cast as an integral part of the crankshaft assembly. The number of notches in the disc matches the number of engine cylinders. Precise crankshaft position information is transmitted to the ECM, which in turn transmits it to the C3I ignition coils.

In this simplified schematic, based upon the signal received from the crankshaft position sensor as well as the other monitored parameters from the various other engine/vehicle sensors, the ECM would refer to a look-up table (see Fig. 3-35) and determine the correct spark advance.

The ECM outputs a signal on either output line 1–4 or 2–3 to cause the ignition circuit to interrupt current flow in only half of the "primary" winding of the coil. Depending upon which half of the coil primary circuit has been interrupted, the secondary coil winding (the upper half) will be energized with a given polarity. Specifically, if the ECM activates circuit 1–4, it causes the coil secondary terminal A to be positive in relation to coil secondary B.

This allows current to flow through diodes D1 and D4 to fire spark plugs 1 and 4, with either 1 or 4 receiving the major spark, and with the other receiving the "waste spark" on its exhaust stroke. During this same time, diodes D2 and D3 are in a reverse biased mode due to the secondary voltage; therefore, no current can flow to spark plugs 2 and 3.

When the ECM outputs a signal on line 2–3, the lower-half of the coil primary is interrupted to cause the coil secondary terminal B to be positive in relation to terminal A. This allows current to flow through diodes D2 and D3 to fire spark plugs in cylinders No. 2 and No. 3. Again, only one receives full power; the other receives the "waste spark."

Refer once more to Fig. 6-34, which illustrates the ECM and ignition module for the GM C3I system employed on the 3.8L V6 ported fuel-injection engine. The same basic reaction that occurred in the simplified system just described would also occur in this GM C3I system. When the

Hall-effect crankshaft sensor switch is activated, it grounds the signal line to the C3I module, pulling the crank signal line's applied voltage low between terminal D on the ignition module and terminal B3 on the ECM. (See Fig. 6-34.) It is therefore interpreted as a crank signal. When the crankshaft sensor signal is high, terminal C on the ignition module relays the signal to terminal B5 on the ECM. This high-low signal is used to trigger the C3I module for ignition at each of the three dual cylinder coils, as well as by the ECM to calculate fuel-injection timing.

NOTE: Both the crankshaft and camshaft sensor signals are either in HIGH or LOW mode; in other words, their signals are a square wave, similar to a digital signal (ON or OFF). Three signal pulses will be generated (120 degrees apart) for every revolution of the engine from the metal interruptor ring located on the harmonic balancer at the front of the crankshaft. (See Fig. 4-48.)

The crank sensor signal is used by the C3I module under the coils to create a reference signal to advise the ECM of the engine speed and also crankshaft position (relative piston position in each cylinder). Should one spark plug lead become disconnected from its plug, the coil is still capable of firing the other plug that is connected to it. The disconnected plug lead acts as one plate of a capacitor, while the engine block acts as the other, and therefore both plates would be charged as current arcs across the connected spark plug. The plates would then be discharged as this secondary energy dissipates in the form of an oscillating current across the gap of the spark plug that is disconnected.

Due to the direction of current flow in the coil primary and secondary windings, one plug will fire from the center electrode to the side electrode, while the other will fire from the side electrode to the center electrode.

Note the bypass circuit 424 shown in Fig. 6-34. When the engine speed reaches approximately 400 rpm, the ECM applies 5 volts to this bypass circuit to switch control of the spark timing from the C3I ignition module to the ECM. Should an open or grounded bypass circuit ever exist, then a Code E042 would be stored in ECM memory. This would cause the engine to operate in a back-up ignition timing situation, known as module timing, which is a calculated timing value. This backup, although providing limp-home capability for the vehicle, would decrease the performance as well as cause poor fuel economy because the ignition timing would not be optimized for different speeds under such a condition.

Also shown in Fig. 6-34 is an EST (electronic spark timing) circuit 423. This circuit does not come into operation at engine speeds lower than 400 rpm. During this time, the C3I ignition module controls the ignition timing. At speeds higher than 400 rpm, the ECM applies a 5 volt reference signal to the "bypass line 424" which causes the

ECM to take over this control function (EST — electronic spark timing).

Should an open or ground ever exist in circuit 423, the engine stalls and a Code E042 is stored in ECM memory, just as the ECM does with an open or ground in the bypass circuit 424. If the engine is restarted, it operates in a backup mode similar to that described for an open/ground in the bypass circuit 424.

The cam sensor circuit 630 in Fig. 6-34 tells the ECM where the No. 1 piston is on its compression stroke. This is very important for the ECM to know, since it controls the sequential fuel-injection mode. If a signal is lost on line 630, then a Code E041 is stored in ECM memory, and the fuel-injection system shifts to simultaneous injection operation.

ELECTRONIC SPARK TIMING/CONTROL

The distributorless C3I ignition system employs the same EST to ECM circuits that are found with General Motors HEI (high-energy ignition) distributor-type systems. The ECM programs the rate of spark advance into the C3I system based upon data that it receives from the engine temperature sensor, the rpm sensor, the load/vehicle speed sensor, and operating mode. The ignition module, found below the three dual coils, monitors the camshaft and crankshaft Hall-effect sensor signals during cranking and passes them on to the ECM.

Below 400 engine rpm, the ignition module controls spark advance by triggering each of the three coils at a predetermined interval based simply on engine speed alone. At engine speeds above 400 rpm, the C3I module relays the crank signal to the ECM as a reference signal. The ECM then applies a 5 volt signal to the bypass line (Fig. 6-34) to switch the timing to ECM control or EST.

The ECM, which is also receiving voltage inputs from the various other engine/vehicle sensors, now computes and controls the spark timing, a process referred to as EST or electronic spark timing. If an open or a ground exists in either the bypass signal or the EST circuit, a Code E042 is stored in the ECM memory bank, and the engine resorts to a backup ignition timing mode (ignition module) at a predetermined timing value.

The camshaft and crankshaft sensor signals and how they affect the engine operation by interacting with the C3I ignition system were described earlier in this chapter. Both the cam and crank sensors were illustrated (Fig. 4-47) and also discussed in some detail in Chapter 4. Because of varying octane levels of gasoline available at service station pumps, excessive detonation can occur under varying engine/vehicle speed and load conditions.

To control such detonation within the combustion chamber of the engine, an ESC (electronic spark control)

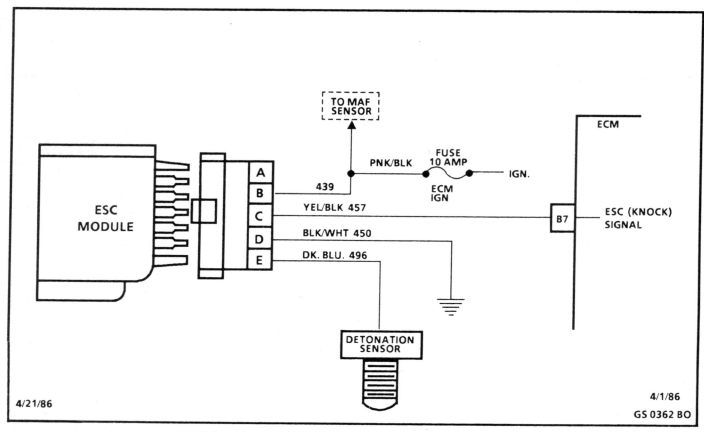

FIGURE 6-36 ESC (electronic spark control) module and detonation sensor. (*Courtesy of Oldsmobile Div. of GMC*)

system is designed to retard ignition timing when detonation is sensed by the detonation sensor (Fig. 4-52). The detonation or knock sensor is a piezo-electric unit located at the rear of the engine that generates electrical impulses in direct proportion to the frequency of the knock detected in the combustion chambers. An electronic buffer switch dampens out all other knock noises except those that occur in the range of combustion chamber detonation. The degree of knock is relayed to the ESC module and then to the ECM to retard the ignition timing. Figure 6-36 illustrates the detonation sensor and ESC module that are used for this purpose.

During engine operation, with no detonation detected by the knock sensor, the ESC module will continue to send an 8 to 10 volt signal to the ECM, and normal spark advance, described earlier from the EST system, will automatically advance ignition timing with respect to engine operation. Should combustion chamber detonation be detected at any time by the knock sensor, the ESC module will turn OFF (zero volts) the voltage circuit to the ECM terminal B7 (Fig. 6-36). This action causes the ECM to retard ignition timing by up to 20 degrees depending upon the severity of detonation.

This retard action happens so quickly that you would have a tough time seeing the zero voltage level if you were monitoring this voltage signal with a DVOM (digital volt/ohmmeter). Instead, you would record a voltage reading

that would be less than the normal 8 to 10 volt signal that feeds to the ECM when no detonation exists. Should the detonation sensor signal be lost for any reason, or if a loss of ground at the ESC module occurred, the voltage signal at the ECM would remain at the normal 8 to 10 volt range resulting in the ECM continuing to control EST (electronic spark timing — advance).

With no ignition retard possible, detonation within the combustion chamber could become severe and create serious piston damage. Therefore, if the ESC signal is lost at speeds above 400 rpm, the ECM becomes aware of this loss on terminal C of the ESC module to terminal B7 on the ECM, and the ECM resorts to a constant retard EST condition. This would certainly ensure engine/vehicle limphome capability, but since there would be no ignition advance, the engine would perform poorly, and a trouble Code E043 would be stored in ECM memory.

The *Check* or *Service Engine Soon* light would illuminate on the instrument panel to warn the driver of a problem. Upon accessing these stored trouble codes, the mechanic/technician realizes that a problem exists in the EST/ESC circuit.

NOTE: In some cases, particularly on earlier model year engines that used different knock sensors, retarded timing can be caused by excessive valve lifter or pushrod noise.

CHAPTER 7

◆

General Motors ECM Systems

INTRODUCTION

Since the 1980 production year and depending upon the model, all domestic General Motors Corporation vehicles are equipped with either FBC (feedback carburetor), TBI (throttle body injection), or MPFI (multi-port fuel injection) systems. Some engines are equipped with a HEI (high-energy ignition) distributor system, while some later model engines are equipped with the C3I (computer-controlled coil ignition) system or what is commonly known as a "distributorless ignition system," since there is no actual conventional distributor used on the engine. (Information on the C3I system can be found in Chapter 6 in this book.) Each system employs a number of engine sensors which are commonly employed on most gasoline automotive engines today to meet EPA or EEC exhaust emissions regulations and also to improve the fuel economy and performance of the car.

General Motors designates its various division vehicles by body type using a letter code system. Figure 7-1 illustrates the various letter codes used and the specific GMC division model cars that fall into each letter code designation.

Although technically referred to as a CCCS (computer command control system), the operational unit is most often known simply as an ECM or "electronic control module." The first digital engine control module manufactured by Delco Electronics was introduced in 1979 for the Cadillac range of vehicles. It featured three separate printed circuit boards that were designed to handle only five functions.

Electronic control modules manufactured for the 1987 GMC passenger cars have only a single compact printed circuit board and are designed to handle/control 27 different functions for both the engine and vehicle systems. For example, the 1987 Cadillac Allante carries a combined computer information systems memory capacity of 90.7 Kbytes, which means that it is capable of holding and storing 90,700 characters of data or information. The 1988 Chevrolet Beretta model passenger car is another example of current electronics technology with its 2.8L V6 multi-port fuel-injected engine featuring a computer-controlled coil ignition (see Chapter 6) and an electronic control module with a brand-new microprocessor that can handle 600,000 commands per second. At the time of writing this book, Delco Electronics was producing and testing 25,000 electronic systems each day, which include music systems, instrument panel clusters, and sophisticated digital engine control computers.

Since the 1980 model year, General Motors has designed and produced over 45 different ECM's and over 2000 PROM's for its various division vehicles. It is imperative for the mechanic/technician to realize this fact. Only a similar ECM (part number) must be used to replace a faulty ECM.

When a service replacement ECM is ordered from a GMC source, it is generally necessary to remove the PROM from all ECM's for replacement into the new service unit. On later model vehicles fitted with a CALPAK, this unit must also be removed and inserted into the service replacement ECM. If, of course, either the PROM or the CALPAK unit is damaged or faulty, then new ones can be or-

BODY DESIGNATION	A	B	C	D	E	F	G	J	K
CHEVROLET	Celebrity	Impala Caprice Classic				Camaro	Monte Carlo	Cavalier	
PONTIAC	6000	Parisienne				Firebird	Bonneville Grand Prix	Sunbird (2000)	
OLDSMOBILE	Ciera	Delta 88	Ninety-Eight		Toronado		Cutlass Supreme	Firenza	
BUICK	Century	LeSabre	Electra		Riviera		Regal	Skyhawk	
CADILLAC			Fleetwood Brougham DeVille	Fleetwood Limousine	Eldorado			Cimarron	Seville
GMC							Caballero		

BODY DESIGNATION	M	N	P	R	S & T Truck	T	X	Y
CHEVROLET	Sprint			Spectrum	Blazer	Chevette	Citation	Corvette
PONTIAC		Grand Am	Fiero			1000	Phoenix	
OLDSMOBILE		Calais					Omega	
BUICK		Somerset Regal					Skylark	
CADILLAC								
GMC					Jimmy			

FIGURE 7-1   GMC vehicle body designation letters/models. (*Courtesy of Kent-Moore Tool Group, Sealed Power Corporation*)

dered. Again, it is very important that only the same P/N replacement assembly be used; otherwise, serious operational damage to the vehicle can occur. In CALPAK equipped vehicles, the engine/vehicle will lapse into a "backup mode" based on a program stored in ROM. This will provide "limp-home" capability, but the vehicle will perform poorly. (For a description of ROM, RAM, PROM, and CALPAK units, see Chapter 3.) For an example of the electronics advancements made in on-board vehicle computers, see Fig. 7-2. Shown on the far right of the illustration is an ECM from a 1980 model year California car. The middle unit shows an ECM from a 1982 vehicle, and the one on the left-hand side shows an ECM from a 1986 model Corvette.

VEHICLE SYSTEMS SENSED

Figure 7-3 illustrates typical operating systems that are sensed by the on-board ECM (electronic control module), which is part of the CCCS (computer command control system), or C3S system. Depending upon the GMC Division that manufactured the vehicle and the particular model of car or light truck, the sensed and controlled systems can vary slightly between makes and models. However, all vehicles employing the CCCS system are controlled by the ECM.

Later GMC Division upscale model passenger cars, such as the Oldsmobile Toronado, Buick, and Cadillac vehicles, also employ a BCM (body control module) in addition to

FIGURE 7-2 Comparative examples of GMC vehicles computer denseness and size reductions from 1980 through 1986. (*Courtesy of Oldsmobile Div. of GMC*)

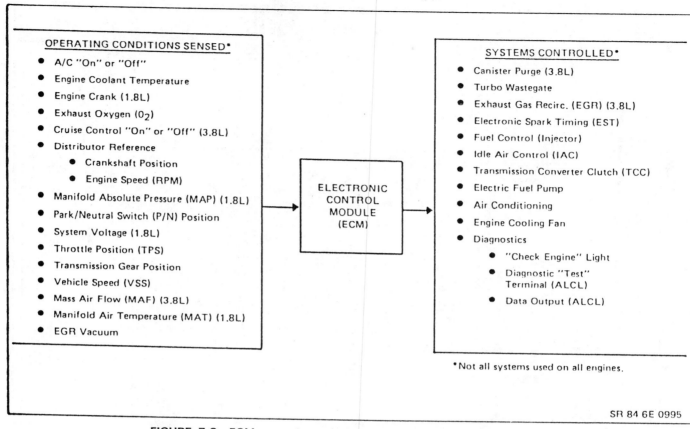

FIGURE 7-3 ECM operating conditions sensed and systems controlled. (*Courtesy of Oldsmobile Div. of GMC*)

the ECM (electronic control module). The ECM monitors and controls the various systems shown in Fig. 7-3 while the BCM is designed to monitor and control most vehicle functions other than the actual ignition and fuel systems which are tied into the ECM.

The location of the various on-board computers will vary between specific GMC car makes and models. However, Fig. 7-4 illustrates an example of a FWD (front wheel drive) vehicle with a 3.8L V6 transversely mounted engine and the location of the various sensors and controlled devices. Figure 7-5 illustrates the same vehicle with its hood open and shows the actual sensors and switches.

SENSORS USED ON GMC VEHICLES

In Chapter 4, all the various types of sensors and switches and their function and operation in the overall control of the engine and other body functions were described in detail. The following list simply indicates what sensors are in use on GM vehicles so that you can readily assimilate how these sensors tie-in with the on-board computer systems.

Keep in mind that the type of fuel system used on the vehicle, its year of manufacture, and the options with which it is equipped will determine just what sensors and switches are in use. Some or all may be found on the vehicle.

Data Sensors List

1. Air conditioner ON switch
2. Barometric pressure sensor (BARO)
3. Coolant temperature sensor (CTS)
4. Crank signal or engine speed sensor
5. E-Cell timer
6. High gear switch
7. Mass air flow sensor (MAF)
8. Manifold absolute pressure sensor (MAP)
9. Manifold air temperature sensor (MAT)
10. Oxygen sensor (02)
11. Park/neutral switch (P/N)
12. Throttle position sensor (TPS)
13. Vacuum sensor

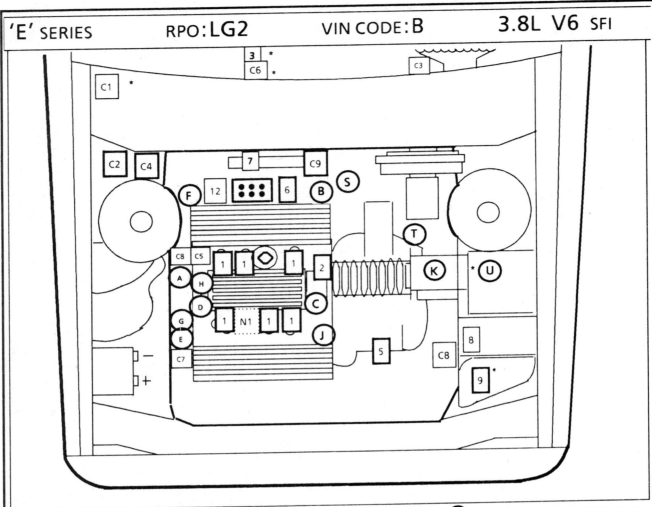

COMPUTER HARNESS

- C1 Electronic Control Module (ECM)
- C2 Engine to dash harness grommet
- C3 "CHECK ENG/SERV ENG SOON" light
- C4 Engine to ECM grommet
- C5 ECM harness ground
- C6 Fuse panel
- C7 Isolated engine/body grd.
- C8 Fuel pump test connector
- C9 Engine/dash harness harness connector

NOT ECM CONNECTED

- N1 Positive crankcase ventilation valve (PCV)

CONTROLLED DEVICES

- 1 Fuel injector
- 2 Idle Air Cntrol valve (IAC)
- 3 Fuel pump relay
- 5 Trans. Converter Clutch connector (TCC)
- 6 (C³I) Ignition module and coil assy.
- 7 Electronic Spark Control module (ESC)
- 8 Underhood relay center
  - A/C clutch control relay
  - Low speed coolant fan relay
  - High speed coolant fan relay (Puller)
  - High speed coolant fan relay (Pusher)
  - Headlamp door relays
- 9 Fuel vapor canister solenoid
- 12 Exhaust Gas Recirculation vacuum solenoid (EGR)

INFORMATION SENSORS

- A Oil pressure sensor or switch
- B Oxygen (0²) sensor
- C Throttle Position Sensor (TPS)
- D Coolant temperature sensor
- E Crank sensor
- F Vehicle Speed Sensor (VSS)
- G Cam sensor
- H Temperature switch
- J ESC detonation (knock) sensor
- K Mass Air Flow (MAF)
- S P.S. pressure switch
- T Gear selector switch
- U Manifold Air Temperature sensor (MAT)

 Exhaust Gas Recirculation valve

* Located beneath the visible component

3/17/86
GS 0289 O

FIGURE 7-4 Component location of various sensors/controlled devices on a 3.8L V6 engine. *(Courtesy of Oldsmobile Div. of GMC)*

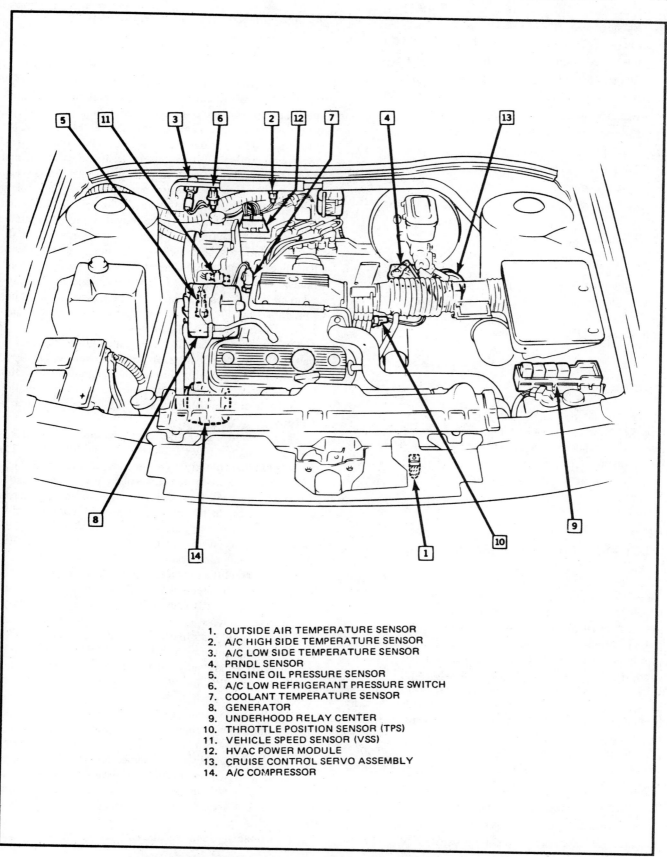

1. OUTSIDE AIR TEMPERATURE SENSOR
2. A/C HIGH SIDE TEMPERATURE SENSOR
3. A/C LOW SIDE TEMPERATURE SENSOR
4. PRNDL SENSOR
5. ENGINE OIL PRESSURE SENSOR
6. A/C LOW REFRIGERANT PRESSURE SWITCH
7. COOLANT TEMPERATURE SENSOR
8. GENERATOR
9. UNDERHOOD RELAY CENTER
10. THROTTLE POSITION SENSOR (TPS)
11. VEHICLE SPEED SENSOR (VSS)
12. HVAC POWER MODULE
13. CRUISE CONTROL SERVO ASSEMBLY
14. A/C COMPRESSOR

FIGURE 7-5 Component reference — underhood view of a 3.8L V6 transversely mounted engine. (*Courtesy of Oldsmobile Div. of GMC*)

14. Vehicle speed sensor (VSS)
15. Idle air control valve (IACV) fuel-injected vehicles
16. Idle speed control (ISC) carbureted models
17. Idle speed module (2.0L TBI models)
18. Air injection reaction (AIR) management system
19. Exhaust gas recirculation valve (EGRV)
20. Evaporative emission control system (EECS)
21. Early fuel evaporation (EFE)
22. Torque converter clutch (TCC)
23. Viscous converter clutch (VCC)
24. High-energy ignition — electronic spark control (HEI — ESC)
25. Electronic spark timing (EST)
26. Canister purge control solenoid (CPCS)

In addition to the list of switches and sensors listed above, refer to the Abbreviations and Glossary of Terms List in Table 7-1. The table alphabetically lists the typical terms used by GM for its vehicles.

SPECIAL TOOLS

Various special tools and equipment are available from both GM dealers and major tool suppliers to assist you in effectively troubleshooting the ECM/BCM systems. These various tools are illustrated and described at the rear of this section, while special diagnostic equipment is described in Chapter 14.

ELECTRONIC CONTROL ARRANGEMENT

The major component in the latest (1985 and up) on-board computer system is the BCM (body computer module), which is usually located behind the glove box and which has an internal microprocessor that is the actual center for linking up and communicating with all the various components of the electronic systems. An example of the location of the BCM and ECM modules for an Oldsmobile Toronado with a 3.8L V6 engine is shown in Fig. 7-6. This same engine is, of course, available to and widely used by a number of other GMC Divisions in their various models of passenger cars.

All vehicle system sensors and switches are monitored directly either by the BCM or one of the five following subsystems:

1. ECM (electronic control module)
2. IPC (instrument panel cluster)
3. ECC (electronic climate control panel)
4. Programmer – Heating – Ventilation – A/C
5. Chime/voice module

Information fed to each of these various subsystems from the various sensors and switches communicates directly to the BCM individually or on a common communications link known as an SDL (serial data line). A memory system is incorporated into the ECM and BCM; therefore, the numerous inputs to the BCM combine with these programmed instructions to ensure continuous and accurate control over these various subsystems. Should any subsystem circuit exceed its previously preprogrammed limits, then a system malfunction will be indicated, and certain backup functions may be provided during this time.

The BCM controls the various subsystems either directly or through transmitted signals along the SDL (serial data line) to one of the other four major electronic components—namely, the ECM, IPC, ECC, and the heating–ventilation–A/C programmer. The data communications link allows the BCM to control the ECM's own self-diagnostic capabilities as well as its own.

To provide additional control capability to the CCCS, the five major components of the computer system listed earlier share information through the communications link process. A detailed description of the actual basic operation of an on-board computer system was discussed earlier in Chapter 3.

The method used to tie these five circuits together is similar to that used by the old style telegraph system. The BCM's internal circuitry is continuously and rapidly switching a circuit between 0 and 5 volts, just as an old style telegraph key used to do with its dots and dashes across miles of wires. In the BCM, the process converts information into a series of pulses to represent coded data messages, in a way similar to how the old Morse code was used on the telegraph system.

These coded data messages are then easily understood by the other subsystems which all have their own address or recognition code. Because of the fact that each subsystem has its own address and recognition code, any code sent out on the serial data line (SDL) which does not match a subsystem's programmed code will simply be ignored. To ensure access and control of the BCM self-diagnostic features, both the IPC and ECC are necessary.

The IPC is part of the vehicle instrument panel cluster, and it offers a 20 character display area commonly called the "Information Center." During normal engine operation, this display can be used as either a tachometer, or it can show the vehicle model name, such as "Toronado." Should a malfunction be sensed at the BCM, then a driver warning light will illuminate in this area to display such messages as *Check Engine Light, Service Engine Soon* or *Now* warnings.

When the mechanic/technician accesses the stored trou-

TABLE 7-1

List of terms and abbreviations used for GMC systems vehicles

LIST OF AUTOMOTIVE ABBREVIATIONS

A/C—Air Conditioning
ADJ—Adjust
A/F—Air Fuel Ratio
AIR—Air Injection Reaction system
ALCL—Assembly Line Communication Link
Alt—Altitude
AMP—Ampere(s)
APS—Absolute Pressure Sensor
AT—Automatic Transmission/Transaxle
ATDC—After Top Dead Center
Auth—Authority

BARO—Barometic Pressure Sensor
Bat—Battery
Bat+—Battery Positive Terminal
Bbl—Barrel
BCM—Body Control Module
BP—Back Pressure
BTDC—Before Top Dead Center

°C—Degrees Celsuis
Calif—California
Cat. Conv.—Catalytic Converter
CCC—Computer Command Control
CCOT—Cycling Clutch Orifice Tube
CCP—Controlled Canister Purge
CID—Cubic Inch Depalcement
CL—Closed Loop
CLCC—Closed Loop Carburetor Control
CO—Carbon Monoxide
Conn—Connector
Conv—Converter
CP—Canister Purge
CPS—Central Power Supply
CV—Constant Velocity
Cyl—Cylinder(s)
C³I—Computer Controlled Coil Ignition

DBM—Dual Bed Monolith
Diff—Differential
Dist—Distributor
DUM—Digital Voltmeter (10 meg.)
DVDV—Differential Vacuum Delay Valve

EAC—Electric Air Control
EAS—Electric Air Switching
ECC—Electronic Climate Control
ECM—Electronic Control Module
ECU—Engine Calibration Unit (PROM)
EECS—Evaporative Emission Control System
EFE—Early Fuel Evaporation
EFI—Electronic Fuel Injection
EGR—Exhaust Gas Recirculation
EGR/TVS—Exhaust Gas Recirculation /
        Thermosatic Vacuum Switch
ELC—Electronic Level Control
ESC—Electronic Spark Control
EST—Electronic Spark Timing
ETR—Electronically Tuned Receiver
EVRV—Electronic Vacuum Regulator Valve
EXH—Exhaust

°F—Degrees Fahrenheit
FED—Federal (All States Except Calif.)
FWD—Front Wheel Drive

g—gram

HC—Hydrocarbons
HD—Heavy Duty
HEI—High Energy Ignition
Hg—Mercury
HiAlt—High Altitude

IAC—Idle Air Control
IC—Integrated Circuit
ID—Identification
   —Inside Diameter
IGN—Ignition
ILC—Idle Load Compensator
INJ—Injection
IP—Instrument Control
IPC—Instrument Panel Cluster

km—kilometer
km/h—Kilometer per hour
kPa—KiloPascals
KV—Kilovolts (thousands of volts)

L—Liter
lbs. ft.—pounds foot
lbs. in.—pounds inch
LF—Left Front
LH—Left Hand
LR—Left Rear
LS—Left Side
L-4—In-line four cyclinder engines

MAF—Mass Air Flow
MAP—Manifold Absolute Pressure
MAT—Manifold Air Temperature
Max—Maximum
M/C—Mixture Control
Min—Minimum
mm—millimeter
MPFI—Multi-Port Fuel Injection
MPG—Miles Per Gallon
MPH—Miles Per Hour
MT—Manual Transaxle/Transmission
MV—Milli Volt

NC—Normally closed
N•m—Newton Meters
NO—Normally open
NOx—Nitrogen, Oxides of

OD—Outside diameter
OHC—Overhead Camshaft
OL—Open Loop
O_2—Oxygen

PAIR—Pulse Air Injection System
P/B—Power Brakes
PROM—Programmable Read Only Memory
P/S—Power Steering
PSI—Pounds per Square Inch
Pt.—Pint
Pri—Primary
PWM—Pulse Width Modulated

Qt—Quart   *(continued)*

G35315-0A-BG

175

TABLE 7-1 (*Continued*)

LIST OF AUTOMOTIVE ABBREVIATIONS

REF—Reference
RF—Right Front
RH—Right Hand
RPM—Revolutions per Minute
RPO—Regular Production Option
RR—Right Rear
RS—Right Side
RTV—Room Temperature Vulcanizing
RVB—Rear Vacuum Break
RVR—Response Vacuum Reducer
RWD—Rear Wheel Drive

SAE—Society of Automotive Engineers
Sec—Secondary
SES—Service Engine Soon
SFI—Sequential-port Fuel Injection
SI—System International
Sol—Solenoid

TAC—Thermostatic Air Cleaner
Tach—Tachometer
TBI—Throttle Body Injection
TCC—Transmission/Transaxle Converter Clutch

TDC—Top Dead Center
Term—Terminal
Thermo— Thermocstatic Air Cleaner
TPS—Throttle Postion Sensor
TV—Throttle Valve
TVRS—Television & Radio Suppression
TVS—Thermal Vacuum Switch

U-Joint—Universal Joint

V—Volt(s)
VAC—Vacuum
VIN—Vehicle Identification Number
V-ref—ECM refernce voltage
VRV—Vacuum Reducer Valve
VSS—Vehicle Speed Sensor
V-6—Six cylinder "V" engine
V-8—Eight cyclinder "V" engine

w/—With
w/b—Wheel base
w/o—Without
WOT—Wide open Throttle

G35316-0A-BG

ble codes of the system (see accessing trouble codes in this section), any BCM or ECM diagnostic codes are immediately displayed, starting with the lowest number first and proceeding on through any other higher numbered codes. The ECM codes will always be displayed first before the BCM codes. The technician can also access the data parameters, discrete inputs and outputs, as well as BCM output override messages on this same instrument panel when called for through the ECC.

The ECC (electronic comfort control) panel provides the controls for both the heating and air conditioning systems, and also functions as the controller for entering the diagnostics mode of the BCM. This access to the trouble codes in the BCM and ECM is achieved by simply pressing the appropriate buttons on the ECC, which allows any data messages to be transmitted over the SDL (serial data line) to the BCM. This action produces a listing of the specific diagnostic features required. Should the technician place the BCM diagnostics into an override mode, then the amount of override is displayed at the ECC, where the normal outside and interior set temperatures are graphically shown.

ENTERING DIAGNOSTIC MODE

Depending upon the year of vehicle manufacture and also upon the particular make and model of car, the diagnostic mode circuit of the ECM, or both the ECM and BCM

systems, will be accessed in different ways. In some vehicles (upscale models), a flashing letter and number, or simply a number, will be illuminated on the instrument panel (ECC type), while on others (ALCL connector type), the technician must carefully watch and monitor the number of times the *Check or Service Engine Soon or Now* light illuminates and for how long in order to determine the stored trouble code(s) in memory.

In order to enter the diagnostic mode and allow the self-diagnostic features of the ECM and/or ECM/BCM to illuminate as a letter and number on the IPC or by the flashing check-engine warning light method, refer to the subheading which relates to the particular type of vehicle that you are working on—namely, one with an IPC/ECC panel or an ALCL diagnostic link. If the vehicle is not equipped with an IPC and ECC (electronic climate control) panel, then the ALCL (assembly line communication link) access mode will be used. If, however, the vehicle is equipped with an IPC and ECC, then various buttons on the ECC panel are pushed simultaneously to cause the ECM and BCM to enter the self-diagnostic code check routine. Only vehicles equipped with ECC (electronic climate control) or upscale models have the capability to self-diagnose problems by pushing certain operational buttons on the facia panel. On units equipped with both an ECM and BCM, the trouble code is preceded by a letter to indicate whether the problem is common to the ECM or BCM. However, special

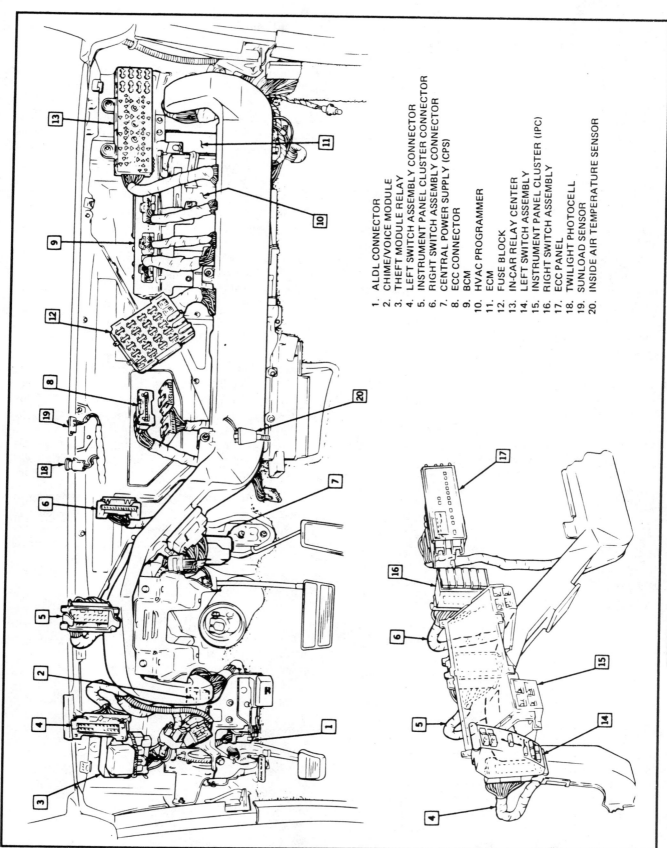

1. ALDL CONNECTOR
2. CHIME/VOICE MODULE
3. THEFT MODULE RELAY
4. LEFT SWITCH ASSEMBLY CONNECTOR
5. INSTRUMENT PANEL CLUSTER CONNECTOR
6. RIGHT SWITCH ASSEMBLY CONNECTOR
7. CENTRAL POWER SUPPLY (CPS)
8. ECC CONNECTOR
9. BCM
10. HVAC PROGRAMMER
11. ECM
12. FUSE BLOCK
13. IN-CAR RELAY CENTER
14. LEFT SWITCH ASSEMBLY
15. INSTRUMENT PANEL CLUSTER (IPC)
16. RIGHT SWITCH ASSEMBLY
17. ECC PANEL
18. TWILIGHT PHOTOCELL
19. SUNLOAD SENSOR
20. INSIDE AIR TEMPERATURE SENSOR

FIGURE 7-6 Component reference — interior view, Oldsmobile Toronado. (*Courtesy of Oldsmobile Div. of GMC*)

test tools and instruments are now available for testing both the ECC equipped vehicles as well as the non-ECC equipped vehicles. Refer to the end of this chapter for information on these tools.

Testing and Battery Power

CAUTION: Operating the vehicle in the diagnosis mode to allow the ECM to flash consecutive trouble codes to either the *Check Engine* or *Service Engine Soon* warning light or to IPC digital readout facia without the engine running for long periods of time can result in a reduction in vehicle battery voltage. Such a condition can cause faulty diagnostic information codes to be relayed, or failure of the engine to start when required. Therefore, should extended diagnostic checks be required, attach a battery charger to the vehicle in a "trickle charge" mode. The recommendation is to do this if the ECM system is to be accessed for periods longer than 30 minutes.

Flashing Warning Light ECM System Accessibility — ALCL Type

On vehicles equipped with an ECM only (does not have the BCM), the sequence for accessing stored trouble codes from the memory system is the same, whether the fuel system is of the feedback carburetor (FBC) type, TBI (throttle body injection), or MPFI (multi-port fuel injection) design. This type of vehicle will not be equipped with an ECC (electronic climate control) system; therefore, if available, the use of a test instrument is preferable to the illuminated *Check Engine* light procedure. The technology and electronic component parts used by the various GMC car divisions can be considered common as far as testing procedures are concerned. Therefore, although minor variations will exist between test specifications for a particular make/model of vehicle, once you have mastered a given test sequence for one GMC vehicle, the same process can be applied to other division models within the GMC stable.

With this system, the *Check Engine* light will come on when the ignition key is turned on, even with the engine not running. This simply confirms that the bulb and system are operational. When the engine is started, this light should go off if no problems are detected by the ECM from the various sensor inputs. If, however, the *Check Engine* light remains illuminated, then the ECM has detected a problem somewhere in the system, and the light remains illuminated to warn the driver of a trouble code now stored in the memory bank of the ECM.

If for some reason the detected problem system were to disappear (intermittent), then the trouble code would be retained in memory within the ECM, although the *Check Engine* light would go out after about 10 seconds. Often these intermittent trouble codes are hard to find when di-

agnosing the engine and system sensors. Often the vehicle will have to be road tested at speeds in excess of 45 mph (72 km/hr) once the trouble codes are cleared from the system to determine if, in fact, the problem recurs or if it was simply an intermittent condition.

To withdraw a trouble code on these types of vehicles, an ALCL (assembly line communication or diagnostic link) connector located in the passenger compartment must be tied together with a jumper wire, thereby causing the ECM to output any stored diagnostic trouble codes. Figure 7-7(a) illustrates the actual location of the ALCL connector in the A, X, and J model GMC cars with FBC or TBI, while Fig. 7-7(b) shows the ALDL connector for a 1986 Oldsmobile Toronado equipped with a 3.8L V6 sequential port fuel-injection engine.

With reference to Fig. 7-7, the diagnostic test terminal is Item B, which can be connected to either terminal A or directly to ground, which will allow the ECM to enter the diagnostic or the field service mode.

Diagnostic Mode — ALCL Connector

Two methods can be used to access the ALCL (assembly line communication link) which is located under the dash on the vehicle. Method A involves using a special tool known as a "mini-scanner," which is plugged into the system to read the trouble codes. Method B simply involves using a jumper wire across the necessary ALCL terminals, which will cause the *Check Engine* light to flash a coded number.

Method A. Terminal E of the ALCL connector located under the vehicle dash is connected to the computer serial data line; therefore, if this terminal is accessed by a special tool such as that shown in Fig. 14-5, it will provide information that is either extremely difficult or impossible to obtain with other equipment.

The mini-scanner tool (Fig. 14-5) plugs into the vehicle ALCL connector and allows the service/technician to read and interpret the ECM data stream. The mini-scanner also provides a visual means of examining computer related parameters such as sensor input voltages, input switch status, solenoid driver commands, mixture control solenoid dwell, and trouble codes.

When a troubleshooting chart within the vehicle service manual calls for a sensor reading, the ALCL tool can be used to read the following components directly:

1. Park/Neutral switch
2. Throttle position sensor (TPS)
3. Manifold absolute pressure sensor (MAP)
4. Coolant temperature sensor (CTS)
5. Vehicle speed sensor (VSS)
6. Oxygen sensor (O2)

When the ALCL tool is plugged in, the *Check Engine* light will flash rapidly, which indicates that the computer information is being transferred to the special mini-scanner.

NOTE: When the mini-scanner tool is plugged into the system, it removes the timer that is used to keep the fuel system in the open-loop mode for a certain period of time. Therefore, the system will go into the closed-loop mode as soon as the engine is started, if all other closed-loop conditions are met. (Closed-loop conditions occur when the computer normally receives voltage signals from the exhaust oxygen sensor.)

If the air management system operation is checked with the mini-scanner tool plugged in during such an override condition, then the air management system will not function in its normal capacity because the air is directed to the catalytic converter as soon as the engine is started. It will not be directed to "ports" for a period of time.

It is also helpful to use the ALCL mini-scanner tool when trying to pinpoint an intermittent operating problem. This can be done by placing the mini-scanner inside the vehicle while driving the car, noting under what condition the light comes on, or noting when the engine driveability seems to be poor for a momentary time period.

If the intermittent problem is one that can be checked with the ALCL tool, then the problem can be checked while driving the vehicle. Any changes to the ALCL tool reading indicate an intermittent problem in that circuit.

Method B. The engine should be stopped when the ALCL is accessed and the ignition key is turned on. The following conditions will occur:

1. If the system is operating correctly, a Code 12 will be indicated at the *Check Engine* light. A Code 12 is indicated by one flash of the light, followed by a short pause, then two flashes in quick succession. The Code 12 will be displayed three times. Then any other codes stored in memory will follow. If, however, no other codes are stored in memory, then Code 12 continues to flash until the jumper wire at the ALCL test terminal is disconnected.

CAUTION: Do not start the engine with the ALCL test terminal connected or grounded, because it may continue to flash a Code 12. Also, if the test terminal is grounded after the engine is running, any stored codes will flash, but Code 12 will flash only if there is a problem with the distributor reference signal.

2. In addition, with the test terminal grounded (ignition on) and the engine stopped, if a trouble code is displayed, the memory is cleared. Then the engine must

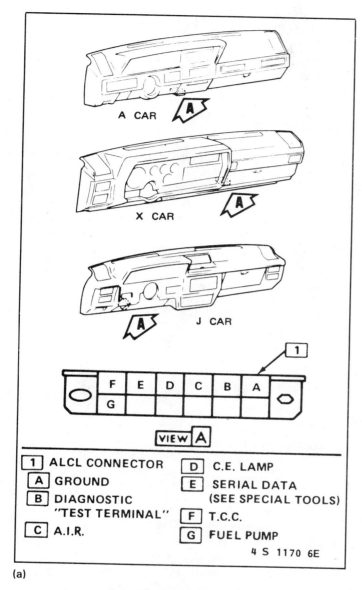

(a)

1	ALCL CONNECTOR	D	C.E. LAMP
A	GROUND	E	SERIAL DATA (SEE SPECIAL TOOLS)
B	DIAGNOSTIC "TEST TERMINAL"	F	T.C.C.
C	A.I.R.	G	FUEL PUMP

4 S 1170 6E

TERMINAL IDENTIFICATION

A	GROUND	F	T.C.C.
B	DIAGNOSTIC TERMINAL	L	} FOR ALDL COVER WITH SERIAL DATA JUMPER
D	"SERVICE ENGINE SOON" LAMP	M	

3/7/86   *GS 0448 BO

(b) **FIGURE 7-7** (a) ALCL (assembly line connecting link) connector — A, X and J vehicles with FBC and TBI engines; (b) ALDL (assembly line diagnostic link) connector — 1986 Toronado SPFI (sequential port fuel injection) engine. (*Courtesy of Oldsmobile Div. of GMC*)

be run to see if the code is a "hard" or "intermittent" failure. Hard failures are located by referring to the manufacturer's vehicle service manual and following a sequence of diagnostic charts to pinpoint the problem. This involves using a digital voltmeter or mini-scanner tool to check the particular terminals of the ECM, as well as the actual sensor and wiring that the flashing *Check Engine* light indicates has as a problem (trouble code) existing in that system/circuit. Intermittent failures, on the other hand, are generally located by the technician physically inspecting the suspected system or systems for loose, taut or corroded connections, damage, etc., or by again using the mini-scanner special tool.

Typical voltage readings obtained from various sensors and contact points of the ECM system for a number of different model vehicles are shown in Figs. 7-10, 7-13, 7-20, and 7-25.

Figures 7-9, 7-12, 7-15, 7-16, 7-18, 7-19, 7-23, and 7-24 illustrate the various wiring diagrams showing the sensor wiring and the tie-in to the ECM terminals for the various FBC, TBI, and MPFI engine/vehicle models.

Figures 7-8, 7-11, 7-14, 7-17, 7-21, and 7-22 will allow you to identify the various locations of the sensors, switches, ECM connections, and ALCL location, both underhood and in the passenger compartment.

3. Energize all ECM controlled relays and solenoids unless otherwise indicated by the vehicle manufacturer in the service manual. If so equipped, also check that the ISC (idle speed control) motor moves back and forward, and that the EGR (exhaust gas recirculation) solenoid is turned on and off.

4. When the ALCL test terminal is grounded with the engine running, the system enters the "field service mode" and the *Check Engine* light indicates whether the system is in open or closed loop.

NOTE In open loop, the ECM ignores voltage signals from the oxygen sensor. In closed loop, the ECM controls the engine air/fuel ratio at stoichiometric (14.7:1), while receiving and acting upon the voltage signals from the exhaust oxygen sensor.

In open loop, the *Check Engine* light flashes 2.5 times per second, while in closed loop, the light will flash once per second. In addition, while in closed loop, the light will stay out most of the time if the system is too lean. It stays on most of the time if the system is too rich.

CAUTION: On engines using an unheated exhaust oxygen sensor and with the engine running at an idle rpm for a short time, the exhaust cools off, and the engine enters an open-loop mode. In order to restore the engine back into the closed-loop mode, run the engine at part throttle and accelerate from idle to part throttle a few times in order to allow the system to go back into closed loop.

TROUBLE CODES

Depending upon the year of manufacture, the engine used, the options on the vehicle, etc., all trouble codes are not the same on every vehicle, although many are common. Figure 7-26 lists the various trouble code numbers used with the FBC (feedback carburetor) equipped vehicles. Cars equipped with either TBI (throttle body injection) or MPFI (multi-port fuel injection) also use these same basic numbers, with the following exceptions:

TBI Engine/Vehicle

- Code 32: Not used
- Code 33: MAP—Low Voltage
- Code 43: Not used

MPFI Engine/Vehicle

- Code 32: EGR system
- Code 33: MAF sensor
- Code 34: MAF sensor
- Code 52: CALPAK
- Code 55: ECM

The trouble codes shown in Fig. 7-26 and above are for vehicles equipped with ECM systems only and do not contain a BCM (body control module). For informational codes related to the BCM system, refer to the subheaded section in this chapter that treats the combination ECM/BCM systems which are used on later-model upscale GMC division cars.

Clearing Trouble Codes

To clear stored trouble codes from the ECM memory effectively, it is necessary to remove battery voltage for a period of 10 seconds. This can be done by disconnecting the ECM harness from the positive battery pigtail for 10 seconds with the ignition key off, or by removing the ECM fuse. Note that once the trouble codes have been cleared from memory, the ECM's learning ability must start all over again. Therefore, once memory has been cleared, you may notice a change in the vehicle's initial performance. To reinitiate the ECM, simply ensure that the engine is at normal operating temperature, and drive the vehicle at part

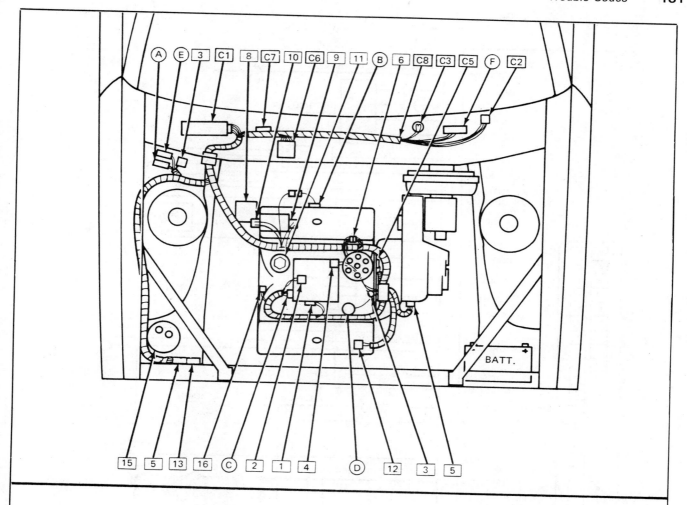

"X" SERIES
2.8L (173 CID) V6   RPO:LE2/LH7   V.I.N. CODE:X/1

COMPUTER SYSTEM

C1	Electronic Control Module (ECM)
C2	ALCL Connector
C3	"CHECK ENGINE" Light
C5	System Ground
C6	Fuse Panel
C7	Lamp Driver
C8	Computer Control Harness

AIR/FUEL SYSTEM

1	Mixture Control
2	Throttle Kicker Vacuum Solenoid
3	EFE Heater Switch
4	Heated Grid EFE
5	Throttle Kicker Relay

TRANSMISSION CONVERTER CLUTCH CONTROL SYSTEM

| 5 | Trans. Conv. Clutch Connector |

IGNITION SYSTEM

| 6 | Electronic Spark Timing Connector |

AIR INJECTION SYSTEM

8	Air Injection Pump
9	Air Control Solenoid Valve
10	Air Switching Solenoid Valve

EXHAUST GAS RECIRCULATION CONTROL SYSTEM

| 11 | Exhaust Gas Recirculation Valve |
| 12 | Exhaust Gas Recirculation Solenoid Valve |

FUEL VAPOR CONTROL SYSTEM

13	Canister Purge Solenoid Valve
15	Vapor Canister
16	Fuel Bowl Vent Solenoid

SENSORS/SWITCHES

A	Differential Pressure Sensor
B	Exhaust Oxygen Sensor
C	Throttle Position Sensor
D	Coolant Sensor
E	Barometric Pressure Sensor
F	Vehicle Speed Sensor

SR 84 6E 0201A

FIGURE 7-8 Component locations — 2.8L X series vehicle. (*Courtesy of Oldsmobile Div. of GMC*)

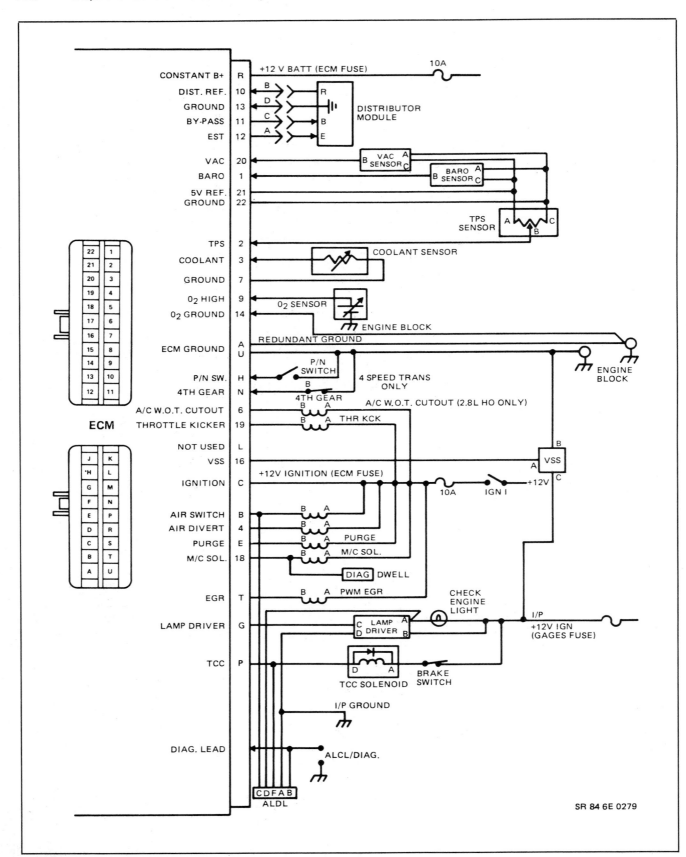

FIGURE 7-9 ECM wiring diagram — 2.8L engine. (*Courtesy of Olds-mobile Div. of GMC*)

ECM TERMINAL VOLTAGE
2.8L A, X

THIS ECM VOLTAGE CHART IS FOR USE WITH A DIGITAL VOLTMETER TO FURTHER AID IN DIAGNOSIS. THESE VOLTAGES WERE DERIVED FROM A KNOWN GOOD CAR. THE VOLTAGES YOU GET MAY VARY DUE TO LOW BATTERY CHARGE OR OTHER REASONS, BUT THEY SHOULD BE VERY CLOSE.

THE FOLLOWING CONDITIONS MUST BE MET BEFORE TESTING:

- ENGINE AT OPERATING TEMPERATURE
- CLOSED LOOP
- ENGINE IDLING (FOR "ENGINE RUN" COLUMN)
- TEST TERMINAL NOT GROUNDED
- SCANNER NOT INSTALLED

Voltage Key "ON"	Voltage Engine Run	Voltage Circuit Open		#	#		Voltage Key "ON"	Voltage Engine Run	Voltage Circuit Open
0	0	0	SENSOR RETURN	22	1	BARO SENSOR SIGNAL DECREASES WITH ALTITUDE	4.75	4.75	*.5
5	5	5	5V REFERENCE	21	2	TPS SENSOR SIGNAL	*1.0 †5.0	*1.0	5.0
.5-.65	2–3	*.5	VACUUM SENSOR OUTPUT	20	3	COOLANT TEMP. SENSOR SIGNAL	*2.5	*2.5	5.0
12	14	*.5	THROTTLE KICKER (IDLE SPEED SOLENOID)	19	4	AIR CONTROL SOLENOID	12	*1.0	*.5
12	5–10 (var.)	*.5	M/C SOLENOID	18	5	DIAGNOSTIC TEST TERM	5	5	5
			NOT USED	17	6	A/C W.O.T. CUTOUT IF USED	12	14	*.5
**10	**11	10	VSS SIGNAL	16	7	COOLANT TEMP. SENSOR RETURN	0	0	0
			NOT USED	15	8	NOT USED			
*.5	*.5	1.7	OXYGEN SENSOR – LO	14	9	OXYGEN SENSOR – HI	.3-.45	.1–.9 (var.)	.3-.45
*.5	*.5	*1.0	DIST. REF. PULSE – LO	13	10	DIST. REF. PULSE – HI	*.5	1–2 (var.)	*.5
*.5	1–2 (var.)	*.5	EST	12	11	IGN. MODULE BY-PASS	*.5	3.7	*.5

			NOT USED	J	K	NOT USED			
*.5 P/N 12 D/R	*.5 P/N 14 D/R	12	PARK/NEUTRAL SWITCH	H	L	NOT USED			
10	*.5	*.5	"CHECK ENGINE" LAMP	G	M	NOT USED			
			NOT USED	F	N	4TH GEAR SWITCH IF USED	*.5	*.5	12
12	*.5	*.5	PURGE	E	P	TRANS CONVERTER CLUTCH SOLENOID	12	14	*.5
			NOT USED	D	R	TROUBLE CODE MEMORY POWER	12	14	*.5
12	14	*.5	IGN. 1 POWER	C	S	NOT USED			
12	14	*.5	AIR SWITCHING SOLENOID	B	T	EGR	12	*1	*.5
0	0	0	GROUND (TO ENGINE)	A	U	GROUND (TO ENGINE)	0	0	0

* = Value Shown or Less Than that Value
† = Wide Open Throttle
(var.) = variable
P/N = Park or Neutral
D/R = Drive or Reverse
** = If less than 1V Rotate Drive Wheel to Verify.

SR 84 6E 0457

FIGURE 7-10 ECM Connector terminal end view — 2.8L engine. *(Courtesy of Oldsmobile Div. of GMC)*

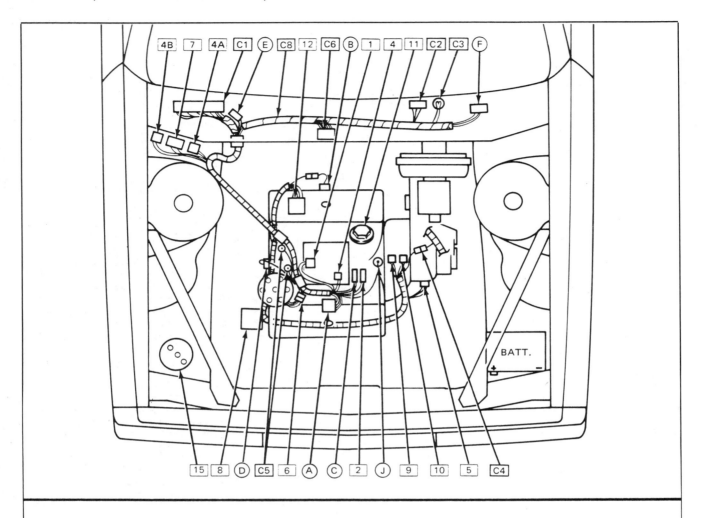

"A" SERIES
3.0L (186 CID) V6   RPO: LK9   V.I.N. CODE: E

COMPUTER SYSTEM

C1	Electronic Control Module (ECM)
C2	ALCL Connector
C3	"CHECK ENGINE" Light
C4	System Power
C5	System Ground
C6	Fuse Panel
C8	Computer Control Harness

AIR/FUEL SYSTEM

1	Mixture Control
2	Idle Speed Control
4	Heated Grid EFE
4A	EFE Relay
4B	A/C Compressor Relay

TRANSMISSION CONVERTER CLUTCH CONTROL SYSTEM

5	Trans. Conv. Clutch Connector

IGNITION SYSTEM

6	Electronic Spark Timing Connector
7	Electronic Spark Control (ESC)

AIR INJECTION SYSTEM

8	Air Injection Pump
9	Air Control Solenoid Valve
10	Air Switching Solenoid Valve

EXHAUST GAS RECIRCULATION CONTROL SYSTEM

11	Exhaust Gas Recirculation Valve
12	Exhaust Gas Recirculation Solenoid Valve

FUEL VAPOR CONTROL SYSTEM

15	Vapor Canister

SENSORS/SWITCHES

A	Manifold Pressure Sensor
B	Exhaust Oxygen Sensor
C	Throttle Position Sensor
D	Coolant Sensor
E	Barometric Pressure Sensor
F	Vehicle Speed Sensor
J	ESC Sensor (Knock)

SR 84 6E 0225

FIGURE 7-11 Component locations — 3.0L A series vehicle. (*Courtesy of Oldsmobile Div. of GMC*)

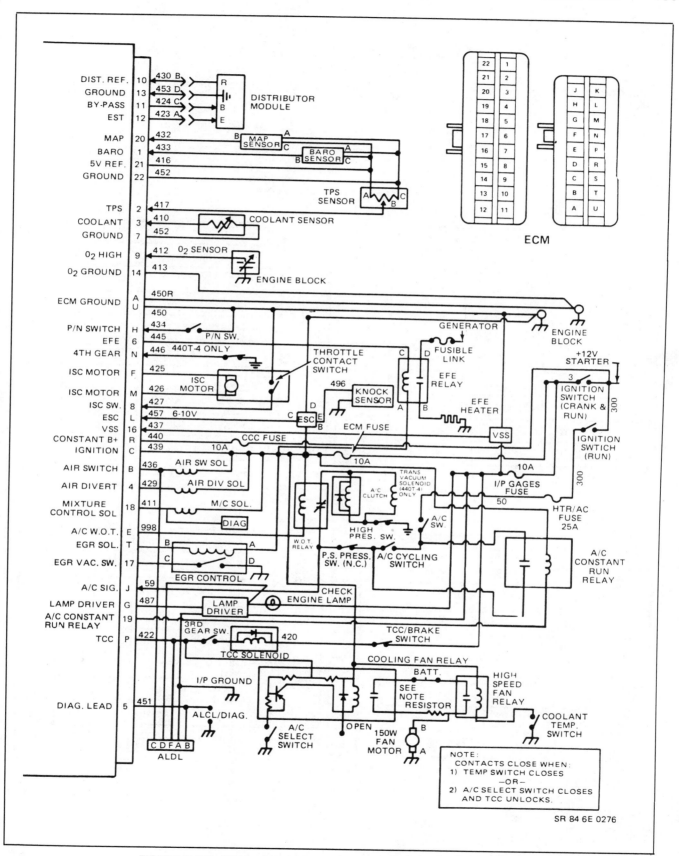

FIGURE 7-12 ECM wiring diagram — 3.0L A series vehicles. (*Courtesy of Oldsmobile Div. of GMC*)

ECM TERMINAL VOLTAGE
3.0L, A SERIES

THIS ECM VOLTAGE CHART IS FOR USE WITH A DIGITAL VOLTMETER TO FURTHER AID IN DIAGNOSIS. THESE VOLTAGES WERE DERIVED FROM A KNOWN GOOD CAR. THE VOLTAGES YOU GET MAY VARY DUE TO LOW BATTERY CHARGE OR OTHER REASONS, BUT THEY SHOULD BE VERY CLOSE.

THE FOLLOWING CONDITIONS MUST BE MET BEFORE TESTING:

- ENGINE AT OPERATING TEMPERATURE ●
- CLOSED LOOP ●
- ENGINE IDLING (FOR "ENGINE RUN" COLUMN) ●
- TEST TERMINAL NOT GROUNDED ●
- SCANNER NOT INSTALLED ●

Voltage Key "ON"	Voltage Engine Run	Voltage Circuit Open	Description	Terminal
0	0	0	SENSOR RETURN	22
5	5	5	5V REFERENCE	21
4.75	1.5	*.5	MAP SENSOR OUTPUT VARIES WITH ALTITUDE	20
12	14	*.5	A/C CONSTANT RUN RELAY	19
12	5–10 (var.)	*.5	M/C SOLENOID	18
12	14	12	EGR VACUUM SWITCH	17
**10	**11	10	VSS SIGNAL	16
			NOT USED	15
*.5	*.5	1.7	OXYGEN SENSOR – LO	14
*.5	*.5	*1.0	DIST. REF. PULSE – LO	13
*.5	1–2 (var.)	*.5	EST	12

Terminal	Description	Voltage Key "ON"	Voltage Engine Run	Voltage Circuit Open
1	BARO SENSOR SIGNAL DECREASES WITH ALTITUDE	4.75	4.75	*.5
2	TPS SENSOR SIGNAL	*1.0 †4+	*1.0	5.0
3	COOLANT TEMP. SENSOR SIGNAL	*2.5	*2.5	5.0
4	AIR CONTROL (DIVERT) SOLENOID	12.5	*1.0	*.5
5	DIAGNOSTIC TEST TERM	5	5	5
6	EFE RELAY	12	14 HOT *1 COLD	*.5
7	COOLANT TEMP. SENSOR RETURN	0	0	0
8	ISC SWITCH SIGNAL O.T. C.T.	12 *.5	14 *.5	12
9	OXYGEN SENSOR – HI	.3–.45	.1–.9 (var.)	.3–.45
10	DIST. REF. PULSE – HI	*.5	1–2 (var.)	*.5
11	IGN. MODULE BY-PASS	*.5	3.7	*.5

Voltage Key "ON"	Voltage Engine Run	Voltage Circuit Open	Description	Terminal
*.5 OFF 12 ON	*.5 OFF 14 ON	*.5	A/C "ON" SIGNAL	J
*.5 P/N 12 D/R	*.5 P/N 14 D/R	12	PARK/NEUTRAL SWITCH	H
10	*.5	*.5	"CHECK ENGINE" LAMP	G
			ISC (EXTEND)	F
12	14	*.5	A/C W.O.T. CUTOUT	E
			NOT USED	D
12	14	*.5	IGN. 1 POWER	C
12	14	*.5	AIR SWITCHING SOLENOID	B
0	0	0	GROUND (TO ENGINE)	A

Terminal	Description	Voltage Key "ON"	Voltage Engine Run	Voltage Circuit Open
K	NOT USED			
L	ESC SIGNAL	7–10	7–10	*.5
M	ISC (RETRACT)			
N	4TH GEAR SWITCH IF USED	*.5	*.5	12
P	TRANS CONVERTER CLUTCH SOLENOID	6–7	14	*.5
R	TROUBLE CODE MEMORY POWER	12	14	*.5
S	NOT USED			
T	EGR SOLENOID	12	14	12
U	GROUND (TO ENGINE)	0	0	0

* = Value Shown or Less Than that Value
† = Wide Open Throttle
C.T. = Closed Throttle
O.T. = Open Throttle
(var.) = Variable
P/N = Park or Neutral
D/R = Drive or Reverse
** = If less than 1V Rotate Drive Wheel to Verify.

4S 0454-6E A

FIGURE 7-13 ECM connector terminal end-view — 3.0L A series vehicles. (*Courtesy of Oldsmobile Div. of GMC*)

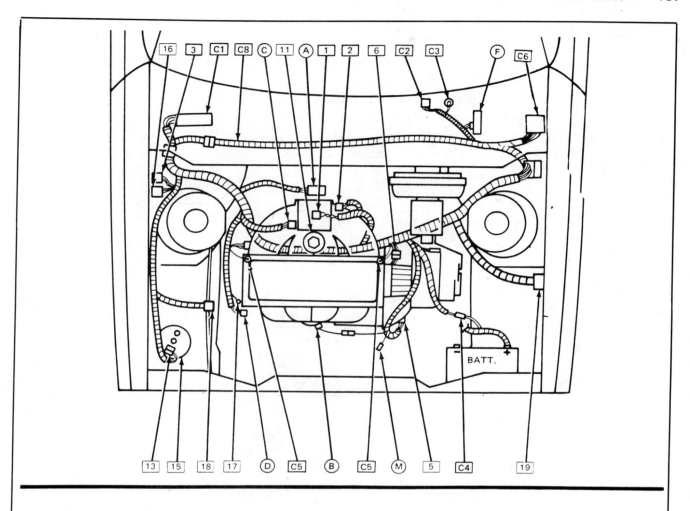

"J" SERIES
1.8L (111 CID) L4 RPO: LH8 V.I.N. CODE: 0

COMPUTER SYSTEM		IGNITION SYSTEM		SENSORS/SWITCHES	
C1	Electronic Control Module (ECM)	6	Electronic Spark Timing Connector	A	Manifold Pressure Sensor
C2	ALCL Connector			B	Exhaust Oxygen Sensor
C3	"CHECK ENGINE" Light	**EXHAUST GAS RECIRCULATION CONTROL SYSTEM**		C	Throttle Position Sensor
C4	System Power	11	Exhaust Gas Recirculation Valve	D	Coolant Sensor
C5	System Ground			F	Vehicle Speed Sensor
C6	Fuse Panel	**FUEL VAPOR CONTROL SYSTEM**			
C8	Computer Control Harness	13	Canister Purge Solenoid Valve	M	Fuel Pump Test Connector
		15	Vapor Canister		
AIR/FUEL SYSTEM					
1	Throttle Body Injection	**FAN AND A/C SYSTEM**			
2	Idle Air Control	16	A/C Compressor Control Relay		
3	Fuel Pump Relay	17	Coolant Fan Switch		
		18	A/C Fan Pressure Switch		
TRANSMISSION CONVERTER CLUTCH CONTROL SYSTEM		19	Coolant Fan Relay		
5	Trans. Conv. Clutch Connector				

SR 84 6E 0246

FIGURE 7-14 Component locations — 1.8L engine. (*Courtesy of Oldsmobile Div. of GMC*)

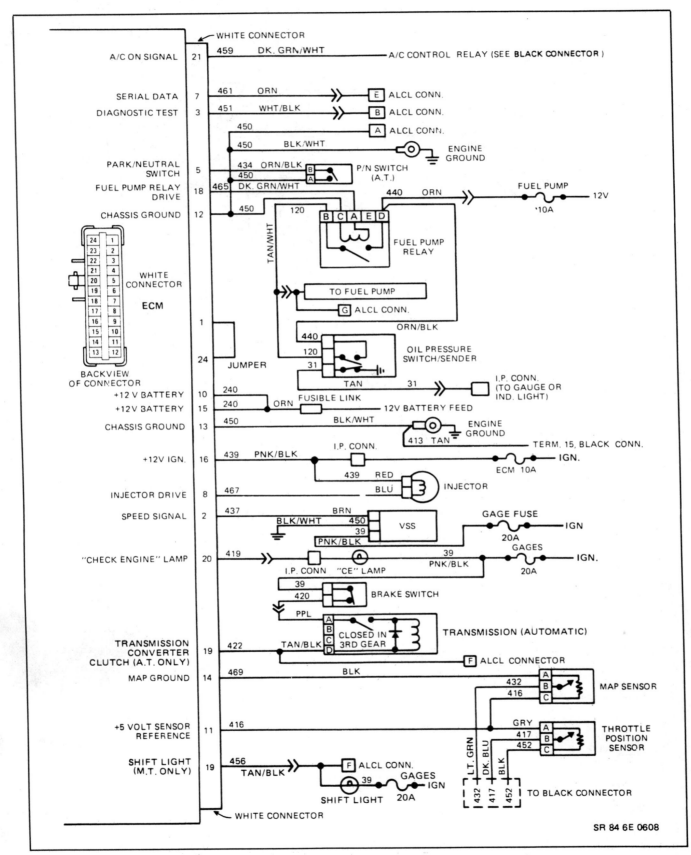

FIGURE 7-15 ECM wiring diagram — 1.8L-white connector. (*Courtesy of Oldsmobile Div. of GMC*)

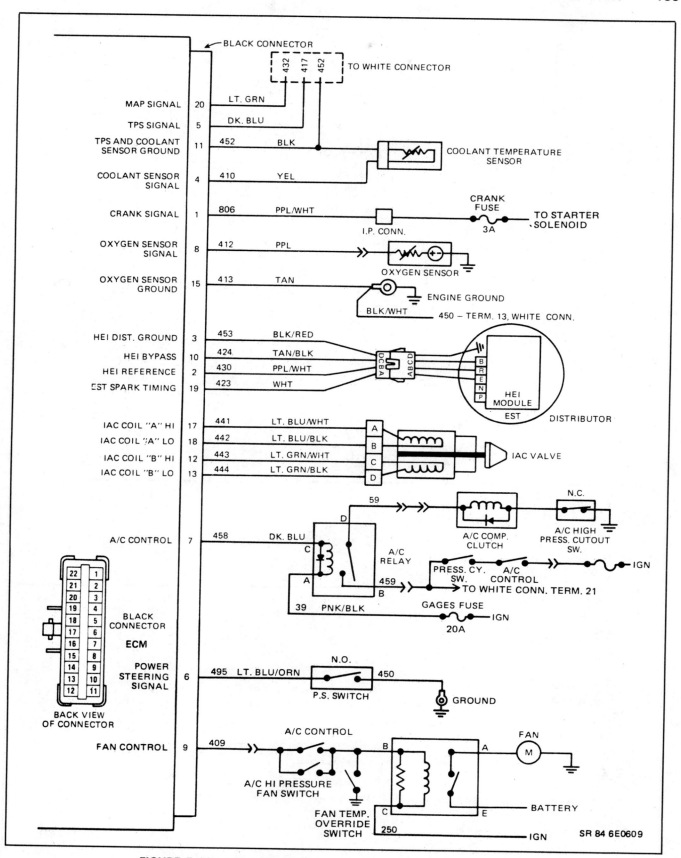

FIGURE 7-16 ECM wiring diagram — 1.8L-black connector. (*Courtesy of Oldsmobile Div. of GMC*)

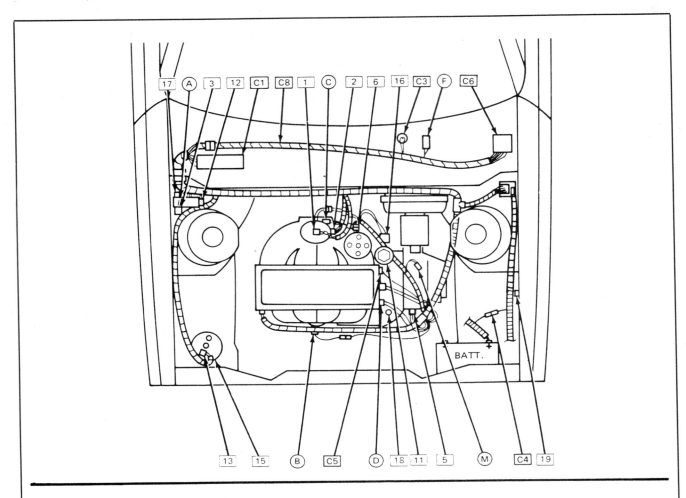

"J" SERIES
2.0L (121 CID) L4   RPO: LQ5   V.I.N. CODE: P

COMPUTER SYSTEM

C1	Electronic Control Module (ECM)
C2	ALCL Connector
C3	"CHECK ENGINE" Light
C4	System Power
C5	System Ground
C6	Fuse Panel
C8	Computer Control Harness

AIR/FUEL SYSTEM

1	Throttle Body Injection
2	Idle Air Control
3	Fuel Pump Relay

TRANSMISSION CONVERTER CLUTCH CONTROL SYSTEM

5	Trans. Conv. Clutch Connector

IGNITION SYSTEM

6	Electronic Spark Timing Connector

EXHAUST GAS RECIRCULATION CONTROL SYSTEM

11	Exhaust Gas Recirculation Valve
12	Exhaust Gas Recirculation Solenoid Valve

FUEL VAPOR CONTROL SYSTEM

13	Canister Purge Solenoid Valve
15	Vapor Canister

AIR INJECTION CONTROL SYSTEM

16	Pulse Air Control

FAN AND A/C SYSTEM

17	A/C COMPRESSOR CONTROL RELAY
18	COOLANT FAN SWITCH
19	COOLING FAN RELAY

SENSORS/SWITCHES

A	Manifold Pressure Sensor
B	Exhaust Oxygen Sensor
C	Throttle Position Sensor
D	Coolant Sensor
F	Vehicle Speed Sensor
M	Fuel Pump Test Connector

SR 84 6E 0243

FIGURE 7-17 Component locations — 2.0L engine. (*Courtesy of Oldsmobile Div. of GMC*)

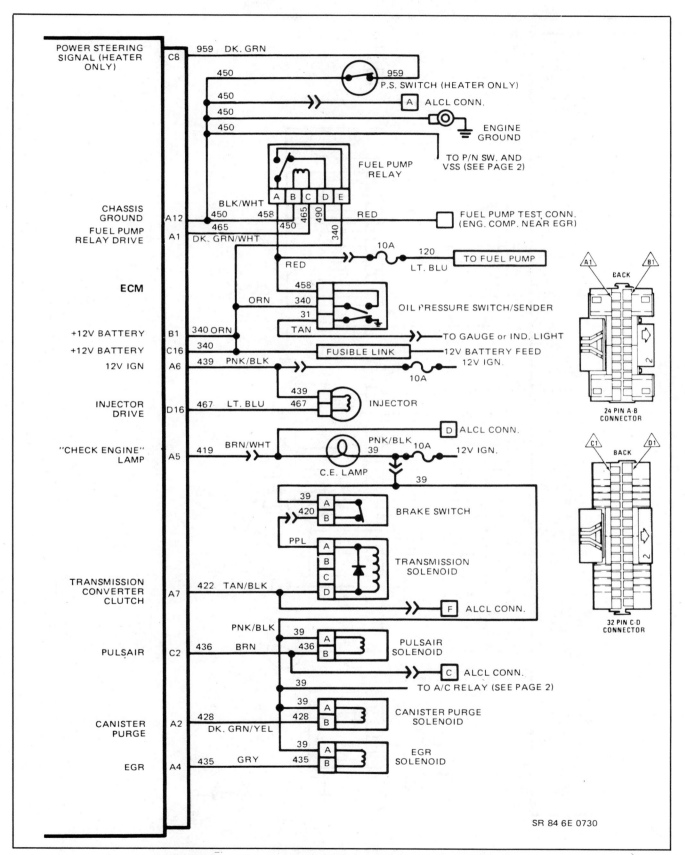

FIGURE 7-18 ECM wiring diagram number 1 — 2.0L engine. (*Courtesy of Oldsmobile Div. of GMC*)

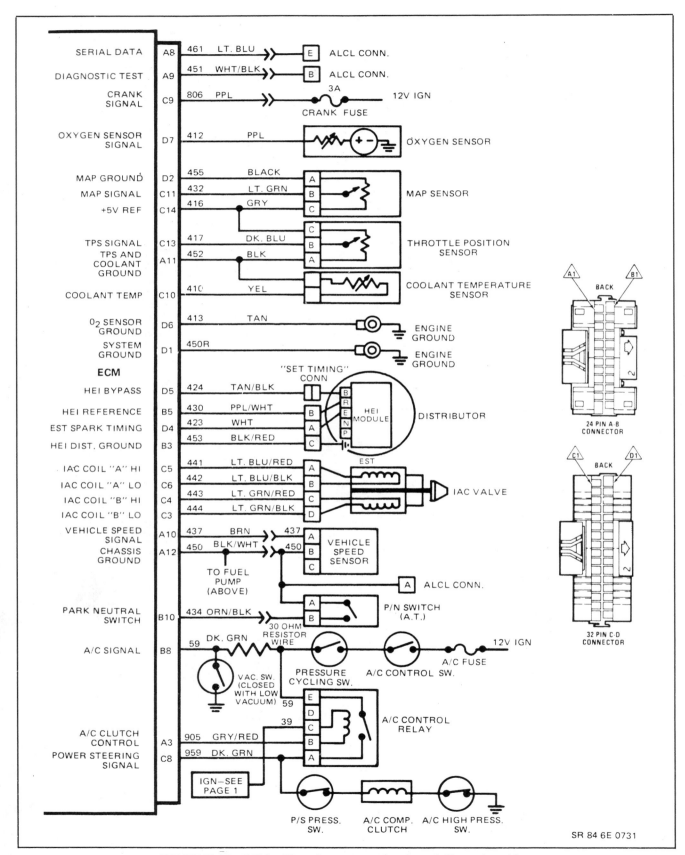

FIGURE 7-19 ECM wiring diagram number 2 — 2.0L engine. (*Courtesy of Oldsmobile Div. of GMC*)

FUEL INJECTION ECM CONNECTOR IDENTIFICATION

THIS ECM VOLTAGE CHART IS FOR USE WITH A DIGITAL VOLTMETER TO FURTHER AID IN DIAGNOSIS. THE VOLTAGES YOU GET MAY VARY DUE TO LOW BATTERY CHARGE OR OTHER REASONS, BUT THEY SHOULD BE VERY CLOSE. <u>THE FOLLOWING CONDITIONS MUST BE MET BEFORE TESTING:</u>
● ENGINE AT OPERATING TEMPERATURE ● ENGINE IDLING IN CLOSED LOOP (FOR "ENGINE RUN" COLUMN) ●
● TEST TERMINAL NOT GROUNDED ● ALCL TOOL NOT INSTALLED ●

VOLTAGE

	KEY "ON"	ENG. RUN (1)	OPEN CRT.	CIRCUIT	PIN
(2)	0	13.45		FUEL PUMP RELAY	A1
	0	0		CANISTER PURGE	A2
(4)	12.1	13.8		A/C RELAY	A3
	0	0		EGR	A4
	0	13.7		"CHECK ENGINE LAMP"	A5
	12.3	13.7		12V IGN	A6
	0	0		TCC	A7
	(6)	(6)		SERIAL DATA	A8
	5.0	5.0		DIAGNOSTICS	A9
(5)	0 or 12.3	0 or 13.7		VSS	A10
	0	0		COOLANT AND TPS GROUND	A11
	0	0		SYSTEM GROUND	A12

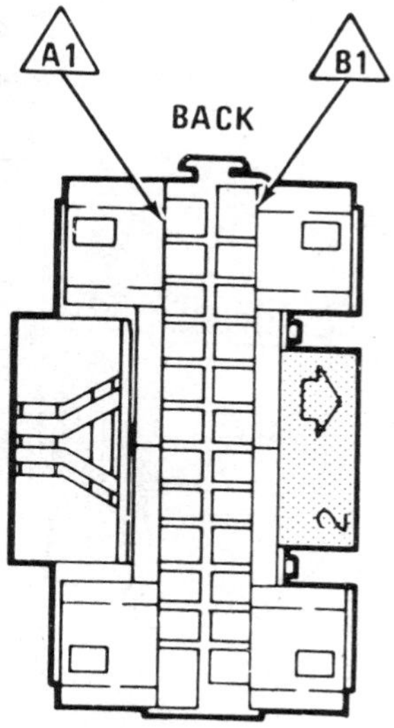

24 PIN A-B CONNECTOR
BACK

VOLTAGE

PIN	CIRCUIT	KEY "ON"	ENG. RUN (1)	OPEN CRT.	
B1	BATTERY	12.4	13.6		
B2					
B3	HEI GROUND	0	0		
B4					
B5	HEI REFERENCE	0	.6		
B6					
B7					
B8	A/C SIGNAL	0	0		(4)
B9					
B10	P/N SWITCH	0	0		(3)
B11					
B12					

	KEY "ON"	ENG. RUN	OPEN CRT.	CIRCUIT	PIN
					C1
	0	0		PULSAIR	C2
	(6)	(6)		IAC "B" LO	C3
	(6)	(6)		IAC "B" HI	C4
	(6)	(6)		IAC "A" HI	C5
	(6)	(6)		IAC "A" LO	C6
					C7
(4)	0	0		POWER STEERING SIGNAL	C8
	0	0		CRANK	C9
	.7	.8		COOLANT	C10
	4.91	1.19		MAP	C11
					C12
	.6	.6		TPS	C13
	5.0	5.0		5 VOLT REFERENCE	C14
					C15
	12.4	13.6		BATTERY	C16

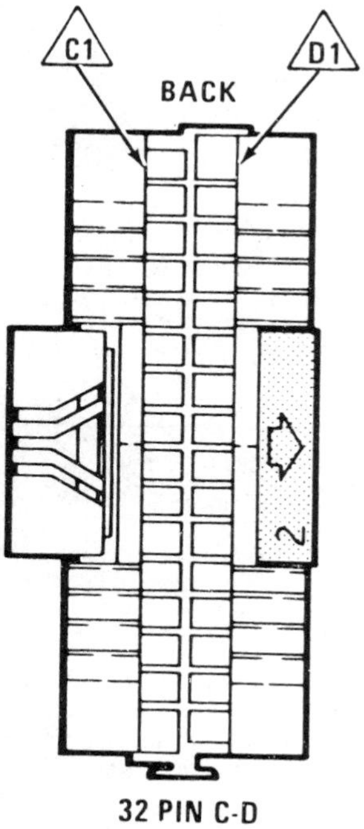

32 PIN C-D CONNECTOR
BACK

PIN	CIRCUIT	KEY "ON"	ENG. RUN	OPEN CRT.
D1	SYSTEM GROUND	0	0	
D2	MAP GROUND	0	0	
D3				
D4	EST	0	.9	
D5	BYPASS	0	4.5	
D6	OXYGEN SENSOR GROUND	0	0	
D7	OXYGEN SENSOR SIGNAL	0	varies	
D8				
D9				
D10				
D11				
D12				
D13				
D14				
D15				
D16	INJECTOR DRIVE	12.4	13.6	

(1) ENGINE RUNNING IN PARK, AT IDLE, NORMAL OPERATING TEMPERATURE, IN CLOSED LOOP.
(2) ALL VOLTAGES SHOWN AS "0" SHOULD READ LESS THAN 1.0 VOLT WITH DIGITAL VOLT-OHM METER SUCH AS J-29125.
(3) READS BATTERY VOLTAGE IN GEAR.   (4) A/C OFF   (5) VARIES FROM 0 TO 12 VOLTS DEPENDING ON POSITION OF DRIVE WHEELS
(6) NOT USEABLE.

ENGINE ___2.0L___

CARLINE ___J___

SR 84 6E 0727

FIGURE 7-20 ECM Connector terminal end-view — 2.0L engine.
(Courtesy of Oldsmobile Div. of GMC)

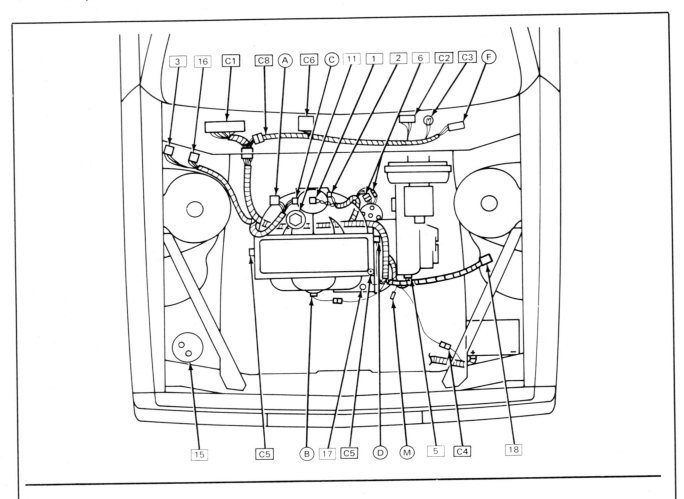

"A" SERIES
2.5L(151 CID)L4   RPO: LR8   V.I.N. CODE: R

COMPUTER SYSTEM

C1 Electronic Control Module (ECM)
C2 ALCL Connector
C3 "CHECK ENGINE" Light
C4 System Power
C5 System Ground
C6 Fuse Panel
C8 Computer Control Harness

AIR/FUEL SYSTEM

1 Throttle Body Injection
2 Idle Air Control
3 Fuel Pump Relay

TRANSMISSION CONVERTER CLUTCH CONTROL SYSTEM

5 Trans. Conv. Clutch Connector

IGNITION SYSTEM

6 Electronic Spark Timing Connectors

EXHAUST GAS RECIRCULATION CONTROL SYSTEM

11 Exhaust Gas Recirculation Valve

FUEL VAPOR CONTROL SYSTEM

15 Vapor Canister

FAN AND A/C SYSTEM

16 A/C Control Relay
17 Coolant Fan Switch
18 Cooling Fan Relay

SENSORS/SWITCHES

A Manifold Pressure Sensor
B Exhaust Oxygen Sensor
C Throttle Position Sensor
D Coolant Sensor
F Vehicle Speed Sensor
M Fuel Pump Test Connector

SR 84 6E 0249

FIGURE 7-21 Component locations — 2.5L A series vehicles. (*Courtesy of Oldsmobile Div. of GMC*)

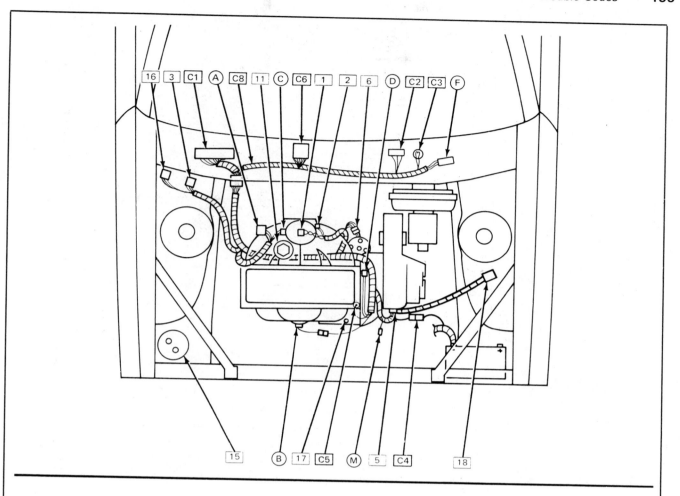

"X" SERIES
2.5L(151 CID)L4   RPO: LR8   V.I.N. CODE: R

COMPUTER SYSTEM

C1	Electronic Control Module (ECM)
C2	ALCL Connector
C3	"CHECK ENGINE" Light
C4	System Power
C5	System Ground
C6	Fuse Panel
C8	Computer Control Harness

AIR/FUEL SYSTEM

1	Throttle Body Injection
2	Idle Air Control
3	Fuel Pump Relay

TRANSMISSION CONVERTER CLUTCH CONTROL SYSTEM

| 5 | Trans. Conv. Clutch Connector |

IGNITION SYSTEM

| 6 | Electronic Spark Timing Connector |

EXHAUST GAS RECIRCULATION CONTROL SYSTEM

| 11 | Exhaust Gas Recirculation Valve |

FUEL VAPOR CONTROL SYSTEM

| 15 | Vapor Canister |

FAN AND A/C SYSTEM

16	A/C Compressor Control Relay
17	Coolant Fan Switch
18	Fan Control Relay

SENSORS/SWITCHES

A	Manifold Pressure Sensor
B	Exhaust Oxygen Sensor
C	Throttle Position Sensor
D	Coolant Sensor
F	Vehicle Speed Sensor
M	Fuel Pump Test Connector

SR 84 6E 0252

FIGURE 7-22 Component locations — 2.5L X series vehicles. (*Courtesy of Oldsmobile Div. of GMC*)

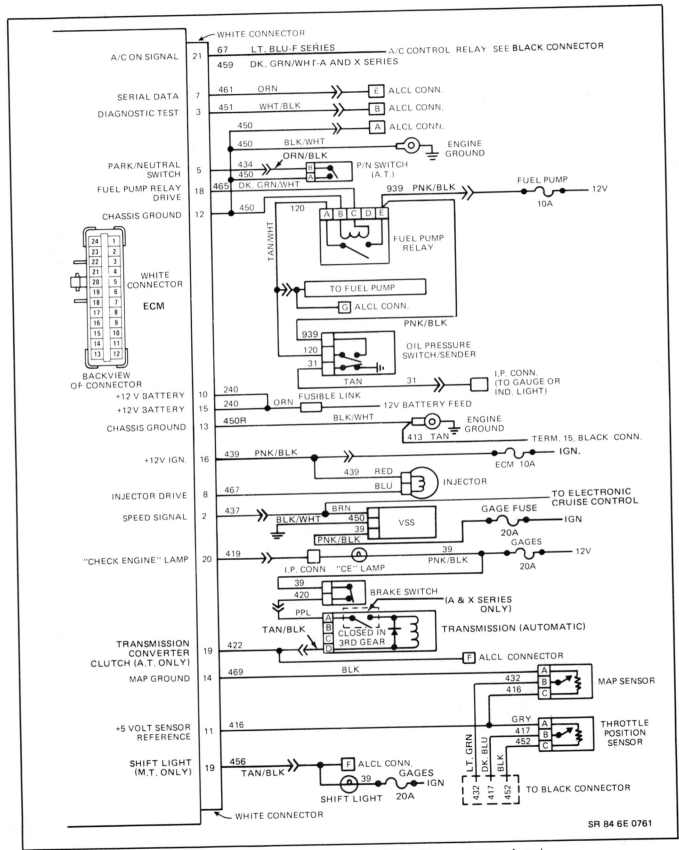

FIGURE 7-23 ECM wiring diagram — 2.5L-white connector, A and X vehicles. (*Courtesy of Oldsmobile Div. of GMC*)

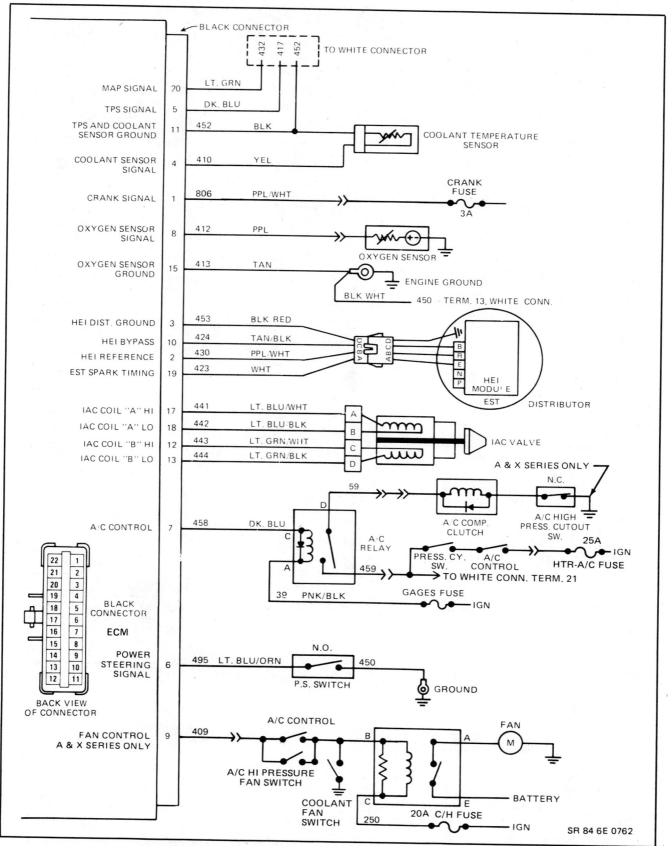

FIGURE 7-24 ECM wiring diagram — 2.5L-black connector, A and X vehicles. (Courtesy of Oldsmobile Div. of GMC)

FUEL INJECTION ECM CONNECTOR IDENTIFICATION

THIS ECM VOLTAGE CHART IS FOR USE WITH A DIGITAL VOLTMETER TO FURTHER AID IN DIAGNOSIS. THE VOLTAGES YOU GET MAY VARY DUE TO LOW BATTERY CHARGE OR OTHER REASONS, BUT THEY SHOULD BE VERY CLOSE.

THE FOLLOWING CONDITIONS MUST BE MET BEFORE TESTING:
- ENGINE AT OPERATING TEMPERATURE ● ENGINE IDLING IN CLOSED LOOP (FOR "ENGINE RUN" COLUMN) ●
- ● TEST TERMINAL NOT GROUNDED ● ALCL TOOL NOT INSTALLED ●

WHITE CONNECTOR

VOLTAGE KEY "ON" ①	VOLTAGE ENGINE RUN ②	WIRE COLOR						VOLTAGE KEY "ON"	VOLTAGE ENGINE RUN	WIRE COLOR	
5.1	5.5		SPARE	24	1	SPARE		4.8	4.9	`	
			NOT USED	23	2	VEHICLE SPEED SENSOR		11.6	13.4	BRN	⑤
11.3	13.2		NOT USED	22	3	DIAGNOSTIC TEST ALCL		5.2	5.3	WHT/BLK	
④ 0	0	DK. GRN	A/C CLUTCH	21	4	NOT USED					
0	14.1	BRN/WHT	CHECK ENGINE LIGHT	20	5	PARK/NEUTRAL SWITCH		0	0	ORN/BLK	③
0	0	TAN/BLK	TCC OR SHIFT LIGHT	19	6	NOT USED					
0	14.0	DK. GRN/WHT	FUEL PUMP RELAY DRIVE	18	7	SERIAL DATA		5.0 — VARIES —	4.6	ORN	
			NOT USED	17	8	INJECTOR		12.3	14.2	BLU	
12.3	14.3	PNK/BLK	SWITCHED IGNITION	16	9	NOT USED					
12.3	14.3	ORN	BATTERY	15	10	BATTERY		12.3	14.3	ORN	
0	0	BLK/ORN	MAP GROUND	14	11	5 VOLT REFERENCE		5.3	5.3	GRY	
0	0	BLK/WHT	ECM GROUND	13	12	ECM GROUND		0	0	BLK/WHT	

BACK VIEW OF CONNECTORS

BLACK CONNECTOR

VOLTAGE KEY "ON"	VOLTAGE ENGINE RUN	WIRE COLOR						VOLTAGE KEY "ON"	VOLTAGE ENGINE RUN	WIRE COLOR	
0	0		NOT USED	22	1	CRANK SIGNAL		0	0	PPL/WHT	
5.2	5.3		NOT USED	21	2	HEI REFERENCE		0		PPL/WHT	
5.1	1.5	LT. GRN	MANIFOLD ABSOLUTE PRESSURE SIGNAL	20	3	HEI DIST. GROUND		0	0	BLK/RED	
0	1.8	WHT	EST SIGNAL	19	4	COOLANT SENSOR SIGNAL		1.3	.6	YEL	
⑥	⑥	LT. BLU BLK	I.A.C. COIL "A" LO	18	5	T.P.S. SIGNAL		.81	.81	DK. BLU	
⑥	⑥	LT. BLU WHT	I.A.C. COIL "A" HI	17	6	POWER STEERING SIGNAL		12.3	12.3	LT. BLU/ORN	
			NOT USED	16	7	AC CLUTCH RELAY		12.3	14.3	DK. BLU	④
0	0	TAN	OXYGEN SENSOR GROUND	15	8	OXYGEN SENSOR SIGNAL		.3	VARIES .3 to .7	PPL	
			NOT USED	14	9	COOLING FAN		0	0	LT. BLU/BLK	④
⑥	⑥	LT. GRN BLK	I.A.C. COIL "B" LO	13	10	EST BYPASS		0	4.2	TAN/BLK	
⑥	⑥	LT. GRN WHT	I.A.C. COIL "B" HI	12	11	COOLANT & TPS GROUND		0	0	BLK	

DIAGNOSTIC TEST TERMINAL

T.C.C.   GROUND

F	E	D	C	B	A
G	H	J	K	L	M

J AND P SERIES   ALCL CONNECTOR

ENGINE ____1.8L AND 2.5L____

CARLINE ____ALL____

① ENGINE RUNNING IN PARK, AT IDLE, NORMAL OPERATING TEMPERATURE, IN CLOSED LOOP.
② ALL VOLTAGES SHOWN AS "0" SHOULD READ LESS THAN 1.0 VOLT WITH A DIGITAL VOLT-OHM METER SUCH AS J-29125.
③ READS BATTERY VOLTAGE IN GEAR.   ④ A.C. OFF   ⑤ VARIES FROM 0 to 12 VOLTS DEPENDING ON POSITION OF DRIVE WHEELS
⑥ NOT USEABLE.

SR 84 6E 0344

FIGURE 7-25 ECM connector terminal end-view — 1.8L and 2.5L engines (*Courtesy of Oldsmobile Div. of GMC*)

TROUBLE CODE IDENTIFICATION

The "CHECK ENGINE" light will only be "ON" if the malfunction exists under the conditions listed below. It takes up to five seconds minimum for the light to come on when a problem occurs. If the malfunction clears, the light will go out and a trouble code will be set in the ECM. Code 12 does not store in memory. If the light comes "on" intermittently, but no code is stored, go to the "Driver Comments" section. Any codes stored will be erased if no problem reoccurs within 50 engine starts. A specific engine may not use all available codes.

The trouble codes indicate problems as follows:

TROUBLE CODE 12   No distributor reference pulses to the ECM. This code is not stored in memory and will only flash while the fault is present. Normal code with ignition "on," engine not running.

TROUBLE CODE 13   Oxygen Sensor Circuit — The engine must run up to four minutes at part throttle, under road load, before this code will set.

TROUBLE CODE 14   Shorted coolant sensor circuit — The engine must run two minutes before this code will set.

TROUBLE CODE 15   Open coolant sensor circuit — The engine must run five minutes before this code will set.

TROUBLE CODE 21   Throttle Position Sensor (TPS) circuit voltage high (open circuit or misadjusted TPS). The engine must run 10 seconds, at specified curb idle speed, before this code will set.

TROUBLE CODE 22   Throttle Position Sensor (TPS) circuit voltage low (grounded circuit or misadjusted TPS). Engine must run 20 seconds at specified curb idle speed, to set code.

TROUBLE CODE 23   M/C solenoid circuit open or grounded.

TROUBLE CODE 24   Vehicle speed sensor (VSS) circuit — The vehicle must operate up to two minutes, at road speed, before this code will set.

TROUBLE CODE 32   Barometric pressure sensor (BARO) circuit low.

TROUBLE CODE 34   Vacuum sensor or Manifold Absolute Pressure (MAP) circuit — The engine must run up to two minutes, at specified curb idle, before this code will set.

TROUBLE CODE 35   Idle speed control (ISC) switch circuit shorted. (Up to 70 % TPS for over 5 seconds.)

TROUBLE CODE 41   No distributor reference pulses to the ECM at specified engine vacuum. This code will store in memory.

TROUBLE CODE 42   Electronic spark timing (EST) bypass circuit or EST circuit grounded or open.

TROUBLE CODE 43   Electronic Spark Control (ESC) retard signal for too long a time; causes retard in EST signal.

TROUBLE CODE 44   Lean exhaust indication — The engine must run two minutes, in closed loop and at part throttle, before this code will set.

TROUBLE CODE 45   Rich exhaust indication — The engine must run two minutes, in closed loop and at part throttle, before this code will set.

TROUBLE CODE 51   Faulty or improperly installed calibration unit (PROM). It takes up to 30 seconds before this code will set.

TROUBLE CODE 53   Exhaust Gas Recirculation (EGR) valve vacuum sensor has seen improper EGR vacuum.

TROUBLE CODE 54   Shorted M/C solenoid circuit and/or faulty ECM.

09-02-83Z
SR 84 6E 0340

FIGURE 7-26 Trouble code identification numbers. (*Courtesy of Oldsmobile Div. of GMC*)

throttle with moderate acceleration and idle speed conditions.

CAUTION: Always ensure that the ignition key is in the off position when either connecting or disconnecting battery power to the ECM, whether or not these procedures involve the battery cable, jumper cables, ECM fuse, or ECM pigtail.

IMPORTANT SERVICING PRECAUTION: Prior to performing any type of service on electronic systems or IC's (integrated circuits), you MUST discharge yourself of static electricity or ESD (electrostatic discharge) by touching a good vehicle ground, such as the door post or vehicle shift lever. Failure to do so can result in damage to voltage sensitive electronic components. If, for any reason, you leave the vehicle during servicing, after re-entering to continue work, you MUST again ground yourself of ESD in order to drain any static electrical charge. Also, if you are performing control head/radio type checks on a new vehicle, remove the plastic seat covers, since they increase the possibility of creating a static charge.

COMPUTER PRECAUTIONS: Care must be exercised at all times when working around computers, since damage frequently attributable to poor work habits can cause serious and expensive harm to these components.

The computer system is designed to withstand normal current draws such as those that normally occur during vehicle operation. Overloading a circuit can result in damage.

When you are testing for opens or shorts in a circuit, NEVER ground or apply voltage to any of the circuits, unless the service manual or diagnostic procedure specifically calls for such action.

When testing computer circuits, voltage readings are normally very small; therefore, these circuits should only be tested using a high impedance multimeter, such as the Kent-Moore Tool P/N J-29125A or equivalent, if they remain connected to either one of the on-board computers.

CAUTION: Before removing/connecting battery cables, fuses, or harness wire connectors, ALWAYS turn the ignition key to the "Lock" position. Power should never be applied or removed to any one of the on-board computers when the ignition key is in the on position.

GMC—ECM/BCM SYSTEM DIAGNOSIS

Delco Electronics supplies equipment to all General Motors passenger car divisions. Many similarities therefore exist among different model vehicles, although the ECM or ECM/BCM units are not the same for each and every vehicle. Because of similarities of design and incorporation of the ECM/BCM into these upscale GMC division vehicles, the information and procedural checks to access these systems can be considered similar, if not common, in all such models.

The ECM/BCM computer systems on these vehicles have the capability to self-diagnose themselves when certain procedures are followed. Therefore, special tools (Fig. 7-59) and mini-scanners (Chapter 14) such as those that would be used on an ALDL system described earlier for ECM only equipped vehicles, are not required.

A systematic diagnostic check of the ECM/BCM computer system can be initiated "on-board" by manipulation of various ECC button selections. Vehicles that employ this ECC system are the Cadillac, Oldsmobile, and major Buick models, as well as top of the line models from GM's other two divisions—namely, Chevrolet and Pontiac.

For example, current model vehicles for Cadillac Eldorado and Seville were completely redesigned for 1986 and beyond to incorporate the most advanced, integrated electronic control system existing on any passenger cars in the world. On these vehicles, the integration of all the on-board computers into a single data bus called the Universal Asynchronous Receiver Transmitter, or UART data circuit, was a major technological advance. To coordinate control of all powertrain and passenger compartment comfort, lighting, and display functions, the ECM, BCM, the climate control and driver information center (CCDIC), the instrument panel controller (IPC), and HVAC (heating, ventilation, air conditioning) programmer are all in high speed communication.

Beginning with the 1980 and later model year, full-size upscale models of GMC cars were equipped with a HVAC system known as ECC (electronic climate control). These vehicles were equipped with an ECM. In 1985, a BCM (body computer module) was added to the electronics package. These ECM/BCM modules have the capability to transmit serial data information to the ECC panel, IPC (instrument panel cluster), or CCP (climate control panel).

In the 1982 through 1985 longitudinal vehicles (rear wheel drive), the microcomputer in the ECC panel decodes the serial data and displays the information on the FDP (fuel data panel) or on the ECC display if a diagnostic mode is selected through manipulation of various panel control buttons.

In 1985 and later years, FWD (front wheel drive) C model vehicles, the ECM transmits and receives serial data to and from the BCM (body computer module), which in turn compiles and transmits this information to the ECC and FDC (fuel data center). The lines that carry the information between the BCM and FDP/ECC panels are called "data lines." (Refer to Chapter 3 for more information on data lines.)

In FWD vehicles, display of the diagnostic information is done on both the FDC and ECC panels. To activate and access this system requires that the mechanic/technician depress one or more of the control buttons on the ECC control panel. The diagnostic features for both the longitudinal and front-wheel-drive-type vehicles are listed below:

1982–85 Longitudinal Vehicles

- Display of stored malfunction codes
- Discrete input tests
- Parametric display
- Discrete output tests
- Status light indicators
- Fixed spark mode

1985 On FWD C Model Vehicles

- Display of stored ECM and BCM malfunction codes
- ECM input discrete tests (switch tests)
- ECM parameter value display
- BCM parameter value display
- ECM output discrete tests
- ECM status indicator lights
- BCM status indicator lights
- BCM program number control
- BCM cooling fans override

The BCM, which is usually located behind the glove box (see Fig. 7-6), is the heart of the on-board computer system. It has an internal microprocessor to which is fed all the information from all the other components in the system.

The five other components in contact with the BCM are:

1. ECM (electronic control module)
2. IPC (instrument panel cluster)
3. ECC (electronic climate control)
4. HVAC (heating, ventilation, and air conditioning programmer)
5. C/V (chime/voice module)

When an engine/vehicle malfunction is sensed by the BCM, a driver warning message is displayed in the information center, which is part of the IPC. In order for the mechanic/technician to withdraw information stored in the computer memory bank, as well as to provide the controls for the heating and air conditioning systems, the ECC panel buttons become the controller to enter memory and access the BCM self-diagnostics, which will then display all stored information to the instrument panel.

Data messages are sent to the BCM via the serial data line to access the desired information by pressing the appropriate ECC buttons. Because of the commonality of their design and operation, diagnostic sequence checks for these systems are described in this chapter for an Oldsmobile Toronado, as well as for the Cadillac DeVille, Eldorado, and Seville models, all of which represent the latest advancements in on-board computer technology.

ECM DATA

To more fully understand the function of the ECM, let's look at the type of data that is continually being monitored at the ECM from all of the various engine and vehicle sensors, and what type of message that these individual units are sending. Each sensor in the system is allocated a ''parameter number'' so that it can be identified by the computer system. The signal generated from each sensor can be in millivolts, volts, degrees, milliseconds, grams per second, off/on, rpm, mph, or counts or steps. Therefore, to assist you in understanding all of these various parameters, refer to Fig. 7-27. All of these various sensors and switches, which total 21 data messages, and the range value of each are listed.

A similar parameter number sequence is also used for the BCM, an example of which can be reviewed in the 1986 Oldsmobile and Cadillac diagnostic procedure, described later in this chapter. Note that the ECM/BCM diagnostic trouble code numbers in Figs. 7-28 and 7-29 are preceded by the letter ''E'' (ECM) or ''B'' (BCM).

The ECM/BCM diagnostic trouble codes can be displayed on the IPC (instrument panel cluster) in addition to other service-related information, such as:

1. ECM data, such as that shown in Fig. 7-27.
2. ECM inputs. (Four input switches can be monitored for their *high* or *low* status; refer to Figs. 7-31 and 7-42.)
3. ECM output cycling. (The ECM can cycle the components shown in Figs. 7-31 and 7-42 as on and off.)

SERVICE DIAGNOSTICS

Both the ECM and BCM are continually monitoring the various engine and vehicle sensors during operation. When emissions or vehicle driveability problems are encountered, the ECM/BCM can therefore detect the sensed component malfunction by comparing all system conditions against preprogrammed standard acceptable operating limits. When a malfunction is detected, a driver warning message and/or the *Check Engine Soon or Now* light will illuminate on

ECM DATA

Idle / Upper Rad. Hose Hot / Closed Throttle / Park or Neutral / Closed Loop / Acc. Off / Shop Temp. 60-100°F

Data Number	Description	Message	Typical Data Value	Units Displayed
ED01	Throttle Position	TPS	350 – 450	Millivolts
ED04	Coolant Temperature	COOLANT	85 – 105	°C - *Metric Selected*
ED05	Air Temperature	MAT	Variable Value	°C - *Metric Selected*
ED06	Injector Pulse Width	INJ PW	1 – 6 (Varying)	Milliseconds
ED07	Oxygen Sensor Voltage	OXY	1 – 1000 (Varying)	Millivolts
ED08	Spark Avance	SPARK	Variable Value	Degrees
ED09	Transaxle Convertor Clutch	TCC	0	0 = OFF / 1 = ON
ED10	Battery Voltage	VOLTS	13.5 – 14.5	VOLTS
ED11	Engine RPM	RPM	700 – 800	RPM
ED12	Vehicle Speed	MPH	0	MPH
ED15	Closed or Open Loop	MODE	1	0 = OL / 1 = CL
ED16	ESC (Knock Retard)	ESC	0	Degrees
ED17	OLDPA3 (Knock Signal)	OLDPA3	0 – 255 (Fixed Value)	Counts
ED18	Cross Counts 0^2	X CTS	N/A For Diagnosis	Counts
ED19	Fuel Integrator	INT	Variable Value	Counts
ED20	Block Learn Memory (Fuel)	BLM	118 – 138	Counts
ED21	Air Flow	AIR FLOW	3 – 6	Grams Per Sec.
ED22	Idle Air Control	IAC	10 – 50	Steps
ED23	LV8 (Engine Load)	LV8	Variable Value	Counts
ED98	Ignition Cycle Counter	IGN C	0 – 50	Key Cycles
ED99	ECM PROM ID	PROM	0 – 999 (See 6E3-11)	CODE #

ECM DISCRETE INPUTS

Input Number	Description	Message	Input Circuit State	Units Displayed
EI60	EVRV- EGR Vac. Switch	EVRV	HI = No Vac / LO = Vac	HI/LO
EI74	Park/Neutral Switch	P/N	HI = D/R / LO = P/N	HI/LO
EI78	Power Steering Press. Sw.	PS	HI = Low / LO = High	HI/LO
EI82	Fourth Gear Switch	4TH	HI = In 4th / LO = Out 4th	HI/LO

ECM OUTPUT CYCLING

Output Number	Description	Message	Commanded State	Units Displayed
EO00	No Outputs	None	None	None
EO01	Canister Purge Solenoid	Purge	HI = Off / LO = On	HI/LO
EO02	TCC Solenoid	TCC	HI = Off / LO = On	HI/LO
EO04	EGR Solenoid	EGR	HI = Off / LO = On	HI/LO
EO07	IAC Motor Set	IAC	Pintle Extended To Seat	HI/LO
EO08	A/C Clutch	A/C Clutch	HI = Off / LO = On	HI/LO
EO09	Coolant Fan Relay	Fan	HI = Off / LO = On	HI/LO

GS O495-BO 5-2-86

FIGURE 7-27 ECM data and relative display signals. (*Courtesy of Oldsmobile Div. of GMC*)

ECM DIAGNOSTIC CODES

CODE	DESCRIPTION	COMMENTS
E013	Open O$_2$ Sensor Circuit (*Canister Purge)	A
E014	Coolant Sensor Circuit - High Temperature	A – B
E015	Coolant Sensor Circuit - Low Temperature	A – B
E016	System Voltage Out Of Range (*All Solenoids)	A
E021	TPS Circuit Failure – Signal Voltage High (*TCC)	A
E022	TPS Circuit Failure – Signal Voltage Low (*TCC)	A
E024	Vehicle Speed Sensor Circuit Failure (*TCC)	A
E029	Fourth Gear Switch Circuit Open	A
E032	EGR Vacuum Control System Fault	A
E033	Mass Air Flow Sensor Frequency High	A
E034	Mass Air Flow Sensor Frequency Low	A
E037	MAT Sensor Circuit - High Temperature	A
E038	MAT Sensor Circuit - Low Temperature	A
E040	Power Steering Pressure Switch Circuit Open - (*A/C Clutch and Cruise)	A
E041	CAM Sensor Circuit - C^{3}I Module to ECM	A
E042	C^{3}I Electronic Spark Timing Or Bypass Circuit Failure	A – D
E043	Electronic Spark Control System Failure	A
E044	Lean Exhaust Indication	A – C
E045	Rich Exhaust Indication	A – C
E047	ECM–BCM Data - (*A/C Clutch and Cruise)	A
E051	ECM PROM Error	A – D – E
E052	Calpak Error	A
E055	ECM Error	A

DIAGNOSTIC CODE COMMENTS

"A"	"Service Engine Soon" Message Displayed
"B"	Forces Cooling Fans "ON"
"C"	Forces Open Loop Operation
"D"	Causes System to Operate in Bypass Spark Mode
"E"	Causes System to Operate in Back up Fuel Mode

* Functions are disengaged while specified malfunctions remain current.

5/1/86

GS 0493 BO

FIGURE 7-28 ECM diagnostic trouble codes. (*Courtesy of Oldsmobile Div. of GMC*)

BCM DIAGNOSTIC CODES

Code	Circuit Affected	Code	Circuit Affected
B110	Outside Temp Sensor	B409	Generator
B111	A/C Hi Side Temp SEnsor	B411	Battery Low
B112	A/C Lo Side Temp SEnsor	B412	Battery High
B113	In–Car Temp Sensor	B440	Air Mix Door
B115	Sunload Temp Sensor	B445	A/C Clutch
B118	Door Ajar / Jamb Switch	B446	Low Refrigerant Warning
B119	Twilight Photocell	B447	Very Low Refrigerant Problem
B120	Twilight Delay Pot	B448	Low Refrigerant Pressure
B122	Panel Lamp Dimming Pot	B449	A/C HI Temp
B123	Courtesy Light Switch	B450	Coolant HI temp – A/C
B124	VSS	B552	BCM Memory Reset
B127	PRNDL Sensor	B556	E² Prom
B131	Oil Pressure Sensor	B660	Cruise – Not In Drive
B132	Oil Pressure Sensor	B663	Cruise – Speed Difference
B334	ECM Data	B664	Cruise – Acceleration
B335	ECC Data	B667	Cruise – Switch Shorted
B336	IPC Data	B671	Cruise – Position Sensor
B337	Programmer Data	B672	Cruise – Vent Solenoid
B338	Chime / Voice Data	B673	Cruise – Vacuum Solenoid

FIGURE 7-29 BCM diagnostic trouble codes. (*Courtesy of Oldsmobile Div. of GMC*)

the IPC. A three-digit numerical trouble code is then stored in computer memory to allow the service technician to re-call it when the diagnostic system is activated.

Should a problem arise whereby unacceptable system operation results, the self-diagnostic system attempts to minimize this condition by taking what is commonly known as ''failsoft'' action. What this means is that the computer will attempt to compensate for a problem, such as an open or shorted sensor, by substituting a fixed input value. The vehicle may not operate at peak efficiency, and the *Check Engine Soon or Now* light will be on, but this action does allow vehicle ''limp-home'' capability.

When the system is activated into ECM diagnosis, the IPC will display the following information:

1. ECM data
2. ECM inputs
3. ECM output cycling
4. ECM diagnostic codes

SELF-DIAGNOSTICS/PRECHECKS

When engine/vehicle problems occur, they are generally initiated by one of the following conditions:

1. The instrument panel *Service Engine Soon or Now* light warns the driver of a problem.

2. Vehicle performance is poor.
3. Engine will crank, but may not run, or it will run, but very poorly.

NOTE: Often engine/vehicle problems may have nothing at all to do with a faulty sensor or ECM/BCM unit, but they get blamed for the problem anyway. Prior to perform-ing the diagnostic check on the vehicle, always raise the hood, remove the air cleaner, and carefully inspect for signs of disconnected, pinched, or cut vacuum hoses. Also, visually inspect all wiring and connections for possible signs of chafing, burning, or looseness. In other words, pursue the diagnosis procedure in the same way that you would tackle a noncomputer-equipped vehicle problem. Spend a few minutes assuring yourself that the problem is not one that can be corrected by a few simple checks and/or minor adjustments.

The vehicle should be brought to normal operating tem-perature before proceeding with the systematic diagnosis check; otherwise, the problem may not reflect itself fully, or it may be that the problem is intermittent in nature. Also, if the engine is cold, the system will be in open loop. The ECM/BCM will ignore the oxygen sensor feedback signal. When the vehicle engine is in open loop, a 0 display will show on the IPC facia, while if in closed loop, a number 1 will be illuminated.

ENTERING DIAGNOSTIC SERVICE MODE

Minor variations in both the procedural check and the actual codes employed by each GMC car division will vary slightly. However, the procedure used, for example, on BCM equipped Oldsmobile and Cadillac vehicles, described below with the aid of tables and code charts, will systematically lead you through the correct sequence.

Figures 7-31 and 7-42 illustrate a typical IPC and ECC panel, along with information regarding what buttons to push to enter ECM/BCM self-diagnostics. To enter the diagnostic mode, proceed as follows:

Procedure

1. Turn the ignition key on.
2. Simultaneously push and hold the off and warm buttons on the ECC panel for about 3 seconds until a segment check is displayed on the facia.
3. Any trouble codes stored in computer memory will now be displayed. Refer to Fig. 7-28, which illustrates the various trouble codes for each sensed system.
4. If no ECM trouble codes are stored, then the IPC will display a *No ECM Codes* message for about a two-second time period. If, however, there are stored trouble codes in memory, then the ECM codes will appear before any BCM codes. ECM codes will be preceded by the letter E, while BCM codes will be preceded by either the letter B, or by the letter F in some GMC division vehicles.
5. Stored ECM codes will appear for two-second intervals, starting with the lowest code, and proceeding towards the highest one retained in memory.
6. When all ECM codes have been shown, the BCM codes will also appear for two-second intervals, unless of course a *No BCM Codes* message appears, indicating there are none in memory. Any in memory, however, will start from the lowest numeral and work towards the highest. If the word *Current* follows the BCM code number, this indicates that the problem still exists. This word will *not* appear with any ECM codes since the ECM is incapable of making such a determination.

CAUTION: If at any time during the display of the ECM/BCM codes the LO fan button is pressed on the ECC, this action will cause all trouble codes to be bypassed. In addition, if the BI-LEV button is pressed, the BCM will exit the diagnostic service mode and revert back to normal vehicle operation.

Displayed diagnostic trouble codes can be determined by reference to the various diagnostic code charts within this section. In addition to self-diagnosing trouble codes,

the ECM/BCM computer system can also be triggered to supply information on:

1. ECM/BCM data
2. ECM/BCM input
3. ECM/BCM output
4. Override displays

More detailed information on these other three checks follows:

1. *ECM/BCM Data:* When troubleshooting a system malfunction, the ECM and BCM data display can be used to compare the vehicle problems with a car that is functioning correctly. Refer to the various ECM and BCM data charts in this section for specific code numbers.
2. *ECM/BCM Input:* When troubleshooting any malfunction, the ECM, BCM, or IPC input display can be used to determine if the switched inputs can be properly interpreted. When one of the various input tests is selected, the state of that device is displayed as either HI or LO, which individually refer to the input terminal voltage for that particular circuit. In addition, the display also indicates if the input signal changed state, so that the service technician can activate or deactivate any listed device and return to the display to see if it changed state. If a change did occur, an X would appear once per selected input (Oldsmobile) next to the HI/LO indicator on the IPC. The HI/LO indication will continue to change with a changing input signal. Since some tests are momentary, the appearance of the X would signify that a change has occurred in that circuit.
3. *ECM/BCM Output:* When troubleshooting a system malfunction, the ECM and BCM output cycling can be used to determine if the output tests can be actuated regardless of the inputs and normal program instructions. Once an output test has been selected, except for ECM IAC, the test will display HI or LO for three seconds in each state to indicate the command and output terminal voltage.
4. *Override Displays:* When troubleshooting a malfunction, the BCM override feature allows testing of certain system functions regardless of normal program instructions.

A service diagnostics system overview is illustrated in Fig. 7-30, which is the procedure recommended for the 1986 Oldsmobile Toronado 3.8L SFI V6 engine/vehicle. Before going on with the specific diagnostic information for an Oldsmobile or Cadillac vehicle, study the illustration chart so that you have a better understanding of just what is required to initiate the ECM/BCM diagnostic procedural check.

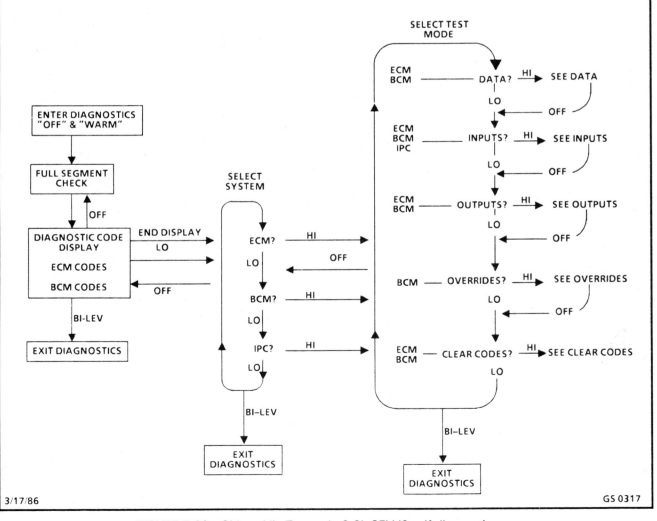

FIGURE 7-30 Oldsmobile Toronado 3.8L SFI V6 self-diagnostic system flow chart. (*Courtesy of Oldsmobile Div. of GMC*)

CADILLAC ECM/BCM DIAGNOSTIC PROCEDURE

The sequence to initiate computer self-diagnosis on the ECM/BCM equipped vehicles is very similar regardless of the car model. However, since there are minor variations involved in not only the procedural steps but also in the code numbers and the number of codes used, the information that follows is broken into separate procedural checks:

1. 1980–85 longitudinal mounted engine vehicles
2. 1985–86 transverse mounted engine DeVille
3. 1986 Eldorado and Seville

The 1980–85 longitudinally mounted engine vehicle diagnostic procedure, although similar in many areas to the 86's, had fewer monitored systems, and therefore less codes were utilized. There is also some variation in the code numbers between these various model years.

The procedures for the 85/86 and up transverse mounted engine DeVilles are the same. Although the procedures for the 86 Eldorado and Seville are similar to that for the 1986 Oldsmobile Toronado, the actual trouble codes differ slightly. Figure 7-31 illustrates the CCDIC (climate control driver information center) buttons and display areas for the self-diagnostic feature of the vehicle.

The actual entry into self-diagnostic checks is illustrated in a series of flow charts that follows. (See Figs. 7-32 to 7-38). Note that by depressing the appropriate ECC buttons, you will be able to enter and exit the various testing modes at will.

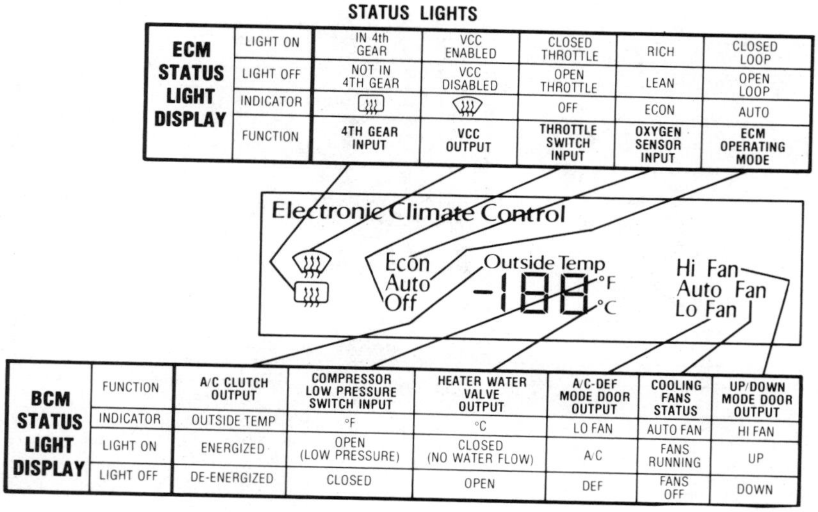

7-31 Cadillac Eldorado and Seville CCDIC self-diagnostic panel. (*Courtesy of Cadillac Motor Car Div. of GMC*)

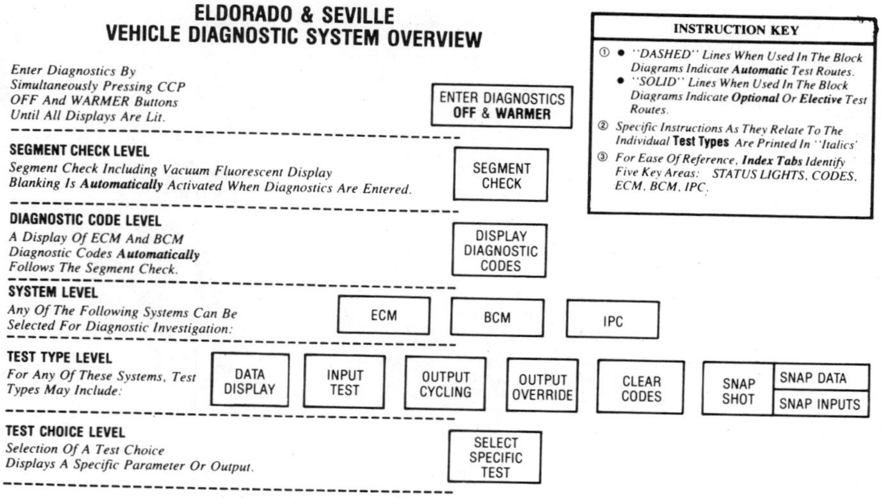

FIGURE 7-32 Systematic procedural check for initiating self-diagnostic check of ECM/BCM system—Eldorado and Seville. (*Courtesy of Cadillac Motor Car Div. of GMC*)

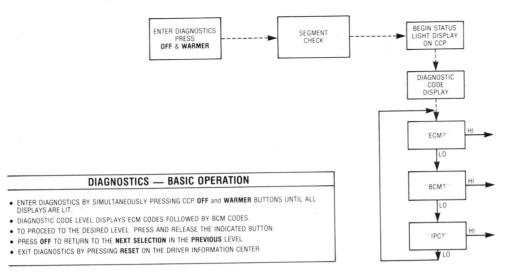

DIAGNOSTICS — BASIC OPERATION

- ENTER DIAGNOSTICS BY SIMULTANEOUSLY PRESSING CCP **OFF** and **WARMER** BUTTONS UNTIL ALL DISPLAYS ARE LIT.
- DIAGNOSTIC CODE LEVEL DISPLAYS ECM CODES FOLLOWED BY BCM CODES.
- TO PROCEED TO THE DESIRED LEVEL, PRESS AND RELEASE THE INDICATED BUTTON.
- PRESS **OFF** TO RETURN TO THE **NEXT SELECTION** IN THE **PREVIOUS** LEVEL.
- EXIT DIAGNOSTICS BY PRESSING **RESET** ON THE DRIVER INFORMATION CENTER.

FIGURE 7-33

ECM DIAGNOSTIC CODES

CODE	DESCRIPTION	COMMENTS	CODE	DESCRIPTION	COMMENTS
E012	No Distributor Signal	Ⓐ	E031	Shorted MAP Sensor Circuit [AIR]	Ⓐ
E013	Oxygen Sensor Not Ready [AIR, CL & Canister Purge]	Ⓑ	E032	Open MAP Sensor Circuit [AIR]	Ⓐ
E014	Shorted Coolant Sensor Circuit [AIR]	Ⓑ Ⓙ	E034	MAP Sensor Signal Too High [AIR]	Ⓐ
E015	Open Coolant Sensor Circuit [AIR]	Ⓑ Ⓙ	E037	Shorted MAT Sensor Circuit [AIR]	Ⓑ
E016	Generator Voltage Out Of Range [All Solenoids]	Ⓐ Ⓕ	E038	Open MAT Sensor Circuit [AIR]	Ⓑ
E018	Open Crank Signal Circuit	Ⓑ	E039	VCC Engagement Problem	Ⓑ
E019	Shorted Fuel Pump Circuit	Ⓑ	E040	Open Power Steering Pressure Switch Circuit	Ⓑ
E020	Open Fuel Pump Circuit	Ⓐ	E044	Lean Exhaust Signal [AIR, CL & Canister Purge]	Ⓐ
E021	Shorted Throttle Position Sensor Circuit	Ⓑ	E045	Rich Exhaust Signal [AIR, CL & Canister Purge]	Ⓑ
E022	Open Throttle Position Sensor Circuit	Ⓑ	E047	BCM — ECM Data Problem	Ⓑ
E023	EST/Bypass Circuit Problem [AIR]	Ⓑ Ⓔ	E048	EGR System Fault [EGR]	Ⓑ
E024	Speed Sensor Circuit Problem [VCC]	Ⓑ Ⓕ	E051	ECM PROM Error	Ⓐ Ⓙ
E026	Shorted Throttle Switch Circuit	Ⓑ	E052	ECM Memory Reset Indicator	Ⓓ
E027	Open Throttle Switch Circuit	Ⓑ	E053	Distributor Signal Interrupt	Ⓓ
E028	Open Third Or Fourth Gear Circuit	Ⓑ	E055	TPS Misadjusted	Ⓓ
E030	ISC Circuit Problem	Ⓑ	E059	VCC Temperature Sensor Circuit Problem	Ⓓ

DIAGNOSTIC CODE COMMENTS

Ⓐ	Displays "SERVICE NOW" Message And Turns On "ENGINE CONTROL SYSTEM" Light.		Ⓕ	Disengages VCC For Entire Ignition Cycle.
Ⓑ	Displays "SERVICE SOON" Message And Turns On "ENGINE CONTROL SYSTEM" Light.		Ⓖ	Displays Square Box Around Each PRND321 Position On IPC.
Ⓒ	Displays Status Message On DIC.		Ⓗ	Displays 'Error' In Season Odometer.
Ⓓ	Does Not Turn On Any Telltale Light Or Display Any Message.		Ⓘ	Switches ECC Mode To ECON.
Ⓔ	Causes System To Operate On Bypass Spark.		Ⓙ	Forces Cooling Fans On Full Speed.
			[ ]	Functions Within Bracket Are Disengaged While Specified Malfunction Remains Current.

FIGURE 7-34

BCM DIAGNOSTIC CODES

CODE	DESCRIPTION	COMMENTS	CODE	DESCRIPTION	COMMENTS
B110	Outside Air Temperature Circuit Problem		B441	Cooling Fans Problem	Ⓒ
B111	A/C High Side Temperature Circuit Problem	Ⓙ	B446	Low A/C Refrigerant Condition Warning	Ⓒ
B112	A/C Low Side Temperature Circuit Problem [A/C Clutch]	Ⓒ	B447	Very Low A/C Refrigerant Condition Warning [A/C Clutch]	Ⓒ Ⓘ
B113	In-Car Temperature Circuit Problem		B448	Very Low A/C Refrigerant Pressure Condition [A/C Clutch]	Ⓒ Ⓘ
B115	Sunload Temperature Circuit Problem		B449	A/C High Side Temperature Too High [A/C Clutch]	Ⓒ
B119	Twilight Sentinel Photosensor Circuit Problem				
B120	Twilight Sentinel Delay Pot Circuit Problem		B450	Coolant Temperature Too High [A/C Clutch]	Ⓒ
B121	Twilight Sentinel Enable Circuit Problem		B552	BCM Memory Reset Indicator	
B122	Panel Lamp Dimming Pot Circuit Problem		B556	BCM EEPROM Error	Ⓗ
B123	Panel Lamp Enable Circuit Problem		B660	Cruise - Transmission Not In Drive [Cruise]	
B124	Speed Sensor Circuit Problem [Cruise]		B663	Cruise - Car Speed And Set Speed Difference Too High [Cruise]	
B127	PRND321 Sensor Circuit Problem [Cruise]	Ⓖ	B664	Cruise - Car Acceleration Too High [Cruise]	
B128	Incandescent Reference Circuit Problem		B665	Cruise - Coolant Temperature Too High [Cruise]	
B334	Loss Of ECM Data [Cruise]	Ⓒ Ⓙ	B666	Cruise - Engine RPM Too High [Cruise]	
B335	Loss Of CCDIC Data	Ⓒ	B667	Cruise - Cruise Switch Shorted During Enable [Cruise]	
B336	Loss Of IPC Data [Cruise]	Ⓒ			
B337	Loss Of Programmer Data [A/C Clutch]	Ⓒ	B671	Cruise - Servo Position Sensor Circuit Problem [Cruise]	
B410	Charging System Problem	Ⓒ			
B411	Battery Volts Too Low [Cruise]	Ⓒ	B672	Cruise - Vent Solenoid Circuit Problem [Cruise]	
B412	Battery Volts Too High [Cruise]	Ⓒ	B673	Cruise - Vacuum Solenoid Circuit Problem [Cruise]	
B420	Relay Circuit Problem				
B440	Air Mix Door Problem				

FIGURE 7-35

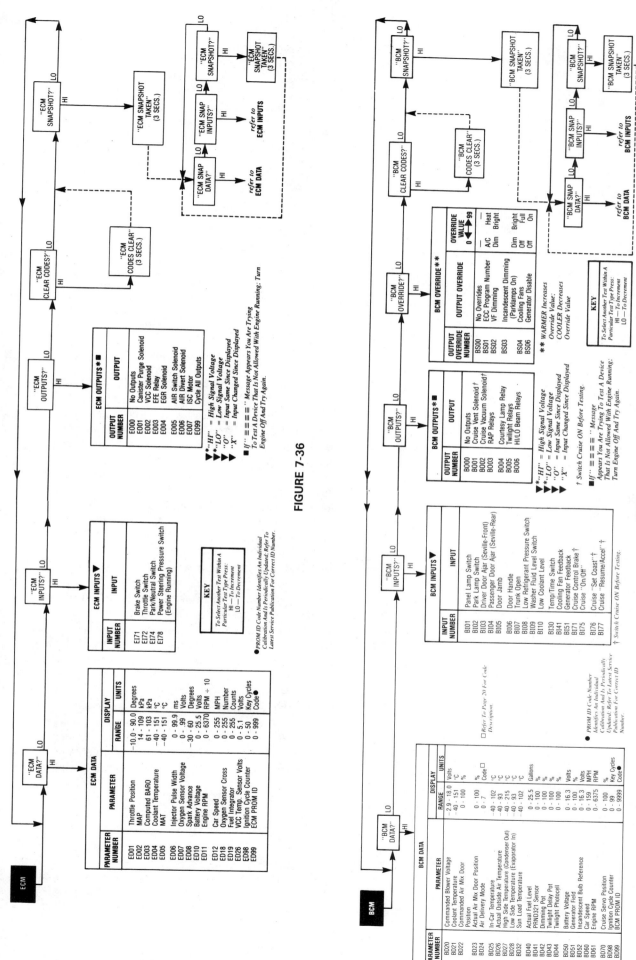

ECM

ECM DATA

PARAMETER NUMBER	PARAMETER	DISPLAY RANGE	UNITS
ED01	Throttle Position	-10.0 - 90.0	Degrees
ED02	MAP	14 - 109	kPa
ED03	Computed BARO	61 - 103	kPa
ED04	Coolant Temperature	-40 - 151	°C
ED05	MAT	-40 - 151	°C
ED06	Injector Pulse Width	0 - 99.9	ms
ED07	Oxygen Sensor Voltage	0 - 99	Volts
ED08	Spark Advance	-30 - 60	Degrees
ED10	Battery Voltage	0 - 25.5	Volts
ED11	Engine RPM	0 - 6370	RPM ÷ 10
ED12	Car Speed	0 - 255	MPH
ED18	Oxygen Sensor Cross	0 - 255	Number
ED19	Fuel Integrator	0 - 255	Counts
ED26	VCC Temp. Sensor Volts	0 - 5.1	Volts
ED98	Ignition Cycle Counter	0 - 50	Key Cycles
ED99	ECM PROM ID	0 - 999	Code●

ECM INPUTS ▼

INPUT NUMBER	INPUT
EI71	Brake Switch
EI72	Throttle Switch
EI74	Park/Neutral Switch
EI78	Power Steering Pressure Switch (Engine Running)

KEY

To Select Another Test Within A Particular Test Type Press:
HI — To Increment
LO — To Decrement

● *PROM ID Code Number Identifies An Individual Calibration And Is Periodically Updated. Refer To Latest Service Publication For Correct ID Number.*

ECM OUTPUTS *■

OUTPUT NUMBER	OUTPUT
E000	No Outputs
E001	Canister Purge Solenoid
E002	VCC Solenoid
E003	EFE Relay
E004	EGR Solenoid
E005	AIR Switch Solenoid
E006	AIR Divert Solenoid
E007	ISC Motor
E099	Cycle All Outputs

▶*"HI" = High Signal Voltage*
▶*"LO" = Low Signal Voltage*
▶*"O" = Input Same Since Displayed*
▶▶*"X" = Input Changed Since Displayed*

■ *If "■ ≡ ≡ ≡ ■" Message Appears You Are Trying To Test A Device That Is Not Allowed With Engine Running: Turn Engine Off And Try Again.*

FIGURE 7-36

BCM

BCM DATA

PARAMETER NUMBER	PARAMETER	DISPLAY RANGE	UNITS
BD20	Commanded Blower Voltage	-2.9 - 18.0	Volts
BD21	Coolant Temperature	-40 - 151	°C
BD22	Commanded Air Mix Door	0 - 100	%
BD23	Actual Air Mix Door Position	0 - 100	%
BD24	Air Delivery Mode	0 - 7	Code □
BD25	In-Car Temperature	-40 - 102	°C
BD26	Actual Outside Air Temperature	-40 - 93	°C
BD27	High Side Temperature (Condenser Out)	-40 - 215	°C
BD28	Low Side Temperature (Evaporator In)	-40 - 93	°C
BD32	Sun Load Temperature	-40 - 102	°C
BD40	Actual Fuel Level	0 - 25.5	Gallons
BD41	PRND321 Sensor	0 - 100	%
BD42	Dimming Pot	0 - 100	%
BD43	Twilight Delay Pot	0 - 100	%
BD44	Twilight Photocell	0 - 100	%
BD50	Battery Voltage	0 - 16.3	Volts
BD51	Generator Field	0 - 100	%
BD52	Incandescent Bulb Reference	0 - 16.3	Volts
BD60	Car Speed	0 - 159	MPH
BD61	Engine RPM	0 - 6375	RPM
BD70	Cruise Servo Position	0 - 100	%
BD98	Ignition Cycle Counter	0 - 99	Key Cycles
BD99	BCM PROM ID	0 - 9999	Code●

□ *Refer To Page 20 For Code Description*

● *PROM ID Code Number Identifies An Individual Calibration And Is Periodically Updated. Refer To Latest Service Publication For Correct ID Number.*

BCM INPUTS ▼

INPUT NUMBER	INPUT
BI01	Panel Lamp Switch
BI02	Park Lamp Switch
BI03	Driver Door Ajar (Seville-Front)
BI04	Passenger Door Ajar (Seville-Rear)
BI05	Door Jamb
BI06	Door Handle
BI07	Trunk Open
BI08	Low Refrigerant Pressure Switch
BI09	Washer Fluid Level Switch
BI10	Low Coolant Level
BI30	Temp/Time Switch
BI41	Cooling Fan Feedback
BI51	Generator Feedback
BI71	Cruise Control Brake †
BI75	Cruise "On/Off"
BI76	Cruise "Set Coast" †
BI77	Cruise "Resume/Accel" †

† *Switch Cruise ON Before Testing.*

BCM OUTPUTS *■

OUTPUT NUMBER	OUTPUT
B000	No Outputs
B001	Cruise Vent Solenoid †
B002	Cruise Vacuum Solenoid †
B003	RAP Relays
B004	Courtesy Lamp Relay
B005	Twilight Relays
B006	HI/LO Beam Relays

▶*"HI" = High Signal Voltage*
▶*"LO" = Low Signal Voltage*
▶*"O" = Input Same Since Displayed*
▶▶*"X" = Input Changed Since Displayed*

† *Switch Cruise ON Before Testing.*

■ *If "■ ≡ ≡ ≡ ■" Message Appears You Are Trying To Test A Device That Is Not Allowed With Engine Running: Turn Engine Off And Try Again.*

BCM OVERRIDE **

OUTPUT OVERRIDE NUMBER	OUTPUT OVERRIDE	OVERRIDE VALUE 0 ◀▲▶ 99
BS00	No Overrides	
BS01	ECC Program Number	A/C — Heat
BS02	VF Dimming	Dim — Bright
BS03	Incandescent Dimming (Parklamps On)	Dim — Bright
BS04	Cooling Fans	Off — Full
BS06	Generator Disable	Off — On

** *WARMER Increases Override Value;*
COOLER Decreases Override Value

KEY

To Select Another Test Within A Particular Test Type Press:
HI — To Increment
LO — To Decrement

FIGURE 7-37

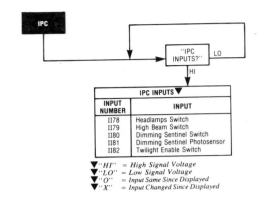

IPC INPUTS ▼	
INPUT NUMBER	INPUT
II78	Headlamps Switch
II79	High Beam Switch
II80	Dimming Sentinel Switch
II81	Dimming Sentinel Photosensor
II82	Twilight Enable Switch

▼ *"HI"* = *High Signal Voltage*
▼ *"LO"* = *Low Signal Voltage*
▼ *"O"* = *Input Same Since Displayed*
▼ *"X"* = *Input Changed Since Displayed*

```
        KEY
To Select Another Test Press:
  HI — To Increment
  LO — To Decrement
```

FIGURE 7-38

OLDSMOBILE TORONADO—ECM/BCM DIAGNOSTIC CHECK

The sequence used on the 1986 Olds Toronado equipped with the 3.8L V6 sequential port fuel-injected engine is similar to that given for the 4.1L V8 Cadillac vehicles, with some minor variations peculiar to each vehicle and system. (Refer to Fig. 7-4 for an illustration of the component location of the computer harness, the controlled devices, and the information sensors on the 3.8L V6 transversely mounted engine package.)

Although the ECM/BCM computer system is capable of self-diagnosis through manipulation of the various ECC buttons, it may be necessary to have to check out the individual voltage signals for each circuit once the ECM/BCM self-diagnostic feature has confirmed that a problem exists in that particular circuit. By this means the exact cause of the problem can be pinpointed. Figure 7-39 illustrates the ECM connector identification for the ECM terminals when viewed "end-on" from the back of the connector. The various voltage readings, as well as the conditions for the test, must be closely followed when systematically troubleshooting with this procedure. In addition, the individual ECM pin connectors, wire color, and circuit number for the back view of the ECM system are shown in Fig. 7-39, while Fig. 7-40 illustrates the vehicle wiring diagram for this same model vehicle (1986 Olds Toronado). Also shown in Fig. 7-41 is the back view of the BCM connector.

Diagnostic Procedure Check

The sequence to initiate computer self-diagnosis on the ECM/BCM equipped vehicles is illustrated in a flow-chart arrangement. These charts enable you to view how to enter and exit the various testing modes at will by depressing the appropriate ECC buttons.

Figure 7-42 illustrates the IPC (instrument panel cluster) and ECC (electronic climate control) panels for the 1986 Oldsmobile Toronado, together with their various control buttons and display areas.

Figures 7-43 through 7-50 describe and lead you through the various sequences necessary to initiate and pursue information stored in the computer memory for both the ECM/BCM diagnostic mode, input and output cycling, and override features.

Detailed Trouble Code Analysis

Use a digital high impedance multimeter and the various charts in this section for checking trouble code circuits, when they are confirmed by the computer. Check and compare these circuits to see whether they fall within the voltage range listed. Generally, this is a straightforward case of the circuit being "in" or "out" of specification.

For a thorough step-by-step procedure to correct any such problem, always refer to the latest manufacturer's service information manual, where you may find several hundred pages containing information listing detailed checks and tests for all of the ECM and BCM trouble codes, as well as information relating to the input/output phases of the computer.

ON-CAR SERVICE—ECM

The ECM (electronic control module) or controller is the heart of the computer diagnostic system unless, of course, the vehicle is a 1985 and later model. These later units were interfaced with a BCM (body control module). The

ECM CONNECTOR IDENTIFICATION

This ECM voltage chart is for use with a digital voltmeter to further aid in diagnosis. The voltages you get may vary due to low battery charge or other reasons, but they should be very close.

THE FOLLOWING CONDITIONS MUST BE MET BEFORE TESTING:
- Engine at operating temperature
- Engine idling in closed loop (for "Engine Run" column)
- Test terminal not grounded
- ALDL tool not installed
- A/C Off

VOLTAGE					
KEY "ON"	ENG. RUN	CIRCUIT	PIN	WIRE COLOR	
.01	B+	FUEL PUMP RELAY	A1	GRN/YEL	④
.01	0	A/C CLUTCH CONTROL	A2	GRN/YEL	⑤
B+	B+	CANISTER PURGE CONTROL	A3	GRN/YEL	
B+	B+	EGR SOLENOID	A4	GRY	
.79	B+	"SERVICE ENGINE SOON" LIGHT	A5	BRN/WHT	
B+	B+	IGNITION FEED	A6	PNK/BLK	
B+	B+	TCC CONTROL	A7	TAN/BLK	
2.3 3.6	2.3 3.6	SERIAL DATA	A8	TAN	
5.0	4.9	ALDL DIAG. TERMINAL	A9	WHT	①
B+	B+	VSS SIGNAL	A10	BRN	
.0	6.8	CAM SIGNAL (SFI)	A11	BLK	
.0	.02	GROUND	A12	TAN/WHT	
		NOT USED	C1		
		NOT USED	C2		
NOT USEABLE		IAC "B" LO	C3	GRN/BLK	
NOT USEABLE		IAC "B" HI	C4	GRN/WHT	
NOT USEABLE		IAC "A" HI	C5	BLU/WHT	
NOT USEABLE		IAC "A" LO	C6	BLU/BLK	
		NOT USED	C7		
.0	.0	4TH GEAR SWITCH SIGNAL	C8	LT BLU	
		NOT USED	C9		
2.24	1.75	COOLANT TEMP. SIGNAL	C10	YEL	②
2.2	1.75	MAT SIGNAL	C11	TAN	
B+	B+	INJECTOR 6	C12	BLK/YEL	
.45	.45	TPS SIGNAL	C13	DK BLU	
5.0	4.9	TPS 5 VOLT REFERENCE	C14	GRY	
B+	B+	INJECTOR 2	C15	BLK/GRN	
B+	B+	BATTERY	C16	ORN	

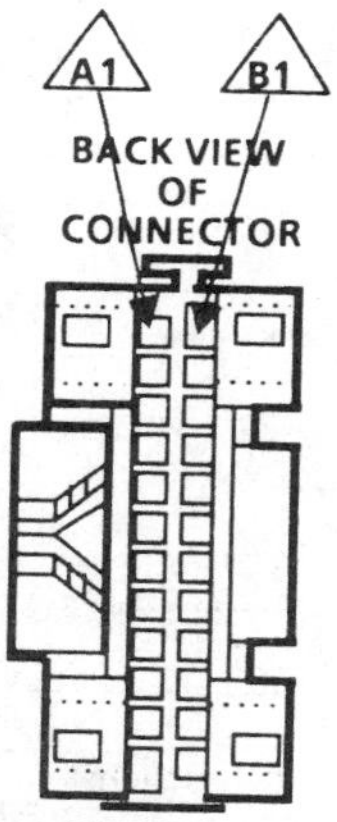

BACK VIEW OF CONNECTOR

24 PIN A-B CONNECTOR

WHEN TWO VALUES ARE GIVEN, THE VOLTAGE SIGNAL WILL CYCLE BETWEEN THE TWO VALUES

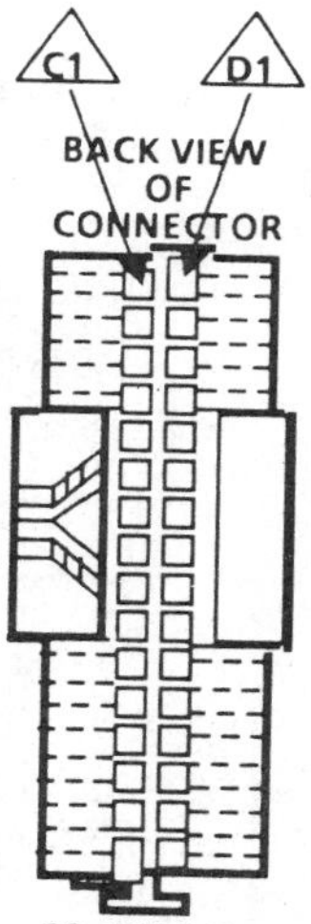

BACK VIEW OF CONNECTOR

32 PIN C-D CONNECTOR

WIRE COLOR	PIN	CIRCUIT	VOLTAGE		
			KEY "ON"	ENG. RUN	
	B1	NOT USED			
	B2	NOT USED			
BLK/RED	B3	REFERENCE LOW	.0	.0	
WHT	B4	EST CONTROL	.04	1.2	
PNK/WHT	B5	REFERENCE SIGNAL	.0	4.0	
YEL	B6	MASS AIR FLOW SENSOR SIGNAL	3.0	2.6	③
YEL/BLK	B7	ESC SIGNAL	9.2	9.2	
	B8	NOT USED			
	B9	NOT USED			
ORN/BLK	B10	PARK/NEUTRAL DRIVE/REVERSE	.0	.0	
	B11	NOT USED			
BLK/WHT	B12	INJECTOR 5	B+	B+	
BLK/WHT	D1	GROUND	0	0	
DK/GRN	D2	LOW SPD. COOLING FAN CONTROL	B+	1.57	
	D3	NOT USED			
	D4	NOT USED			
TAN/BLK	D5	BYPASS SIGNAL	.0	4.85	
TAN	D6	(O₂) GROUND	.0	.0	
PPL	D7	O₂ SENSOR SIGNAL	.42	.25 1.0	③
	D8	NOT USED			
RED	D9	EVRV DIAG. SWITCH	B+	B+	
BLK/WHT	D10	GROUND	.0	.0	
BLU/TAN	D11	POWER STEERING PRES. SW. SIGNAL	B+	B+	
BLK	D12	MAT, COOLANT & TPS GROUND	.0	.0	
	D13	NOT USED			
BLK	D14	INJECTOR 1	B+	B+	
BLK/PPL	D15	INJECTOR 3	B+	B+	
BLK/RED	D16	INJECTOR 4	B+	B+	

① Varies from .60 to battery voltage depending on position of drive wheels.
② Normal operating temperature.
③ Varies
④ 12 V only for first 2 seconds unless engine is cranking or running (System will not reenergize if fuel rail pressure is high)
⑤ 6.62 with A/C On

ENGINE ___3.8L___

CARLINE ___E___

4/23/86
GS 0388 BO

FIGURE 7-39 Oldsmobile Toronado 3.8L V6 SFI engine ECM terminal end-view, pin connector cavity circuit number, and wire color chart. (*Courtesy of Oldsmobile Div. of GMC*)

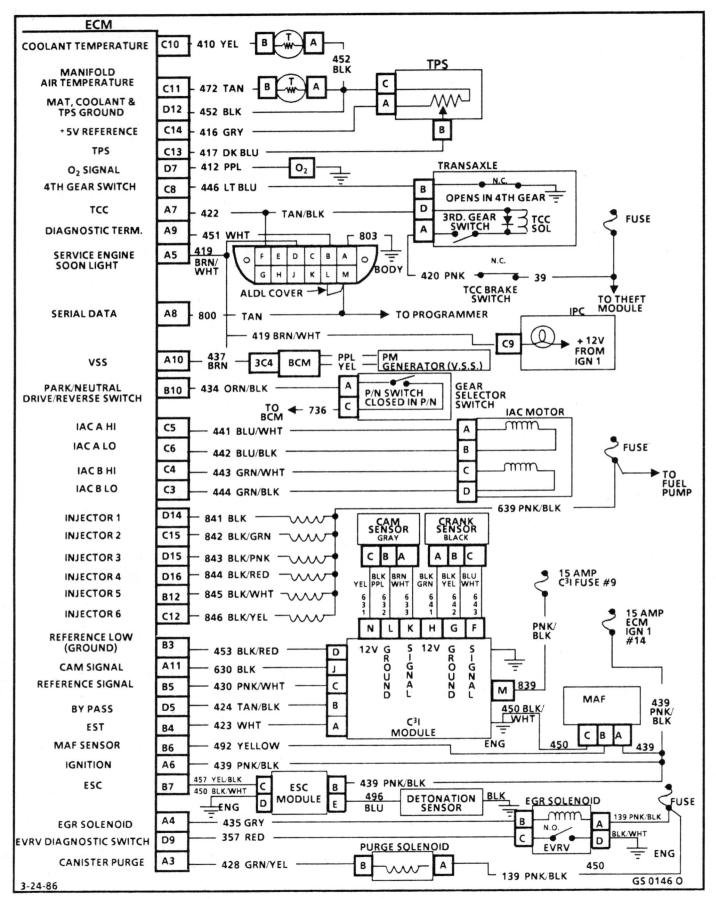

FIGURE 7-40 (a) ECM wiring diagram (1 of 2) for 1986 Oldsmobile Toronado 3.8L SFI V6 engine; (b) ECM wiring diagram (2 of 2) for 1986 Oldsmobile Toronado 3.8L SFI V6 engine. (*Courtesy of Oldsmobile Div. of GMC*)

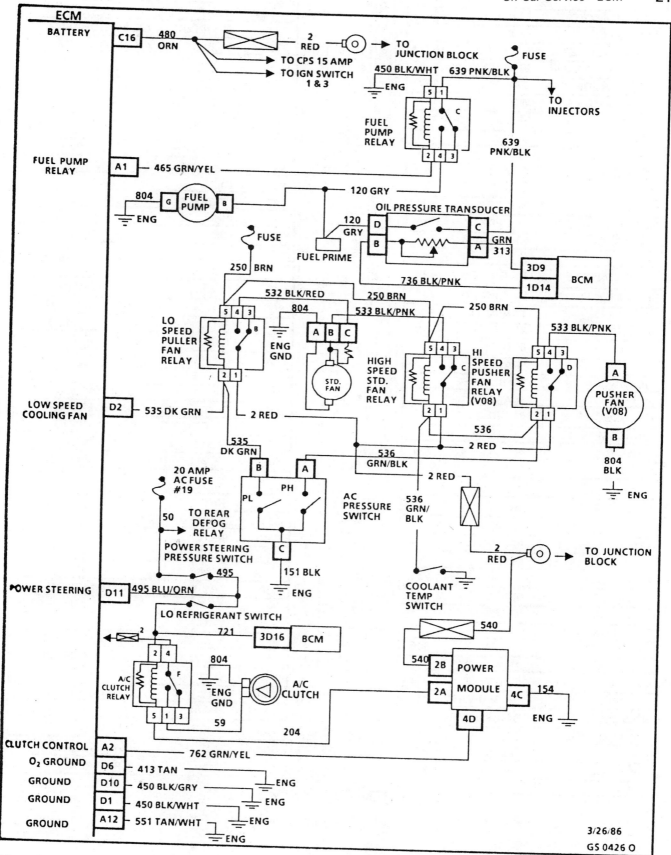

FIGURE 7-40 (Continued)

CKT DESC	WIRE COL	CKT NO
VSS RETURN	PPL	401
SPARE		
TAIL LAMP OUT	LT BLU/BLK	519
VSS TO ECM	BRN	437
EXPORT JUMPER	DK BLU/WHT	937
SUNLOAD SENSOR	LT BLU/YEL	590
DOOR HANDLE SW	GRY	157
DOOR JAMB SW	WHT/DK GRN	156
SPARE		
VSS FEED	YEL	400
IGNITION OFF	WHT	343
DRIVER DOOR AJAR	GRY/BLK	147
KEY IN IGNITION	LT GRN	80
PASS. DOOR AJAR	BLK/ORN	158
SEAT BELT SW	BLK/PNK	238
PARK SIGNAL	LT GRN/BLK	275
RADIO MUTE	DK GRN/ORN	626
IN CAR TEMP	DK GRN/WHT	734
VOICE ACTIVE	TAN/WHT	553
WASHER FLUID LEV	BLK/WHT	99
COURTESY LT SW	BRN/YEL	685
SPARE		
HEADLAMP OUT	DK BLU/YEL	539
SPARE		
CPS GROUND	BLK/RED	801
CRUISE SERVO LO	LT BLU/BLK	399
VF DIMMING	PPL/YEL	724
SPARE		
CRUISE BRAKE SW	BRN	86
BRAKE FLD LEV SW	TAN/WHT	33
STOP LAMP OUT	PPL/WHT	549
C.C. SET/COAST SW	DK/BLU	84
PARK BRAKE SW	TAN/WHT	233
SPARE		
SPARE		
HEADLAMPS ON	YEL	10
CRANK INPUT	PNK/WHT	806
CPS 12 VOLT	RED/WHT	812
CRUISE ON/OFF	GRY/WHT	397
CPS WAKE-UP	DK BLU/WHT	555
REVERSE INPUT	DK GRN/WHT	24
C.C. RESUME/ACCEL	GRY/BLK	87
CPS 7 VOLT	PPL/WHT	807
CPS 7 VOLT	PPL/WHT	807

11-05-85

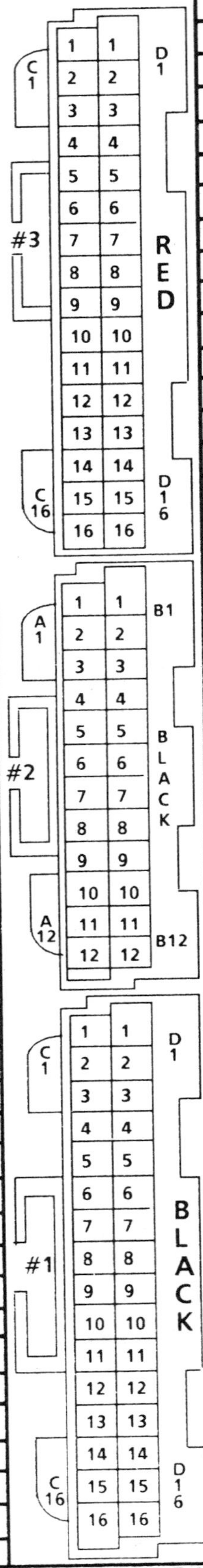

CKT NO	WIRE COL	CKT DESC
	SPARE	
	SPARE	
	SPARE	
731	GRY/RED	A/C LO SIDE TEMP
732	DK BLU	A/C HI SIDE TEMP
	SPARE	
39	PNK/BLK	IGNITION REF
278	WHT/BLK	TWI PHOTOCELL
313	LT GRN	OIL PRESSURE
800	TAN	SERIAL DATA
23	GRY/WHT	GEN F TERMINAL
686	TAN/BLK	DIM CONTROL
69	GRY	COOLANT LEVEL
735	LT GRN/BLK	OUTSIDE TEMP
25	BRN	GEN I TERMINAL
721	WHT	LO REF PRESSURE
	SPARE	
402	LT GRN	CRUISE VAC ON
900	YEL	P/N CRANK INPUT
271	PPL	TWILIGHT DELAY
800A	TAN	SERIAL DATA
356	GRY/BLK	PRNDL
	SPARE	
30	PPL	FUEL LEVEL WIPER
398	TAN	CRUISE SERVO HI
529	DK GRN/YEL	PARK LAMP OUT
	SPARE	
403	DK BLU/WHT	CRUISE VENT ON
	SPARE	
651	PPL/YEL	CHIME 1
652	PPL/WHT	CHIME 2
733	LT BLU	MIX DR. WIPER
	SPARE	
308	GRY/BLK	PARKLAMPS ON
343	WHT	IGNITION OFF
	SPARE	
992	BLK/PNK	TWILIGHT PK REL
760	PPL/WHT	BLOWER CONTROL
692	BLK/PNK	TWILIGHT H/L REL
690	GRY/BLK	COURTESY LT REL
	SPARE	
736	BLK/PNK	5V RETURN (GND)
801	BLK/RED	CPS GROUND
705	TAN	5V REFERENCE

GS 0427 Q

BCM CONNECTOR BACK VIEW

FIGURE 7-41 Toronado BCM connector back view. (*Courtesy of Oldsmobile Div. of GMC*)

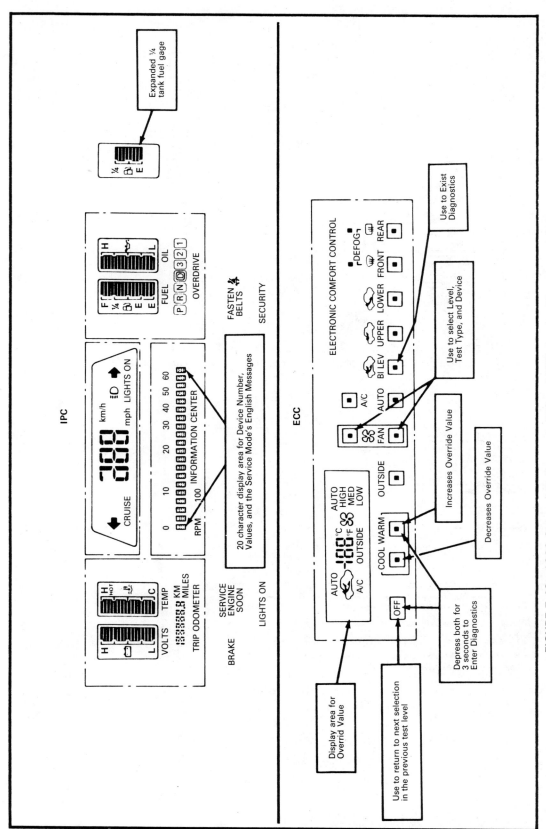

FIGURE 7-42 1986 Oldsmobile Toronado IPC and ECC panels. (*Courtesy of Oldsmobile Div. of GMC*)

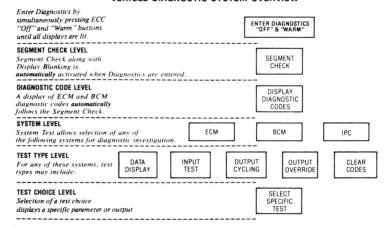

FIGURE 7-43 Systematic procedural check of ECM/BCM self-diagnostic system—Oldsmobile Toronado. (*Courtesy of Oldsmobile Div. of GMC*)

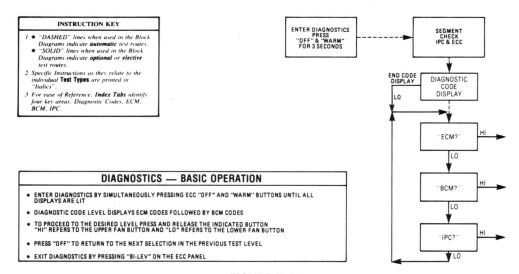

FIGURE 7-44

ECM DIAGNOSTIC CODES

CODE	DESCRIPTION	COMMENTS	CODE	DESCRIPTION	COMMENTS
E013	Open Oxygen Sensor Circuit [Canister Purge]	(A)	E037	MAT (ATS) Sensor Temperature Too High	(A)
E014	Coolant Sensor Temperature Too High	(A)/(F)/(M)	E038	MAT (ATS) Sensor Temperature Too Low	(A)
E015	Coolant Sensor Temperature Too Low	(A)/(F)/(M)	E040	Open Power Steering Pressure Switch Circuit [A/C Clutch]	(A)
E016	System Voltage Out of Range [All Solenoids]	(A)	E041	Cam Sensor Circuit -(C³I)	(A)
E021	Throttle Position Sensor Voltage Too High [TCC]	(A)	E042	Ignition System -(C³I)	(A)/(J)
E022	Throttle Position Sensor Voltage Too Low [TCC]	(A)	E043	ESC System	(A)/(I)
E024	Speed Sensor Circuit [TCC]	(A)	E044	Lean Exhaust Signal	(A)/(I)
E029	Open Fourth Gear Circuit	(A)	E045	Rich Exhaust Signal	(A)
E032	EGR System Fault	(A)	E047	BCM-ECM Communication [A/C Clutch & Cruise]	(A)
E033	MAF Sensor Voltage High	(A)	E051	ECM PROM Error	(A)/(J)/(K)
E034	MAF Sensor Voltage Low	(A)	E052	Calpak Error	(A)
			E055	ECM Error	(A)

DIAGNOSTIC CODE COMMENTS

(A)	"Service Engine Soon" Indicator Lights	(I)	Forces OL Operation
(B)	Displays Diagnostic Message on IPC	(J)	Causes System to Operate on Bypass Spark
(C)	No Indicator Light or Message	(K)	Causes System to Operate on Back-Up Fuel
(D)	Displays "Error" in Season Odometer	(L)	ECC Displays 3 Dashes
(E)	Switches A/C Compressor "OFF", if in AUTO	(M)	Appropriate Segments Flash on IPC
(F)	Forces Cooling Fans On	[ ]	Functions within Bracket are Disengaged While Specified
(G)	Displays "Electrical Problem" on IPC		Malfunction Remains Current
(H)	Disables ECI		

FIGURE 7-45

BCM DIAGNOSTIC CODES

CODE	DESCRIPTION	COMMENTS	CODE	DESCRIPTION	COMMENTS
B110	Outside Air Temperature Circuit	(B)/(H)	B411	Battery Volts Too Low [Cruise]	(B)
B111	A/C High Side Temperature Circuit	(B)	B412	Battery Volts Too High [Cruise]	(B)
B112	A/C Low Side Temperature Circuit [A/C Clutch]	(B)/(E)	B440	Air Mix Door	(B)
B113	In-Car Temperature Circuit	(B)	B445	Compressor Clutch Engagement [A/C Clutch]	(B)/(E)
B115	Sunload Temperature Circuit	(B)	B446	Low A/C Refrigerant Condition Warning	(B)
B118	Door Jam/Ajar Circuit	(C)	B447	Very Low A/C Refrigerant [A/C Clutch]	(B)/(E)
B119	Twilight Sentinel Photosensor Circuit	(C)	B448	Very Low A/C Refrigerant Pressure Condition [A/C Clutch]	(B)/(E)
B120	Twilight Sentinel Delay Pot Circuit	(B)	B449	A/C High Side Temperature Too High [A/C Clutch]	(C)/(E)
B122	Panel Lamp Dimming Pot Circuit	(B)	B450	Coolant Temperature Too High [A/C Clutch]	(C)/(E)
B123	Courtesy Lamps On Circuit	(B)	B552	BCM Memory Reset Indicator	
B124	Speed Sensor Circuit [Cruise]	(H)	B556	BCM EEPROM Error	(D)
B127	PRNDL Sensor Circuit [Cruise]	(M)	B660	Cruise - Transmission Not In Drive [Cruise]	(C)
B131	Oil Pressure Sensor Circuit	(M)	B663	Cruise - Car Speed and Set Speed Difference Too High [Cruise]	(C)
B132	Oil Pressure Sensor Circuit	(M)	B664	Cruise - Car Acceleration Too High [Cruise]	(B)
B334	Loss of ECM Serial Data [Cruise and A/C Clutch]	(A)/(B)/(E)/(G)	B667	Cruise - Cruise Switch Shorted [Cruise]	(B)
B335	Loss of ECC Serial	(B)/(G)/(L)	B671	Cruise - Servo Position Sensor Circuit [Cruise]	(B)
B336	Loss of IPC Serial Data	(B)/(G)	B672	Cruise - Vent Solenoid Circuit [Cruise]	(B)
B337	Loss of Programmer Serial Data [A/C Clutch]	(B)/(E)/(G)	B673	Cruise - Vacuum Solenoid Circuit [Cruise]	(B)
B338	Loss of Voice Serial Data	(B)/(G)			
B409	Generator Detected Condition	(B)			

FIGURE 7-46

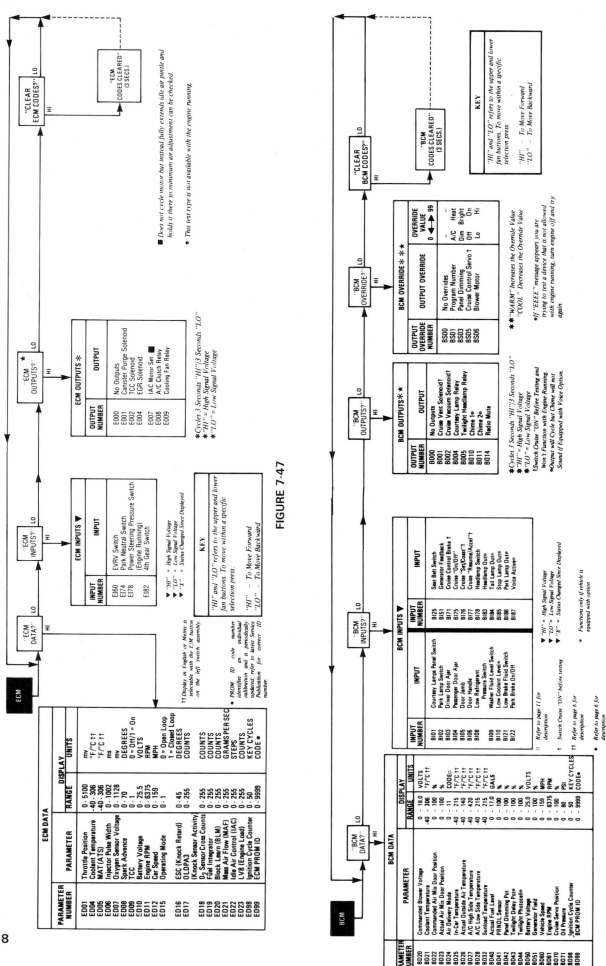

FIGURE 7-47

FIGURE 7-48

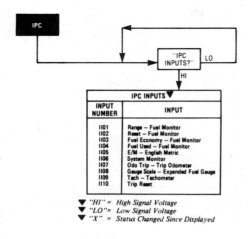

IPC INPUTS ▼	
INPUT NUMBER	**INPUT**
1101	Range – Fuel Monitor
1102	Reset – Fuel Monitor
1103	Fuel Economy – Fuel Monitor
1104	Fuel Used – Fuel Monitor
1105	E/M – English Metric
1106	System Monitor
1107	Odo Trip – Trip Odometer
1108	Gauge Scale – Expanded Fuel Gauge
1109	Tach – Tachometer
1110	Trip Reset

▼ *"HI" = High Signal Voltage*
▼ *"LO"= Low Signal Voltage*
▼ *"X" = Status Changed Since Displayed*

KEY
"HI" and "LO" refers to the upper and lower fan buttons. To move within a specific selection press:
"HI" – To Move Forward
"LO" – To Move Backward

FIGURE 7-49

ABBREVIATIONS					
A/C	Air Conditioning	ECM	Engine Control Module	MAT	Manifold Air Temperature
A/D	Analog to Digital	EEPROM	Electronically Erasable Programmable	MS	Milliseconds
ATS	Air Temperature Sensor		Read Only Memory	MV	Millivolts
BCM	Body Computer Module	EGR	Exhaust Gas Recirculation	O2	Oxygen
BLM	Block Learn Multiplier	ESC	Electronic Spark Control	OL	Open Loop
C3I	Computer Command Control Ignition	EST	Electronic Spark Timing	PROM	Programmable Read Only Memory
CL	Closed Loop	EVRV	Electronic Vacuum Regulator Valve	POT	Potentiometer (Varible Resistor)
ECC	Electronic Climate Control	IAC	Idle Air Control	TCC	Transaxle Converter Clutch
ECCP	Electronic Comfort Control Panel	IPC	Instrument Panel Cluster	TPS	Throttle Position Sensor
ECI	Extended Compressor at Idle	MAF	Mass Air Flow	VF	Vacuum Fluorescent

AIR DELIVERY MODE			
BCM Air Delivery Mode is Parameter BD24 of BCM Data and is displayed as a numerical code as follows:			
CODE NO.	**MODE**	**CODE NO.**	**MODE**
0	Auto-Recirc/Max A/C	6	Normal Purge
1	Auto-A/C (Vents)	7	Cold Purge
2	Auto-Bi-Level	8	Defog
3	Auto-HTR-DEF	9	Forced Lower
4	Auto-Max Heat	10	Forced Upper
5	Off	11	Forced Bi-Level

TEMPERATURE CONVERSION							
°C	°F	°C	°F	°C	°F	°C	°F
– 40	– 40	25	77	75	167	140	284
– 30	– 22	30	86	80	176	150	302
– 20	– 4	35	95	85	185	160	320
– 10	14	40	104	90	194	170	338
– 5	23	45	113	95	203	180	356
0	32	50	122	100	212	190	374
5	41	55	131	105	221	200	392
10	50	60	140	110	230	210	410
15	59	65	149	120	248	215	419
20	68	70	158	130	266		

FIGURE 7-50

physical location of both the ECM and BCM will vary slightly among GMC division vehicles, but generally these items can be found under the instrument panel on the passenger side.

Figure 7-51 illustrates the ECM location for A and X series GMC division vehicles. Identification of A and X model vehicles can be determined by referring to Fig. 7-1. Figure 7-6 (Item 11) shows the location of the ECM on the Oldsmobile Toronado, which is an E body vehicle. The Buick Riviera and the Cadillac Eldorado are equipped with the ECM in a similar location. When so equipped, the BCM is located in the same general area. (See Fig. 7-6, Item 9 and 11.) In order to allow one model of ECM to be used for many different cars, a device called a calibrator or PROM (programmable read only memory) chip is used.

If an ECM or BCM code indicates that there is an ECM or ECM/PROM error after initiating the computer diagnostic check, then either the PROM must be removed and replaced, or if the problem lies with the ECM itself, then a new ECM has to be installed.

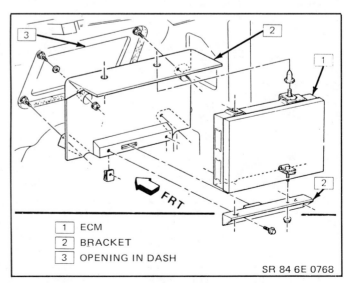

1	ECM
2	BRACKET
3	OPENING IN DASH

SR 84 6E 0768

FIGURE 7-51 ECM location, A and X series vehicles. (*Courtesy of Oldsmobile Div. of GMC*)

CAUTION: PROM units should *never* be interchanged among different vehicles since each PROM has specific information on that vehicle's weight, engine, transmission, axle ratio, and other assorted components.

Inserting the wrong PROM into an ECM can result not only in poor vehicle performance but also in possible computer damage. When a new replacement service ECM is ordered, it is necessary to remove the PROM unit as well as the CALPAK unit, which is used on some model vehicles. These units must be inserted into the replacement ECM, which does not come equipped with either the PROM or CALPAK.

The CALPAK shown in Fig. 7-55 allows a programmed substitution engine fuel control when a signal loss from the crankshaft and camshaft sensors is lost to the ECM, or other parts of the ECM are damaged. If the CALPAK is missing, it will result in a "no start" and run condition. On the 1986 Oldsmobile Toronado, for example, if the CALPAK is missing from the ECM, then a Code EO52 is set into the ECM memory. If there was a PROM error, a Code EO51 would have been set, while an ECM error would have triggered a Code EO55.

From earlier information describing "how to access" the stored trouble codes from memory, you will recall that upscale vehicles flash the trouble codes directly onto the instrument panel, while lower scale vehicles employ the ALDL (assembly line diagnostic link) which, when activated, causes the *Check Engine Light* to illuminate on and off to indicate the actual trouble code.

FBC (feedback carburetor) engines are equipped with a RTLD (remote trouble lamp driver) as shown in Fig. 7-52. This is a small circuit board located in a plastic holder taped to the harness near the ECM. The RTLD turns the *Check Engine* light on any time that the ignition key is on and the ECM is not pulling terminal C of the lamp driver to ground. This normally occurs with the ignition on and the engine not running. The main advantage of the RTLD is the *Check Engine* light will come on to indicate a fault if the ECM loses power.

If the self-diagnostic or ALDL test confirms that there is an ECM problem, you should always first doublecheck to ensure that the ECM and the PROM are the correct ones for that vehicle. In addition, when a Code 51 (PROM problem) is confirmed, check the PROM installation for bent pins, or pins not fully seated in the socket. If this check confirms that the PROM was in fact installed correctly and a Code 51 is still retained in memory, then replace the PROM. The procedure for changeout of both the PROM and the CALPAK is described below.

CAUTION: Always ensure that the ignition key is in the off/lock position when disconnecting/connecting battery power to the ECM. Follow this procedure not only when using the battery cables, but also for the ECM pigtail, the ECM fuse, or even when using booster cables to start an engine.

NOTE: Should it become necessary to replace the original factory installed ECM with a service replacement assembly and in order to ensure that positive identification of ECM parts will always be possible throughout the life of the vehicle, always transfer the *broadcast* code and original factory installed ECM production number onto the replacement ECM cover. *Do not,* however, record this number on the ECM cover with an electric marking pencil or by any other means.

ECM Replacement Procedure

1. Ignition off; disconnect negative battery cable.
2. Locate the ECM on the vehicle, which is usually found either under the instrument panel lower hush panel or the right-hand hush panel.
3. Refer to Fig. 7-53 and remove the connectors from the ECM.
4. Remove the ECM mounting hardware.
5. Carefully remove the ECM from the passenger compartment.
6. Refer to Fig. 7-53, Item 3, and remove the access cover.
7. Refer to Fig. 7-54 and remove the PROM assembly with the "special tool." (First read the Caution stated below.) Gently engage the hook-end of the tool with the PROM carrier, as is shown in Fig. 7-54. Applying gentle pressure to the vertical bar end of the tool, rock

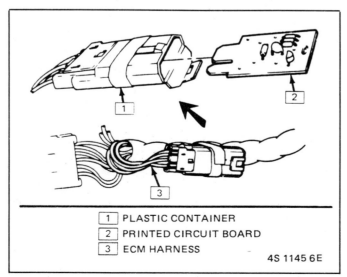

1	PLASTIC CONTAINER
2	PRINTED CIRCUIT BOARD
3	ECM HARNESS

4S 1145 6E

FIGURE 7-52 FBC remote lamp driver printed circuit board. (*Courtesy of Oldsmobile Div. of GMC*)

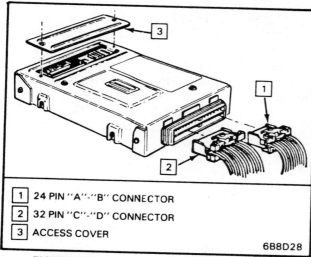

1 | 24 PIN "A"-"B" CONNECTOR
2 | 32 PIN "C"-"D" CONNECTOR
3 | ACCESS COVER

6B8D28

FIGURE 7-53 ECM access covers and connectors. (*Courtesy of Oldsmobile Div. of GMC*)

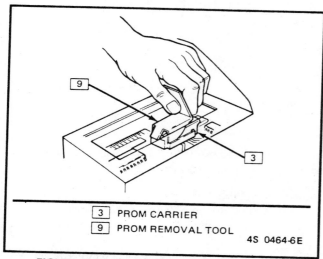

3 | PROM CARRIER
9 | PROM REMOVAL TOOL

4S 0464-6E

FIGURE 7-54 PROM removal tool. (*Courtesy of Oldsmobile Div. of GMC*)

back and forward on the engaged end of the tool until the PROM carrier comes up as far as possible. Switch to the other end of the PROM carrier with the tool, and repeat the same procedure. It may be necessary to switch back and forward to each end of the PROM carrier until it is free of the PROM socket. Then remove the PROM carrier with the PROM that is in it away from the PROM socket.

CAUTION: Exercise extreme care when attempting to remove the PROM or CALPAK unit from the ECM, and use only the special tool shown as Item 9 in Fig. 7-54. Do not exert undue force to pop the PROM unit out of the socket holder. Clean, dry hands are an important part of this ser-

vice procedure, with some manufacturers suggesting that clean cotton gloves be worn during PROM removal and installation to avoid static electricity from the human body coming into contact with the PROM unit.

8. Refer to Figs. 7-55 and 7-56, and remove the CALPAK assembly in the same basic manner that was used for the PROM.

PROM/CALPAK INSTALLATION

The installation procedure for both the PROM and CALPAK is the same. Prior to installing either the PROM or the CALPAK unit into the ECM, check the pins to make sure that they are not bent. If they are, extreme caution must be exercised in attempting to straighten them. Any sign of a cracked or broken pin is sufficient reason to replace

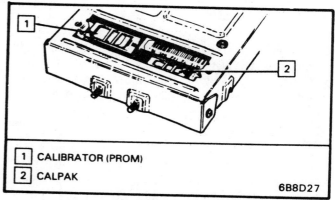

1 | CALIBRATOR (PROM)
2 | CALPAK

6B8D27

FIGURE 7-55 PROM and CALPAK location. (*Courtesy of Oldsmobile Div. of GMC*)

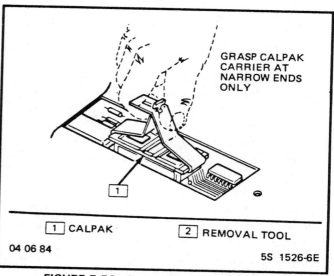

GRASP CALPAK CARRIER AT NARROW ENDS ONLY

1 | CALPAK   2 | REMOVAL TOOL

04 06 84

5S 1526-6E

FIGURE 7-56 Removing the CALPAK. (*Courtesy of Oldsmobile Div. of GMC*)

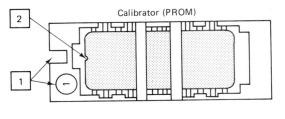

Calibrator (PROM)

| 1 | Carrier locator notch and circle |
| 2 | Calibrator (PROM) locator notch |

6B8D26

FIGURE 7-57 PROM and carrier locator notch. (*Courtesy of Oldsmobile Div. of GMC*)

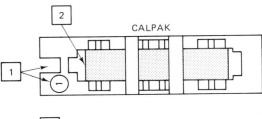

CALPAK

| 1 | Carrier locator notch and circle |
| 2 | CALPAK locator dot |

6B8D25

FIGURE 7-58 CALPAK and carrier locator notch. (*Courtesy of Oldsmobile Div. of GMC*)

the unit with a new one. If a new **PROM** or **CALPAK** is required, be sure that the replacement unit has the same part number as the old one. Remember, **PROM**'s are designed to suit a particular weight of vehicle, engine, transmission, axle ratio, etc.

Procedure

NOTE: The PROM and CALPAK both have a female ''locator notch'' as shown in Figs. 7-57 and 7-58. Before attempting to install either of these units, check the ECM so that you are aware of where the matching male prong is. If these units are installed backwards, they will be immediately damaged and will require replacement. Also, if the ignition switch is turned on with the PROM unit installed backwards, its circuitry will be destroyed immediately.

1. Carefully blow out any dust or dirt that may be present in the PROM or CALPAK mounting bores. Ensure that there are no signs of damage.

2. Gently position the PROM or CALPAK unit over its matching ECM so that the matching notches are in alignment.

3. Apply firm but careful pressure to the PROM or CAL-PAK ''carrier only'' until it is firmly and fully seated in its socket.

4. Replace the access cover back onto the ECM.

5. Replace the ECM assembly back into its mounting position.

6. Before attaching the ECM connectors, make sure that the ignition key is off and that the battery negative cable

is disconnected. Then snap the connectors into position.

7. Replace the necessary ECM protective hush panel.

8. With the ignition key off, reconnect the negative battery cable.

Checkout Procedure

To functionally test that the PROM replacement service has been successful, proceed as follows:

1. Turn the ignition key on.

2. Initiate the self-diagnostic procedure check by:
   (a) Using a jumper wire between the ALDL terminals,
   (b) Depressing the off and warmer buttons on the ECC panel.
   Refer to the detailed procedure for this self-diagnostic check described earlier.

3. If the PROM has been installed correctly with no damage, then the information displayed on the IPC should read ''no ECM codes.'' Similarly, on an ALDL system, a Code 12 indicates there are no codes stored in memory.

4. However, if a Code 51 occurs or if the *Service Engine Soon or Now* light is on continually with no codes set, the problem can be traced to one of the following conditions:
   (a) The PROM has been installed backwards. (If so it is now damaged beyond repair and must be replaced.)
   (b) The PROM is not fully seated.
   (c) The PROM pins are bent, cracked, or damaged.
   (d) The PROM is malfunctioning.

TOOLS NEEDED TO SERVICE THE SYSTEM

A tachometer, test light, ohmmeter, digital voltmeter with 10 megohms impedance (J34029-A-), vacuum gage and jumper wires are required foir diagnosis. A test light or voltmeter must be used when specified in the procedures. They must NOT be interchanged.

SPECIAL TOOLS

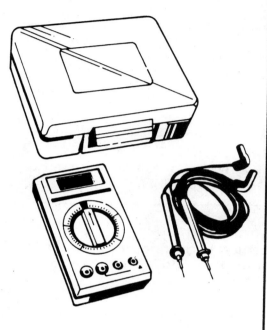

HIGH IMPEDANCE MULTIMETER
(DIGITAL VOLTMETER-DVM)
J34029-A

VOLTMETER - Voltage Position Measures amount of voltage. When connected in parallel to an existing circuit. A digital voltmeter with 10 meg ohm input impedence is used because some circuits require accurate low voltage readings, and some circuits in the ECM have a very high resistance.

AMMETER - When used as ammeter, this meter also accurately measures extremely low current flow. Refer to meter instructions for more information.
- Selector must be set properly for both function and range. DC is used for most automotive measurements.

OHMMETER - Measures resistance of circuit directly in ohms. Refer to meter for more information.
- OL Display in all ranges indicates open circuit.
- Zero display in all ranges indicates a short circuit.
- Intermittent connection in circuit may be indicated by digital reading that will not stabilize on circuit.
- Range Switch.
  - 200Ω – Reads ohms directly
  - 2K,20K,200KΩ – Reads ohms in thousands
  - 2M and 20MΩ - Reads ohms in millions

J23738

VACUUM PUMP (20 IN. HG. MINIMUM)
Use gage to monitor manifold engine vacuum and check vacuum sensors, solenoids and valves with hand pump.

UNPOWERED TEST LIGHT
Used to check wiring for complete circuit and short to ground or voltage. Connect lead to good ground. Probe with test prod to connector or component terminal. Bulb will light if voltage is present.

TACHOMETER
Use inductive trigger signal pickup type.

(continued)

GS 0494 O

FIGURE 7-59 Special tools and equipment. (*Courtesy of Oldsmobile Div. of GMC*)

SPECIAL TOOLS

J26792/BT7220-1	**SPARK TESTER** Use to check available secondary ignition voltage . Also called ST125.
J36101	**MASS AIR FLOW (MAF) SENSOR TESTER** Used for static test of MAF Sensor on vehicle.
J36179	**CRANKSHAFT SENSOR ALIGNMENT TOOL (C3I SYSTEMS)** Used to properly align crank or combination sensor to harmonic balancer interrupter.
J35616	**CONNECTOR TEST ADAPTER KIT** Used to make electrical test connections in current Weather Pack, Metri - Pack and Micro-Pack style terminals.
J34636	**CIRCUIT TESTER** Used to check all relays and solenoids before connecting them to a new ECM. Measures the circuit resistance and indicates pass or fail via green or red LED. Amber LED indicates current polarity. Can also be used as a non-powered continuity checker.
J28687-A/BT8220	**OIL PRESSURE TRANSDUCER WRENCH** Used to remove or install oil pressure transducer on engine.
J35689	**METRI-PACK TERMINAL REMOVER** Used to remove 150 series Metri-Pack "pull-to-seat" terminals from connectors. Refer to wiring harness service for removal procedure.
J28742/BT8234-A	**WEATHER PACK TERMINAL REMOVER** Used to remove Terminals from Weather Pack connectors. Refer to wiring harness service for removal procedure.
J33095/BT8234-A	**ECM CONNECTOR TERMINAL REMOVER** Used to remove terminal from Micro-Pack connectors. Refer to wiring harness service for removal procedure. GS 0494 O

SPECIAL TOOLS

J29533A/BT8127	**OXYGEN SENSOR WRENCH** Used to remove or install the oxygen sensor.
J33031/BT8130	**IDLE AIR CONTROL WRENCH** Used to remove or install IAC valve on throttle body.
J34730-A	**PORT FUEL INJECTION DIAGNOSTIC KIT** Used to diagnosis and service port fuel injection systems. The kit includes: • Fuel Pressure Gage - to check fuel pump pressure and compare injector pressure drop for equal fuel distribution. • Test Light - to check electrical impulses to an injector. • Injector Tester - top evaluate each injector's pressure drop using pressure gage.
J34730-1	**FUEL PRESSURE GAGE** Used to check and monitor fuel line pressure of port fuel system. Part of Diagnostic Kit J34730-A
J34730-2	**INJECTOR TEST LIGHT** Used to check port fuel injector signal from ECM. Part of Diagnostic Kit J34730-A
J34730-3	**INJECTOR TESTER** Used to perform injector balance trest in CHART C-2A. Part of Diagnostic Kit J34730-A.

3-27-86
GS 0494 O

CHAPTER 8

♦

Ford EEC Systems

The words EEC and MCU are synonomous with Ford Motor Company produced vehicles. The EEC (electronic engine control) is a computer-directed system of engine control that has progressed from the model EEC-1 to the current EEC-IV system. These systems can be described as follows:

1. *EEC 1:* Designed to control engine spark timing.
2. *EEC 11:* Designed to control both engine ignition timing and fuel systems fitted with a FBC (feedback carburetor).
3. *EEC 111:* Feedback carburetor descendant of EEC 11.
4. *EEC 111-CFI:* CFI (central fuel injection—throttle body type) controls engine ignition timing and fuel distribution with EFI (electronic fuel injection).
5. *EEC 1V:* Is a descendant of the EEC 111 with a FBC, CFI, and EFI control system, and is designed to control the air/fuel ratio system, the ignition system, and, with these subsystems working together, the exhaust emissions.

EFI designates that the engine is equipped with a multiport fuel-injection system. CFI (central fuel injection) indicates that the engine is equipped with throttle body injection, which usually consists of two electronically controlled injectors, while port injection systems have one injector per cylinder. (See Chapter 5 for more detail on these types of systems.) Other common terms related to Ford systems are the following:

The ECA (electronic control assembly), is a vehicle computer consisting of a calibration assembly containing the computer memory and thus its control program and a processor assembly, which is the computer hardware. The calibration assembly plugs into the microprocessor, which in turn is connected to the vehicle wiring harness.

The MCU (microprocessor control unit) is an integral part of the electronically-controlled feedback carburetor system, which uses a TWC (three-way catalyst) exhaust system. Various engine sensors monitor mode conditions with the MCU system, as they do with the ECA or EEC systems.

The center of the EEC-1V system is the ECA, which continually receives information via voltage signals from all of the engine/vehicle sensors, relays, and switches. Along with this information and the operation program (PROM) in the ECA's memory, the ECA generates output voltage signals to control various relays, solenoids, and other actuators for engine operation. The processor samples input data and performs output control several times a second. The calibration assembly of the ECA is a permanent memory device (both ROM and PROM). Figure 8-1 illustrates the ECA used with the EEC-1V system.

The ECA in the EEC-1V system is a microprocessor similar to that found in other Ford EEC systems, with the one significant difference being that in this ECA unit, the calibration module is located internally within the ECA assembly rather than externally as in the EEC-111 system. (See Fig. 8-2.)

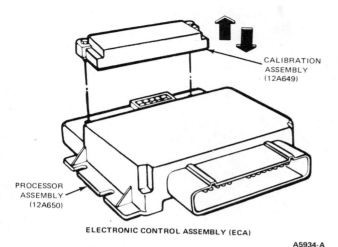

FIGURE 8-1 EEC 111 ECA Unit with external calibration unit. (*Courtesy of Ford Motor Company, Dearborn, MI.*)

The actual location of the ECA will vary among different model Ford vehicles. On the Thunderbird, for example, the ECA is located in the passenger compartment under the dash on the right-hand kick panel, while on the Mustang and Capri, the ECA is mounted under the front passenger seat.

ECA INPUTS AND OUTPUTS

An example of the various inputs and outputs to the ECA microprocessor for both the 2.3L EFI (port fuel injected) engine as well as for the 3.8L CFI (throttle body injected)

engine is illustrated in Figs. 8-3 and 8-4. The actual location of the various sensors for the 1.6/2.3L EFI engines as well as the 3.8L V6 engine can be seen in Figs. 8-5 and 8-6.

IMPORTANT SERVICING PRECAUTION: Before performing any type of service on electronic systems or IC's (integrated circuits), you *must* discharge yourself of static electricity or ESD (electrostatic discharge) by touching a good vehicle ground, such as the door post or vehicle shift lever. Failure to do so can result in damage to voltage sensitive electronic components. If, for any reason, you leave the vehicle during servicing, after re-entering to continue work, you *must* again ground yourself of ESD in order to drain any static electrical charge. Also, if you are performing control head/radio type checks on a new vehicle, remove the plastic seat covers, since they increase the possibility of creating a static charge.

SYSTEM DIAGNOSIS—SPECIAL TOOLING

Accessing the ECA system memory and withdrawing the various trouble codes can be accomplished in three ways:

1. By using an analog volt-ohmmeter (VOM) with a 0 to 20v d.c. scale.

2. By using a Rotunda STAR (Self-test Automatic Readout) tester instrument, Part Number 07-0004, with its cable assembly P/N 07-0010.

3. By using a Kent-Moore or OTC Monitor 2000 test instrument or a digital automotive systems "Conquest" tester.

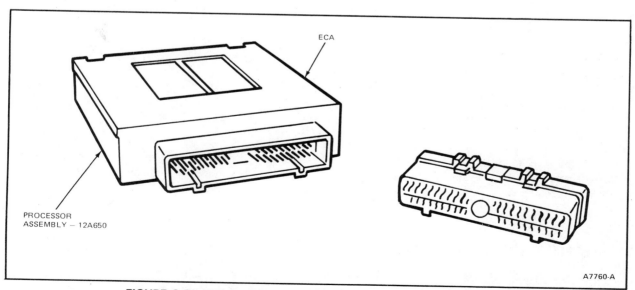

FIGURE 8-2 EEC-1V ECA Unit with internal calibration unit. (*Courtesy of Ford Motor Company, Dearborn, MI.*)

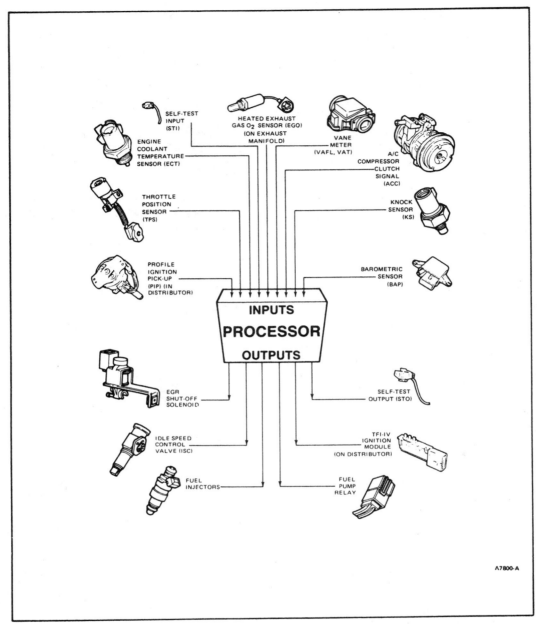

FIGURE 8-3 ECA system inputs/outputs for the 2.3L EFI TC engines.
(*Courtesy of Ford Motor Company, Dearborn, MI.*)

NOTE: Tools noted in Items 1 and 2 are illustrated at the end of this chapter, while tools in Item 3 can be found in Chapter 14 of this textbook.

QUICK TEST LISTING PROCEDURE

The sequence for a "quick test" of the EEC-1V system is the same for all vehicles regardless of the engine size and whether it is a FBC system or a fuel-injected system of CFI or EFI design. The functional test of the EEC-1V system requires that the following steps be followed in sequence to prevent the possibility of misdiagnosis or the replacement of nonfaulty components.

Quick Test Steps

1. Always conduct a visual check of the engine compartment and wiring harnesses and connections for signs of apparent damage just as you would on an engine/vehicle that is not equipped with an electronic control system.

2. Equipment hookup prior to initiating the test.

3. Service codes. Note if they are fast codes, engine identification codes, engine service codes, continuous codes.

4. Ignition key on, engine off test, which allows a static check of the microprocessor inputs and outputs.

5. Continuous self-test to check the sensor inputs for opens and shorts while the vehicle is in actual operation.

NOTE: An "open" is defined as any resistance reading greater than 5 ohms, unless otherwise specified by the manufacturer. A "short" is defined as any resistance reading less than 10,000 ohms to ground, unless otherwise specified by the manufacturer.

6. Output cycling test allows the processor to activate all outputs when the throttle is cycled for additional diagnostics.

7. Computed timing check verifies that the ignition system is able to maintain a "fixed spark timing" during the self-test.

8. Engine running self-test, which is a dynamic procedural check to test all of the sensors and actuators under actual operating conditions.

9. A wiggle test of all wires during testing to ensure that there is not a poor connection or fault at a snap-in harness connector or wire.

10. Pinpoint routine requires a systematic check of a suspected area to confirm exactly where the problem lies.

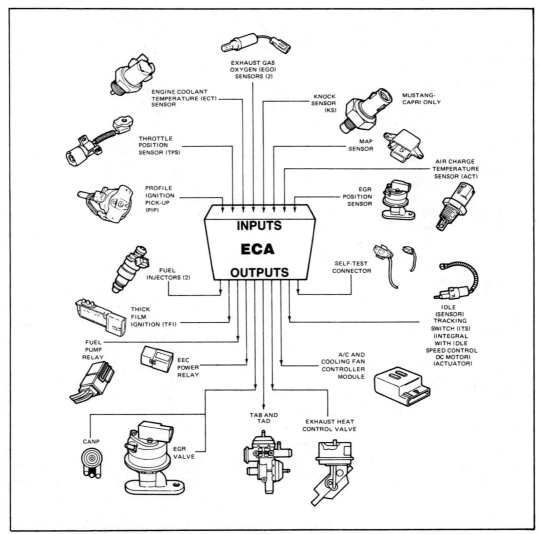

FIGURE 8-4 ECA system inputs/outputs for the 3.8L V6 CFI engines. (*Courtesy of Ford Motor Company, Dearborn, MI.*)

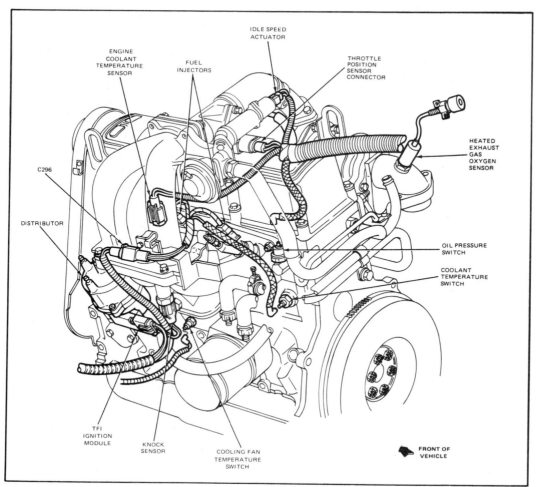

FIGURE 8-5   Sensor location, 1.6L/2.3L EFI engines. (*Courtesy of Ford Motor Company, Dearborn, MI.*)

SELF-TEST DESCRIPTION

The EEC system is capable of self-diagnosing once the system has been activated by the mechanic/technician, just as other such systems do on most electronically equipped vehicles produced today. The microprocessor stores the self-test program in its permanent memory or ROM/PROM system.

When the self-test system is activated, it checks the EEC-1V system by testing its memory integrity and processing capability, and verifies that various sensors and actuators are connected and operating properly. The self-test activation on the EEC system is basically divided into three distinct and specialized test procedures, which are:

1. Ignition key on, engine off test.
2. Engine running test.
3. Continuous testing.

This self-testing process by the EEC system microprocessor is not an all-encompassing test by itself. Although the system can direct you to a particular problem area by reference to a trouble code number, you then have to systematically pinpoint the specific problem with a follow-up sequence of tests to confirm component failure, be it in the sensor, a switch, an actuator, wiring, or the ECA system itself. This self-test procedure by the microprocessor is part of what is commonly referred to as a "Quick Test" diagnostic procedure.

NOTE: Intermittent versus continuous faults indicate whether the problem existed prior to the self-test. If it did, then this is commonly referred to as a "hard fault," since continuous testing is an on-going test. It's done by the microprocessor, which stores fault information for retrieval at any time that the self-test is initiated.

If however the fault is intermittent and it is not repeated

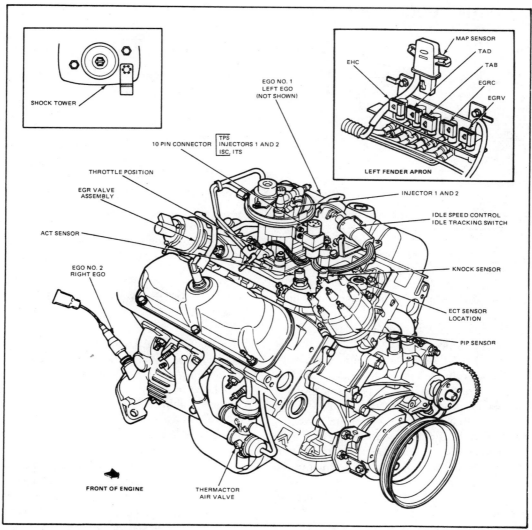

FIGURE 8-6 Sensor location, 3.8L V6 CFI engine. (*Courtesy of Ford Motor Company, Dearborn, MI.*)

on a regular basis, then it may not appear in memory. During the key on, engine off, and engine running tests, these are functional tests which are only detected and present at the time of the self-test procedure.

SERVICE-CODE ACCESS OPTIONS

The service or trouble codes for the system are two-digit numbers representing the results of the self-test procedure. The codes have been activated from the memory system of the EEC-1V ECA, which communicates service information either to the analog volt-ohmmeter, the Rotunda STAR tester, the Kent-Moore or OTC Monitor 2000 unit, or to the digital automotive systems ''Conquest'' monitor. Regardless of the test instrument used to access these service

trouble codes, the ECA outputs them in the form of timed pulses.

This pulse format can best be described by referring to Figs. 8-7 and 8-8, which illustrate clearly the time interval between voltage pulse signals for the two typical test sequences called for by Ford Motor Company.

When using an analog volt-ohmmeter, each voltage pulse will reflect itself as one sweep of the needle across the dial face of the gauge. If using the Rotunda STAR tester or similar digital test instrument, a code number as shown will flash on the readout scale of the meter.

It is infinitely harder to determine trouble codes when you use an analog volt-ohmmeter rather than a STAR tester or one of the other available test instruments which flash an actual trouble code number, since the pulses occur rather quickly across the dial face of the voltmeter. Reference to

SELF-TEST OUTPUT CODE FORMAT*
KEY ON, ENGINE OFF

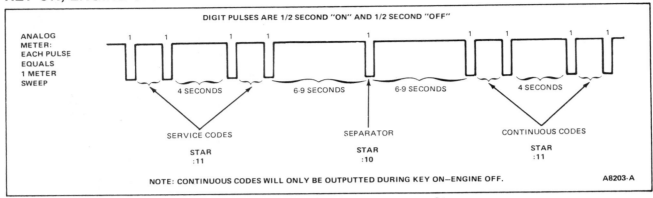

FIGURE 8-7   Key on, engine off self-test output code format. (*Courtesy of Ford Motor Company, Dearborn, MI.*)

Fig. 8-9 may help you to interpret this function a little easier.

As stated earlier, the service trouble codes are represented by a two-digit number such as 2-3 (23), which is easily interpreted on the STAR tester or equivalent instrument. When using the voltmeter method, the 2-3 would be interpreted by watching for two needle pulses or sweeps; then, after a two-second pause, the needle will pulse (sweep) three more times. Continuous testing codes are separated from the functional codes by a six-second delay, a half-second sweep, and another six-second delay, and are produced on the voltmeter dial face in the same manner as the functional codes.

Figure 8-10 illustrates the hookup required when using an analog volt-ohmmeter, as well as the Rotunda STAR tester. In both cases the self-test connector is located in the engine compartment and can be seen in the vehicle electrical schematic as the VIP (vehicle in process) connector.

USING ROTUNDA STAR TESTER OR EQUIVALENT

If a Rotunda STAR (self-test automatic readout) tester or equivalent is readily available, the self-test procedure will be accomplished much more quickly and easily than it would be by using an analog volt-ohmmeter, such as was described above.

The STAR tester can be seen under special tools at the end of this chapter, while the other special tools and equipment are illustrated in Chapter 14 of this text. Figure 8-10 illustrates the hookup required to connect the STAR tester as well as the analog volt-ohmmeter. In both cases the hookup is to the self-test connector located in the engine compartment and identified as the VIP (vehicle in process) connector, as is shown in each of the electrical diagrams for both the 1.6L/2.3L EFI engines as well as the 3.8L CFI engine, respectively in Figs. 8-11, 8-12, and 8-13.

SELF-TEST OUTPUT CODE FORMAT*
KEY ON, ENGINE RUNNING

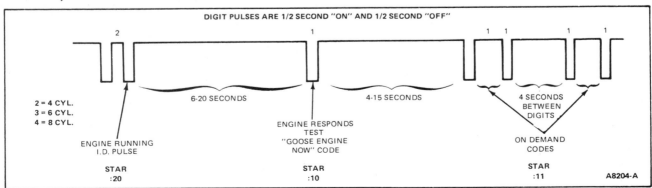

FIGURE 8-8   Key on, engine running self-test output code format. (*Courtesy of Ford Motor Company, Dearborn, MI.*)

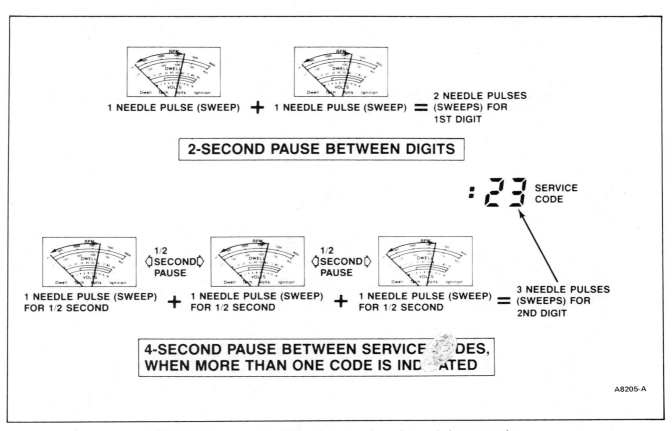

FIGURE 8-9 Analog voltmeter functional service code interpretation. (*Courtesy of Ford Motor Company, Dearborn, MI.*)

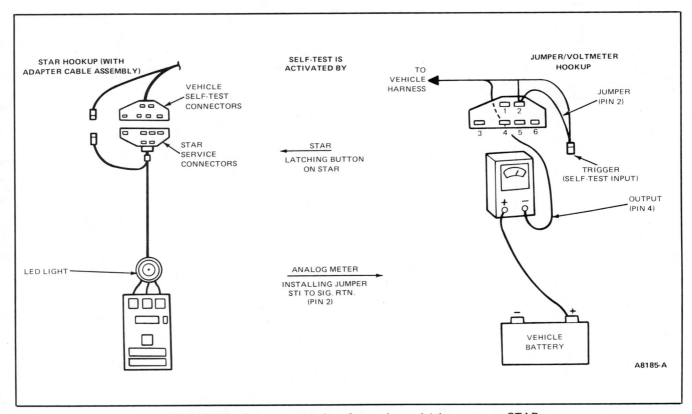

FIGURE 8-10 Quick test hookup for analog volt/ohmmeter or STAR tester. (*Courtesy of Ford Motor Company, Dearborn, MI.*)

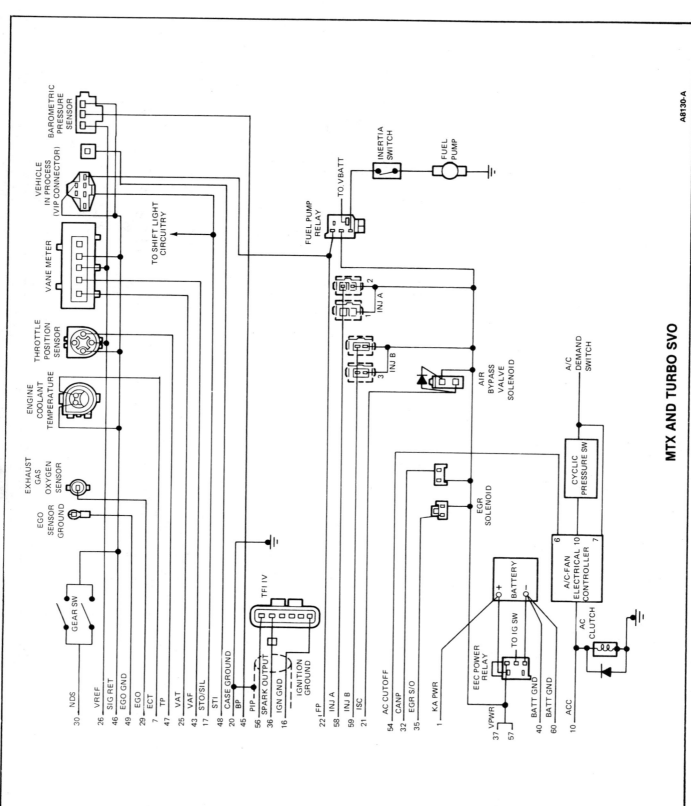

FIGURE 8-11 Electrical schematic for 1.6L EFI T/C engine with manual transaxle and turbo SVO. (*Courtesy of Ford Motor Company, Dearborn, MI.*)

MTX AND TURBO SVO

A8130-A

234

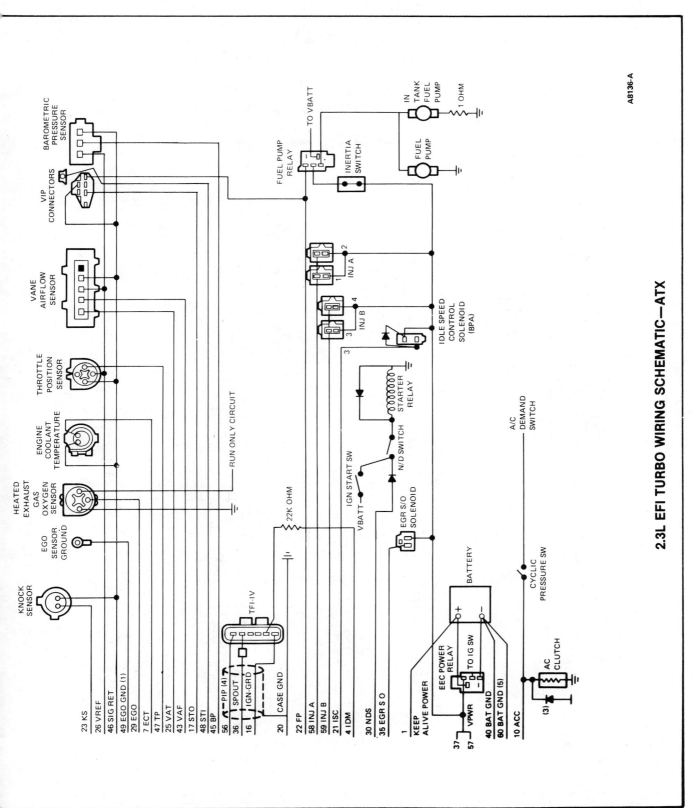

FIGURE 8-12 Electrical schematic for 2.3L EFI turbo SVO vehicle with automatic transaxle. (*Courtesy of Ford Motor Company, Dearborn, MI.*)

2.3L EFI TURBO WIRING SCHEMATIC—ATX

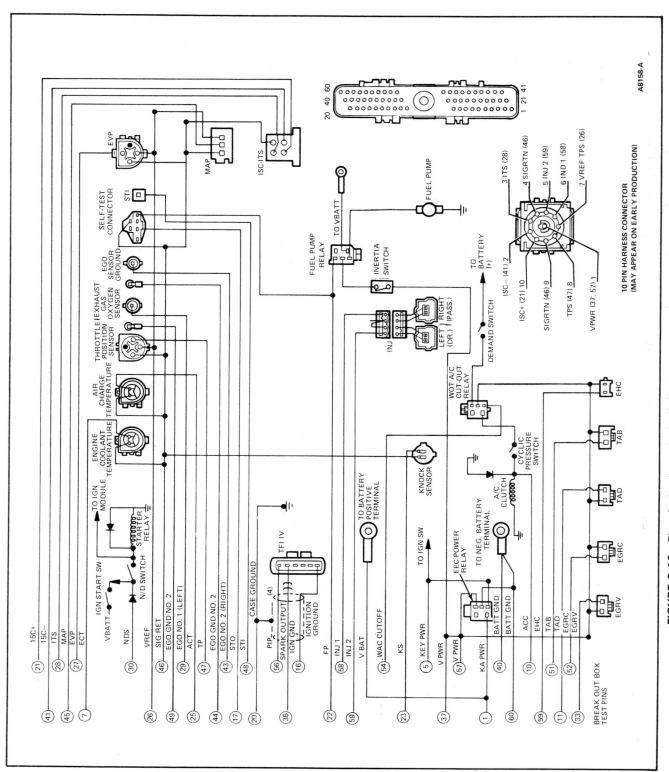

FIGURE 8-13 Electrical schematic for 3.8L V6 CFI vehicle. (*Courtesy of Ford Motor Company, Dearborn, MI.*)

NOTE: Minor variations exist among the vehicle electrical schematics (wiring diagrams) for various models of Ford cars, as well as for different cars of the same model. These variations are dependent upon the size of engine the cars use, and whether or not the vehicles are fitted with a standard or automatic transmission or transaxle. These differences do not, however, create any change to the procedure and systematic checks required to self-test the system.

Reading STAR Tester Codes

When the STAR tester is hooked up to the vehicle self-test connector (Fig. 8-10) and the on switch is depressed, the tester will automatically proceed into a system check and the numerals "88" will begin to flash in the display window, as shown in Fig. 8-14.

Shortly after the number 88 has flashed, the system will resort to a "nonflashing" 00, which signifies that the STAR tester is ready to begin self-test and interpret the stored service codes. In order to withdraw stored service codes, a "colon" (Fig. 8-14) must be displayed, which is achieved by pressing down the pushbutton at the front of the tester until it latches down. Should the LO BAT indicator glow steadily at any time during testing, turn STAR tester's power switch off and replace the 9 volt battery inside the tester.

The following information describes the various checks and tests that can be performed by the STAR tester or an analog volt-ohmmeter:

1. Key on, Engine off
2. Fast codes (factory checkout only)
3. Separator pulse
4. Continuous codes
5. Engine running test
6. Engine identification codes
7. Dynamic response check
8. Continuous monitor test
9. Output state check

A more detailed explanation of the nine tests listed above follows:

1. *Key on, Engine off:* In order for the self-test actually to detect errors during this procedure, the fault must be present at the time of testing. For intermittent faults, refer to the continuous testing procedure. Figure 8-15 illustrates the codes that would be apparent on both the STAR tester and the analog volt-ohmmeter. A fault is indicated when the STAR LED (light emitting diode) turns off or VOM deflection is 10.5 volts or greater.

2. *Fast Codes:* The STAR tester has been designed to disregard these codes, although some test instruments available from tool suppliers can detect these fast codes as a short burst of information (slight meter needle deflection). These codes are used mainly for final vehicle assembly line checks, similar to checks used with the ALDL hookup on GMC vehicles. They therefore serve no useful purpose for the technician in the field and can be disregarded.

   Although fast codes contain the same information as the regular service codes, they always appear before the regular display. They are called fast codes because they are transmitted 100 times faster than the normal rate. (See Fig. 8-16.)

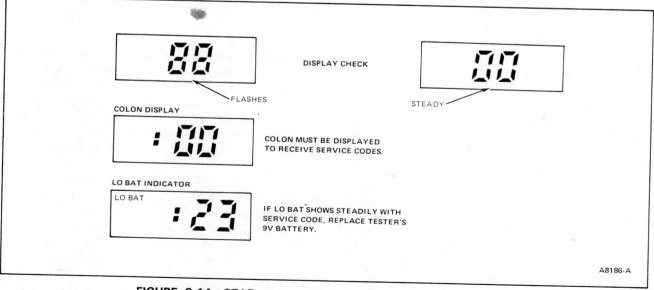

FIGURE 8-14 STAR tester self-test output code display format. (*Courtesy of Ford Motor Company, Dearborn, MI.*)

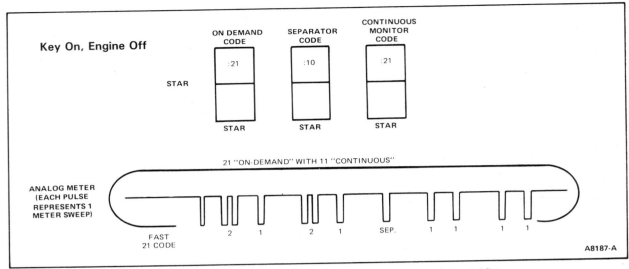

FIGURE 8-15   Key on, engine off format. (*Courtesy of Ford Motor Company, Dearborn, MI.*)

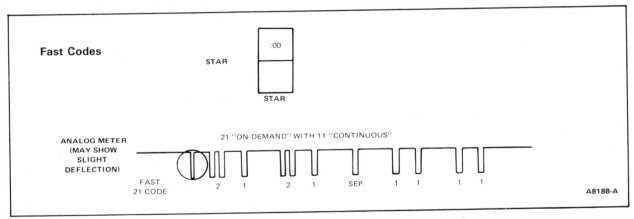

FIGURE 8-16   Fast codes format. (*Courtesy of Ford Motor Company, Dearborn, MI.*)

3. *Separator Pulse:* Approximately 6–9 seconds after the last functional test code (key on, engine off) has been flashed, a single half-second separator pulse is issued. After another 6–9 seconds, continuous codes will then be pulsed to the STAR tester, the analog volt-ohmmeter, or other similar test instruments. Figure 8-17 illustrates the STAR code as well as the reaction at the analog volt-ohmmeter needle.

4. *Continuous Codes:* During normal vehicle operation, the ECA or microprocessor is continually monitoring the various sensed systems. Hard codes, which are failures that are detected during this time, are stored in memory and will be displayed to the technician during the key on, engine off testing and after the separator code format. An example of the STAR code and the analog volt-ohmmeter display for continuous codes is shown in Fig. 8-18.

5. *Engine Running Test:* As the name implies, this test is one which involves starting and running the engine in order to allow all the EEC-1V system sensors to be checked in a mode that represents an engine at normal operating temperature. In addition, the various actuators are also checked during this test. Figure 8-19 illustrates typical STAR tester and analog volt-ohmmeter results. A system fault is indicated when the STAR LED (light emitting diode) turns off or the VOM is 10.5 volts or greater.

6. *Engine ID (identification) Codes:* In order to verify that the correct microprocessor is installed for the vehicle/engine combination and that the self-test has been entered, engine ID codes are displayed at the start of the "engine running test." These displays consist of one digit numbers only and are represented by the number of pulses sent out. The engine ID codes are equal to

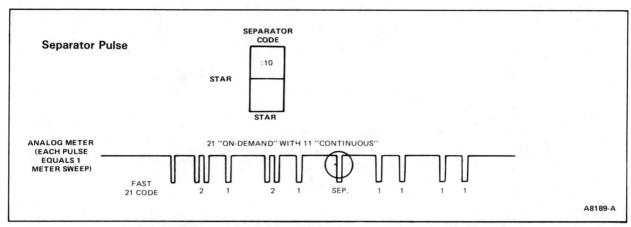

FIGURE 8-17 Separator pulse format. (*Courtesy of Ford Motor Company, Dearborn, MI.*)

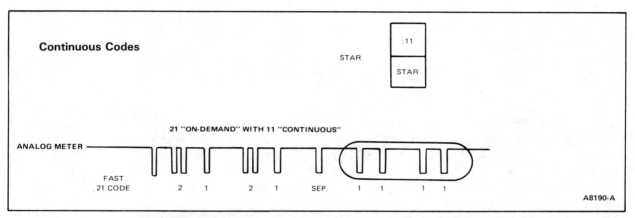

FIGURE 8-18 Continuous codes format. (*Courtesy of Ford Motor Company, Dearborn, MI.*)

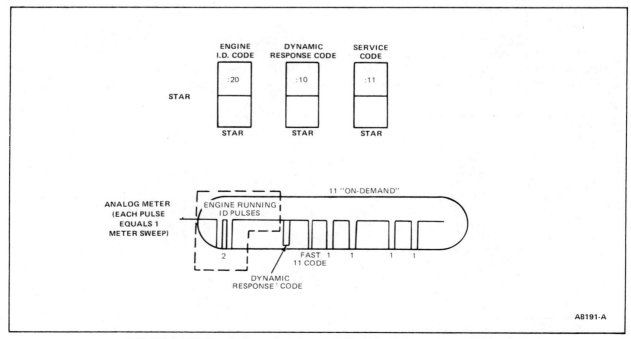

FIGURE 8-19 Engine running test format. (*Courtesy of Ford Motor Company, Dearborn, MI.*)

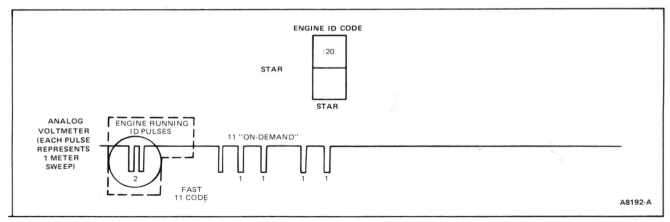

FIGURE 8-20 Engine ID codes format. (*Courtesy of Ford Motor Company, Dearborn, MI.*)

only ½ the number of engine cylinders; in other words, a 4-cylinder engine would have two pulses, and a V6 engine would have three pulses. (See Fig. 8-20.)

7. *Dynamic Response Check:* During the engine running test, a single analog meter needle pulse or alternately a Code 10 on the STAR tester indicates that the operator should perform a brief WOT (wide open throttle) test (dynamic response check) in order to confirm the operation of the TP (throttle position) sensor, VAF (vane air flow) meter, and MAP (manifold absolute pressure) sensor. Figure 8-21 illustrates the STAR number and analog volt-ohmmeter conditions.

8. *Continuous Monitor Test:* Figure 8-22 illustrates the analog volt-ohmmeter or STAR tester format for this mode. During this test, intermittent failures in the sensor input circuits can be diagnosed by continually monitoring inputs to the processor for opens and shorts.

NOTE: If continuous service codes are not retrieved, on the twenty-first engine temperature warm-up cycle, these codes will automatically be erased from memory. Another method in which continuous codes can be erased at any time during testing is by deactivating "quick test" while the service codes are being outputted. This can be done simply by turning off the ignition key, pressing the STAR tester pushbutton once to unlatch it, and then pressing the button again to latch it down.

The self-test output is energized whenever the continuous test mode senses a fault. It is de-energized when the system checks OK! With the STAR tester (or equivalent instrument) or analog volt-ohmmeter connected to the vehicle self-test output (Fig. 8-10), proceed into the continuous monitor test as follows:

1. With ignition key on, engine off, verify that the self-test is not activated, and then turn the key to the engine run position.
2. If a continuous fault is detected in a sensed system and a trouble code is stored in memory, then the self-test mode is automatically brought into action.

NOTE: Approximately two minutes after starting and running the engine, and after the service codes have been dis-

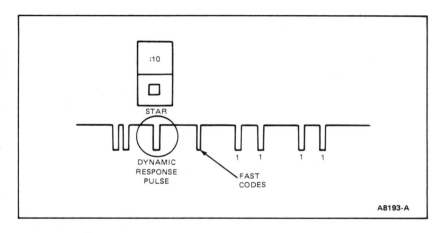

FIGURE 8-21 Dynamic response check format. (*Courtesy of Ford Motor Company, Dearborn, MI.*)

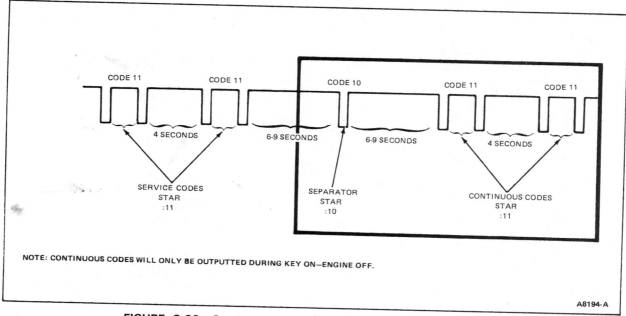

FIGURE 8-22 Continuous monitor self-test output code format. (*Courtesy of Ford Motor Company, Dearborn, MI.*)

played in Step 2 cited above, the system will enter the continuous engine running monitor test. (See Step 5 cited above.) To go directly to this mode of operation after starting the engine, and to eliminate having to wait for the self-test mode to complete its cycle, enter the engine running test right away. Then exit, and re-enter. (Do not shut the engine off.) This action will put you in the engine running continuous monitor test.

3. If the STAR tester or equivalent instrument or analog volt-ohmmeter indicates a system fault (short or open), a service trouble code will be stored in memory. A fault is indicated when the STAR LED (light emitting diode) turns off or the VOM needle deflection is 10.5 volts or greater.

NOTE: An "open" is defined as any resistance reading greater than 5 ohms unless otherwise specified by the manufacturer. A "short" is defined as any resistance reading less than 10,000 ohms to ground, unless otherwise specified.

The following example might best explain how to use the "continuous test" on a systematic basis:

Procedure

1. Let's assume that a Code 51 is displayed on the STAR tester or equivalent tester or analog volt-ohmmeter dial face.

2. This indicates that a fault has been detected in the engine coolant temperature sensor. This may be due to low voltage at the wiring harness, connections, or the sensor itself, or may be caused by a fault in the actual sensor. Voltage and resistance readings of the wiring harness pins should only be done with the aid of the Rotunda Breakout Box (Fig. 8-34).

3. Initiate the continuous monitor test, as described earlier. As well as having the STAR tester hooked into the system, hook up the volt-ohmmeter also.

4. It is good practice to tap the sensor lightly by flicking your finger against its surface to see if there is any change at the STAR tester or VOM.

5. Carefully inspect the wiring and harness to the sensor on the engine by pulling/pushing lightly on it to check for loose or poor connections. Repeat this inspection process by continuously wiggling the wire harness as you proceed from the sensor connector up towards the dash panel and then onto the processor.

6. If no change occurs at the VOM while performing Step 5 above, this indicates a continuous problem. If, however, the VOM reading flickers or changes while doing a wire harness check, this usually indicates an intermittent problem.

7. Disconnect the wire harness from the sensor and remove the terminals from the connector. Carefully inspect the terminals at the harness and the sensor itself for signs of corrosion, bad crimps, poorly seated terminals, or other signs of damage.

8. Reconnect the wire harness to the sensor.

9. Repeat the same procedure at the opposite end of the sensor wiring harness, namely at the processor end.

10. If a positive intermittent reading is not achieved at the VOM, reconnect the connector and erase the continuous test service codes as follows:

    (a) Initiate key on, engine off self-test.

    (b) Remove the jumper wire from the self-test input terminal as soon as the first service code is received (even if an 11 is the first code).

    (c) Rerun the self-test with a jumper wire to confirm that these service codes have, in fact, been erased.

11. To check the CTS (coolant temperature sensor) itself while on the engine, the ignition key should be off. Since the construction of the CTS is basically that of a ''thermistor,'' its resistance will decrease as the engine coolant temperature increases, and its resistance will increase as the coolant temperature drops. (Refer to Chapter 4 for more information and also for a description of common faults in shorts and opens for 2- and 3-wire type sensors.)

12. Disconnect the wire harness from the CTS sensor. Then place the DVOM (digital volt-ohmmeter) on the 200,000 ohm scale, and measure the resistance across the CTS. The resistance should read as follows if it is OK:

    (a) 1300 ohms (240°F) to 7700 ohms (140°F), with the engine off.

    (b) 1550 ohms (230°F) to 4550 ohms (180°F), with the engine running.

    Figure 8-23 illustrates typical resistances that might be found when checking between test pin 7 and 46 for the CTS (coolant temperature sensor). See Breakout Box information given below regarding test pin number identification.

9. *Output State Check:* This check allows the mechanic/technician to energize/de-energize most of the system output actuators. Turn EGR solenoid and self-test output (STO) power on and off/on-command. Once all codes have been received from ignition key on, engine off, on-demand, and continuous testing modes, the STO

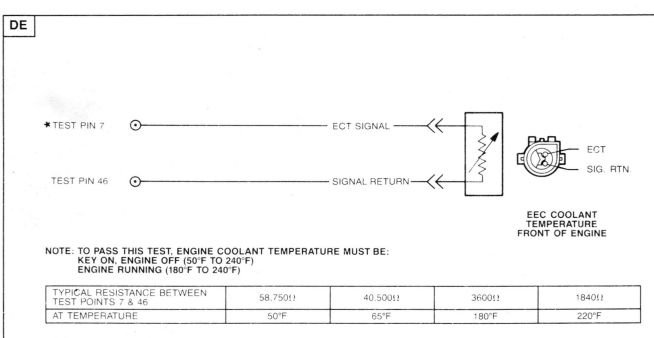

FIGURE 8-23   CTS test readings. (*Courtesy of Ford Motor Company, Dearborn, MI.*)

is entered by leaving the self-test mode activated and by depressing the throttle. Each time that the throttle is depressed, the output actuators will change state (on to off, or off to on). The sequence is as follows:

(a) Enter self-test
(b) Code output ends
(c) Do brief WOT test
(d) Output actuators energized
(e) Next brief WOT test
(f) Output actuators are de-energized

BREAKOUT BOX

The Rotunda Breakout Box P/N T83L-50 EEC-1V or equivalent, illustrated under special tools at the end of this chapter, is an EEC-1V test device that can be connected in series with the ECA (electronic control assembly) and the ECA harness to permit voltage measurements of sensor inputs and outputs from the ECA.

CAUTION: Attempting to probe the 60 pin connector of the ECA with a DVOM probe will result in permanent damage to the pin connectors. Therefore, the use of the Breakout Box with its mating plug-in harness connector will prevent this from happening.

The EEC-1V module connector pin-usage identification is shown in Fig. 8-24 for the 1.6L EFI and TC SVO vehicle, while Fig. 8-25 lists the ID for the 2.3L EFI turbo vehicle with automatic transaxle. Figure 8-26 lists the pin connector ID and relevant sensor/switch connection for the 3.8L CFI engine/vehicle.

The vehicle electrical wiring schematics shown earlier in Figs. 8-11, 8-12, and 8-13 can be used in conjunction with the EEC-1V Module Connector pin identification diagrams when tracing down a sensor/switch/actuator fault in the system.

When a problem exists in the system and the service trouble code has indicated a number, reference to the trouble codes listing in this section will direct you to the general area requiring closer inspection. This procedure then involves a systematic check of the sensor/switch/actuator to find out if the reason for the complaint is related to one of the following:

1. Low voltage supply
2. High voltage supply
3. High circuit resistance due to corrosion, loose connections, or damaged wiring or vacuum hoses
4. Burned fusible link
5. Faulty sensor/switch or actuator
6. Faulty ECA

NOTE: If access to the manufacturer's service literature regarding specific minimum and maximum voltages and resistances is not readily available, always compare the sensor values on the vehicle with a new unit that is known to be good.

For more detailed analysis of pinpoint testing and troubleshooting for various EEC-1V Ford manufactured vehicles, always refer to the manufacturer's latest up-to-date car shop manual and review the Engine/Emissions Diagnosis/chapter that deals specifically with pinpoint testing. Information contained within approximately 250 pages will systematically lead you to the various causes and remedies for each and every sensor/switch and actuator.

KEY ON/ENGINE OFF SELF-TEST CODE FORMAT

The various trouble codes stored in the computer memory determine what route to take when you first access the system. These routes are as follows:

1. Key on/engine off self-test
2. Check timing
3. Engine running self-test
4. Continuous monitor mode (wiggle test)

Once the self-test process has been initiated by connecting up the STAR tester or VOM to the engine compartment (Fig. 8-10), one of the following outputs will occur as shown in the table.

Pin	Circuit	Wire Color	Application	Abbreviations
1	37	Y	Keep Alive Memory	KAM
7	354	LG/Y	Engine Coolant Temperature	ECT
10	347	BK/Y H	A/C Clutch	ACC
16	259	BK/O	Ignition Ground	IGN. GND.
17	201	T/R	Self-Test Output/Shift Indicator Light	STO/SIL
20	57	BK	Case Ground	CASE GND.
21	68	O/BK	Idle Speed Control	ISC
22	97	T/LG D	Fuel Pump Control	FP
25	357	LG/P	Vane Air Temperature	VAT
26	351	O/W	Voltage Reference	V. REF.
29	94	DG/P H	Exhaust Gas Oxygen Sensor	EGO
30	614	GY-O	Neutral Drive Switch	NDS
30	359	BK/W	(SVO Only NDS Input Grounded)	NDS
32	101	GY-Y H	Canister Purge Solenoid	CANP
35	362	Y	EGR Shut Off	EGR S/O
36	324	Y/LG D	Ignition Module Signal	IMS
37	361	R	Vehicle Power	V PWR
40	60	BK-LG D	Battery Ground	BATT. GND.
43	200	W-BK	Vane Air Flow	VAF
45	358	LG/BK	Barometric Pressure	BP
46	359	BK/W	Signal Return	SIG. RET.
47	355	DG/LG	Throttle Position Sensor	TPS
48	100	W/R D	Self-Test In	STI
49	89	O	EGO Ground	EGO GND.
54	73	O-LB H	Wide Open Throttle A/C Cut-Off	WAC
56	349	DB	Distributor Output Signal	DOS
57	361	Red	Vehicle Battery	V BATT.
58	95	T/R D	Injector A	INJ. A
59	96	T/O D	Injector B	INJ. B
60	60	BK-LG D	Battery Ground	BATT. GND.

Pin locations given for reference only. Probing 60 pin connector with DVOM probe will result in permanent damage to the pin connectors. Always probe as directed, using the Breakout Box.

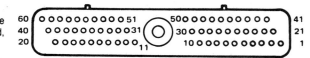

CA8133-A

1.6L EFI and 1.6L EFI TC SVO

FIGURE 8-24   EEC-1V module connector pin I.D. for the 1.6L EFI T/C SVO vehicles. (*Courtesy of Ford Motor Company, Dearborn, MI.*)

Pin	Circuit	Wire Color	Application	Abbreviations
1	37	Y	Keep Alive Memory	
4	11	DG-Y D	Ignition Diagnostic Monitor	KAM
7	354	LG Y	Engine Coolant Temperature	IDM
10	348	LG/P H	A/C Clutch	ECT
16	259	BK LG D	Ignition Ground	ACC
17	201	T R	Self-Test Output	IGN. GND.
20	60	BK LG H	Case Ground	STO
21	68	O BK	Idle Speed Control	CASE GND.
22	97	T LG D	Fuel Pump Control	ISC
23	310	Y R D	Knock Sensor	FP
25	357	LG/P	Vane Air Temperature	KS
26	351	O W	Voltage Reference	VAT
29	94	DG/P H	Heated Exhaust Gas Oxygen Sensor	V. REF.
30	60	BK/LG H	Neutral Drive Switch	HEGO
35	362	Y	EGR Shut Off	NDS
36	324	Y/LG D	Ignition Module Signal	EGR S/O
37	361	R	Vehicle Power	IMS
40	60	BK/LG H	Battery Ground	V PWR
43	200	LG/P	Vane Air Flow	BATT. GND.
45	358	LG/BK	Barometric Pressure	VAF
46	359	BK/W	Signal Return	BP
47	355	DG/LG	Throttle Position Sensor	SIG. RET.
48	100	W/R D	Self-Test In	TPS
49	89	O	EGO Ground	STI
56	349	DG	Distributor Output Signal	EGO GND.
57	361	Red	Vehicle Power	DOS
58	95	T/R D	Injector A	V PWR
59	96	T/O D	Injector B	INJ. A
60	60	BK/LG H	Battery Ground	INJ. B
				BATT. GND.

Pin locations given for reference only. Probing 60 pin connector with DVOM probe will result in permanent damage to the pin connectors. Always probe as directed, using the Breakout Box.

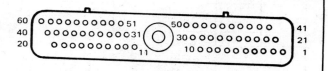

CA8139-A

EFI TURBO—ATX

FIGURE 8-25 EEC-1V module connector pin I.D. for the 2.3L EFI T/C ATX vehicles. (*Courtesy of Ford Motor Company, Dearborn, MI.*)

Pin	Circuit	Wire Color	Application	Abbreviations
1	38	BK/O	Keep Alive Power	KAPWR
5	16	R/LG	Key Power	KPWR
7	354	LG/Y	Engine Coolant Temperature	ECT
10	347	BK/Y	A/C Clutch	ACC
11	99	LG/BK	Air Management — TAD	AM2
16	259	BK/O	Ignition Ground	IGN. GND.
17	382	Y/B	Self-Test Output	STO
20	57	BK	Case Ground	CSE. GND.
21	376	Y/R	Idle Speed Control (LT/MQ, M/C)	ISC +
	382	Y/BK	Idle Speed Control (T/X)	ISC +
22	97	T/LG	Fuel Pump	FP
23	310	Y/R	Knock Sensor (M/C Only)	KS
25	357	LG/P	Air Charge Temperature	ACT
26	351	O/W	Reference Voltage	V. REF.
27	352	BR/LG	EGR Valve Position	EVP
28	265	LG/W	Idle Tracking Switch	ITS
29	94	DG/P	Exhaust Gas Oxygen Sensor — Left	EGO 1
30	199	LB/Y	Neutral Drive Switch	NDS
33	360	DG	Exhaust Gas Recirculation Vent	EGRV
36	324	Y/LG	Spark Output	SPOUT
37	361	R	Vehicle Power	V. PWR.
40	60	BK/LG	Power Ground	PWR. GND.
41	264	W/LB	Idle Speed Control	ISC −
43	90	DB/LG	Exhaust Gas Oxygen Sensor — Right	EGO 2
44	91	GY/R	Exhaust Gas Oxygen Ground — Right	EGOG 2
45	358	LG/BK	Manifold Absolute Pressure (LTD/MQ AND T/X)	MAP
	356	DB/LG	Manifold Absolute Pressure (M/C)	MAP
46	359	BK/W	Signal Return	SIG RTN
47	355	DG/LG	Throttle Position Sensor	TP
48	209	W/R	Self-Test Input	STI
49	89	O	Exhaust Gas Oxygen Ground — Left	EGOG 1
51	100	W/R	Air Management — Tab	AM1
52	362	Y	Exhaust Gas Recirculation Control	EGRC
54	73	O/LB	W.O.T. A/C Cut Off	WAC
55	377	W	Exhaust Heat Control	EHC
56	349	DB	Profile Ignition Pick-Up	PIP
57	361	R	Vehicle Power	V. PWR.
58	95	T/R	Injector 1	INJ 1
59	96	T/O	Injector 2	INJ 2
60	60	BL/LG	Power Ground	PWR. GND.

Pin locations given for reference only. Probing 60 pin connector with DVOM probe will result in permanent damage to the pin connectors. Always probe as directed, using the Breakout Box.

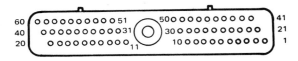

CA8159-A

FIGURE 8-26 EEC-1V module connector pin I.D. for the 3.8L V6 CFI vehicles. (*Courtesy of Ford Motor Company, Dearborn, MI.*)

NOTE: The STAR tester displays a 10 in place of a 1 for the single digit separator code. Therefore the separator code is expressed in the results column as a 10.

RESULT			ACTION TO TAKE
	Code Format		
On-Demand	Separator	Continuous	
11	1(0)	11	Key on, Engine off; on-demand and continuous tests indicate a pass. Therefore, proceed directly to engine timing quick test. If vehicle will not start, check for voltage to the processor and also check that the fuel system inertia switch has not activated (reset switch usually located in the trunk).
Any codes	1(0)	11	Key on, Engine off; on-demand test indicates a fault. Record on-demand codes, then proceed to the key on, engine off self-test routine.
Any codes	1(0)	Any codes	Key on, Engine off; on-demand and continuous tests indicate a fault. Record on-demand and continuous codes, then proceed to the key on, engine off self-test procedure.
11	1(0)	Any codes	Continuous test indicates a fault. Record continuous code(s). Proceed to engine timing check.
	No codes outputted		Check battery power supply to processor, and check for corroded or bent pins. Also check EGO sensor ground circuit.

On-demand codes that will appear during a Key on, Engine off self-test for various engines are as follows:

ON-DEMAND CODES — Key ON, Engine OFF Self-Test

1.6 EFI 1.6 EFI TC 2.3 EFI TC	2.3L OHC	2.3L HSC	3.8L CFI	5.0L CFI
15	15	15	15	15
21	21	21	21	21
22	22	22	22	22
23	23	23	23	23
24		24	24	24
26				
		31	31	31
51	51	51	51	51
53	53	53	53	53
54		54	54	54
56				
61	61	61	61	61
63	63	63	63	63

(continued)

ON-DEMAND CODES — Key ON, Engine OFF Self-Test (continued)

1.6 EFI 1.6 EFI TC 2.3 EFI TC	2.3L OHC	2.3L HSC	3.8L CFI	5.0L CFI
64		64	64 65	64
66 67	67 68		68	
				81
				82
				83
				84
				85
				86
				87
				88

CAUTION: When more than one service code is flashed, always record the different codes and begin your systematic check of the system with the first code that was received. When a repair is made, repeat the test procedure to ensure that the problem and trouble code has been erased. Should the engine fail to start, check for voltage at the processor as well as checking that the fuel system inertia switch (rollover/accident protection) in the trunk has not been triggered. If so, push the reset button. If the engine still fails to start, proceed through the customary checks that you would do on a non-EEC-IV equipped engine.

Check Timing

Key off, wait 10 seconds. Restart the engine after verifying that the self-test trigger has been activated. Check engine timing while in the self-test mode (two minutes from time that last self-test code was flashed). Check and compare timing with VECI decal in engine compartment and adjust if necessary.

Engine Running Self-Test

Deactivate self-test by switching engine off for at least 10 seconds. In order to warm up the exhaust oxygen sensor, start and run the engine at 2000 rpm for two minutes. Turn the engine off and wait 10 seconds before activating the self-test procedure again. Start the engine, and the test proceeds as follows:

1. Engine ID Code. This is equal to half the number of cylinders. A code of 2 equals a 4-cylinder engine, etc., except when using the STAR tester, which adds a zero to all single digit readings. (For example, 20 equals a 4-cylinder engine.)
2. Run test.
3. When the dynamic response ready code occurs (77), perform a brief WOT (wide open throttle) action. The STAR tester displays a 10 in place of a 1 for single separator code. Therefore, the dynamic response code is expressed in the results column as 10.
4. Engine running service codes that will appear will be as shown in the following table:

ENGINE RUNNING SELF-TEST SERVICE CODES

1.6L EFI 1.6L EFI TC 2.3L EFI TC	2.3L OHC	2.3L HSC	3.8L CFI	5.0L CFI
12	12	12	12	12
13	13	13	13	13
			16	16
			17	17
21	21	21	21	21
22	22	22	22	22
23	23	23	23	23
24		24	24	24
25			25	
26				
		31	31	31
		32	32	32
		33	33	33
34		34	34	34
		35	35	35
41		41	41	41
42		42	42	42
	43	43	43	43
	44	44	44	44
	45	45	45	45
	46	46	46	46
				47
			48	
	58		58	
	72	72	72	72
73		73	73	73
76				
77		77	77	77
			91	
			92	
			93	
			94	
			95	
			96	

Carefully note and record all of the flashed service codes. One of the following outputs shown in the chart will exist.

RESULT			ACTION TO TAKE
CODE FORMAT			
Engine ID	Dynamic Response	On-Demand	
2(0)	1(0)	11	Indicates a pass. If intermittent code, initiate continuous testing mode. If the drive symptom is present, proceed to a

(continued)

RESULT			ACTION TO TAKE
CODE FORMAT			
Engine ID	Dynamic Response	On-Demand	
			systematic check of the particular system symptom or code as per the listed trouble code charts in this section. Otherwise, testing is complete, and the EEC-1V system is OK.
2(0)	1(0)	Any codes	This indicates a fault. Therefore, proceed to the engine running self-test mode.
No codes outputted			Repeat the self-test mode and verify that no service codes are present. Then proceed to determine if a 15 (invalid code) is present. Check for battery power to the processor system. Connect Breakout Box to check system. Connect DVOM between EGO ground point on the engine and test pin 49 on the Breakout Box. If less than 5 ohms, inspect for corrosion, damaged pins, etc., at B/O box and processor. If greater than 5 ohms, check and service EGO sensor ground wire or open circuit · bad connection.

CONTINUOUS MONITOR MODE (Wiggle Test)

Continuous service codes are as follows in the accompanying chart:

CONTINUOUS MONITOR MODE WIGGLE TEST CODES

1.6L EFI 1.6L EFI TC 2.3L EFI TC	2.3L OHC	2.3L HSC	3.8L CFI	5.0L CFI
11	11	11	11	11
			13	
14			14	14
	15	15	15	15
18				18
21	21	21	21	21
22	22	22	22	22
		31	31	31
41		41		41
42				42
51	51	51	51	51
53		53	53	
54		54	54	54
56				
61	61	61	61	61
63	63	63	63	
64		64	64	64
			65	
66				

Connect a STAR tester or similar test instrument to the EEC-1V system output as per Fig. 8-10. The self-test should be deactivated. Refer to the codes recorded under the key on, engine off mode, listed above. If any repairs are required, perform them. Then, with the self-test deactivated, turn the ignition key to the on position (engine off), which will put the system into the continuous monitor code (wiggle test mode). Star test output or equivalent will be activated whenever a fault is detected. This is indicated when either the STAR LED turns off or the VOM needle deflection is 10.5 volts or greater.

Start the engine, activate the self-test, and perform an engine running quick test. After the service code output has been completed and two minutes after a Code 11 has been flashed, the system will enter and remain in continuous monitor mode until self-test is deactivated, or the engine is turned off. STO (self-test output) will be activated whenever a fault is detected; i.e., when the STAR LED turns off, or the VOM needle deflection is 10.5 volts or greater.

FORD SERVICE TROUBLE CODES — EEC-1V SYSTEM

Code Number	Sensor/Switch/Actuator Unit
11	On FBC (feedback carburetor) engines, treat a Code 11 as a Code 44 (see below).
12	RPM test (d.c. motor control): throttle kicker
13	ISC (idle speed control) bypass air: rpm not returning to normal speed. Throttle kicker.
14	Erratic ignition: code indicates that two successive erratic profile ignition pick-up (PIP) pulses occurred, resulting in a possible engine miss or stall. Check EEC-1V and ignition system for loose wires/connectors, arcing secondary ignition components (coil, cap, rotor, wires, plugs), on-board transmitter (two-way radio). Check distributor. Check EEC-1V harness and processor connectors.
15	Invalid codes — Continuous test: check power to processor.
16, 17	Fuel control — CFI system check: see detailed explanation under Codes 91 through 98.
18	IDM (ignition diagnostic monitor): check TFI (thick film ignition) module, EEC-1V harness, and processor and harness connectors for corrosion or bent pins.
21	Check engine operating temperature and ECT (engine coolant temperature sensor). Check continuity and signal return voltage, and ECT signal for shorts. Check sensor resistance, which should be between 1300 ohms (240°F) to 7700 ohms at 140°F, with the engine off; should be between 1550 ohms at 230°F to 4550 ohms (180°F), with engine running. Test drive vehicle.
22	BP (barometric pressure sensor) or MAP (manifold absolute pressure sensor): BP voltage check is digital in nature. Check all voltage inputs and outputs, connections, and processor/harness connector. Continuity and shorts. Use continuous monitor mode and observe VOM or STAR LED (light emitting diode) with vacuum pump on the BP/MAP sensor. Apply and release vacuum source to see if a fault is indicated. Check vacuum lines. Enter continuous monitor test and replace sensor if fault indicated.

E5ZF-9B989-AA

4 L 28C

Code Number	Sensor/Switch/Actuator Unit
23	TPS (throttle position sensor): check for a Code 58, 68, 31, or 41 before servicing a Code 23. Attempt to close throttle completely in key on, engine off mode; if Code 23 present, check for stuck throttle plate; no Code 23, do not adjust TPS if EEC system functioning correctly. If Code 63 present during key on, engine off test, replace TPS. If no Code 63 present, replace processor. If service Code 53 and with key off, connect DVOM test leads to +, and signal return at TPS harness; if 10V or greater, connect DVOM leads to TPS and signal return at harness connector; and if voltage less than 4V and with TP harness disconnected, perform key on, engine off self-test; if Code 63 present, replace TPS. If no Code 63, replace processor. Also check signal return for opens and shorts to power.
24	Check VAT (vane air temperature) sensor or ACT (air charge temperature) signal to signal return voltage, key off. Check continuity of circuits. Check for shorts. VAT sensor check (harness disconnected from vane meter; ambient temperature must be greater than 50°F, key off) and measure resistance of VAT sensor, VAT signal pin to signal return pin; if reading is from 125 ohms (240°F) to 3700 ohms (50°F), then replace processor. If reading is not between these figures, replace vane meter.
25	Engine KS (knock sensor): engine running self-test and induce rap/tap on exhaust manifold (4 ounce hammer or wrench) above sensor when the dynamic response signal is given. Fifteen seconds later a code will be generated; if no Code 25, system OK. If Code 25, test knock circuit for voltage. Check continuity of KS and signal return circuits. Check KS circuit for short to ground or to voltage. Test processor with substitute new knock sensor.
26	VAF (vane air flow) sensor: check for contamination, such as oil residue and other foreign material that might impede VAF sensor vane movement, after removing air cleaner assembly. There are no opens or shorts in the circuit; otherwise, a Code 56 (voltage signal always high) or Code 66 (signal always low) would have been generated. Install Breakout Box and measure voltage between test pins 43 and 46 with new unsharpened pencil or similar instrument pushed through VAF meter to hold it wide open; if 2.8V to 3.7V, then Code 26 has been caused by incorrect engine rpm or vacuum leak. If voltage not between 2.8V and 3.7V, replace processor.
31	EVP (EGR valve position sensor): engine running quick test with EGR vacuum signal line disconnected at EGR valve. Check EVP sensor resistance; if less than 100 ohms or greater than 5500 ohms, replace it. Check EVP movement. Measure VREF signal return and input voltage. Check EVP signal for shorts to ground or power; if greater than 10,000 ohms, replace processor. Use continuous test mode and observe STAR LED or VOM for fault indication. Check EEC-1V harness and process connectors.
32, 33, 34	EVP (EGR valve position sensor): measure EGR vent and EGR control solenoid resistance; if EGRC and EGRV readings are less than 30 ohms or greater than 70 ohms replace EGR. Check EGR solenoids for electrical and vacuum cycling. Check vacuum lines. Check EVP resistance while applying vacuum to EGR valve and if reading gradually decreases from no more than 5500 ohms to no less than 100 ohms, replace the processor. While manually exercising EVP sensor if reading decreases smoothly from 5500 ohms to no less than 100

Code Number	Sensor/Switch/Actuator Unit

ohms, replace EGR valve. If reading does not decrease smoothly or changes abruptly, replace EVP. While checking EGRV and EGRC signals for shorts to power and if all readings are more than 10,000 ohms, replace processor.

35 EVP/EGR system: rpm too low for EGR test. Retest at 1500 rpm. If Code 35 still present, replace processor. Check VREF circuit to ground. Check signal return to VREF. Check EVP circuit voltage. Check EVP voltage signal short to ground. Check EVP voltage signal for opens. Substitute EVP sensor with new one. If Code 31 still present, replace processor. Check EVP signal short to power. If Code 31 present, measure EVP signal voltage while exercising EVP sensor. Also check EEC-1V harness and process connectors.

41, 42, 43, 47 Fuel control circuit: Code 41 always lean (for more than 15 seconds); Code 42 always rich (for more than 15 seconds); Code 43 with warm engine, check exhaust leaks and idle quality; Code 42/47 on a FBC, check choke.

If a Code 41, then check for:

- leaking vacuum actuator (e.g., A/C control motor)
- engine sealing
- EGR system
- PCV system
- unmetered air leak between air meter and throttle body
- lead contaminated EGO (exhaust gas oxygen) sensor

If a Code 42, check for:

- fuel contamination
- ignition caused misfire
- CANP (canister purge solenoid) problems

44, 45, 46 AIR (air management system): Code 45 TAD (thermactor air diverter solenoid) only; Code 46 TAB (thermactor air bypass solenoid) only. Always verify correct vacuum line routing first. Measure TAB/TAD solenoid resistance; if resistance is between 50 and 100 ohms, OK; if either resistance is less than 50, or greater than 100 ohms, replace TAB/TAD solenoid assembly. Check TAB/TAD solenoid electrical operation and for vacuum cycling. Check voltage of VPWR and TAB/TAD circuits. Check for short to power or ground.

48 Fuel Control-CFI: refer to detail under Codes 91 to 98.

51 ECT (engine coolant temperature): check sensor, harness, and processor connectors. Enter continuous test sequence.

53 TPS, key off and TPS harness disconnected: jumper VREF to TPS signal and perform key on, engine off self-test. If Code 53 present, replace TPS; if no Code 53, replace processor. Service Code 53, check signal return for open. Check continuity of TPS and VREF circuits. Also perform continuous monitor test and observe VOM or STAR LED while moving throttle to WOT and back position. While

Code Number	Sensor/Switch/Actuator Unit
	using a DVOM and using key on, engine off test mode, if fault occurs below 4.25V, replace TPS if connections are OK. Check EEC-1V harness and processor connectors.
54	VAT sensor or ACT sensor: induce opposite code; check continuity of VAT or ACT signal and signal return. Use continuous monitor code to observe STAR LED; check EEC-1V harness/connectors.
56	Check voltage signal return, check continuity, check for short. Using continuous monitor test, observe STAR LED or VOM for fault indication. Check EEC-1V harness and processor connectors.
58	Idle tracking switch: key off and press on ISC DC motor to simulate throttle contact; perform key on, engine off self-test. If Code 68, check for short to ground. Install Breakout Box and check resistance of test pin 28 to 40, 46 and 60. If all greater than 10,000 ohms, replace processor.
61	ECT (engine coolant temperature): enter continuous test and if voltage greater than 5 volts or STAR LED is off, check terminals and connectors, EEC-1V harness, and processor connectors; if good, replace ECT sensor. Also, when checking ECT signal for a short, if readings are 10,000 ohms or greater, replace processor.
63	TPS (throttle position sensor): check for VREF to TPS signal input. Check resistance of TPS to ground. Using continuous monitor test mode, observe VOM or STAR LED for indication of a fault while moving to WOT and back. If fault indicated, clean and inspect connections. If still faulty, replace TPS after checking EEC-1V harness and processor harness.
64	VAT or ACT sensor: induce opposite code; check VAT or ACT signal for shorts, key off. Also use continuous mode test and observe STAR LED or VOM; check EEC-1V harness and connectors.
65	Key power check: Code 65 in continuous memory; perform key on, engine off quick test and record continuous modes.
66	VAF (vane air flow) sensor: check VREF (voltage reference) signal return voltage; check for shorts and continuity. Use continuous monitor mode and observe STAR LED and VOM for fault indication. Check EEC-1V harness and processor connectors.
67	Neutral drive switch A/C input check: turbo boost switch, install Breakout Box attached and check voltage at circuit 30 to ground. For A/C circuit, measure voltage at test pin 10 to ground. Check resistance from pin 30 to 46 and check for grounds.
68	Idle tracking switch: key off. Move throttle away from ISC DC motor shaft and perform key on, engine self-test. If Code 68 present (key off), disconnect harness from ISC and use jumper wire between ISC harness connector pins 3 and 4. Key on, engine off self-test: if Code 68 present, check ITS and signal return circuits for continuity. If continuity of test pin 46 to signal return circuit and pin 28 to ITS circuit is less than 5 ohms, replace processor.
73	TPS moves in engine response test: this code indicates that the TPS did not exceed 25 percent of its rotation in the engine response check. With Breakout Box connected, perform engine running quick test; if DVOM exceeds 3.5 volts, replace processor; if not, verify that TPS is properly attached to throttle body; if so, replace it.

Code Number	Sensor/Switch/Actuator Unit
76	VAF (vane air flow) sensor: check for voltage increase in VAF signal return.
77	Dynamic response test: system failed to recognize brief WOT (wide open throttle).
81, 82	Output circuit check (thermactor): measure TAB/TAD solenoid resistance. Voltage of V PWR circuit. Continuity of TAB/TAD circuit. Check for shorts to power or ground. Use Breakout Box and DVOM.
83, 84	EGRV/EGRC (exhaust gas recirculation vent solenoid/exhaust gas circulation control solenoid) output circuit check: use Breakout Box and DVOM.
85	Output circuit check, canister purge: measure CANP solenoid resistance. Check voltage of V PWR circuit. Check continuity of CANP circuit, as well as for shorts to power or ground. Use Breakout Box and DVOM.
86	Output circuit check, WOT A/C cut-off: measure WAC solenoid resistance. Voltage of V PWR circuit. Continuity of WAC circuit, and short to power or ground. Use Breakout Box and DVOM.
87	Fuel pump circuit and inertia switch: check V power to processor. Power to pumps. Fuel pump circuit check to V battery. Check resistance of fuel pump relay. Check continuity of fuel pump circuit and inertia switch. Check for shorts to power or ground. Use Breakout Box and DVOM.
88	Output circuit check-idle speed control TK (throttle kicker): measure TK solenoid resistance. Voltage of V PWR circuit. Continuity of TK circuit. Shorts to power or ground. Use Breakout Box and DVOM.
89	Output circuit check, EHC (exhaust heat control): measure EHC solenoid resistance. Check voltage of V PWR circuit. Check continuity of EHC circuit. Check for short to power or ground. Use Breakout Box and DVOM.
91 to 98	Fuel control — CFI system check. The following non-EEC areas may be at fault with these codes:

- ignition coil
- distributor cap
- distributor rotor
- fouled spark plugs
- spark plug wires
- CANP problems
- PCV valves
- EGR valve and gasket
- air filter
- fuel contamination, engine oil
- poor power ground
- fuel pressure
- manifold leaks, intake/exhaust
- engine not at normal operating temperature

If all systems listed above for Codes 91 through 98 are OK, diagnose the following areas:

- EGO sensor
- EGO signal and ground circuits
- EGO sensor connection
- vacuum systems
- fuel injectors
- processor assembly
- thermactor impact

NOTE: Fuel contaminated engine oil can affect Code 4-1, 4-2, and 4-3 service codes. Therefore, remove the PCV from the valve cover and rerun the quick test listed earlier. If the problem is corrected, then change the oil and filter.

FORD MCU (MICROPROCESSOR CONTROL UNIT)

The MCU system is common only to the 5.8L FBC (feedback carburetor) V8 engine used in police cruisers and Canadian Trailer Tow vehicles. It is designed to control only the fuel system and to maintain a stoichiometric air/fuel ratio (14.7:1), which will ensure maximum exhaust system catalyst efficiency.

The system employs a MCU and carburetor that is equipped with a FBCA (feedback carburetor actuator) and exhaust gas oxygen sensor. The MCU is located on the left fender panel underhood, as shown in Fig. 8-27, which also illustrates the various positions of the system sensors on the 5.8L V8 FBCA engine.

As with the Ford EEC-1V system, the MCU system operates in either open- or closed-loop mode. In an open loop, the MCU module sends out a fixed signal to the FBCA. This condition occurs when the engine is cold or the exhaust temperature is not yet high enough to initiate a voltage signal from the oxygen sensor. Closed loop, on the other hand, occurs when the oxygen sensor is warm enough to send a voltage signal back to the MCU module. The MCU module then sends a varying signal to the FBCA to change the air/fuel ratio setting in order to keep it as close to stoichiometric (14.7:1) as possible under all modes of operation. For more detail on the oxygen sensor, refer to Chapter 4, which discusses the topic of sensors.

Other sensors employed with the MCU system are the CTS (coolant temperature), manifold vacuum, and rpm. Other areas controlled by the MCU are canister purge (CANP), TAD (thermactor air diverter), TAB (thermactor air bypass), TK (throttle kicker), and the spark retard system, or spark retard through the use of a KS (knock sensor). All these various sensors were described in more detail in Chapter 4.

Test Instruments

The test instruments that can be used to access the MCU system are similar to those used for the EEC-1V Ford systems — namely, either an "analog voltmeter," or a Rotunda STAR tester, both of which are illustrated at the end of this chapter, under "Special Tools." A detailed description of both these instruments was given in the section on EEC-1V system access and test procedures.

MCU CIRCUIT ACCESS

In order to access stored information from the MCU memory, a self-test connector is the output point for the MCU system. It is similar to the one found on EEC-1V vehicles and is located on either the left or right fender apron, when viewing these from the driver's seat. (See Fig. 8-28.)

MCU PRETEST CHECKS

As with the EEC-1V system, it is very important that a number of general checks be made of the engine compartment prior to actually attempting to access the MCU memory system for any possible stored trouble codes. Often the problem of poor performance can be attributed directly to minor causes rather than to an actual problem with a sensor or MCU system. The following checks should be conducted prior to accessing the MCU system:

1. Check all vacuum lines for cracks or breaks and proper connections.
2. Check the electrical harness for corroded, loose, frayed, broken, or burned connections, and check that all terminals are correctly seated.

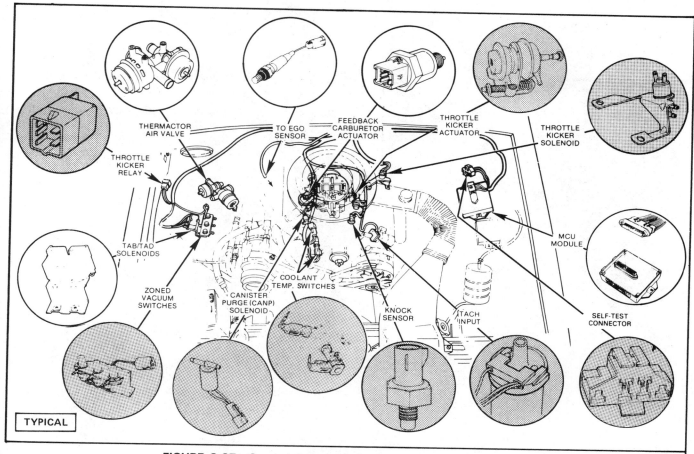

FIGURE 8-27 General layout of the MCU 5.8L V8 FBCA system. (*Courtesy of Ford Motor Company, Dearborn, MI.*)

A. Turn the ignition key Off.

B. Locate the Self-Test connector near MCU module (left or right fender apron as viewed from driver's seat).

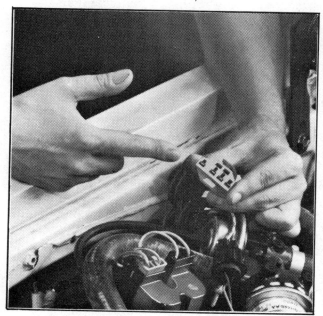

FIGURE 8-28 MCU system self-test connector location. (*Courtesy of Ford Motor Company, Dearborn, MI.*)

3. Check the engine coolant level.

4. Transmission must be in Park or Neutral.

5. Set the parking brake and block the wheels.

6. Turn accessory electrical loads off on the instrument panel.

7. Check that vacuum hoses are, in fact, connected to the air cleaner.

8. If using an "analog voltmeter," make sure that there is power to the carburetor choke (engine must be running).

9. Start and run the engine until it is up to normal operating temperature. Then allow it to idle.

10. Turn the ignition key off and locate the MCU self-test connector under the hood and on the fender apron (Fig. 8-28).

MCU QUICK TEST SETUP AND CHECK

Figures 8-29 and 8-30 illustrate the hookup requirements for both the "analog voltmeter" and STAR tester arrangement. Make sure that the ignition key is off when connecting the voltmeter or STAR tester to the self-test connector. When using the analog voltmeter, connect a jumper wire or paper clip from the self-test Trigger (circuit 201) to ground (circuit 60), as shown in Fig. 8-29.

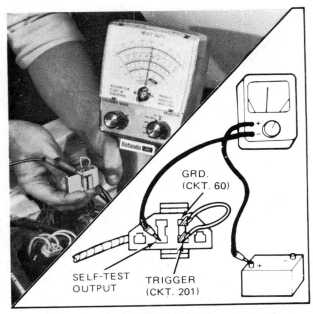

FIGURE 8-29 MCU analog voltmeter hookup to the self-test connector. (*Courtesy of Ford Motor Company, Dearborn, MI.*)

When using the STAR tester or equivalent, hook it up as shown in Fig. 8-30, and refer to the additional instructions on the back of the tester. With the test instrument connected as shown, perform the following procedures:

1. Remove the PCV unit from the breather cap on the valve rocker cover.

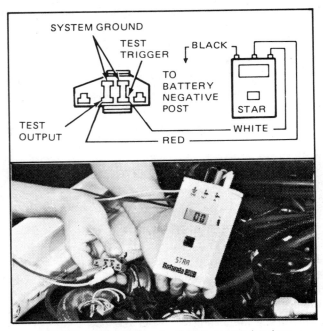

FIGURE 8-30 Rotunda STAR tester hookup to the self-test connector. (*Courtesy of Ford Motor Company, Dearborn, MI.*)

2. Tee a vacuum gauge into the canister purge solenoid valve hose on the carbon canister side of the hose.

3. On engines fitted with a vacuum delay valve, as shown in Fig. 8-31, the retrictor must be uncapped during the quick test. Be sure to recap it after you have finished the test.

MCU TEST STEPS

These test steps are not unlike those used with the EEC-1V system described earlier in this chapter, in that a key on, engine off and engine running test procedure is employed.

Procedure: key on, engine off

1. Ignition key off.

2. Turn key to on, with engine off.

3. Carefully monitor the voltmeter or the STAR tester.

4. Proceed with necessary service once the first code has been received. If more than one code is flashed, always start service with the first code received.

On 5.8L engine calibrations with a vacuum delay valve, there is a Tee and restrictor in the Thermactor Bypass Vacuum Control line. The restrictor must be uncapped during the Quick Test. Recap it after the Quick Test is completed.

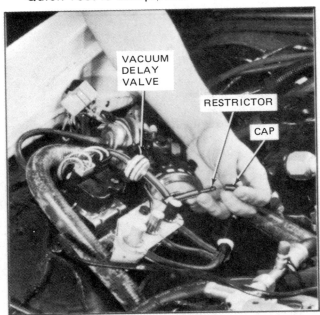

FIGURE 8-31 Carburetor vacuum delay valve and restrictor. (*Courtesy of Ford Motor Company, Dearborn, MI.*)

Refer to the Trouble Code Listings Chart for the MCU system to determine a starting point for service.

Procedure: engine running quick test

1. Engine MUST be at normal operating temperature.

2. Run engine at 2000 rpm for 2 minutes; turn key off; immediately restart engine and allow to idle.

3. Check voltmeter and vacuum gauge after engine restart to ensure that needle pulses are evident. The throttle kicker will extend at this time and remain on throughout the test (rpm increase) for 90 seconds.

4. If the vehicle is equipped with a knock sensor, after the first 4 initial voltmeter pulses, quickly simulate spark knock by tapping lightly (small hammer or wrench) on the intake manifold near the base of the knock sensor for about 15 seconds.

5. If no knock sensor is fitted to the engine, after the first 4 initial voltmeter pulses, record the various voltmeter pulses and convert these to a code number, or alternately, read the codes directly from the STAR tester.

6. Always start service with the first trouble code received.

NOTE: If the engine doesn't start, follow the procedure normally used to verify first, that the problem is non-MCU related, and then check the MCU and circuitry for battery voltage supply. Also check for corroded and loose wiring connections, etc., at the MCU and wiring harness connections. If there are no initialization pulses on the voltmeter, erroneous codes, or pulses on the vacuum gauge, check the MCU system connections, etc.

MCU SERVICE CODES

A service Code 1-1 will appear on vehicles operating below 4000 feet elevation, and a Code 6-2 will appear for vehicles operating above 4000 feet.

Code Number	System Checkout
1-1	Indicates vehicle is operating below 4000 feet. If in fact it isn't, check barometric pressure switch operation.
1-2	RPM check: check carburetor idle speed adjustments; refer to VIN decal and adjust, if necessary, and retest. Check vacuum lines between throttle kicker solenoid and actuator for leaks, blockage, or improper connections.
2-5	Knock sensor: make sure KS is torqued into manifold to 12–18 lb-ft (16–24 Nm). Check circuit 310 for resistance. Check circuit 60 for continuity between KS and MCU. Repeat Step 4 of engine running test after disconnecting KS from vehicle harness. After 4 initialization pulses occur, continually tap circuit 310 (wiring harness connector), as shown in Fig. 8-32 with the probe end of tester lamp for 5 seconds. If a service Code 2-5 still exists, replace the MCU and retest. For any other codes, replace knock sensor.
4-1	Fuel always lean: although the following items are not MCU-controlled, they can cause a Code 4-1 to appear:

- malfunctioning carburetor
- low fuel pressure (fuel line kink, fuel pump problem)
- vacuum leaks (EGR gasket, head gasket, cracked hoses)
- canister purge solenoid
- bowl vent
- PCV

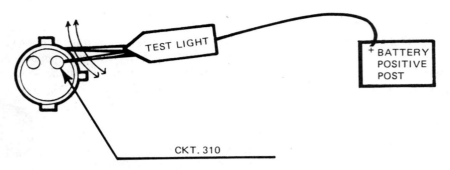

CKT. 310

A6330-A

FIGURE 8-32 Knock sensor test light hookup. (*Courtesy of Ford Motor Company, Dearborn, MI.*)

Code Number	System Checkout

MCU-controlled EGO sensor (use only a voltmeter with an input impedence of 10 megohms or greater); check resistance of EGO leads and harness; check FBCA motor and harness; check TAD/TAB solenoids.

4-2   Fuel always rich: non-MCU items that could cause a Code 4-2 are the following:

- malfunctioning carburetor (high float level, no power to choke cap)
- misfiring spark plugs (coil, distributor)
- restricted air cleaner
- restricted PVS
- air pump not working (malfunctioning pulley, broken belts)
- throttle kicker stuck on
- PCV

Check for power to choke cap and that choke is off; check EGO sensor and circuit as in Code 4-1; check FBCA motor and harness, and also for shorts to ground.

4-4   Thermactor check: non-MCU components that could cause a Code 4-4 are:

- retard delay valve (RDV)
- TVS (temperature vacuum switch)
- malfunctioning carburetor (same conditions as listed for a Code 4-2)

Check for manifold vacuum at input to TAB/TAD solenoids; check TAB/TAD solenoid circuits for short to ground, resistance, continuity, etc.

4-5   Thermactor air switching (air always upstream): non-MCU systems that might affect this code are:

- broken or loose belts
- crimped, pinched, or missing hoses, plugged restrictor
- malfunctioning vacuum delay valve

Check TAD solenoid and circuit for resistance, continuity, and short to ground.

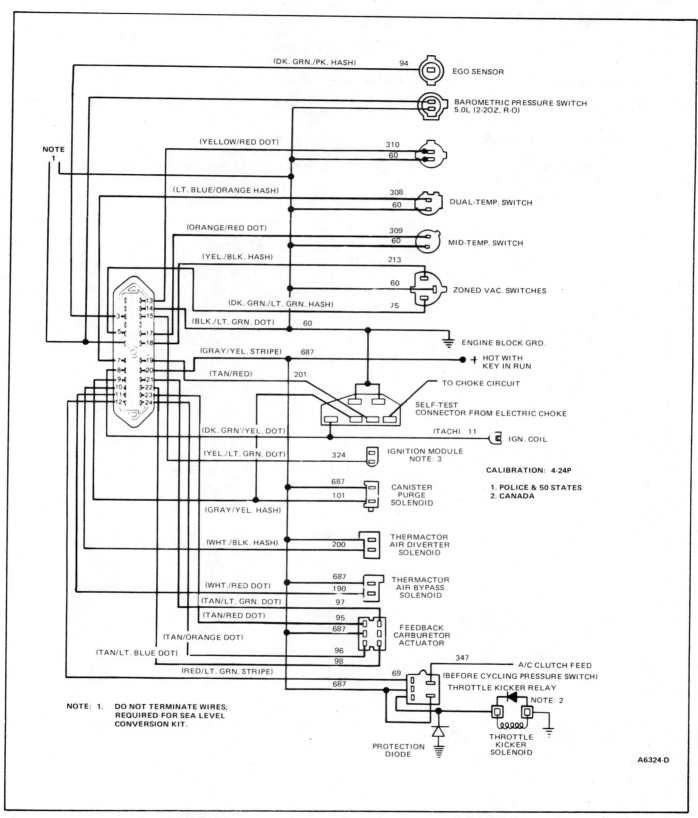

FIGURE 8-33 Electrical schematic for MCU 5.8L V8 FBC engine system. (*Courtesy of Ford Motor Company, Dearborn, MI.*)

Test Equipment

EQUIPMENT REQUIRED:

- Rotunda Self-Test Automatic Readout (STAR), No. 07-0004 with cable assembly No. 07-0010. Refer to STAR operation.
- Analog volt-ohmmeter (VOM), 0 to 20v DC, (alternate to STAR). Refer to Appendix A.

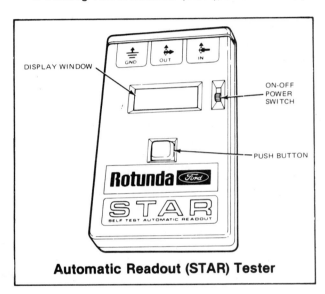

Automatic Readout (STAR) Tester

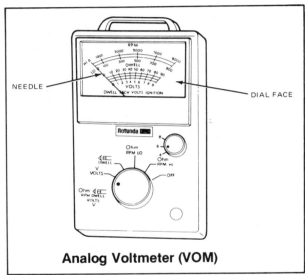

Analog Voltmeter (VOM)

- Jumper wire.
- Vacuum gauge, Rotunda 59-0008 or equivalent. Range 0-30 in. Hg. Resolution 1 in. Hg.

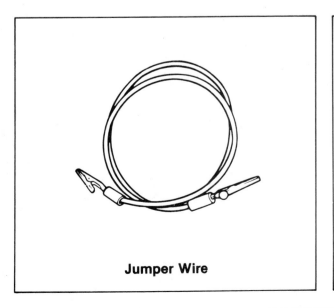

Jumper Wire

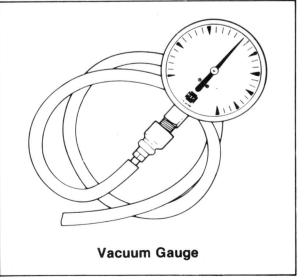

Vacuum Gauge

FIGURE 8-34 Special tools and test equipment. (*Courtesy of Ford Motor Company, Dearborn, MI.*)

Test Equipment

- Tachometer, Rotunda No. 59-0010 or equivalent. Range 0-6,000 rpm. Accuracy ± 40 rpm. Resolution 20 rpm.
- Breakout Box, Rotunda T83L-50 EEC-IV or equivalent.

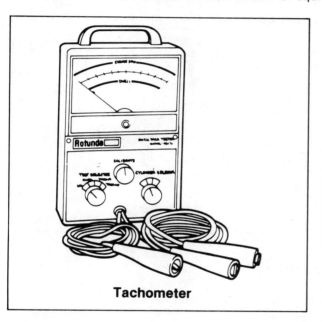

Tachometer

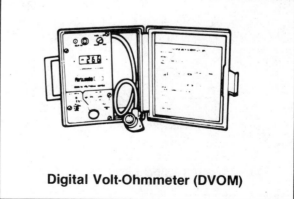

Breakout Box

- Vacuum pump, Rotunda No. 21-0014 or equivalent. Range 0-25 in. Hg.
- Digital volt-ohmmeter (DVOM), Rotunda No. 15-0031 or equivalent. Input impedance 10 Megaohm minimum.

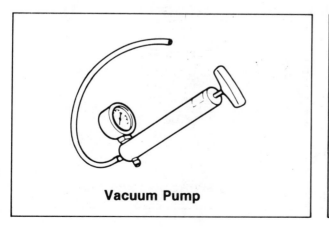

Vacuum Pump

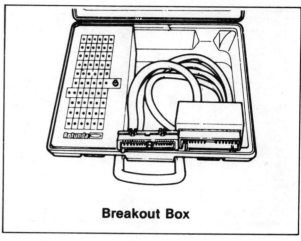

Digital Volt-Ohmmeter (DVOM)

Test Equipment

- Electronic Fuel Injection Pressure Gauge EFI/CFI only, Rotunda No. T80L-9974-A or equivalent.
- Spark tester Tool D81P-6666-A or equivalent.

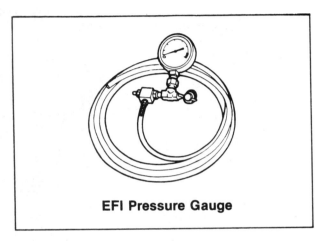

EFI Pressure Gauge

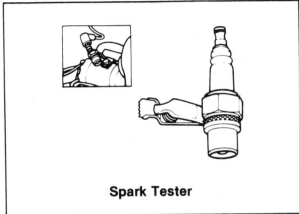

Spark Tester

- Timing light, Rotunda Tool No. 27-0001 or equivalent.
- Non-powered Test lamp.

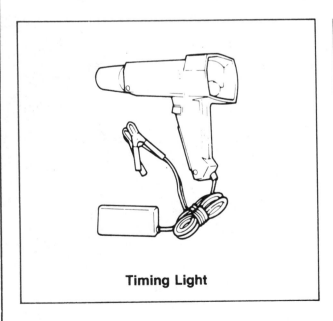

Timing Light

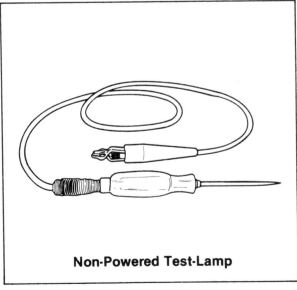

Non-Powered Test-Lamp

Code Number	System Checkout
4-6	Thermactor air always not bypassing: non-MCU items that could affect system are the same as for a Code 4-5. Check TAB solenoid and circuit for resistance, continuity, and short to ground.
5-3 or 5-4	Electrical temperature switch "open": use ohmmeter and check circuit after ensuring that coolant temperature is between 60–93°C (140–200°F).
5-1 or 5-5	Zoned vacuum switch: check for vacuum at switches, and that the switch assembly holds vacuum. Check for resistance and continuity of circuit.
6-1 or 6-5	Zoned vacuum switch: vacuum switch closed. Connect ohmmeter across MIDVAC switch terminals and measure circuit resistance from circuit 213 to 60. Disconnect vehicle harness from MCU, and check resistance from vehicle harness circuit 213 and ground.
6-2	Vehicle operating above 4000 feet: if it isn't, check barometric pressure switch operation.

Figure 8-33 depicts a typical wiring schematic for the MCU 5.8L V8 FBC engine system. Test equipment recommended for troubleshooting Ford vehicles is illustrated in Fig. 8-34.

CHAPTER 9

◆

Chrysler Electronic Engine Controls

TBI AND PFI SYSTEMS—INTRODUCTION

Current Chrysler-produced vehicles employ either a (CPI) central point injection (throttle body injection) system with one fuel injector, or EFI (electronic fuel injection) with (MPI) multi-point port fuel injection that uses one fuel injector per cylinder. Turbocharged vehicles all use port fuel injection, while the TBI unit is generally employed on all other vehicles. Engines discussed here and using these systems are the 2.2L (134 cu.in.) and 2.6L (156 cu.in.) four-cylinder engines. The computerized engine controls on these engines are designed to handle the fuel, ignition, and exhaust emissions systems.

Various engine and vehicle sensors are employed that are designed to monitor each facet of the systems operation on a continuous basis when it is in the closed-loop mode, which is the operating period when the engine exhaust is hot enough to generate a voltage feedback signal from the exhaust gas oxygen sensor to the on-board computer system. The computer then determines the characteristics of ignition and injector pulse-width (time energized to inject fuel) in order to maintain a stoichiometric air/fuel ratio (14.7:1) under all conditions of load and speed. In this way, the best fuel economy, exhaust emissions, and vehicle performance are achieved.

The two types of systems, along with their respective sensors, input and output devices, and logic and power modules, are illustrated in Fig. 9-1 for the nonturbo engine, while Fig. 9-2 depicts the system used with the turbocharged vehicle engines.

LOGIC MODULE

In both the CPI (central point injection) and MPI (multipoint injection) systems, a digital, preprogrammed computer, known as a logic module (LM), regulates ignition timing, air/fuel ratio, emission control devices, and idle speed. The various signals sent to the LM from the system switches, sensors, and components are compared with a preprogrammed system (PROM and ROM), and the LM computes the necessary fuel-injector pulse-width, spark advance, ignition coil dwell, idle speed, and purge and EGR solenoid cycles from this information.

Since the various engine sensors continuously send their respective voltage signals back to this LM, it has the ability to constantly update and revise its programming in order to meet the various conditions required to maintain the air/fuel ratio at stoichiometric (14.7:1) under all operating conditions, thereby ensuring a minimum exhaust emission output, and excellent fuel economy and vehicle performance. The sensors employed with each system are illustrated in each of the diagrams related to the nonturbocharged and turbocharged engines. A detailed description of these various sensors can be found in Chapter 4.

All input signals to the LM are converted into signals that are then sent to the PM (power module), which is designed to carry the electrical loads necessary to activate the fuel flow at the injector(s), as well as the ignition timing.

The LM, like other computer-equipped vehicles, has the capability to monitor or test many of its own input and

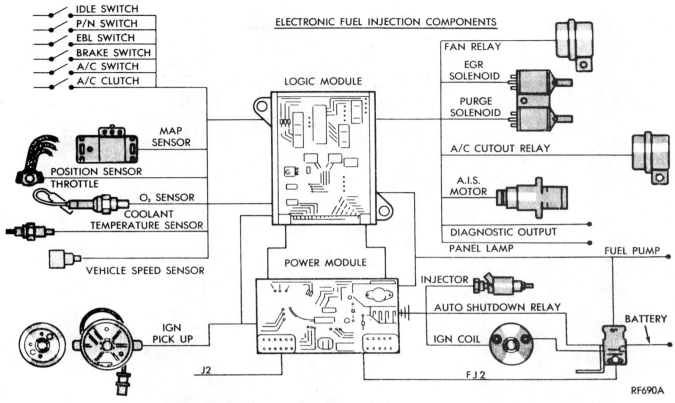

FIGURE 9-1 Electronic fuel injection components for the 2.2L four-cylinder CPI nonturbocharged engine. (*Courtesy of Chrysler Corporation*)

output voltage signals from the various sensors. Should the LM sense a fault condition in a major circuit or system, then this information will be stored in the LM memory system. This information can be retrieved at any time by a service technician by means of the instrument panel power loss lamp, or alternately by connecting a diagnostic readout tool (Chrysler P/N C-4805), a Kent-Moore or OTC Monitor 2000, or a digital automotive systems "Conquest" readout instrument. These alternative instruments are discussed in Chapter 14. The LM appears illustrated as part of the overall system in Figs. 9-1 and 9-2, but for clarity it is shown by itself in Fig. 9-3, where its 21 pin connector is clearly visible. In addition, Fig. 9-4 clearly shows where the LM is normally located in the vehicle itself.

POWER MODULE

The PM (power module) is the workhorse of the system, since it contains the necessary circuits required to carry the high current to power or operate the ignition coil and fuel injector(s). The PM is isolated from the LM to minimize any "electrical noise" or interference between the two units, and therefore the PM is generally located underhood and mounted on the fender apron on the driver's side. The PM

location is shown in Figs. 9-1 and 9-2 (engine sensors location). The PM is also used to energize the ASD (automatic shutdown) relay, which is used specifically to activate both the ignition coil and electric fuel pump as well as to power its own internal circuitry. The ASD relay is shown in Fig. 9-4, where it appears just above the logic module. Figure 9-5 illustrates the PM which uses both a 10 pin and 12 pin harness connector arrangement.

The PM receives a voltage signal from the ignition distributor which is used to indicate to the electronic control system that the engine is cranking and then running. This signal *must* be received at the PM; otherwise, the ASD relay will not be activated, and power will be shut off from both the fuel pump and the ignition coil. Within the PM is a voltage converter which is used to reduce battery voltage down to a regulated output to the system of 8 volts in order that it may power both the ignition distributor and the internal circuitry of the PM itself.

AUTOMATIC SHUTDOWN RELAY

The ASD (automatic shutdown) relay is energized from the PM at 8 volts once the PM receives a cranking signal from the ignition distributor. The PM will then ground the ASD,

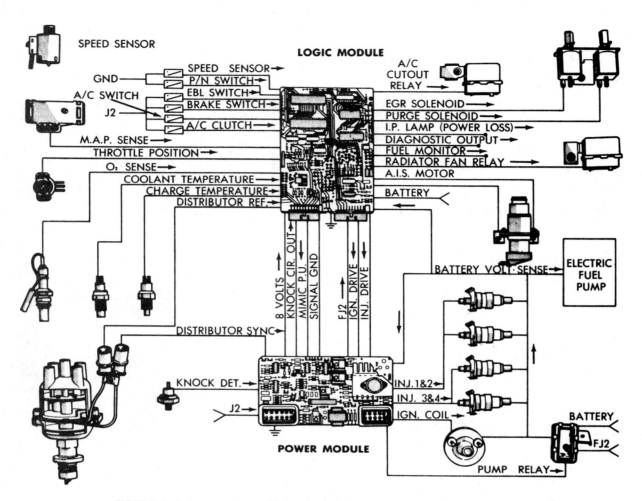

FIGURE 9-2   Electronic fuel injection components for 2.2L four cylinder engine MPI turbocharged engine. (*Courtesy of Chrysler Corporation*)

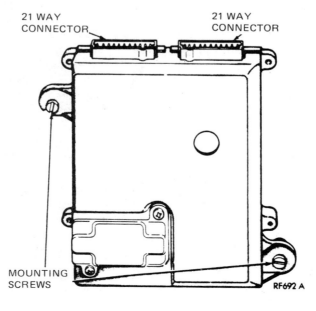

FIGURE 9-3   ECU logic module assembly. (*Courtesy of Chrysler Corporation*)

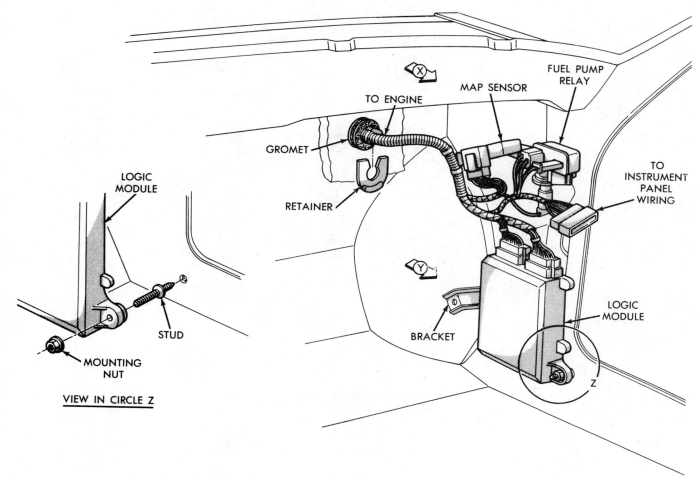

FIGURE 9-4 Logic module location in vehicle. (*Courtesy of Chrysler Corporation.*)

thereby closing its contacts and completing the circuit for the electric fuel pump, PM circuitry, and ignition coil. Should the distributor signal be lost at any time, then within 1 second, the ASD circuit will lose its ground path, the fuel and ignition systems will be de-energized, and the engine will shut down.

SENSORS

The various sensors used will not be discussed in detail here. (For comprehensive information regarding sensors, refer to Chapter 4.) However, note the location of the various sensors used with these engines in Figs. 9-6 and 9-7.

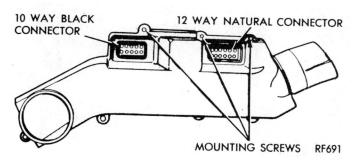

FIGURE 9-5 Electronic control system power module. (*Courtesy of Chrysler Corporation*).

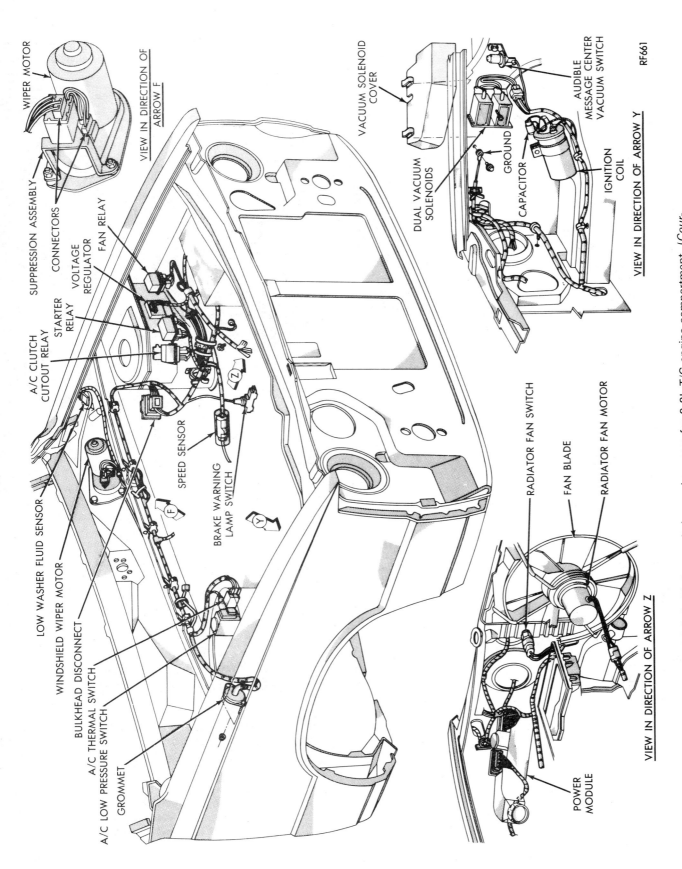

WIPER MOTOR

VIEW IN DIRECTION OF
ARROW F

SUPPRESSION ASSEMBLY
CONNECTORS
VOLTAGE REGULATOR
FAN RELAY

A/C CLUTCH CUTOUT RELAY
STARTER RELAY

LOW WASHER FLUID SENSOR
WINDSHIELD WIPER MOTOR
BULKHEAD DISCONNECT
A/C THERMAL SWITCH
A/C LOW PRESSURE SWITCH
GROMMET

SPEED SENSOR

BRAKE WARNING LAMP SWITCH

VACUUM SOLENOID COVER

DUAL VACUUM SOLENOIDS

GROUND
CAPACITOR

AUDIBLE MESSAGE CENTER VACUUM SWITCH

IGNITION COIL

RF661

VIEW IN DIRECTION OF ARROW Y

RADIATOR FAN SWITCH
FAN BLADE
RADIATOR FAN MOTOR

POWER MODULE

VIEW IN DIRECTION OF ARROW Z

FIGURE 9-6 Various switches and sensors for 2.2L T/C engine compartment. (*Courtesy of Chrysler Corporation*)

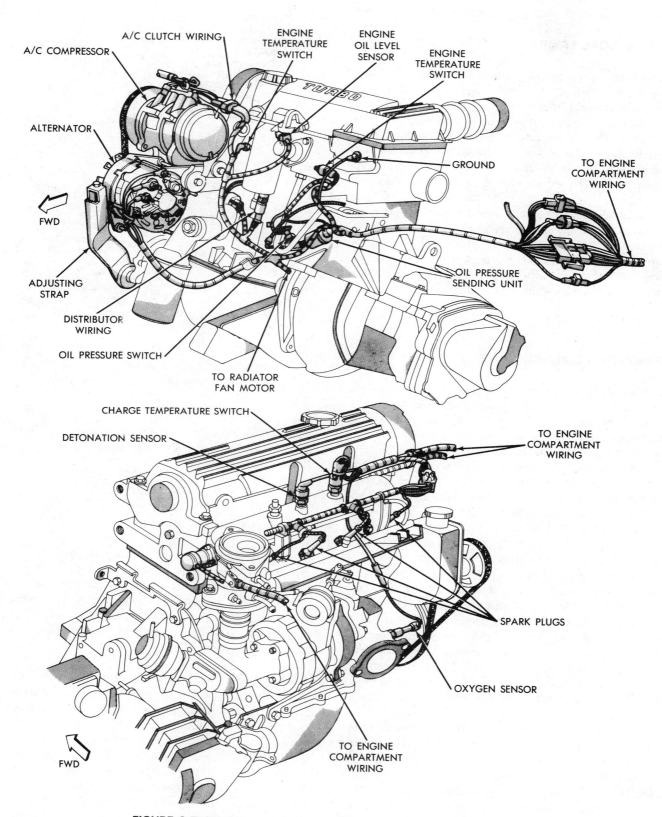

A/C COMPRESSOR

A/C CLUTCH WIRING

ALTERNATOR

ENGINE TEMPERATURE SWITCH

ENGINE OIL LEVEL SENSOR

ENGINE TEMPERATURE SWITCH

TURBO

GROUND

TO ENGINE COMPARTMENT WIRING

FWD

ADJUSTING STRAP

DISTRIBUTOR WIRING

OIL PRESSURE SWITCH

TO RADIATOR FAN MOTOR

OIL PRESSURE SENDING UNIT

CHARGE TEMPERATURE SWITCH

DETONATION SENSOR

TO ENGINE COMPARTMENT WIRING

SPARK PLUGS

OXYGEN SENSOR

TO ENGINE COMPARTMENT WIRING

FWD

FIGURE 9-7 Engine-mounted switches and sensors for 2.2L Turbo K-Body C-V 22-27-41 E Body E-T 4. (*Courtesy of Chrysler Corporation*)

POWER LOSS LAMP

Each time the ignition key is turned on, the PLL (power loss lamp) comes on for a few seconds to indicate that the bulb is operational. If at any time the logic module receives an incorrect or no signal condition from either the CTS, MAP, or TPS sensors, the PLL on the instrument panel will be illuminated as a warning to the driver that the LM has detected a fault and has resorted to a backup or limp-home mode. The vehicle should be serviced as soon as possible.

In addition, the PLL can be used to display fault codes stored in the computer memory system when activated by the service technician. This is simply done by turning the ignition key on/off, on/off, and on within a 5 second time period to activate the withdrawal from LM memory of any stored trouble codes which will be displayed/flashed.

PURGE AND EGR SOLENOIDS

Figure 9-6 illustrates both the EGR and purge solenoids. These are identified as dual vacuum solenoids in the diagram. They appear next to the "voice alert" and the "audible message center vacuum switch." Both solenoids are operated from the logic module with the purge solenoid switch being grounded (to energize) anytime that the engine coolant temperature is below 61°C (145°F). (See Fig. 9-1.) This action prevents engine vacuum from drawing stored fuel vapors from the charcoal canister valve, which would create a rich air/fuel mixture. Once the engine attains a temperature of 145°F or higher, the LM de-energizes the purge solenoid valve by breaking its path to ground. This now allows engine vacuum to pull fuel vapors through the canister purge valve and into the throttle body. The EGR solenoid is energized (grounded and closed) from the LM anytime that the engine coolant temperature is below 21°C (70°F) in order to prevent ported engine vacuum from reaching the EGR valve. When the engine warms up to the trigger point of the EGR valve, the LM breaks the ground path for the solenoid, thereby de-energizing it, and allows ported engine vacuum from the throttle body to pass through the EGR valve.

At an idle or WOT (wide open throttle) condition, the solenoid is energized (grounded through the LM) to prevent EGR operation. If not, the oxygen sensor would erroneously detect a rich condition, since recirculation of exhaust gases displace air (oxygen), and the sensor would signal the logic module to provide less fuel in order to lean out the air/fuel ratio.

Under all other engine operating conditions, EGR is programmed by the use of a back pressure transducer (Fig. 9-8). The back pressure transducer measures the amount of

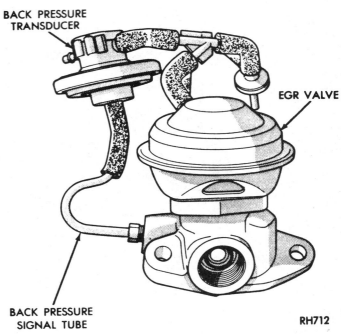

FIGURE 9-8 EGR and back-pressure transducer. (*Courtesy of Chrysler Corporation*)

exhaust back pressure on the exhaust side of the EGR valve and varies the strength of the vacuum signal applied to the EGR valve.

AIR CONDITIONING RELAY

The ACCR (air conditioning cut-out relay) is illustrated in Fig. 9-6. The ACCR is wired in series with the cycling switch and low pressure cut-out switch. Normally, the ACCR contacts are closed (on) when the engine is running. If, however the LM senses WOT through the TPS, it will energize the relay, thereby opening its contacts to prevent air conditioning clutch engagement.

IMPORTANT SERVICING PRECAUTION: Before performing any type of service on electronic systems or IC's (integrated circuits), you *must* discharge yourself of static electricity or ESD (electrostatic discharge) by touching a good vehicle ground, such as the door post or vehicle shift lever. Failure to do so can result in damage to voltage sensitive electronic components. If for any reason, you leave the vehicle during servicing, after re-entering to continue work, you *must* again ground yourself of ESD in order to drain any static electrical charge. Also, if you are performing control head/radio type checks on a new vehicle, remove the plastic seat covers, since they increase the possibility of creating a static charge.

ECU SYSTEM ACCESS AND DIAGNOSIS

When a problem is indicated by illumination of the instrument panel power loss lamp, first perform an underhood check before accessing the system to ensure that there are no loose, disconnected, or damaged vacuum hoses, or poor or damaged electrical connections. Once you have satisfied yourself that these systems are OK, proceed to access the logic module memory circuit at the engine compartment self-test connector, which is usually located near the right-side suspension strut tower.

LM access and stored trouble codes can be read directly from the Chrysler diagnostic readout Tool P/N C-4805 or from other special tools used for this purpose, such as the Kent-Moore and OTC Monitor 2000, or the digital automotive systems "Conquest" instrument, all of which are illustrated in Chapter 14. If none of these test instruments are available to you, then these stored trouble codes can be read directly from the flashing instrument panel power loss lamp as it flashes on and off, once the self-test connector has been activated.

The diagnostic connector and its relationship to the logic module and the other components of the system can best be described by reference to Fig. 9-9, which is a wiring diagram for a 2.2L EFI turbocharged four cylinder engine. The diagnostic connector is shown at the bottom of the diagram, midway between the center and right-hand side of the illustration.

In addition the two 21 pin logic module plug-in harness connectors' pin identifications are shown in Fig. 9-10 for connector 1, and in Fig. 9-11 for connector 2. These are the logic module connectors and they are shown, together with their circuit number, wire color, wire gauge, and function.

With the diagnostic readout box tool connected to the system, start the engine (if possible) and move the transmission selector lever through its various selective positions. If the vehicle is equipped with an air conditioner system, cycle the A/C switch on and off several times.

To initiate the self-diagnostic service access, quickly turn the ignition switch on/off, on/off, and on within 5 seconds, and monitor and record all of the trouble codes that flash on the readout tool. A Code 88 will flash first, which indicates the start of the diagnostic readout process. In addition, make sure that the instrument panel power loss lamp illuminates for 2 seconds, which will confirm that the bulb is operational.

Quick Check Procedure List:

1. Underhood check for loose vacuum hoses, wires, etc., or any signs of mechanical problems, such as oil, fuel, or vacuum leaks.

2. Connect self-diagnostic readout box to underhood (right strut tower) connector.

3. Cycle transmission selector and A/C switch.

4. Turn ignition switch on/off, on/off, and on within 5 seconds.

5. Record all diagnostic trouble codes. A Code 55 indicates that all stored codes have been flashed.

6. Refer to the fault code description chart which lists all of the trouble code numbers, along with an explanation of the system to check.

NOTE: If no fault codes are displayed, although the power loss lamp has illuminated for its 2 second period to confirm bulb serviceability, but engine performance problems are evident, then the problem is more than likely to be a mechanical rather than electronic one.

CAUTION: If any service is to be performed on the fuel-injection system, it must be depressurized before loosening off any lines, etc. The CPI (central point injection — throttle body type) is under a constant pressure of 36 psi (250 kPa), while the MPI (multi-point injection — individual cylinder injectors) system is under a constant pressure of 53 psi (380 kPa). This can be done as follows:

1. Loosen the gas tank cap to release any in-tank pressure.

2. Remove the wiring harness connector from any injector, and ground one terminal with a jumper wire.

3. Connect a jumper wire to the other terminal of the injector, and touch the battery positive post for a maximum time period of 10 seconds.

4. Remove the jumper wires. System pressure has now been released.*

SWITCH TEST

Once a Code 55 flashes to indicate the end of diagnostic readout, the following component switches should be actuated/released to see if the test instrument digital display does, in fact, change from a Code 55. Failure to change from this code indicates a possible malfunction at one of the following switches:

1. Brake pedal.

2. Gear shift selector from Park, Reverse, Park.

3. A/C switch, if the vehicle is so equipped.

4. Electric backlight switch, if applicable.

---

*More detailed discussion and service information for all the various fuel-injection systems (gasoline and diesel) for passenger cars and light pickup trucks can be found in my text, *Automotive and Small Truck Fuel-Injection Systems, Gas and Diesel,* published by Prentice-Hall, Inc., Englewood Cliffs, New Jersey, 07632, U.S.A.

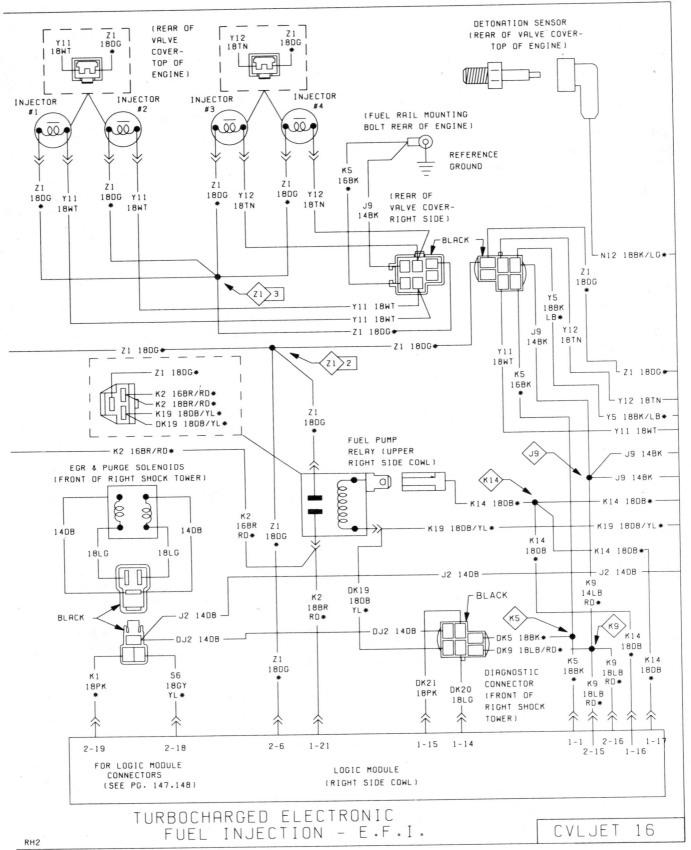

TURBOCHARGED ELECTRONIC
FUEL INJECTION - E.F.I.

CVLJET 16

RH2

FIGURE 9-9 Wiring diagram for a 2.2L EFI (port fuel injected) turbocharged engine. (*Courtesy of Chrysler Corporation*)

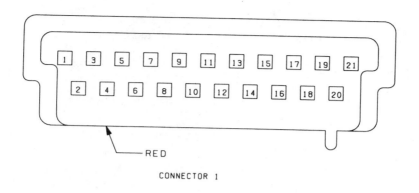

CONNECTOR 1

CAV	CIRCUIT	GAUGE	COLOR	FUNCTION
1	K5	18	BK*	SIGNAL GROUND
2	N5	18	BK/LB*	SIGNAL GROUND
3	N6	18	OR	7.5 VOLT SUPPLY FROM POWER MODULE
4	K8	18	VT*	5.0 VOLT SUPPLY FROM M.A.P. SENSOR
5	K16	18	VT/YL*	INJECTOR OFF CONTROL SIGNAL
6				
7	K15	18	YL	IGNITION CONTROL SIGNAL
8	Y1	18	GY/	INJECTOR ON SIGNAL
9	K12	18	YL/RD*	DETONATION SENSOR SIGNAL
10				
11	N7	18	GY*	DISTRIBUTOR REFERENCE SIGNAL
12	G7	20	WT/OR*	TRANSMISSION READ SWITCH SIGNAL
13	Z6	20	LB*	FUEL MONITOR OUTPUT SIGNAL
14	DK20	18	LG	DIAGNOSTIC INTERFACE
15	DK21	18	PK	DIAGNOSTIC INTERFACE
16	K14	18	DB*	FUSED IGNITION FEED-J2
17	K14	18	DB*	FUSED IGNITION FEED-J2
18	C27	18	DB/PK*	RADIATOR FAN RELAY
19	Y7	18	TN/YL*	DISTRIBUTOR SYNC PICKUP SIGNAL
20	K6	18	OR/WT*	5.0 VOLT SUPPLY FOR THROTTLE POT
21	K2	18	BR/RD*	FUSED BATTERY FEED

LOGIC MODULE CONNECTOR
TURBOCHARGED-EFI

CVLJET 147

RH2

FIGURE 9-10 Logic module connector 1 pin I.D. for 2.2L EFI turbocharged engine. (*Courtesy of Chrysler Corporation*)

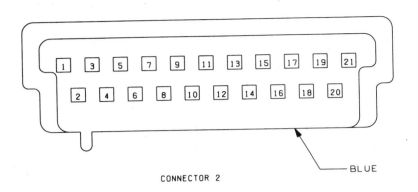

CONNECTOR 2 — BLUE

CAV	CIRCUIT	GAUGE	COLOR	FUNCTION
1	S4	18	BR/YL*	PARK/NEUTRAL SWITCH SIGNAL
2	C16	18	LB/YL*	HEATED REAR WINDOW SIGNAL
3	K4	18	DG/RD*	MANIFOLD ABSOLUTE PRESSURE SIGNAL
4	K4	18	DG/RD*	MANIFOLD ABSOLUTE PRESSURE SIGNAL
5	K7	18	OR/DB*	THROTLE POSITION SIGNAL
6	Z1	18	DG*	FUEL PUMP SIGNAL
7	C2	18	BR	AIR CONDITIONING CLUTCH SIGNAL
8	K10	18	TN*	COOLANT TEMPERATURE SENSOR SIGNAL
9	C2	18	DD/BK*	AIR CONDITIONING SWITCH SIGNAL
10	K13	18	BK/RD*	AIR TEMPERATURE SENSOR SIGNAL
11	N13	18	DB/OR*	WIDE OPEN THROTTLE A/C CUTOUT SIGNAL
12	N1	18	GY/RD*	AUTOMATIC IDLE SPEED OPEN SIGNAL
13	D4	18	WT/TN*	BRAKE SWITCH SIGNAL
14	N2	18	BR*	AUTOMATIC IDLE SPEED CLOSE SIGNAL
15	K9	18	LB/RD*	POWER GROUND
16	K9	18	LB/RD*	POWER GROUND
17	K3	20	GY/OR*	POWER LOSS LAMP
18	S6	18	GY/YL*	EXHAUST GAS RECIRCULATOR SIGNAL
19	K1	18	PK*	EGR SOLENOID SIGNAL
20				
21	N11	18	BK	OXYGEN SENSOR SIGNAL

LOGIC MODULE CONNECTOR
TURBOCHARGED-EFI

CVLJET 148.

RH2

FIGURE 9-11 Logic module connector 2 pin I.D. for 2.2L EFI turbo-charged engine. (*Courtesy of Chrysler Corporation*)

ACTUATOR TEST MODE (ATM)

This test is designed to check the following three facets of operation:

1. When the ignition coil fires 3 times, it indicates—
   (a) Coil is operational;
   (b) Logic module (LM) is operational;
   (c) Power module (PM) is operational;
   (d) Interface between the LM and PM is operational.
2. AIS (automatic idle speed motor) is operational.
3. Injector fuel pulse into throttle body indicates —
   (a) Fuel injector is operational;
   (b) Fuel pump is operational;
   (c) Fuel lines are intact.

The electronic fuel-injection system must be evaluated/diagnosed from all of the information obtained from the following tests:

1. Start/no start;
2. Fault codes flashed to the diagnostic readout tool;
3. Loss of power lamp illumination (on or off), which will cause the logic module to revert to limp-home capability. The LM substitutes a programmed operational sequence into the system.
4. ATM (actuator test mode) results, such as:
   (a) Spark, yes or no,
   (b) Fuel delivery, yes or no,
   (c) AIS (automatic idle speed) motor movement, yes or no.

Perform the test instrument actuator test mode (ATM) as follows:

ATM Procedure

1. Remove ignition coil high tension wire from the coil and place it no more than ¼″ from ground; otherwise, power module damage can result.
2. Remove the air cleaner assembly.

NOTE: When the ATM button on the diagnostic readout tool is pressed, a Fault Code 42 will be flashed, because the ASD (automatic shutdown) relay is bypassed. DO NOT use this code for diagnostics after ATM operation.

3. Press the ATM button on the diagnostic readout box and check for:
   (a) 3 sparks from the coil wire to ground,
   (b) And listen carefully for 2 AIS motor movements (1 open, 1 close).
4. With ATM button still depressed, install a jumper wire between pins 2 and 3 of the gray distributor synchronous connector, and listen for a click which confirms that one set of fuel injectors have been activated. Remove the jumper wire, and the second set of injectors should now be activated. Reconnect the distributor wire connector.

NOTE: The ATM test will last for only 5 minutes after the ignition switch is turned on. Therefore, if you require longer than this time to check the system, cycle the ignition key on and off three times, and ending, of course, with the ignition key in the on position.

FAULT CODE NUMBERS

Number	System Affected
11	Ignition distributor circuit. Logic Module has not sensed a distributor voltage signal.
12	Direct memory feed (standby) circuit interruption to the logic module.
13	MAP sensor pneumatic system problem. Code triggered when vacuum level doesn't change between start and start/run transfer speed (500–600 rpm).
14	MAP sensor voltage signal too low (less than 0.02 volts), or too high (above 4.9 volts).
	Vehicle speed sensor (VSS) circuit. Code appears if engine is at idle and speed is less than 2 mph while moving.
21	Exhaust gas oxygen sensor circuit. This code will appear if no oxygen sensor voltage signal has been received by the logic module for at least 5 seconds, and if the engine coolant temperature is above 77°C (170°F) and with a speed above 1500 rpm. (Refer to Chapter 4 on Sensors for a test of this unit.)

Number	System Affected
22	CTS (coolant temperature sensor) circuit.
23	T/C engine only. Problem is in the charge temperature circuit.
24	TPS (throttle position sensor) circuit. Code appears if the voltage is below 0.16 volts or above 4.7 volts.
25	AIS (automatic idle speed) system. An open motor or harness will not activate this code. Normally caused by lack of proper voltage feed.
31	CPS (canister purge solenoid) circuit. Code appears when open or shorts are evident. Improper voltage at solenoid.
32	PLL (power loss lamp) circuit is open or shorted. The problem is improper voltage.
33	Problem in the air conditioning wide-open-throttle cut-out-relay circuit. Open or shorted system.
34	EGR (exhaust gas recirculation) solenoid circuit. Open or shorted.
35	Fan relay circuit. Code appears if fan is not operating, or is operating at the wrong time.
41	Charging system problem. Code appears if battery voltage from the ADS (automatic shutdown) relay is below 11.75 volts.
42	ADS (automatic shutdown) relay circuit. Code appears if during cranking, battery voltage from the ASD relay is not present for at least ⅓ of a second after the initial ignition distributor pulse; or if after engine stall, the battery voltage is not off within 3 seconds after last distributor pulse.
43	Indicates a problem in the interface circuit between the logic and power modules. Code appears if the anti-dwell or injector control signal is not present.
44	Logic module problem. Possibly, incorrect PROM installed in logic module.
45	Turbocharged engine only with problem in the overboost shutoff circuit. Code appears if the MAP sensor electrical signal increases beyond a 10 psi (68.95 kPa) boost.
51	Closed-loop fuel system problem. A closed-loop condition exists when the logic module is receiving and responding to the voltage signal from the oxygen sensor. Code 51 will appear if, during closed loop, the voltage signal from the oxygen sensor is low or high for more than 2 minutes.
52, 53	Internal failure in logic module.
54	Problem in the synchronization pickup circuit. Code appears if, at start/run transfer speed, the reference pickup signal is present, but the synchronization pickup signal is missing at the logic module.
55	Indicates that all codes have been flashed and end of trouble code transfer.
88	This code always appears at the start of diagnostic readout (access).

CHAPTER 10

♦

American Motors
ECU System

Chapter 4 dealt in detail with the function, operation, and description of the various sensors and switches/solenoids used on engines and vehicles today. The various sensors used on the Alliance/Encore four-cylinder engine vehicles are shown in Fig. 10-2, while Fig. 10-1 illustrates the various inputs and outputs to the ECU (electronic control unit) for these systems.

ALLIANCE AND ENCORE VEHICLES

Figure 10-2 illustrates the typical arrangement of the engine and associated sensors and switches used with these vehicles, with the engine control system being divided into six main subsystems. These are:

1. The ECU (electronic control unit), which on these vehicles is located below the glove box near the fuse panel.
2. Sensors and switches as shown in Fig. 10-2.
3. Fuel control: incorporates an in-tank electric fuel pump which delivers fuel to the throttle body containing the fuel pressure regulator and the electronically controlled centrally-mounted fuel injector. Fuel pressure in excess of 14.5 psi (1 kg/cm2) is returned via a return line to the tank. Injector pulse-width time is controlled from the ECU.
4. Emission control: both EGR and fuel vapor canister purge are controlled by the ECU. No EGR occurs until the engine reaches a predetermined operating temperature in order to improve cold driveability. The charcoal canister purge system does not operate until the oxygen sensor reaches approximately 600°F.
5. Idle speed control: an idle speed control motor changes the throttle stop angle based upon information fed from the ECU. When the engine is cold, the throttle is held open for a longer time than it would be when a hot engine is started. Engine idle speed is controlled from the ECU, which determines this rpm based upon the various sensor inputs.
6. Ignition advance control: the ignition control module and the ECU are connected through two switching circuits. Under certain engine operating conditions, the ignition advance curve will be modified for optimum performance.

IMPORTANT SERVICING PRECAUTION: Before performing any type of service on electronic systems or IC's (integrated circuits), you *must* discharge yourself of static electricity or ESD (electrostatic discharge) by touching a good vehicle ground, such as the door post or vehicle shift lever. Failure to do so can result in damage to voltage sensitive electronic components. If, for any reason, you leave the vehicle during servicing, after re-entering to continue work, you *must* again ground yourself of ESD in order to drain any static electrical charge. Also, if you are performing control head/radio type checks on a new vehicle, remove the plastic seat covers, since they increase the possibility of creating a static charge.

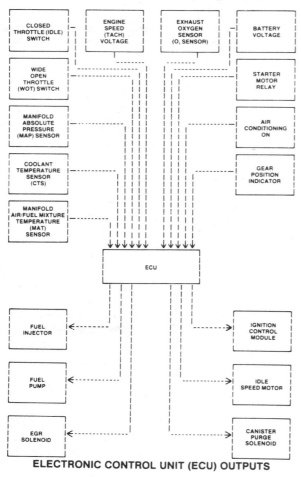

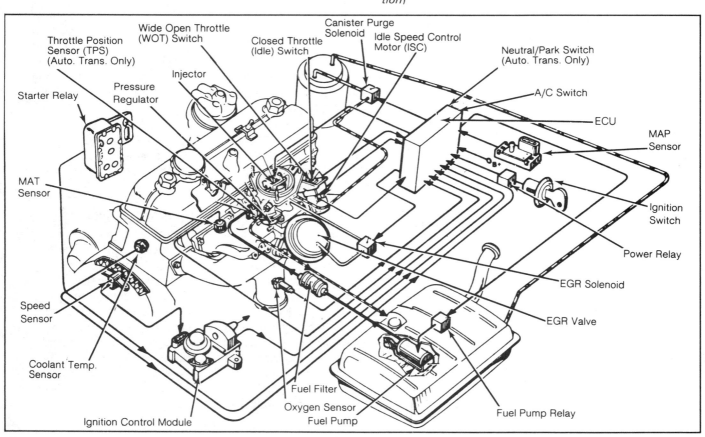

ELECTRONIC CONTROL UNIT (ECU) OUTPUTS

FIGURE 10-1 Typical inputs/outputs for the Alliance/Encore ECU system. (*Courtesy of American Motors Corporation*)

ECU ACCESS

Figure 10-3 illustrates the location of and the terminal identification for the diagnostic connector on these vehicles, while Fig. 10-4 depicts the wiring diagram for the ECU system and the various diagnostic connectors. Use this wiring diagram to assist you when checking various sensors and switches for resistance, voltage, and shorts and opens between problem areas in the system.

When it becomes necessary to access the ECU trouble code memory bank, install a No. 158 test bulb or equivalent between pin 2 and 4 of the diagnostic connector D2, as shown in Fig. 10-3. With the test bulb installed and to activate the system, push the WOT switch lever on the throttle body as well as the ISC motor plunger closed. Turn the ignition switch on and closely watch the test bulb, which should illuminate for a short time and then go out. Failure of the bulb to light indicates that there is a problem with the ECU. Therefore, whether or not there are any trouble codes stored in the memory bank of the ECU, the initial illumination of the test light confirms that the ECU is, in fact, operational.

FIGURE 10-2 AMC Alliance/Encore TBI engine component locations. (*Courtesy of American Motors Corporation*)

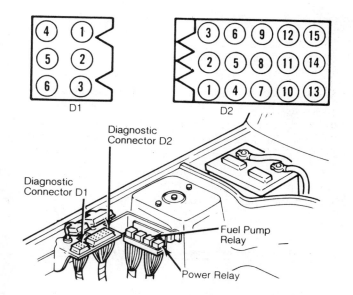

FIGURE 10-3 Alliance/Encore diagnostic connector location and terminal identification. (*Courtesy of American Motors Corporation*)

FIGURE 10-4 Alliance/Encore TBI system wiring diagram for ECU sensors/switches. (*Courtesy of American Motors Corporation*)

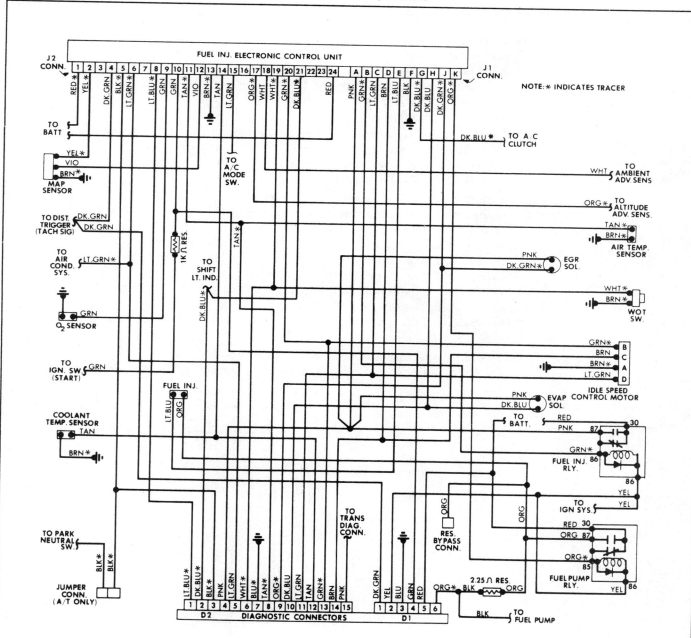

Should the test bulb fail to flash, ensure that the test bulb is not faulty and that voltage is, in fact, available to the bulb. Also check that a minimum battery voltage of 11.5 volts is apparent at the ECU, with the ignition key on. Check for a good ground at the ECU as well. Finally, check that both the WOT switch and coolant temperature switch are making contact. After the initial illumination of the test light bulb, the ECU will cause any trouble codes to appear as a series of brief flashes at the test bulb. For example, if a Code 4 is stored in the ECU memory bank, then the test light bulb will flash four times. If more than one trouble code is stored in the ECU, then after a slight pause, the test bulb will flash again to indicate the other trouble code in memory. The ECU always indicates first the trouble code which has been stored the longest. After a longer pause, the cycle of trouble codes will repeat as long as the test light bulb remains in place.

TROUBLE CODES

Code 1   Check the MAT sensor resistance after disconnecting the wiring harness. It should be between 300–300,000 ohms or 10,000 ohms if at room temperature; otherwise, replace the sensor. Also test the wiring harness resistance for a maximum reading in excess of 1 ohm between pin 13 of the ECU harness connector J2 and the sensor connector, as well as between pin 11 and the sensor connector.

Code 2   Check coolant temperature sensor resistance for the same values as that in Code 1. Check harness resistance between pin 14 of ECU connector J2 and sensor connector. Check resistance between pin 11 of connector J2 and sensor connector. Check harness for open circuits.

Code 3   Check WOT (wide open throttle) switch, wiring and harness connectors for corrosion, bent pins, damaged wiring, shorts or grounds. Infinite resistance should be seen when WOT switch is closed. When wide open, resistance value should be low. Also check for zero voltage with WOT switch fully open, and more than 2 volts in all other positions between pin 6 and 7 (ground) of diagnostic connector with ignition switch on.
Zero voltage continuously: check for short to ground in harness or switch. Check for opens between pin 19 of ECU connector J2 and switch connector.
Greater than 2 volts continuously: check for opens between the switch and ground.

Code 4   This indicates a simultaneous closed throttle switch and MAP sensor failure. Check both units for resistance in wiring, opens or grounds, corrosion, loose

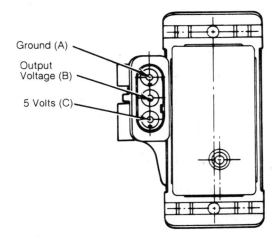

Ground (A)
Output Voltage (B)
5 Volts (C)

FIGURE 10-5 MAP sensor terminal I.D. (*Courtesy of American Motors Corporation*)

connections, etc. If voltage is always zero, check for a short circuit to ground, and if always 2 volts or more, check for an open circuit between the ECU and switch connector.

Code 5   WOT switch and MAP sensor problem. Check as in Code 4. MAP sensor output voltage should be between 4 and 5.5 volts with a voltage drop of between 0.5 to 1.5 volts with a hot engine at idle. Figure 10-5 illustrates the terminals on the MAP sensor.

Code 6   Oxygen sensor problem. Refer to Chapter 4 for details on sensor test. In addition, test that fuel pressure is correct in system. Check EGR and canister purge control systems. Check secondary ignition circuit. Check PCV circuit.

JEEP CHEROKEE—WAGONEER, AND COMANCHE VEHICLES MCU/CEC SYSTEM

Jeep vehicles are available with either an in-line four- or six-cylinder gasoline engine, or with a 2.8L 60-degree V6 gasoline engine of GMC manufacture. A four-cylinder 2.1L (128 cu. in.) turbodiesel is also optional. AMC has gone to a full computer system on the 2.5L four-cylinder 1986 engine used in the Cherokee and Comanche vehicles with TBI (throttle body injection). In addition to cycling the fuel injector (pulse-width time, on/off), the engine control computer also determines ignition timing, idle speed, exhaust gas recirculation, and canister purge. The GM 2.8L V6 engine is equipped with a two-barrel feedback carburetor containing an electronically-operated mixture control solenoid similar to the system used on the in-line four- and six-cylinder FBC engines found on nonfuel-injected Jeep vehicles.

NOTE: For information dealing with the 2.8L V6 engine and its CCC (computer command control) system, refer to Chapter 7, which discusses GMC vehicles.

The four-cylinder (2.5L/153 cu. in.) and six-cylinder (4.2L/258 cu. in.) in-line gasoline engines use an electronically-controlled system designed to manage the air/fuel ratio, idle rpm, and ignition timing. This system is known as a CEC (computerized emission control) arrangement, and it consists of the following subsystems:

1. Fuel control
2. Microcomputer control unit (MCU)
3. Various data sensors
4. Catalytic converter
6. Idle speed control
7. Pulse air injection control
8. Ignition advance control

Both the in-line four- and six-cylinder engines are equipped with FBC (feedback carburetors), which contain an electronically-controlled MC or mixture control solenoid on the four-cylinder and a stepper motor on the six-cylinder engine. (See Figs. 5-1 and 5-2.)

The MC solenoid on the four-cylinder engine controls the amount of air that is allowed to mix with the fuel, while on the six-cylinder engine, the stepper motor controls metering pins, which in turn vary the size of both the idle and main bleed orifices in the carburetor body. The stepper motor has the ability to move the pins in or out in 100 increments, although when it operates under normal conditions, the stepper motor places the pins in the middle position.

Moving (stepping) the metering pins into the orifices results in a richer air/fuel ratio, whereas stepping the pins out of these same orifices will result in a leaner air/fuel ratio. This system is similar to that discussed in Chapter 5 for GMC and its FBC equipped engines. For information on sensors used with these engines and the function of sensors, refer to Chapter 4. In the open-loop mode, the MCU ignores the exhaust oxygen sensor signals, and sets a preprogrammed air/fuel mixture.

In the closed-loop engine operating mode, the MCU receives the oxygen sensor voltage signals and then determines the correct air/fuel ratio, based upon the amount of oxygen flowing through the exhaust system. Because of the ability of the exhaust gas oxygen sensor to respond rapidly to changing oxygen conditions flowing through the system, closed-loop operation is characterized by continual movement of the MC (mixture control) solenoid plunger (four cylinder), or by the metering pins on the six-cylinder FBC engines.

Other engine sensors which are also feeding information back to the MCU allow the air/fuel mixture to be kept as close to stoichiometric (14.7:1) as possible. The MCU alters ignition timing based upon signals its receives from the knock sensor.

The throttle position determines whether air injection is routed ''downstream'' or ''upstream'' at any given moment. The pulse air injection system is switched from upstream to downstream injection (or both) by the MCU. This

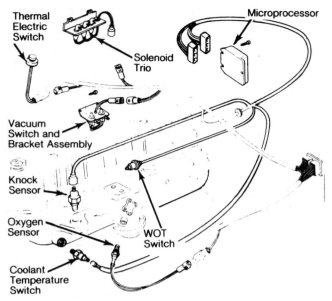

FIGURE 10-6 Jeep CEC (computerized emission control) system. (*Courtesy of American Motors Corporation*)

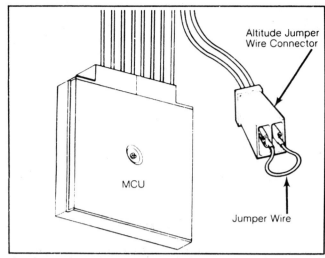

Jumper wire must be installed as shown for vehicle operated above 4000 feet.

FIGURE 10-7 Jumper wire connection — four-cylinder engine shown. (*Courtesy of American Motors Corporation*)

is achieved through the use of two electrically-operated vacuum solenoid valves, with one valve being employed for upstream and the other for downstream control routing. These solenoid control valves are mounted on a bracket on the left-fender panel for the four-cylinder engine, or on top of the valve rocker cover for the six-cylinder engine.

Figure 10-6 illustrates an example of the CEC system, on Jeep vehicles. The MCU on the four- and six-cylinder engines is located behind the right-hand kick panel in the passenger compartment. When checking the system for a complaint cause, first perform the normal checks and tests that you would run on a non-CEC equipped vehicle, before assuming that the CEC system is malfunctioning. Check all vacuum hoses for proper routing, looseness, or disconnections, as well as all electrical wires and harness connectors. Also ensure that the carburetor is correctly adjusted, the ignition system is sound, that there are no leaking manifold gaskets, and that the engine compression pressure, etc., is acceptable. Often, these simple checks will uncover the reason for the problem, without your having to resort to more detailed checks.

ALTITUDE JUMPER WIRE

Poor engine/vehicle performance may be a direct result of geographical location. If the vehicle is operated at altitudes above 4000 feet, an altitude jumper wire must be grounded (see Fig. 10-7) and an emission control information update label must be installed. The label can be obtained from your local Jeep dealer.

The connection for the jumper wire on the four-cylinder engine is next to the MCU, while on the six-cylinder engine, the jumper wire is taped to the CEC system wiring harness in the engine compartment. The jumper wire can be grounded as shown in Fig. 10-7 for the four-cylinder engine, while for the six-cylinder engine, physically connect the ground wire to a noninsulated screw.

TESTING EQUIPMENT

On the four- and six-cylinder CEC equipped engines, typical tools required include:

1. Tachometer.
2. Hand-operated vacuum pump and gauge.
3. Dwell meter for the four-cylinder engine only.
4. DVOM (digital volt/ohmmeter) with a minimum 10 megohm impedance.
5. Assorted jumper wires.
6. Clear plastic air cleaner cover (¼″ thick) for use on the six-cylinder engine in order to observe both the operation and position of the metering pins. (The metering pins operate in tandem, with only the upper pin visible). Figure 10-8 illustrates how to fabricate a clear plastic cover that can be installed in place of the regular air cleaner cover. Retain this cover with the air cleaner wing nut for testing purposes.

Checks and tests of these two systems involve systematically checking the various vacuum controls and electrical

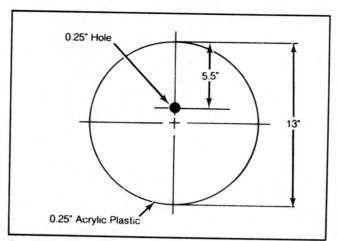

0.25" Hole

5.5"

13"

0.25" Acrylic Plastic

FIGURE 10-8 Clear plastic air cleaner cover dimensions — six-cylinder engine only. (*Courtesy of American Motors Corporation*)

Fabricate cover to allow observation of metering pins.

connections and circuits for signs of opens, shorts, corroded terminals, loose connections, continuity between the CEC electronic control unit, and the various sensors and switches.

Figure 10-9 illustrates a typical wiring diagram for the four- and six-cylinder CEC engines. Figure 10-10 shows the CEC electronic control unit connector pin locations.

TEST SEQUENCE — FOUR- AND SIX-CYLINDER ENGINES

The following lists the typical tests that are performed on the four-cylinder FBC engines.

Test Number	Condition
1	Operational test of system
2	Switch test
3	Closed-loop test
4	Knock test
5	Oxygen sensor and closed-loop test
6	Downstream solenoid test
7	Upstream solenoid test
8A	Bowl vent test
8B	PCV shutoff test
8C	Anti-diesel system test
9	Idle speed control system test
10	Solenoid vacuum switching relay test
11	Basic engine test

The following test sequence is performed on the six-cylinder engines:

Test Number	Condition
1	Operational test
2	Initialization test
3	Open-loop switch test

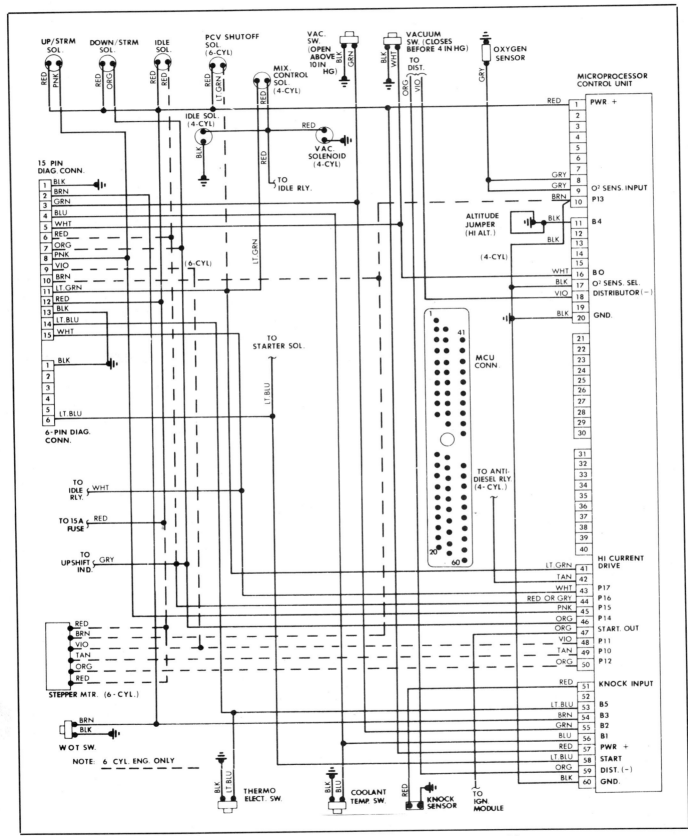

FIGURE 10-9   Jeep four- and six-cylinder CEC wiring diagram. (*Courtesy of American Motors Corporation*)

Test Number Condition

4	Closed-loop operational test
5	Electronic ignition retard test
6	Oxygen sensor and closed-loop test
7	Downstream solenoid test
8	Upstream solenoid test
9	Idle speed control system test
10	Solenoid vacuum switching solenoid test
11	Solenoid vacuum idle speed relay test
12	Basic engine test

Index to Connector Pins (Figure 10-10)

D1 Connector

1. Tachometer
2. Electric choke
3. Ground
4. Starter circuit
5. Idle control solenoid
6. Not used

D2 Connector

1. PCV shutoff solenoid
2. Shift light (4 cylinder)
   Idle solenoid (6 cylinder)

3. Altitude jumper wire
4. Power supply
5. Downstream air-injection solenoid
6. WOT switch
7. Ground
8. Upstream air-injection solenoid
9. 10-inch Hg (mercury) vacuum switch
10. Thermal electric switch
11. Mixture control solenoid vacuum (4-cylinder engine);
    Stepper motor on the 6-cylinder engine.
12. Coolant temperature switch
13. Idle speed relay
14. Mixture control solenoid (4-cylinder engine); Stepper motor on the 6-cylinder engine.
15. 4-inch Hg (mercury) vacuum switch

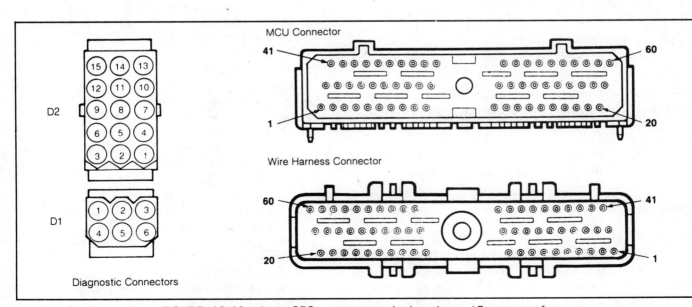

FIGURE 10-10 Jeep CEC connector pin locations. (*Courtesy of American Motors Corporation*)

An electronic fuel feedback tester AMC P/N ET 501 is available to assist the technician in diagnosing system complaints. In addition, several other major tool suppliers offer similar tools for quick troubleshooting of the system. For more information on these diagnostic tools, refer to Chapter 14. If the feedback tester is not available, then systematically perform tests 1, 3, 4, 6, 8A, 8B, and 9, which will confirm where the problem might be. For detailed analysis of the following systematic checks, refer to the respective AMC service manual.

CHEROKEE/COMANCHE 2.5L TBI SYSTEM

The TBI 2.5L four-cylinder engine employs thirteen sensors and switches to monitor engine operation through the ECU (electronic control unit), which is a microprocessor-based computer.

The following sensors and switches/relays are used with this TBI system:

1. Exhaust gas oxygen sensor
2. MAT (manifold air temperature) sensor
3. CTS (coolant temperature sensor)
4. MAP (manifold absolute pressure) sensor
5. Knock sensor
6. Speed sensor
7. Starter motor relay
8. WOT (wide open throttle) switch
9. Closed throttle idle switch
10. Transmission gear position indicator switch
11. Power steering pressure switch
12. A/C switch
13. Idle speed actuator motor
14. Fuel pump control relay
15. System power relay
16. Load swap relay (works in conjunction with the power steering pressure switch to disengage the A/C compressor clutch)

Figure 10-11 illustrates the wiring diagram for the 2.5L four-cylinder TBI (throttle body injection) system.

Basic System Description

An in-tank electric roller cell fuel pump, which is controlled by the ECU, delivers fuel to the combination fuel pressure regulator/fuel injector. Both are integral components of the throttle body assembly. The fuel pressure regulator is a spring-loaded device that controls fuel pressure in the system to 17.3 psi, after which time it bypasses excess pressure/fuel back to the fuel tank through a return line. The fuel injector is controlled by the ECU, which determines its pulse-width time (on/off), based upon voltage signals from the various engine/vehicle sensors.

In open-loop operating mode, the ECU ignores the feedback signal from the exhaust gas oxygen sensor, while in the closed-loop mode, the ECU responds to the oxygen sensor signal and varies the injector pulse-width time to maintain as near a stoichiometric air/fuel ratio as possible under all operating conditions.

SENSOR CHECKS

CAUTION: When working around on-board computer systems, it is imperative that you always exercise extreme care when connecting or disconnecting hot wires. Therefore *never* remove or attach a wire/connector with the ignition switch in the on position. Turn it off first. *Never* induce a voltage higher than 12 volts to the system or terminals. *Always* disconnect the battery terminals before charging the battery. If at any time the vehicle is to be repainted and dried in a drying chamber where the baking temperature will exceed 176°F (80°C), remove the ECU from the vehicle. The ECU is located in the passenger compartment below the glove box.

1. *MAT and CTS sensor checks:* Both the MAT and CTS can be checked in the same manner and should have the same resistance values. To check these two sensors, disconnect the wiring harness connector and connect a high impedance digital type ohmmeter across the sensor terminals. If the resistance value is not between 185 and 100,700 or 3400 ohms at 70°F (21°C); 1600 ohms at 100°F (38°C), then replace the sensor. With the engine warm, the sensor resistance should be less than 1000 ohms.

2. *MAP sensor:* The MAP sensor is located on the intake manifold. (See Fig. 10-12.) If the vacuum hoses appear to be tight and properly routed, check the sensor as follows:
   (a) Connect a voltmeter to the MAP sensor terminal B, similar to that shown in Fig. 10-12, with the ignition key on, but the engine stopped. If the reading is between 4.0 and 5.0 volts, then the sensor is OK. Another check to confirm that the MAP sensor is operational is one with the engine at operating temperature/idling, and with this voltage reading decreasing to between 0.5 and 1.5 volts.
   (b) To ensure that the wiring harness to the MAP sensor is operational, test the voltage between pin 33 of the ECU connector (Fig. 10-14), which should register between 4.0 and 5.0 volts.

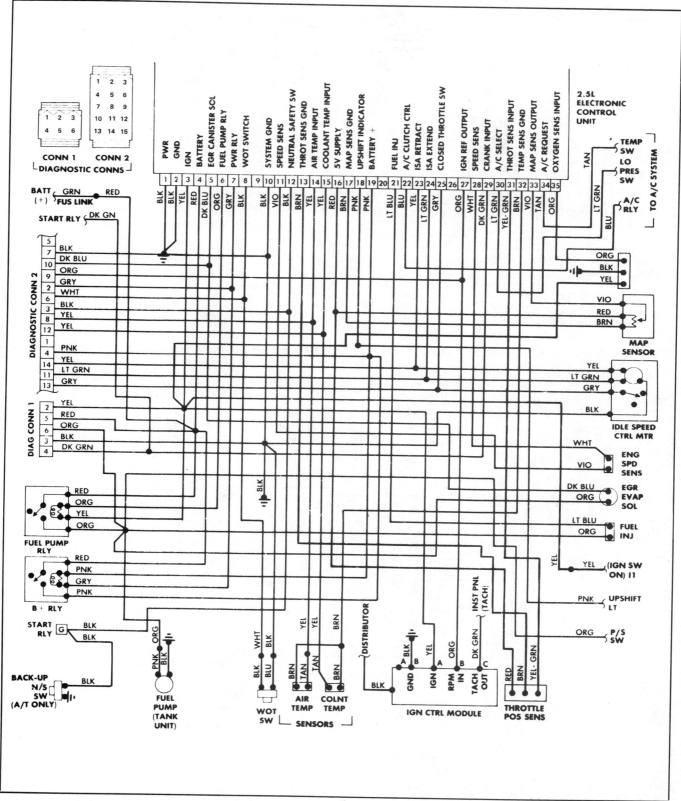

FIGURE 10-11 Jeep 2.5L TBI system wiring diagram. (*Courtesy of American Motors Corporation*)

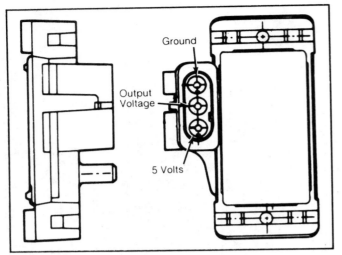

If markings on MAP sensor vary from illustration, use markings on sensor.

FIGURE 10-12 MAP sensor — 2.5L four-cylinder TBI engine. (*Courtesy of American Motors Corporation*)

(c) Ignition key on: check sensor connector pin C for between 4.5 and 5.5 volts. This reading should also be registered at pin 16 of the ECU connector. Also ensure that a ground exists between pin 17 of the ECU connector and pin A of the sensor connector.

(d) With an ohmmeter attached between pin 17 of the ECU connector and pin 2, make sure that a ground

exists. If an open circuit is indicated, check for a possible sensor ground on the flywheel housing close to the starter motor assembly. Should a good ground be indicated on the ohmmeter, check first of all to see if pin 17 of the ECU connector is shorted to the battery voltage supply (12 volts). If it is, then attempt to repair the fault; otherwise, the ECU will require replacement.

3. *WOT switch check:* WOT switch can be checked by using an ohmmeter across the switch terminals with the wiring harness disconnected, and by manually opening and closing the throttle switch. Resistance should be infinite at a closed position and have a low resistance at a wide open position; otherwise, replace the switch.

   With the wiring harness connected to the throttle switch, turn the ignition key on, and connect a voltmeter across pins 6 and 7 of the diagnostic connector D2. (See Fig. 10-13.)

   No voltage should register on the voltmeter with the switch in the wide open position, or be greater than 2 volts in any other position. The wiring harness requires repair or replacement if the voltage always registers zero, since a possible short to ground in either the harness or switch is probably the cause. To check for an ''open'' circuit, connect the volt/ohmmeter between pin 8 of the ECU connector and the switch connector.

   Should the voltage at the WOT switch always be in excess of 2 volts, then test for an open wire or connector between the switch and ground.

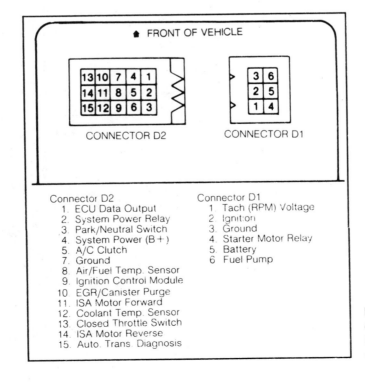

FIGURE 10-13 Identification of diagnostic connectors D1 and D2. (*Courtesy of American Motors Corporation*)

4. Closed throttle switch check: Make sure that the ISA (idle speed actuator) motor plunger is in the fully extended position when conducting this test. If you have to pull out the ISA plunger manually, then the ISA motor has more than likely failed, especially if voltage feed to the terminals is confirmed.

Proceed as follows:

(a) Ignition on: connect the positive lead (red) of the voltmeter to pin 13 of the diagnostic connector D2. (See Fig. 10-13.) Connect the black negative lead to pin 7. Zero to minimum voltage should be evident at a closed throttle position, and it should always be higher than 2 volts in any other position.

(b) Voltage always at zero: test for a short to ground in either the wiring harness or switch. Test for an "open" between pin 25 of the ECU connector (Fig. 10-14) and throttle switch.

(c) Voltage always in excess of 2 volts: test for an "open" in the wiring harness between the ECU and switch connector, as well as between the switch connector and ground.

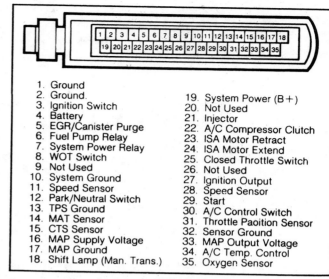

1. Ground
2. Ground.
3. Ignition Switch
4. Battery
5. EGR/Canister Purge
6. Fuel Pump Relay
7. System Power Relay
8. WOT Switch
9. Not Used
10. System Ground
11. Speed Sensor
12. Park/Neutral Switch
13. TPS Ground
14. MAT Sensor
15. CTS Sensor
16. MAP Supply Voltage
17. MAP Ground
18. Shift Lamp (Man. Trans.)
19. System Power (B+)
20. Not Used
21. Injector
22. A/C Compressor Clutch
23. ISA Motor Retract
24. ISA Motor Extend
25. Closed Throttle Switch
26. Not Used
27. Ignition Output
28. Speed Sensor
29. Start
30. A/C Control Switch
31. Throttle Paoition Sensor
32. Sensor Ground
33. MAP Output Voltage
34. A/C Temp. Control
35. Oxygen Sensor

FIGURE 10-14 Identification of ECU connector terminals. (*Courtesy of American Motors Corporation*)

CHAPTER 11

Toyota (TCCS) Computer-Controlled System

TROUBLE CODE ACCESS

Toyota Motor Corporation manufactures a number of different passenger car and truck models that are equipped with an on-board diagnostic computer for improved engine/vehicle performance. The on-board diagnostic computer used on these vehicles is known as a TCCS system or Toyota Computer-Controlled System and is designed to control the ignition timing as well as the amount of fuel injected by means of an ECU (electronic control unit). Models using the TCCS system include the Camry, Supra, Cressida, Celica, Corolla, and MR2 two-seat sports car.

On vehicles equipped with automatic transmissions, such as the Camry, the Supra, and the Cressida, an ECT (electronically controlled transmission) system is used. This electronic system controls the transmission shift points and the operation of the lock-up clutch. There is a separate on-board vehicle computer for the ECT system, so that both a TCCS and ECT computer are found on these vehicles. Note the illustrations for the various models of vehicles that appear in this chapter.

Special Tools

A number of special tools are required for quick and accurate diagnosis of the ECM system, as well as the engine and fuel-injection system. Figure 11-1 illustrates typical special tools recommended by Toyota Motor Corporation for this purpose. Minor variations exist between the number of service jumper wires required to test out the fuel-injec-

tion system on various model vehicles, but the rest of the tools are basically the same.

FUEL-INJECTION SYSTEM

Ported fuel-injection systems employed on Toyota cars are of Robert Bosch L-Jetronic design. (Refer to Chapter 5 for a comprehensive treatment of the more specific operations of the Robert Bosch systems.) Specific examples of these various fuel system arrangements are illustrated in Figs. 11-2 through 11-4.

ENGINE SENSOR AND SWITCH LOCATIONS

The actual location of the various engine sensors and switches found on the various models of Toyota vehicles are illustrated in Figs. 11-5 through 11-9.

Figures 11-5 and 11-6 illustrate the system layout for the Corolla and MR2 vehicles respectively, while Fig. 11-7 shows the layout for the Celica 3S-GE engine vehicle. The layouts for the Cressida and Supra 5M-GE engine vehicles are shown in Figs. 11-8 and 11-9.

The test sequences for the Corolla, MR2 and Celica are basically the same, while the connection point for the Cressida and Supra differs slightly.

NOTE: The battery voltage must be above 11 volts in order to ensure a diagnostic code output.

NECESSARY TOOLS AND EQUIPMENT

CIRCUIT TESTERS

Digital Type   Analog Type

 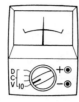

NOTE:

Use a circuit tester with a high-impedance (10kΩ/V minimum).

COMPRESSION GAUGE
(SST 09992-00023)

SOUND SCOPE

INJECTION MEASURING TOOL SET (SST 09268-41045)

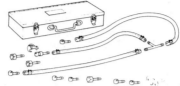
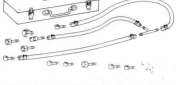

FUEL PRESSURE GAUGE
(SST 09268-45011)

SPARK PLUG WRENCH

SERVICE WIRE

For checking oxygen sensor operation
(SST 09842-14010)

For checking injector operation
(SST 09842-30020)

(SST 09842-30050)

Short-circuiting wire

Clip type jumper wire

FIGURE 11-1 Recommended special tools and equipment. (*Courtesy of Toyota Motor Corporation*)

CAUTION: Any diagnostic codes stored in the memory of the ECU will be erased when the battery cable is removed. Therefore, if it becomes necessary to remove the battery cable for any reason before troubleshooting a vehicle, withdraw the diagnostic codes first.

The following procedure describes the sequence of events required to access the stored trouble codes on these vehicles.

IMPORTANT SERVICING PRECAUTION: Before performing any type of service on electronic systems or IC's (integrated circuits), you *must* discharge yourself of static electricity or ESD (electrostatic discharge) by touching a good vehicle ground, such as the door post or vehicle shift lever. Failure to do so can result in damage to voltage sensitive electronic components. If, for any reason, you leave the vehicle during servicing, after re-entering to continue work, you *must* again ground yourself of ESD in order to drain any static electrical charge. Also, if you are performing control head/radio type checks on a new vehicle, remove the plastic seat covers, since they increase the possibility of creating a static charge.

COMPUTER ACCESS AND DIAGNOSTIC CONNECTOR LOCATIONS

When a sensed system exhibits a condition outside of the closely monitored ECU parameters, a *Check Engine* light on the instrument panel will illuminate (flash) to warn the driver of a problem with a sensed system.

In order to withdraw stored information trouble codes from the ECU, a test procedure involving the installation of a service jumper wire to activate the flashing check engine light is used. An ''analog-type'' voltmeter can be used when working under the hood. This voltmeter will provide you with the same information, if you watch the number of times that the needle deflects on the face scale.

NOTE: On later Cressida and Supra model cars, an optional super monitor display is located on the dashboard. (See Fig. 11-10.) With the ignition switch on, but the engine stopped, the technician must simultaneously push and hold the SELECT and INPUT M buttons for approximately 3 seconds.

The letters DIAG will appear on the screen to indicate that the self-diagnosis function of the computer is ready for

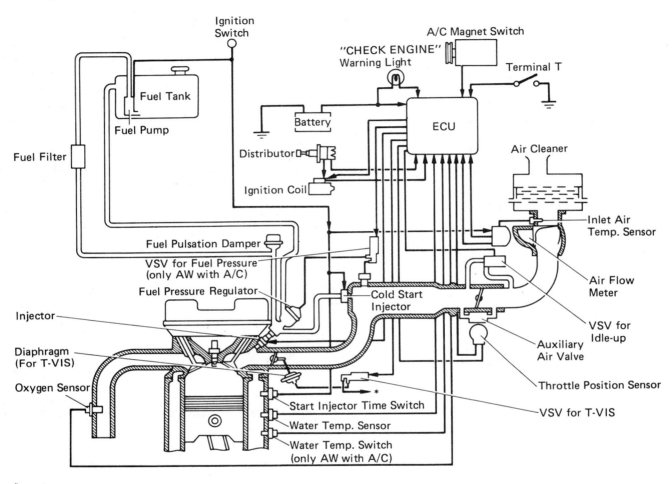

FIGURE 11-2 Corolla and MR2 fuel-injection system. (*Courtesy of Toyota Motor Corporation*)

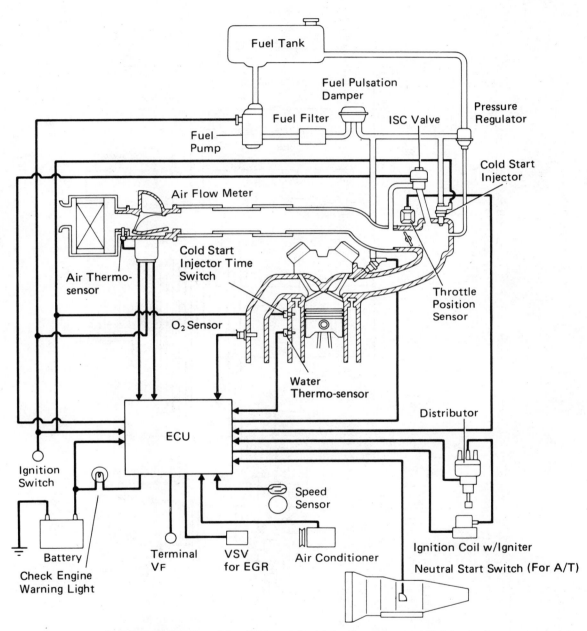

FIGURE 11-3 Cressida and Supra fuel-injection system. (*Courtesy of Toyota Motor Corporation*)

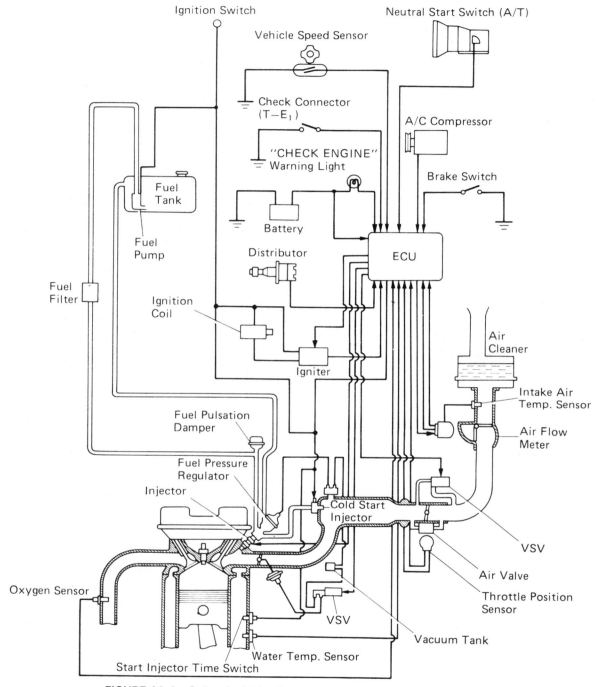

FIGURE 11-4   Celica fuel-injection system arrangement. (*Courtesy of Toyota Motor Corporation*)

SYSTEM LAYOUT — 4A-GE ENGINE

COROLLA

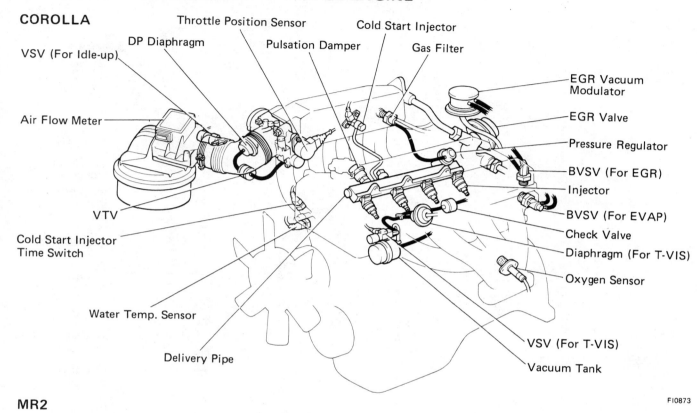

VSV (For Idle-up)

DP Diaphragm

Throttle Position Sensor

Pulsation Damper

Cold Start Injector

Gas Filter

Air Flow Meter

EGR Vacuum Modulator

EGR Valve

Pressure Regulator

BVSV (For EGR)

Injector

BVSV (For EVAP)

Check Valve

Diaphragm (For T-VIS)

Oxygen Sensor

VTV

Cold Start Injector Time Switch

Water Temp. Sensor

Delivery Pipe

VSV (For T-VIS)

Vacuum Tank

MR2

FI0873

FIGURE 11-5 System layout for the Corolla. (*Courtesy of Toyota Motor Corporation*)

MR2

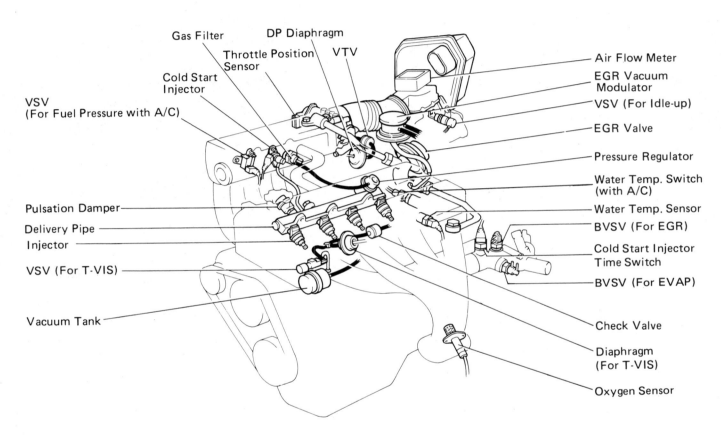

Gas Filter

DP Diaphragm

Throttle Position
Sensor

VTV

Cold Start
Injector

Air Flow Meter

EGR Vacuum
Modulator

VSV
(For Fuel Pressure with A/C)

VSV (For Idle-up)

EGR Valve

Pressure Regulator

Water Temp. Switch
(with A/C)

Pulsation Damper

Water Temp. Sensor

Delivery Pipe

BVSV (For EGR)

Injector

Cold Start Injector
Time Switch

VSV (For T-VIS)

BVSV (For EVAP)

Vacuum Tank

Check Valve

Diaphragm
(For T-VIS)

Oxygen Sensor

FI0874

FIGURE 11-6 System layout for the MR2 vehicle. (*Courtesy of Toyota Motor Corporation*)

SYSTEM LAYOUT — 3S-GE ENGINE

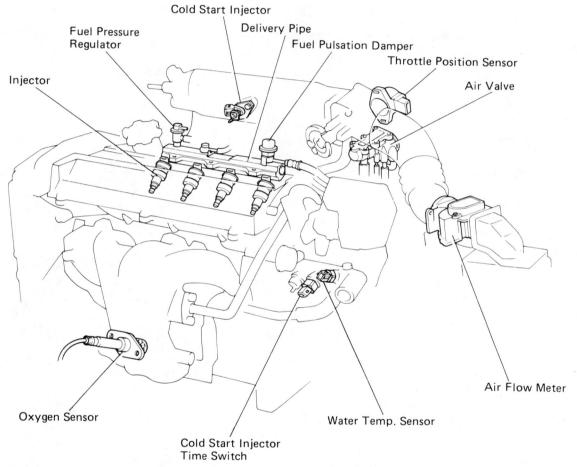

FIGURE 11-7 System layout for the Celica 3S-GE vehicle. (*Courtesy of Toyota Motor Corporation*)

SYSTEM LAYOUT — CRESSIDA

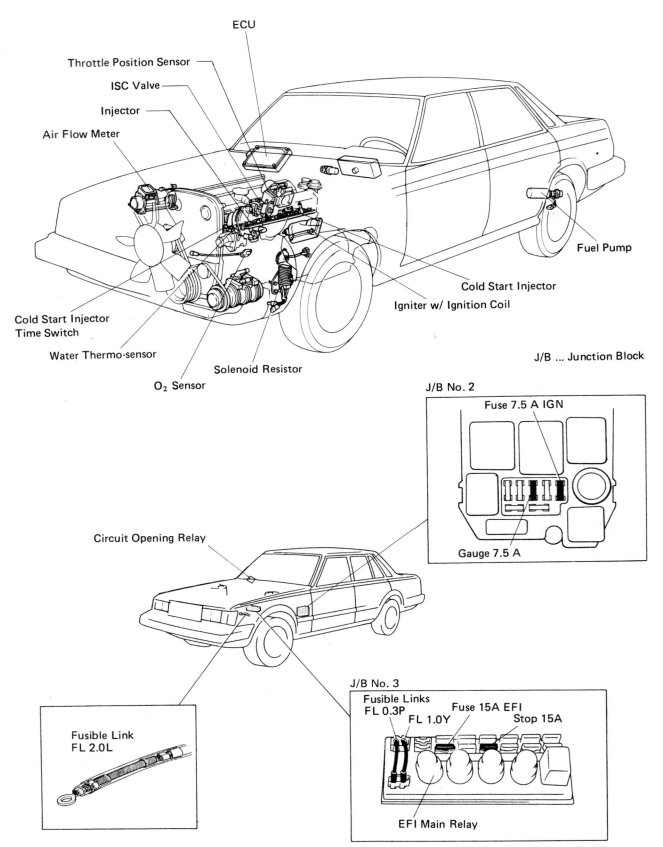

FIGURE 11-8 System layout for the Cressida. (*Courtesy of Toyota Motor Corporation*)

SYSTEM LAYOUT — SUPRA

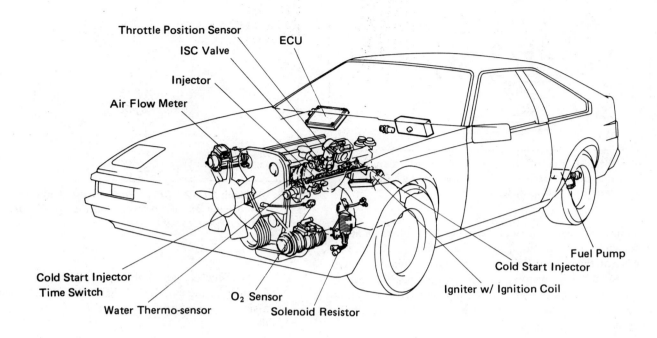

Throttle Position Sensor

ECU

ISC Valve

Injector

Air Flow Meter

Cold Start Injector
Time Switch

Water Thermo-sensor

O₂ Sensor

Solenoid Resistor

Igniter w/ Ignition Coil

Cold Start Injector

Fuel Pump

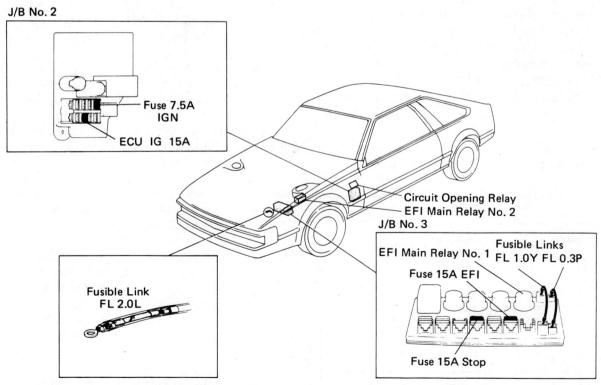

J/B No. 2

Fuse 7.5A
IGN

ECU IG 15A

Circuit Opening Relay
EFI Main Relay No. 2
J/B No. 3

Fusible Link
FL 2.0L

EFI Main Relay No. 1

Fusible Links
FL 1.0Y FL 0.3P

Fuse 15A EFI

Fuse 15A Stop

FIGURE 11-9 System layout for the Supra. (*Courtesy of Toyota Motor Corporation*)

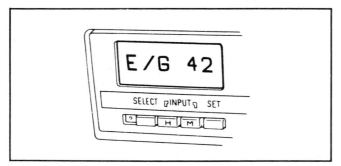

FIGURE 11-10 Super monitor digital display unit on the Cressida and Supra models. (*Courtesy of Toyota Motor Corporation*)

action. After a short pause, hold in the SET button for about 3 seconds. If the system is normal, the letters E/G OK will appear on the screen. If there is a malfunction in the system or one that has been stored in memory, the respective code number will appear on the screen. There will be a three second pause between trouble codes stored in memory as they flash on the screen.

Procedure

1. Battery voltage check should confirm that there are at least 11 volts flowing in the circuit.
2. The throttle valve should be fully closed to ensure that the throttle sensor contacts are closed.
3. The transmission should be in Park on automatic transmission equipped vehicles, and in Neutral on standard transmission equipped vehicles.
4. If so equipped, turn the air conditioner switch off.
5. Turn the ignition switch on, but do not start the engine.
6. Visually inspect that the *Check Engine* warning light comes on. (Refer to Figs. 11-11 and 11-12.)

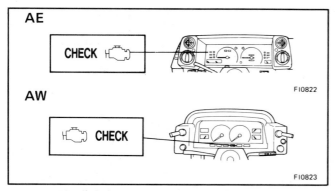

FIGURE 11-11 *Check Engine* light location (AE) — Corolla, and (AW) for the MR2 4A-GE engine. (*Courtesy of Toyota Motor Corporation*)

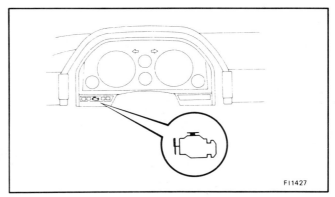

FIGURE 11-12 *Check Engine* light location for the Celica 3S-GE engine. (*Courtesy of Toyota Motor Corporation*)

7. If the *Check Engine* light fails to come on, refer to Chart 1 for the Corolla and MR2 vehicles. However, a similar procedure can be used for the other vehicle models.
8. If the *Check Engine* light is, in fact, illuminated, is a normal condition code available at this time? See the code charts for various model vehicles under the heading Toyota Diagnostic System Troubleshooting Codes (Figs. 11-16, 11-17, and 11-18).
9. To initiate the self-diagnostic capability of the ECU, refer to Fig. 11-13, which illustrates the method used for the Corolla and MR2 vehicles, while Fig. 11-14 shows the connections required for the Celica 3S-GE engine. Figure 11-15 is the method that is used for the Cressida and Supra 5M-GE engine vehicles.

NOTE FOR DIAGNOSTIC CONNECTIONS: Refer to Fig. 11-13. When using a service jumper wire, short the terminals of the check connector located near the wiper motor for the AE Corolla, and the terminals T to E1 near the air cleaner for the AW MR2 vehicle. A jumper wire, as shown in Fig. 11-14, is used to activate the diagnostic codes for the Celica 3S-GE vehicle.

For the Cressida and Supra 5M-GE engine vehicles, insert a jumper wire (Fig. 11-15) to short terminals T and E1 of the check connector near the ignition distributor assembly, and connect an analog voltmeter to the service connector, set to the 5 to 20 volt scale range.

10. Turn the ignition switch to on, but DO NOT start the engine.
11. On the Corolla, MR2, and Celica 3S-GE engine vehicles, carefully note how many times the *Check Engine* light blinks to determine what code or codes are stored in the ECU trouble code memory. If an analog voltmeter is being used underhood and connected to

CHART 1 — No "CHECK ENGINE" warning light

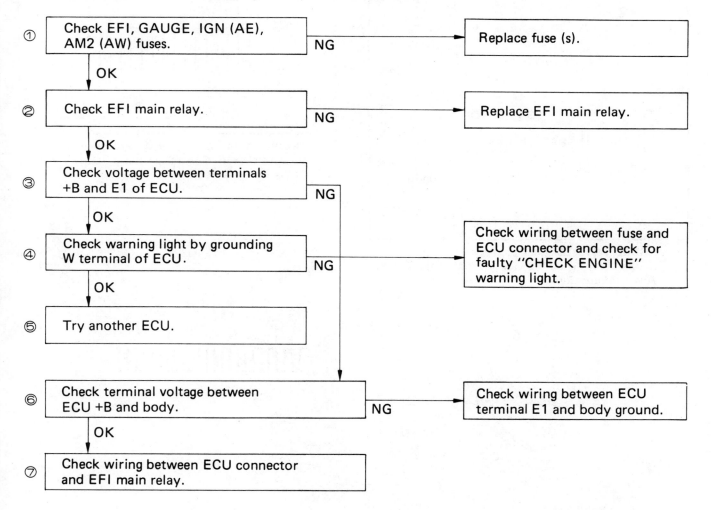

① Check EFI, GAUGE, IGN (AE), AM2 (AW) fuses. — **NG** → Replace fuse (s).

| OK

② Check EFI main relay. — **NG** → Replace EFI main relay.

| OK

③ Check voltage between terminals +B and E1 of ECU. — **NG**

| OK

④ Check warning light by grounding W terminal of ECU. — **NG** → Check wiring between fuse and ECU connector and check for faulty "CHECK ENGINE" warning light.

| OK

⑤ Try another ECU.

⑥ Check terminal voltage between ECU +B and body. — **NG** → Check wiring between ECU terminal E1 and body ground.

| OK

⑦ Check wiring between ECU connector and EFI main relay.

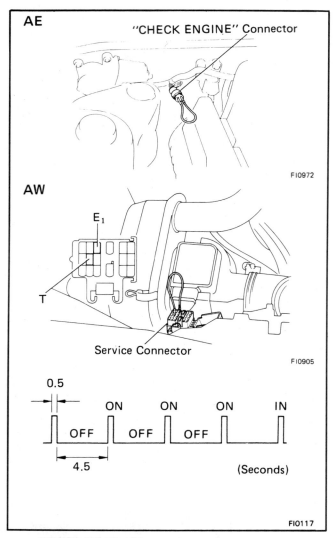

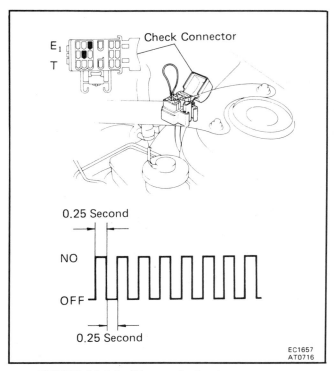

FIGURE 11-14 Diagnostic service connector for the Celica 3S-GE engine vehicle. (*Courtesy of Toyota Motor Corporation*)

FIGURE 11-13 Diagnostic service connector for the Corolla and MR2 vehicles. (*Courtesy of Toyota Motor Corporation*)

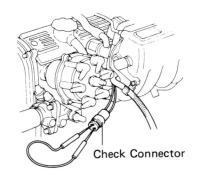

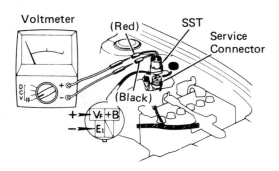

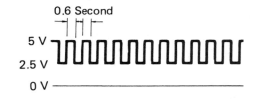

FIGURE 11-15 Diagnostic service connector for the Cressida and Supra 5M-GE engine vehicle. (*Courtesy of Toyota Motor Corporation*)

the check connector, closely monitor the number of needle deflections.

12. On the Cressida and Supra 5M-GE vehicles, carefully monitor and note how many times the voltmeter needle deflects or fluctuates between 5 volts and then is followed by a 2.5 volt deflection in order to determine the actual trouble code number.

ECU TROUBLE CODE ANALYSIS

To determine and analyze the meaning of either the flashing *Check Engine* light or the analog voltmeter needle deflection, refer to the Diagnostic System Code Charts in this chapter. (Figs. 11-16, 11-17, and 11-18.)

Once one or more codes have been determined, it then becomes necessary to refer to the vehicle shop service manual or TCCS Diagnosis Manual for a systematic procedural check to determine what the cause or causes of this code condition might be. This check generally involves carefully examining all wiring harnesses and plug-in connections first to determine if they are loose or connected with too much tension in the wire harness (like a bow string — too taut). Also, carefully check that the interconnecting terminals between the male and female harness connections have not spread apart internally, thereby causing loose contacts.

Another good procedural check is carefully to check each sensor, signal, and relay in the system (See the various engine and vehicle diagrams in this chapter.) Lightly flick each unit with your finger. If this action causes the problem to disappear intermittently, then replace the faulty unit before proceeding further with the procedural check as outlined in the respective service diagnosis manual.

The following information indicates how the flashing *Check Engine* light or analog voltmeter needle deflections can be interpreted.

TOYOTA DIAGNOSTIC SYSTEM TROUBLE CODES

The diagnostic codes, listed in Figs. 11-16, 11-17, and 11-18 for particular vehicles, may be indicated (if a problem is stored in memory) when the service jumper wire is inserted. This procedure has been described in the section headed Computer Access.

The *Check Engine* light will blink and/or the analog voltmeter needle will deflect, if the voltmeter is used and hooked into the system. The length of time that the light blinks (illuminates), or that the needle fluctuates between signals, will vary depending upon the specific model of vehicle being accessed. This duration will vary and depends upon whether the system is flashing a normal operation trouble code or a sensed system problem code. On some

systems (Celica 3S-GE engine), the light alternately blinks on and off for 0.25 second intervals, while in the normal system mode. On the Corolla and MR2 vehicles, the light blinks on for 0.5 second at the end of every 4.5 second period. On the Cressida and Supra 5M-GE engine vehicles, the voltmeter needle fluctuates between 5 volts and 2.5 volts every 0.6 seconds while in the normal mode.

When a trouble code has been set into memory by a problem in the system and it is once activated, the ECU will cause the *Check Engine* light to blink once every 4.5 seconds on the Corolla and MR2, as shown in the trouble code chart for these engines. If, however, more than one code is stored, then there will be a 2.5 second interval between the different numbered trouble codes. This time limit varies between Toyota car models, but once all stored trouble codes have each been flashed once, the ECU starts the same process all over again. Probably, you will need to make several attempts at deciphering the time between flashes or voltmeter needle deflections before you will readily be able to interpret whether one or more trouble codes have actually been stored in memory.

IDENTIFICATION OF ECU CONNECTORS

ECU locations for the various models of Toyota vehicles are illustrated in Figs. 11-8, 11-9, and 11-19 through 11-21. When it becomes necessary to check the ECU system and the various sensors systematically, an analog type multimeter is used to check for either a voltage reading or a resistance reading between the various sensors in the system and their respective ECU connectors.

CAUTION: DO NOT probe the connecting wires with a pointed test lead from a voltmeter. If the insulation is punctured or broken, corrosion of the wires or a short circuit can occur.

See Figs. 11-22 through 11-24 for identification of the various ECU connectors. The voltage and resistance values for different models of vehicles will not all be the same. However, the basic test procedure can be considered common in most cases. To give you a better understanding of just what tests are performed, and what voltage and resistance values are considered acceptable, the following information describes typical tests run on either the Corolla or MR2 models of Toyota cars.

COROLLA AND MR2 VOLTAGE CHECKS

1. Refer to Fig. 11-25, which illustrates the wiring diagrams for both the Corolla and the MR2. Use an analog type voltmeter between terminals +B and E1 of

Code No.	Number of blinks "CHECK ENGINE"	Item	Diagnosis	"CHECK ENGINE" Warning Light
1	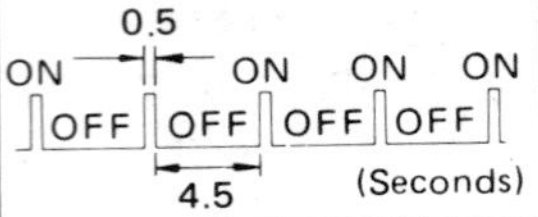 ON — 0.5 — ON ON ON / OFF OFF OFF OFF / 4.5 (Seconds)	Normal condition	—	—
2	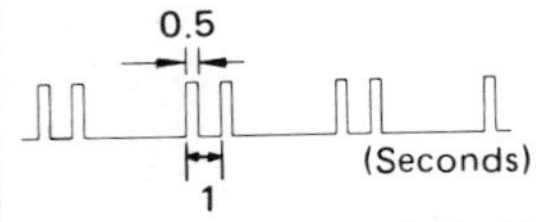 0.5 / 1 (Seconds)	Air flow meter signal	• Open circuit in Vc, Vs, V_B or E_2. • Short circuit in Vc.	ON
3		Ignition signal	No signal from igniter four times in succession.	ON
4		Water temp. sensor signal	Open or short circuit in coolant temperature sensor signal.	ON
5		Oxygen sensor signal	Open circuit in oxygen sensor signal. (only lean indication)	ON
6		RPM signal	No Ne, G signal to ECU within several seconds after engine is cranked.	ON
7		Throttle position sensor signal	Open or short circuit in throttle position sensor signal.	OFF
8		Intake air temp. sensor signal	Open or short circuit in intake air temperature sensor.	OFF
10		Starter signal	No STA signal to ECU when engine is running over 800 rpm.	OFF
11		Switch signal	Air conditioner switch ON or idle switch OFF during diagnosis check.	—

NOTE: 1. Including "Normal," the ECU is programmed with the 10 diagnostic codes shown above.

2. When 2 or more codes are indicated, the lowest number (code) will appear first.

3. All detected diagnostic codes, except 11, will be retained in memory by the ECU from the time of detection until cancelled out.

4. Once the malfunction has gone out, the "CHECK ENGINE" warning light on the instrument panel will go out but the diagnostic code(s) will remain stored in the ECU memory (except for code no. 11).

5. For the code numbers that have "OFF" in the "CHECK ENGINE" Warning Light column, the "CHECK ENGINE" light does not go on if the indicated malfunction occurs. However, the trouble codes (except for code no.11) are still stored in the memory of the ECU.

6. Diagnosis code No.10 will be indicated if the vehicle is push started.

FIGURE 11-16 ECU malfunction trouble code chart for the Corolla and MR2 vehicles. (*Courtesy of Toyota Motor Corporation*)

Code No.	Number of "CHECK ENGINE" blinks	System	Diagnosis	Trouble area	"CHECK ENGINE" Warning Light
—	ON ⎍⎍⎍⎍⎍ OFF F11401	Normal	This appears when none of the other codes (11 thru 51) are identified.	—	—
11	⎍⎍ F11388	ECU (+B)	Wire severance, however slight, in +B (ECU).	1. Main relay circuit 2. Main relay 3. ECU	OFF
12	⎍⎍⎍ F11389	RPM signal	No Ne, G signal to ECU within several seconds after engine is cranked.	1. Distributor circuit 2. Distributor 3. Starter signal circuit 4. ECU	ON
13	⎍⎍⎍⎍ F11390	RPM signal	No Ne signal to ECU within several seconds after engine reaches 1,000 rpm.	Same as Code No. 12.	ON
14	⎍⎍⎍⎍⎍ F11391	Ignition signal	No signal from igniter 8 ~ 11 times in succession.	1. Igniter circuit (+B, IGt, IGf) 2. Igniter 3. ECU	ON
21	⎍⎍⎍ F11400	Oxygen sensor signal	Open circuit in oxygen sensor signal (only lean indication).	1. Oxygen sensor circuit 2. Oxygen sensor 3. ECU	ON
22	⎍⎍⎍⎍ F11392	Water temp. sensor signal	Open or short circuit in water temp. sensor signal.	1. Water temp. sensor circuit 2. Water temp. sensor 3. ECU	ON
24	⎍⎍⎍⎍⎍⎍ F11571	Intake air temp. sensor signal	Open or short circuit in intake air temp. sensor	1. Intake air temp. sensor circuit 2. Intake air temp. sensor 3. ECU	OFF
31	⎍⎍⎍⎍ F11394	Air flow meter signal	Vc circuit open or Vs − E2 short circuit.	1. Air flow meter circuit 2. Air flow meter 3. ECU	ON
32	⎍⎍⎍⎍⎍ F11395	Air flow meter signal	E2 circuit open or Vc − Vs short circuited.	Same as Code No. 31, above.	ON
41	⎍⎍⎍⎍ F11396	Throttle position sensor signal	Open or short circuit in throttle position sensor signal.	1. Throttle position sensor circuit 2. Throttle position sensor 3. ECU	OFF
42	⎍⎍⎍⎍⎍ F11397	Vehicle speed sensor signal	Signal informing ECU that vehicle stopped has been input to ECU for 5 seconds with engine running between 2,500 − 6,000 rpm.	1. Vehicle speed sensor circuit 2. Vehicle speed sensor 3. ECU	OFF
43	⎍⎍⎍⎍⎍⎍ F11398	Starter signal	No STA signal to ECU when vehicle stopped and engine running over 800 rpm	1. Main relay circuit 2. IG switch circuit (starter) 3. IG switch 4. ECU	OFF
51	⎍⎍⎍⎍⎍⎍ F11399	Switch signal	Air conditioner switch ON, idle switch OFF or shift position other than P or N range during diagnosis check.	1. Air con. S/W 2. Throttle position sensor circuit 3. Throttle position sensor 4. Neutral start switch 5. ECU	OFF

NOTE: 1. When 2 or more codes are indicated, the lowest number (code) will appear first.
   2. All detected diagnostic codes, except 51, will be retained in memory by the ECU from the time of detection until cancelled out.
   3. Once the malfunction has gone out, the "CHECK ENGINE" warning light on the instrument panel will go out but the diagnostic code(s) will remain stored in the ECU memory (except for code no. 51).
   4. For the code numbers that have "OFF" in the "CHECK ENGINE" Warning Light column, the "CHECK ENGINE" light does not go on if the indicated malfunction occurs. However, the trouble codes (except for code no. 51) are still stored in the memory of the ECU.

FIGURE 11-17 ECU malfunction trouble chart for the Celica 3S-GE engine. (*Courtesy of Toyota Motor Corporation*)

Code No.	System	Voltage Pattern	Diagnosis	"CHECK ENGINE" Diagnostic Light
—	All	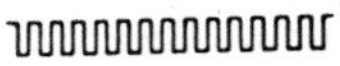 ⎍⎍⎍⎍⎍⎍⎍⎍⎍	Normal: this appears when none of the other codes (11 thru 51) are indicated.	Off
11	ECU Power Supply	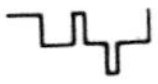	Wire severance, however temporary, in power supply of ECU.	↑
12	RPM Signal	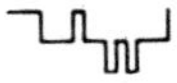	No Ne or G signal to ECU while engine is cranked.	On
13	RPM Signal	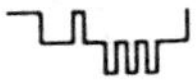	No Ne signal to ECU within several seconds after engine reaches 1,000 RPM.	↑
14	Ignition Signal		No signal from ignitor six times in succession.	↑
21	O_2 Sensor Signal	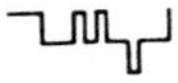	O_2 sensor gives a lean signal for several seconds even when coolant temperature is above 50°C and engine is running under high load conditions above 1,500 RPM.	↑
22	Water Thermo-sensor Signal	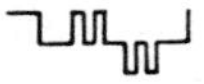	Open or short circuit in coolant temperature sensor signal.	↑
23	Intake Air Thermo-sensor Signal	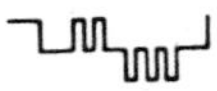	Open or short circuit in intake air temperature sensor.	Off
31	Air Flow Meter Signal		Open circuit in Vc; or Vs and E_2 short circuited when idle contacts are closed.	On
32	Air Flow Meter Signal	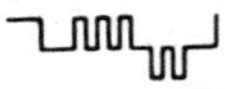	Open circuit in E_2; or Vc and Vs short-circuited.	↑
41	Throttle Position Sensor Signal		Simultaneous IDL and PSW signal to ECU	Off
42	Vehicle Speed Sensor Signal		A/T: No signal for over 5 seconds when vehicle is travelling under 1.7 km/h (1 mph), engine running over 2,500 RPM and shift lever is in other than N or P range. M/T: No signal for over 5 seconds when vehicle is travelling under 1.7 km/h (1 mph), and engine running over 2,500 RPM.	↑
43	Starter Signal	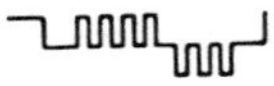	No STA signal to ECU when engine is running over 800 RPM.	↑
51	Switch Signal		Neutral start switch off or air conditioner switch on during diagnostic check.	↑

NOTES: 1. Including "Normal", the ECU is programmed with the 14 diagnostic codes shown above.

2. When 2 or more codes are indicated, the lowest number (code) will appear first. However, no other code will appear along with code No. 11.

3. All detected diagnostic codes, except 51, will be retained in memory by the ECU from the time of detection until cancelled out.

4. Once the malfunction is cleared, the "CHECK ENGINE" warning light on the instrument panel will go out but the diagnostic code(s) will remain stored in the ECU memory (except for code 51).

5. For the code numbers that have "Off" in the "CHECK ENGINE" Diagnostic Light column, the CHECK ENGINE light does not go on if the indicated malfunction occurs. However, the trouble codes (except for code no. 51) are still stored in the memory of the ECU.

FIGURE 11-18 ECU malfunction trouble code chart for the Cressida and Supra 5M-GE engine. (*Courtesy of Toyota Motor Corporation*)

SYSTEM LAYOUT — COROLLA

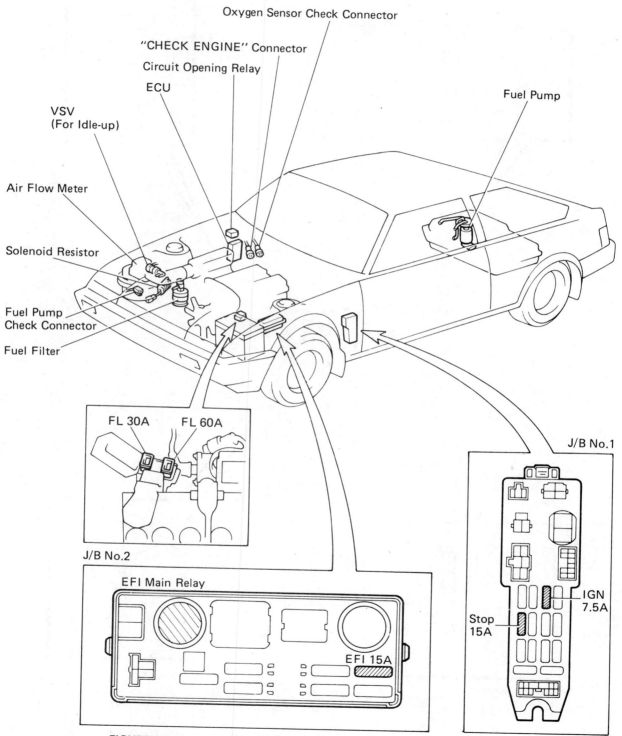

FIGURE 11-19 System layout and ECU location — Corolla. (*Courtesy of Toyota Motor Corporation*)

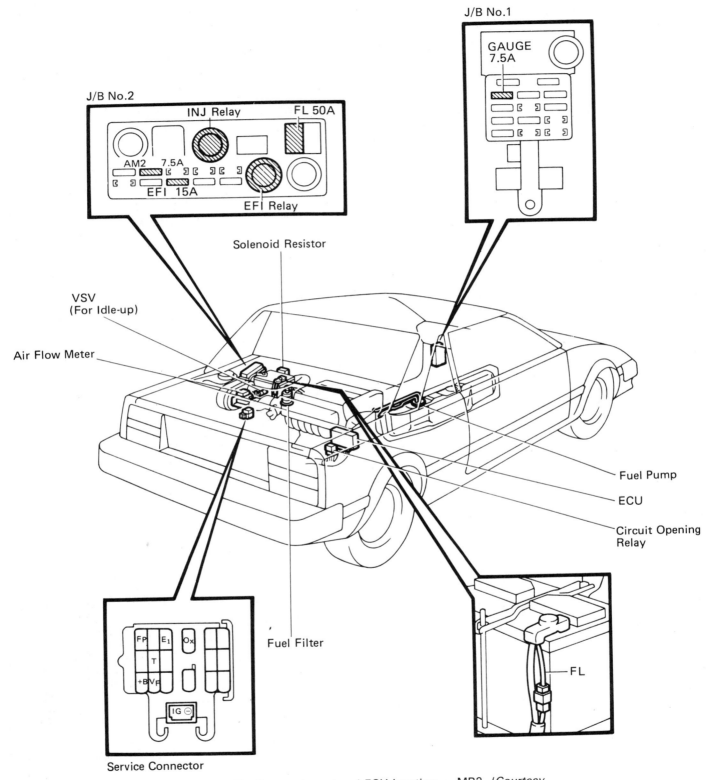

FIGURE 11-20 System layout and ECU location — MR2. (*Courtesy of Toyota Motor Corporation*)

SYSTEM LAYOUT — CELICA

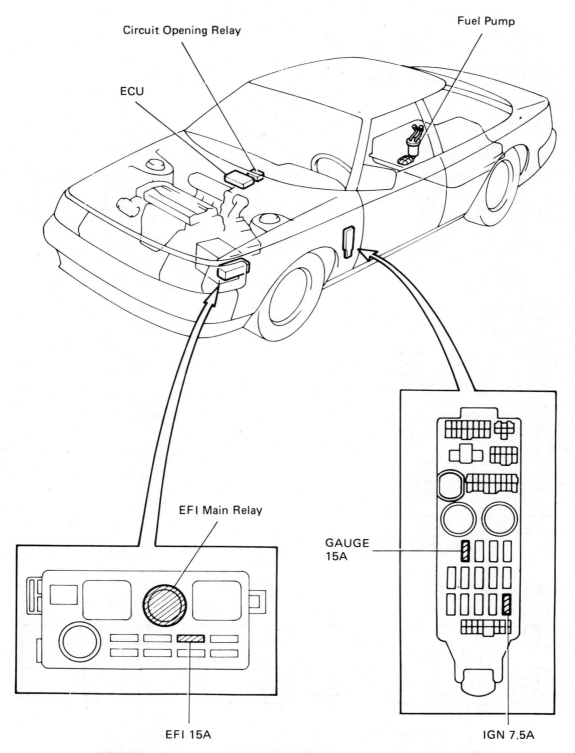

FIGURE 11-21 System layout and ECU location — Celica. (*Courtesy of Toyota Motor Corporation*)

ECU CONNECTORS

Symbol	Terminal Name	Symbol	Terminal Name
E01	ENGINE GROUND	E2	SENSOR GROUND
E02	ENGINE GROUND	G ⊖	ENGINE REVOLUTION SENSOR
No. 10	NO. 3, 4 INJECTOR	OX	OXYGEN SENSOR
No. 20	NO. 1, 2 INJECTOR	G ⊕	ENGINE REVOLUTION SENSOR
STA	STARTER SWITCH	VCC	THROTTLE SENSOR
IGT	IGNITER	VTA	THROTTLE SENSOR
VF	CHECK CONNECTOR	NE	ENGINE REVOLUTION SENSOR
E1	ENGINE GROUND	THW	WATER TEMP. SENSOR
S/TH	VSV for T-VIS	VC	AIR FLOW METER
★ FPU	VSV for fuel pressure up system	E21	SENSOR GROUND
V-ISC	VSV for idle speed control system	VS	AIR FLOW METER
W	WARNING LIGHT	THA	AIR TEMP. SENSOR
T	CHECK CONNECTOR	SPD	SPEEDOMETER
★ TSW	WATER TEMP. SWITCH	BATT	BATTERY
IDL	THROTTLE SENSOR	+B1	MAIN RELAY
A/C	A/C MAGNET SWITCH	+B	MAIN RELAY
IGF	IGNITER		

★ AW vehicles only

ECU Connectors

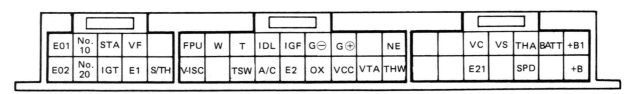

FIGURE 11-22 ECU connector identification for the MR2 and Corolla vehicles. (*Courtesy of Toyota Motor Corporation*)

ECU CONNECTORS

Symbol	Terminal Name	Symbol	Terminal Name
E_{01}	ENGINE GROUND	IDL	THROTTLE SWITCH
E_{02}	ENGINE GROUND	IDf	IGNITER
No. 10	INJECTOR	O_2	O_2 SENSOR
No. 20	INJECTOR	THW	WATER THERMO-SENSOR
STA	STARTER SWITCH	E_2	SENSOR GROUND
IGt	IGNITER	E_1	ENGINE GROUND
EGR	EGR VSV	M-REL	MAIN RELAY COIL
E_1	ENGINE GROUND	A/C	A/C MAGNET SWITCH
N/C	NEUTRAL START SWITCH (A/T)	SPD	SPEEDOMETER
	CLUTCH SWITCH (M/T)	W	WARNING LAMP
ISC_1	ISC MOTOR NO. 1 COIL	THA	AIR THERMO-SENSOR
ISC_2	ISC MOTOR NO. 2 COIL	Vs	AIR FLOW METER
ISC_3	ISC MOTOR NO. 3 COIL	Vc	AIR FLOW METER
ISC_4	ISC MOTOR NO. 4 COIL	BAT	BATTERY +B
G $\ominus$	SENSOR*	IG S/W	IGNITION SWITCH
VF	CHECK CONNECTOR	+B	MAIN RELAY
G	CRANKSHAFT ANGLE SENSOR	ECT	ECT COMPUTER
T	CHECK CONNECTOR	S_1	ECT COMPUTER
PSW	THROTTLE SWITCH	S_2	ECT COMPUTER
Ne	ENGINE SPEED SENSOR	OIL	OIL PRESSURE SWITCH

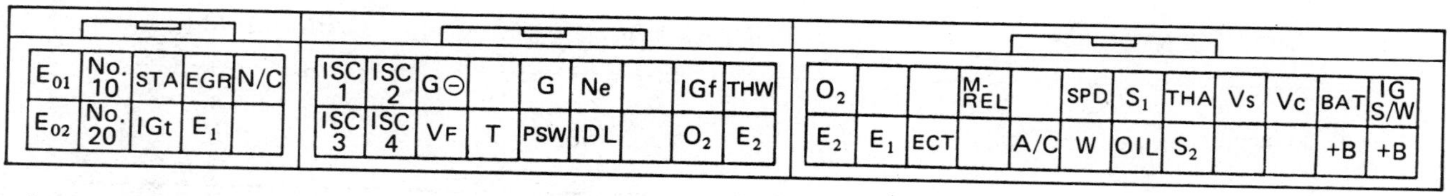

E_{01}	No. 10	STA	EGR	N/C
E_{02}	No. 20	IGt	E_1	

ISC_1	ISC_2	G $\ominus$		G	Ne		IGf	THW
ISC_3	ISC_4	VF	T	PSW	IDL		O_2	E_2

O_2			M-REL		SPD	S_1	THA	Vs	Vc	BAT	IG S/W
E_2	E_1	ECT		A/C	W	OIL	S_2			+B	+B

* Connector for crankshaft angle and engine RPM sensors.

FIGURE 11-23   ECU connector identification for the Cressida and Supra. (*Courtesy of Toyota Motor Corporation*)

ECU CONNECTORS

Symbol	Terminal Name	Symbol	Terminal Name	Symbol	Terminal Name
E_{01}	ENGINE GROUND	G_1	ENGINE REVOLUTION SENSOR	L_1	ECU ECT
E_{02}	ENGINE GROUND	T	CHECK CONNECTOR	L_3	ECU ECT
STA	STARTER SWITCH	G_2	ENGINE REVOLUTION SENSOR	L_2	ECU ECT
IGt	IGNITER	VTA	THROTTLE POSITION SENSOR	OD_1	ECU ECT
STJ	COLD START INJECTOR	Ne	ENGINE REVOLUTION SENSOR	A/C	A/C MAGNET SWITCH
E_1	ENGINE GROUND	IDL	THROTTLE POSITION SENSOR	SPD	SPEED SENSOR
NSW	NEUTRAL START SWITCH	V–ISC	ISC–VSV	W	WARNING LIGHT
T–VIS	T–VIS VSV	IGf	IGNITER	STP	STOP LIGHT SWITCH
No. 1	INJECTOR	Ox	OXYGEN SENSOR	THA	AIR FLOW METER
No. 2	INJECTOR	THW	WATER TEMP. SENSOR	Vs	AIR FLOW METER
No. 3	INJECTOR	E_2	SENSOR GROUND	Vc	AIR FLOW METER
No. 4	INJECTOR	Ox_1	OXYGEN SENSOR	BATT	BATTERY
$G\ominus$	ENGINE REVOLUTION SENSOR	E_{22}	SENSOR GROUND	+B	MAIN RELAY
VF	CHECK CONNECTOR	E_{11}	ENGINE GROUND	$+B_1$	MAIN RELAY

ECU Connectors

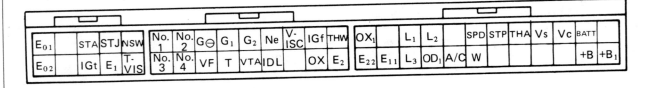

FIGURE 11-24 ECU connector identification for the Celica 3S-GE engine. (*Courtesy of Toyota Motor Corporation*)

COROLLA

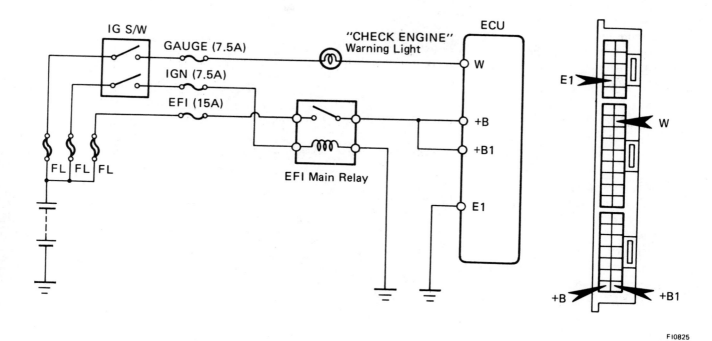

MR2

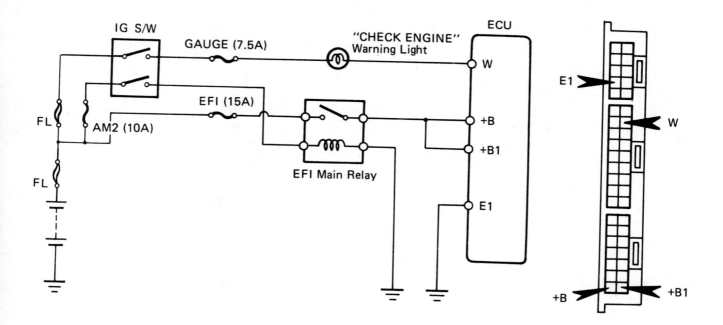

FIGURE 11-25 Corolla and MR2 ECU, main relay, and ignition switch wiring diagram. (*Courtesy of Toyota Motor Corporation*)

the ECU connector, and then between terminal +B of the ECU and ground. Both readings should indicate battery voltage with the ignition switch on.

2. Refer to Fig. 11-26, which illustrates the wiring diagram for the air inlet meter and fuel system. Three voltage checks are required here, with the ignition switch on.

   The voltage—

   (a) Between both terminals of the fuel pump connector should read 11 volts or more;

   (b) Between +B terminal of fuel pump circuit opening relay and body should read battery voltage;

   (c) Between the STA and E1 terminals of the fuel pump circuit opening relay should read between 8 and 12 volts.

3. Refer to Fig. 11-27 for these checks. Two checks are required here, and these are done with the analog voltmeter and the ignition switch on.

   (a) Between the +B terminal of the injector solenoid resistor and body, which should read battery voltage;

   (b) Between the ECU terminal No. 10 and/or 20 and E01 or E02, which should read battery voltage.

4. Refer to Fig. 11-28, and perform the following check. Check the voltage between +B terminal of the VSV (vacuum switching valve) and body (ground), with the headlights or heater blower fan or defogger switch turned on. Battery voltage should be read on the face of the voltmeter.

5. Refer to Fig. 11-29, and perform the following checks to the air flow meter circuit with the ignition switch turned on:

   (a) Between the Vc and E2 terminals of the air flow meter, which should measure between 6 and 10 volts.

   (b) Between the Vs and E2 terminals of the air flow meter, which should read between 2 and 7 volts as you gently push the air flow meter valve (measuring plate inside the housing) from its closed to fully open position with a screwdriver or similar object. There should be a gradual voltage increase here — not a sudden jump from 2 to 7 volts. Otherwise, the voltage signal to the ECU will be irregular and cause the ECU to output a voltage signal to the injectors that will result in too much fuel (injector pulse-width time) even though the throttle is not, in fact, at a wide open position. The air flow meter operates on a variable resistance concept. Therefore, the voltage gradually increases as the driver opens up the throttle to allow greater air flow into the engine.

   (c) Between the Vs and E2 terminals of the ECU. The voltage reading should be between 2 and 7 volts as you perform the same opening of the air flow meter measuring plate (Figs. 4-31 through 4-33), just as you did for Check (b), above.

   (d) Between terminal Vc and E2 of the air flow meter connector (snap-in connector removed from its harness on the air flow meter body). Use a digital voltmeter (illustrated under the Special Tools section of this chapter); you should get a reading of between 6 to 10 volts.

   (e) Place a voltmeter between the Vc and E2 terminals of the ECU, 6 to 10 volts.

6. To confirm that an ignition signal is being sent to the ECU, perform the following two checks. Refer to Fig. 11-30 first.

   (a) With the engine running at idle, check the voltage between the IGT and E1 terminal of the ECU, which should be approximately 1 volt.

   (b) With the engine stopped, but the ignition switch on, check between the ignition coil terminal and the igniter body, which should show approximately 12 volts.

7. Refer to Fig. 11-31, and check the voltage reading between the THW and E2 terminals of the ECU with the ignition switch on. It is acceptable if the voltage is neither 0 nor 5 volts.

8. Refer to the wiring diagram shown in Fig. 11-32 for the voltage hookups required for these checks and tests of the throttle position sensor system with the ignition switch turned on:

   (a) Between the Vcc and E2 terminals of the TPS (throttle position sensor), there should be a reading of 4 to 6 volts.

   (b) Between the VTA and E2 terminals of the TPS connector. While slowly opening the throttle from a closed to a wide open position, the voltmeter should register between 0.1 volt with the throttle closed up to about 5 volts wide open.

   (c) Between the VTA and E2 terminals of the ECU connector, while slowly opening the throttle as per the instructions in Step (b) above. This should result in the same voltage readings. Failure of the voltage to increase gradually and smoothly is an indication that the TPS is faulty.

   (d) Between the Vcc and E2 terminals of the TPS connector, which should read between 4 and 6 volts.

   (e) Between the Vcc and E2 terminals of the ECU, which should read 4 to 6 volts.

9. Refer to Fig. 11-33, and check the resistance of the

COROLLA

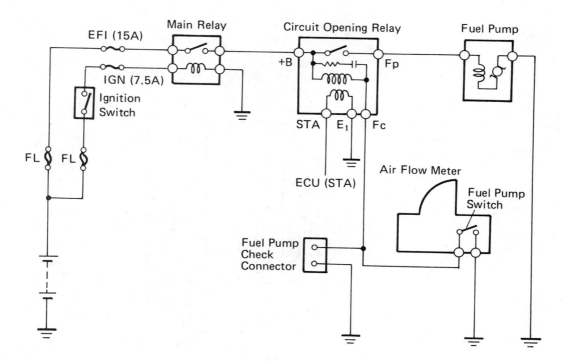

MR2

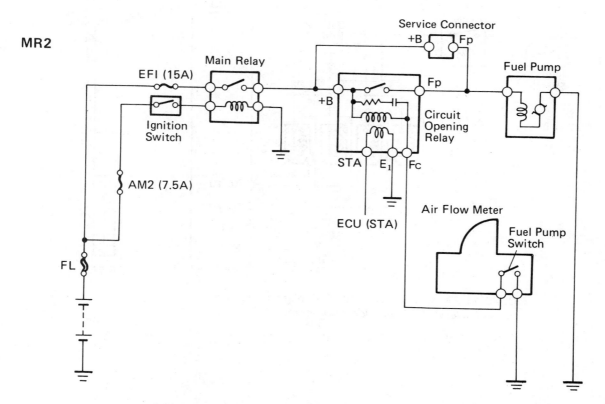

FIGURE 11-26 Corolla and MR2 fuel system wiring diagram. (*Courtesy of Toyota Motor Corporation*)

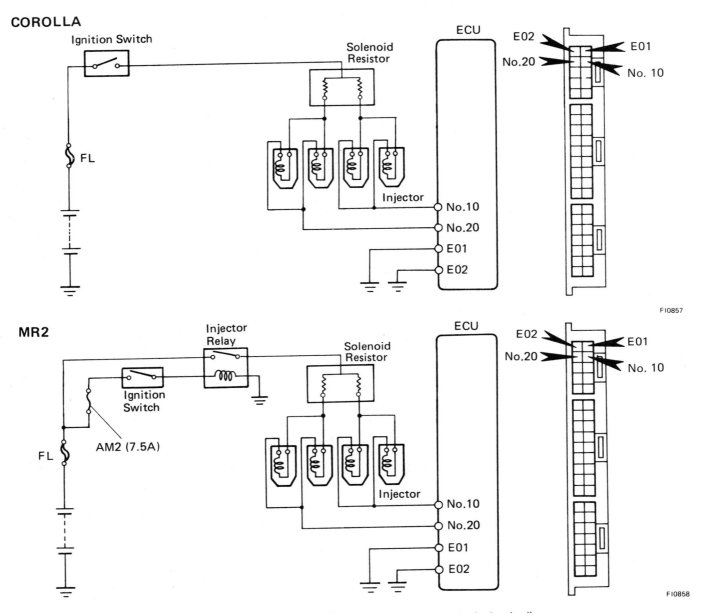

FIGURE 11-27 Corolla and MR2 fuel injector electrical circuit diagram. (*Courtesy of Toyota Motor Corporation*)

COROLLA

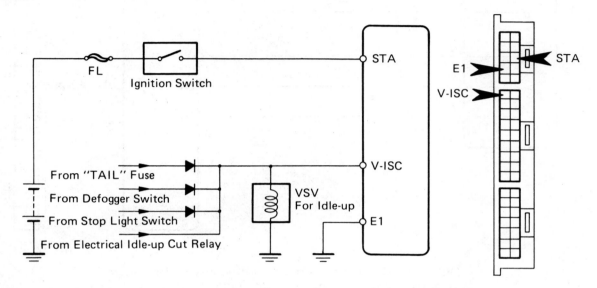

MR2

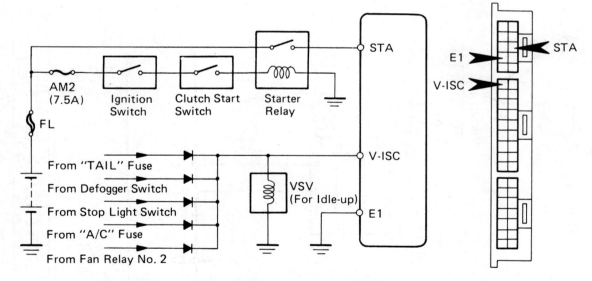

FIGURE 11-28 Corolla and MR2 ECU, VSV and ignition system wiring diagram. (*Courtesy of Toyota Motor Corporation*)

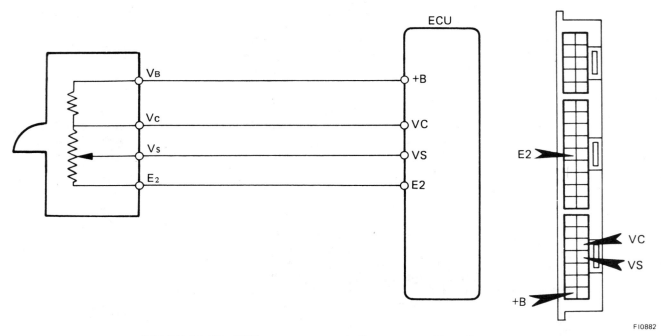

FIGURE 11-29 ECU connector to air flow meter wiring diagram — Corolla and MR2. (*Courtesy of Toyota Motor Corporation*)

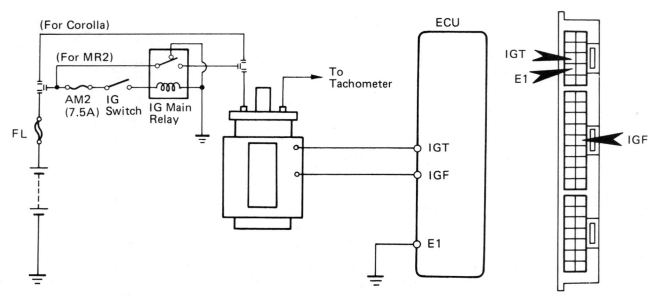

FIGURE 11-30 Wiring diagram for the ignition and coil circuit — Corolla and MR2 vehicles. (*Courtesy of Toyota Motor Corporation*)

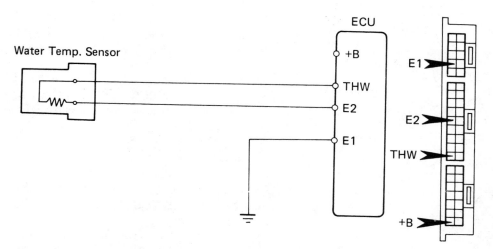

FIGURE 11-31 Water temperature sensor circuitry — Corolla and MR2 vehicles. (*Courtesy of Toyota Motor Corporation*)

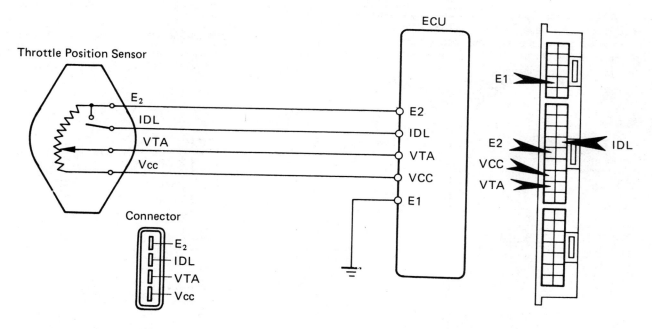

FIGURE 11-32 TPS (throttle position sensor) and ECU wiring circuit — Corolla and MR2 vehicles. (*Courtesy of Toyota Motor Corporation*)

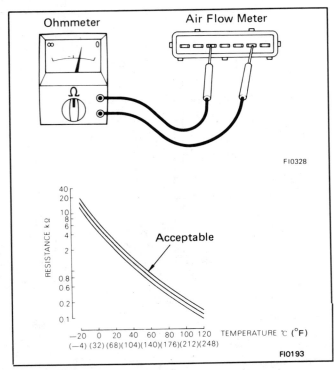

FIGURE 11-33 Acceptable resistance values in ohms for the intake air temperature sensor on the Corolla and MR2 vehicles. (*Courtesy of Toyota Motor Corporation*)

intake air temperature sensor with the connector disconnected. The acceptable values are shown in the illustration.

10. Refer to Fig. 11-34, and check to ensure that there are between 9 and 11 volts at the STA (50) terminal of the starter motor, with the ignition switch in the start position.

Then check the voltage between the STA and E1 terminals of the ECU, with the ignition switch at the start position. The voltmeter should register between 6 and 12 volts.

RESISTANCE CHECKS OF COROLLA AND MR2 VEHICLES ECU SYSTEM

A number of ECU circuit resistance checks are required to determine if a problem exists somewhere in the system. Always check that all snap-in wire connectors are not too tight or too loose, that the internal terminals are not damaged or corroded, and that the wires haven't been punctured, perhaps by a previous technician who has serviced the system.

A number of checks and tests are required for all the various ECU-controlled systems. Follow each check after first referring to the respective wiring diagram, if available.

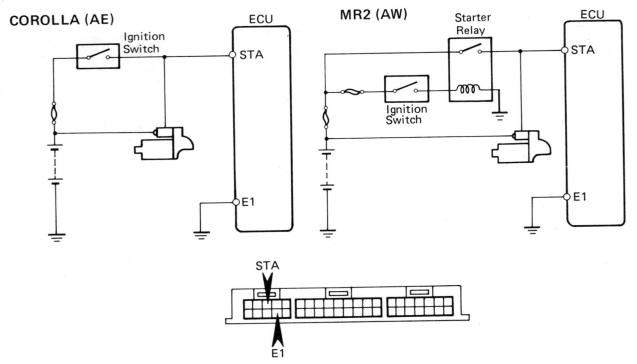

FIGURE 11-34 Corolla and MR2 starter circuit wiring test points. (*Courtesy of Toyota Motor Corporation*)

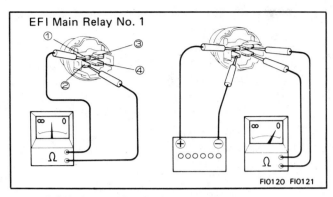

FIGURE 11-35 Test lead connections for checking the resistance values of the EFI main relay on the Corolla and MR2 vehicles. (*Courtesy of Toyota Motor Corporation*)

1. All fuses should show a resistance of 0 ohms.

2. All individual high tension spark plug wire leads should not exceed 25 K (25,000) ohms.

3. Refer to Fig. 11-25. It illustrates the wiring circuitry for the ECU system, main relay, and ignition switch. Check the EFI (electronic fuel injection) main relay plug-in harness (Fig. 11-35), and check for the following maximum resistance values:

   (a) 60 to 90 ohms between terminals 1 and 2.

   (b) 0 ohms between terminals 3 and 4.

4. Checks 4, 5, and 6 and their location in the wiring circuit are shown in Fig. 11-26.

   Also refer to Fig. 11-36 and check the resistance of the fuel pump circuit opening relay between terminals B and Fp, with current from the battery flowing between terminal STA and E1. The value should be 0 ohms.

5. Refer to Fig. 11-37, and check the air flow meter pump switch, with the connector disconnected. With the measuring plate closed inside the housing, the resistance value should read infinity, while with the

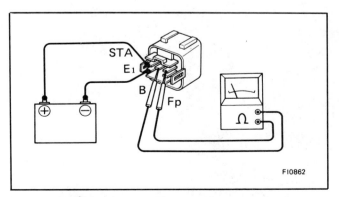

FIGURE 11-36 Ohmmeter connection for checking the fuel pump circuit opening relay resistance on the Corolla and MR2 vehicles. (*Courtesy of Toyota Motor Corporation*)

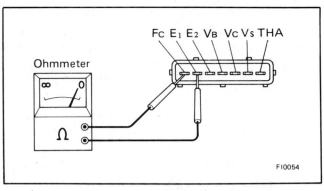

FIGURE 11-37 Air flow meter pump switch resistance check. (*Courtesy of Toyota Motor Corporation*)

measuring plate slightly open, a zero ohms resistance should be read, with the ohmmeter connections between terminals Fc and E1.

6. Refer to Fig. 11-38 and check the resistance of the fuel system circuit opening relay connector between terminals B and Fc, which should show a value of between 88 and 132 ohms.

7. Refer to Fig. 11-39. With the injector solenoid resistor connectors removed, check the resistance between the +B and other illustrated terminals, which should have a maximum resistance of 3 ohms.

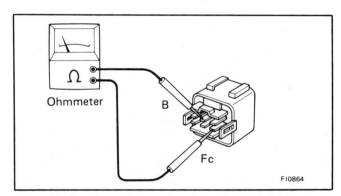

FIGURE 11-38 Checking circuit opening relay connector resistance. (*Courtesy of Toyota Motor Corporation*)

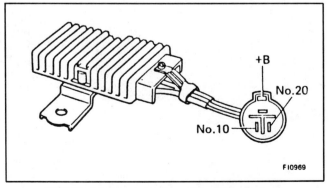

FIGURE 11-39 Injector solenoid resistor connector resistance check. (*Courtesy of Toyota Motor Corporation*)

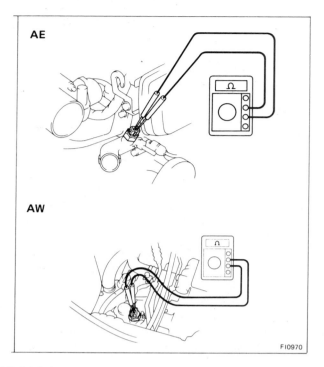

8. Refer to Fig. 11-40. With the cold start injector connector disconnected, measure the resistance between the following terminals:

(a) Between STA and STJ, 20–40 ohms with a coolant temperature below 35°C (95°F).

(b) Between STA and STJ, 40–60 ohms with a coolant temperature above 35°C (95°F)

(c) Between STA and ground, 20–80 ohms

9. With the CSI (cold start injector) wiring connector removed, insert the ohmmeter leads across both terminals of the CSI, which should read between 3 and 5 ohms.

10. With the wire harness connectors removed from the individual injectors, place the ohmmeter leads across each injector connection one at a time. The resistance value should be between 1.5 and 3 ohms each.

11. Check the ignition coil primary resistance after dis-

FIGURE 11-40 Cold start injector and time delay switch connector resistance check and wiring schematic. (*Courtesy of Toyota Motor Corporation*)

COROLLA

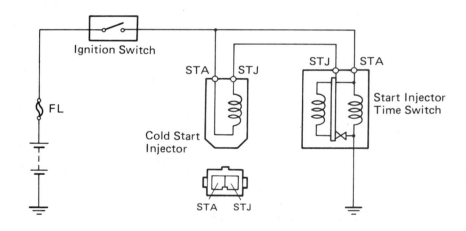

MR2

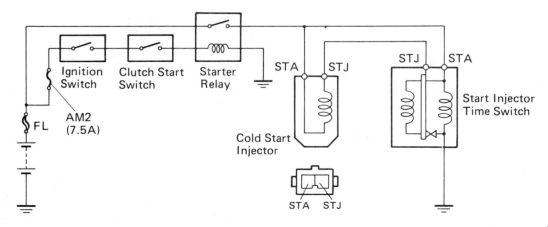

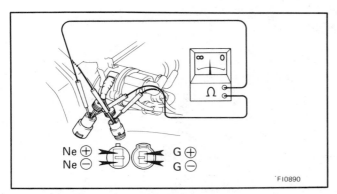

FIGURE 11-41 Ohmmeter connections for distributor pick-up coils resistance check. (*Courtesy of Toyota Motor Corporation*)

connecting the leads between the coil and the igniter. Using an ohmmeter, check the resistance between the + and − terminals, which should give a cold value of between 0.5 and 0.7 ohms.

12. Check the coil secondary resistance after disconnecting the leads between the coil and igniter. Place the ohmmeter leads between the + terminal and high tension terminal (center electrode of the coil). A cold resistance of 11 to 16 ohms is normal.

13. Refer to Figs. 11-41 and 11-42. Check the pickup coils in the distributor with the connector disconnected. With the ohmmeter between G+ and G− and

between Ne+ and Ne−, there should be a resistance in both cases of between 140 and 180 ohms.

14. Refer to Fig. 11-42. Check the resistance of the distributor pickup coils at the ECU connections, with the ignition switch turned to the lock position and the wiring connectors disconnected from the ECU.

    Measure the resistance between terminals G+ and G−, which should be between 140 and 180 ohms. Between terminals Ne and E1, the value should be 210 to 250 ohms.

15. Refer to Fig. 11-33. Check the resistance of the intake air temperature sensor, and compare the values with those shown in the chart of the figure.

ENGINE EXHAUST OXYGEN SENSOR CHECK

When a problem exists in the oxygen sensor circuit, a trouble code will be stored in the computer memory bank. This will be indicated by a Code 5 for the Corolla and MR2 vehicles, and by a Code 21 in the Cressida, Supra, and Celica vehicles.

In all cases, start by checking the oxygen sensor (see Chapter 4) and connector to ensure that they are not loose or damaged. Also make certain that there are no loose connections between the oxygen sensor and the ECU connector. Then refer to Table 11-1, which shows the preferred sequence to use when logically checking out the reason for a possible Code 5 or 21.

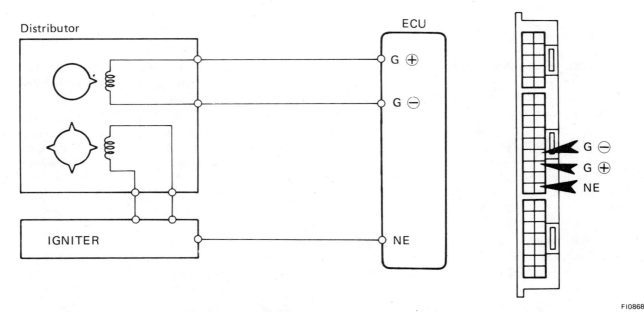

FIGURE 11-42 ECU and distributor pick-up coil wiring circuit. (*Courtesy of Toyota Motor Corporation*)

CODE 5 — Open circuit in oxygen sensor circuitry

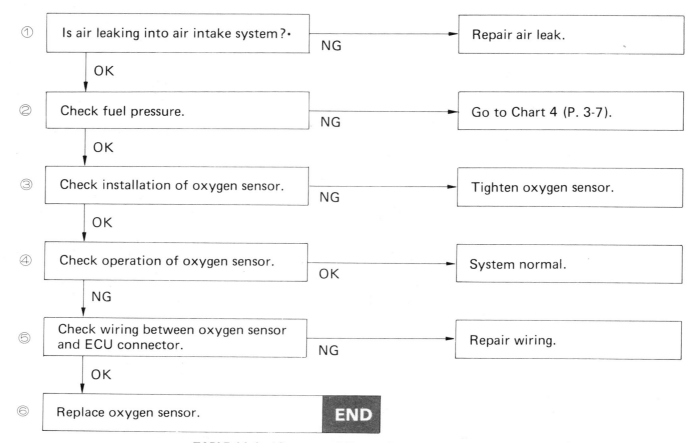

TABLE 11-1   *(Courtesy of Toyota Motor Corporation)*

Check Sequence — Oxygen Sensor

Follow the sequence given below for a systematic check of the actual oxygen sensor itself.

1. Ensure that the engine is at normal operating temperature.
2. Refer to Figs. 11-43 and 11-44. Short out the respective ''Check Engine Connector'' (AE) or terminals T-E1 of the service connector (AW), depending on whether the vehicle is a Corolla or MR2 model.
3. On AE Corolla vehicles, using special tool SST (09842-14010), connect an analog voltmeter (Fig. 11-43) to the service connector and set the switch dial to the 5–20 volt range.
4. Refer to Fig. 11-43. On AW MR2 vehicles, connect the analog voltmeter + terminal to the Vf terminal on the service connector, with the other voltmeter lead to a good clean ground. Set the switch dial of the voltmeter to the 5–20 volt range.

5. Run the engine to operating temperature at 2500 rpm for about two minutes to ensure a stabilized exhaust oxygen sensor reaction.
6. Look at the face plate of the voltmeter and carefully note how many times the needle fluctuates between 0 and 5 volts within a 10 second period and with the engine still running at 2500 rpm. If the needle indicates a minimum of 8 fluctuations every 10 second period, then the oxygen sensor is operational. Any less than this is sufficient cause to replace the oxygen sensor assembly.

CLEAR ECU MEMORY

Anytime that a systematic check of the ECU trouble codes has been performed, the ECU memory should be cleared. To do this, the ignition switch should be turned off to the lock position, and the respective fuse removed. Refer to Fig. 11-45 for the location of the EFI/ECU fuse in the

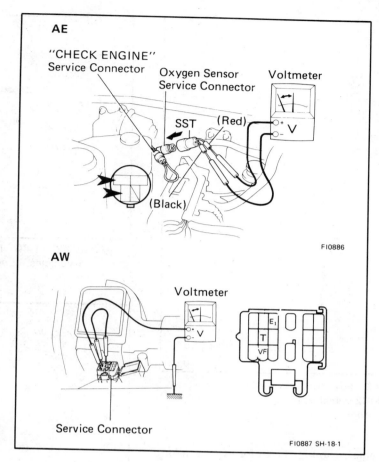

FIGURE 11-43 Oxygen sensor test hookup. (*Courtesy of Toyota Motor Corporation*)

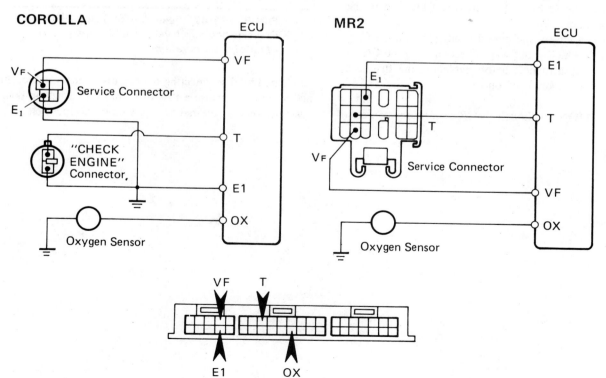

FIGURE 11-44 Oxygen sensor circuit wiring arrangement for the Corolla and MR2 vehicles. (*Courtesy of Toyota Motor Corporation*)

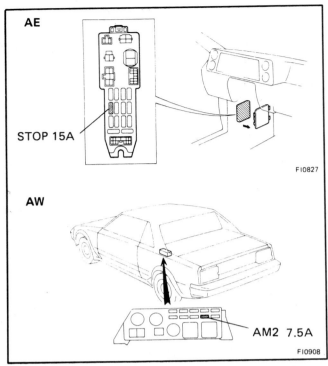

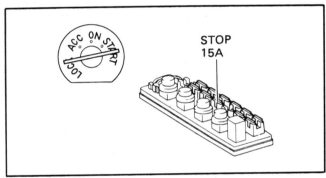

FIGURE 11-46 Fuse location for ECU on Celica vehicles. (*Courtesy of Toyota Motor Corporation*)

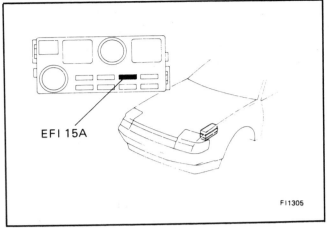

FIGURE 11-45 Fuse location for ECU on the Corolla and MR2 vehicles. (*Courtesy of Toyota Motor Corporation*)

FIGURE 11-47 Fuse location for ECU on Cressida and Supra vehicles. (*Courtesy of Toyota Motor Corporation*)

Corolla and MR2 vehicles, to Fig. 11-46 for ECU location in the Celica, and to Fig. 11-47 for ECU location in the Cressida and Supra vehicles.

Generally, a ten-second period is adequate on the Corolla and MR2 vehicles, but wait 30 seconds on the Celica and Cressida/Supra models before replacing the fuse and turning the ignition key back on.

NOTE/CAUTION: Although the ECU memory can also be cleared by disconnecting the negative battery cable, this action will also cause a loss of memory to other on-board systems, such as the radio, trip computer, clock, etc.

CHAPTER 12

◆

Nissan 300 ZX ECCS System

BASIC ARRANGEMENT OF ECCS SYSTEM

Nissan is another prominent name in passenger cars, since it produces, along with many other manufacturers, a truly excellent product. In the U.S. the company is now known as Nissan Motor Corporation U.S.A., while in Canada it is known as Nissan Automobile Company (Canada) Ltd. For years, of course, everyone knew the company as Datsun, since this name was the marque commonly used to identify its vehicles.

Nissan has been involved in automotive electronics for many years, and has contributed to the development of everything from electronically-controlled fuel injection in 1971 with Robert Bosch Corporation, the introduction of the Electronic Concentrated Engine Control System (ECCS) in 1979, digital instrument displays in 1980, electronically-controlled suspension with sonar road surface sensor technology in 1984, to a variable nozzle turbocharger concept in 1985.

The ECCS system is now employed on a number of Nissan passenger cars, with the Maxima, 200 SX Turbo, and 300 ZX, and 300ZX Turbo all employing this same basic system. Since this system is common to all of these vehicles, let's look at the basic system employed on the 280 ZX Turbo, 300 ZX, and 300 ZX Turbo passenger cars. Latest model Maxima models also employ the same basic engine and electronic control system as the one used in the 280 and 300 ZX models.

Each engine used in these vehicles employs the basic Bosch LH-Jetronic gasoline fuel-injection system. (Refer to Chapter 5.) The basic system and components for the 280 ZX and 300ZX are illustrated in Figs. 12-1 and 12-2.

The ECCS system is designed to control both the ignition and fuel control systems, as well as the exhaust emissions. In this respect it is therefore similar in operation to the Bosch Motronic system. (Refer to Chapter 5.) Figure 12-3 illustrates the basic fuel-injection system and vacuum line arrangement for the 300ZX.

The ECCS control unit receives various sensor voltage signal inputs based upon the various operating conditions of the engine, just as other computer equipped vehicles that are discussed in this book do. (For a detailed description of operation of these various sensors, refer to Chapter 4.)

IMPORTANT SERVICING PRECAUTION: Before performing any type of service on electronic systems or IC's (integrated circuits), you *must* discharge yourself of static electricity or ESD (electrostatic discharge) by touching a good vehicle ground, such as the door post or vehicle shift lever. Failure to do so can result in damage to voltage sensitive electronic components. If, for any reason, you leave the vehicle during servicing, after re-entering to continue work, you *must* again ground yourself of ESD in order to drain any static electrical charge. Also, if you are performing control head/radio type checks on a new vehicle, remove the plastic seat covers, since they increase the possibility of creating a static charge.

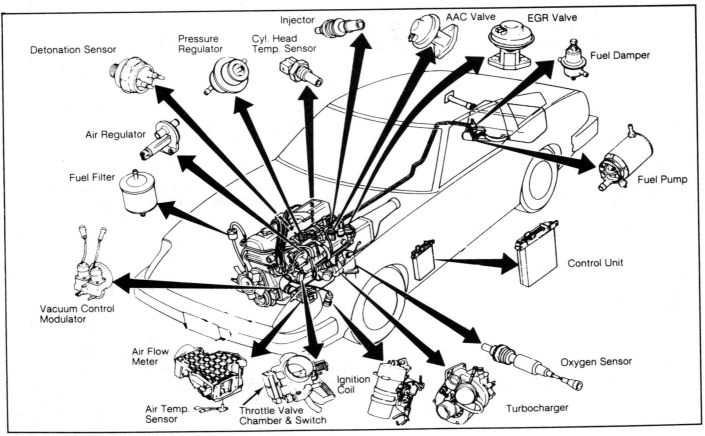

FIGURE 12-1   Nissan 280ZX Turbo ECCS system. (*Courtesy of Nissan Motor Co. Ltd.*)

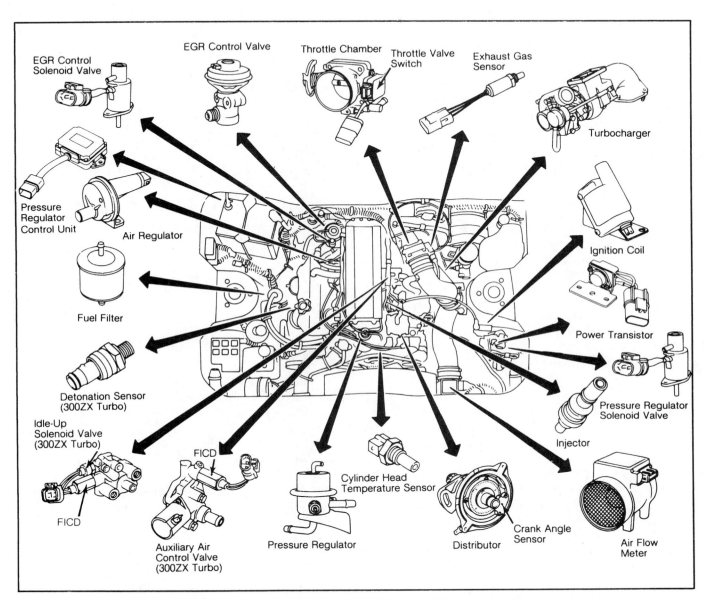

FIGURE 12-2 Nissan 300ZX and 300ZX Turbo ECCS system. (*Courtesy of Nissan Motor Co. Ltd.*)

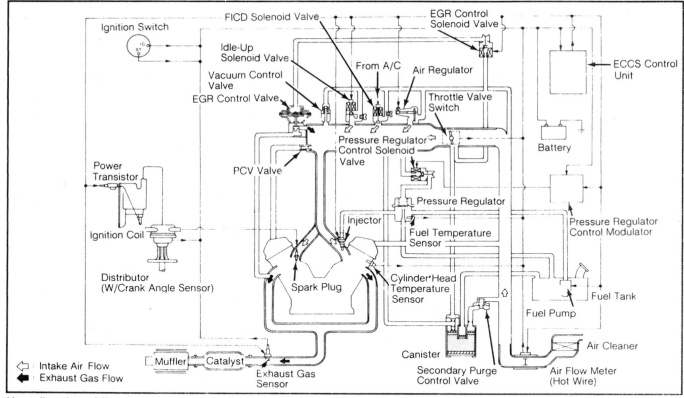

Note direction of flow.

FIGURE 12-3 Nissan 300ZX ECCS and fuel system schematic. (*Courtesy of Nissan Motor Co. Ltd.*)

TESTING AND DIAGNOSIS

The ECCS control unit (computer) is located behind the passenger side kick panel on the 300ZX and 300ZX Turbo models, while on the Maxima, it is located under the left side of the dash. On the 200SX, the computer is located behind the driver's side kick panel.

A monitor lamp is provided on the lower side of the ECCS control unit (Fig. 12-4) to allow the technician to check the system. Should a sensed and monitored system malfunction, then a *Check Engine* light on the instrument panel warns the driver of a system malfunction.

A special tester (Nissan ECCS Analyzer P/N J28835) is required to access and fully diagnose the ECCS system. If, however, this tool is not available, the system will self-diagnose itself when the mode selector switch shown on the side of the computer in Fig. 12-4 is turned CW.

To monitor the system by noting the number of bulb flashes on the computer (Fig. 12-4), proceed as follows:

Procedure

1. Engine should be at normal operating temperature.
2. Make *sure* that the ignition key is off, and disconnect the ECC harness connector.
3. Ensure that the diagnosis mode selector knob is turned fully CCW; then turn the ignition switch on.

4. Inspection lamps on the computer control unit shown in Fig. 12-4 should stay on. If they don't, check the harness for battery power. If there is battery power, then a fault exists in the computer control unit.
5. If the computer lights stay on, turn the diagnosis mode selector knob fully CW and note the number of blinks/flashes of the lights on the side of the computer.

NOTE: The LED's (light emitting diodes) on the side of the computer are colored red and green. The red LED followed by the green LED will blink to indicate a trouble code. For example, two red LED blinks followed by five green LED blinks indicates a Code 25.

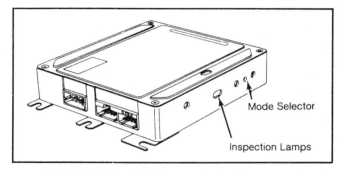

FIGURE 12-4 ECCS control unit. (*Courtesy of Nissan Motor Co. Ltd.*)

6. Normal conditions flash a Code 23, then 24 (300ZX Turbo), Code 31 and 32 (200SX). If some other sequence flashes, write down the codes as they appear.

7. A technician writes down these codes as they flash and then refers to the appropriate service manual to determine the circuit at fault.

TROUBLE CODES

The following codes indicate a problem in a particular circuit:

Code Number	Circuit
11	Crank angle switch
12	Air flow meter
14	Vehicle speed sensor
21	Ignition signal
22	Fuel pump
23	Throttle valve switch
24	Neutral/Park switch
31	Air conditioner
32	Start signal
34	Detonation sensor
41	Fuel temperature sensor

ECCS MEMORY ERASURE

When all stored trouble codes in memory have been withdrawn, the computer memory is cleared as follows:

1. Turn the ignition key switch on.

2. Rotate the diagnosis mode selector on the side of the computer control unit (Fig. 12-4) fully CW and leave it there for at least 2 seconds.

3. Turn the diagnosis mode selector fully CCW and leave it there for at least 2 seconds.

4. Turn the ignition key switch back to the off position.

TRACING SYSTEM FAULTS

When a system fault is indicated by a stored trouble code in memory, where the fault lies in the basic system can be found by referring to the trouble code charts. This, in itself, directs the technician to the circuit where the problem is suspected; however, it DOES NOT necessarily pinpoint the exact cause of the problem.

It now becomes necessary for the technician systematically to check out the condition of the plug-in harness connectors and the respective pins for signs of damage or bent pins. In addition, high circuit resistance due to corrosion, poor contact between the wiring harness connector and the ECU are frequent other causes for trouble codes to appear in memory.

You should also carefully check all vacuum hoses for signs of crimping, which would cause a restriction or blockage, and for signs of holes or burning from contact with a hot exhaust or engine component: You should also ensure that no vacuum lines or wires have come loose and that, in fact, all vacuum lines are properly routed.

In many instances, failure of a system to operate correctly can often be traced to a mechanical problem rather than an electrical cause. Too often the computer system or a sensor receives the blame for a problem, and consequently these are replaced haphazardly without rectifying the original cause of the problem.

A digital volt-ohmmeter with at least a 10 megohm impedance can be used across the various connector pins of the harness and computer terminals. These readings can be compared to the manufacturer's specifications to determine if a problem exists in that circuit.

Figure 12-5 illustrates the wiring schematic for the 300 ZX and 300ZX Turbo vehicle, showing all the various numbered connections at the electronic control module, and numbered wires extending out through the wiring harness to the various sensors and relays.

TROUBLE CODE CHECKS

Code 12   *Air flow meter* problem (300ZX and Maxima engines)

1. Disconnect the wiring harness from the air flow meter as shown in Fig. 12-6, and apply battery voltage to terminals D and E.

2. On a digital volt/ohmmeter, the reading should be between 1.5 and 1.7 volts; otherwise, a fault in the air flow meter is indicated, and it should be replaced.

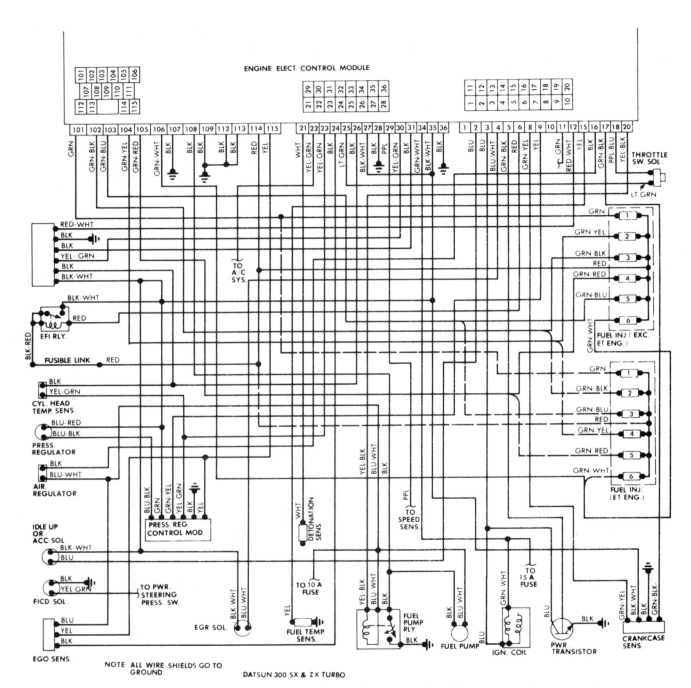

FIGURE 12-5 300ZX and 300ZX Turbo vehicle wiring schematic.
(*Courtesy of Nissan Motor Co. Ltd.*)

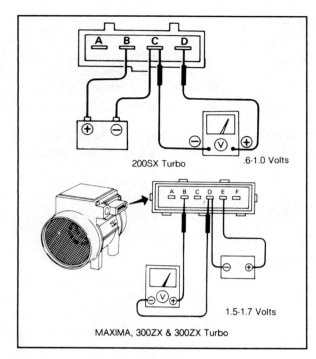

200SX Turbo

.6-1.0 Volts

MAXIMA, 300ZX & 300ZX Turbo

1.5-1.7 Volts

FIGURE 12-6 Air flow meter test connections. (*Courtesy of Nissan Motor Co. Ltd.*)

Water Temperature Sensor

This sensor plays an important role in the overall performance of the engine, since the computer varies the pulse-width signal to the fuel injectors based upon this signal.

To check this sensor, you disconnect the 16 pin connector harness, which is the one in the center of the ECU. (See Fig. 12-5.)

1. Measure the resistance between terminals 23 and 26 with the digital ohmmeter.

2. The resistance values should be below 2100 ohms when the coolant temperature is just below 68°F (20°C), or below 2900 ohms with the coolant temperature just above 68°F (20°C).

3. If the resistance readings are within the specifications shown below at the five test temperatures, replace the control unit (ECU).

4. If the resistance readings are not within specifications, check the harness and connector pins for signs of damage (bent pins), poor connections, corrosion, etc.

5. If no damage is found at the harness, proceed to check the actual sensor resistance by suspending it in a beaker of heated water, just as you would check a thermostat assembly. Do not allow the sensor to rest on the bottom of the container; otherwise, it will give a false reading. Agitate the water (stir it) while it is being heated, and with an accurate thermometer suspended in the container (not on the bottom), note the temperature of the water and the resistance reading across the sensor as per the following information for the 300ZX/Turbo and Maxima.

Water Temperature/Resistance Relationship (ohms)

14°F (10°C)	7000–11,400 ohms
68°F (20°C)	2100–2900 ohms
122°F (50°C)	680–1000 ohms
176°F (80°C)	260–390 ohms
212°F (100°C)	180–200 ohms

Code 14   *Vehicle Speed Sensor*

1.   Disconnect the speedometer cable from transmission.
2.   With ECU 16 pin connector disconnected from the ECU (center harness), check continuity from terminal number 29 to ground as you slowly rotate the speedometer cable.
3.   An on/off pulse should be noted on the volt/ohmmeter needle.

NOTE: The ignition switch should be off if an analog (needle) type speedometer is used; if a digital unit is used, the ignition switch should be turned on during this check.

4.   If there is no visible pulse at the volt/ohmmeter during this check, a closer inspection of the wiring harness and vehicle speed sensor is warranted.
5.   If there is a pulse at the volt/ohmmeter needle, then replace the ECCS control unit (ECU).

Code 21   *Ignition Signal*

1.   Disconnect the 20 pin connector from the ECU as shown on the top right-hand side of Fig. 12-5.
2.   Check for continuity between terminals 3, 5, and ground.
3.   If no continuity is evident, repair/replace the harness.
4.   If continuity is indicated, check the power transistor, as shown in Fig. 12-7, by placing the ohmmeter positive lead (red) on terminal 1. Continuity should be evident at terminals 3 and 2.

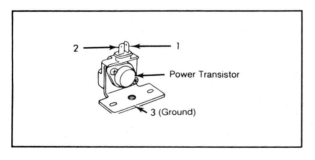

FIGURE 12-7   Power transistor terminals (Code 21). (*Courtesy of Nissan Motor Co. Ltd.*)

5.   With the positive lead at terminal 2, continuity should be evident at terminal 3.
6.   If continuity is confirmed in Steps 3 and 4 above, then replace the ECCS control unit (ECU).

Code 22   *Fuel Pump*

1.   With the ignition key switch on, carefully listen for the sound of the electric fuel pump motoring for about a five second interval.
2.   If pump performance is confirmed, then replace the ECCS control unit (ECU).
3.   If no sound is heard from the pump in Step 1, disconnect the ECCS 15 pin connector (Fig. 12-5, top left-hand side).
4.   Check for voltage between terminal 108 and ground with the ignition switch on.
5.   If there is continuity, proceed to Step 6. If no continuity exists, check the wiring harness for continuity. If evident, proceed to Step 6; otherwise repair the harness problem.

6. On the Maxima, check the fuel pump relay for continuity between terminals 1-2 and 3-4, as shown in Fig. 12-8. Continuity should exist between terminals 1 and 2, but there should be none between terminals 3 and 4.

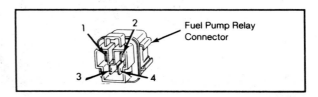

FIGURE 12-8 Connector terminals for continuity check of fuel pump relay. (*Courtesy of Nissan Motor Co. Ltd.*)

7. Apply 12 volts to terminals 1 and 2, and continuity should now exist between terminals 3 and 4. If there is not, then replace the fuel pump relay. If continuity does exist, then proceed to Step 8.

8. Check the fuel pump for continuity on all models, and if continuity is confirmed, replace the ECCS control unit (ECU). If there is no continuity, replace the fuel pump.

Code 23 *Throttle Valve Switch or TVS (See Fig. 12-9)*

1. Always check the harness first for continuity, and repair if necessary.

2. Check the throttle valve switch for continuity between terminals 18 and 25 on the 300 ZX and 300ZX Turbo. On the Maxima (and 200SX Turbo), check for continuity between terminals 29 and 30. If there is no continuity, then proceed to Step 3.

3. Adjust the TVS by disconnecting the AAC (auxiliary air control) valve wiring harness connector on the 300ZX Turbo only. On all other models,

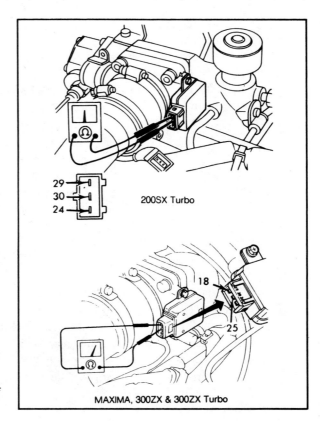

FIGURE 12-9 Throttle valve switch connector. (*Courtesy of Nissan Motor Co. Ltd.*)

run the engine speed to the following rpm's by manipulation of the throttle valve:

   (a) 300ZX Turbo engine, 800–850 rpm

   (b) 300ZX and Maxima, 850–950 rpm

   (c) 200SX Turbo, 850–950 rpm

4. Adjust the idle switch carefully, until the idle switch actually turns on between the rpm's shown in Step 3.

5. If switch adjustment cannot be achieved, then replace the TVS.

NOTE: If during the procedure in Step 1, continuity existed, check for continuity between terminals 18, 25 and ground on the 300ZX and 300ZX Turbo. Check between terminals 29, 30 and ground on the Maxima and 200SX Turbo. If there is continuity, replace the TVS. If there is no continuity, replace the ECCS control unit (ECU).

Code 24   *Neutral/Park Switch or NPS*

1. Check the wiring harness for continuity, and repair as necessary.

2. If continuity exists, check the NPS.

3. With the NPS plunger depressed, there should be no continuity.

4. With the NPS in its free-position, there should be continuity.

5. If the NPS fails Step 2 or 3 above, replace it.

6. If the NPS passes Step 2 and 3 above, then replace the ECCS control unit (ECU).

Code 31   *Air Conditioner System or ACS*

1. To check the compressor operation, start the engine and turn the A/C switch on.

2. If the compressor is operational, stop the engine and disconnect the 16 pin connector shown in Fig. 12-5 at the top center.

3. With the ignition on, measure the voltage between terminal 22 and ground; if there is no battery voltage indicated on the voltmeter, check and repair the harness.

4. If battery voltage is evident on the voltmeter, then replace the ECCS control unit (ECU).

Code 32   *Start Signal*

1. Check that the vehicle starting system is operational.

2. If it is, disconnect the starter motor S terminal.

3. Disconnect the 20 pin connector from the ECU (top right-hand side plug in Fig. 12-5), and measure the voltage between terminal 9 and ground. If there is no battery ground, repair the harness.

4. If there is a ground, replace the ECCS control unit (ECU).

Code 34   *Detonation Sensor*

1. Disconnect the detonation sensor wiring harness connector.

2. Start the engine and manually increase the speed while checking the engine timing as per the EPA underhood sticker.

3. Note that the ignition timing automatically retards by 5 degrees when the engine speed has increased more than 2000 rpm.

4. If timing doesn't retard by 5 degrees, then replace the ECCS control unit (ECU).

5. If the timing does retard by 5 degrees, check the wiring harness for continuity, and if continuity is confirmed, then replace the detonation sensor.

Code 41 *Fuel Temperature Sensor*

1. Disconnect the 20 pin connector at the ECU (top right-hand side of Fig. 12-5).
2. Using a digital ohmmeter, measure the resistance between terminal number 15 and ground.
3. When the fuel temperature is below 68°F (20°C), resistance should be above 2100 ohms; when the temperature is higher than 68°F (20°C), the resistance should be below 2900 ohms.
4. If the resistance values are within specifications, replace the ECCS control unit (ECU).
5. If the resistance values are outside of the specifications, check the wiring harness for continuity and repair as necessary.
6. If the wiring harness is serviceable, then check the resistance of the fuel temperature sensor.

NOTE: The actual resistance change of the fuel temperature sensor will vary with temperature rise. The resistance value for the fuel temperature sensor is the same as that shown earlier for the water temperature sensor.

7. If the fuel temperature sensor resistance values are within the specifications shown for the water temperature sensor, then replace the ECCS control unit (ECU).
8. If the resistance values for the sensor are outside of the specifications, replace the fuel temperature sensor and fuel pressure regulator as an assembly.

AUXILIARY AIR CONTROL VALVE (AAC)

1. Disconnect the 20 pin connector shown at the top right-hand side of the ECU as shown in Fig. 12-5.
2. Check the voltage between terminal number 2 and ground when the ignition is on. This can be done between terminal 2 of the 20 pin connector, and terminal number 28 or 36 of the 16 pin connector on the ECU, or connect the voltmeter leads between terminal 2 and ground.
3. If battery voltage is read on the voltmeter, then the test is complete.
4. If no battery voltage is evident, then check the wiring harness and repair as necessary. If the harness is serviceable, check the fuel pump relay as described under Code 22 earlier.
5. Check for continuity between terminals 1–2 and 3–4 of the 20 pin connector. There should be continuity only between terminals 1–2, but not at 3–4.
6. Apply 12 volts to terminals 1–2, and continuity should now exist between terminals 3–4.
7. If no continuity exists between terminals 3–4, replace the relay.
8. If continuity is evident, proceed to Step 9.
9. Check the AAC valve for continuity between its terminal and ground. If there is no continuity, then replace the AAC valve.

EXHAUST GAS RECIRCULATION VALVE (EGR)

1. Disconnect the 20 pin connector at the top right-hand side of the ECU (Fig. 12-5).
2. Check for voltage between terminal number 4 and ground when the ignition key is turned on.
3. If battery voltage is evident on the voltmeter, the test is complete. If, however, there is no voltage reading, then check the wiring harness for continuity and repair as necessary.
4. If continuity does exist at the wiring harness, check the EFI (electronic fuel injection) relay for continuity be-

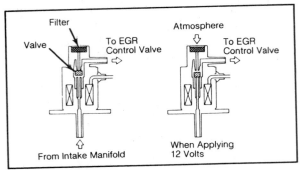

FIGURE 12-10 300ZX and Turbo EGR valve operation. (*Courtesy of Nissan Motor Co. Ltd.*)

tween terminals 1–2 and 3–4 of the 20 pin connector. There should be continuity between terminals 1–2, but not at 3–4.

5. Apply 12 volts to terminals 1–2, and continuity should now exist between terminals 3–4.

6. If no continuity exists, replace the EFI relay.

7. If continuity exists, proceed to Step 8.

8. Check the EGR valve for continuity between two terminals of the wiring connector. If no continuity exists, replace the EGR control valve.

9. If continuity exists, check the EGR control valve for proper operation and replace it if it fails to perform satisfactorily. Figure 12-10 illustrates the reaction/operation of the EGR control valve.

AIR REGULATOR CHECK

1. Disconnect the 20 pin connector at the top right-hand side of the ECU, as shown in Fig. 12-5.

2. Check for voltage between terminal number 16 and ground when the ignition key is on.

3. If battery voltage is evident, then the test is complete.

4. If no voltage or low battery voltage is observed, then check the wiring harness and repair as necessary.

5. If the harness is serviceable, then check the air regulator assembly.

6. Check for continuity between the two terminals of the connector.

7. If no continuity exists, replace the air regulator assembly.

8. If continuity is evident, remove the air regulator assembly and visually check the shutter opening with the aid of a mirror held alongside the valve.

9. The shutter should be open when the engine is cold (bypass air) and should be closed when the engine is warm.

10. Carefully insert a small screwdriver into the valve to check that it does, in fact, open smoothly.

FUEL INJECTOR TESTS

1. The fuel injector circuits on the 280ZX are numbered according to cylinder number. For example, injector power circuit number 103 signifies that it goes to injector number 3, etc.

2. Disconnect the 15 pin connector located on the top left-hand side of the ECU (Fig. 12-5).

3. On the 300ZX and Turbo, as well as the Maxima, check voltage between ground and terminals 101, 102, 104, 105, 106 and 114. On the 200SX Turbo, check between 101, 102, 104 and 105, and ground.

4. If battery voltage is evident, then the test is complete.

5. If there is no battery voltage, check each injector for continuity between two terminals of the injector connector.

6. If continuity is evident, then check the wiring harness and repair if necessary.

7. If there is no continuity, replace the injector.

BATTERY POWER SOURCE AND GROUND CONFIRMATION

1. On the 300ZX and 300ZX Turbo as well as the Maxima, ensure that the diagnosis mode selector switch on the side of the ECCS (ECU), shown in Fig. 12-4, is turned fully CCW.

2. Turn the ignition on and confirm that both the red and green LED's on the ECU remain illuminated. If they do, then the test is complete.

3. If the red and green LED's do not remain on, check the wiring harness for continuity and repair as necessary.

4. If continuity exists at the wiring harness, check the EFI relay as described earlier under the EGR check.

5. If no continuity exists, replace the EFI relay.

6. If the EFI relay is OK, then replace the ECCS control unit (ECU).

7. On the 200SX Turbo, disconnect the 16 pin connector from the ECU, which is on the left-hand side.

8. Check for voltage between terminals 27–28, 27–36, 35–36, and 35–28 when the ignition is on. If there is battery voltage, then the test is complete.

9. If no battery voltage is evident, then check and repair the wiring harness. If the harness is serviceable, then the test is complete.

10. If the battery voltage is not evident now, check the EFI relay as described earlier under the EGR check.

EXHAUST GAS OXYGEN SENSOR HEATER (300ZX/TURBO AND MAXIMA)

1. Disconnect the 15 pin ECU connector (top left of Fig. 12-5) and check for voltage between terminal 115 and ground with the ignition key on.
2. If battery voltage is evident, then the test is complete.
3. If no battery voltage is visible, measure the resistance of the exhaust gas sensor heater. The resistance value should be between 2.62–3.12 ohms.
4. If the resistance value is within specifications, then check the wiring harness.
5. If the resistance value is not within specifications, then replace the exhaust gas oxygen sensor.

NOTE: For detailed information on the exhaust gas oxygen sensor, refer to Chapter 4.

EXHAUST GAS OXYGEN SENSOR (200SX TURBO)

1. Disconnect battery ground cable.
2. Disconnect the exhaust gas sensor harness connector, and connect the center terminal to ground.
3. Disconnect the 16 pin ECU connector and check for continuity between terminal 24 and ground.
4. If continuity doesn't exist, check the ECCS wiring harness; and if the harness shows continuity, replace the exhaust gas oxygen sensor.

IDLE-UP SOLENOID VALVE (200SX TURBO AND 300 ZX)

1. Disconnect the 20 pin connector from the ECU.
2. Check for voltage between terminal number 2 and ground, with the ignition key switch on.
3. On the 300ZX, if battery voltage is evident, then the test is complete; therefore, proceed to Step 5.
4. On the 200SX Turbo, if voltage is evident, check for voltage between terminal 19 and ground; then proceed to Step 9.
5. If no battery voltage is present, check the wiring harness, and repair as necessary.
6. If the harness is serviceable, then check the EFI relay

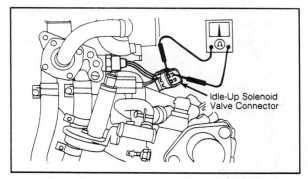

FIGURE 12-11 Idle-up solenoid valve continuity check. (*Courtesy of Nissan Motor Co. Ltd.*)

for continuity, as described earlier under the EGR check.

7. If the EFI relay fails the test, replace it.
8. If the EFI relay is serviceable, check the idle-up solenoid valve for continuity as shown in Fig. 12-11. If no continuity exists, replace the idle-up solenoid valve.
9. On the 200SX, turn the ignition key switch on, as well as the heater fan.
10. If there is no voltage, check the diodes for signs of an open circuit. Check all switches and repair, and then backtrack to Step 4.
11. If there is voltage, check the idle-up solenoid for continuity, as shown in Fig. 12-11.
12. If there is no continuity, replace the idle-up solenoid.
13. If there is continuity, check the EFI relay as per the description given earlier under the EGR check.
14. If the EFI relay does not meet the specifications, replace the relay.

AIR INJECTION CONTROL VALVE (AIV)

1. Disconnect the cylinder head temperature sensor wiring harness connector, and connect a 2500 ohm resistor between the terminals of the sensor and the wiring harness connector.
2. Start the engine and listen carefully for the sound of the AIV operating. If the AIV sounds OK, the test is complete.
3. If the AIV doesn't appear to be operating, disassemble the AIV, clean it out carefully, and check it for successful operation. If it still fails to operate, replace it.
4. Check the voltage ECU between terminals 14, 28, and 36 of the 16 and 20 pin connectors with the ignition on.
5. If there is battery voltage, then the test is complete.

6. If no battery voltage is evident, check the wiring harness for continuity and repair as necessary.

7. If the wiring harness is serviceable, then check the EFI relay for continuity as described earlier under the EGR check.

8. Replace the EFI relay if it fails the check.

9. If the EFI passes the check, then check the AIV solenoid control valve for continuity, which should have a resistance of approximately 30 ohms.

PRESSURE REGULATOR SOLENOID VALVE

1. Disconnect the cylinder head temperature sensor harness connector, and insert a jumper wire between the terminals of the sensor harness connector.

2. Disconnect the vacuum hose between the pressure regulator and solenoid valve.

3. Start the engine and ensure that vacuum does not occur for at least three minutes. If so, the system is OK, the test is complete.

4. If vacuum does occur within the three minute time period, check voltage ECU between terminals 14, 28, and 36 of the 16 and 20 pin connectors, with the ignition on. If there is battery voltage, the test is complete.

5. If no battery voltage is evident, check and repair the wiring harness.

6. If continuity exists at the harness, check the EFI relay for continuity, as was described earlier under the EGR check. If the relay fails to meet the specifications, replace the relay.

7. If the relay meets the specifications, check the pressure regulator solenoid valve for continuity, which should have a resistance value of approximately 30 ohms.

CHAPTER 13

♦

Isuzu ECM/MCU Systems

Typical Isuzu vehicles employing electronically controlled fuel systems, are the I-Mark model, Pickup trucks, and Trooper II, as well as the newer Impulse model car, which employs port fuel injection. The I-Mark and Pickup trucks employ an ECM (electronic control module) system, while the Impulse uses an MCU (microprocessor control unit) system.

The I-Mark, Pickups, and Trooper II models are equipped with a FBC (feedback carburetor) fuel system and catalytic converter. The Impulse car is equipped with a Bosch multi-port fuel injection (one injector per cylinder) system. (See Chapter 5.) For information on sensors used on these engines, their function, and a description of their operations refer to Chapter 4.

ECM SYSTEM

Figures 13-1 and 13-2 illustrate the inputs and outputs used with the ECM system to control the air/fuel ratio of the engine via the FBC. The ECM controls the air/fuel ratio by sending a signal to a vacuum control solenoid. This control signal cycles the solenoid on and off rapidly in order to maintain the air/fuel ratio as close to stoichiometric (14.7:1) as possible when in the closed-loop condition, in which state the oxygen sensor is at operating temperature and constantly sending a voltage signal back to the ECM to determine air/fuel ratio settings.

Figure 13-3 illustrates an example of the vacuum-operated fuel control actuators for the I-Mark, Pickups, and

Trooper II engines. Engine sensors continuously feed signals back to the ECM, which in turn sends an electrical signal to a vacuum control valve that converts these signals into vacuum signals to operate the actuators.

The vacuum control valve consists of a regulator and a control solenoid, with the regulator controlling the varying engine manifold vacuum conditions into constant vacuum

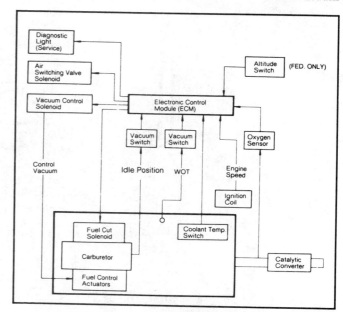

FIGURE 13-1 Isuzu ECM (electronic control module) I-Mark closed loop emission control system.

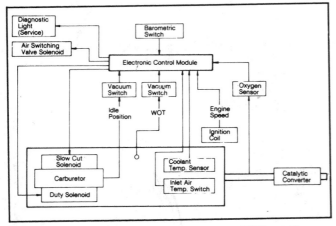

FIGURE 13-2 Isuzu California P'UP and Trooper II engine/fuel vacuum closed loop emission control system.

levels. The ECM-controlled solenoid then employs the vacuum signals to operate the fuel actuators.

DIAGNOSTIC TOOLS

Tools required to diagnose/troubleshoot the system are:

1. A dwell meter. This tool is connected to the green connector situated near the carburetor. This connector is not connected to any circuit unless the dwell meter is used. Care should be exercised with this green terminal connector to avoid its coming into contact with a ground or even a rubber hose.

The dwell meter is used to measure the time that the vacuum control solenoid is on or off, which signifies how accurately the fuel control system is operating, as well as indicating its lean or rich state. If you notice an appreciable change in the engine's operation when you connect the dwell meter, you may have to use another brand/type to avoid a noncompatibility problem with the electronic system.

Anytime that the engine is at operating temperature and running at an idle rpm, the dwell meter needle will move up and down the scale if the ECM is in a closed-loop mode. If the oxygen sensor has not yet reached its operating temperature (open loop), then the ECM will control the engine air/fuel ratio from a preprogrammed setting, and therefore the dwell meter needle will not move.

2. A tachometer, Mag pickup digital type.

3. Test light.

4. Ohmmeter, which can be part of DVOM in 5.

5. Digital voltmeter, with 10 megohms impedance (minimum).

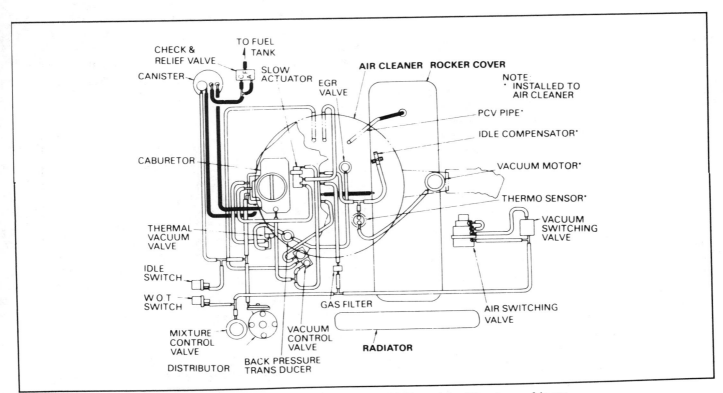

FIGURE 13-3 Vacuum diagram for P'UP models. (*Courtesy of Isuzu Motors of America.*)

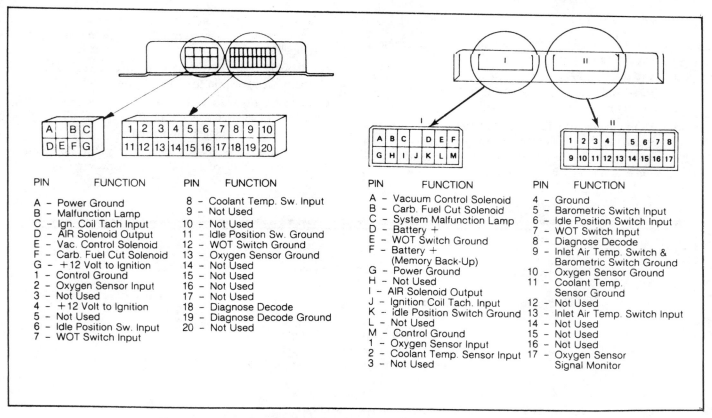

FIGURE 13-4 Isuzu I-Mark and P'UP model ECM connector identification.

6. Vacuum pump and gauge (e.g., Kent-Moore or Mityvac).

7. Assorted jumper wires.

Typical ECM terminals and identification for both the I-Mark and P'UP units are shown in Fig. 13-4.

DIAGNOSTIC FORMAT

Before beginning ECM diagnostics, always check underhood for any signs of loose, crimped, damaged, or missing vacuum lines, and also that these lines are correctly routed. Similarly, check all engine wiring and connections for signs of frayed, loose, corroded, or burned wiring.

As with most electronic diagnostic systems in use today, the Isuzu system will alert the driver to a problem by illuminating the amber-colored *Check Engine* lamp on the instrument panel. This same light will illuminate any time that the engine ignition switch is initially turned on to confirm that the system and bulb are serviceable. This light will go out within 1 to 4 seconds after engine startup. Interpretation of the trouble code number follows the regular sequence, with the lamp flashing on and off to indicate a specific code number. For example, a flash, pause, flash/flash/flash/flash indicates a Code 14, and so on.

IMPORTANT SERVICING PRECAUTION: Before performing any type of service on electronic systems or IC's (integrated circuits), you *must* discharge yourself of static electricity or ESD (electrostatic discharge) by touching a good vehicle ground, such as the door post or vehicle shift lever. Failure to do so can result in damage to voltage sensitive electronic components. If, for any reason, you leave the vehicle during servicing, after re-entering to continue work, you *must* again ground yourself of ESD in order to drain any static electrical charge. Also, if you are performing control head/radio type checks on a new vehicle, remove the plastic seat covers, since they increase the possibility of creating a static charge.

ACCESSING DIAGNOSTIC CODES

To enter the diagnostic mode, first locate the "diagnostic terminal connector," which is simply taped onto the wiring harness close to the ECM. If the *Check Engine* light fails to illuminate when the ignition key is turned on, check the bulb condition.

Procedure

1. Tape the two ends of the diagnostic connector terminals together, and start the engine.

2. Any stored trouble codes in ECM memory will be released and identified as a two-digit flashing *Check Engine* light.

3. All trouble codes will be flashed starting with the lowest, and progressing to the highest numbered code, with each code repeating three times before the next code stored in memory begins to flash.

4. Codes will continue to flash as long as the ignition key is on and the diagnostic connector terminals are tied together.

5. Trouble codes and their respective sensor/switch/circuits are shown in the tables below.

6. To clear trouble codes from memory, turn the ignition key off, and remove the positive battery cable; then disconnect the diagnostic terminals.

7. To exit the diagnostic mode, simply turn the ignition key off, and disconnect the diagnostic terminals.

I-MARK ECM TROUBLE CODES AND CIRCUITS

Code Number	System Affected
12	Idle position switch, high voltage output.
13	Idle position switch, low voltage output.
14	WOT (wide open throttle) switch, high voltage output.
15	WOT switch, low voltage output.
21	Vacuum control solenoid, high output.
22	Vacuum control solenoid, low output.
23	Oxygen sensor circuit problem.
24	Coolant temperature switch circuit problem.
25	ECM/RAM (random access memory) error.

P'UP ECM Trouble Codes and Circuits

Code Number	System Affected
12	No ignition reference pulse to ECM.
13	Oxygen sensor circuit problem.
14	Shorted coolant temperature sensor circuit.
15	Open coolant temperature sensor circuit.
21	Idle switch circuit, either open or WOT switch circuit shorted.
22	Fuel cutoff solenoid circuit, open or grounded.
23	Vacuum control solenoid circuit, open or grounded.
25	Air switching solenoid circuit, open or grounded.
31	No ignition reference pulse to ECM.
44	Oxygen sensor circuit, lean signal.
45	Oxygen sensor circuit, rich signal.
51	Shorted fuel cutoff solenoid circuit or faulty ECM.
52	Faulty ECM/RAM (random access memory).
53	Shorted air switching solenoid or faulty ECM.
54	Shorted vacuum control solenoid or faulty ECM.
55	Faulty ECM (A/D = Analog to Digital) converter.

NOTE: Since the same basic ECM is used on the Isuzu P'UP as on the GMC S series trucks, the same codes listed above for the Isuzu P'UP apply to all GMC California model S trucks with the 1.9L four-cylinder engine. Because of the difference in the fuel system control (vacuum on Isuzu, and an M/C solenoid on GMC), the only exception for this application is that a Code 23 on the GMC truck indicates that the mixture control solenoid circuit is open or grounded, and a Code 54 that there is a shorted mixture control solenoid and/or faulty ECM.

ISUZU IMPULSE MCU SYSTEM

The four-cylinder model Impulse is equipped with an electronically-controlled port fuel injection system (one injector per cylinder). Commonly referred to as the I-TEC system by Isuzu, a MCU (microcomputer control system) controls both the fuel injection and ignition systems in order to ensure stoichiometric (14.7:1) air/fuel ratio under all closed-loop operating conditions. An example of the I-TEC system is illustrated in Fig. 13-5.

The MCU is located under the instrument panel for protection, and it continually receives voltage inputs from the various engine sensors so that it can control the transistorized ignition coil, the individual fuel injector pulse-width time, as well as the VSV (vacuum switching valve). The VSV, which is located in the engine compartment close to the ignition coil, controls the fuel pressure regulator, based upon intake manifold vacuum and the MCU signals. This system uses a fuel cutoff feature during engine deceleration on a warm engine in order to reduce exhaust emissions by having the MCU reduce the pulse-width time of the injectors.

DIAGNOSTIC CODES AND SYSTEM FORMAT

A *Check Engine* light on the instrument panel is the signal to the driver that a problem has occurred in the engine system. This problem will be stored in computer memory until accessed by the mechanic/technician. (See Fig. 13-6.) The *Check Engine* light flashes on and off to indicate a specific code stored in memory, with the lowest numbered codes being flashed first. For example a flash/flash/flash, pause, followed by five other flashes, indicates a Code 35, and so on.

Each code is repeated three times, before the next code begins to flash. Once all codes have been flashed, the system will repeat itself, until you exit diagnostics by turning the ignition key off. Once you have finished your diagnosis, however, it is advisable to clear the computer memory by disconnecting the No. 4 fuse in the fuse box, connecting the diagnostic terminals together (Fig. 13-6), turning the ignition on, and making certain that only a Code 12 is displayed (normal condition). Once this is done, disconnect the diagnostic terminals.

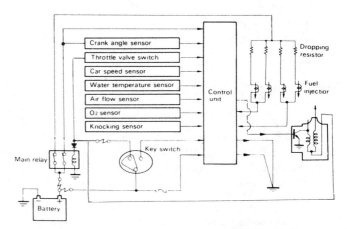

FIGURE 13-5 Impulse I-TEC control system.

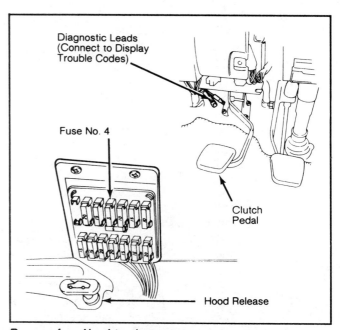

Remove fuse No. 4 to clear memory.

FIGURE 13-6 Diagnostic connector location — Impulse.

Trouble codes and their related systems/switch/circuits are listed below.

Diagnostic Tools

Tools required are:

1. A tachometer (mag-pick up or photo digital type),
2. DVOM (digital volt/ohmmeter),
3. 1.5 volt battery,
4. Assorted jumper wires.

Diagnostic System Access

Before beginning self-diagnostics, always check that the *Check Engine* light on the instrument panel comes on when the ignition key is turned on, but before starting the engine. After starting the engine, the light should go off within 1 to 4 seconds. You should also do an underhood check. Pay particular attention to such items as vacuum hoses and electrical wiring for signs of damage. Check for:

1. Loose or improperly routed vacuum hoses,
2. Cracked or broken vacuum hoses,
3. Corroded wires and terminals,
4. Loose or burned wires or connections,
5. Any other obvious signs of a possible problem area, such as leaking fuel lines, injectors, etc.
6. Make sure that the idle rpm and the ignition timing are set correctly.

Refer to Fig. 13-6. After locating the MCU under the instrument panel, find the diagnostic connector leads and connect the brown and black/yellow wires together. With the ignition key on, the MCU will automatically start to flash the various stored trouble codes in memory to the *Check Engine* light on the instrument panel. All codes are flashed three times; then the system repeats itself.

IMPULSE TROUBLE CODES

Code Number	System/Circuit Affected
12	No ignition, normal condition.
13	Oxygen sensor circuit open.
14	Coolant sensor circuit shorted.
15	Incorrect coolant sensor circuit.
16	Coolant sensor circuit open.
21	Throttle position switch circuits connected at same time.
22	Starter signal circuit.
23	Output terminal to ignition coil grounded.
25	Output terminal to vacuum switching solenoid circuit open or grounded.
33	Fuel injector circuit open or grounded.
35	Ignition power transistor open.
41	Crank angle sensor, poor or incorrect signal.
43	No idle position signal.
44	Oxygen sensor, lean signal.
45	Oxygen sensor, rich signal.
51 and 52	Faulty MCU.
53	Vacuum switching valve.
54	Bad ignition transistor or ground.
55	Faulty MCU.
61 and 62	Air flow sensor circuit bad.
63	No vehicle speed sensor signal.
64	Fuel injector transistor or ground.
65	Continuous signal from throttle position switch.
66	Open or shorted knock sensor circuit.

Wiring Diagram and Connector Identification

Figure 13-7 illustrates a typical wiring diagram schematic for the Impulse I-TEC MCU system, while Fig. 13-8 illustrates the MCU connector terminal pin identification.

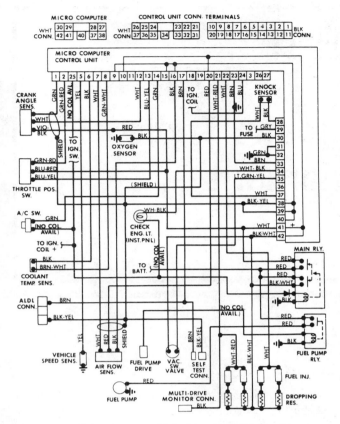

FIGURE 13-7 Impulse I-TEC MCU wiring schematic.

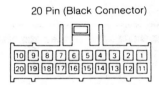

20 Pin (Black Connector)

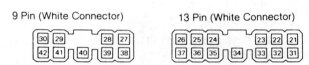

9 Pin (White Connector)   13 Pin (White Connector)

FIGURE 13-8 I-TEC connector terminal pin number identification.

CHAPTER 14

♦

Special Diagnostic Tools and Equipment

COMPUTER COMMUNICATION DIAGNOSTIC PROGRAMS

A wide variety of special tools and equipment for accessing on-board vehicle computer systems — namely the ECM (electronic control module) for the engine management function, and the BCM (body computer module) for vehicle and accessory management control — are illustrated in this chapter. These special instruments are a tremendous asset to the service technician, for they remove much of the guesswork associated with electronic engine and vehicle controls troubleshooting analysis.

A number of technicians tend to curse the invention and the advent of multiple electronic control systems on passenger cars and trucks, usually because they have, at some time or another, been involved with a particularly tough and repetitive problem that could not be pinpointed without their having to change almost every component on the system. Granted, the electronics explosion has forced service technicians into situations that were previously unknown to them. It is only since the 1980 model year that on-board electronic computers have become an accepted normal component of mass-produced passenger cars in North America. Other technicians have tended to shy away from vehicles fitted with such mind-boggling technology, usually because they fear the unknown, a normal fear in human nature and one that we have all had to deal with at some time in our lives.

A technician today, however, doesn't have to be an expert in all phases of electronics in order to understand

and service on-board computer systems. However, he or she must have a solid grounding in basic electricity and be familiar with the various meanings of such terms as volts, ohms, amperes, diodes, transistors, resistors, opens, grounds, shorts, circuits, and with the use of basic tools, such as test lights, analog and digital volt/ohmmeters, etc. There is really nothing forbidding about testing or accessing an on-board computer system, as you have probably realized from reading the various descriptions of manufacturers' different systems in this textbook.

You certainly require various special test instruments in order to successfully access and interpret the meaning of the trouble codes that are stored in the vehicle's computer memory system, and you also must follow systematically the vehicle manufacturer's step-by-step procedures in order to pinpoint exactly where and what the cause of the problem might be.

The fact that you are reading this textbook is reason enough to compliment yourself on your own desire and ability to learn these various complex systems. In a short time, you will find that systems applications become second nature to you, and you will be able to apply this new-found knowledge and put it into practice at the shop-floor level.

Before connecting a test instrument to the on-board computer self-diagnostic system, always perform the normal routine checks that you would usually do on a non-computer-equipped vehicle. Details on this check are referenced in the various individual vehicle chapters of this textbook, as well as in this chapter under the heading "Special Tools and Diagnostic Equipment."

Failure to follow these prechecks could cause you to spend unwarranted time and effort in attributing a problem to the electronic computer system or sensors, when, in fact, the problem might simply be, for example, a loose or disconnected vacuum line. When a test instrument is connected to the on-board computer system, it simply follows a preprogrammed series of tests in order to record and withdraw the information that has been continuously fed to it from the various sensors, switches, and solenoids during engine/vehicle operation. Specific manufacturers' service trouble codes can then be referred to in order to guide you towards the system or circuit that might be causing the problem.

Although the service trouble code will not always lead you directly to the exact component or problem, it will narrow down within a close area one or more components or systems that are causing the complaint. Troubleshooting then becomes a systematic process of checking and eliminating those areas that are suspected of causing the problem until you locate the source. In many instances, it is necessary to substitute a known good component during a test to isolate/confirm whether the original component is either serviceable or nonserviceable.

Descriptions of the various special tools and equipment will help you see just how valuable these items can be in your day-to-day diagnosis of electronic system problems.

Since this book was designed to clarify the details of on-board computer systems and digital instrumentation, no attempt has been made to supply detailed information dealing with either electronic ignition systems, or fuel-injection systems.*

FACTORY INTERFACE

The latest development now coming on stream to aid the service/technician become more familiar with and to improve his/her ability in effectively and efficiently pinpointing electronic on-board computer system problems is a factory interface system that is continually updated on a daily basis. It is one in which the technician can phone for direct assistance at any time, when he/she faces a problem occurring with a vehicle equipped with a self-diagnosing computer system. At the time of writing this chapter, three companies have pioneered this direct line (interface) from the dealer's shop floor back to the source (factory).

These companies are the Oldsmobile and Buick Divisions of General Motors Corporation, located in Lansing and Flint, Michigan, respectively, and the Ford Motor Company in Dearborn, Michigan. On-going research is actively being pursued by these three companies, as well as a number of other car manufacturers; inevitably, changes in this on-line system will occur with increasing rapidity.

Most manufacturers involved in this on-line system between shop floor and a factory mainframe computer system project that these systems will be truly cost effective and of major assistance to the technician and dealers in one to three years' time. Obviously, each manufacturer who is pursuing this system of data transmission and troubleshooting assistance has designed the system to respond to problems related to his own make of vehicle. For example, having an on-line connection with the Ford system would be of little help to you if you are troubleshooting a Buick or an Oldsmobile, and vice versa.

The three systems presently available to respective manufacturers' dealers are:

1. FORD OASIS system (on-line automotive service information system)
2. OLDSMOBILE OASIS system (Oldsmobile automated sales/service information system)
3. BUICK CAMS system (computerized automotive maintenance system)

The FORD system is available nationally to dealers as of 1986, while Buick intends to have its system available by 1987 to its respective dealer personnel.

The Oldsmobile and other General Motors Divisions systems are projected for delivery close to the Buick date for release of a similar system. Although information at this time indicates that the Oldsmobile system will be more wide-reaching than that offered by Buick, it's possible that eventually a fairly standardized system will be used for all GMC division vehicles. Olds and Cadillac dealers will not be able to obtain information on Chevs and Pontiacs from their own system, and vice versa; however, this may change as time goes on.

Buick's system, at this time, is designed strictly for on-car-electronics. Although it offers greater detailed coverage than that currently offered by Ford, it doesn't cover as many areas of access. On the Buick system, the technician also enters the VIN (vehicle identification number) and answers yes/no to a series of introductory questions probing what accessories are actually fitted to the vehicle about to be diagnosed. Typical questions follow. Does the vehicle have air conditioning? An automatic transmission? Power steering?

The technician then connects up the necessary terminals from the CAMS system to the battery and the ALDL (assembly line data link), located under the instrument panel. (See Chapter 7.) If the technician has identified other problems, these can be entered into the computer system, and the CAMS does the rest. It automatically runs through lit-

*For detailed coverage of electronic fuel-injection systems, refer to a textbook titled, *Automotive and Small Truck Fuel-Injection Systems—Gas and Diesel,* written by this same author, and available through Prentice Hall in Englewood Cliffs, New Jersey, 07632, U.S.A.

erally hundreds of tests of the ECM, as well as analyzing input data from the various sensors.

After a diagnosis is made by the CAMS system, a printed technique of repair will be flashed on the monitor (TV screen) for the technician to follow. The system is designed to be "user friendly." If the technician requires assistance at any time, he can simply push a "help" button that will clarify and simplify the procedure. Once the repair has been carried out, the CAMS system will run through a self-check to determine if any other problems exist and if, in fact, the repair has been successful.

Should a problem exist that is not capable of being picked up while the vehicle is stationary in the service shop, then a VSM (vehicle service monitor), can be installed on the vehicle while it is being road tested. (This monitor is similar to the digital automotive systems "Conquest" monitor, which is described below under special tools and equipment.) This monitor will detect and record any problem areas. Once back in the shop, with the car again connected up to the CAMS system, this information can be withdrawn, and the problem determined.

All information relayed into these types of systems with their factory interface is recorded. An on-going library of problems is accumulated at the factory level, which expands the available knowledge that can be replied to by the dealer-network technicians. Since Buick feeds new and update information into the CAMS system from the dealerships overnight, the system is always as up-to-date as possible.

Granted that at the present time these systems are designed for the manufacturer's field and sales/service personnel to access the factory mainframe computer when an unusual problem presents itself. However, the intent is that these computers will be readily available to the car manufacturer's dealer personnel within the next one to three years. An example of how the shop floor minicomputer is hooked into the on-board vehicle computer is shown in Fig. 14-1. (A typewritten hard-copy of the identified problem and the suggested repair answer from the factory source is sent back to the dealership.)

Other systems will use a monitor (TV screen) to flash the information to the service technician and to present a systematic step-by-step repair procedure. Although these systems present and display written information only at this time — the Buick system can supply schematics — future systems will possibly be capable of supplying graphics as well.

In the interim, however, the technician will have to refer to the service or parts manual information when details of components are required. Each one of these systems uses a new approach to on-board computer self-diagnostics and repair. Basically, the system employs a small-shop computer that can be placed on the vehicle and attached to the

FIGURE 14-1 Minicomputer diagnostic tool connected into the on-board vehicle computer for troubleshooting purposes. (*Courtesy of Motor Magazine, Des Moines, Iowa*)

self-test connector of the on-board computer, while it is connected via a shop hookup directly to the mainframe computer at the factory level.

The service technician enters the VIN (vehicle identification number) and a problem symptom code that is chosen from a factory-supplied code sheet which lists complaint areas by category. As an example, the Ford code sheet is given below:

1. Engine/performance/driveability
2. Noise/vibration
3. Automatic transmission
4. Manual transmission/transfer case
5. Steering/suspension/handling/tire wear
6. Brakes
7. Heating/ventilation/air conditioning
8. Leaks (water, oil, coolant, fuel, or other fluids)
9. Electrical and accessories
10. Body/trim/chassis/miscellaneous

Once the system is accessed, the trouble code in the service manual leads you to the system or sensor that is creating the problem. If, however, you run into a problem that creates an on-going complaint, you can type in the question on the small-shop computer. The factory system will respond to simple problem statements within a 7 to 8 second time span. If the problem is more detailed, then it might take the factory computer from 2 to 3 minutes to reply.

Each of the 10 categories of engine/vehicle problems that Ford uses is broken down further into subsystem complaints. Step 6, Brakes is further divided into 9 subsystem complaints, for example. These are:

1. Brakes ineffective
2. Vehicle pulls when brakes are applied
3. Brakes lock up or grab
4. Brake drag
5. Abnormal pedal feel
6. Noisy brakes
7. Brake warning light illuminates
8. Parking brake problem
9. Fluid leakage

After studying the list of brake complaints, the service technician selects a listed code number for the problem and enters it into the computer. Within a short time, the computer responds with information similar to the following:

1. Numbers of all service information bulletins released by the Ford factory that are related to the specific prob-

lem entered by the technician into the computer terminal.

2. Suggested possible causes for the complaint.
3. A list of necessary parts if repair is required.
4. Any special service information released by Ford.
5. If there had been a recall because of this problem, then such information would be supplied.
6. Warranty status of the vehicle.
7. Vehicle description.
8. Engine calibration number.

The service access line to the factory is via a telephone hookup (modem), and the dealer would be charged for only a local phone call, since the factory pays for long distance calls. This feature will be available 24 hours a day, seven days a week. The only time that the interface hookup will not be available is when the main system at the factory is being updated with new information. Initially, the factory plans on maintaining only a five year history and information retrieval system, and therefore any vehicle older than five years will not be accessible on this system.

MULTIMETERS AND COMPUTER CODE ACCESS

Although many special tools and equipment are readily available today to assist you in effectively determining the possible problem area on the vehicle, one of the most important tools that you will use in troubleshooting automotive electrical systems is the "multimeter," so named because of its ability to measure amperage (current), voltage (pressure), and resistance (ohms).

The common automotive multimeter has been in wide use for many years, but now with the advent of the various electronic controls such as sensors and on-board computers, the more elaborate multimeters of today have features that can check such things as frequency and temperature, as well as make diode tests. Older multimeters do not have the appropriate scales and functions to handle computer-equipped vehicle testing.

Not only is the common analog type multimeter inadequate in many instances when checking automotive electrical and electronic circuitry, but it can also damage delicate computer circuitry. Because of their low internal resistance (input impedance), most analog multimeters draw too much power from the component being tested on computer-equipped vehicles. In addition, many analog multimeters employ 9 volt battery power for their operation, and this voltage is sufficient to destroy sensitive digital components when these multimeters are used to perform a resistance test.

The latest types of digital multimeters (DMM's) are constructed so that they have a much higher input impedance than analog multimeters. This impedance is generally 10 meg (million) ohms in order to ensure that the multimeter will draw very little power from the component under test. Test voltages for resistance checks are usually well below 5 volts, and so selecting a multimeter that has a voltage lower than a 5 volt setting is desirable.

Various models of Fluke analog/digital multimeters are illustrated in Fig. 14-2 and 14-3. All of these Fluke DMM's have test voltages of 3.5 volts, which therefore greatly re-duces the chance of damage when testing an electrical/electronic circuit or component.

The one problem in the past with digital readouts for the mechanic/technician was that the numbers displayed didn't give any indication whether the value was increasing or decreasing. Or technicians may have experienced the typical frustration associated with attempting to read ever-changing temperature values when monitoring a digital exhaust gas or an engine analyzer.

Fluke multimeters overcome this problem by providing a combination display which provides the accuracy of a

Fluke Analog/Digital Multimeters

The Fluke 70 Series introduced the analog/digital concept in a handheld package. Combining the best of both systems with exceptional ease of use, durability and low price, the three multimeter models in the 70 Series made sophisticated test equipment affordable to everyone.

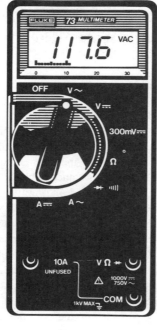

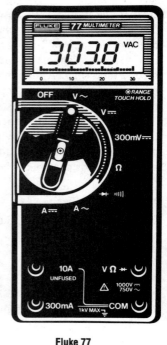

Fluke 73

Analog bar graph
3200 count display
0.7% basic dc accuracy
10A
Autoranging only
Three year warranty

Fluke 75

Analog bar graph
3200 count display
0.5% basic dc accuracy
Autoranging with Range Hold
10A + autoranged mA ranges
Continuity and diode test beeper
Three year warranty

Fluke 77

Analog bar graph
3200 count display
0.3% basic dc accuracy
Autoranging with Range Hold
10A + autoranged mA ranges
Continuity and diode test beeper
Touch-Hold™
Three year warranty

FIGURE 14-2 Fluke 70 series analog/digital multimeters. (*Courtesy of John Fluke Mfg. Co., Inc., Everett, WA.*)

digital readout with the dynamic measurement capabilities of an analog meter. The Fluke analog/digital multimeters have the following major features which make them ideal for use in automotive troubleshooting techniques:

1. Analog/Digital Display: A combined 31 segment analog bar graph and a 3200 count digital display.
2. Touch Hold Feature: The meter display "freezes" a reading until you are ready to look at it.
3. Automatic Polarity and Range Selection: This feature permits the meter to select the range and polarity automatically for the best possible reading.
4. Continuity Beeper: An audible tone beeper provides easy testing for continuity, shorts, and diode tests.
5. Rugged Construction: A tough plastic case resists the possibility of damage when working in the day-to-day hazards of a shop environment.

Successful operation of a gasoline automotive engine and its accessories is to a large degree dependent upon the

The Fluke 20 Series offers additional safety with fuses on all current inputs and optional high visibility yellow cases. The Fluke 25 and 27 are totally sealed against dirt, dust, and airborne contaminants. They are impervious to water, oil, grease, antifreeze and gasoline, making them ideal for shop use.

John Fluke Mfg. Co., Inc.
P.O. Box C9090, Everett, WA 98206
Tel. 206-347-6100

For more product information—
or where to buy Fluke products call;

800-426-0361 (toll free) in most of U.S.A.
206-356-5400 from AK, HI, WA
and 206-356-5500 from other countries

Fluke (Holland) B.V.
P.O. Box 2269, 5600 CG,
Eindhoven, The Netherlands
Tel (040) 458045, TELEX 51846

Phone or write for the name of your local Representative.

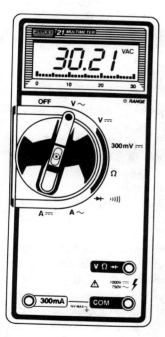

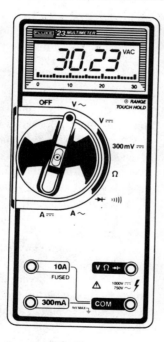

Fluke 21

Safety yellow case
Fluke 75 features and specs, less 10A input

_____
_____
_____
_____
_____
_____
_____

Fluke 23

Safety yellow case
Fluke 77 features and specs, plus fused 10A input

_____
_____
_____
_____
_____
_____

Fluke 25

Charcoal or yellow case
Analog/Digital display
0.1% basic dc accuracy
100 µV to 1000V ac & dc
0.1 µA to 10A, all fused
−15°C to 55°C operation
Touch-Hold™
Two year warranty

Fluke 27

Charcoal or yellow case
Analog/Digital display
0.1% basic dc accuracy
100 µV to 1000V ac & dc
0.1 µA to 10A, all fused
−15° to 55°C operation
Touch-Hold™
Relative (difference) mode
Min/Max recording mode
Two year warranty

FIGURE 14-3　Fluke 20 series analog/digital multimeters. (*Courtesy of John Fluke Mfg. Co., Inc., Everett, WA.*)

electrical energy stored in the battery. On computer-equipped vehicles, it is very important that the state of charge of the storage battery always be maintained at an acceptable level. Many battery and car manufacturers specify that the battery must be between 2.075 to 2.08 volts per cell prior to conducting a high-rate discharge or a full-load battery test. A cell reading of 2.08 volts corresponds to an electrolyte specific gravity of 1.230, which places the battery into the 75% state of charge category.

Multimeter Computer Code Access

Although there are special diagnostic tools shown in this chapter that allow you to quickly and efficiently access the various stored trouble codes retained in ECM memory, should one of these tools not be readily available to you, then a digital multimeter, such as those manufactured by John Fluke Manufacturing Company, can be used instead. A perfect example of this relates to the Ford EEC-IV system described in Chapter 8. The system requires the use of a STAR tester (Fig. 8-34a) to access the computer codes. Should a STAR tester not be available, Ford recommends that an analog meter be used, since it will respond to the various voltage pulses sent out from the on-board computer memory system.

Most digital multimeters will not operate if connected to the computer; however, Fluke analog/digital multimeters have both digital and analog displays, with the analog bar graph being capable of responding to these computer-generated pulses. An example of a Fluke multimeter that can be used to check these pulses via a bar-graph pattern is illustrated in Fig. 14-4.

SPECIAL TOOLS AND DIAGNOSTIC EQUIPMENT

Since the beginning of the 1980's, vehicle manufacturers have had to respond to tough governmental exhaust gas regulations, as well as CAFE (Corporate Average Fuel Economy) standards. These regulations can only be met through the use of sophisticated on-board vehicle electronics, in the form of individual sensors feeding information to microprocessor-controlled systems.

These technological breakthroughs have placed great emphasis on technician training to ensure that not only are they capable of understanding the electronics componentry on cars and trucks today, but also that they are able to access, diagnose, and interpret these microprocessor systems with the use of the very special diagnostic tools and equipment now on the market. This rapidly-changing automotive technology has produced a family of diagnostic instruments and software that enables the technician to

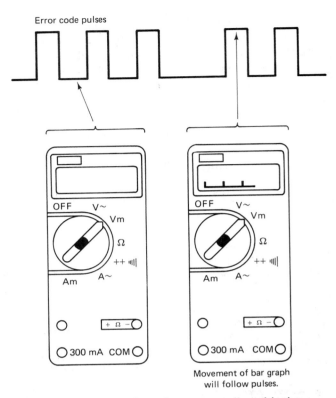

FIGURE 14-4 Counting error codes with the analog bar graph on a fluke multimeter for a Ford EEC-IV system. (*Courtesy of John Fluke Mfg. Co., Inc., Everett, WA.*)

communicate directly with on-board computers, thereby eliminating guesswork when troubleshooting.

Although there are a number of commonly-available and widely-used mechanics tools that can be adapted for use when accessing and troubleshooting electrical and electronic systems on today's cars and trucks, many of these tools are just not capable of withdrawing the information that the mechanic/technician requires from the on-board computer system.

Serious damage can result to the computer system if precautions highlighted by a vehicle manufacturer are not followed closely. It is very important that you, the service technician, be aware of the wide variety of special tools and instruments that are available at your disposal that can make your job of diagnosis, evaluation, and troubleshooting that much easier and satisfying, both for you and the customer.

Certainly, there are still a number of common tools that can be used, such as:

1. Test light
2. Analog ohmmeter
3. Analog voltmeter
4. DVOM (digital volt/ohmmeter)

5. Vacuum pump and gauge
6. Tachometer
7. Dwell meter
8. Jumper wires
9. Timing light

Many problems that exist today, and that the service technician is presented with, have nothing to do with the electronic sensors or the electronic control modules used, though more often than not, they are blamed. In fact, many of these problems can be directly attributable to such simple, but often overlooked, items such as:

1. Vacuum lines, loose, cracked, disconnected, routed wrongly, plugged or restricted.
2. Wiring, corroded connections, bent pins, harnesses too tight, harnesses too loose, broken or burned wires.
3. Fuel system, plugged filters, leaking lines, faulty pump, etc.
4. Plugged air cleaner, PCV valve, etc.
5. Ignition timing incorrect.
6. Idle speed set incorrectly.

It is always wise to perform the above series of checks prior to condemning the on-board computer system, unless after accessing the system, you are able to quickly pinpoint the reason for the problem directly from a flashed trouble code.

In many instances the stored trouble code in the computer memory will lead you to the general area of the problem, but it will not necessarily pinpoint the exact cause or item that is at fault; however, it does isolate the problem to one or more areas that require further checking. Opens or grounds, high resistance values, etc., often are the reason for a circuit problem.

With the use of these special tools and test instruments, your mechanic/technician's job becomes diagnostic-specific, and with repeated use, you will quickly become comfortable and confident in your daily task of accessing and pinpointing troubles related to sensors, switches, solenoids, etc., in all the various engine systems.

In order to quickly, safely, and effectively withdraw various stored trouble codes from the computer memory system, the vehicle manufacturers or major tool and instrument manufacturers produce a wide assortment of tools that can be used specifically for this purpose. The details of how to access each manufacturer's vehicle system are described and explained within the various chapters of this textbook. For example, more than one tool supplier now offers one particular instrument, readily available from several sources, that can be used on all General Motors, Ford, and Chrysler Corporation vehicles to access the various trouble codes stored in the memory bank of the on-board vehicle computer.

To do so means using three different "plug-in" cartridges, with a different one required for each make of vehicle. This feature allows a company to purchase one test instrument and expand its use to cover all three makes of cars with minimal additional cost.

At the end of most of the chapters in this textbook dealing with individual vehicle computers and systems, "special tools" are shown that are recommended by the manufacturer in order to facilitate and assist the mechanic/technician in diagnosing the many possible causes of electronic system failure or problem areas related to feedback carburetor and fuel-injected engines on their specific vehicles.

Use this chapter and the tool listings at the rear of other various chapters in this book to advantage by becoming familiar with all the tools and instruments that are available to make your task that much easier.

Kent-Moore Products

Kent-Moore Tool Group is part of the Sealed Power Corporation and is one of the larger and more widely-known suppliers of specialized tools and equipment for passenger cars, trucks, and heavy equipment. A number of special tools from Kent-Moore that are available for use on passenger car and truck electronic systems are highlighted, along with a description of their function and purpose.

OTC Products

OTC is also a division of Sealed Power Corporation. Consequently, many of the special tools and equipment manufactured by both Kent-Moore and OTC are the same, only they are available under a different part number. One good example of this is the Monitor 2000 diagnostic tester illustrated in Fig. 14-5.

Monitor 2000

The Monitor 2000 with a GM Starter Kit is illustrated in Fig. 14-5. Figures 14-6 and 14-7 illustrate the Starter Kits required for use on both Ford and Chrysler vehicles. This special hand-held electronic tester is available with special software cartridges "tailor-made" for specific makes of vehicles and computer systems that allow the full function Monitor 2000 to read virtually any manufacturer's on-board computer with a diagnostic connector hookup feature.

NOTE: This same tool is available from the OTC Tool Division, which is also part of the Sealed Power Corporation.

The various cartridges, which are the real brains of the system, plug into the Monitor 2000 and are about the size

FORD STARTER KIT

No. 211356—Contains all the information needed to troubleshoot 1980-1986 MCU and EEC-IV on-board computer systems. Included are: Ford cartridge, diagnostic connector, battery adapter and instruction manual. Terminal capability available in the spring of 1987. Wt., 12 oz.

FIGURE 14-6   Monitor 2000 Ford starter kit. (*Courtesy of OTC Division, Sealed Power Corporation*)

MONITOR 2000 KITS

GM Starter Kit

No. 212544—Fully dedicated to GM C-3/P-4 computerized automotive systems. This kit allows you to "read" all existing C-3/P-4 systems from 1981-1987, including both carbureted and EFI systems. Set includes a GM cartridge with printer/terminal capabilities, 5-pin adapter block, vehicle cable, and instruction manual. Wt., 12 oz.

GM Software Kit

No. 212522—1981-1987 GM cartridge with printer/terminal capabilities, instruction manual and 5-pin adapter block. Wt., 9 oz.

The MONITOR 2000 combines hand-held convenience with built-in flexibility to make it the most versatile diagnostic tool you can own. Using state-of-the-art technology, the MONITOR 2000 represents a revolutionary new concept in on-board computer diagnostics. Special software cartridges "tailor-made" for specific makes of vehicles and computer systems allow the *full-function* MONITOR 2000 to "read" virtually *any* manufacturer's on-board computer with a diagnostic connector.

Simply plug in the software cartridge for the vehicle on which you are working, attach the adapter cables to the vehicle's computer output terminal and power supply and go to it! By pressing a few membrane-type switches, you can instantly access "trouble" codes, read sensor output voltages and perform an *infinite* number of diagnostic functions.

No. 3280—Monitor 2000 Tester. Wt., 1 lb., 10 oz.

FIGURE 14-5   Monitor 2000 diagnostic tool set for use with GMC, Ford, and Chrysler computer systems. (*Courtesy of Kent-Moore Tool Group, Sealed Power Corporation*)

CHRYSLER STARTER KIT

No. 211357—Thoroughly diagnose 1983-1986 Chrysler vehicles with on-board computers. Kit includes a Chrysler cartridge, vehicle cable, battery adapter, operating manual, and quick reference card. Printer/terminal capabilities available in the spring of 1987. Wt., 12 oz.

FIGURE 14-7   Monitor 2000 Chrysler starter kit. (*Courtesy of OTC Division, Sealed Power Corporation*)

of a book of matches. Each cartridge is designed for a specific computer system, thereby giving you not only the most up-to-date diagnostic information possible, but also the capability to read new systems as they are developed by each vehicle manufacturer.

The Monitor 2000 is capable of performing 54 separate diagnostic tests and generates more than 80 different displays, including simultaneous test result readouts and eight status lights. In addition, on many vehicles the use of the P/N 3280 (Monitor 2000) tester will also help determine if transmission problems are mechanical or electronic.

To operate the Monitor 2000, you simply plug in the software cartridge for the type of vehicle you are working on, attach the furnished adapter cables to the vehicle's computer output terminal and power supply, and the Monitor 2000 is ready to access the stored trouble codes in the onboard computer memory system. By pressing a few membrane-type switches, instant access to the trouble codes is assured, as well as being able to read sensor output voltages and perform an infinite number of diagnostic functions. The Monitor 2000 can also be programmed for different communication rates to "talk" to almost any computer system.

Two simultaneous alphanumeric and eight LED status readouts help you do a thorough job of troubleshooting quickly and effectively. Typical checks and tests that can be accomplished by the Monitor 2000 for these three makes of vehicles, are:

GM Applications

1. Battery voltage
2. Trouble codes
3. PROM ID number
4. Closed/open loop and rich/lean status
5. Oxygen voltage
6. Air cleaner divert and air switch solenoid
7. EGR and carbon canister purge solenoid
8. Park/neutral switch and A/C clutch
9. Throttle position sensor (rpm and volts)
10. Nose switch and WOT switch
11. rpm and mph
12. rpm and torque converter clutch
13. mph and torque converter clutch
14. Third and/or fourth gear switch
15. MAP (kPA and volts)
16. Barometric pressure (kPA and volts)
17. Coolant temperature and idle air control
18. Knock retard and throttle body backup
19. rpm and mixture control dwell
20. Ignition switch and crank

21. Power steering
22. Block learn and integrator
23. Turbo boost and oxygen cross-counter
24. Start-up enrichment
25. Exhaust pressure regulator
26. ALCL vote and M/C solenoid dwell
27. Altitude switch and temperature switch
28. Open-loop regulator and M/C solenoid dwell
29. Present diagnostic state
30. Fan solenoid and early fuel evaporation solenoid
31. Spark advance reference and idle speed control
32. Elapsed time battery cell
33. Hi/low battery status
34. Quasi asynchronous and asynchronous
35. Manifold air temperature and fan
36. Air flow and load variable
37. Proper step taken
38. Clear flood mode
39. Selected diagnostic state
40. O/D disable and fourth gear delay
41. A/C head pressure
42. Injector base pulse-width
43. Vacuum and wastegate bypass control
44. Ignition spark
45. Engine temperature, warm and hot
46. Electronic spark timing
47. Rear vacuum brake and A/C freon pressure low
48. Diesel EGR, min. and max.
49. EGR pressure desired and actual

Ford Applications

1. Wiggle test (EEC-1V)
2. Key on, Engine off test
3. Computed timing test
4. Engine running self-test
5. Clear memory procedure
6. Outputs state test

Chrysler Applications

1. Spark fire actuator
2. Injector fire actuator
3. Auto. idle speed
4. Radiator fan relay actuator
5. A/C cut-out relay actuator
6. Auto/shutdown relay actuator
7. Canister purge solenoid actuator

8. Baro. read solenoid actuator
9. Wastegate solenoid actuator
10. EGR solenoid actuator
11. MAP sensor test
12. Throttle body sensor test
13. Coolant sensor test
14. Throttle position sensor test
15. Peak knock test
16. Battery voltage test
17. Brake pedal switch test
18. A/C switch test
19. Gear shift (P/N) switch test
20. Speed sensor switch test
21. Backlight switch test

NOTE: Items 1–4, 8–15, 17, 19, and 40 on the GMC list relate to transmission applications. All other items for GMC, Ford, and Chrysler relate to engine applications.

Additional products such as "The Anticipator," which is a road-test memory storage and retrieval device, allow the technician to capture diagnostic information prior to the occurrence of a problem.

A typical software and starter kit for Chrysler vehicles is shown in Fig. 14-8. It is used with the Anticipator and communicator 2000 system in conjunction with a telephone modem. With this kit, the mechanic/technician can transmit vehicle data to local shops, other experts, or factory service representatives that also have a communicator.

You can increase the speed and accuracy of your diagnosis by using an IBM PC Jr., PC, XT, or AT as a diagnostic display terminal that can show up to 14 different data displays simultaneously. If an IBM PC is unavailable to you, you can also use a recommended VT-100 terminal

ANTICIPATOR/COMMUNICATOR KITS

ANTICIPATOR 2000

No.3282—Quickly and accurately diagnose intermittent problems in Chrysler and GM vehicles. Using the Monitor 2000 and special software, the Anticipator will store a 30 second running history of vehicle operation. By simply pressing a button when a problem arises, the Anticipator will store a 15 second running history of the vehicle's performance prior to the problem, and 15 seconds of vehicle data after the problem

has occurred. The Anticipator's solid-state memory captures up to four vehicle tests and lets the technician review the data later in the shop. Comes complete with a GM Anticipator/Communicator Starter Kit. This kit includes everything you need to solve intermittent problems in all existing 1981-1987 C-3 systems, including carbureted, EFI, and P-4 systems.

COMMUNICATOR 2000

No. 3284—Same as the Anticipator 2000; however, the Communicator features a telephone modem that allows the technician to transmit vehicle data to local shops or experts that also have a Communicator. Included is a 1981-1987 GM Anticipator/Communicator Starter Kit. It contains the information you need to solve intermittent problems in all existing C-3 systems, including carbureted, EFI, and P-4 systems.

GM Anticipator/Communicator Software Kit

No. 212526—Software and instruction manual only. For diagnosing intermittent problems on 1981-1987 GM C-3 systems, including carbureted, EFI, and P-4 systems. Has printer/terminal capabilities. Wt., 11 oz.

Chrysler Anticipator/Communicator Starter Kit

No. 212548—Diagnose intermittent problems on 1983-1987 Chrysler vehicles with on-board computers. Includes cartridge with Anticipator/Communicator and printer/terminal capabilities, adapter cables, and instruction manual. Wt., 14 oz.

Chrysler Anticipator/Communicator Software Kit

No. 212547—Cartridge and instruction manual only. For diagnosing intermittent problems on 1983-1987 Chrysler vehicles with on-board computers. Has printer/terminal capabilities. Wt., 11 oz.

FIGURE 14-8 Anticipator/communicator 2000 Chrysler starter and software kit. (*Courtesy of OTC Division, Sealed Power Corporation*)

with the Monitor 2000, and its special software cartridges with terminal capabilities. You can get hard-copy printouts of the vehicle problem areas through the use of a computer printer.

In addition, a factory interfacing system which is now being used at various General Motors and Ford dealerships will allow a service repair center using this equipment to interface with the shop's personal business computer terminal for ultrafast storage and retrieval of a full-range of information, or with manufacturer's and other data sources via telephone modems or, possibly, satellite links.

The Monitor 2000 is available from Kent-Moore under P/N 3280, and from OTC under P/N OT 3280. The cartridge P/N's are as follows:

1. General Motors Software Cartridge Kit, P/N 211-355
2. Ford Software Cartridge Kit, P/N 211-356
3. Chrysler Software Cartridge Kit, P/N 211-357

When using the Monitor 2000 tester, it is necessary to use the correct wiring adapters to prevent any damage to sensor/computer pins. Figures 14-9, 14-10, 14-11 illustrate three typical testing adapter sets required for use when setting/adjusting various engine switches.

The OTC Division is a part of the Sealed Power Corporation, which is also the parent company of Kent-Moore

C-3 TESTING ADAPTERS

No. 3457—Throttle position sensor adjustment cable. For use with OTC 3390 Digital Multimeter. Permits proper, damage-free testing and setting of the Throttle Position Sensor on GM vehicles with C-3 systems. Complete with instructions. Wt., 2 oz.

14-10 GMC C3 system TPS testing harness adapters. (*Courtesy of OTC Division, Sealed Power Corporation*)

C-3 TESTING ADAPTERS

No. 3456—Idle speed control cable. Allows technician to check and adjust both the base (minimum authority) and high (maximum authority) idle r.p.m. settings on GM vehicles with C-3 systems. Also permits checking idle speed control nose switch. Complete with instructions. Wt., 5 oz.

FIGURE 14-9 GMC C3 system idle testing harness adapters. (*Courtesy of OTC Division, Sealed Power Corporation*)

C-3 TESTING ADAPTERS

No. 3458—C-3 test lead kit. Includes jumper wire used to complete a circuit by bypassing an open, and jumper wires used to insert between WeatherPack connector terminals for circuit checking. Wt., 4 oz.

FIGURE 14-11 GMC C3 system jumper wire and weatherpack connector terminal testing harness adapters. (*Courtesy of OTC Division, Sealed Power Corporation*)

Tool Group. The following special tools from OTC are highlighted along with a description of their purpose for use in accessing computers and fuel-injection and ignition systems.

Remember that both the fuel-injection system as well as the ignition system are controlled by signals received from the on-board computer, which itself relies on voltage input signals from the various engine and vehicle sensors. (For more information on sensors, see Chapter 4. For an example that shows their location, see both Fig. 4-1 and Fig. 2-2.)

Ultrasonic Leak Detector

Figure 14-12 illustrates an electronic leak detector which is used to locate hard-to-find air leaks. It is not unusual for a technician to suspect that the cause of a complaint originates with the electronic computer system, when in fact the problem can be traced directly to such simple items as leaking vacuum lines, etc.

Always check the routing of vacuum lines, as well as their tightness and signs of kinking, plugging, etc., before you condemn the computer system. This tool can help you locate hard-to-find leaks.

Oxygen Sensor Tester

The closed-loop stoichiometric air/fuel ratio (14.6:1) of the engine is controlled directly by the exhaust gas oxygen sensor; therefore, a problem with this sensor can have a dramatic effect not only upon vehicle performance but also on fuel economy and exhaust gas emissions. The sensor continually sends a voltage signal to the on-board vehicle computer during its closed-loop phase of operation. (Refer to Figs. 4-17 and 4-18 in Chapter 4 for a description of both the open- and closed-loop operating cycles.)

The oxygen sensor tester illustrated in Fig. 14-13 provides a fast and easy way to troubleshoot GMC, Ford, Chrysler, AMC, and all Robert Bosch electronic fuel-injected vehicle systems. The sensor can be left in place in the engine exhaust manifold or down pipe, while the tester checks the oxygen sensor voltage levels and switching times. A built-in safety feature prevents adapters from being hooked up improperly, which might otherwise burn out a good sensor. The tester is available from OTC under P/N 3472.

Digital Photo Tachometer

A photo sensitive tach that works along with retro-reflective tape applied to the crankshaft damper or pulley is illustrated in Fig. 14-14. Aim the tach at the rotating member and within 2 seconds an accurate digital readout of + or − 1 rpm is achieved. This type of tach, recommended by almost all engine manufacturers, is available from OTC under P/N 3344.

ULTRASONIC LEAK DETECTOR

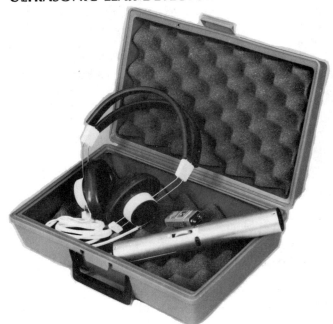

OTC's Model 3200 Ultrasonic Leak Detector will locate those hard-to-find air leaks that could result in costly accidents and downtime. The compact unit indicates the precise location of leaks and their relative magnitude. Ultrasonic energy, when listened to with the OTC detector produces a rushing sound in the headset. The detector hears only ultrasound created by the leak. To operate, plug the earphones into the receptacle at the rear of the unit and place them on your ears. Turn the unit on and adjust volume to a comfortable level. In a matter of minutes, the air lines, hoses, valves, tires, etc., can be checked for leaks. The 3202 Ultrasonic Tone Generator is used in conjunction with the Leak Detector to find small holes or cracks in nonpressurized compartments or containers. The 3201 Snubber is used on the Leak Detector when trying to locate directional leaks in a confined area.

No. 3200—Ultrasonic leak detector, complete with 9 volt battery and plastic carrying case. Wt., 1½ lbs.

No. 3202—Ultrasonic generator, complete with four 1.5 volt Penlight cells, type AA. Not included with 3200. Wt., ½ lb.

No. 3201—Snubber attachment for 3200 leak detector. Not included with 3200. Wt., 2 oz.

Specifications

Model 3200 Ultrasonic Leak Detector: 1½" diameter by 9" long; powered by—9 volt battery; headset—lightweight plug-in type.

FIGURE 14-12 Ultrasonic leak detector. (*Courtesy of OTC Division, Sealed Power Corporation*)

OXYGEN SENSOR TESTER

Fast, easy way to trouble-shoot oxygen sensors! While sensor stays in place, the 3472 checks oxygen sensor voltage levels and switching times. New tip jack allows you to hook unit directly to digital multimeter for true oxygen sensor voltage readings. Runs off vehicle battery and has high temperature cables to resist high heat engine conditions. Includes connecting and extension cables, 2 GM adapters, case & instructions. Adapters available for Ford, AMC, Chrysler and Bosch systems. Adapters can't be hooked up improperly which might burn out a good sensor.

No. 3472—Oxygen sensor tester with extension cables, battery adapter and 2 adapters for GM vehicles. Packed in molded plastic case. Wt., 3¼ lbs.

No. 302831—Sensor adapter for Bosch vehicles. Wt., 6 oz.

No. 302832—Sensor adapter for Chrysler vehicles. Wt., 6 oz.

No. 302833—Sensor adapter for AMC and Ford vehicles. Wt., 6 oz.

Specifications

Tester Size .... 3¼" × 6" × 1½" deep
Case Size .... 13¼" × 5" × 9¼" deep
Power Supply .... 12V vehicle battery
Switch Positions .... Rich-Normal-Lean
LED Indicators .... Rich-Lean-Pass-Fail
Connectors .... One to sensor, 58" long; sensor cable extension, 70" long; lighter plug, 36" long; lighter plug to battery, 11" long

> **FIGURE 14-13** Oxygen sensor tester. (*Courtesy of OTC Division, Sealed Power Corporation*)

DIGITAL PHOTO TACHOMETER

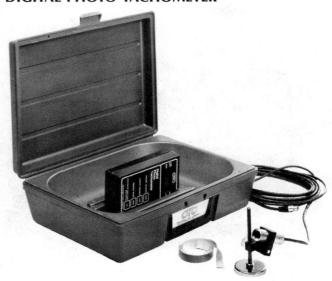

Engine speed accuracy: It's crucial for getting maximum efficiency from today's finely balanced truck tractor engines as well as stationary power units. Even a variation of just a few RPMs from specifications during tuning can make the engine work harder, reducing horsepower and fuel economy. You get the accuracy you need: ± 1 RPM, with OTC's No. 3344 Digital Photo Tachometer. The 3344's memory feature lets you check critical governor high limits without holding that high RPM for an extended period of time. The memory catches RPM in just two seconds. The light source is held in place securely with its magnetic base, freeing both your hands for required engine adjustments. Retro-reflective tape is furnished; you merely apply a piece of this tape to the engine component rotating at crankshaft speed, and aim the light source at it. The unit's membrane-type power switch (with automatic shut-off after one-minute of no signal input) makes tach operation and set-up easy. This diagnostic device can also be used to verify accuracy of the vehicle's on-board tach; a 15' cable lets you bring the No. 3344 into the cab with you for a check.

No. 3344—Digital photo tachometer. With memory, photo probe assembly, magnetic light base and 108" of reflective tape, plus molded plastic storage/carrying case. Wt., 4 lbs. 8 oz.

No. 204666—Replacement retro-reflective indicator tape. 108" long × ½" wide. Wt., 1 oz.

No. 39811—Replacement magnetic light base assembly. Wt., 5 oz.

No. 45329—Replacement photo probe assembly. Wt., 6 oz.

Specifications

Readout: Liquid crystal display; (4) .4" high digits; low battery indicator; memory mode indicator; high and low RPM memory mode indicator. **Range:** 200 to 9999. **Accuracy:** ± 1 digit. **Update Time:** 3/4 second. **Power Switch:** Membrane switch (automatic shut-off after one minute of no signal input). **Power Source:** 9 volt alkaline battery. **Light Source:** Infra-red with 15' cable. **Light Holder Ass'y.:** 30 lb. rated magnet; 2" dia. × 1/4" high (4" high overall with post).

> **FIGURE 14-14** Digital photo tachometer. (*Courtesy of OTC Division, Sealed Power Corporation*)

MULTIMETER PLUS

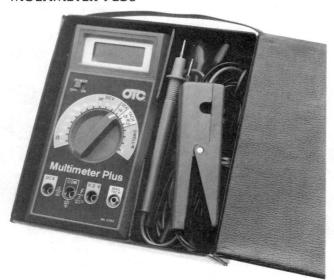

The new hand-held OTC Multimeter Plus provides all the necessary test ranges to check the performance of computer-controlled vehicle systems. With its special "clamp-on" secondary tachometer, you can run r.p.m. tests. And, a separate set of leads allows you to measure dwell with just a flick of a switch without disconnecting test leads. In addition, the Multimeter Plus features a 2 amp scale to measure DC current and diagnose leakage on vehicles equipped with a computer that has constant current draw, a separate diode test, and an audible circuit that "beeps" when you have continuity. Of course its rugged design withstands tough shop use. All diagnostic information is displayed in digital read-out form for truly accurate results.

No. 3390—Multimeter Plus with carrying case, one set of test leads (convertible alligator clips), clamp-on secondary tach pick up and operating instructions. Wt., 1 lb., 14 oz.

> **FIGURE 14-15** Multimeter plus kit. (*Courtesy of OTC Division, Sealed Power Corporation*)

Mulitmeter Plus

The multimeter illustrated in Figure 14-15 from OTC not only can be used to check the computer system, but it also doubles as a clamp-on tachometer and a dwell-tester. It can be used in conjunction with testing adapter No. 3457 (Fig. 14-10) for setting the throttle position sensor on GM vehicles equipped with C3 systems.

Electronic Injector Pulse Tester

The injector pulse tester shown in Fig. 14-16 can be bought separately. It is also included in the test kit illustrated in Figs. 14-21 and 14-23. This tool is a must when injectors are suspected of being at fault when a performance complaint is registered.

PULSE TESTER

The 3398 is the only true way to do a cylinder balance test when injectors are suspect in engine performance problems. This vehicle-powered electronic tool fires individual fuel injectors in ½-second increments in three different ranges: 1 pulse of 500 milliseconds, 50 pulses of 10 milliseconds, and 100 pulses of 5 milliseconds. Power light and output light tell you when test is in activation. Complete instructions. This tester is included in Kit No. 7210.

No. 3398—Pulse tester with three pulse ranges. Includes wiring harness adapter. Wt., 8 oz.

> **FIGURE 14-16** Injector pulse tester. (*Courtesy of OTC Division, Sealed Power Corporation*)

"NOID-LITE" HARNESS TESTER

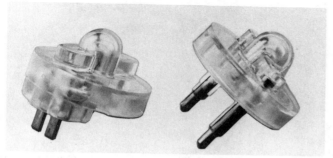

Instantly checks the injector harness for power. This can be a three-hand, two-person operation if you lack this inexpensive little tester. The test is possible with a voltmeter, but harness terminals are recessed and hard to get at. To use "Noid-Lite," just disassemble harness from solenoid, plug tester into harness and turn ignition on. From the passenger compartment, you'll be able to see if tester light is flashing (indicating normal pulsing voltage) or steady or off, revealing an electrical problem.

No. 7187—Tester for GM TBI. Wt., 2 oz.

No. 7188—Tester for Bosch. Wt., 2 oz.

FIGURE 14-17 Injector harness "noid-lite" tester. (*Courtesy of OTC Division, Sealed Power Corporation*)

Noid-lite Tester

Although the major passenger car manufacturers in North America use some form of Bosch fuel-injection system, special tools shown in this chapter are designed specifically for most of these engines. However, for any engine equipped with a Robert Bosch Corporation gasoline fuel-injected system, this noid-lite will allow you to quickly check the condition of the injector harness to ensure that power is in fact flowing to each injector assembly. This tester is illustrated in Fig. 14-17.

Electronic Ignition Analyzer

There are a number of special electronic ignition tester/analyzers on the market which often consist of a base unit. This OTC analyzer can be expanded to cover other types of ignition systems by the addition of special adapters. It is illustrated in Fig. 14-18. This particular unit is not designed for use with GM's distributorless ignition systems (C3I), where the base ignition timing, on the 3.8L V6 engine for example, is preset when the engine is manufactured. No adjustment is possible, although the crankshaft sensor to interruptor ring gap can be adjusted. Timing advance and retard on the C3I system is accomplished through the ECM with EST (electronic spark timing) and ESC (electronic spark control). This analyzer is also not for use with Ford's TFI (thick film ignition) system which also employs

ELECTRONIC IGNITION ANALYZER

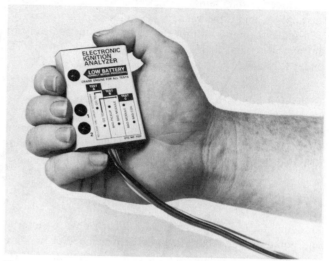

Electronic ignition analysis at your fingertips! Troubleshooting has never been easier. The 7200-K detects problems on Ford, GM and Chrysler cars thru 1983 with electronic ignitions and all 1978 and newer AMC cars. (Not for use on Ford thick film ignitions or GM vehicles with Hall effect distributor.) It quickly checks the function of the battery, magnetic pickup, module and coil primary circuit. Only four simple connections are required for trouble-shooting. You do not even have to look up voltage and resistance levels. The analyzer's solid state design provides instant LED readout. The analyzer is equipped with extra-long color coded leads which make for easy, one man operation. With the carrying case you can take the analyzer to a customer's disabled car and know what the problem is before leaving the driveway. Use it to verify repairs and guard against customers coming back.

No. 7220-K—Electronic ignition, analyzer set. Complete with analyzer unit with 8' and 9' leads, detailed instructions, No. 7230 Calibrated spark plug and No. 7225 Adapter for Omni and Horizon (both shown at right). In 8½" × 7" × 3¼" plastic carrying case. Wt., 1¾ lbs.

NOTE: The spark tester and Omni/Horizon adapter are included with the 7220-K but may also be ordered separately.

FIGURE 14-18 Electronic ignition analyzer. (*Courtesy of OTC Division, Sealed Power Corporation*)

a TFI module and a Hall effect vane switch stator assembly. No distributor calibration is required, and initial timing is not a normal adjustment.

GMC AC Custom Cruise 111 Tester

This instrument illustrated in Fig. 14-19 tells you if cruise sets properly, maintains speed, turns off when the brakes are applied, and if the vacuum system is working properly. Ten indicator lights inform the technician immediately of any problems and their location. It's available from OTC under P/N 3475, plus Pontiac Fiero adapter P/N 45349.

GMC TBI Injection Tester Kit

This kit can be used on all General Motors TBI (throttle body injection) systems from 1982 and up. The kit is illustrated in Fig. 14-20.

Port Fuel-Injection Tester Kit

Designed for testing port fuel-injection systems (both turbo and nonturbo versions) via static or running fuel pressure tests and cylinder balance tests in conjunction with the OTC 3398 pulse tester, this test kit will handle all types of fuel injectors, including all the Robert Bosch units. It is illustrated in Fig. 14-21 and is available from OTC under P/N 7210.

Injector Harness Tool

Shown in Fig. 14-22, this simple tool is designed for removing and installing injector wiring harnesses without damaging the connections. It can be used on all multiport fuel-injection systems and will save you time, because you will not have to remove excess parts when the injector cannot be reached. It's available from OTC under P/N 7216.

Fuel-Injection Tool Kit

Illustrated in Fig. 14-23, this tester kit covers GM, Ford, and Chrysler engines and can be used in conjunction with the Monitor 2000 computer test tool shown in Fig. 14-5.

Feedback Carburetor Tool Kit

Although most newer engines are now equipped with either TBI or port fuel injection systems, there are still many FBC (feedback carburetor) vehicles on the road. This kit, illustrated in Fig. 14-24, can be used on GM FBC engines in conjunction with the Monitor 2000 series test instrument (Fig. 14-5).

GM AC CUSTOM CRUISE III TESTER

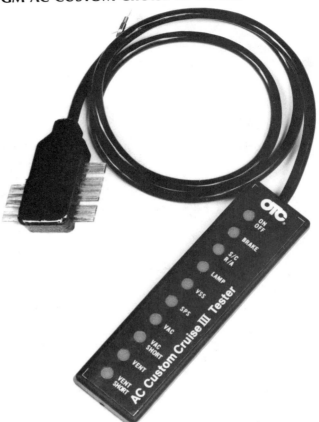

Trouble-shooting the GM AC Custom Cruise III cruise control system is fast, simple and accurate with the new 3475! Ten indicator lights tell you everything you need to know. It tells you if cruise sets properly, maintains speed, turns off when brakes are applied, and if vacuum system is working properly. For working on Pontiac Fiero and other GM vehicles with digital instrument panels, adapter No. 45349 is available separately.

No. 3475—GM AC Custom Cruise III tester. For troubleshooting 1983 GM light trucks and GM cars and light trucks since 1984. Wt., 12 oz.

No. 45349—Adapter for using No. 3475 to trouble-shoot AC Custom Cruise III systems on Pontiac Fiero. Wt., 6 oz.

FIGURE 14-19 GM AC custom cruise 111 tester. (*Courtesy of OTC Division, Sealed Power Corporation*)

THROTTLE BODY INJECTION TESTER KIT

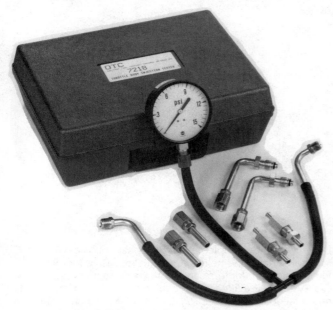

For use on all throttle bodies in the 1982 thru current GM line. This kit inludes No. 7219 Gauge, No. 7221 adapters for the Pontiac J2000/6000 engines, No. 7222 adapters for 1.8L throttle body fuel injection systems and No. 7223 adapter for 4.3 V6 engines. The kit comes in a sturdy, molded plastic storage box and includes all necessary instructions.

No. 7218—Throttle body fuel injection tester kit with adapters. Wt., 3 lbs., 10 oz.

Contents of Kit 7218:
Tester Gauge & Hose

Remove fuel line and replace with this gauge and hose assembly to test TBI systems. Large 3½" dia., 0-15 p.s.i. gauge is extremely accurate and easy to read. Instructions are included.

No. 7219—Tester gauge & hose, Wt., 1 lb.

Adapter Set

These adapters are for use with No. 7219 tester. Includes adapters for Pontiac J2000/6000 models.

No. 7221—Adapter set for Pontiac J2000/6000. Wt., 6½ oz.

Adapter Set

These adapters are for use with No. 7219 tester. These are needed on 1.8L engines and the pair is required.

No. 7222—Adapter set for 1.8L engines. Wt., 6½ oz.

Adapter Set

This set of adapters are new fittings required on 4.3L V6 engines. Two pair (included) are required in some applications.

FIGURE 14-20 Throttle body injection tester kit. (*Courtesy of OTC Division, Sealed Power Corporation*)

ELECTRONIC FUEL INJECTION TESTER KIT

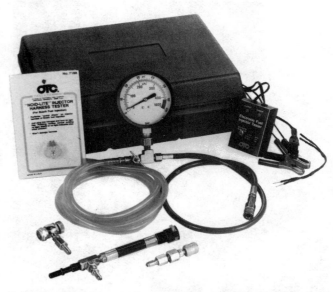

Features everything you need to test port fuel injection systems (both turbo and non-turbo versions) via static or running fuel pressure tests and cylinder balance tests. Instructions are included and kit comes in a rugged, molded plastic carrying case lined with protective foam rubber.

No. 7210—EFI Tester Kit. Wt., 1 lb., 13 oz.

FIGURE 14-21 Electronic fuel-injection tester kit. (*Courtesy of OTC Division, Sealed Power Corporation*)

INJECTOR HARNESS TOOL

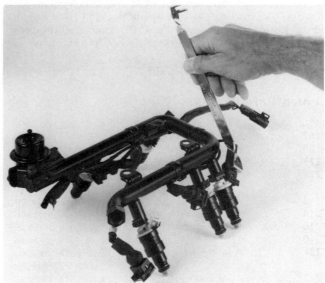

The No. 7216 removes and installs injector wiring harness without damaging the connections. For use on all multiport fuel injection injectors, this tool saves time by not having to remove excess parts when the injector cannot be reached.

No. 7216—Injector Harness Remover/Installer Tool. Wt., 2½ oz.

FIGURE 14-22 Injector harness removal/installation tool. (*Courtesy of OTC Division, Sealed Power Corporation*)

FUEL INJECTION TOOL KIT

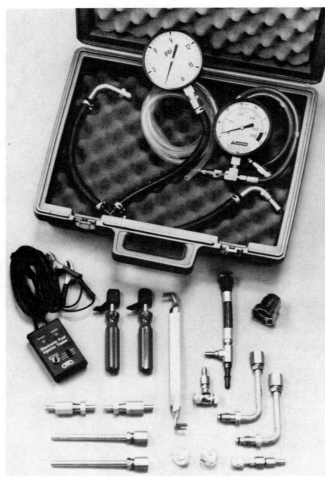

We've assembled everything you need to repair electronic fuel injection systems into one convenient package. This set is to be used in conjunction with the OTC Feedback Carburetor Tool Kit and Monitor 2000. Comes packed in a sturdy plastic carrying case.

No. 7233—Fuel injection tool kit. Wt., 7 lbs., 11 oz.

Contents of Kit 7233:

3398 .... Pulse tester for cylinder balance tests.
7187 ...... "Noid-Lite" injector harness tester for GM TBI.
7188 .... "Noid-Lite" injector harness tester for Bosch.
7211 .... Gauge assembly and hose.
7272 .... Ford adapter with Schroeder valve for central and port EFI systems.
7213 .... Ford CFI adapter.
7214 .... GM/Chrysler adapter for port EFI systems.
7216 .... Injection harness remover/installer tool.
7219 .... Tester gauge and hose for TBI systems.
7221 .... Adapter set for Pontiac J2000/6000 models. To be used with 7219 tester.
7222 .... Adapter set for 1.8L engines. To be used with 7219 tester.
7223 .... Adapter set for 4.3L V6 engines. To be used with 7219 tester.
7226 .... Idle air control socket.
7234 .... Idle air inlet plugs.
7236 .... Ford EFI fuel pressure adapter.

FIGURE 14-23 Fuel-Injection tool kit. (*Courtesy of OTC Division, Sealed Power Corporation*)

FEEDBACK CARBURETOR TOOL KIT

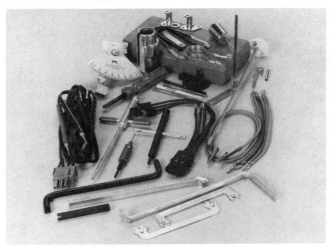

Designed as a complementary tool set for use with OTC Monitor series hand-held testers, this extensive tool kit is the ideal basic shop kit for repair work on present and *future* GM C-3 systems. Provided is everything you need to thoroughly repair feedback carburetor systems on GM vehicles. This is a "must have" set of tools for feedback carburetor work. Comes with protective carrying case and instructions.

No. 7232—Feedback carb. tool kit. Wt., 7 lbs., 8 oz.

Contents of Kit 7232:

Part No.	Description	Part No.	Description
3456	Idle speed control cable	7184	Terminal remover
3457	Throttle position sensor adjustment cable	7186	Solenoid/idle air gauge set
3458	C-3 test lead kit	7190	Bleed valve adjuster
7094	Choke angle gauge	7194	Carburetor linkage bending tool set
7153	Carburetor adjustment tool		
		7227	Float positioning tool kit
7181	Float level set	7228	Universal float scale
7182	Adjustment tool for Rochester DualJet and QuadraJet and VaraJet carburetors	7229	Idle adapter spanner wrench set
		7231	Universal oxygen sensor wrench
7183	Adjustment tool for Rochester DualJet and QuadraJet carburetors		

FIGURE 14-24 Feedback carburetor tool kit. (*Courtesy of OTC Division, Sealed Power Corporation*)

Alcohol Detection Kit

Often poor engine performance is blamed upon the computer, when, in fact, the computer has nothing at all to do with the problem. In many US states, a blend of gasoline and alcohol is readily available at the pumps. Excess amounts of alcohol in this mixture can result in swelling of both rubber and plastic parts within the fuel system. This test kit will allow the technician to determine the percentage of alcohol in the fuel mixture (Fig. 14-25).

DIGITAL AUTOMOTIVE SYSTEMS CONQUEST TESTER

DAS recently presented a breakthrough in diagnostic testing of today's on-board vehicle computer systems with the release of an access instrument known as the Conquest.

It differs from other computer access tools on the market at the moment, in that unlike the simple ALCL (assembly line connector or diagnostic link) scanners which passively read a slow and limited stream of data from the under dash connector, the Conquest taps directly into the heart of the ECM's engine computer.

Major features of the Conquest tool are troubleshooting functions, transient-trapping functions, engine reprogramming, and engine taping. Designed initially for all General Motors ECM-equipped cars, units will be available shortly for both Ford and Chrysler cars.

Figure 14-26 illustrates this particular instrument, which is a hand-held unit, while Figure 14-27 shows the complete DAS Conquest analyzer package in its carrying case. Components in this package include the Conquest unit, a tape recorder, a printer, and all the necessary parts to hook up and fully utilize the Conquest system.

The Conquest unit is available with various plug-in cartridges, not unlike the concept design used with the Kent-Moore and OTC Monitor 2000 units. Since 1980, GMC has used over 45 different ECM's and over 2000 PROM's in their various division vehicles; therefore, the Conquest has different cartridges that plug into the base unit, somewhat like a video game part, to handle these various ECM's and PROM's.

Additional options available with the Conquest are a tape recorder that will record all engine conditions while the vehicle is being driven, and which can be played back at any time, whether the Conquest instrument is in the vehicle or not.

A printer is also available that interfaces with the Conquest and will give a written explanation of the various engine functions for use by the service technician, or as an aid to give the customer a description of the vehicle problem.

ALCOHOL DETECTION KIT

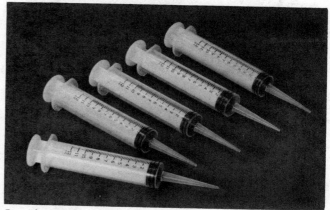

Provides a fast, simple method of checking for excessive alcohol in gasoline mixtures. An excessive alcohol content will cause swelling of rubber and plastic parts. It also cleans fuel systems to such a degree that accumulated rust and corrosion at low points in the system are dislodged and distributed throughout the system, causing plugging and damage. This detection kit includes five easy to use syringes, and instructions with a table showing the percentage of allowable alcohol in the fuel mixture.

How the Kit is Used:

One container is filled with gasoline, another with clean water. A syringe is used to withdraw 3 cc of water. Gasoline is drawn into the syringe until the 12 cc mark is reached. The syringe is shaken vigorously to mix the liquids, and set aside for one minute on a flat surface with the nozzle pointing up. If alcohol is present in the fuel, it will separate from the gasoline and join the water in the lower part of the syringe. A reading is then taken at the boundary of the two liquids and the table is consulted.

No. 7224—Alcohol detection kit. Wt., 8 oz.

FIGURE 14-25 Alcohol detection kit. (*Courtesy of OTC Division, Sealed Power Corporation*)

When the Conquest is hooked into the on-board vehicle computer PROM connection, the service technician can see 45 different functions going on in the engine, although only four different things can be shown on the screen at one time.

The Conquest monitors and updates engine information 10 times a second, and with the push of a button, the Conquest will indicate what trouble codes are stored in the ECM. Normal readout on an ALCL or similar readout instruments is once every 1 to 2 seconds; therefore, the speed of the Conquest allows the technician to see surges, dropouts, loose connections, and other transient conditions that testers and scopes are too slow to catch. Unlike most testers which display information values in volts or other similar modes, the Conquest can show displays, such as those for

FIGURE 14-26 Conquest hand-held diagnostic computer tool. (*Courtesy of Digital Automotive Systems, Inc.*)

vehicle. The technician can connect up the Conquest with one plug to the car's ECM, find past trouble codes stored in memory, and press the correct key to display the current trouble area on the screen. While driving the vehicle on the road, let's assume that both the MAP and BARO sensors go to zero, and the rpm and ignition timing fluctuate. It's possible that this condition could be caused by some loose connections at the sensors; therefore, in order to confirm this fact, the technician could press the TRAP mode on the Conquest panel. Upon returning to the shop area, the technician can use the Conquest to determine what actually occurred when both sensor signals dropped to zero during the road test.

Other functions of the Conquest are that the technician can advance or retard ignition timing, increase or decrease engine idle rpm, richen or lean out the fuel mixture as well as turning on or off the various solenoids for the air conditioning system, torque converter lockup phase, EGR valves, and diverter valves without ever having to open the vehicle hood. This control function is designed to operate for only a three-minute time period, after which the system returns to normal.

Should you have trouble following the test sequence or lose your place, the "user-friendly" Conquest offers a Help key button. When it is pressed, Conquest will systematically guide the technician out of trouble, as well as showing him/her how to achieve the function desired. Unlike most scopes which require the attachment of sensors and probes to numerous engine connections, the Conquest requires only one hookup.

Conquest Hookup

The Conquest diagnostic tool differs from ALCL (assembly line communication link) testers in that ALCL test tools tap into an external line leading out of the computer system, while the Conquest taps directly into the heart of the onboard computer system.

This is done by the technician first of all lowering the ECM (electronic control module) from below the dash, attaching an "anti-electrical" surge device by strapping it to the ECM, and then very carefully removing the PROM (programmable read only memory) chip assembly as described in Chapter 7 for GMC vehicles. Once the PROM assembly is removed, the Conquest wiring harness is connected directly to the vehicle computer PROM connector pin holes.

An example of a typical Conquest printer hard-copy is shown in Fig. 14-28. The left-side of the diagram displays a representative shot of over 30 different functions that the ECM is performing at a particular instant, while the right-hand side of the diagram illustrates three different functions in seven-second increments.

manifold pressure, in inches of mercury (Hg), psi, or kilopascals (kPA).

An example of two different functions that can be seen simultaneously on the Conquest screen are the MAP (manifold absolute pressure) sensor and the BARO (barometric pressure sensor), since these two sensors are connected to the same wiring harness.

A feature of the Conquest is that the engine systems can be monitored while actually driving/road testing the

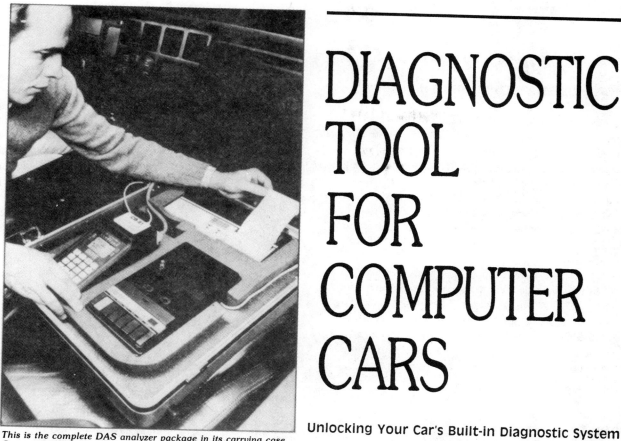

This is the complete DAS analyzer package in its carrying case. Components include Conquest unit, tape recorder, printer, and all other parts to hook up and fully utilize the Conquest.

DIAGNOSTIC TOOL FOR COMPUTER CARS

Unlocking Your Car's Built-in Diagnostic System

FIGURE 14-27 Complete Conquest diagnostic package. (*Courtesy of Digital Automotive Systems, Inc.*)

```
Ready to SNAPSHOT, TRACK, and PLOT.
------------------------------------
SNAPSHOT:
  MAP: KPA  =   87    MAP:INHG = 26.0
  MAP: PSI  = 12.8    VAC: KPA =   20
  VAC:INHG  =  5.9    VAC: PSI =  2.9
  BARO:KPA  =  107    BAROINHG = 31.9
  BARO:PSI  = 15.6      MPH    =   33
  KM/HOUR   =   53    TEMP: F  =  113
  TEMP: C   =   45    RUN TIME =  207
  TPS: %    =   51      RPM    = 1225
  SPARK     =   42    SPKDWELL =   18
  KNOCKRTD  =   .0     KNOCKS  =  188
  STARTUPS  =    0    CROSSCNT =    0
  MC DUTY   =   10    MC DWELL =    6
  O2:VOLTS  =  .33    BATTERY  = 13.8
  TPS: V    = 2.55    MAPVAC:V = 1.64
  S-TCODES  =   42
  C-TCODES  =   42

LIGHT  =on ; TCC sol=off: O2 hot =on
CLoop  =on ; Rich   =off: A/C Req=off
A/C  on=off; ISC/IAC=off; AIRCTRL=off
AIR SW =off; EGR    =on
------------------------------------
```

FIGURE 14-28 Typical Conquest printer readout information sheet. (*Courtesy of Digital Automotive Systems, Inc.*)

```
Each sample will take 007 seconds to
print.

How many seconds between each sample?
Enter as 3 digits (005, not 5):
           007
Press # to stop.
----------=============----------
  RUN TIME =  461    VAC: PSI =  2.9
  BAROINHG = 31.9      RPM    = 1100
----------=============----------
  RUN TIME =  468    VAC: PSI =  2.9
  BAROINHG = 31.9      RPM    = 1100
----------=============----------
  RUN TIME =  475    VAC: PSI =  2.9
  BAROINHG = 31.9      RPM    = 1100
----------=============----------
  RUN TIME =  482    VAC: PSI =  2.9
  BAROINHG = 31.9      RPM    = 1100
----------=============----------
  RUN TIME =  489    VAC: PSI =  2.9
  BAROINHG = 31.9      RPM    = 1100
----------=============----------
  RUN TIME =  496    VAC: PSI =  2.9
  BAROINHG = 31.9      RPM    = 1100
----------=============----------
  RUN TIME =  503    VAC: PSI =  2.9
  BAROINHG = 31.9      RPM    = 1100
----------=============----------
  RUN TIME =  510    VAC: PSI =  2.9
  BAROINHG = 31.9      RPM    = 1100
----------=============----------
  RUN TIME =  517    VAC: PSI =  2.9
  BAROINHG = 31.9      RPM    = 1100
----------=============----------
  RUN TIME =  524    VAC: PSI =  2.9
  BAROINHG = 31.9      RPM    = 1100
```

CRT (CATHODE RAY TUBE) TESTER

The recent introduction of a CRT (cathode ray tube) style of vehicle instrumentation system on the 1986 Buick Riviera allows the driver of the vehicle command of a variety of menu selections through touch sensitive technology. This system is described in Chapter 16. A similar system that is available in the Japanese domestic market is used in the Toyota Soarer series passenger cars. In addition, the Lincoln Continental Mark V11 Comtech car also features a DIS (driver information system) employing a CRT touch screen arrangement.

To isolate faults in this type of a system requires that a special CRT membrane switch tester be used, such as the Kent-Moore J34914 unit shown in Fig. 14-29. This diagnostic unit is used to substitute for the CRT controller, either at the CRT or at the wiring harness connector. A fault can be pinpointed in the CRT picture tube, membrane switch circuitry, or wiring harness.

J 34914
CRT MEMBRANE SWITCH TESTER

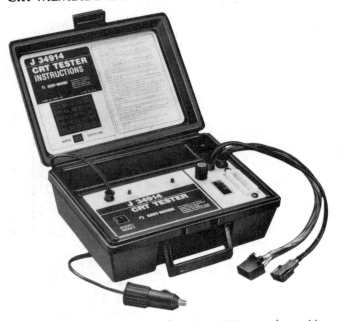

This unit is used to isolate faults in the CRT, a touch sensitive TV screen which is a multifunction driver information center, standard on the 1986 Buick Riviera.

By substituting this tester for the CRT controller, either at the CRT or at the wiring harness connector, a fault can be pinpointed in the CRT picture tube, membrane switch circuitry, or wiring harness.

FIGURE 14-29 CRT (Cathode Ray Tube) membrane switch tester. (*Courtesy of Kent-Moore Group, Sealed Power Corporation*)

FIGURE 14-30 Digital Brainmaster 11 on-board computer tester. (*Courtesy of ALLTEST, Division of Triplett Corporation*)

ALLTEST DIAGNOSTIC EQUIPMENT

Another popular manufacturer of electronic diagnostic test equipment for both passenger cars and diesel-equipped pickup and heavy-duty trucks is Alltest. It offers a wide range of diagnostic tools for checking out gasoline fuel-injected engine computer systems, electronic ignition systems, diesel equipped trucks, and a broad range of general electrical test tools. A wide range of computer diagnostic tools is available, and the purchaser simply has to decide whether he requires an all encompassing tool, such as the Model 3256 Digital Brainmaster illustrated in Fig. 14-30. The Brainmaster is capable of accessing and testing General Motors, Ford, and Chrysler products. A Model 3226 is a similar model tester, which can also be used on the big three electronic systems.

Figure 14-31 illustrates Alltest's Model 3707/3710 Digital Engine Analyzers, which with one hookup allows the mechanic/technician to access both domestic or imported vehicles, and quickly and effectively troubleshoot the computer system.

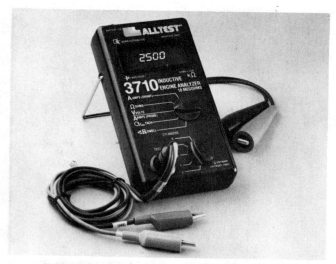

FIGURE 14-31 Digital engine analyzers. (*Courtesy of ALLTEST, Division of Triplett Corporation*)

Also shown in Fig. 14-32 is the Alltest Model 4300 Portable Digital Electronic Ignition Tester, designed specifically to test modules without removing any parts. It is adaptable to domestic, European, and Japanese import vehicles from the 1972 model year through to current production vehicles.

In addition to the computer and ignition test instruments, Alltest offers other special tools, such as a digital mag timing tester, digital multimeter, charging system analyzers, inductive d.c. amp probe, automatic range temperature probe, advance timing lights for both gasoline and diesel engines, and heavy-duty truck/trailer portable light testers and digital diesel engine tachs.

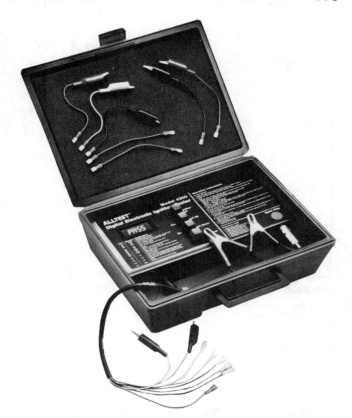

FIGURE 14-32 Portable digital electronic ignition tester. (*Courtesy of ALLTEST, Division of Triplett Corporation*)

PINOUT BOX

Checking the plug-in harness connectors and pins to the on-board computer for resistance checks/voltage cannot be done with jumper wires, or by simply placing the leads of an ohmmeter across the connecting pins, for burning and damage to the pin connectors will result.

A "Pinout Box," such as that illustrated in Fig. 14-33, must be used for all computer harness/pin checks. Some manufacturers refer to this instrument as a "Breakout Box." (See Fig. 8-34b for the instrument used on Ford vehicles.)

Generally the pinout/breakout box has numbers below each hole on the face of the instrument to allow the probe lead of a DVOM to register the resistance of a particular circuit being checked. The Pinout Box shown in Fig. 14-33 is designed to plug into the controller harness and is used to diagnose the TEVES Anti-Skid Brake System (discussed in Chapter 21), and also on Cadillac passenger cars.

FIGURE 14-33 On-board computer harness/pin connector Pinout Box. (*Courtesy of Kent-Moore Tool Group, Sealed Power Corporation*)

CHAPTER 15

♦

Electrical Test Routines

ACCESSING STORED TROUBLE CODES

Since electricity is an invisible source and cannot be seen inside an operating component, it becomes imperative to approach electrical/electronics component troubleshooting in a systematic fashion, since it is not practical for the mechanic/technician to dismantle so many electrical/electronics components to determine whether or not they are operating properly. Replacing electronic sensors, switches, solenoids, and relays is not only time consuming, but it is very expensive as well. Vehicle manufacturers report that well over half of all on-board computers that have been removed under the suspicion of being at fault are, in fact, perfectly functional.

This procedure becomes a very expensive repair job for the customer. Moreover, if a computer is replaced when it is operating correctly, the same problem is bound to occur again and again. Sooner or later the customer will challenge his high repair costs, particularly inasmuch as the vehicle problem will not be solved by computer replacement. It isn't hard for the mechanic/technician to access the stored trouble codes held in memory by the computer, but once these trouble codes have been determined, the mechanic/technician must then be capable of tracing the trouble source to its starting point as quickly and effectively as possible.

Once the on-board computer diagnostic connector link has been jumper-wired, or the self-diagnostic features of the computer have been initiated, taking the make of vehicle

into account, the stored trouble codes in memory can be determined by the following steps:

1. Counting the number of pulses of the *Check Engine* light and their duration.
2. Watching the red and green flashing lights on the side of the computer housing on some import vehicles (e.g., Nissan vehicles).
3. Simply reading the trouble code number which is flashed on the instrument panel of the vehicle (e.g., Cadillac, Oldsmobile, Buick).
4. Reading the trouble code number from the connected special troubleshooting tool. (See Chapter 14 on special tools; e.g., Monitor 2000, and Conquest instruments.)

Once the trouble code has been flashed, the mechanic/technician must then consult the vehicle service manual to determine what circuit, sensor, or switch is affected, and then systematically check the manufacturer's sequence for either a voltage or resistance reading in most cases. In doing these checks, be sure that you use a multimeter that has at least 10 meg (million) ohms of resistance minimum or greater; otherwise, severe damage to electronic componentry can occur. Resistance checks made with an analog multimeter can damage or destroy expensive computer circuitry, so always use a multimeter that will protect these systems, in addition to providing you with the range of readings that you desire.

TYPES OF MEASUREMENTS

The vehicle manufacturer will always indicate in the service/test procedure just what type of test/reading is to be accessed. Typically, voltage, current, and resistance are used to confirm the operating condition of an electrical/electronic component.

Voltage, however, is normally the most helpful measurement when checking out an electrical system, since readings will provide you with answers to the following questions:

1. Is there voltage present at the test point? If there is, it is an indication that the wiring, circuitry, and various system components are, in fact, capable of delivering voltage to the item suspected of being at fault.
2. What voltage reading is present? Compare the voltage reading to specifications to determine whether it is too high or too low.
3. Is there a voltage drop across the component being tested? The voltage drop tells you how much voltage is being consumed by that component.

PROBLEM AREAS

Various problems in an electrical or electronic system can appear in more than one system. Often, the problem may appear in one system, while the symptoms may appear in yet another, which can cause you to follow the wrong path for correction.

Break the systems down so that you can logically follow the problem to its source. Typical automotive electrical systems can be broken down as follows:

1. Ignition system
2. Charging system
3. Starting system
4. Sensors and switches
5. On-board computers
6. Cooling system

Problems existing in these systems are often the direct result of current drains, shorts, and poor ground connections. (See Fig. 15-1 for examples of voltage, current, and resistance locations on a typical passenger car/truck application.)

CAUTION: Self-powered test lights should never be used on a circuit or component that contains solid-state devices, since damage to these components can result as a consequence of the battery voltage used with these testers.

System/Component	Voltage Presence & Level	Voltage Drop	Current	Resistance	Temperature
CHARGING SYSTEM					
Alternators	●		●		
Regulators	●				
Diodes		●		●	
Connectors	●	●		●	
STARTING SYSTEM					
Batteries	●	●			
Starters		●	●		
Solenoids	●	●			
Connectors		●		●	
Interlocks	●				
IGNITION SYSTEM					
Coils	●			●	
Connectors	●	●		●	
Condensors				●	
Contact Set (points)	●			●	
Distributor Caps				●	
Plug Wires				●	
Rotors				●	
Magnetic Pick-up	●			●	
LIGHTING & ACCESSORIES					
A/C Condensors					●
A/C Evaporators					●
Compressor Clutches	●		●		
Lighting Circuits	●	●	●	●	
Relays	●	●			
Transmissions					●
COOLING SYSTEM					
Connectors	●	●		●	
Fan Motors	●		●		
Relays	●	●			
Temperature Switches	●	●		●	●
Radiators					●

FIGURE 15-1 Typical electrical system component and measurement type. (*Courtesy of John Fluke Mfg. Co., Inc. Everett, WA.*)

NOTE: It is recommended that only a digital multimeter with at least 10 megohms or higher impedance be used on electronic circuits for cars.

TEST TOOLS

Typical electrical test tools that are commonly used when checking electrical and electronic systems of computer-equipped passenger cars and trucks are the following ones:

1. Fused jumper wire
2. Short finder
3. Fuse tester
4. Analog/digital multimeter, with at least a 10 megohm impedance value
5. Unpowered test light

Examples of where and how these test tools are used are shown in the illustrations herein.

FIGURE 15-2 Model J-8681 short finder (*Courtesy of Kent-Moore Tool Group, Sealed Power Corporation*)

1. *Fused Jumper Wire:* Although a nonfused jumper wire is often suitable for many uses when testing circuits, an in-line 5 amp fuse should be employed for bypassing open circuits. Care should be exercised when using a fused jumper wire, since the fuse will be blown if it is placed across any load motors or current draw device.

2. *Short Finder:* The short finder (Fig. 15-2) is ideal for locating shorts to ground, since it creates a pulsing magnetic field in the shorted circuit, and indicates to the mechanic/technician the location of the short, either through the vehicle body trim or sheet metal.

   See Fig. 15-3. When using the short finder, such as a Kent-Moore P/N J-8681 or equivalent, follow the sequence given below:
   (a) With the battery connected, remove the blown fuse from its socket and connect the short finder across the fuse terminals.
   (b) Close all of the switches in the circuit that you are troubleshooting.
   (c) Operate the short finder in order to create a pulsing magnetic current to the short which will cause a pulsing magnetic field to surround the circuit wiring between the fuse block and the short.
   (d) Moving the short meter slowly along the suspected wiring from the fuse block will cause the needle to pulse back and forth. When the meter needle

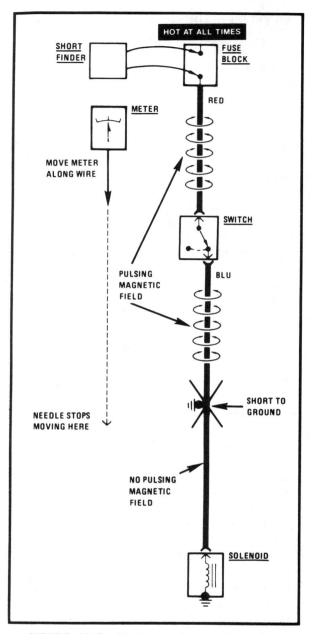

FIGURE 15-3 Finding a short with a short finder. (*Courtesy of Oldsmobile Div. of GMC*)

stops moving, it indicates there is a break or short in the wire at that point or in that general area.

3. *Fuse Tester:* This handy tool tests, removes, and installs both blade- and glass-type automotive fuses (Fig. 15-4). This tool features adjustable contacts and a red LED which glows upon contact with a bad fuse (open). When checking a fuse, the tester is applied directly to the fuse while it is in position in its fuse block seat. Two probes contact the fuse either into the slots of a flat plastic fuse or to the metal ends of a glass fuse.

J34764
AUTO FUSE TESTER & REMOVER/INSTALLER

This handy tool tests, removes, and installs both blade and glass type automotive fuses. It features adjustable contacts and a red light which glows upon contact with a bad fuse. This slender hand tool makes it easy for the technician to check and service fuses within the tight confines of the fuse block area.

FIGURE 15-4 Model J-34764 fuse tester, remover, and installer. (*Courtesy of Kent-Moore Tool Group, Sealed Power Corporation*)

4. *Analog/digital Multimeter:* The key to using a multimeter on an electronic system is that it have an impedance of at least 10 meg (million) ohms so that the solid-state devices will not be damaged. Many multimeters are available on the market under various brand names; the well-known and widely-used Fluke models were illustrated in Fig. 14-2. Another widely-used digital multimeter is the Kent-Moore J-34029-A or J-35500. Figure 15-5 illustrates the J-34029-A unit, which has a 22 meg (2.2 million) ohm input impedance. In addition, a current clamp J-35590 (shown in Fig. 15-6) can be plugged into either one of these multimeters for up to a 600 amp reading in 0.1 amp increments. This addition is particularly helpful in identifying problems with low power accessories.

When measuring resistance with a digital multimeter, either the vehicle battery or the ignition switch

J 34029-A DIGITAL MULTIMETER

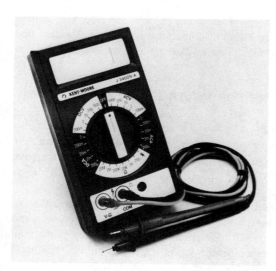

The J 34029-A is designed for years of dependable service under the most rugged shop conditions. The single rotary dial incorporates a patented design eliminating friction wear which reduces the life of typical wafer type switches. Other superior design features include extra overload protection, 100% factory testing of all ranges and functions, a specially designed case which seals out contaminants encountered in the field.

Features:

● In Circuit Diode Test ● 0.50% Basic DCV Accuracy ● Easy Read LCD 0.5'' High Digits ● 2000 Hour Battery Life ● Standard 9 Volt ● Audible Continuity Beeper ● 22 Mega

Ohm Input Impedance ● In Circuit Measurements ● Spare Fuse ● Test Leads With Alligator Clips ● Patented Long Life Rotary Dial ● Built-In Multiposition Tilt Bail ● Plastic Storage/Carrying Case ● Complete Instructions

Accessories for J 34029-A
J 34029-15
EZ Mini-hook Test Lead Set

Contains a red and black 36'' long spring-loaded hook end which can be used to fit over up to .059 diameter components when continuous hook up is required.

J 34029-248
Deluxe Test Lead Kit

Includes safety designed test leads with push-on probe plus banana plug extensions insulated alligator clips, extension probe tips, medium size hook type prods, large size hook type prods all in a rugged cordura nylon pouch with velcro closures.

J 34898
High Current Shunt

J 34898 is an inexpensive calibrated resistance wire which is connected in series with the electrical accessory to be tested and plugged into the J 34029 Multimeter. The multimeter range switch is set on the 200 MV DC scale. This will provide a direct readout of the accessory current draw in .1 amp increments. From 0 to 99 amps.

J 35590
Current Clamp (See Feature)

FIGURE 15-5 Model J-34029-A digital multimeter. (*Courtesy of Kent-Moore Tool Group, Sealed Power Corporation*)

J 35590
CURRENT
CLAMP
(0-600 AMPS)

J 35590 is used with a digital multimeter (such as J 34029-A or J 35500) to precisely measure DC current flow (AMPS) in 0.1 AMP increments without breaking into the circuit or affecting the operation of the circuit. During operation the inductive pick-up type jaws of the J 35590 are simply clamped around the vehicle battery cable or a wire leading to the accessory to be tested. A readout of the current draw will be indicated on the multimeter digital display. J 35590 is especially helpful in identifying problems with low power accessories because it will measure 0 to 200 AMPS in 0.1 AMP increments.

FIGURE 15-6 Model J-35590 current clamp (multimeter). (*Courtesy of Kent-Moore Tool Group, Sealed Power Corporation*)

or component control switch must be disconnected in order to prevent a false reading. Digital multimeters apply such a low voltage when measuring resistance that the presence of voltages can give a false resistance reading. The use of diodes and solid-state components in electronic circuits can cause an ohmmeter to register an incorrect value.

If you reverse the leads of the multimeter/ohmmeter and the readings on the component you are checking differ, then the solid-state device is affecting the measurement.

The vehicle manufacturer's service manual procedure should always be your guide when taking voltage or resistance reading checks of any electronic circuit or component.

5. *Unpowered Test Light:* An unpowered test light is required to perform many of the diagnostic procedures on electronic control systems of most passenger cars and trucks. Figure 15-7 illustrates a typical unpowered test light J-34142A. It is manufactured by the Kent-Moore Tool Group. The unpowered test light is used on a live circuit to determine if power is flowing, whereas a self-powered test light is used only on an unpowered circuit to determine if continuity exists (no breaks).

J 34142-A
UNPOWERED TEST LIGHT (MICRO-PACK
COMPATIBLE)

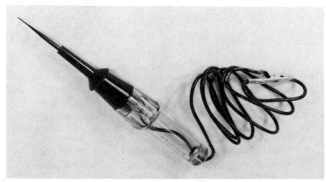

A test light such as J 34142-A is required to perform many of the diagnostic procedures on General Motors electronic control systems. J 34142-A has a unique specially shaped probe tip which will plug directly into female Micro-Pack connectors minimizing danger of over expansion. This durable unit is built of high strength material and includes a 48″ long lead.

FIGURE 15-7 Model J-34142-A unpowered test light. (*Courtesy of Kent-Moore Tool Group, Sealed Power Corporation*)

CAUTION: Never use a self-powered test light when checking a circuit containing solid-state devices; doing so may result in severe damage to these components.

TESTING FOR VOLTAGE

Either a test light or a voltmeter can be used when checking a circuit for voltage. An example of a hookup for a voltage check is illustrated in Fig. 15-8. Make sure that the voltmeter's black lead (negative) is connected to the ground source.

Illumination of the test light will confirm that voltage is present; however, the voltmeter tells you just how much voltage, and this reading can be compared to the manufacturer's specifications. As a general rule of thumb, if the voltage reading is more than one volt less than battery voltage, there is a problem. Of course, this does not hold true for electronic systems that use 5 volt sensors and for very low current draw components.

VOLTAGE DROP CHECK

A voltmeter can be placed into the circuit, similar to the way it is shown in Fig. 15-8. The positive lead (red) is connected to the top of the circuit, which in this case is the lower side of the fuse block. The black (negative lead) is connected to the solenoid at the lower side of the illustrated circuit. Operate the circuit, and the voltmeter will indicate

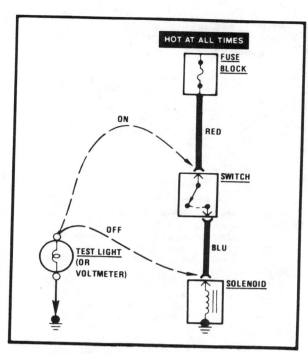

FIGURE 15-8 Typical hookup for a voltage check. (*Courtesy of Oldsmobile Div. of GMC*)

the difference in voltage passing through the circuit/switch in relation to battery power.

TESTING FOR SHORTS

A short circuit means that the circuit is being completed by electricity finding its way to ground, thereby creating a shorter path than that which was designed for the circuit. These shorts can usually be caused by defective components in the circuit, or by some form of insulation (wire or component) that has rubbed or chafed through. Shorts that end up blowing fuses can generally be found by following the same troubleshooting techniques that are used to find current (amperage) drains, even though the symptoms may be different.

Use the same process that is used to find ''current drains'' when finding shorts, except switch the digital multimeter to the d.c. volts function, and hook it up in series with the battery. This method will self-limit the actual current flowing in the system, thereby avoiding an excessive amount of blown fuses. When using this check, keep in mind that the alternator diodes do leak some current; therefore, disconnect the alternator wiring to remove this possible sensed condition. If there is current draw for whatever reason, the meter will record battery voltage.

The cause of a battery discharging overnight is often attributed to a short, although the cause is actually related to current drains. On electronic computer systems and dig-

ital circuitry, the normal electrical procedure of using the multimeter and setting it to volts is not acceptable practice, since some devices/components are always in the on position, and the voltmeter will reflect battery voltage when the system is normal.

Figure 15-9 illustrates one example of checking for a short with either a nonpowered test light or a voltmeter. The blown fuse should be removed first and the load disconnected.

Starting at the fuse block, wiggle the wiring harness from side to side, and repeat this action about every six inches. If the test light glows or the voltmeter registers, then there is a short to ground in the wiring near that point.

LOCATING CURRENT DRAINS

Current drains cause the battery to be in a continual low charge condition, so that often there is not enough amperage available to crank the engine over first thing in the morning. Although the condition can be caused by a low charging rate, often it can be traced to an underhood, trunk, or domelight that was left on overnight.

If you are working on a computer-equipped vehicle and if the service procedure requires you to activate the self-diagnostic feature of the system to withdraw trouble codes, keep in mind that a trickle charger should be applied to the battery if this time period exceeds 30 minutes, as it does in most cases. Underhood or domelight switches can be

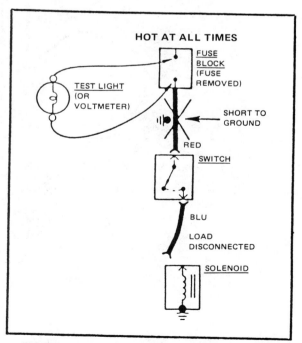

FIGURE 15-9 Testing for a short with a test light or voltmeter. (*Courtesy of Oldsmobile Div. of GMC*)

isolated by placing a small piece of tape over the switch plunger.

NOTE: When using a multimeter, it is wise to select the 10 amp rating until you are sure that the current draw is less than 320 mA (milliamps); otherwise, you could blow the multimeter's protective fuse.

Never crank the engine or operate accessories that draw more than the selected ampere rating on the multimeter; otherwise, severe damage to the meter could result.

When checking the entire electrical system for current drains, the digital multimeter should always be connected in *series* with the battery. The scale on the digital multimeter can be set to 10 amps; once the current draw has been determined to be less than 0.3 amps, the selector switch can be placed in the 320 mA range in order to determine the total current drain across a circuit.

Figure 15-10 illustrates the correct hookup for a current leakage check of an alternator, while Fig. 15-11 shows a

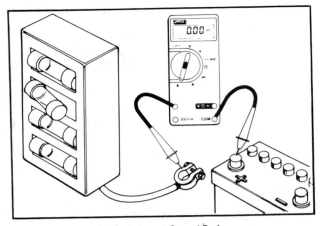

—Isolating the Circuit Causing A Current Drain
CAUTION—*Do not crank the engine or operate accessories that draw more than 10 amps. You could damage the meter, possibly beyond repair. Connect the DMM in series with the battery using the current function. Isolate the circuit causing the current drain by pulling one fuse after another while watching the multimeter.*

The current reading will drop to 0 when the fuse in the offending circuit is pulled. Reinstall the fuse and disconnect the components in that circuit one at a time to find the defective component. Again, keep in mind that on modern cars there are many computer circuits that draw current normally and they may not all be on the same fuse.

FIGURE 15-11 Digital multimeter hookup for isolating a circuit causing a current drain. (*Courtesy of John Fluke Mfg. Co., Inc., Everett, WA.*)

typical hookup for isolating the circuit that may be causing a continual current drain in the system.

BAD GROUNDS

Often, many problems associated with electrical and electronic systems can be directly attributed to poor connections in the live part of the circuit; and very often the circuit cannot be completed because of a bad ground connection. Poor or loose connections create a high circuit resistance since they can produce a wide range of symptoms, particularly with snap-in and weather-pack type connectors.

Examples of poor grounds are lights that do not illuminate as brightly as they should, lights that may illuminate when they are not supposed to, gauges that change their value when another switch is turned on, and lights that fail to illuminate. Many manufacturers recommend that conductive grease be applied to various connections before they are reassembled to minimize the growth of corrosion.

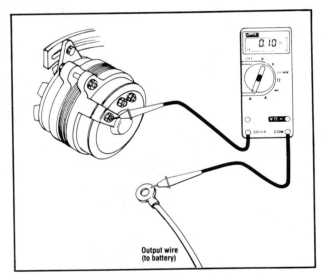

—Alternator Leakage Current
To check alternator diode leakage, connect the multimeter in series with the alternator output terminal with the car not running. Leakage current should be on the order of a couple of milliamps at most, and more often will be on the order of 500 microamps or less.

FIGURE 15-10 Digital multimeter hookup for checking alternator current leakage. (*Courtesy of John Fluke Mfg. Co., Inc., Everett, WA.*)

CHAPTER 16

♦

Electronic Instrumentation Systems

INTRODUCTION TO ACTIVE AND PASSIVE DISPLAYS

Recent changes in automobile design include a reduction in the overall size, weight, and bulk of the passenger car, and an increase in performance from smaller displacement engines. These changes have created problems for the stylists. New automotive interior needs have been created. Meeting these needs requires:

1. An overall reduction in the size of the instrument panel.
2. Elimination of daytime glare (readability factor of instruments).
3. Elimination of window and driver windshield reflections, particularly during nighttime driving.
4. A desire for greater information on the part of the vehicle driver about the various systems on the vehicle.
5. A demand by the mechanic/technician for easier access to the various sensors and electronic systems on the vehicle. This need is especially important for monitoring and troubleshooting the various electronic systems.

With the space age adventures that we are subjected to in our everyday lives, there is a demand for new technology and information-gathering that is displayed electronically through colored graphics in digitized form, rather than in the long-used analog style of instrumentation. Manufacturers have been able to design and manufacture instrument panel clusters that not only incorporate the five major design features listed above but also improve the appearance of the vehicle itself. Electronic instrumentation offers unique performance features and an improved appearance compared to dial-gauge types of instrumentation. Conventional analog instrumentation generally employs pointers and scales to feed the information to the car driver in a passive mode (not constantly updated).

Two basic categories of electronic instrumentation are available, which are:

1. Active displays
2. Passive displays

The active display arrangement employs VFD (vacuum fluorescent displays), LED (light emitting diodes), CRT (cathode ray tubes) employed by both Buick (1986) and Toyota in 1985, as well as gas discharge displays which are self-illuminating, with the light source also being the information source. LCD (liquid crystal displays) are similar to the conventional analog-type of instrumentation in that they are passive and rely on an external, auxiliary lighting source in order for the driver to be able to read and interpret the information.

One of the major advantages of electronic instrumentation is that it provides a much greater range of information, and can do so within a smaller overall space than an analog arrangement. Reader enhancement is provided through the use of multicolored information displays.

Although analog type instrumentation and gauges are still in wide use in many makes of passenger cars and trucks, there is a growing trend towards the wide use of digital

LCD (liquid crystal display) dashboard displays. Speed-ometers, tachometers, and a driver information center containing oil pressure, fuel consumption, trip recorder times and fuel used, coolant temperature, an instant readout on miles per gallon, fuel reserve in the tank, etc., are just some of the options now being incorporated into the displays of many passenger cars and trucks.

Ford Motor Company first introduced the use of an electronic display instrument panel in 1978. General Motors Corporation and Chrysler Corporation followed in 1980; Toyota and Nissan, in 1981; and Mitsubishi and Honda joined the trend towards electronic display of vehicle/engine operation in 1982. With the increasing desire for more information feedback to the driver of a vehicle, coupled with the need for effective and efficient electronic ignition and fuel-injection control, the use of on-board microprocessors, sensors, and control systems has become prominent on almost all vehicles in use today.

In terms of information density and resolution, a cathode ray tube (CRT) is the preferred choice of automotive display device; however, this arrangement has several significant drawbacks. The CRT is heavier and thicker compared to other types of available flat displays, such as LCD (liquid crystal display), LED (light emitting diode), EL (electro-luminescence), and VF (vacuum fluorescent). Recent trends offer various styles and configurations of instrument clusters that employ one of the above types of flat displays.

In order to reduce glare from electronic instrumentation clusters, various methods have been used; however, one popular method is to employ what is called an LCF (light

control film). Figure 16-1 illustrates typical vehicle interior uses for LCF.

The LCF is a thin plastic film which is optically transparent and which contains uniformly-spaced microlouvers to control light both entering and leaving the display area of the panel. (See Fig. 16-2 for an example.) The louvers are used to hood or shield the unwanted external light sources so that the driver can easily see the information displayed on the panel. Figure 16-3 illustrates the instrument panel contrast improvement and light reflection control when employing LCF (light control film).

LCD (liquid crystal displays) are gaining popularity over the VFD (vacuum fluorescent display) and the LED (light emitting diode) in many passenger cars and trucks for instrumentation purposes. In 1980, Ford Motor Company of Dearborn, Michigan, applied VFD's on the instrument panels of their luxury cars; however, these VFD's had size limitations and also consumed a lot of power. In 1984, Chevrolet superseded the VFD method in their Corvette, with the adoption of LCD technology. In 1985, Ford also switched to this method of instrumentation in their Thunderbird model passenger car. The reasons behind the adoption of LCD technology were based mainly upon its low cost, small size, low weight, and high reliability.

Today, the most commonly-used form of LCD is the "twisted nematic display," on which dark figures appear against a light background. Polarizers on the front and rear of the display "sandwich" long rod-like molecules of an organic fluid which are twisted through 90 degrees from one polarizer to the other. When no electrical power is supplied to the panel, light will pass through from the front

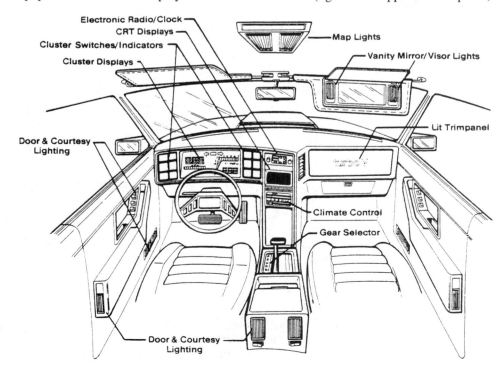

FIGURE 16-1 Light control film uses in a typical passenger car interior. (*Reproduced from the Conference Proceedings, "Automotive Electronics," 1985, by permission of the Council of the Institution of Mechanical Engineers*)

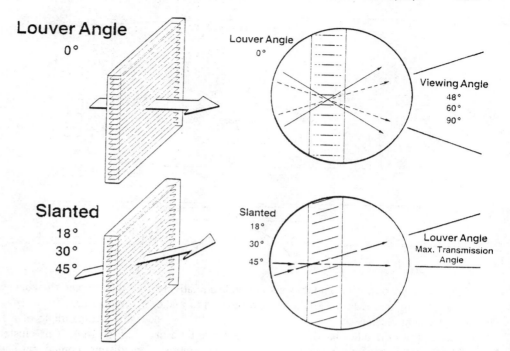

FIGURE 16-2 Light control film louver orientation. (*Reproduced from the Conference Proceedings, ''Automotive Electronics,'' 1985, by permission of the Council of the Institution of Mechanical Engineers*)

to rear polarizer plate, but it does so in a twisted motion or light reflection process.

When light reaches the rear polarizer plate, it is reflected back towards the front of the cell via a multipurpose surface that acts as a reflector during daylight hours. On its way back to the front of the cell, the light is twisted again, and it emerges at the front polarizer to create a light spot on a bright background, and therefore no image is visible.

When electrical power is supplied to the instrument panel circuit board, the rod-like molecules are altered so that the light is no longer twisted. The net result is that the rear polarizer plate absorbs the light, and a dark spot now appears on the light background of the rear polarizer. Cur-

rent technology employs color segments added with back-lighting for large instrument cluster/panel displays, although often the panel clock will not use any color. It will appear as simply a black and white color.

Current colors in use by various manufacturers depend upon the model of vehicle. Ford, for example, employs what is known as Ford signal green for most of its vehicles. LCD technology is used on the recent Ford Taurus and Mercury Sable vehicles.

LCD instruments have greater functional options than mechanical gauges and are employed in Ford's fuel computer, which is just not available in any other form. Although in wide use, LED's have the disadvantage of being

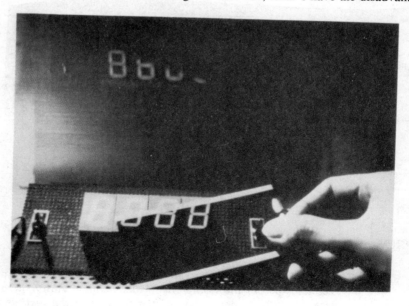

FIGURE 16-3 Use of light control film to improve both enhancement and reflection control of instrumentation. (*Courtesy of 3M Company, Minnesota, and Society of Automotive Engineers, Inc., copyright 1986*)

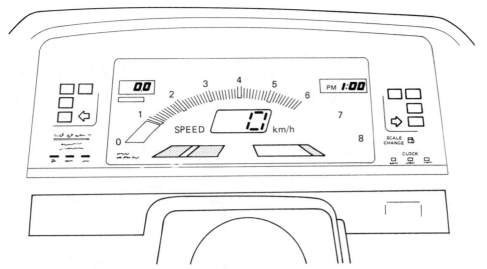

FIGURE 16-4 Typical LCD instrument panel. (*Courtesy of Toyota Motor Corporation*)

high consumers of power, and they also provide a relatively small lighting area. Many LED's have to be used to make an instrument cluster.

LCD's, on the other hand, have slow response time in cold ambient operating temperatures and have low contrast. It is also difficult to tune color on them. Their plus features are that they have low power consumption, exhibit good legibility under strong sunshine conditions, have the ability to display complex patterns, and have a simple circuitry, because they are driven by signal processing IC's (integrated circuits). In addition, they are compatible with CMOS LSI's, and their thin construction makes them highly suitable for automotive displays.

A CRT (cathode ray tube), on the other hand, can also display complex information in many colors, but a CRT requires a large space to accommodate it and a fairly high voltage to drive it. (For a description of a CRT instrument cluster, refer to the Buick Riviera CRT System section in this chapter.) Toyota used a similar system in its 1985 Soarer model car.

An example of a LCD instrument cluster is shown in Fig. 16-4. This cluster is divided into the following three distinct component parts:

1. The LCD assembly
2. The electronic circuit
3. Telltales and odometer

The instrument panel illustrated in Fig. 16-4 is shown in block diagram form in Fig. 16-5. Its major components include:

1. A signal processor to control the functions of the speedometer, the tachometer, twin trip meter, clock, fuel gauge, and water temperature gauge.

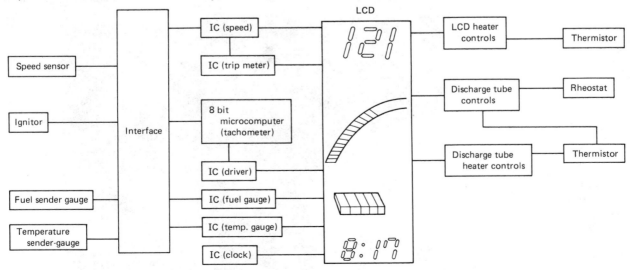

FIGURE 16-5 Block diagram of a typical LCD instrument panel. (*Reproduced from the Conference Proceedings, "Automotive Electronics," 1985, by permission of the Council of the Institution of Mechanical Engineers*)

2. A discharge tube controller.
3. A heater controller.
4. A LCD driver.

DISPLAY MODES OF LCD's

Some of the problems with electronic LCD instrument panels are the visibility of the display, electrical connections between the LCD panel and the circuit board, reliability under severe environmental conditions, suitable production processes for a large area display panel, and LCD operational temperature range. Major advantages of LCD's, however, are their low driving voltage, low power consumption, good legibility, and versatility in design.

In order to optimize LCD character visibility for the driver for both day and night operation, what is commonly known as the "transmissive mode" is widely used. This system employs a dark background, while the LCD number or letter is transmissive or optically clear. The color used for the letter or number can, of course, be chosen by the manufacturer. It might be clear (white), orange, green, red, yellow, etc. The two types of LCD's now in wide use in automotive instrument clusters are the following:

1. A full dot-matrix in multiplexing drive is widely used because conventional methods of manufacturing of positive/reflective mode similar to that now in use in consumer information devices can be employed. In addition, high density information in a large sized LCD cell is possible.
2. An active matrix (embedding or enclosing mass) LCD

in TFT (thin film transistor) drive. This type of LCD cannot display high density information in a large sized LCD cell.

In North America, one example of a LCD instrument panel is the one found on current model Chevrolet Corvettes. Figure 16-6 illustrates a number of these LCD instrument clusters. During manufacture, each cluster undergoes extensive hot and cold cycling tests in an environmental test chamber to ensure that it is acceptable for installation into the vehicle.

FLUORESCENT INDICATOR PANELS

The fluorescent indicator panel (FIP) is widely used in automotive electronic instrumentation displays because of its flexibility in graphic design. FIP displays are pleasing to the eye and are easy to read and interpret.

Latest advances in the use of FIP's now allow a three-dimensional design to be used; the design is based upon a concept known as a CIG FIP (chip-in-glass fluorescent indicator panel). Compared to the standard FIP, the CIG FIP has a simpler electronic control circuit and a smaller printed circuit board.

An example of the advantages of a CIG FIP over a standard FIP display can be seen on a typical one-line, 40 character illuminated display (letters and numbers). The conventional FIP printed circuit board dimensions typically measure 2.75 × 10 inches and contain 82 leads, while the same instrumentation layout using a CIG FIP measures only 2 × 10 inches and contains only 18 leads.

FIGURE 16-6 Chevrolet Corvette LCD (liquid crystal display) instrument cluster on test. *(Courtesy of AC Spark Plug Div. of GMC, Flint, MI.)*

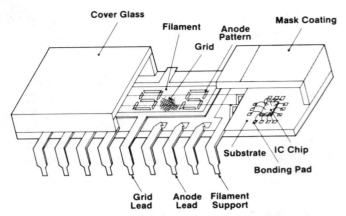

FIGURE 16-7 CIG FIP (chip-in-glass fluorescent indicator panel) structural arrangement. (*Courtesy of Society of Automotive Engineers, Inc., copyright 1986*)

Figure 16-7 illustrates a chip-in-glass FIP (CIG FIP) which employs integrated circuit (IC) chips internally mounted on the glass substrate through a process known as die-bonding or wire bonding technology.

An operational block diagram of the CIG FIP, with its IC's wired directly to the anode and grid electrodes inside the package, is shown in Fig. 16-8. The display numbers/letters are controlled by a serial signal from the on-board vehicle computer. In the not too distant future, indications are that even the microcomputer will be inside the FIP

structure, and the display information will communicate directly with the vehicle's own main computer.

Three methods employed with the CIG FIP to obtain the three-dimensional appearance of letters/numbers are in the selection of colors (phosphor material) used, through aperture variation, and also through a combination of colored filters. To obtain a particular color on the display panel, a combination of filter materials is printed on the inside or outside surface of the glass package.

When current is applied to the grid, the phosphor-coated numbers/letters emit light. The light output from the FIP can be filtered to any color through the use of filters placed over the phosphor. Multicolored instrument panels use five, six, seven, or eight phosphor materials printed on the segment anodes, or have various filters printed on the glass surface of the CIG FIP structure.

Typical colors now in use on automotive digital instrument panels are red, orange, amber, yellow, yellow green, blue green, blue, and sky blue. One or more of these colors are directly attainable through phosphor selection and filtering.

One of the most widely-used phosphors is zinc-oxide-zinc (ZnO:Zn), which produces the standard blue-green color so prevalent in many electronics components. It is the most efficient phosphor and has a wide spectral output. As a result, it is easily filterable from blue to red.

The FIP is one of the best methods for producing a first-class flat light source for backlighting a LCD (liquid crystal display). White light can be generated by a bar segment

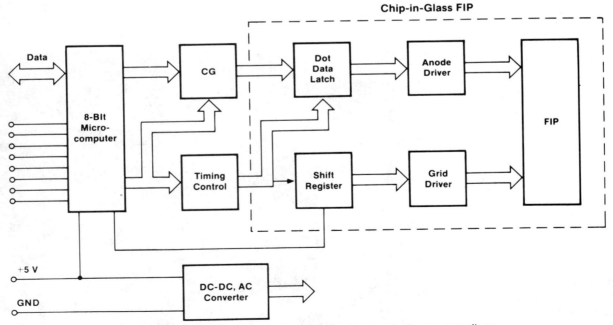

FIGURE 16-8 CIG FIP (chip-in-glass fluorescent indicator panel) operational block diagram. (*Courtesy of Society of Automotive Engineers, Inc., copyright 1986*)

FIGURE 16-9 Chevrolet Cavalier Special Z-24 VFD (vacuum fluorescent display) instrument cluster. (*Courtesy of AC Spark Plug Div. of GMC, Flint, MI.*)

anode printed with closely spaced and alternating blue, green, and red phosphors; and then, by employing various filters, various colors can be produced.

Two examples of VFD (vacuum fluorescent display) instrument panel clusters are illustrated. See Fig. 16-9 for the VFD on the Chevrolet Cavalier Special Edition Z-24, and Fig. 16-10 for the one on the 1986 Oldsmobile 98.

Regardless of the type of display used, the digital instrument cluster, also referred to as the digital instrument meter, receives signals from various sensors and converts these signals into a graphic display to inform the driver of such things as:

1. Vehicle speed
2. Engine rpm
3. Oil pressure
4. Coolant temperature
5. Alternator charging rate
6. Fuel level
7. Trip time
8. Turbocharger boost

In order for this information to be displayed graphically in digital form, it must first of all be processed by the onboard vehicle microcomputer and various IC (integrated circuit) devices. A typical example of how an instrumentation cluster with its various sensors, processing, and display data actually functions is illustrated in Fig. 16-11.

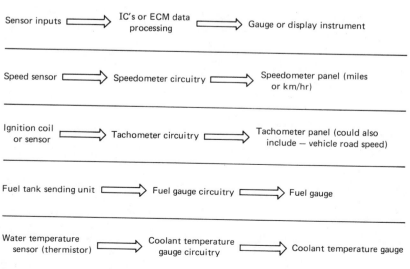

FIGURE 16-10 Oldsmobile 98 VFD (Vacuum Fluorescent Display) instrument cluster. (*Courtesy of AC Spark Plug Div. of GMC, Flint. MI.*)

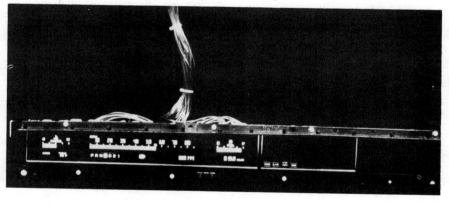

Sensor inputs ⟹ IC's or ECM data processing ⟹ Gauge or display instrument

Speed sensor ⟹ Speedometer circuitry ⟹ Speedometer panel (miles or km/hr)

Ignition coil or sensor ⟹ Tachometer circuitry ⟹ Tachometer panel (could also include — vehicle road speed)

Fuel tank sending unit ⟹ Fuel gauge circuitry ⟹ Fuel gauge

Water temperature sensor (thermistor) ⟹ Coolant temperature gauge circuitry ⟹ Coolant temperature gauge

FIGURE 16-11 Block diagram of a typical instrument panel arrangement using a digital readout and monitoring the vehicle speed, engine rpm, fuel level in the tank, and coolant temperature.

IPC

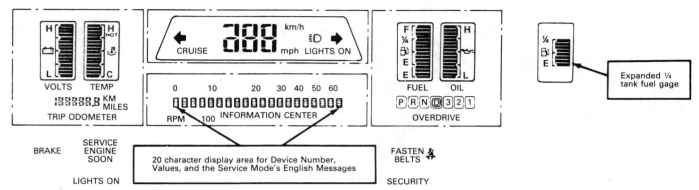

FIGURE 16-12 Location of four bar-graph type gauges on the vehicle instrument panel cluster. (*Courtesy of Oldsmobile Div. of General Motors Corporation*)

BAR GRAPH INSTRUMENTS

In addition to the use of VFD (vacuum fluorescent display) electronic instrument clusters, vehicle information is displayed by a variety of indicators which includes digital and bar-graph type indicator lights. One example of the use of bar-graph type warning gauges in a vehicle is that used by both Oldsmobile and Toyota in a number of their car models. In the Oldsmobile Toronado, mounted on the in-strument cluster, there are two bar graph gauges to the left, and two to the right of the digital speedometer on the panel (Fig. 16-12).

Figure 16-13 illustrates these bar-graph type gauges, which include information on voltage charge (battery), engine coolant temperature, engine oil pressure, and fuel level remaining in the tank. Below the symbols for these warning gauges on the illustration is an enlargement of the bar-graph type gauge. Note that a 16-segment display is used on each

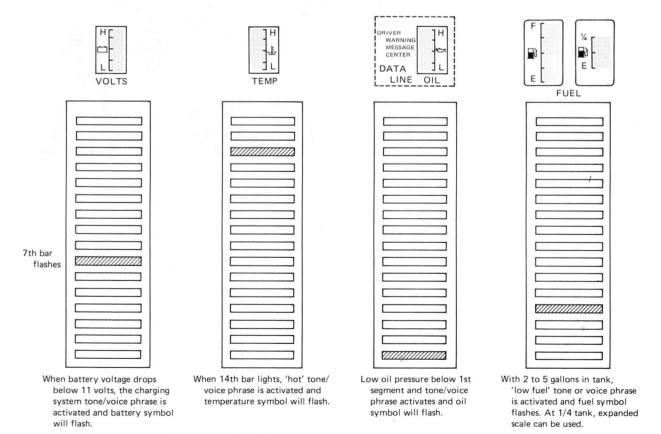

FIGURE 16-13 Bar-graph type gauges and their function.

bar. These bar-graph type gauges are arranged as follows in the Oldsmobile Toronado:

1. When the battery voltage drops below 11 volts, which corresponds to the 7th bar segment lighting up, the "charging system" tone or voice phrase will activate, and the battery symbol will flash to warn the driver of a low charging condition.

2. When the engine overheats, the 14th bar segment will illuminate, and the "hot" tone or voice phrase will be activated along with the temperature symbol flashing to warn the operator of a problem condition.

3. When engine oil pressure drops below the level of the first bar segment, the "low oil pressure" tone or voice phrase will activate, and the oil symbol will flash to warn the operator of a problem.

4. When the quantity of fuel in the tank drops below the

¼ tank level, and with between 2 and 5 gallons remaining, the "low fuel" tone or voice phrase will be activated, as well as the flashing fuel symbol. In addition, a fuel "gauge scale" button can be pushed, which allows an expanded ¼ tank scale to be read for a ten-second period.

Toyota also uses this bar-graph type gauge concept in a number of its passenger cars.

In both the Oldsmobile and Toyota vehicles, the fuel tank float assembly construction for the digital unit is similar to that for an "analog type" of instrument. The sequence of operational events, however, that occurs when the fuel level in the tank drops below the ¼ tank zone is listed below. The digital instrument system uses bar-graph type gauges.

Trigger Unit	*Resultant Action*
1. Fuel tank float/sending unit receives a voltage from the on-board computer (BCM).	Voltage applied to sending unit is divided, and approximately 2.5v is sent to the A/D (analog/digital) converter in the BCM (body control module — Oldsmobile).
2. Within the BCM, the following operations take place:	
(a) Fuel tank float level sending unit voltage is converted from an analog to a digital value.	A/D converter converts the voltage signal into a numbered pulse signal that corresponds to about 128 pulses.
(b) Within the CPU (central processing unit) of the BCM, the ALU (arithmetic logic unit) computes these pulse counts; for example, 128 counts.	Due to fuel slosh in a moving vehicle, an average pulse count is computed over a time period of several minutes. A neutral value is equal to 128 counts (no change) or an average value.
(c) Within the BCM temporary memory storage register, the new average value pulse count is compared and inserted into storage if it differs from the previous average value.	The 128 pulse counts is compared with the previous average reading of say 144 counts.
(d) Within the BCM CPU control section, the operation decoder will determine, from the 128 pulse counts, how many bar graph segments will be illuminated.	The CPU decoder uses a look-up table, equates that 128 pulses is equal to a given volume of fuel remaining in the tank, and sends out a voltage signal to the bar graph segments.
(e) BCM decoder relays the desired information for the fuel level gauge on the instrument panel.	The required number of bar graph segments are illuminated.

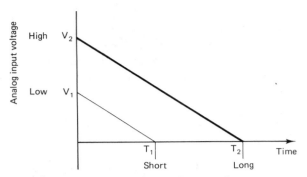

FIGURE 16-14 Analog voltage pulse versus time.

The procedure described above for the operation of the fuel level bar-graph type gauge is further clarified in Figs. 16-14 and 16-15. Since the fuel level gauge outputs an analog type signal, it is changed into digital format through the A/D (analog/digital) converter within the computer, so that the computer can process the information. (This basic system of analog to digital was discussed earlier; for example, see Figs. 2-11 and 2-12, and also Fig. 3-8.) There is more than one way in which these analog signals can be converted into digital signals. The method used for the digital fuel gauge is illustrated in Fig. 16-14. Here the analog input voltage V1 and V2 is attenuated (reduced in intensity, force, amount, or value by artificial shaping) at a constant rate by special circuitry within the computer, with the length of time T1 and T2 reaching zero volts being proportional to the actual input voltage.

Refer to Fig. 16-14. At the same time that the analog input voltage is being input to the computer A/D converter, a pulsed signal is generated within the computer from another special circuit that is in direct conjunction with the input voltage attenuation; therefore, the number of pulses is noted by the counter circuit until the input voltage reaches zero. The fewer the voltage pulses, the shorter the duration

Segment number	Temperature	
	°F	°C
10	Over 248	120
9	239-248	115-120
8	230-239	110-115
7	221-230	105-110
6	185-221	85-105
5	158-185	70-85
4	149-158	65-70
3	140-149	60-65
2	122-140	50-60
1	Below 122	50

FIGURE 16-16 Bar-graph type coolant temperature scale readout and equivalent temperature readings.

of the digital signals; while the greater the pulses, the longer the digital signals will be. (See Fig. 16-15).

The engine coolant temperature bar-graph type scale is similar to that for the fuel level gauge just described. The difference between the two is that a sensor probe (thermistor, thermometer/resistor) is located in the water jacket of the cylinder head. The resistance of the sensor changes in relation to the temperature of the coolant, which is reflected by successive segment bars lighting up as per the temperature scale design of the instrument/vehicle manufacturer.

Figure 16-16 illustrates one example of a coolant temperature bar-graph type gauge used on Toyota vehicles with a 10-segment bar graph design. As with the Oldsmobile bar graph system (Fig. 16-13), this system triggers a tone/voice control module and flashing light system to warn the driver of an overheating condition in the engine.

DIGITAL SPEEDOMETER OPERATION

The input signal for an electronic digital-type speedometer can either be through conventional cable drive from the transmission output shaft, or alternately, a permanent magnet type sensor, (Fig. 4-46) can be used to output a pulsed voltage signal to an analog/digital converter within the onboard computer.

The vehicle speed sensor shown in Fig. 18-5 is located at the rear of the transmission, with the sensor sending electrical pulses to the BCM (body computer module) at the rate of 4000 pulses per mile in the 1986 Oldsmobile Toronado, for example. The BCM buffers this signal and computes speed and total miles travelled. In this system, seasonal odometer data is stored in the nonvolatile memory

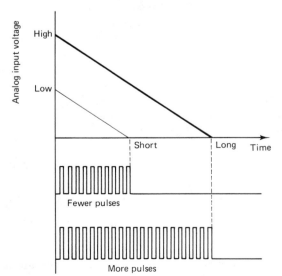

FIGURE 16-15 Analog voltage versus digital pulses.

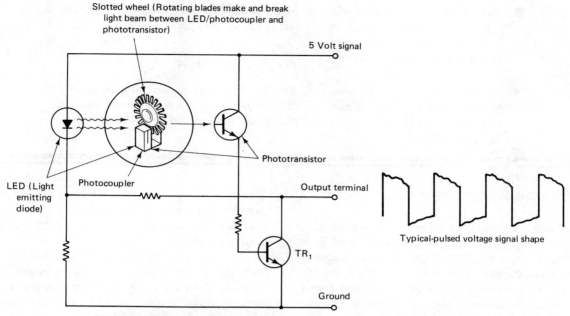

FIGURE 16-17 Example of a rotating vaned (fan) wheel type vehicle speed sensor.

of the computer, while trip odometer data is stored in the resettable keep-alive memory. When the ignition switch is in the run position, voltage is applied to the ignition-off input line of the BCM, which then sends data line information to the IPC (instrument panel cluster), where vehicle speed, total accumulated miles, and trip miles are displayed.

Other options for speedometer monitoring include a design similar to that shown in Fig. 2-34, which illustrates an optical-crankshaft-position type sensor, and a permanent magnet type sensor shown in Fig. 18-5.

If the conventional speedometer cable drive mechanism is employed, the cable can drive a small slotted wheel at its top end, which looks like a small fan assembly (Fig. 16-17). This type of arrangement is sometimes referred to as an interruptor disc (vaned wheel) and is similar to that found in some optical ignition systems.

In the system illustrated in Fig. 16-17, a small LED (light emitting diode) and a photoelectric cell or photocoupler allow the speed sensor to output pulsed electrical signals as the vaned wheel passes between the LED and the phototransistor.

The rate of these voltage pulses will vary in proportion to vehicle road speed, and they are relayed to the computer, where IC's and their associated circuitry perform the necessary analog to digital conversion. Electrical signals from the IC's are sent to the instrument cluster display in order to illuminate the necessary decimal segments.

In Fig. 16-17, the rotating vaned wheel will continually break the beam of light that passes between the LED and the phototransistor. The net result is that the phototransistor will alternately turn transistor TR1 on and off.

Transistor TR1 outputs a pulsed voltage signal to the computer, with its duration varying in direct relation to vehicle road speed.

Most digital instruments today are usually capable of displaying either mph or km/hour, simply by selecting the position of a speed switch on the instrument panel. Various digital-type speedometers are illustrated in Figs. 16-6, 16-9, and 16-10.

A description listing follows of what occurs when a vehicle's speed decreases because of a driver moving the throttle pedal, or the vehicle travelling up an incline.

Trigger Unit	*Response*
1. Vehicle slows from 55 mph (88.5 km) to 50 mph (80.5 km/hr).	Speedometer cable slows rotational speed of vaned wheel.
2. Decrease in pulsed signals from output terminal of photocoupler.	Computer IC's recognize a reduction in pulse signals.

3. The computer ALU (arithmetic logic unit) continually monitors (counts) and compares the input voltage pulses with the previous signal.

New pulse signal count is stored in memory if signal differs from previous one.

4. The decoder unit in the computer determines pulse signal variations. This decoder acts as an output interface.

The decoder relays positive voltage signals to the appropriate segments on the instrument display panel to allow them to light up.

DIGITAL TACHOMETER OPERATION

The digital tachometer registers engine speed on a bar-graph type panel which is constructed of a printed circuit board that includes a series of LED's (light emitting diodes) arranged in a semicircular fashion or in a straight line, depending upon the manufacturer's esthetic design layout. The tachometer is combined with the on-board computer system so that the number of voltage pulses per second can be continually monitored. These voltage pulses are generally output from either the ignition coil negative terminal or, alternately, from a crankshaft sensor.

The range of engine rpm monitored is coupled to the engine design speed; however, rpm's monitored generally fall between 5000 to 8000 rpm for most mass produced engines/vehicles.

Since the ignition system is tied to how often the spark plug fires, using the ignition coil as a sending unit is very common for a tachometer input signal; however, either a camshaft or crankshaft sensor can also be used to monitor engine speed.

The colors of the LED's are selected by the vehicle manufacturer, and these can be yellow, orange, green, red, blue, etc. Normally, only one color is used and illuminated up to the usual ''redline'' or maximum recommended speed for a particular engine. When an unsafe speed range is encountered, generally red LED's will illuminate to warn the driver of an unsafe engine speed condition.

The number of LED's employed in a digital-type tachometer layout is determined by the engine/vehicle manufacturer. How many LED's illuminate for a given speed range is also determined by the instrument designer. An example of how many LED's are illuminated for a given engine rpm is given below.

Engine RPM Range	Number of LED's Illuminated
0 – 250	Minimum of 1
250 – 300	3 illuminated
300 – 2000	1 additional LED illuminated for each 100 rpm beyond 300
2000 – 8000	1 additional LED illuminated for each 200

Therefore, if an engine is redlined at 6000 rpm, then it requires a total of 41 LED's to be illuminated to show this speed. Analog voltage signals from the negative side of the ignition coil are converted into digital pulses within the A/D (analog/digital) unit, which rectifies or squares-off the number of pulses, stores the calculated data, decodes this information, and then displays the data as an rpm by having the computer output a 5 volt signal to the corresponding number of tachometer LED's. This rectification inside the computer can best be listed as a sequence of steps. These are:

Trigger Unit	Response
1. Ignition coil or crankshaft sensor sends out a number of pulsed voltage signals per second.	Pulses sent to the computer.

2. Analog/digital converter within the computer changes voltage pulses to digital (squared off).

3. The computer decoder circuit determines if a change has occurred since the last average reading.

Computer ALU (arithmetic logic unit) calculates the time between the beginning of each pulse and stores an average length based upon 3 or 4 pulse-widths.

If a change to the average reading (voltage pulses) has taken place, the decoder signals additional or less LED's to illuminate by feeding a 5 volt reference voltage to show the new engine speed.

CRT (CATHODE RAY TUBE) INSTRUMENTATION

Graphic displays on automobile instrument panels have advanced well beyond the gimmicky stage and the early attempts to make them appear like video arcade centers.

One of the most advanced applications of electronic instrumentation can be found in the 1986 Buick Riviera, which uses a video display terminal in the form of a cathode ray tube that is very similar to the main viewing tube in your home TV set or computer system. The video terminal is part of the vehicle dash/instrument panel, and it is used to control the car's sound and climate control systems (heating, ventilation, and air conditioning) as well as the on-board trip computer.

The driver or the passenger can operate the systems by simply touching one of the symbols displayed on the CRT screen; therefore, the term ''touch technology'' is often used to describe this type of system. A similar system to that now being used by Buick was adopted by Toyota in their 1985 luxury model Soarer series passenger car, which is sold in the Japanese market only. This system is called the ''Toyota Electro Multivision.''

Although still in the early stages of adoption, the CRT display offers many advantages for use in automobiles and trucks. ''Touch input'' by the operator of the vehicle allows an easy interface with the on-board computer system, similar to the interface now available with some home computers. In addition, regardless of worldwide user language differences, the CRT touch technology concept can be easily adapted for use in different countries. Furthermore, the touch technology system provides a fast and easy method of accessing computer information without having to use a host of special instruments and tools.

Various examples of touch screen applications outside the automotive market that are well known are the Xerox 5700 laser printer, the Hewlett-Packard Touchscreen (formerly the HP 150) used both in office and home computers, as well as the touch machines at your local bank.

This same basic technology is now moving into the automotive market. Because of low volume production, the cost factor is still high at this time. However, with the potential for high volume production in the future, there should be significant cost reductions and a greater penetration of the automotive market as a result. Both the Buick and Toyota CRT systems are described below.

Touch Technology Basic Operation

Prior to looking at both the Buick and Toyota CRT touch technology systems, let's discuss the basic operational concept of such a system. Three main types of touch technology are presently available and used by a number of commercial manufacturers. These are:

1. The conductive membrane method
2. The capacitive method
3. The scanning infrared beam method

These three types of systems differ in the method employed to relay the human finger touch from the CRT screen to the on-board computer, which will then carry out the necessary functional command.

One method involves the use of two metallized mylar sheets with a grid of electrodes etched onto their respective surfaces, with one pattern running in what is commonly referred to as the X direction, and the other pattern running at right angles to the first, or in a Y direction. These two mylar sheets are then placed together in a sandwich fashion, with the respective X and Y electrodes physically separated by a simple air gap between them to prevent continuous contact.

When the operator applies light pressure to any spot on the CRT screen, the top mylar sheet deflects and causes a short between the X and Y electrodes at the contact point, thereby creating an electrical path back to the computer system. Since all of the grid coordinate (positions) lines are numbered, the computer is able to determine what information is being called up whenever any part of the CRT screen is touched.

A second type of touch screen is illustrated in Fig. 16-18 and is known as a ''resistive membrane system.'' With this system, a resistive coating is applied either to the display screen itself or on a glass implosion shield fitted to the display with a sheet of metallized embossed mylar placed over the glass. An air gap exists between the two layers,

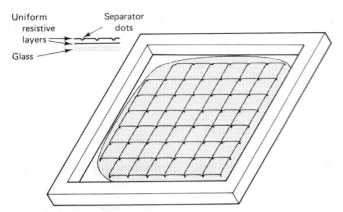

FIGURE 16-18 Resistive membrane touch screen arrangement. (*Courtesy of Society of Automotive Engineers Inc., copyright 1986*)

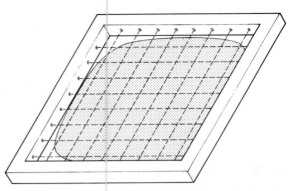

FIGURE 16-19 Scanning infrared touch screen arrangement. (*Courtesy of Society of Automotive Engineers, Inc., Copyright 1986*)

similar to the one referred to in the first type, to prevent continuous contact between the grid contacts. Again, similar to the conductive membrane type discussed above, there is an X and Y pattern. Voltage is then alternately applied to the glass surface of the screen.

When someone touches the soft mylar sheet, light pressure causes this sheet to contact the glass screen, where the two electrically conductive surfaces create a short circuit. As a result, both an X and a Y voltage is sent to the controller/computer. The computer is able to determine what information is being called up by using a voltage divider principle.

Membrane type systems used on CRT's are fairly inexpensive, but the mylar layer can be damaged by scratches or abrasion. It is also possible for the conductive surfaces either to wear or become oxidized over time. This action leads to dead spots that no longer respond to touch commands. Information is displayed with these systems through the use of liquid crystal or electroluminescence.

Capacitive systems, on the other hand, have a thin layer of neutral density dielectric electro-deposited over the face of the implosion shield, and their response to human touch tends to be much slower compared to other CRT systems.

The third type, or infrared system, is illustrated in Fig. 16-19. This system employs LED (light emitting diode) emitters and phototransistor detectors mounted on opposite sides of the display screen in an X and Y pattern similar to the other two types described.

Voltage pulses to the LED's produce a grid of infrared light beams in front of the display screen surface; therefore, touching the screen lightly with the human finger causes an obstruction to the path of light at the contact area, and the light beam does not reach its corresponding phototransistor detectors. The microcomputer is able to effectively determine what part of the screen was touched by constantly monitoring the small voltage output of the various phototransistors. The relevant information is then flashed on the screen's surface.

Of the three types of touch screen systems in use, the infrared style is the most rugged of them all, since it uses 100% solid-state electronic componentry, and since the optical devices are protected by an infrared transparent bezel within the display cabinet.

TOYOTA ELECTRO MULTIVISION INSTRUMENTATION SYSTEM

A major technical breakthough in automotive electronics occurred in 1985 when Toyota Motor Corporation decided to employ a color CRT (cathode ray tube) as the instrumentation display system on their upscale Soarer model vehicle, which is a luxury class passenger car available only in the Japanese market.

Although not widely used at this time, many industry executives insist that many more CRT systems will appear over the next few years in a number of automobiles. Figure 16-20 illustrates this CRT system and the location of its components in the Soarer model car. In addition, a block diagram of the system (Fig. 16-21) illustrates the various inputs to the computer from other monitored systems on the vehicle.

The CRT is installed into the instrument panel as shown

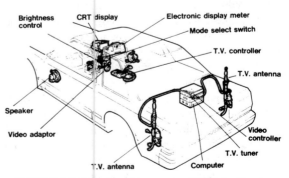

FIGURE 16-20 Arrangement of CRT (cathode ray tube) system components. (*Courtesy of Society of Automotive Engineers Inc., Copyright 1986*)

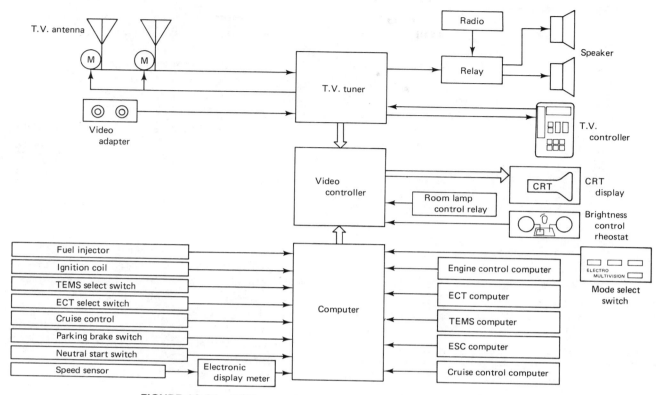

FIGURE 16-21   CRT operational block diagram. (*Courtesy of Society of Automotive Engineers, Inc., copyright 1986*)

in Fig. 16-22, with the CPU (central processing units) being mounted in the trunk or luggage compartment of the vehicle.

As well as serving as a vehicle interactive monitor system, the Toyota system CRT can also be used as a television set that activates when the ignition key is in the ACC (accessory) position. To prevent battery drain when using the CRT in the TV mode, the system is arranged so that the CRT shuts off automatically when:

1. The TV (CRT) has been operated for more than one hour with the ignition key in the ACC position,
2. The battery voltage has dropped to just below 11.7 volts; this action is necessary to ensure that the engine will, in fact, crank and start.

Before automatically turning itself off, the system displays a warning message to the driver/operator to start the engine and keep the battery from going dead. Should the engine not be started within 15 seconds of this warning message, then 10 seconds later the CRT will shut off automatically.

The Toyota CRT system is capable of three different informational displays, which are:

1. Colored computer graphics

2. Television viewing mode
3. Accessibility for diagnosing system faults and trouble codes

Warning messages will automatically be displayed on the CRT screen at any time a sensed and monitored system on the engine or vehicle fails.

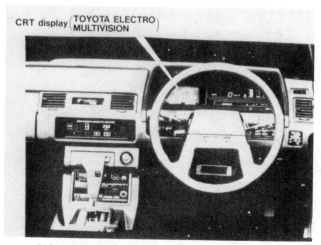

FIGURE 16-22   Front view of Toyota Soarer instrument panel. (*Courtesy of Society of Automotive Engineers, Inc., copyright 1986*)

BUICK RIVIERA CRT SYSTEM

A CRT system is used in the 1986 Buick Riviera luxury sedan, which is designated as the graphic control center or GCC. All types of information transmittal systems were considered by Buick for display on the CRT monitor including infrared, capacitance, accoustical, and transparent membrane. The type of system employed with Buick's CRT is of the transparent membrane style. The three types of touch technology systems in use were described earlier in this chapter.

The transparent membrane type of CRT system was selected by Buick over the IR (infrared light beam switch) because it is the easiest system for a driver to use. The driver simply places his or her finger on the screen, and then presses the surface. Prototype tests indicated that the membrane type switch activation system was superior to other types now in use.

The CRT touch screen uses a free format display as opposed to segmented displays. Figure 16-23 illustrates the three major subassemblies of the CRT display unit, which are the monitor, the front face assembly, and the necessary decoding electronics package. Figure 16-24 shows the CRT monitor with its protective case, electronic circuit boards, and necessary support brackets. The CRT monitor measures

5 inches diagonally and is 140 mm × 140 mm × 150 mm deep (5.5 inches × 5.5 inches × 5.9 inches) in overall dimensions, and it is situated within the vehicle instrument panel.

The front face assembly shown in Fig. 16-23 consists of a transparent membrane switch mounted in front of the monitor, with six selections possible, namely:

1. Climate control (heater, ventilation, air conditioning)
2. Summary
3. Radio/tape deck
4. Trip monitor
5. Diagnostic readout
6. Gauges

When a touch screen selection is made from the above list, a displayed page menu of information appears on the CRT screen. Examples of these various informational pages or menus, together with a number of available options, are illustrated in Fig. 16-25. For example, the vehicle gauge page graphics display shows both analog and digital readings for engine rpm, oil pressure, battery voltage, and coolant temperature.

If the driver touches the "summary" heading on the

CRT ASSEMBLY

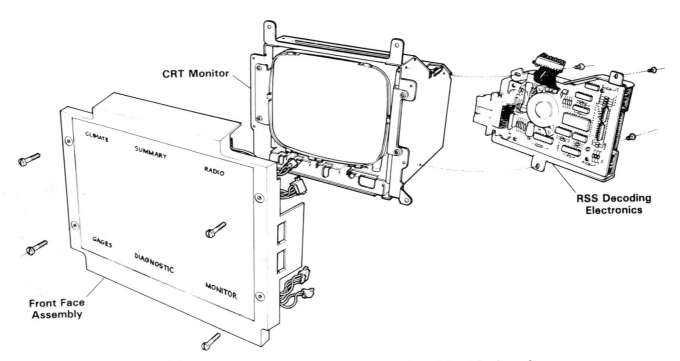

FIGURE 16-23 Buick Riviera CRT assembly. (*Copyright of Society of Automotive Engineers, Inc., copyright 1986*)

CRT MONITOR

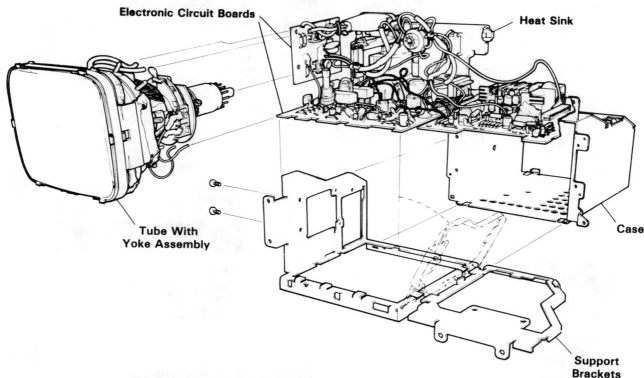

FIGURE 16-24 Buick Riviera CRT monitor arrangement. (*Courtesy of Society of Automotive Engineers, Inc., copyright 1986*)

screen, the computer will display all the primary controls and selective information from all access areas. The summary screen selection touch control is one of the most often used access areas of the system, since the primary controls page shows those items that are required for the normal operation of driving the vehicle.

In order to accommodate continuous product improvements, the CRT display is completely software driven; therefore, any changes required to the system in the future can be done simply by reprogramming the CRT controller. The vehicle electrical system is used to interface with the CRT system via a universal asynchronous receiver transmitter (UART) data link. The CRT is fully integrated with the vehicle electrical system and therefore depends upon the networked logic system for its successful operation. The vehicle's central logic processing module (computer) interfaces (works in harmony with) other modules of the vehicle electrical system via the UART data link.

Various engine and vehicle sensors are used to monitor the numerous systems. Sensor signals are fed either to the ECM (electronic engine control module) or the BCM (body control module). The CRT needs the BCM to display the

diagnostics and vehicle status information. (For more information on both the ECM and BCM, refer to Chapter 7.)

The CRT system is activated when the vehicle driver's door handle is operated by someone entering the vehicle. The CRT monitor receives a voltage signal from the microprocessor controller, which starts a preheat mode of the CRT's filament. This action causes the CRT to enter its "wake-up" or turn-on mode. By the time the driver has entered the car and closed the door, both the instrument cluster and the CRT monitor have been triggered into operation. The controller triggers a relay within the CRT monitor, and the words, *Riviera by Buick,* are displayed on the screen. By the time that the engine has been started, the CRT is ready to deliver selected information by activation of the touch control buttons on the outer periphery of the screen.

The use of a central logic controller (computer) allows wider utilization of the microprocessors, since individual processors are not necessary for every individual feature on the vehicle. The CRT controller employs a master (Motorola 6803 unit) and slave microprocessor (Motorola 6801 unit) system that is capable of addressing a total of 50K of

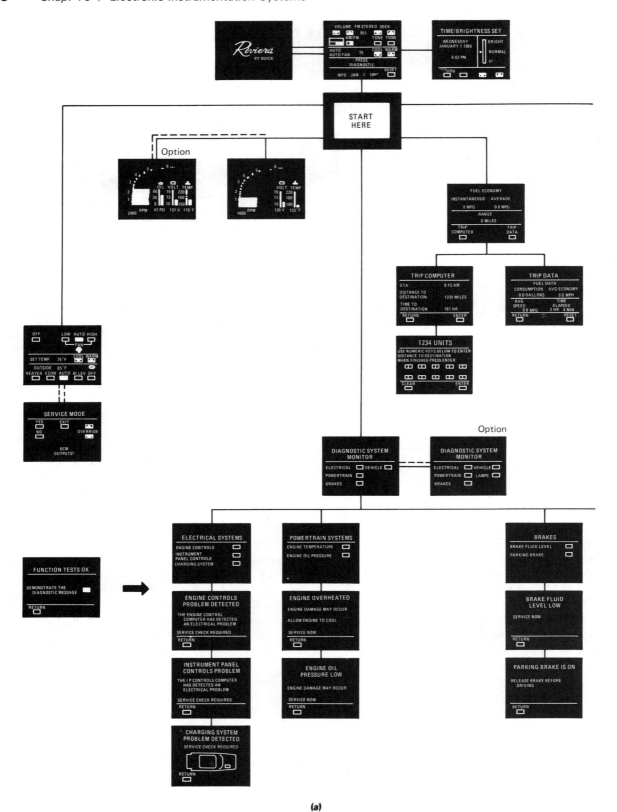

(a)

FIGURE 16-25 1986 Buick Riviera graphic control center display pages. (*Courtesy of Society of Automotive Engineers, Inc., copyright 1986*)

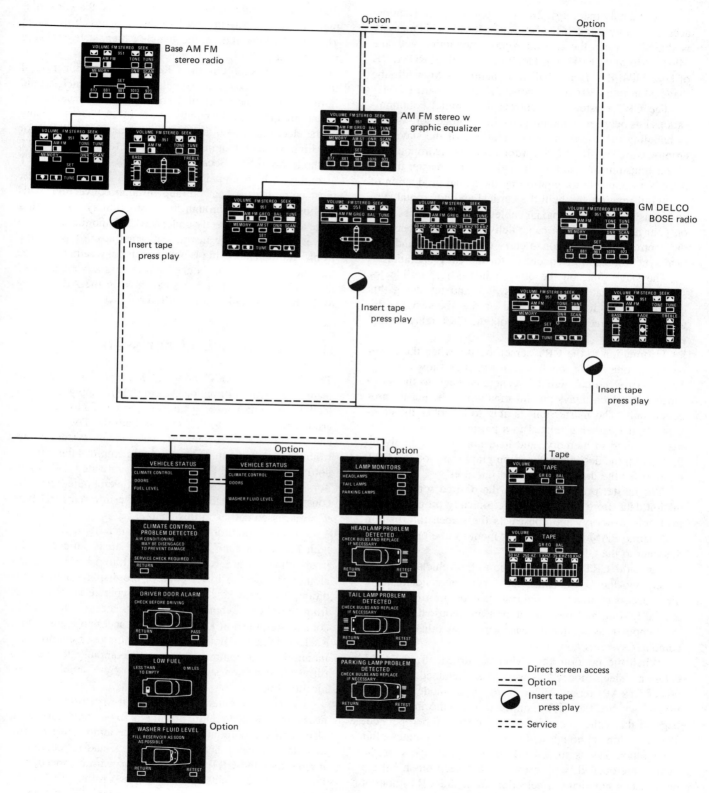

(b)

ROM (read only memory), 2K of keep-alive RAM (random access memory), and 16K of dynamic RAM. This memory is shared between the two microprocessor units, with the Master Motorola 6803 unit handling 48K of EPROM, 2K of keep-alive RAM, and 16K of dynamic RAM, while the Slave Motorola 6801 unit handles 2K of on-board ROM.

The CRT master unit controls the parallel communications bus between it and the slave microprocessor, as well as handling the communications required of the slave microprocessor on the UART (universal asynchronous receiver transmitter) data bus. In addition, the master unit is directly responsible for controlling the actual production of video information and both the vertical and horizontal synchronous pulses. Two coaxial cables, similar to those used on your home TV set for cable delivery, are used between the controller and monitor to carry the horizontal and vertical synchronization frequencies for the CRT operation.

The slave unit, on the other hand, is responsible for scanning the matrix membrane switch and retrieving this data when the driver closes one of the six switches by touching the screen. It also controls the CRT relay on and off function.

Information to the CRT screen occurs when the driver depresses one of the touch screen switches shown in Fig. 16-23. An electrical signal is generated back to the slave processor, which relays this information to the master processor unit. The master unit is able to decipher the command signal as being related to a particular page of information stored in memory, and it responds accordingly by flashing up the desired information graphically on the CRT monitor for the driver to read and interpret.

The master processor obtains the desired screen information/data from EPROM (electronically-programmable read only memory) and constructs the screen information in dynamic RAM (random access memory) before flashing this data to the CRT monitor.

Since the CRT system is linked to the vehicle electrical system via the UART link, the service technician has a direct access route into stored trouble code information. No special tooling and instrumentation are required to access the computer, as is often the case with many other on-board computer systems now in use.

When the ignition key switch is turned off, the CRT enters a "sleep mode," as well as a "retained accessory power" (RAP) mode. When in the RAP mode, the controller switches the CRT monitor to the radio information page so that either the radio or tape deck can be operated. This function, although active for up to 10 minutes after the ignition key is turned off, or until the doors of the vehicle are opened, will resort to the "sleep mode" if the driver does not make a selection from the CRT monitor within 30 seconds. The driver then has to "wake-up" the monitor by touching the radio information page hard switch.

During this standby state of selection, only the CRT filament is kept warm in order to allow access for instant graphics. By these means, the vehicle battery state of charge is maintained.

The power supply to the CRT monitor is a function of the state of charge of the vehicle battery, which would normally be in the range of 13.5 d.c. volts. However, internal circuitry transforms this power to 24 VDC for many of the electronic functions, and as high as 13,000 VDC for the high voltage requirements needed to drive the CRT (cathode ray tube). Because of this high voltage the CRT assembly, which contains in excess of 250 components, must be cooled of heat buildup through convection. This cooling is achieved through the ventilation system, with a large air flow hole directly under the CRT monitor and with louvers located on the instrument panel at the top and the front. Additional cooling is obtained in hot weather anytime that the air conditioner is on, by directing a percentage of this cool air flow through a small hole in the AC ducting to the rear heat sink of the CRT monitor.

LINCOLN CONTINENTAL CRT SYSTEM

The 1985 ½ Lincoln Continental Mark V11 Comtech car features a driver information system (DIS) employing a CRT (cathode ray tube) based system consisting of a touch screen arrangement similar to that used in both the Toyota Soarer and the Buick Riviera vehicles. The Lincoln system differs from the Buick one in that the Lincoln employs the infrared dot matrix LED (light emitting diode) activated CRT monitor and the Buick uses the transparent membrane type. The construction and basic operation of the infrared LED type was discussed earlier in this chapter.

The CRT monitor on the Lincoln is a 3" × 6" screen, with 12 "touch zone" or "soft key" areas defined by the intersections of a 3 × 4 matrix of infrared LED's located along one side and lower edge of the display area. In addition, 10 "hard keys," which are separate switch inputs from the CRT keyboard, are used to access a feature; in comparison, the soft keys are used to access options within a selected feature. Both the soft and hard key actuations are monitored and communicated by a computer to the DIS (driver information system) computer by a serial communication link.

The DIS computer is responsible for performing all the necessary selected feature arithmetic logic computations. It also maintains communication with the temperature control module (automatic heating, ventilation, and air conditioning) system and CRT monitor, sensor warning speed, fuel flow, fuel level inputs, providing video information to the CRT monitor, as well as providing "keep alive memory" features.

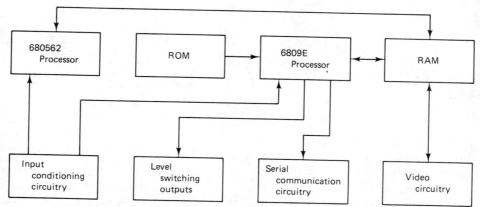

FIGURE 16-26 Lincoln Continental driver information system layout.
(*Courtesy of Society of Automotive Engineers, Inc., copyright 1986*)

The CRT monitor contains a microcomputer to determine when a LED light beam intersection (X and Y) has been broken; this action serves as a command to the microcomputer to provide the information requested. Major features of the CRT DIS soft key selection are:

1. Automatic temperature control (heating, ventilation, and air conditioning).
2. Readout of fuel used, distance-to-empty, as well as instantaneous and average fuel economy.
3. Readout of trip odometer, average speed, distance-to-destination, ETA (estimated time of arrival), and total trip time.
4. Readout of time features, such as the time, day, date, year, elapsed time, and time alarm.
5. Readout of a calendar feature which will display any month from January 1900 to December 2099.
6. Readout of vehicle speed alarm control, service reminder, reset control, trunk ajar warning enable/disable control, and tone enable/disable control.
7. Vehicle information, such as scheduled maintenance, capacities, and special features.
8. System checkout displays, such as oil pressure, oil level, engine temperature, charge system, suspension system, low beam headlamps, tail lamps, brakelamps, distance-to-empty, doors, trunk, service reminder, and windshield washer fluid level.
9. English/metric control of displayed features.
10. Standby screen feature to provide a visually-quiet screen if desired.
11. Reformattable displays that allow for animated information which can be used for warnings or the display of information graphically as well as digitally.

Figure 16-26 illustrates in block diagram form the basic layout of the components that make up the DIS (driver information system). The 6805G2 Motorola processor and CMOS RAM keep track of real time as well as rapid input pulse counting. The remainder of the components are non-active until the ignition key switch is turned on.

In order to handle additional processing power, a 6809E Motorola processor was added to the system. Communication between the CPU's occurs by passing information in RAM using direct memory access. Controlled access is accomplished by the 6805G2 processor periodically stopping the 6809E unit. When a pending problem condition occurs in the engine or vehicle sensor monitored systems, two priorities for warning items include "intermittent" and "singular" warnings flashed onto the CRT screen.

Intermittent warnings are displayed about once per minute and indicate a potential serious operating condition. These warnings include the following:

1. Charging system failure
2. Suspension failure
3. Oil pressure loss
4. Coolant temperature problem
5. Speed alarm
6. Door ajar
7. Trunk ajar

NOTE: Soft key functions are disabled during the display of a warning message.

Singular warnings, which are less serious conditions, are displayed only once until the engine is restarted. These warnings include the following:

1. Low windshield washer fluid level
2. Low headlight beams out

3. Tail lamps out
4. Brakelamps out
5. Low oil level
6. Service reminder time alarm
7. Low fuel tank level
8. Destination reached alarm

The serial communication section of the DIS (driver information system) consists of a master/slave arrangement that is similar in some respect to the Buick Riviera system. This arrangement is illustrated in Fig. 16-27. The DIS (master) transmits commands to the two system slaves, which are the temperature controller and switch monitor.

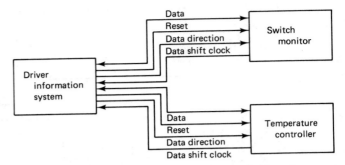

FIGURE 16-27 Lincoln Continental driver information system serial interface. (*Courtesy of Society of Automotive Engineers, Inc., copyright 1986*)

CHAPTER 17

◆

Electronic Climate Control Systems

BASIC AUTOMATIC HEATING SYSTEM OPERATION

A number of well-known makes of upscale passenger cars commonly employ a system that automatically controls the heating, ventilation, and air conditioning systems within the passenger compartment. These systems are controlled through either an ECU/ECM or a BCM (body control module) that receives input signals from switches on the instrument panel as well as a number of sensors. The BCM interfaces with the ECM (electronic control module), which receives inputs from a variety of engine sensors to control the fuel-injection system. On some vehicles, the ECM and BCM regulate the ignition and fuel control systems together. The number of sensors used on a vehicle is dependent upon the degree of automatic control desired, such as for heating, ventilation, or air conditioning.

If automatic temperature control of only the heating system is required, then basically three sensors are employed: namely, one sensor to determine the engine coolant temperature; one for monitoring the interior temperature of the passenger compartment; and one to monitor the temperature of the discharge air (warm) from the in-car heater. For additional control of an air conditioning system, both a low and high side refrigerant temperature sensor are used, as well as a sunload sensor, particularly in warm climates.

The basic automatic electronic control system is illustrated in Fig. 17-1. A complete heating, ventilation, and air conditioning system for an Oldsmobile Toronado passenger car is described later in this chapter. In the basic automatic heating system shown in Fig. 17-1, two sensors are employed. These are Item 3 for the car interior unit and Item 7, which is the actual blower heater discharge temperature sensor. In addition, a solenoid valve that controls the engine coolant flow through the heat exchanger core is illustrated in Fig. 17-2. This solenoid valve is identified as Item 4 in Fig. 17-1.

In order to achieve automatic control of the heating system, an electronic control unit is required which receives voltage signals from both of the in-car sensors (Items 3 and 7 in Fig. 17-1). A diagrammatic layout of the electronic control unit is illustrated in Fig. 17-3.

Within the electronic control unit is a regulated power supply, an evaluation network and amplifier, a sawtooth voltage generator and comparator, a driver and output stage, and a desired temperature potentiometer (variable resistor) with a limit switch.

Operation

Both in-car temperature sensors function as thermistors, which are devices that change their resistance values as temperature changes. An increase in temperature causes a resistance decrease, while a temperature decrease results in a resistance increase.

NOTE: For more detailed information on a thermistor, refer to Chapter 4 in this book dealing with types and operation of various sensor units.

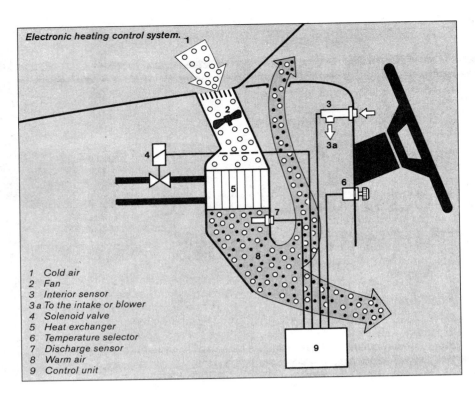

1 Cold air
2 Fan
3 Interior sensor
3a To the intake or blower
4 Solenoid valve
5 Heat exchanger
6 Temperature selector
7 Discharge sensor
8 Warm air
9 Control unit

FIGURE 17-1 Basic layout of an electronically controlled heating system. (*Courtesy of Robert Bosch Corporation*)

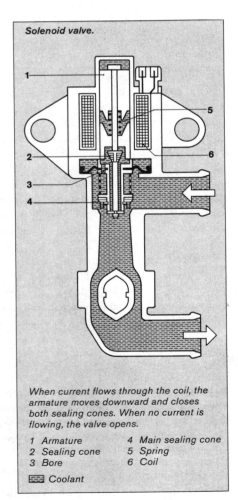

Solenoid valve.

When current flows through the coil, the armature moves downward and closes both sealing cones. When no current is flowing, the valve opens.

1 Armature   4 Main sealing cone
2 Sealing cone   5 Spring
3 Bore   6 Coil
▨ Coolant

FIGURE 17-2 Coolant solenoid valve. (*Courtesy of Robert Bosch Corporation*)

These varying resistances cause a voltage signal to be sensed at the electronic controller evaluation network. The strength of the signal is based upon the actual difference of the in-car temperature and the warm air leaving the heater outlet. The desired in-car temperature is selected by the driver/passenger by rotating either a temperature selector switch or dial on the vehicle instrument panel. This adjustment is basically a potentiometer (variable resistance) adjustment.

An electrically-operated solenoid valve (see Fig. 17-2) in the engine coolant system controls the flow of hot water to the heater core and thus the degree of heat blown into the passenger compartment.

The voltage signals relayed to the electronic control unit pass through what is known as an "evaluation network/amplifier," in which the driver-selected in-car temperature signal from the potentiometer is added to the two sensor signals. (See Fig. 17-3.) In the comparator of the electronic control unit, these varying voltage signals are compared to the predetermined reference signal provided by the saw-tooth voltage generator.

These differing voltages cause a voltage pulse to be created within the driver unit of the ECU. There, the output stage of the system switches this small current flow (approximately 1 ampere) that is required to drive the coolant flow solenoid valve open and closed at predetermined time intervals. On one vehicle, this time interval may possibly be 4 seconds; on others, it may be shorter or longer. This pulsing current, which opens and closes the valve automatically, controls the flow rate of hot coolant through the heater core and therefore is able to maintain a set interior temperature within the passenger compartment. Turning the selector switch completely one way results in the heater

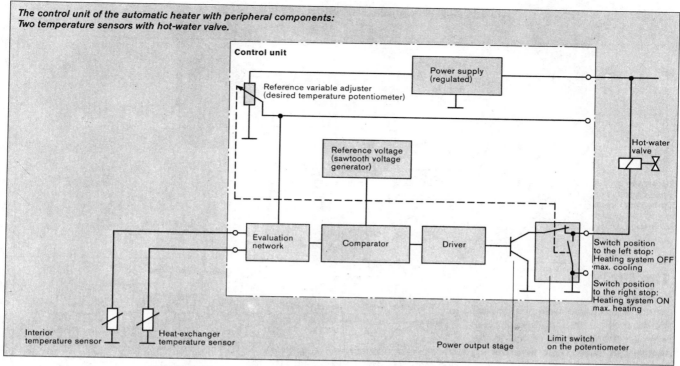

FIGURE 17-3 Automatically controlled heater control unit operational diagram. (*Courtesy of Robert Bosch Corporation*)

being turned off, while turning it in the other direction results in the heater producing its maximum heating value.

OLDSMOBILE ELECTRONIC CLIMATE CONTROL SYSTEM

A number of upscale model passenger cars employ a fully-automated electronic climate control system, which controls not only the in-car temperature when heating is desired in cold weather, but also a preselected cool temperature in hot weather.

Such a system is employed on many General Motors Corporation cars, as well as those manufactured by Ford and Chrysler. In addition, many of the imported manufac-

turers' models, such as Mercedes-Benz, BMW, and Audi, just to name a few, also use a similar type of system.

One such example of this ECC (electronic comfort control) or climate control system is discussed and illustrated below and is typical of the systems in use on Oldsmobile upscale models, such as the Toronado. This system is similar to those in use on the Cadillac and Buick cars, as well as on the top-of-the-line models in other General Motors Corporation divisions.

The electronic comfort control panel for the Oldsmobile Toronado, with its various buttons, is shown in Fig. 17-4, while its underhood components are shown in Fig. 17-5.

The ECC system automatically regulates and controls both the heating and air conditioning system within one degree increments (F° or C° is optional) up or down each

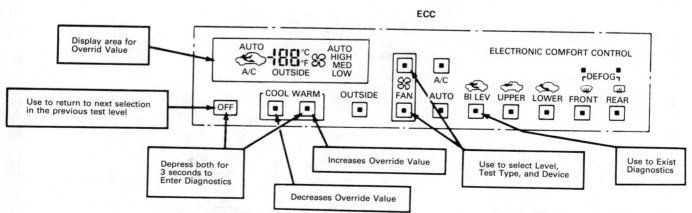

FIGURE 17-4 ECC (electronic comfort control panel). (*Courtesy of Oldsmobile Div. of GMC*)

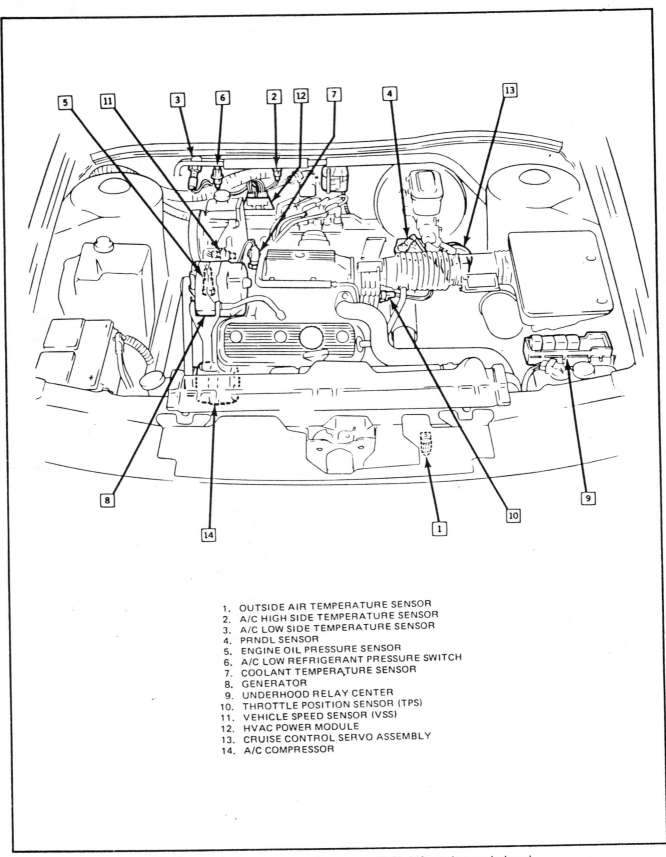

FIGURE 17-5 Component reference — 3.8L V6 engine underhood view. (*Courtesy of Oldsmobile Div. of GMC*)

1. OUTSIDE AIR TEMPERATURE SENSOR
2. A/C HIGH SIDE TEMPERATURE SENSOR
3. A/C LOW SIDE TEMPERATURE SENSOR
4. PRNDL SENSOR
5. ENGINE OIL PRESSURE SENSOR
6. A/C LOW REFRIGERANT PRESSURE SWITCH
7. COOLANT TEMPERATURE SENSOR
8. GENERATOR
9. UNDERHOOD RELAY CENTER
10. THROTTLE POSITION SENSOR (TPS)
11. VEHICLE SPEED SENSOR (VSS)
12. HVAC POWER MODULE
13. CRUISE CONTROL SERVO ASSEMBLY
14. A/C COMPRESSOR

time that the cool or warm ECC buttons are pushed. The range of set temperatures is within a scale of 60° to 90°F or 15.5° to 32°C, which represents the maximum cooling and heating values respectively of the system. The one degree increment settings range from 65° to 85°F (18° to 29°C), and the increase or decrease in temperature setting from 85° to 90°F, or from 65° to 60°F, is made in one jump. Any selected temperature range is illuminated in the VF (vacuum fluorescent) display of the ECC panel. Temperature within the passenger compartment is maintained by varying the position of an air mix door shown as Item 1 in Fig. 17-11. The position of this door is controlled by a signal from the BCM which in turn monitors system requirements based upon the various signals it receives from the ECC panel push buttons and system sensors. The air mix door controls the blend of evaporator core and heater core air being fed into the passenger compartment. The main components that make up the complete ECC system are:

1. BCM (body control module)
2. ECM (engine control module)
3. HVAC (heating, ventilation, and air conditioning) module
4. HVAC programmer
5. HVAC power module
6. Refrigeration system
7. Six temperature sensors

For information on the BCM and ECM modules, refer to Chapter 7.

SENSORS

The six temperature sensors used in the system are monitored by the BCM at all times, and since they are basically of the thermistor design, their resistance decreases as they get hotter. Their functions are the following:

1. *In-Car Temperature Sensor*—This sensor (Item 2 in Fig. 17-6) is located under the center air conditioning outlet. In-car air drawn through an aspirator (Item 6) mounted on top of the HVAC module is designed to create a slight vacuum at one end of this aspirator, and air flows across this sensor (thermistor). The resistance of the sensor is sent to the BCM and is used in ECC calculations.

2. *Outside Temperature Sensor*—On the Oldsmobile Toronado, this sensor is located in a small protective housing at the immediate rear of the radiator grille, as is shown in Fig. 17-7. Because of the possibility of radiated heat from the engine compartment acting on

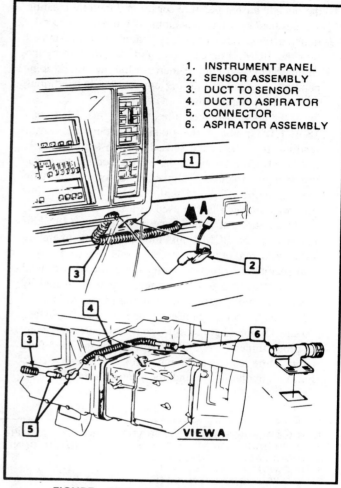

1. INSTRUMENT PANEL
2. SENSOR ASSEMBLY
3. DUCT TO SENSOR
4. DUCT TO ASPIRATOR
5. CONNECTOR
6. ASPIRATOR ASSEMBLY

VIEW A

FIGURE 17-6 In-car temperature sensor. (*Courtesy of Oldsmobile Div. of GMC*)

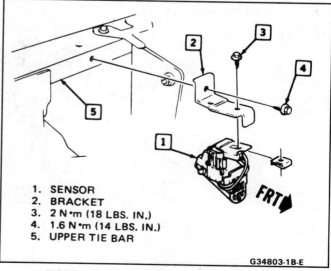

1. SENSOR
2. BRACKET
3. 2 N•m (18 LBS. IN.)
4. 1.6 N•m (14 LBS. IN.)
5. UPPER TIE BAR

G34803-1B-E

FIGURE 17-7 Outside air temperature sensor. (*Courtesy of Oldsmobile Div. of GMC*)

the outside air temperature sensor and thereby creating a false reading of actual ambient temperature conditions, a temperature memory feature is programmed into the BCM. For example, radiated heat from the engine block will tend to increase the underhood temperature, particularly during engine restart conditions after a short shutoff time.

If the coolant temperature of the engine is less than 18°F (10°C) above the outside temperature sensor reading, then the actual sensed outside temperature is displayed. Conversely, if the engine coolant temperature is higher than 18°F above the sensor reading, then the "memorized" BCM temperature of when the engine was operated last is used as a reference point.

In addition, at vehicle speeds of 20 mph (32 km/hr) or less, the BCM limits the displayed temperature value to a maximum increase of one degree F every 100 seconds in order to compensate for the artificial and false reading around the sensor that is created by heavy city traffic and accompanying idling periods.

When the car is again accelerated to speeds between 20 and 45 mph (32–72 km/hr), a two-minute time delay is programmed into the system to prevent any false temperature readings that may result. In this way, cooling air circulating around the sensor from the faster moving vehicle allows a stable reading to exist. At speeds in excess of 45 mph, there is no delay, and outside temperature sensor readings are displayed as soon as they occur.

3. *Coolant Temperature Sensor*—This sensor is located in one of the intake manifold coolant passages. Since this is actually an engine-mounted sensor, its changing resistance value is monitored by the ECM rather than by the BCM. However, this sensor's changing value is relayed from the ECM to the BCM.

4. *A/C High Side Temperature Sensor*—This sensor is illustrated in Figs. 17-5 and 17-8. It is located in the high pressure refrigerant line between the condensor and orifice tube. The BCM receives a changing signal from this sensor so that the pressure based upon this temperature relationship of the R12 liquid is known.

5. *A/C Low Side Temperature Sensor*—(Refer to Figs. 17-5 and 17-8.) This sensor is located in the low pressure refrigerant line between the orifice tube and evaporator. The BCM also receives a changing voltage signal from this sensor in order to determine the low side pressure through the same method as that for the high side pressure sensor.

Also located in the low pressure refrigerant line is

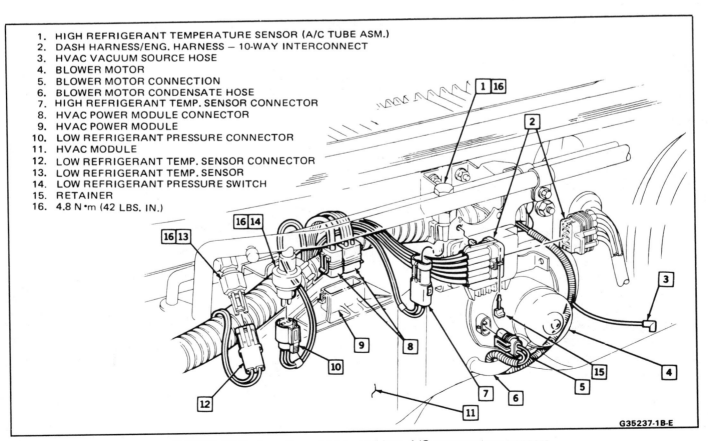

1. HIGH REFRIGERANT TEMPERATURE SENSOR (A/C TUBE ASM.)
2. DASH HARNESS/ENG. HARNESS — 10-WAY INTERCONNECT
3. HVAC VACUUM SOURCE HOSE
4. BLOWER MOTOR
5. BLOWER MOTOR CONNECTION
6. BLOWER MOTOR CONDENSATE HOSE
7. HIGH REFRIGERANT TEMP. SENSOR CONNECTOR
8. HVAC POWER MODULE CONNECTOR
9. HVAC POWER MODULE
10. LOW REFRIGERANT PRESSURE CONNECTOR
11. HVAC MODULE
12. LOW REFRIGERANT TEMP. SENSOR CONNECTOR
13. LOW REFRIGERANT TEMP. SENSOR
14. LOW REFRIGERANT PRESSURE SWITCH
15. RETAINER
16. 4.8 N·m (42 LBS. IN.)

G35237-1B-E

FIGURE 17-8 Location of high and low A/C temperature sensors. (*Courtesy of Oldsmobile Div. of GMC*)

a low pressure switch that allows the ignition circuit to feed power to the compressor clutch coil as long as the refrigerant pressure is above 5 psi plus or minus 3. If the pressure is below this value, then the switch opens and the BCM detects this change. The driver is advised of this problem by the fact that a *Low Refrigerant* warning is illuminated on the instrument panel. A B108 trouble code is also stored in memory so that when the BCM is accessed during the self-diagnostic check routine, the mechanic/technician is able to key in on the problem area. In addition, if a problem exists in a sensor or sensor circuit, the BCM will activate and display an *A/C System Problem* on the instrument panel, as well as storing in memory one or more trouble codes. Self-diagnostics are initiated when the off and warm buttons on the ECC panel are depressed simultaneously for 3 seconds. (See Figs. 7-42 through 7-50.)

6. *Sunload Sensor*—The sunload sensor is a thermistor that senses the heat load radiating into the passenger compartment. It is located under the defogger grille, which is centered at the base of the windshield. (See Fig. 17-9.) The BCM compares the sunload sensor value with that from the ''in-car'' temperature sensor in order to determine just how much cooling is necessary to maintain the selected in-car temperature.

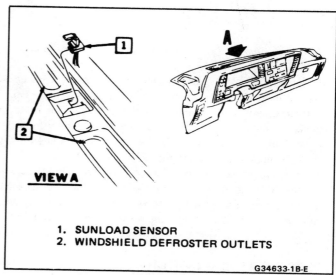

1. **SUNLOAD SENSOR**
2. **WINDSHIELD DEFROSTER OUTLETS**

G34633-1B-E

FIGURE 17-9 Location of sunload temperature sensor. (*Courtesy of Oldsmobile Div. of GMC*)

Sensor-BCM Relationships

All the various sensors that control the automatic temperature setting of the ECC system are connected back to the BCM as illustrated in Fig. 17-10. All the various sensors shown are ''thermistors'' that control the signal voltage to the BCM. This voltage varies between 5 volts (open circuit) and down to zero volts (shorted circuit), depending upon

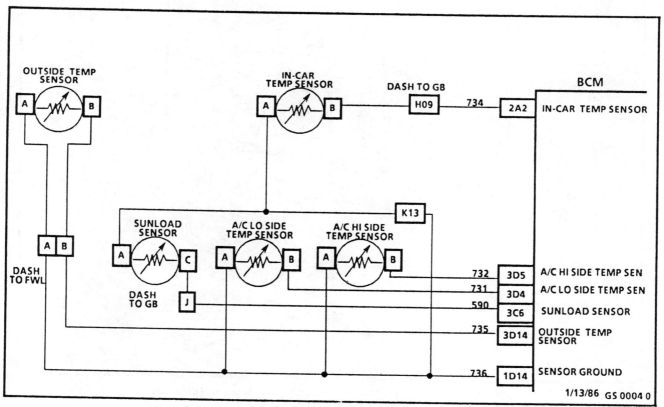

CODE B110

FIGURE 17-10 ECC (electronic climate control) sensor schematic. (*Courtesy of Oldsmobile Div. of GMC*)

the temperature of the sensor. The BCM applies a voltage to each individual thermistor on its own discrete line. This is to terminal B in all cases, with the exception of the sunload sensor, which receives its input through terminal J and terminal C. Note that all sensors have a common ground from terminal A to line number 736.

When all sensors are cold, their resistance is high, causing the BCM to interpret a high signal voltage. As each sensor warms, its resistance becomes less, and the signal voltage is pulled low through the sensor ground circuit 736.

POWER STEERING SWITCH

Illustrated in Fig. 17-14 (system schematic) is a power steering cutout switch which is naturally located in the power steering line. This switch is a normally-closed (NC) unit in order to allow ignition circuit feed to the compressor clutch coil. During conditions of high load—e.g., parking a vehicle in a tight position causes the power steering system pressure to exceed 300 psi—the switch will open the ignition circuit to the compressor clutch in order to relieve

engine load at low rpm and thereby avoid engine stalling. In addition, an idle-up speed control makes an adjustment to the idle speed control motor in order to increase engine idle speed when the ECM receives the air conditioning clutch engagement signal from the BCM. This is necessary because of the additional load placed on the engine under this operating condition.

A circuit to the ECM monitors this system and stores a trouble code E040 in memory for diagnostic purposes when the power steering pressure circuit is in an open-loop mode.

PROGRAMMER/HVAC MODULE

The programmer for the ECC system is shown in Fig. 17-11 as Item 2, and also in the ECC electrical schematic in the center of the diagram. A more simplified arrangement of the programmer, the power module, blower, and BCM is illustrated in Fig. 17-12. The programmer is actually attached to the HVAC module assembly and is located behind the glove box, with both electrical and vacuum connectors attached to it.

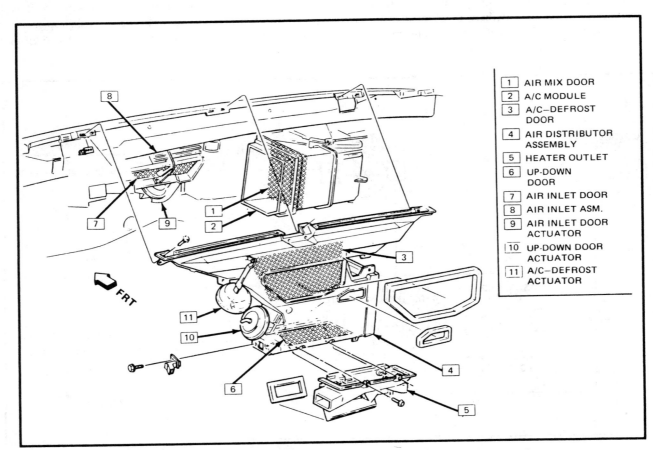

1	AIR MIX DOOR
2	A/C MODULE
3	A/C–DEFROST DOOR
4	AIR DISTRIBUTOR ASSEMBLY
5	HEATER OUTLET
6	UP-DOWN DOOR
7	AIR INLET DOOR
8	AIR INLET ASM.
9	AIR INLET DOOR ACTUATOR
10	UP-DOWN DOOR ACTUATOR
11	A/C–DEFROST ACTUATOR

FIGURE 17-11 HVAC Module and control mechanism. (*Courtesy of Oldsmobile Div. of GMC*)

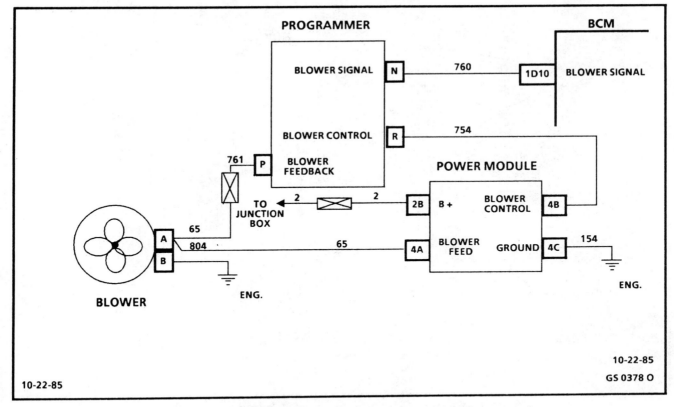

FIGURE 17-12 Programmer/Power module schematic. (*Courtesy of Oldsmobile Div. of GMC*)

The electronic circuit board of the programmer receives BCM data signals that are based upon the various selected conditions and the information being generated from the different vehicle sensors. The programmer then initiates the necessary controls required for automatic temperature regulation of the passenger compartment. It energizes a small reversible d.c. motor that progressively opens and closes the air mix door flap position in order to blend both the cold and warm air flows. The motor continuously provides a sensor reference signal regarding its actual position to the BCM to let it know the position of the air mix door flap at all times. (See Fig. 17-11, Item 1.)

The programmer printed circuit board also controls the four vacuum solenoids which direct vacuum to an air inlet recirculation door, an A/C and defrost door, as well as to a two position actuator for the movement of the up and down door. (See Fig. 17-13.)

Additional functions of the programmer unit are to relay a BCM signal to the power module for fan blower speed operation. When the blower motor is running, a voltage feedback signal to the programmer board allows actual regulation of the variable blower voltage feed signal and, therefore, of the fan speed. This blower fan speed is illuminated on the VF (vacuum fluorescent) display at the left of the ECC panel. It can be in one of the five following modes:

1. Low
2. Medium low
3. Medium
4. Medium high
5. High

This fan speed is selected by depressing the up or down fan buttons on the ECC panel, or alternately by depressing the auto mode button, which allows automatic BCM control of the system.

When the blower fan speed is selected on the ECC panel, the speed signal is relayed from the ECC via the serial data line to the BCM, which calculates a "blower voltage" based upon the selected blower speed (button) and the preprogrammed operating number within the BCM from 0 to 99. The PWM (pulse-width modulated signal similar to a fuel-injector time-on signal) is then sent from the BCM to the HVAC programmer on a discrete signal wire (individual wire) and not on the serial data line. The programmer relays this signal to the power module, which amplifies and carries the current necessary to drive the motor.

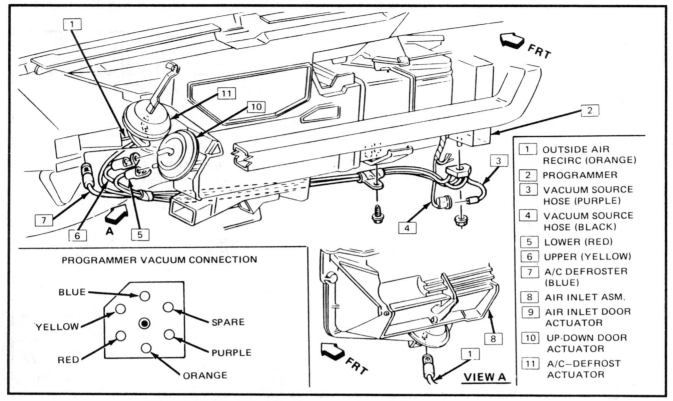

FIGURE 17-13 HVAC mode control doors. (*Courtesy of Oldsmobile Div. of GMC*)

Another added function of the programmer is to provide the ground circuit required to activate the rear defogger when this system is selected. The BCM is programmed to determine how much heating or cooling is required to maintain the selected temperature within the passenger compartment. It determines this from the following various input signals that it receives:

1. The set temperature on the ECC
2. The outside air temperature
3. The in-car temperature
4. The sunload sensor temperature

The BCM is programmed to control the position of the air mix door, the actual air delivery mode, and fan blower speed, which as a group are able to maintain the selected in-car temperature within close tolerances. The program within the BCM is arranged so that the number 0 represents maximum system cooling, and the number 99 represents maximum system heating.

During the self-diagnostic check of the HVAC system (see Fig. 7-30 and Fig. 7-42), which is initiated when the off and warm buttons on the ECC are simultaneously depressed for 3 seconds, the mechanic/technician can monitor the HVAC program number. The technician can also man-

ually override the program number by depressing the cool and warm buttons on the ECC panel which will move the 0 through 99 numbers up or down in order to determine the system's operating mode throughout the complete range. Pressing the off button on the ECC panel allows an exit from this override condition.

POWER MODULE

The transistorized power module is shown in the electrical schematic in Fig. 17-14; it is also shown as Item 9 in Fig. 17-8. A discrete drive signal is relayed from the ECM to the power module which in turn supplies the high current required to activate the A/C compressor clutch. However, the BCM actually controls the cycling (on/off) of this clutch based upon the various sensor input signals.

As the name implies, the power module supplies the necessary power or current to drive both the compressor clutch and blower motor assemblies. The programmer supplies a drive signal from the blower to the power module which it then amplifies (increases) in direct proportion to the strength of this input signal in order to provide variable blower speed control. Due to the reasonably high current values created within the power module, a large heat sink (finned body) is exposed to the evaporator air stream so that the generated heat can be extracted and dissipated.

COLD PURGE

In cold purge, the blower is turned off, and any air flow is directed to the front defog outlets in order to prevent breath humidity from the driver or passengers fogging the windshield. Cold purge only occurs when the system is turned on in any mode except defog or off, and when the engine coolant temperature is below 28°F (−2°C).

The system resorts to normal operation (purge) within several seconds of engine startup if:

1. The program number results in a cooling mode.
2. Engine coolant temperature is above 110°F (43°C).

If neither condition is present within a one minute time frame because of a low ambient temperature, then the BCM automatically resumes normal system control as described below.

NORMAL PURGE

In normal purge (operation), the blower fan is turned off and any air flow is directed to the heater outlets, with a small amount of bleed air going to the A/C outlets to prevent any moist air from clouding the windshield. This is further facilitated by the fact that the BCM will operate the blower fan at low speed for several seconds just before entering normal operation.

As with the cold purge condition described above, if the system is turned on in any operating mode other than defog or off, and the selected program number would not result in cooling or intermediate modes, and the engine coolant temperature is above 110°F (43°C), then normal operation can be initiated. If, however, neither of the above-stated conditions 1 or 2 is present within approximately one minute because of the ambient temperature, then the BCM automatically triggers a normal operating mode.

COMPRESSOR CLUTCH CONTROL

Operation of the air-conditioning compressor clutch is controlled automatically by the various ECC selection buttons, as well as by the various input signals received from the different engine/vehicle sensors. Ultimately, the compressor clutch is directly activated from the BCM through the ECM.

The following inputs are typically fed to both the ECM and BCM units in an on-going basis:

ECM (electronic engine control module) Inputs

1. BCM data
2. Power steering cutout switch
3. Engine coolant temperature
4. Engine rpm
5. Throttle position sensor

BCM (body control/computer module) Inputs

1. ECM data
2. ECC settings
3. Outside (ambient) air temperature
4. In-car temperature
5. Sunload temperature
6. Vehicle speed
7. Low refrigerant pressure switch
8. A/C high-side temperature
9. A/C low-side temperature

In order for the air conditioning compressor clutch to receive power at any time, the power steering and low refrigerant switches must be closed to allow a completed circuit to the assembly via the HVAC fuse. These two switches are shown in Fig. 17-14.

When all of the above-listed BCM input signals 1 through 9 are within the calibrated values, the BCM turns on or signals the ECM via the data line to engage the compressor clutch. The ECM, however, does not carry the high current required to actually engage the compressor clutch, but instead sends a discrete voltage signal to the power module to complete the ground circuit to activate the compressor clutch. Therefore, the power module handles the current to activate the clutch. In this way, the compressor clutch can only be engaged if:

1. The climate control is set to A/C, automatic, bi level, or defog.
2. The ambient (outside) temperature is above 45°F (7°C).

Once the compressor clutch has been activated by the BCM signal, the speed of the vehicle (VSS = vehicle speed sensor) determines how long the clutch will stay engaged.

These two conditions of operating time are as follows:

1. An extended idle mode which will ensure a minimum compressor-on (engaged) time up to about 45 seconds anytime that the vehicle speed falls below 15 mph (24 km/hr) in order to ensure a smoother transition to idle rpm.
2. A minimum compressor-on time of between 2 to 6 seconds anytime that the vehicle operates above 15 mph (24 km/hr) before the BCM will allow compressor clutch disengagement.

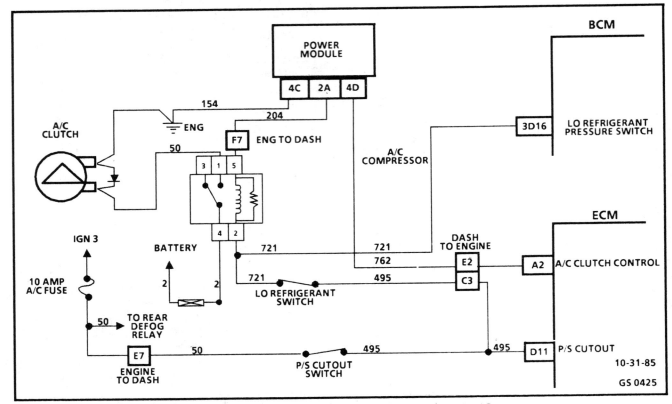

FIGURE 17-14 Power module, ECM, and BCM schematic. (*Courtesy of Oldsmobile Div. of GMC*)

Disengagement of the compressor clutch after condition 1 or 2 above will be done by the BCM only if the low-side temperature is below 30°F (−1°C). Then, depending upon the outside (ambient) air temperature, the BCM will go into a sleep mode until the low-side temperature climbs to between 45° and 50°F (7° and 10°C).

Automatic compressor clutch disengagement by either the BCM or the ECM will occur when any of the following operating conditions are encountered:

BCM Disengagement:

1. A/C low pressure switch is open
2. A/C low-side temperature is below 30°F (−1°C)
3. A/C high-side temperature is above 199°F (93°C)
4. Coolant temperature is above 259°F (93°C)
5. Open or shorted A/C low-side sensor circuit.

ECM Disengagement

1. Wide open throttle signal from the TPS (throttle position sensor)
2. System overvoltage
3. System undervoltage
4. Power steering cutout switch opens

NOTE: The wide open throttle condition will only keep the compressor off for a maximum time period of 20 seconds, while all of the other conditions will maintain a compressor disengagement (off) condition until the condition has been corrected.

Figure 17-15 shows in schematic form the complete ECC (electronic climate control) layout with all of its various components.

FORD ELECTRONIC EATC

Ford employs an EATC (electronic automatic temperature control) system in its 1984 and up model year Continental, Mark V11, Cougar, and T-Bird vehicles. The major difference between the EATC system versus other systems is that in EATC there is no need for engine vacuum to operate air conditioning/heater doors. Therefore, there are no vacuum switches, servos, and reservoirs. In their place a new electronic computer situated in the dash incorporates automatic control of air temperature, air routing, blower speeds, and refrigerant compressor engagement.

For troubleshooting this system, the use of a multimeter, various jumper wires, and a wiring schematic from the

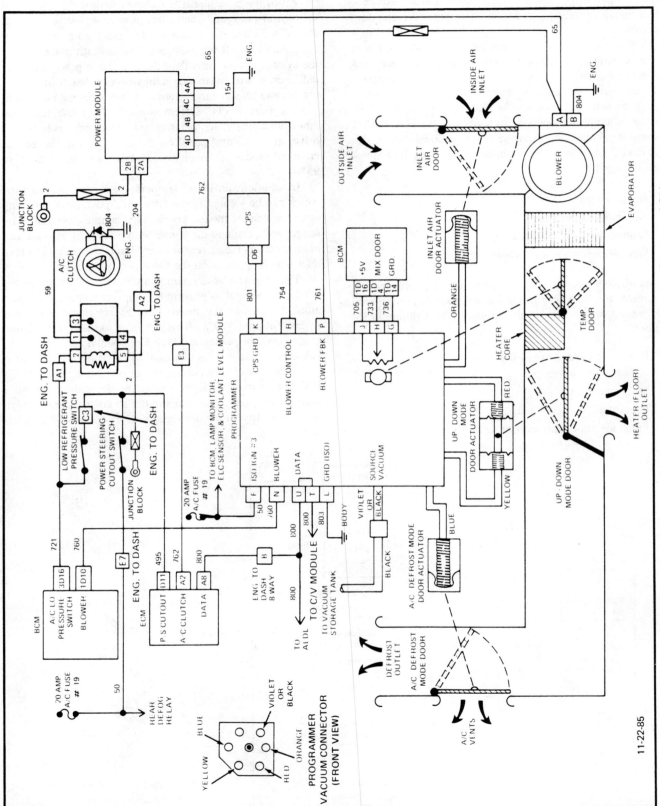

FIGURE 17-15 ECC (electronic climate control) system schematic. (*Courtesy of Oldsmobile Div. of GMC*)

model vehicle service manual are the tools that are required, rather than a vacuum gauge and hand or motor driven pump assembly.

A major feature of the computer for the EATC system is that it contains a self-test mode for diagnostic purposes similar to the engine computer, plus a keep-alive memory that eliminates the need to reset the temperature control system each time the vehicle is restarted. Figure 17-16 illustrates a simplified operational layout for the Ford EATC system. It operates on a three-way informational flow mode. The EATC computer receives information from the following four inputs:

1. In-car sensor
2. Ambient temperature sensor
3. Engine coolant temperature
4. Operator selected temperature

Based upon the signals received from the input sensors just described, the ECA (electronic control assembly) computes the desired output data to the following five different actuators:

1. Blower fan speed controller
2. Air blend door actuator
3. Mode door actuator
4. Panel/defrost door actuator
5. Fresh air recirculation door actuator

All of the actuators listed above, with the exception of the blower fan speed controller, provide signal feedback to the ECA so that it can monitor the exact state of affairs at any given time. If the ECA determines that the reaction of the system is more/less than the initial computed data signal, then it will make fine adjustments to each of the actuators and blower fan system to self-correct the condition.

The Ford EATC system is similar to those found on other luxury cars; temperature selections are made by the driver at the control panel on the dash/console. Seven operational modes are available, covering a range of 60°F to 95°F.

In addition, an in-car temperature sensor (thermistor), which can be located in one of several positions depending upon the vehicle model, continually samples/monitors passenger compartment air temperature. There is also an ambient air temperature sensor located in the outside air intake duct which operates on the thermistor principle.

The engine coolant temperature sensor, on the other hand, is designed to prevent a computer signal from operating the blower fan motor until the engine coolant has reached at least 120°F. This sensor is located in the actual engine coolant passages on the Continental and Mark V11 vehicles, while on the Cougars and T-Birds, it is located in a heater hose. Should the driver or passenger place the EATC system into the auto mode by depressing a control button on the panel, air temperature and distribution as well as the quantity of air delivered will be controlled simultaneously.

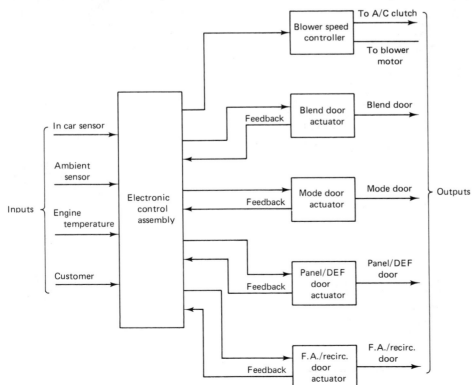

FIGURE 17-16 Electronic automatic temperature control operational diagram. (*Courtesy of Ford Motor Co., Dearborn, MI*)

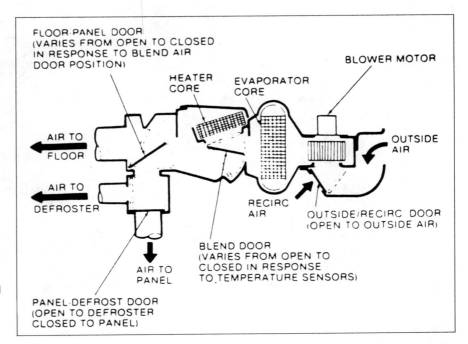

FLOOR-PANEL DOOR
(VARIES FROM OPEN TO CLOSED
IN RESPONSE TO BLEND AIR
DOOR POSITION)

HEATER
CORE

EVAPORATOR
CORE

BLOWER MOTOR

AIR TO
FLOOR

AIR TO
DEFROSTER

OUTSIDE
AIR

RECIRC
AIR

OUTSIDE/RECIRC DOOR
(OPEN TO OUTSIDE AIR)

BLEND DOOR
(VARIES FROM OPEN TO
CLOSED IN RESPONSE
TO TEMPERATURE SENSORS)

AIR TO
PANEL

PANEL-DEFROST DOOR
(OPEN TO DEFROSTER
CLOSED TO PANEL)

FIGURE 17-17 Electronic automatic temperature control plenum doors (total four). (*Courtesy of Ford Motor Co., Dearborn, MI*)

Figure 17-17 illustrates the four various plenum doors that are controlled by the ECA to adjust both air temperature and distribution. Two of these doors are dual position units; that is, they swing fully one way or fully the other until they reach the limit of their respective stops. The remaining two doors, however, can be set at any one of a number of positions throughout their arc of travel.

Basic Operation

During operation, if the selected temperature dialed in by the vehicle operator exceeds ambient, air will flow through the heater core and exit from the floor ducts. Once the vehicle passenger compartment temperature nudges towards the preselected setting, the ECA (computer) will cut back the blower fan speed, as well as actuating the air blend door to allow the cooler outside ambient air to mix with the heated air from the core. On the other hand, should the passenger compartment temperature be higher than ambient (outside air), then the EATC system will switch on the A/C compressor via the blower fan speed controller.

This action causes the mode doors to enter a reset mode, and cooler air conditioner system air will flow out of the instrument panel/dash air ducts in order to reduce the temperature within the passenger compartment. Should a maximum cooling mode be desired, then interior air will be routed through the evaporator core, while the air blend door closes to seal off the heater core, and the blower fan motor would run at its maximum speed setting.

As the interior temperature drops to the preselected range, the ECA (computer) reduces blower fan motor speed and moves the blend door to allow outside air to flow through the heater core. This cool and warm air mixture combination flows out of the dash registers into the vehicle passenger compartment.

A lo or hi mode selection simply changes the blower fan motor speed, while an econ selection will turn off the A/C compressor, and outside ambient air flows through the recirculate/outside air mode door to the dash registers. The lowest temperature that can exist in the passenger compartment during the econ mode selection process is the same as the outside air (ambient) regardless of what temperature selection is chosen.

This means that if the ambient air entering the passenger compartment is cooler than the selected temperature, then it is boosted up as it passes over the heater core on its way into the car. If the mix selector button is activated, air flow is divided between the windshield outlets as well as the floor ducts.

In the off mode, both the A/C compressor and blower fan motor are stopped, and the mode doors open to deliver unheated/uncooled air flow out of the dash registers.

BASIC TROUBLESHOOTING—EATC SYSTEM

The ECA (computer) is capable of self-testing itself when both the off and defrost buttons are pushed together, and the auto button is pushed immediately thereafter. Stored trouble codes within the ECA are then displayed one at a time, along with codes that have been detected during normal vehicle operation. Carefully record the codes which are displayed on the EATC panel. Then, to return it to normal operation, push the cooler button.

The EATC system has three fuses inside the car, which are:

1. A 30 amp fuse for the blower fan motor.
2. A 20 amp fuse for the computer and blower controller.
3. A 4 amp fuse for computer memory (temperature settings) when the ignition key is turned off.

CAUTION: Make sure that the ignition key is off when unplugging or reconnecting system connections.

As with any computer-controlled system, you may have to unplug the control head's electrical connectors (two for EATC) and use a high-impedance multimeter. Check the system wiring interconnecting each unit to the computer.

Locate the connector pins for the voltage supply to the computer, and make certain that sufficient voltage is present, and that all connections are making good contact.

Check the ground circuit for continuity, since the EATC's computer grounds through the connector.

Check the in-car and ambient temperature sensor resistances as per the values given in the respective service manual. However, the resistance values are always higher at a lower temperature, and they drop as the temperature rises.

Check the sensor for continuity. If acceptable, then check the wiring harness.

The four servo motors that move the mode doors can be checked by using a jumper wire to the motor's voltage feed wires. They should operate between 9 and 12 volts with the ignition key on. Jumper the motor wire only as long as it takes to note a movement of the motor arm, usually about 1 second or so.

Check the motor harness for continuity, as well as the motor's feedback resistance circuits to the ECA.

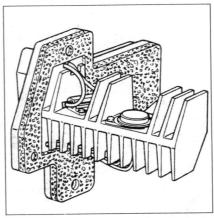

FIGURE 17-18 EATC blower motor controller heat sink. (*Courtesy of Ford Motor Co., Dearborn, MI*)

If the system operates, but the in-car temperature differs more than 4°F from that of a known accurate thermometer placed inside the passenger compartment, make a minor calibration adjustment through a hole in the side of the computer.

A small electrical screwdriver can be inserted through the cooler decal in the housing. For every 15 degrees that you rotate the screwdriver (either clockwise or counterclockwise), the temperature setting within the passenger compartment will change by approximately 1°F.

Both the blower motor and the A/C clutch circuits can be checked also for continuity, voltage, and resistance with the multimeter.

Figure 17-18 illustrates the blower motor's controller heat sink, which is designed to operate as a power amplifier. Therefore, it will get fairly hot when the system is in operation, although it is placed in the systems plenum box to allow air to flow over it.

CHAPTER 18

♦

Cruise Control Systems

CC PURPOSE AND FUNCTION

One of the most popular options available today not only on passenger cars but also on heavy-duty trucks and buses is speed setting or, as it is more commonly called, the ''Cruise Control'' system. Anyone who has ever driven a vehicle equipped with a cruise control option will readily testify to the advantages inherent in such a system. These advantages include the following:

1. Close control over a set vehicle road speed from usually a low setting of 25–30 mph (40–48 km/hr) and up, although this will vary between different makes of vehicles. On some cars, the cruise control can only be engaged at speeds of 35 mph (56 km/hr) and higher.

2. A preselected road speed engagement is stored in computer memory for recall at any time.

3. Lessens driver fatigue, which is partly caused by the driver having to react to constant speed variations caused by changing terrain and road conditions. The cruise control maintains the preselected road speed regardless of uphill or downhill geography.

4. Better fuel economy because of the cruise control system's ability to maintain a preselected speed. Constant up and down movement of the gas pedal is avoided.

5. If used with a standard transmission/clutch arrangement, the tendency for the engine to overrev when the clutch is depressed is eliminated.

Minor variations exist in the actual cruise control circuits between different makes of vehicles; however, an understanding of one circuit can equally be applied to another. Depending upon the year of manufacture of the vehicle in question, the cruise control circuit can be controlled through the ECM (electronic engine control module) or, on later units, the BCM (body control module). In all cases, a vehicle speed sensor which is usually driven off of the transmission output shaft is used to indicate the actual road speed of the car or truck unit.

This sensor signal is relayed to the on-board computer system, which will compare this signal with a preselected speed that has been input to the system by the driver through the use of the steering column mounted multifunction lever. (See Fig. 18-1.) In this particular schematic, both the cruise control features and the windshield wiper/wash system are assembled within this one multifunction lever. In addition, some cars also employ the headlight switch as well as the turn signals in this same stalk lever arrangement. Some cars employ a separate windshield wiper/washer control and headlight control switch on the instrument panel, rather than in the cruise control stalk lever.

The controls for the system are a steering column mounted-stalk type switch for engagement/disengagement/resume for the cruise control, along with the necessary muscle units (relays and servo motors) required to actually move the necessary throttle linkage and hold it at a set position. The Bosch system illustrated in this section shows a system that would be used on a clutch/standard transmission ar-

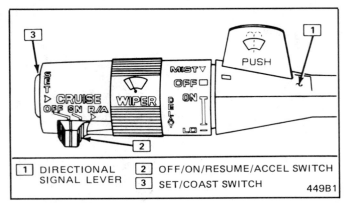

FIGURE 18-1 Multifunction lever mounted on steering column. (*Courtesy of Oldsmobile Div. of GMC*)

rangement employing an electrically-operated servo motor to change the speed setting. The Oldsmobile system, on the other hand, employs a vacuum operated servo unit to operate the throttle in response to the signals from the BCM (body computer module).

These two cruise control circuits are discussed and illustrated in this section. The one manufactured by Robert Bosch Corporation is widely used on many European vehicles, while the one used by the Oldsmobile Division of General Motors Corporation is similar to those found on other GMC division vehicles, and other North American cars.

OLDSMOBILE CRUISE CONTROL CIRCUIT

Electronic cruise control requires the following major components to facilitate engagement at a minimum road speed condition:

1. Mode control switches
2. BCM (body computer module)
3. Servo unit
4. Vehicle speed sensor
5. Vacuum supply from the engine or a storage tank
6. Electrical and vacuum release switches
7. Necessary electrical wiring

Each of the above items is discussed below in greater detail so that you can understand their individual actions within the overall cruise control system's effective operation.

1. Mode Control Switches

The mode control switch is a steering column mounted unit that also incorporates the vehicle directional turn signals,

similar to that shown in Fig. 18-1. The cruise control engage/disengage switch is a dual function arrangement that is best understood by referring to Figure 18-1.

One part of this switch incorporates a slider control that can be placed in either the off, on, or R/A (resume/accelerate) cruise position. The second part of this switch is located on the left-hand side of the lever in the form of a small push button (Item 3) which is used to set the cruise speed once the slider switch has been moved to the on position.

To engage the cruise control function, the driver simply moves the slider switch to the on position, depresses and releases the push button (Item 3). The vehicle will remain at the road speed the car was travelling at when the button was released.

NOTE: The cruise control function will only operate if the vehicle road speed is at or above the minimum cruise engagement speed. This can vary between different vehicles; however, it is normally in the 25–30 mph (40–48 km/hr) category.

The vehicle will maintain the selected cruise speed within 1 to 2 mph maximum variation under all conditions, and will remain there until either the OFF / ON /R/A is moved to the off position, the ignition switch is turned off, or the push button is pushed in and held. If the driver pushes the brake pedal down or depresses the clutch on a standard transmission, the cruise function is released, but the resume mode is held in memory, so that when the driver moves the slider switch to the R/A (resume acceleration) position, the vehicle will again move up to this preselected road speed. If the slider switch is held in the R/A position for longer than 1 second, then the system reverts to an engine acceleration mode in which it will stay until the driver releases the slider switch again. The car will now run at this new cruise control speed.

In some cruise control systems, tapping the slider switch towards the R/A position for no more than one second results in the vehicle road speed increasing by 1 mph (1.6 km/hr) increments per tap, up to a maximum increase of 10 mph (16 km/hr), after which time the cruise system must be reset to a new speed in order to maintain its function.

A "tap-down" mode of vehicle speed deceleration can also be achieved by quickly pressing the push button and releasing it, or by "tapping" it gently. This action will result in a programmed deceleration rate in 1 mph (1.6 km/hr) increments until the system reaches the preprogrammed low speed cutout rate, which is approximately 25 mph.

In addition, if the push button is held fully depressed, then the vehicle speed will decelerate with the throttle pedal released; alternatively, the driver can accelerate to a new speed setting and then release the push button.

2. BCM (Body Computer Module)

The BCM is the major brain cell for the cruise control system. Its electrical tie-in with the cruise system can be seen in Fig. 18-2(a) and (b). (Additional information on the BCM can be found in Chapter 7.)

The BCM signals the servo-motor when to move forward or back in order to set a new cruise speed in response to the driver's commands given from the steering column mounted-stalk lever.

3. Servo Unit

The servo unit is the muscle required to actually move the throttle linkage to a set position and hold it there. Figure 18-3 shows the unit as it would mount on the engine, while Fig. 18-4 illustrates more clearly the actual operating passages within the body.

Within the servo motor is a vacuum operated diaphragm, a NO (normally open) solenoid valve to vent the diaphragm chamber to atmosphere, a NC (normally closed) solenoid valve to connect the diaphragm chamber to the vacuum source, and last but not least, a variable inductance position sensor.

Three major servo positions are encountered during driving conditions, and these are as follows:

1. *Steady Cruise State:* In this mode the cruise system is engaged and operating); Items 2 and 5 (vacuum and vent valves) in Figure 18-4 would be closed to allow vacuum entrapment to be applied to the diaphragm, with no requirements for additional vacuum from the storage tank.

2. *Vehicle Losing Speed:* If the vehicle encounters a steep grade while in the steady cruise mode described above, or should the driver decide to increase the speed of the vehicle by manipulation of the slider or push-button switch on the steering column mounted stalk lever, then the BCM would sense this from either the VSS (vehicle speed sensor) signal decreasing, or the command to increase the speed from the cruise enable switch. This would result in the BCM energizing the vacuum solenoid to open the vacuum valve (Item 2), and the resultant action would draw the diaphragm to a new speed setting which would trigger an increase in throttle opening. The vent valve Item 5 would remain closed during this time.

3. *Vehicle Gaining Speed:* If the vehicle moves down an incline, or if the driver desires to decrease the vehicle road speed by manipulation of the mode control switches, the BCM would sense this from the VSS sensor or the cruise control command switch, and de-energize the vent solenoid (Item 5), and the vent valve would open to atmosphere and allow the throttle return

spring to pull the throttle to a decreased fuel setting. The vacuum valve Item 2 would remain closed during this reaction.

On earlier model cruise control systems, a cable drive from the speedometer cable was used to sense vehicle speed, and these systems maintained a preset cruise speed to within 1 to 2 mph (1.6–3.2 km/hr). However, on later model electronically-controlled systems using the VSS and the BCM, the cruise system can be maintained at a set speed of plus or minus ¼ mph. Because of this very close speed setting tolerance, the BCM will actually pulse the vacuum (speed increase) or vent valve (speed decrease) open as the case may be, in a similar fashion to that which it does for the fuel injector pulse-width signal.

Due to the electronic sensing of vehicle speed at the BCM, should the vehicle road speed exceed the preselected cruise mode by 3 mph (5 km/hr), such as might be encountered when going down a hill, then the vent valve (Fig. 18-4, Item 5) will be held in a constantly open position. On the other hand, if the road speed were to drop below 5 mph (8 km/hr) during normal operating conditions of load, then the vacuum valve (Fig. 18-4, Item 2) would remain in an open position. The servo employs a steel core (Fig. 18-4, Item 6), which moves within a coil (Item 3).

The position of this core for any given throttle position (variable inductance) sends out a voltage signal to the BCM, where it is constantly compared to the VSS (vehicle speed sensor) signal. Should the VSS signal drift outside of the ¼ mph tolerance of the system, then the set signal stored within the BCM, based upon the engagement speed by the driver from the cruise control switch, causes the BCM to send out a corrected pulse-width signal to the servo unit coil to change the position of the throttle linkage either up or down.

The servo unit will go into an open vent valve position when the following conditions are encountered:

1. The brake pedal is applied (depressed).
2. An open variable inductance position sensor coil in the servo unit.
3. A loss of electrical power to the system.
4. The ignition switch/key is turned off.
5. The slider switch on the turn signal lever (Fig. 18-1) is turned off.

4. Vehicle Speed Sensor (VSS)

The VSS uses a PM (permanent magnet) generator (Fig. 18-5), which is gear driven from the transmission/transaxle in order to provide an electrical signal to the BCM so that it can control the preset speed from the cruise control switch. Shown in Figure 18-6 is a simplified wiring schematic for

FIGURE 18-2(A)

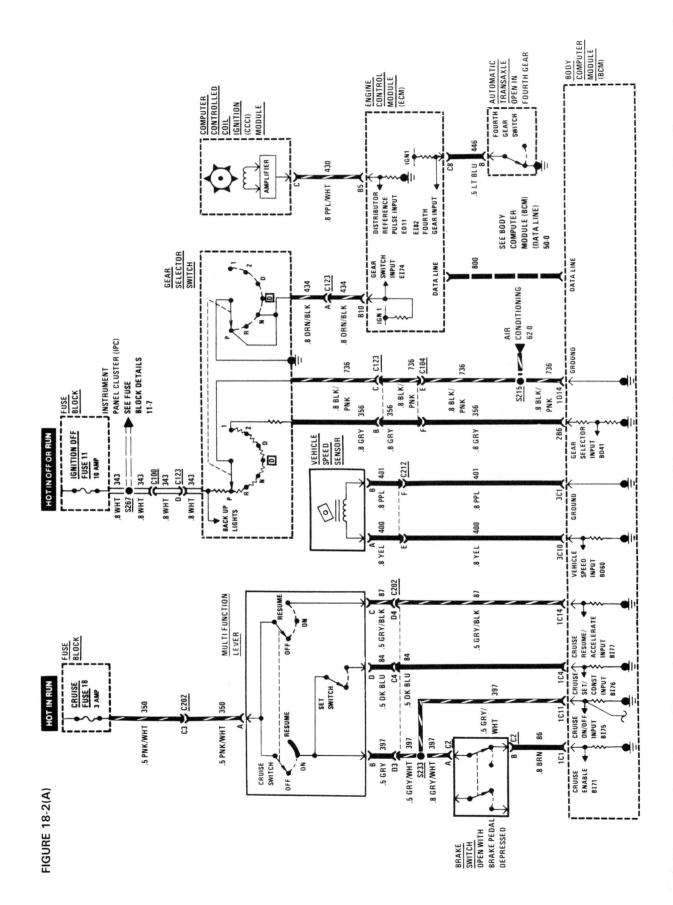

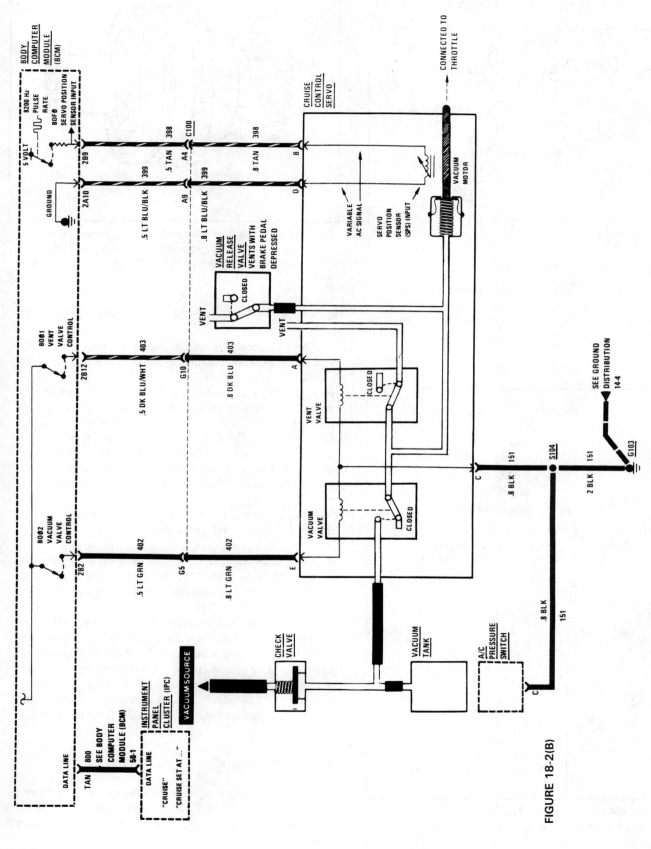

FIGURE 18-2 Cruise control and BCM wiring diagram interface. (*Courtesy of Olds-mobile Div. of GMC*)

FIGURE 18-2(B)

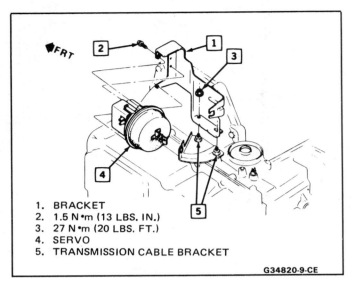

1. BRACKET
2. 1.5 N•m (13 LBS. IN.)
3. 27 N•m (20 LBS. FT.)
4. SERVO
5. TRANSMISSION CABLE BRACKET

G34820-9-CE

FIGURE 18-3 Cruise control servomotor mounting location on the engine. (*Courtesy of Oldsmobile Div. of GMC*)

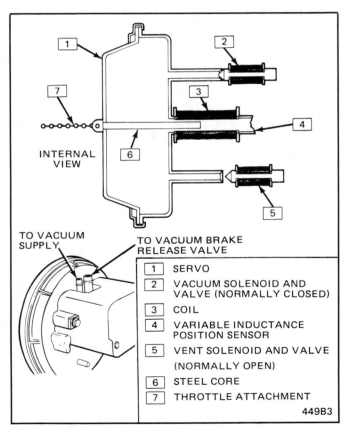

INTERNAL VIEW

TO VACUUM SUPPLY

TO VACUUM BRAKE RELEASE VALVE

1	SERVO
2	VACUUM SOLENOID AND VALVE (NORMALLY CLOSED)
3	COIL
4	VARIABLE INDUCTANCE POSITION SENSOR
5	VENT SOLENOID AND VALVE (NORMALLY OPEN)
6	STEEL CORE
7	THROTTLE ATTACHMENT

449B3

FIGURE 18-4 Operating passages of the cruise control servo unit. (*Courtesy of Oldsmobile Div. of GMC*)

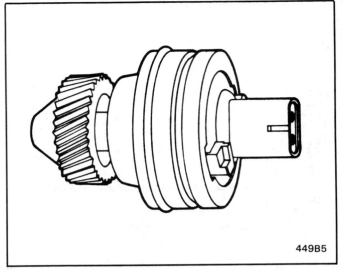

449B5

FIGURE 18-5 VSS (vehicle speed sensor) permanent magnet generator. (*Courtesy of Oldsmobile Div. of GMC*)

the VSS circuit and its tie-in to both the BCM and the ECM computers.

The PM generated voltage signal is brought from the VSS to the BCM on circuit 400 and 401 in Fig. 18-6, with circuit 400 being the VSS HI and 401 being the VSS LO. When the VSS signal reaches the BCM, it is buffered to remove any high frequency oscillations and is then amplified so that the signal will be strong enough to perform its functions. In addition, the generated signal at the VSS is analog (sine wave) in nature; therefore, part of the buffer action in the BCM is to change or convert this analog signal into digital form or a square wave (either on or off).

NOTE: For more information on analog to digital conversion and sensors, refer to Chapter 4.

By determining the length of time between the on and off signals, the BCM is able to determine vehicle speed accurately. The BCM then transmits this data along line (circuit) number 437 to the ECM.

To check the PM generator, raise the front wheels of the vehicle and rotate them manually while a digital voltmeter on the a.c. scale is attached to the PM generator. A voltage reading would confirm that the PM generator and wiring are OK. A problem in the VSS circuit is indicated by a Code B124 stored in BCM computer memory, and may be accompanied by a Code E024 from the ECM as well.

5. Vacuum Supply

The vacuum supply to operate the cruise control servo unit is illustrated in Fig. 18-7. The vacuum tank is usually located in the engine compartment by the left-hand motor rail.

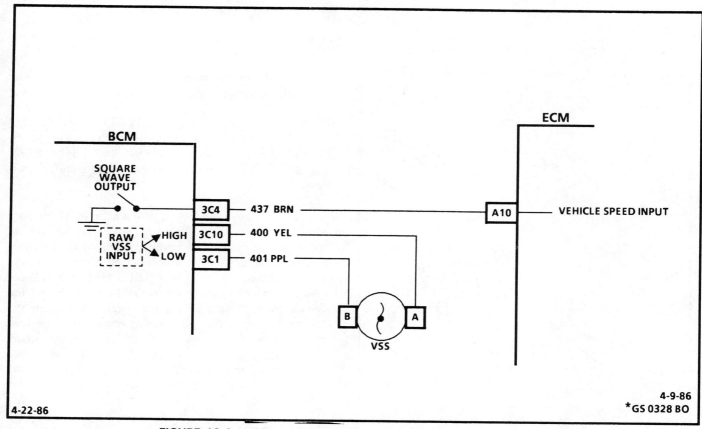

FIGURE 18-6 VSS (vehicle speed sensor) wiring schematic. (*Courtesy of Oldsmobile Div. of GMC*)

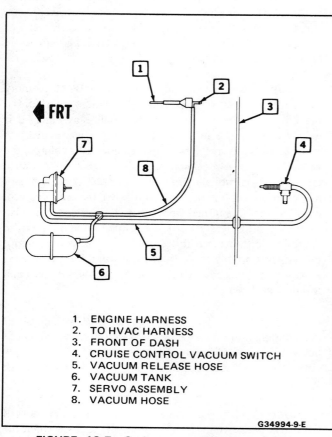

1. ENGINE HARNESS
2. TO HVAC HARNESS
3. FRONT OF DASH
4. CRUISE CONTROL VACUUM SWITCH
5. VACUUM RELEASE HOSE
6. VACUUM TANK
7. SERVO ASSEMBLY
8. VACUUM HOSE

G34994-9-E

FIGURE 18-7 Cruise control vacuum hose routing schematic. (*Courtesy of Oldsmobile Div. of GMC*)

6. Electrical and Vacuum Release Switches

These combination switches are used and mounted on the brake pedal bracket of automatic transmission/transaxle cars; on a standard clutch/transmission arrangement, they are mounted on both the clutch and brake pedals. Both systems are shown in Figs. 18-8 and 18-9. They perform a dual function, which is to disengage the cruise control system in the following ways:

1. The electrical switch disengages the system electrically, when the brake pedal is depressed, by interrupting the flow of current to the BCM.
2. A vacuum release valve also mounted on the brake pedal linkage vents the trapped vacuum in the servo unit assembly to the atmosphere to allow the servo unit to quickly return the throttle linkage to the idle position.
3. On vehicles equipped with manual transmissions, a combination clutch release switch and vacuum valve disengages the cruise control.

7. Necessary Electrical Wiring

A simplified electrical schematic of the cruise control system for the 1986 Oldsmobile Toronado is illustrated in Fig. 18-10, which shows the various circuits by actual identifi-

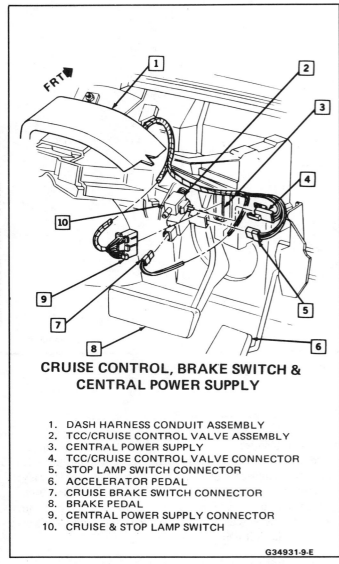

CRUISE CONTROL, BRAKE SWITCH & CENTRAL POWER SUPPLY

1. DASH HARNESS CONDUIT ASSEMBLY
2. TCC/CRUISE CONTROL VALVE ASSEMBLY
3. CENTRAL POWER SUPPLY
4. TCC/CRUISE CONTROL VALVE CONNECTOR
5. STOP LAMP SWITCH CONNECTOR
6. ACCELERATOR PEDAL
7. CRUISE BRAKE SWITCH CONNECTOR
8. BRAKE PEDAL
9. CENTRAL POWER SUPPLY CONNECTOR
10. CRUISE & STOP LAMP SWITCH

G34931-9-E

FIGURE 18-8 Cruise control brake switch and central power supply for an automatic transaxle equipped vehicle. (*Courtesy of Oldsmobile Div. of GMC*)

cation number as well as the tie-in between the various wires, switches, cruise servo, cruise switch, ECM, and BCM. A comparison of this schematic, along with the more detailed arrangement shown earlier in Fig. 18-2, should assist you not only in understanding the system more clearly but also in tracing the flow through the circuit components.

A Code B660 is set in BCM memory if the cruise control is engaged and the BCM receives a PRNDL signal indication that the vehicle is in a park, reverse, or neutral mode. (See Fig. 18-11.) The BCM will automatically disengage the cruise option under any of these gear selector positions. This same Code B660 can also be set into mem-

ory if the driver selects neutral while the cruise control is engaged. Therefore, cruise will be isolated until the driver re-engages it.

Various codes can be set into BCM memory if a fault exists in the cruise control system, as shown in Fig. 18-10. These codes would be B663, B664, B667, B671, B672, and B673. A more detailed explanation of these codes follows.

Code B663. This code will set in BCM memory when the cruise speed difference between the actual road speed and the preselected driver speed is too large. Under this code, the cruise will be disengaged if the actual road speed of the vehicle is 30 mph (48 km/hr) higher or lower than the set speed. Therefore, if the driver accelerates the vehicle by depressing the throttle pedal, and exceeds the set speed by 30 mph or greater, then cruise disengagement occurs. If, however, cruise drop-out/disengagement occurs at accelerated speeds lower than this 30 mph, then a mechanical problem is generally the reason. This code is used to set both the upper and lower limits for successful cruise control operation.

Code B664. This code will set in BCM memory and disengage the cruise control function if the rate of vehicle acceleration exceeds a preset rate which has been calibrated in the BCM. This condition could occur, for example, on slippery roads, during long downhill acceleration, or through a mechanical problem such as slipping clutches in an automatic transmission.

Code B667. This code will set in BCM memory when the set/coast or resume/accel circuit is shorted. To prevent a situation whereby cruise would stay engaged if the set/coast or the resume/accel switches were stuck, or their signal wires to the BCM were shorted to voltage, the BCM would set a Code B667 and disable the cruise control circuit if signal voltage from the set/coast (circuit 84) or the resume/accel (circuit 87) was hi when the cruise control on/off switch was turned from off to on. Cruise would also disengage if the ignition key was turned on and the cruise control on/off switch had been left on. The cruise control remains in a disabled/disengaged state until the BCM reads a lo on both the normally open contacts of the set/coast and resume/accel switches.

Code B671. This code will set in BCM memory if the ignition is on and the servo position sensor signal is below 3 percent. Check for shorts or opens in the feedback circuits or if an open circuit reading is due to the servo or circuits.

Code B672. This code will set in BCM memory if there is a cruise vent solenoid problem, such as when the

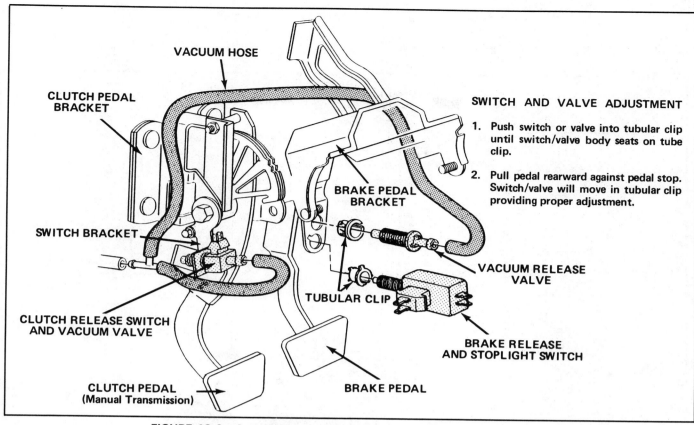

FIGURE 18-9 Cruise control release option for a standard transmission equipped vehicle. (*Courtesy of Oldsmobile Div. of GMC*)

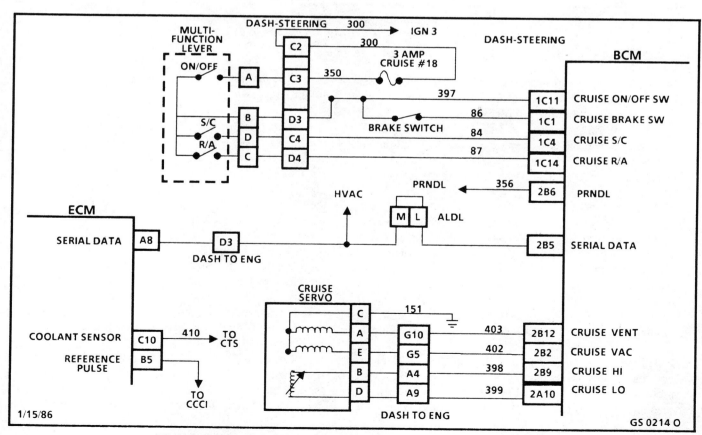

FIGURE 18-10 Cruise control system schematic. (*Courtesy of Oldsmobile Div. of GMC*)

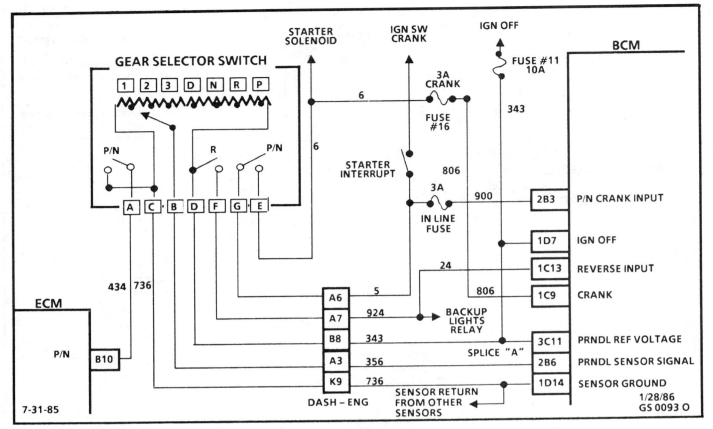

FIGURE 18-11 Cruise control gear selector switch schematic, with cruise control not in drive. (*Courtesy of Oldsmobile Div. of GMC*)

BCM normally energizes the vent solenoid. During this time, the output will be hi and the vacuum is not vented, or it is trapped within the servo chamber.

The code B672 therefore is set in memory if the cruise is on, the brake pedal is not depressed, and the BCM output is hi when it should be lo, or vice versa. The BCM will disable the cruise circuit until it sees the correct output signal.

Code B673. This code will set in BCM memory if there is a cruise vacuum solenoid circuit problem. When the BCM output is hi, the vacuum solenoid is energized, and the vacuum is supplied to the servo unit to increase the speed setting. This code will set therefore if the cruise is on, the brake pedal is not depressed, and the BCM output is hi when it should be lo, or vice versa. The BCM will disengage the cruise until it sees the correct output signal.

NOTE: To enter and exit a computer self-diagnostic mode, both the off and warm buttons on the ECC panel must be pressed at the same time and held for approximately three seconds, and then released. Any stored trouble codes will

be displayed on the ECC/IPC cluster panel beginning with the ECM codes first.

After all codes (both ECM and BCM) have been displayed, and you wish to clear either the ECM or BCM codes, select either ECM or BCM by pressing the hi (yes) fan button after the ECM or BCM message is displayed. Should you only want to clear the BCM codes for example, then you would press the lo (no) fan button after the ECM message, since these codes will always precede the BCM codes in memory.

Once you have accessed the system you desire (either ECM or BCM), test mode messages will be displayed on the panel, and the operator must then respond by repeatedly pressing the lo (no) fan button until the *Clear Codes* message is displayed for the system that you had accessed. You can then press the hi (yes) fan button, which will result in a *Codes Cleared* message.

Next, press the bi-lev button on the ECC panel to exit diagnostics and then re-enter again using the off and warm buttons, which will result in a display of all stored trouble codes in computer memory. (For a more detailed explanation of entering and exiting the diagnostic mode, refer to Chapter 7, and Figs. 7-30 and 7-42.)

Transaxle Converter Clutch

To improve fuel economy on automatic transmission (rear wheel drive), or transaxle (front wheel drive with automatic transmission) cars, a torque converter lockup clutch arrangement is employed. The arrangement is used to provide a mechanical 1:1 drive ratio through the torque converter in order to eliminate power loss (fluid slippage) when the vehicle is in a street or highway cruise condition.

The vehicle does not have to be equipped with a cruise control feature for T/C lockup to occur. Lockup will occur when the vehicle road speed and other conditions listed below are met.

When a predetermined vehicle road speed is reached, the TCC solenoid is energized, which occurs when the transaxle has shifted into 4th gear range. The TCC solenoid is located inside the automatic transaxle and is controlled by the ECM (electronic engine control module).

Figure 18-12 illustrates a typical wiring schematic for a TCC system; Figure 18-2, which depicts the complete ECM/BCM wiring arrangement, shows this 4th gear switch between the ECM and BCM. (See the right-hand side of the diagram.)

The 12 volt battery power supply for the TCC solenoid in the transmission or transaxle flows through a switch located at the brake pedal linkage. This ensures that at any time there is a brake application made, this switch will open and de-energize the TCC solenoid, thereby disengaging the T/C lockup clutch. In addition, if both a 3rd and 4th gear clutch apply switch is employed, it is wired in series between the brake switch and the TCC apply solenoid. This wiring positively prevents T/C lockup until the vehicle is in 3rd gear range (optional), or 4th gear if the vehicle is equipped with this arrangement only.

The TCC solenoid is activated when an internal switch within the ECM is grounded. Although the ECM controls the actual solenoid on/off action, the lockup clutch within the torque converter will not apply until the following conditions are met:

1. Internal transmission fluid pressures are up to specification.

2. Vehicle speed is at a minimum programmed value.

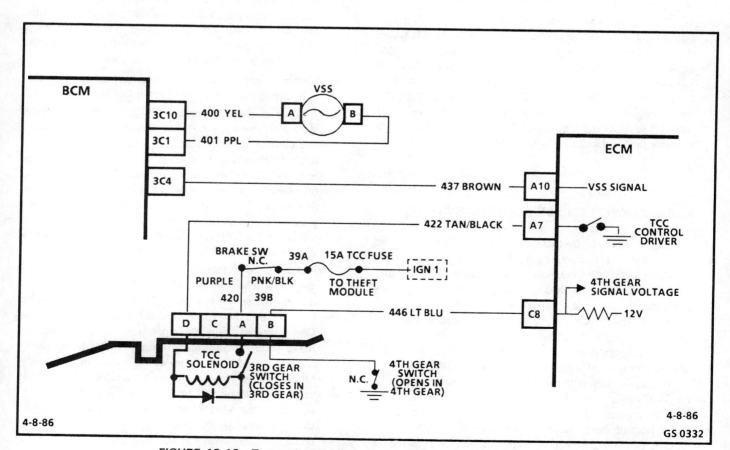

FIGURE 18-12 Transaxle converter clutch (TCC) circuit. (*Courtesy of Oldsmobile Div. of GMC*)

3. Engine coolant temperature is at a minimum programmed value.

4. Gear switch: some vehicles use either a 3rd or 4th gear switch and some use both to indicate to the ECM via a discrete switch (own circuit) when the transaxle or transmission is in a certain gear. For example, if a 4th gear switch is employed, the transmission doesn't have to be in 4th gear for the ECM to energize the TCC solenoid and provide torque converter lockup. The ECM uses the the 4th gear switch input to determine some of the conditions under which the TCC is applied or released.

   If 3rd and 4th gear TCC switches are employed, it simply means that TCC lockup cannot occur until the transmission has shifted up to 3rd gear.

5. TPS (throttle position sensor): once the TCC has been applied and the engine is operating under light load conditions, the ECM recognizes this condition, based upon the voltage signal generated from the TPS, which is after all a potentiometer (variable resistance switch). The ECM, under such a light load condition, would therefore release the torque converter lockup clutch anytime that the vehicle is accelerating or decelerating.

The vehicle speed sensor (VSS) sends a pulsing a.c. (sinusoidal or wave type) voltage signal to the BCM, where it is converted into a digital signal (either on or off) that represents the vehicle speed in either miles per hour or kilometers per hour. This sensor input is mainly used to control the operation of the TCC. (Transmission converter clutch engaged = lockup of pump and turbine for a 1:1 ratio.) The TCC is ECM-controlled when the vehicle is in a cruise mode, thus improving fuel economy.

ROBERT BOSCH CRUISE CONTROL SYSTEM

Most European vehicles that employ a cruise control feature use the system manufactured by Robert Bosch Corporation of W. Germany. The company is a dominant force in many areas of automotive technology, from fuel-injection systems to electrical/electronic components.

The Bosch system is similar in many ways to that employed and manufactured by other major car makers, in that a steering column mounted-stalk type lever is the major control element for activating the cruise control feature.

Familiarization with the cruise control system employed on GMC vehicles that has been discussed and illustrated in this chapter will allow you to compare the similarities between both of these cruise control systems.

The Bosch system can be employed on either a standard clutch-type transmission, or on an automatic-transmission-equipped vehicle. As with the Oldsmobile cruise control system shown in this chapter, the Bosch system employs the following major components:

1. Steering column mounted-stalk type control switch, which is similar to that used on other cruise control systems. Figure 18-13 shows the switch alongside a schematic diagram of the actual ECU used with the cruise control system. Once the stalk switch is pushed to the on position and the small button on the end is depressed, the vehicle will continue to accelerate as long as the button is depressed. Releasing the button will hold the vehicle at a *set* road speed.

   If the brake or clutch pedal is depressed, the system is disengaged, but the previous set speed can be called up again simply by pushing this button once the brake or clutch pedal has been released. If the stalk switch is placed in the off position, the set speed will be held in ECU memory as long as the ignition is still on, and it can be recalled by the reactivate portion of the switch system.

2. Small signal generator mounted directly on the speedometer, which consists of a small coil in a plastic housing to provide a sinusoidal (waveform) alternating voltage. The strength of the signal will vary in proportion to vehicle speed. The Oldsmobile system employs a PM (permanent magnet) generator driven from a gear on the transaxle to monitor vehicle road speed.

3. Electronic control unit (ECU) computer system to initiate engagement or disengagement of the system.

4. A servo motor arrangement similar to the Oldsmobile system. However, the Bosch system employs a reversible electric motor (rather than a vacuum actuated system) to actuate the throttle valve by means of a linkage hookup. While operating, the servo motor operates (electrically pulsed) for only a few tenths of a second to correct an over or underspeed condition, once the preset cruise speed has been selected by the driver. As with the Olds/GMC system, it only takes a few seconds for the servo motor to move the throttle from an idle to a full-throttle position.

5. Safety switches located on the brake pedal for an automatic-transmission-equipped vehicle, or on the brake and clutch pedals for a standard clutch-type transmission-equipped vehicle. Depressing the clutch or the brake pedal results in the cruise system being interrupted. In addition, if the servomotor is mechanically blocked for any reason and does not return, one or both of these switches will interrupt the fuel supply by de-energizing the relay for the electric pump circuit. However, as soon as the driver depresses the accelerator pedal, the drag-switch at this unit will again cause the fuel pump circuit to be reactivated.

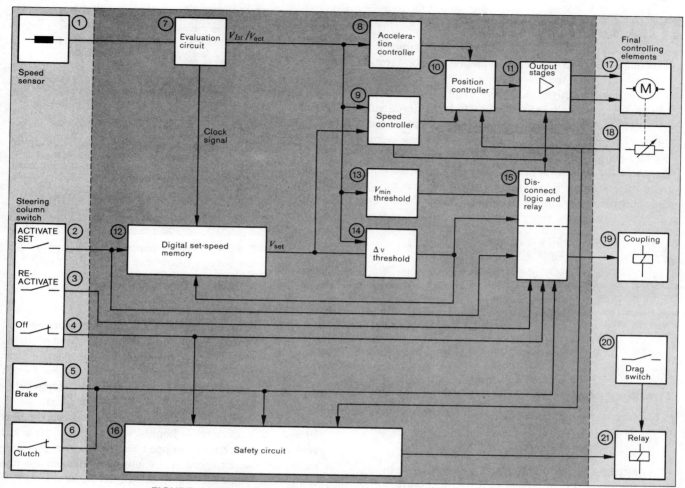

FIGURE 18-13 Cruise control ECU and switch circuit schematic. (*Courtesy of Robert Bosch Corporation*)

System Operation — ECU

In the schematic shown in Fig. 18-13, the cruise control system can only be activated while the vehicle is above the minimum threshold road speed of approximately 22 mph (35 km/hr), the cruise stalk lever is placed in the on position and the small button is depressed on the end and released, and the brake and clutch pedals are not in a depressed position.

The small speed sensor (signal generator) mounted in the speedometer head outputs a wave (analog) alternating voltage signal in proportion to the speed of the vehicle and relays this to the evaluation circuit (7) within the ECU.

The evaluation circuit converts and buffers this analog signal into an on or off form (digital) direct voltage signal that is compared with the preset signal stored in the digital set-speed memory (12) when the driver activated the cruise control system.

The acceleration controller (8) and the speed controller

(9) form a control circuit that generates a comparison between the set cruise speed (steering column switch), and the actual road speed of the vehicle as indicated continuously by the small speed sensor.

If the vehicle road speed were to decrease (e.g., the vehicle going up an incline), the acceleration controller (8) would automatically sense the difference between the set speed and the speed sensor signals, and would output a signal to the servo motor to increase the throttle position.

If, however, the decrease in speed was marginal and remained within the tolerance value of the system when the vehicle slowed down due to road conditions, then the speed controller (9) would output a small pulsed voltage signal to the position controller (10), which would be directly proportional to the change in vehicle road speed based upon the signal variation from the speed sensor unit.

The corrected signal would pass from the position controller (10) to the output stage (11), where it would amplify the current required to activate the servomotor (17), the variable resistor potentiometer (18), and the coupling (19).

The position of the servomotor (17) is determined by the potentiometer (18). Reversal of the servomotor direction is achieved through the output stage (11).

The disconnect logic and relay circuit (15) is tied into the clutch and brake switches on a standard transmission, or simply the brake switch on an automatic transmission. It is also connected to the cruise control steering column mounted-stalk type control switch, so that activation of any of these switches results in a disengagement of the cruise control circuit, thereby providing a safety factor in the systems operation. Regardless of which one of these safety

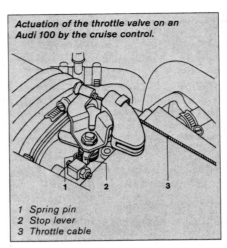

FIGURE 18-15 Cruise control throttle valve actuation linkage. (*Courtesy of Robert Bosch Corporation*)

switches is activated, the result is that the coupling (19) and the servomotor are returned to the idle speed position.

Another safety factor is contained in the system. Item 13 is a minimum speed threshold switch; and Item 14 is a low speed threshold switch. One or both of these switches can return the servomotor (17) to the idle position.

Item 13 will respond if the vehicle speed drops below 19 mph (30 km/hr), while Item 14 will respond if the actual vehicle road speed has dropped well below the tolerance values for the set speed. An example of the linkage and component location for the Robert Bosch cruise control system is illustrated in Figs. 18-14 and 18-15.

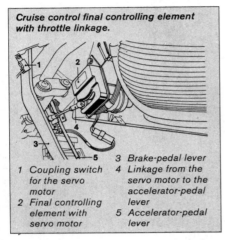

FIGURE 18-14 Linkage and switch location for a Bosch Cruise Control System. (*Courtesy of Robert Bosch Corporation*)

CHAPTER 19

♦

Vehicle Theft Deterrent Systems

TYPES OF SYSTEMS

It is conservatively estimated that in the United States alone, at least 1,000,000 vehicles a year are stolen or broken into. In Europe, this figure is about 750,000. Therefore, the installation of a theft deterrent system, either as a standard factory option or as an aftermarket add-on, has gained increased importance in the last five years, particularly on upscale models of passenger cars.

Various types and degrees of protection desired are offered, both from the factory level as well as at the aftermarket level, so that individuals can choose just how much they wish to spend on protecting their vehicles. An example of a simple theft deterrent system is illustrated in Fig. 19-1. When the system is armed, it is designed to provide both a visual and an audible alarm if either the trunk or door locks are forced open.

When forced entry is attempted, the alarm causes the exterior lights and the horn to pulse on and off for an average of between 2 to 7 minutes, depending upon the make of vehicle and type of alarm system used. The alarm system is also designed to disable the car's starter motor circuit to prevent any attempt to start the engine.

ROBERT BOSCH ALARM SYSTEMS

Robert Bosch offers a variety of vehicle theft alarm systems. These supply added protective features to those already illustrated and discussed in this chapter. The four different types of alarm systems offered from Bosch are the following ones:

1. Protects the car against unwanted opening of any doors, the hood, the trunk lid, and the switching on of the ignition.

2. Covers all of the security features in Item 1, but it also isolates the starter motor circuit.

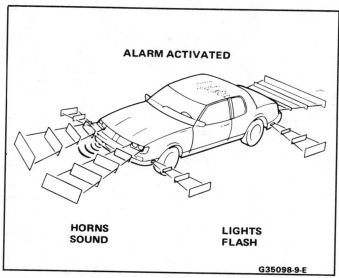

ALARM ACTIVATED

HORNS SOUND **LIGHTS FLASH**

G35098-9-E

FIGURE 19-1 Typical activated theft deterrent warning system reaction. (*Courtesy of Oldsmobile Div. of GMC*)

3. Provides all of the protective features of Items 1 and 2, plus offers protection against wheel theft and against the vehicle being towed or loaded onto another vehicle.

4. Provides all of the features of the first three systems, as well as providing ultrasonic interior protection if a window is broken or a convertible top is tampered with.

Basic System Layout

Figure 19-2 illustrates the basic block diagram of the Bosch car alarm system, with the various optional items related to the Types 1 through 4 systems offered by Bosch.

In the first type, the car alarm switch is located in the passenger compartment. It has one NC (normally closed) and one NO (normally open) contact. When the system is primed, the NO contact energizes the alarm system. The NC contact, on the other hand, simultaneously interrupts the primary power flow to the ignition coil. This first type of system will be live after a period of 30 to 60 seconds once the alarm switch is turned on. Should a car door, hood, or trunk lid be opened, or should someone turn the ignition key on, then the alarm would be triggered.

In the system illustrated in Fig. 19-2, the alarm relay within the control unit is energized through the alarm switch in the door. The priming switch or activation switch shown in the diagram is located at position E.

If the hood contact switch or either door contact is tampered with, then a signal shown at $T-$, $T+$, $S-$, or $S+$

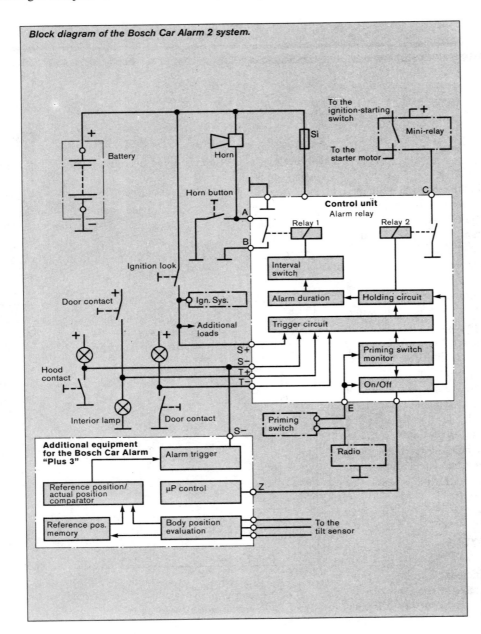

FIGURE 19-2 Block diagram of a typical Bosch Car Alarm 2 system. (*Courtesy of Robert Bosch Corporation*)

in the diagram will cause the alarm to be activated unless the reset/interrupt switch has been deactivated. Even if the system is in the off position, any short circuit or open in the respective leads to the alarm switch triggers the alarm system. Any voltage signal caused by a reaction at the hood or door switches sends these signals to the trigger circuit within the control unit or microprocessor.

The duration of the triggered alarm is dependent upon how long the actual sensing switches at the hood or doors are activated. However, once a signal has been output (alarm energized) by the control unit, each input is placed in a reactivated position so that the alarm would operate again if the doors or hood switches were tampered with.

Once the triggering circuit receives a switch signal, this signal is relayed through the holding circuit to activate the alarm and interval switch, which drives Relay 1 intermittently for a 30 second time period. Contacts A and B in the schematic are used to energize the horn. When an alarm signal is first triggered, Relay 2 is energized and stays in this condition until the alarm switch is reset.

Contact C is used when desired to isolate the starter motor circuit, while terminal Z is used to connect additional car alarm features, such as those used with the Type 3 and 4 systems.

The Type 3 system can be used in conjunction with either or both Types 1 and 2. The major advantage of the Type 3 system is that it contains a "tilt sensor" and electronic relay. Therefore, if someone attempts to jack up the car and remove the wheels, or tries to lift the vehicle on a tow hook, then the fluid-damped weights inside the sensor unit (Fig. 19-3) will cause these weights to act upon a coil within the sensor assembly, resulting in a change to the inductance of the coils.

When the system is placed into the set position by the driver of the vehicle when it is parked, a reference signal is placed in the memory of the electronic relay. The action

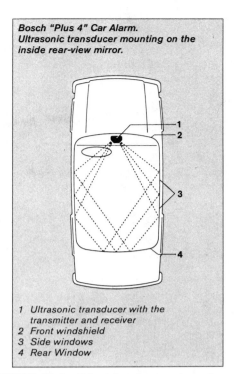

Bosch "Plus 4" Car Alarm.
Ultrasonic transducer mounting on the inside rear-view mirror.

1 Ultrasonic transducer with the transmitter and receiver
2 Front windshield
3 Side windows
4 Rear Window

FIGURE 19-4 Principle of operation of an ultrasonic car alarm system. (*Courtesy of Robert Bosch Corporation*)

of raising the vehicle or lifting it sideways will trigger the alarm system into operation.

In the most advanced of these systems, Type 4, an ultrasonic motion detector, along with the necessary evaluation electronics package, is used to indicate a window being broken or tampered with, as well as a convertible top being cut open or moved in any way. The Type 4 system can also be used in commercial vehicle applications as well as in passenger cars.

Figure 19-4 illustrates the basic arrangement of the Type 4 alarm system, whereby an ultrasonic field is generated using piezo-electric sonic generators to produce sound vibrations exceeding 20 kHz (kilohertz). The concept of operation of this generator or transducer is illustrated in Fig. 19-5. Basically, the transducer/generator consists of a crystal wafer whose thickness varies when it is affected by an electrical field, since this alternating voltage causes the wafer to vibrate. Should the natural frequency of the wafer equal the frequency (cycles per second) of the applied alternating voltage, then these vibrations will become pronounced.

Within the transmitter/transducer shown in Fig. 19-5, a multivibrator drives the piezo-electric transducer using an alternating voltage. Therefore, the crystal wafer will transmit ultrasonic waves with a frequency approaching 40 kHz (kilohertz). These sonic waves due to the resonance created at the wafer radiate outwards against the interior surfaces of the car and are reflected or bounced back to a second transducer.

As long as the car doors and top on a convertible are

FIGURE 19-3 Sectional view of the tilt sensor used with the Type 3 Bosch alarm system. (*Courtesy of Robert Bosch Corporation*)

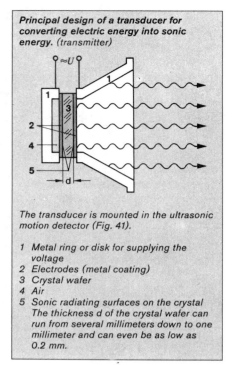

Principal design of a transducer for converting electric energy into sonic energy. (transmitter)

The transducer is mounted in the ultrasonic motion detector (Fig. 41).

1 Metal ring or disk for supplying the voltage
2 Electrodes (metal coating)
3 Crystal wafer
4 Air
5 Sonic radiating surfaces on the crystal
The thickness d of the crystal wafer can run from several millimeters down to one millimeter and can even be as low as 0.2 mm.

FIGURE 19-5 Ultrasonic car alarm vibrating wafer transducer system. (*Courtesy of Robert Bosch Corporation*)

closed, the returning signals will have a specific phase (in harmony) relationship with the original output signal from the vibrating crystal wafer; that is, the frequency (cycles per second) and amplitude (the distance a particle moves from side to side in one vibration) are constant.

The instant that a door or convertible top is opened, however, this constant (balance) is upset and the electrical signal generated by the receiver/transducer is amplified in the HF (high frequency) amplifier, shown in the schematic

in Fig. 19-6. This signal mixture is demodulated or rectified to separate the high frequency 40 kHz (kilohertz) carrier frequency, and the remaining low frequency signals can be attenuated (reduced) to the desired sensitivity by setting the gain as shown in Fig. 19-6. This signal is then fed into a filtering amplifier to stabilize the signal frequency in order to reduce the possibility of setting off the alarm system falsely. This amplified low frequency signal is then used to drive a switching amplifier, which can then trigger the alarm when these signals exceed a predetermined level.

CADILLAC SYSTEM OPERATION

Another example of an excellent theft deterrent system is the one employed by Cadillac on its current vehicles in which a controller (electronic) is located on the right side of the brake pedal mounting bracket and is accessible by removing the lower instrument panel sound panel insert on all C-D car models as shown in Fig. 19-7. On E-K models, the controller is located beneath the instrument panel attached to the accelerator pedal lever cover, and is accessible by removing the instrument panel lower sound panel. Both systems employ a security system indicator lamp located in the tell-tale panel.

Controller Operation

A typical wiring circuit for the theft deterrent system is shown in Fig. 19-8. The controller is designed to function in two stages: the armed stage, and the activated stage. In Fig. 19-8, you will notice that both the left and right front

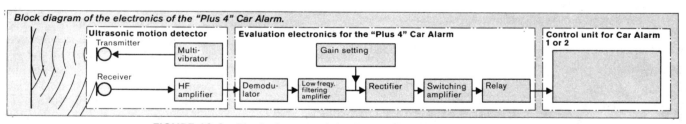

FIGURE 19-6 Block diagram of the Bosch Plus 4 ultrasonic car alarm system. (*Courtesy of Robert Bosch Corporation*)

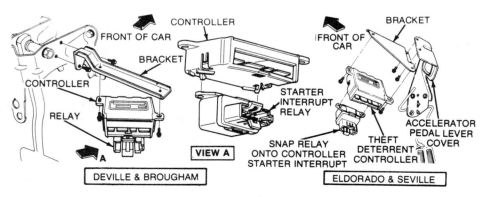

FIGURE 19-7 Theft deterrent electronic controller location. (*Courtesy of Cadillac Motor Car Div. of GMC*)

doors and the left and right rear doors are wired to a door jamb switch; also, the trunk (rear compartment) is fitted with a tamper switch.

Any of these switches can trigger the theft deterrent system if their lock cylinders are opened or tampered with in any way other than normal key opening. The system is protected by one 25 amp fuse between the controller and the horn battery feed, and by a 20 amp fuse between the controller and the external lamp's battery feed.

Within the starter solenoid circuit is contained a starter interrupt relay which is of the NC (normally closed) type. When it is energized from the controller, the relay contacts are opened. Since no current can flow through the open relay contacts, the starter solenoid circuit is inoperative. The theft deterrent system is armed anytime that the driver

turns off the ignition key. When a door is opened, the security lamp in the tell-tale panel will start flashing, but will go out when the door (or the last of the vehicle doors) is closed, thereby arming the system. Note that should the electric door lock switch be placed in lock, this will cause the security lamp to illuminate steadily; therefore, do not do this prior to leaving the vehicle.

Anytime that the system has been placed in the armed position, door or trunk entry can only be made through use of the vehicle key; otherwise, the alarm system will be set off. Once the alarm system has been activated, it can only be shut off by inserting the key in the driver's door to unlock it, or by inserting the key in the ignition and turning it on.

Should the driver wish to leave the system in the unarmed position after using the door lock rocker switch, he

THEFT DETERRENT DIAGNOSIS

Complaint	Probable Cause	Correction
System totally inoperative.	Open in one of the following wires: 1. Ground wire (black) in controller cavity N. 2. Battery feed. 3. Electric door lock wire. 4. Blown fuses. 5. Malfunctioning Controller.	Repair or replace as needed. Same as above. (If fuse in yellow wire is blown, horn only will activate. If fuse in black with red stripe wire is blown, system will not operate.) Replace after investigating previously listed causes.
	Check for loose connectors at controller to instrument panel harness or instrument panel harness to body harness.	Repair or replace as needed.
Inoperative horn and/or headlamps, and/or marker lamps in alarm mode.	Malfunctioning Controller.	Replace after investigating previously listed causes.
Unable to reverse arming process with "UNLOCK" switch.	Open in door "UNLOCK" wire circuit	Inspect circuit from door lock to controller.
	Malfunctioning controller.	Replace after investigating previously listed causes.
"SECURITY SYSTEM" tell-tall light inoperative	Check "Clk Ltr" fuse. Check bulb. Check wiring to bulb for shorts or open condition.	Repair or replace as needed.
System operates normally except does not disarm at one or both doors.	A. Try to disarm system by opening other door lock with key. If system disarms, check for: 1. Open light green wire to problem door. 2. Malfunctioning door key lock switch. 3. Open ground wire inside door. B. If system cannot be disarmed from either door:	Repair or replace as needed. Same as above. Repair as needed.

(Continued on next page)

FIGURE 19-8 Theft deterrent system wiring diagram. (*Courtesy of Cadillac Motor Car Div. of GMC*)

	1. Check for open at grn. lgt. wire at controller with door lock cylinder in unlock position.	Repair or replace as needed.
	2. Malfunctioning controller.	Replace after investigating previously causes.
Security light will not go out upon closing doors, and system will not arm.	LOCK CYLINDER VIOLATED or unwanted ground at door jamb switches, door and trunk tamper switches or pinched wires leading to these components.	Check for unwanted ground in light blue wire (cavity D) in body to dash harness connector. Repair as necessary.
	Door and trunk lock tamper switches out of adjustment.	Readjust or replace as necessary.
Alarm activates when depressing door lock button when equipped with, illuminated lock cylinder option.	Unwanted ground at door jamb switch.	Remove wires from door jamb switch and install wires so that illuminated lock cylinder feed is separated from theft deterrent wiring.
Alarm activates by itself.	Check for too close adjustment of door jamb switches.	Readjust or replace as necessary.
System cannot be armed - tell-tale O.K.	1. Check for ground at body to dash harness connector (cavity C).	Repair or replace as needed.
	2. Courtesy lights do not shut off, also.	Repair grounding condition.
System cannot be armed - tell-tale O.K.	Check for ground at grn-lgt wire at controller.	Repair or replace as needed.
Drivers door only will	Open diode in dash not generate alarm.	Replace diode. harness.
Key buzzer activated by all doors.	Diode shorted.	Replace diode.

FIGURE 19-8
(*continued*)

can do so by moving it to the unlock position prior to closing all of the doors. Another method to cancel the arming process is to rotate the key switch to the on position and then back to lock, since rotating the ignition switch will not in itself cancel the alarm once it is activated. Doors can be locked in one of two ways without arming the theft deterrent system; the lock rocker switch or door key will disarm and deactivate the system. However, the ignition key in the barrel will only disarm the system before the alarm is activated. A damaged lock in the system will cause the security system light to flash when the ignition is off; however, it will not flash with the ignition switch on. Figure 19-9 lists the possible complaints and diagnosis for the theft deterrent system.

CHEVROLET VAN ANTI-THEFT SYSTEM

The anti-theft system employed by Chevrolet differs from that used by Cadillac in that protective switches on the van configuration vehicles are located as shown in Fig. 19-10.

In addition to the switches shown in Fig. 19-10, a hood switch is located at the left-hand front fender, while an anti-theft horn is mounted to the fender inner support, just forward of the battery tray on the right side of the vehicle. To protect the fender mounted arming switch, an anti-tamper switch with a key lock is used. Any forcible entry of this key switch will trigger the alarm system.

Figure 19-11, a wiring schematic of the system, shows two relays, A and B; plus a flasher unit to cycle the horn. These items are located underneath the instrument panel at the left side of the vehicle near the parking brake. Unlike the Cadillac system, which when activated will operate for from three to seven minutes, the Chevrolet system will continue to operate until the system is shut off with the key switch, or the battery is completely discharged.

To arm the system, the driver turns the arm/disarm key switch clockwise, which closes the contacts between the hood switch and terminal 3 of Relay A. It cannot ground the circuit at this time because the hood switch is open and no ground exists between terminal 3 of Relay A. Similarly, anytime that the system key switch is off, all protective

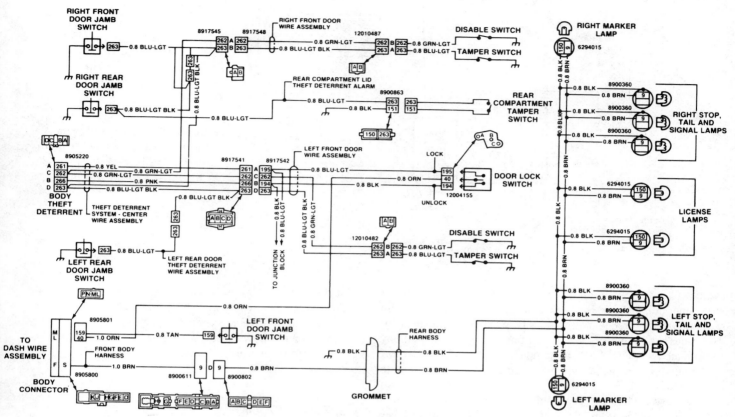

FIGURE 19-9   Theft deterrent diagnosis chart. (*Courtesy of Cadillac Motor Car Div. of GMC*)

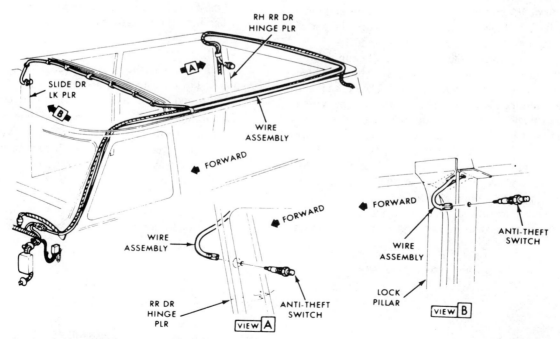

FIGURE 19-10   Chevrolet van anti-theft switch locations. (*Courtesy of Chevrolet Motor Div. of GMC*)

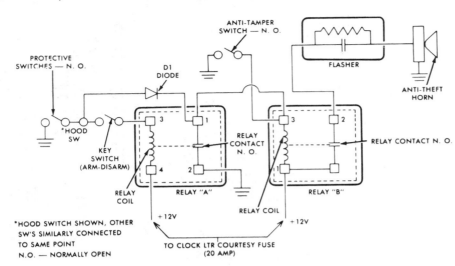

FIGURE 19-11 Chevrolet van anti-theft system wiring diagram. (*Courtesy of Chevrolet Motor Div. of GMC*)

switches are open, and no possible ground path exists for either relay A or B. Note that both relay A and B are connected directly to the battery positive terminal at all times, and therefore are hot on one side only. Should any protective switch now be tampered with, these NO (normally open) switches will close and complete the system to ground.

Two actions can cause the system to operate. The first is by someone attempting to force open the anti-tamper key lock, which would allow this switch to close; however, this action would only allow relay B to be completed to ground. Therefore the horn alarm would activate being completed to ground through terminal 3 of relay B whose relay coil is connected through terminal 2 to the flasher unit and anti-theft horn. To cancel this action, either disconnect the power supply, or depress the anti-tamper switch plunger.

The second way to activate the system, of course, is by someone trying to force open a door or the hood, which will close any of these protective switches. The ground path is completed and the system becomes operable. The wiring diagram does not show all of the door switches; however, these are all tied into relay A and will ground the system in the same manner as that shown for the hood switch. If the switch is activated, it completes a path to ground for the relay coil A, which will close the relay contacts of A and provide a path to ground also for relay B.

If someone attempting to steal the vehicle triggered the system and quickly closed the hood or doors in the hopes

of disarming the horn, this wouldn't work, because diode D1 above relay A provides the holding action. Therefore, in order to disarm the system, the key switch must be activated or the power broken. Figure 19-12 shows the location of the anti-tamper switch.

SPECIAL TOOLING

On the latest microprocessor-controlled theft deterrent systems, such as that now in use on the Chevrolet Corvette, it is necessary to employ an interrogator diagnostic tool such as the Kent-Moore J-35628 unit shown in Fig. 19-13, which has the following four distinct and important diagnostic capabilities:

1. It will determine the electronic code of a key. If duplicate keys are needed, just insert a key in the interrogator, and it will display the electronic code.

2. If there are no keys for the car, the interrogator will input each of the 15 codes into the car. When the car starts, the correct code has been found. Because of the design of the system, this can only be done one code at a time at four minute intervals, on a trial-and-error basis. There is no way to avoid this type of test. The J-35628 tester has a built-in four minute timer to enable this procedure to go as quickly as possible.

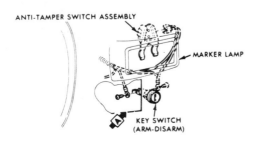

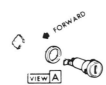

FIGURE 19-12 Chevrolet van anti-theft system anti-tamper switch location. (*Courtesy of Chevrolet Motor Div. of GMC*)

J 35628
V.A.T.S. INTERROGATOR

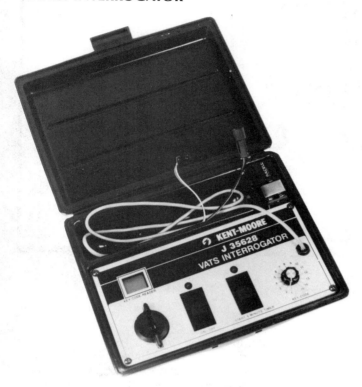

The new Vehicle Anti-Theft System introduced on the 1986 Corvette requires the J 35628 V.A.T.S. Interrogator which has four distinct and important diagnostic capabilities.

1. It will determine the electronic code of a key. If duplicate keys are needed, just insert a key in the Interrogator and it will display the electronic code.

2. If there are no keys for the car, the Interrogator will input each of the 15 codes into the car. When the car starts, the correct code has been found. Because the design of the system, this can only be done one code at a time (at four minutes intervals) on a trial and error basis. There is no way to avoid this type of test. The J 35628 has a built-in four minutes timer to enable this procedure to go as quickly as possible.

3. The Interrogator will determine if there is a fault in the key switch or steering column by reading the key code through these components.

4. A fault downstream of the column or in the V.A.T.S. Module can also be diagnosed with the Interrogator.

FIGURE 19-13   VATS (vehicle anti-theft system) interrogator diagnostic tool. (*Courtesy of Kent-Moore Group, Sealed Power Corporation*)

3. The interrogator will determine if there is a fault in the key switch or steering column, by reading the key code through these components.

4. A fault downstream of the column or in the VATS (vehicle anti-theft system) module can also be diagnosed with the interrogator.

REVIEW QUESTIONS

19-1. What is a theft deterrent system?

19-2. Do all theft deterrent systems shut off automatically?

19-3. How is the theft deterrent system placed in the armed position by the driver?

19-4. Once the alarm system has been activated through a forced entry, how can it actually be shut off or disarmed?

ANSWERS

A19-1. A theft deterrent system is an electronic system that is employed on cars and vans to prevent unwanted opening of the passenger compartment, hood or trunk lids. Trigger switches located at these points of entry will close a circuit to cause the vehicle horn to sound, as well as the vehicle lights to flash should an attempt be made to force open any of these aforementioned areas. In some vehicles, a starter motor interrupt relay is also energized to prevent starting of the vehicle.

A19-2. No; some will shut off automatically after 3 to 7 minutes while others will cycle continuously until the vehicle battery is run down unless the system is disarmed.

A19-3. The theft deterrent system is placed in the armed position anytime that the driver turns off the ignition key and locks the driver's door (as well as all other doors).

A19-4. The alarm system can only be shut off or disarmed by insertion of the ignition key into the system at either the door lock or ignition switch. Disconnecting the battery power supply or depressing the anti-tamper switch (for example, on the Chevy van system) will similarly disarm the system.

CHAPTER 20

♦

Electronic Transmission Control

BASIC LAYOUT AND ARRANGEMENT (ROBERT BOSCH SYSTEM)

Automatic transmissions in passenger cars and trucks both operate on an open-loop hydraulic system concept. A combination of modulator pressure (decreases with an opening throttle) and a transmission driven output shaft mechanical governor pressure acts as a trigger device to push a shift signal valve open against spring pressure. The opening of this valve determines when the next higher or lower clutch is applied and therefore controls the automatic shift sequence of the transmission. Literally, millions of these hydraulic dependent automatic transmissions have been manufactured, and they have provided billions of miles of trouble-free driving for the motoring public.

The use of electronics to control just when these shift points occur allows a reduction in transmission power losses, closer matching of transmission gear ratios, and a reduction in overall vehicle fuel consumption. This same technology has been adapted successfully to the on-highway truck line of Allison heavy-duty automatic models.

Figure 20-1 illustrates an example of the system employed by Robert Bosch Corporation to electronically control the shift sequence of a typical passenger car automatic. In this case, the transmission model is the ZF 4HP-22, which is widely used in the 700 series cars manufactured by BMW (733, 735 etc.). The electronic componentry for the transmission control is actually an integral part of the existing ECU (electronic control unit) for the engine gasoline fuel-injection system, which can be seen in Fig. 20-2.

On the transmission shift selector tower, the various gear ranges are indicated. These are normally 1, 2, 3, D, N, R, and P. Also on this shift selector tower is a three position switch lettered with an S, E or M, although the letters E, C or F may appear on some transmission models. Each one of these selectable shift programs is stored in the ROM unit of the ECU.

Selection of the S letter provides a performance shifting technique, while the E, standing for economy, provides better fuel consumption. The M selection provides the driver with a manual gear selection process for use in winter-type driving conditions.

When the S (performance) selection is made at the program switch located on the shift lever quadrant, the full-load shift points are reached at higher speeds than they would be in the economy program E. This is electronically programmed into the ECU and is designed to function in a manner similar to that which would occur in a straight hydraulically shifted automatic transmission; that is, the shift signal valve is prevented from moving until a higher speed and oil pressure are obtained. Regardless of the selection of either the S, E, or M range, the driver can override the selected operating range and keep the transmission in a first gear mode, or use first and second gears only in order to provide the vehicle with a better engine braking response.

Bosch System Components

The system employs the following major components for successful operation:

1. Engine speed sensor

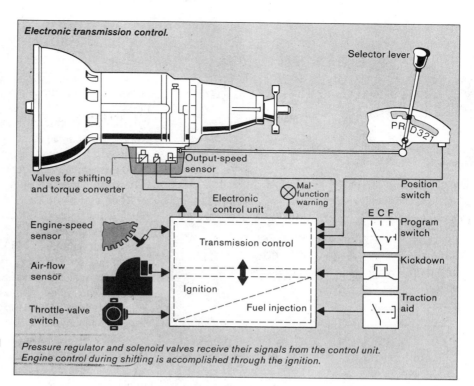

Electronic transmission control.

Selector lever

Output-speed sensor

Valves for shifting and torque converter

Engine-speed sensor

Air-flow sensor

Throttle-valve switch

Electronic control unit

Transmission control

Ignition

Fuel injection

Mal-function warning

Position switch

E C F

Program switch

Kickdown

Traction aid

Pressure regulator and solenoid valves receive their signals from the control unit. Engine control during shifting is accomplished through the ignition.

FIGURE 20-1 Electronic automatic transmission control system. (*Courtesy of Robert Bosch Corporation*)

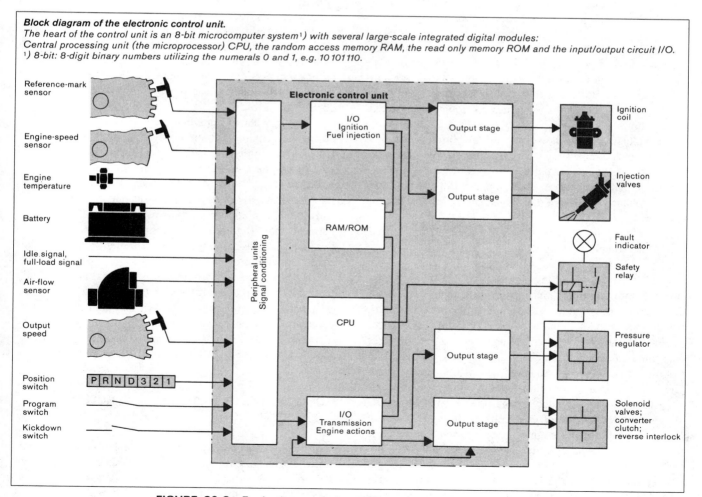

Block diagram of the electronic control unit.

The heart of the control unit is an 8-bit microcomputer system[1]) with several large-scale integrated digital modules: Central processing unit (the microprocessor) CPU, the random access memory RAM, the read only memory ROM and the input/output circuit I/O.
[1]) *8-bit: 8-digit binary numbers utilizing the numerals 0 and 1, e.g. 10 101 110.*

Reference-mark sensor

Engine-speed sensor

Engine temperature

Battery

Idle signal, full-load signal

Air-flow sensor

Output speed

Position switch

Program switch

Kickdown switch

Peripheral units Signal conditioning

Electronic control unit

I/O Ignition Fuel injection

RAM/ROM

CPU

I/O Transmission Engine actions

Output stage

Output stage

Output stage

Output stage

Ignition coil

Injection valves

Fault indicator

Safety relay

Pressure regulator

Solenoid valves; converter clutch; reverse interlock

FIGURE 20-2 Engine/transmission ECU arrangement. (*Courtesy of Robert Bosch Corporation*)

2. Transmission output shaft speed sensor
3. Engine air-flow sensor
4. Throttle valve switch
5. Gear shift lever (1, 2, 3, D, N, R, and P) position switch
6. Transmission program switch (S, E, or M)
7. Throttle kickdown switch
8. Engine coolant temperature sensor
9. Piston reference position sensor
10. Transmission pressure regulator switch
11. Transmission range gear solenoid valves
12. Electrohydraulic control unit
13. Electronic control unit (ECU)
14. Final controlling elements

System Operation

The transmission shaft output speed is sensed by a sensor, and the engine load and speed are also determined by sensors (load through the air-flow sensor, and rpm by a speed sensor). (See Fig. 20-1.) The gear selector position is electronically sensed at the shift tower or quadrant along with the transmission program switch placement (S, E, or M). Finally, the throttle kickdown switch inputs its voltage signal to the ECU. Reference to Fig. 20-2 illustrates that these various sensor input voltage signals are routed to a signal conditioning system within the ECU, where the amplitude of the voltage and the noise filtering are limited. An I/O (input/output) circuit shown in Fig. 20-2 converts the normally analog voltage signal to a digital voltage signal so that the ECU can interpret these signals. Both analog and digital voltage signals and their conversion are explained in Chapter 3.

In addition, the I/O circuit senses switching signals and relays the calculated output signals to the output stages. There, these weak signals are amplified in order to drive (power) the final controlling elements of both the transmission pressure controller and respective solenoid valves so that the electrohydraulic valves will drain pressurized oil from one range clutch and apply the next one in sequence.

From these various input voltage signals, the computer determines a speed for both upshifting and downshifting from the information program stored in ROM, and the difference computed in RAM.

The layout of the microprocessor shown in Fig. 20-2 allows the access by the I/O circuits of the various sensor voltage signals for the engine ignition system, the engine fuel-injection system, and the automatic transmission control circuitry.

Within the ECU, the CPU (central processing unit) is responsible for carrying out the the engine/transmission program stored in memory and is capable of performing the

necessary arithmetic and logic operations for system actuation.

The RAM (random access memory), the temporary working scratchpad for the ECU, is where all computational results and measured values are performed, while the ROM (read only memory) permits the reading of a predetermined pattern of zeros and ones. Accessing of a certain address in ROM results in a predetermined information output. In other words, the ROM contains the control program and the necessary vehicle data required to calculate the necessary output quantities. (For a description of basic computer operations, see Chapter 3.)

The modulation pressure control valve's speed of activation is controlled by the ECU, since the degree of range clutch pressure application determines the harshness of clutch engagement. Therefore this modulation pressure is controlled by using the load signal which is derived from the air-flow sensor and the throttle valve switch.

The safety relay shown in Fig. 20-2 provides engine/transmission overspeed and downshift inhibiting protection through means of the transmission downshift interlock and the reverse interlock by interrupt circuit activation.

These interlocks ensure that shifting into reverse gear range when the vehicle's forward speed is greater than 5 mph (8 km/hr) cannot occur. In addition, a downshift interlock inhibits or prevents a manual downshift by the driver if the vehicle speed is too high to allow a safe automatic downshift.

Further, when an automatic transmission range gear shift occurs, the engine ignition angle is moved from an uncorrected to a corrected position and back through the ECU control program. In other words, the ignition timing is retarded temporarily. This is necessary in order to decrease the torque transfer during a shift sequence to provide easier shifting in conjunction with a reduction in clutch apply slippage rate. Retarding the timing fools the engine into thinking that it is running at part load and therefore makes shifting smoother.

The transmission torque converter is automatically locked up (pump and turbine elements) in both 3rd and 4th gear ranges to eliminate internal slippage and improve fuel economy. The torque converter lockup clutch is applied by a solenoid valve, which reacts in response to both the engine load and transmission output shaft speed.

TOYOTA ELECTRONICALLY CONTROLLED TRANSMISSION

The ECT (electronically controlled transmission) is an automatic transmission that employs electrically controlled solenoid shift valves, rather than the standard hydraulic-type shift valves used in the majority of passenger car automatics.

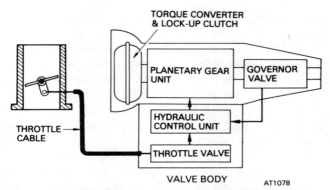

FIGURE 20-3 Typical hydraulically controlled automatic transmission layout. (*Courtesy of Toyota Motor Corporation*)

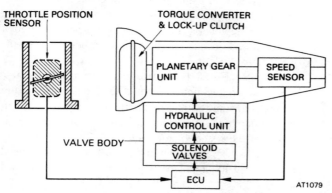

FIGURE 20-4 Electronically controlled automatic transmission layout. (*Courtesy of Toyota Motor Corporation*)

Now widely offered in the Camry, Supra, and Cressida models of Toyota vehicles, the basic system layout, in comparison to a standard hydraulically shifted transmission, is shown in Figs. 20-3 and 20-4.

Before describing the ECT in more detail, we will review the basic operation of both these transmissions.

Basic Operation – Hydraulic Transmission

Shown in Fig. 20-3 are the components which cause the transmission to automatically upshift or downshift. The shift point is controlled by two separate hydraulic pressures. These are:

1. A gear driven governor valve from the output shaft of the transmission that outputs a pressure in direct relation to the speed of the vehicle. In other words, at a low vehicle speed, there is a low governor pressure, and at a higher road speed, the governor pressure increases. This action is achieved by a set of rotating flyweights moving out and pushing a control valve forward inside the governor valve bore. This action de-

creases or restricts the size of the inlet fluid passage coming from the transmission converter oil pump. As the engine rpm increases when the driver pushes the throttle pedal down, so then will the main oil pump pressure. The combination of this rising main oil pressure being forced through a smaller inlet hole at the governor control valve results in a reduction in flow (volume), but an increase in pressure on the outlet side of the governor valve.

The governor pressure is directed to the various range gear shift valves, where it attempts to open each valve against the pressure of a coil spring that is designed to hold each valve closed.

Each shift valve has an adjustment spring to determine the actual speed at which the valve can actually shift or move.

2. The throttle valve is directly connected by cable, or by a vacuum hose on some cars, to a mechanical actuator or vacuum modulator valve bolted to the transmission housing.

Regardless of the type used, the action of moving the throttle results in the following response:

(a) With the engine at an idle rpm, the position of the control valve (modulator) inside the transmission results in the transmission main oil pressure flowing to this valve; therefore, maximum pressure exists at the valve because in this position oil can flow through the valve to the upper-half of the shift signal valves. The oil acting upon these valves will assist the governor pressure at the bottom of the valve in shifting it up against spring pressure.

(b) When the driver pushes the throttle down to accelerate the vehicle, the modulator control valve starts to open. This closes off the supply of main pump oil, while simultaneously dumping the oil from the upper-half of the shift valve body through an exhaust port.

The combination pressures generated at the governor and modulator valves therefore determine when each shift signal valve will move against the force of the valve return spring.

Consequently, when the driver accelerates from a standing position with a gradual opening of the throttle pedal, the vehicle upshifts quickly because both the increasing governor pressure (higher transmission output shaft speed) and the assisting slower dropping modulator pressure allow the shift signal valve to move under the combined action of both these fluid pressures.

If, however, the driver pushes the throttle pedal fully to the floor from a standing vehicle position, all of the modulator pressure at the upper-half of the shift valves is exhausted from the system. In order for a shift to occur, the governor pressure alone must be higher in order to overcome the force of the spring which is holding the shift valve closed. The end result is that a higher vehicle road speed is necessary to cause an upshift.

Once a shift valve is activated, stored main oil pressure at the side of the valve is allowed to flow through to the next range gear clutch, where it applies the multidisc clutches against the compressive force of the clutch release springs. At the same time, oil pressure in the lower clutch is dumped at the same basic rate as the oncoming clutch is being applied. This allows one clutch to slip into engagement, while the other one is sliding out of engagement.

Basic Operation — ECT Transmission

The actual application and release of the internal range gear clutches within the ECT transmission is the same as for the standard hydraulically applied unit described above, in that when a shift valve opens, transmission main fluid pressure is directed to the applying clutch.

The major difference lies in the fact that in the ECT transmission three electrically energized solenoid valves, known as units 1, 2 and 3 and shown in Figs. 20-16 and 20-17, are opened by signals from the ECU. When these solenoid valves are opened in sequence, transmission pump main fluid pressure is directed to the respective applying clutch to control not only shifting but also torque-converter

lock-up clutch timing. (A more detailed description is given in a later part of this chapter.)

Figure 20-5 illustrates the ECT (electronically controlled transmission) system and its respective sensing components, while Fig. 20-6 shows a schematic of the basic inputs and outputs to the ECT ECU.

The major difference between a non-ECT Toyota transmission and an ECT unit is in just how and when the shift sequence is determined:

1. Rather than using a mechanically driven transmission output shaft governor to sense vehicle road speed, the ECT unit employs a VSS (vehicle speed sensor) to send an electrical signal to the transmission ECU (electronic control unit).

   Various VSS's are shown throughout this textbook in various chapters; for a basic description of sensors, refer to Chapter 4. The Toyota ECT system employs two such VSS's, identified as the Number 1 and Number 2 units.

   The No.1 VSS is mounted as shown in Fig. 20-7 and acts as a backup unit should the No.2 sensor at the output shaft fail. Should this particular sensor fail, then it would output four electrical pulses for every revolution of the speedometer cable.

   The No.2 VSS shown in Fig. 20-8 is the main speed sensor, and its signal is the one that is normally used

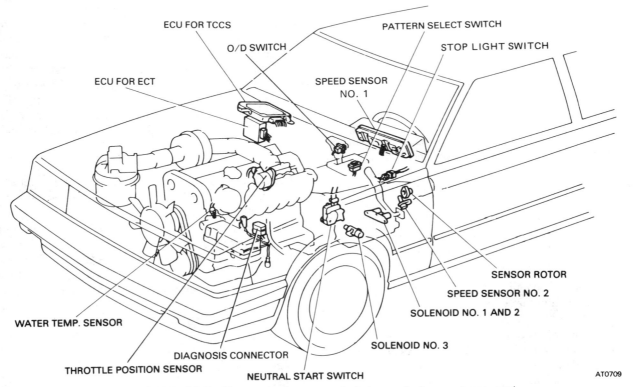

FIGURE 20-5 Electronically controlled transmission sensors and switches. (*Courtesy of Toyota Motor Corporation*)

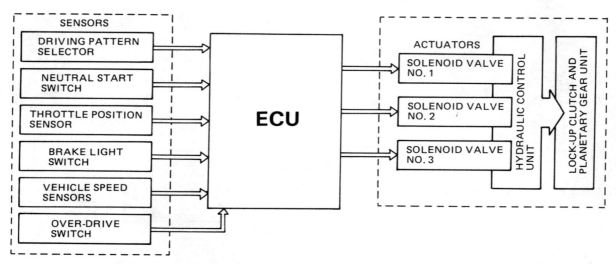

FIGURE 20-6 ECT ECU inputs and outputs. (*Courtesy of Toyota Motor Corporation*)

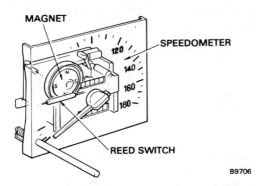

FIGURE 20-7 No. 1 vehicle speed sensor mounted in speedometer. (*Courtesy of Toyota Motor Corporation*)

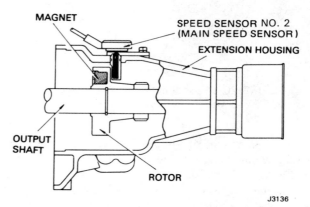

FIGURE 20-8 No. 2 vehicle speed sensor mounted at transmission output shaft. (*Courtesy of Toyota Motor Corporation*)

by the ECU to determine the transmission shift point. The No. 2 sensor on the transmission output shaft therefore takes the place of the mechanically driven governor on a non-ECT equipped vehicle.

2. A TPS (throttle position sensor) mounted on the side of the throttle body and shown in Fig. 20-9 operates on the basis of a varying potentiometer signal as the throttle is opened and closed. (Details of the action of a TPS can be found in Chapter 4.)

Two types of TPS's are used on Toyota vehicles, with one being known as a ''direct-type'' and the other as an ''indirect-type.''

Figure 20-10 illustrates the direct-type, which is used in all vehicles except the 1985 Cressida and Supra models.

Figure 20-11 shows the indirect-type, which is used only on the 1985 Cressida and Supra.

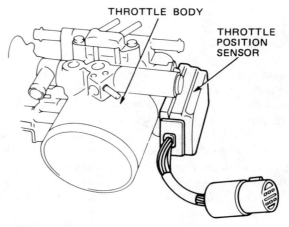

FIGURE 20-9 Location of TPS (throttle position sensor) (*Courtesy of Toyota Motor Corporation*)

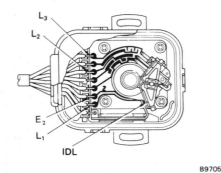

FIGURE 20-10 Direct type TPS. (*Courtesy of Toyota Motor Corporation*)

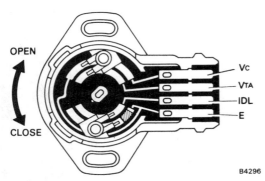

FIGURE 20-11 Indirect type TPS. (*Courtesy of Toyota Motor Corporation*)

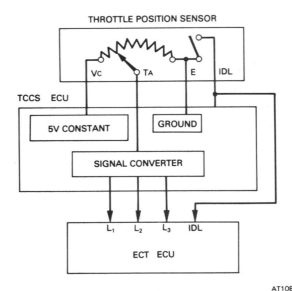

FIGURE 20-12 Indirect type of TPS, wiring schematic. (*Courtesy of Toyota Motor Corporation*)

In the direct-type of TPS, an IDL contact corresponds to a closed throttle position, while three other contacts identified as L1, L2, and L3 correspond to the various intermediate throttle positions. The connections between these four contacts, as well as the ground contact, function to provide a range of nine throttle position signals to the ECU so that a closer feedback signal regarding actual engine rpm position is monitored. In the indirect-type of TPS, there are four terminals, as shown in Fig. 20-11, which are Vc, Vta, IDL, and E.

The Vc terminal receives a constant 5 volt reference signal from the TCCS (Toyota computer-controlled system) ECU (engine fuel and ignition system). The Vta terminal outputs a continuous voltage signal directly proportional to throttle position, while the IDL terminal relays the fully-closed TPS signal to the transmission ECU. The E terminal is simply used as the main ground circuit.

The TCCS ECU receives and then converts the voltage signal from the Vta terminal into one of three signals, namely L1, L2, or L3 (TPS intermediate throttle positions), and then sends these digital signals to the ECT transmission ECU. The indirect-type of TPS electrical schematic is shown in Fig. 20-12.

3. A NTS (neutral start switch) is required with the ECT system as it is with a non-ECT equipped automatic

transmission type vehicle. This is an important switch in the ECT system since it indicates the actual range selector position to the ECT ECU. The NTS is illustrated in Fig. 20-13 and shows the various contact positions for the starter circuit as well as the range gear selector.

The ECT ECU is designed to interpret signals from the NTS only in the No. 2 and L positions, since the interconnection of contacts 2 and E is sensed as the transmission being in 2nd gear range.

The connection of L and E signifies to the ECT ECU that the transmission is in the "low" or 1st gear range, while all other combinations are interpreted by the ECT ECU as the D or drive range (3rd gear).

NOTE: In the 1985 and up Cressida and Supra car models, the ECT ECU senses the signal from the N contact to ini-

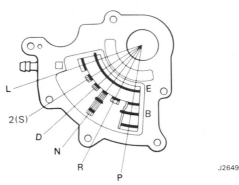

FIGURE 20-13 ECT neutral start switch. (*Courtesy of Toyota Motor Corporation*)

tiate what is known as a "squat reduction" function. This signal shifts the transmission into a 3rd gear or D mode for starting rather than a 1st gear start. This action minimizes the drive-line shock which is normally associated with a range gear selector shift from N to D as the engine torque flows into the transmission when the range gear clutches are applied. This prevents the hug-down effect of the rear of the car as a range gear is selected.

This "squat reduction" feature will only occur if the following three conditions are met:

(a) The vehicle is stopped.
(b) The foot brake is applied.
(c) The accelerator is in the fully closed (idle) position.

A delay feature within the ECU then shifts the transmission from 3rd, back into 1st for starting off from a parked position.

4. A pattern select switch shown in Fig. 20-14 determines the mode initiated by the ECU to control the shift schedule of the transmission. Some vehicles employ a pattern select switch with a power and normal position, while other models may be equipped with a three-position switch with either power, normal, or economy available to the driver.

When the normal pattern is selected, the ECU causes the torque converter lock-up clutch to engage at a lower vehicle road speed to improve fuel economy. When the power pattern is selected, lock-up will occur at a higher vehicle road speed to allow faster acceleration.

5. An overdrive switch allows the transmission to shift into and out of overdrive range, which is basically when the vehicle road speed is at a high enough level and also is in a high enough range gear.

The transmission torque-converter lock-up clutch

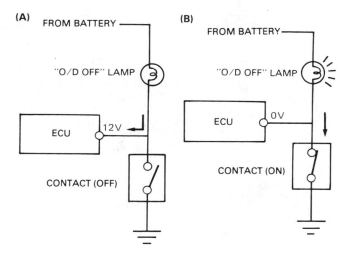

OVERDRIVE SWITCH

FIGURE 20-15 (a) Overdrive switch on circuit; (b) Overdrive switch off circuit. (*Courtesy of Toyota Motor Corporation*)

(turbine and pump are locked together hydraulically to provide a 1:1 direct drive) operates in 2nd, 3rd and O/D (overdrive) ranges by means of the ECT ECU. For lock-up to occur within the torque-converter assembly, the No.3 shift solenoid within the transmission valve body has to be energized by a signal from the ECU, which determines this action from the various sensor signals such as the TPS, the VSS, the pattern-select switch, etc.

In addition, lock-up shift timing is controlled by the ECU in order to reduce shift-shock. When an upshift or downshift occurs, the ECU automatically releases the torque-converter lock-up feature, and then reapplies lock-up once the shift has been completed.

Lock-up is automatically turned off by the ECU anytime that the brake light switch is on in order to ensure that the engine will not "stall out" during a locked drive wheel condition. Also, when the TPS idle contacts indicate a closed throttle position, lock-up disengages so that a smoother deceleration will exist.

When the O/D switch is turned on, as shown in Fig. 20-15, battery current is allowed to flow through the O/D signal lamp on the instrument panel to the ECU. If all conditions are satisfactory, the ECU will allow a shift into an overdrive mode.

When the O/D switch is turned off, battery current flows directly to ground as shown in Fig. 20-15. Therefore, O/D cannot be achieved by the ECU. At the same time, the O/D lamp will illuminate to warn the driver of this condition.

The O/D cancel signal flows from the TCCS ECU and cruise control computer to the O/D1 terminal of

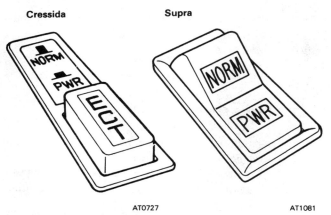

Cressida   **Supra**

AT0727   AT1081

FIGURE 20-14 ECT pattern select switch. (*Courtesy of Toyota Motor Corporation*)

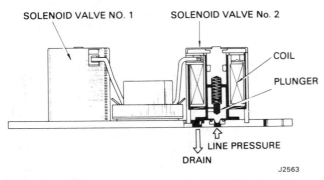

FIGURE 20-16 No. 1 and No. 2 ECT solenoid valves. (*Courtesy of Toyota Motor Corporation*)

the ECU connector where it is grounded out. Grounding of the O/D terminal to prevent this shift mode occurs under the following conditions:

(a) The engine coolant temperature is 158°F (70°C) or less on the Cressida and Supra, and less than 122°F (50°C) on the Camry, which uses a separate water temperature switch.

(b) During a cruise control mode, if the preset vehicle speed is exceeded by more than 4–6 mph (6–10 km/hr).

6. Three solenoid valves are employed with the ECT transmission and are located inside the valve body assembly. The one exception to this is the No. 3 solenoid valve on the Camry model passenger car, which is located on the transmission housing.

Figure 20-16 illustrates solenoid valves 1 and 2, while Fig. 20-17 shows the No. 3 solenoid valve.

In all cases, when either one of the solenoid valves is energized by a signal from the ECU, the valve opens and drains transmission pump main oil pressure from its served circuit. The No. 3 solenoid valve acts to drain line pressure and simultaneously activate the lock-up clutch.

The typical shift pattern that would emanate in the ECT ECU is shown in Fig. 20-18, in addition to what solenoids are activated in each range gear mode of the transmission.

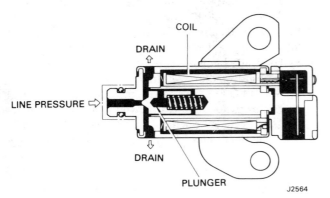

FIGURE 20-17 No. 3 ECT solenoid valve. (*Courtesy of Toyota Motor Corporation*)

SHIFT PATTERN IN ECU

Range \ Pattern	Normal	Power
D	Normal pattern	power pattern
2 (S)	"2" range pattern	←
L	"L" range pattern	←

Solenoid valve \ Gear	1st	2nd	3rd	OD
No. 1	ON	ON	OFF	OFF
No. 2	OFF	ON	ON	OFF

Relationship between the on-off settings of solenoid valves and the selected gear

FIGURE 20-18 ECT ECU shift pattern and applied clutches. (*Courtesy of Toyota Motor Corporation*)

TOYOTA SELF-DIAGNOSTIC FEATURES

The ECT ECU is capable of self-diagnosing a fault in the system, and the ECU will store this trouble code in memory, just as the engine ECU does when a problem exists in any of these circuits.

In the Cressida and Supra model vehicles, this stored trouble code can be determined by watching the number of flashes emanated at the O/D indicator lamp on the instrument panel. (See Fig. 20-19.)

When a problem is detected in the ECT transmission circuitry, the ECU will activate the instrument panel O/D off lamp only on the Cressida and Supra instrument panels. (See Fig. 20-19.) If, however, the O/D switch is off, then the lamp will illuminate steadily, rather than flashing or blinking on/off.

ACCESSING STORED TROUBLE CODES

To recall stored trouble codes from memory on the Cressida and Supra vehicles, a jumper wire has to be inserted as shown in Figure 20-20, across the respective diagnostic connector, and then the ignition key switch must be turned on.

With the jumper wire installed as shown in Fig. 20-20, the O/D lamp will pause for 4 seconds and then enter a

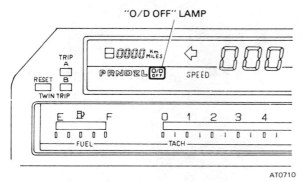

FIGURE 20-19 Cressida/Supra ECT self-diagnosis lamp location. (*Courtesy of Toyota Motor Corporation*)

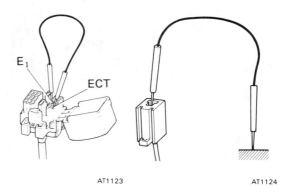

FIGURE 20-20 Cressida and Supra diagnostic connector jumper wire placement. (*Courtesy of Toyota Motor Corporation*)

flashing sequence. If there are no trouble codes stored in memory, the lamp will flash once every 0.25 seconds.

If, however, there are trouble codes stored in memory, then after the 4 second pause, the O/D lamp will flash every 0.5 seconds. The ECU feeds out trouble codes starting with the lowest numbered code first and progressing up to the higher numbers, with a 2.5 second pause between codes.

Once all codes have been flashed, the process repeats itself again. There are only 6 trouble codes for the ECT transmission. The *normal* code would be signified by the O/D lamp flashing every 0.25 second, while the remaining five codes are listed as follows:

Code No.	System Affected
42	Defective No.1 speed sensor (in speedometer head) or a broken wire or short circuit.
61	Defective No.2 speed sensor (transmission output shaft) or a broken wire or short circuit.
62	Faulty No.1 shift solenoid or short circuit or possibly a broken wire or short circuit in the wiring harness.
63	Faulty No.2 shift solenoid or short circuit, or a broken wire or short circuit in the harness.
64	Faulty No.3 shift solenoid or a short circuit, or a broken wire or short circuit in the harness.

A typical *Normal Code* appears as shown in Fig. 20-21 on the O/D lamp, while an example of the flashing code for a Code 62 is illustrated in Fig. 20-22. The ECU is not capable of detecting a mechanical problem in a solenoid valve, such as a sticking plunger.

If both the No.1 and No.2 shift solenoids fail, the ECU allows the transmission to operate in a 1st gear mode only. Since both the No.1 and No.2 solenoids would be defective, the ECU would not flash the instrument panel O/D light on the Cressida and Supra, and it would also not store a trouble code in memory other than *Normal*.

Of course the driver of the vehicle would be aware of the fact that the transmission was stuck in first gear range by the overall performance of the car, but he could safely drive the vehicle by manual selection of the range gear selector lever.

A fail-safe function allows the transmission to shift into 3rd gear, if only solenoid valve No.1 fails and while the vehicle is moving and in 1st gear range (selector in the D position), rather than into an O/D position, which it would want to do otherwise.

A failure in the ECT circuit can be bypassed by dis-

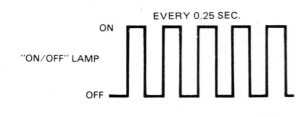

FIGURE 20-21 Normal trouble code O/D lamp flash time. (*Courtesy of Toyota Motor Corporation*)

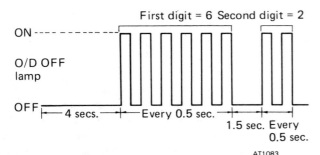

FIGURE 20-22 Trouble code 62 O/D lamp flash time example. (*Courtesy of Toyota Motor Corporation.*)

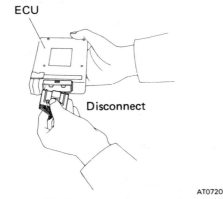

FIGURE 20-23 Disconnecting the ECU for manual transmission operation. (*Courtesy of Toyota Motor Corporation*)

connecting either the ECU connector or the ECT connector in the engine compartment, as shown in Fig. 20-23. During this mode of bypass operation, the transmission would shift in a normal mechanical/hydraulic arrangement to the ranges shown in Fig. 20-24.

VOLTAGE READING DIAGNOSIS METHOD

In all models other than the Cressida or Supra, self-diagnosis is accessed by using a voltmeter placed onto the DG connector or ECT terminal, as shown in Fig. 20-25.

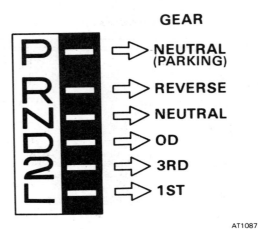

FIGURE 20-24 Range gear positions of the transmission during manual bypass function. (*Courtesy of Toyota Motor Corporation*)

A value of zero volts indicates a normal condition; 4 volts indicates a defective speed sensor; while 8 volts indicates that one or more solenoid valves are defective. If neither 4 volts or 8 volts are recorded, then check the TPS (throttle position sensor). If the TPS is serviceable, then the ECU is at fault. Check all wiring connections, and check the harness for bent pins, etc.

Checking Throttle Position Sensor

The TPS is a variable potentiometer. Therefore, at a closed position, no voltage is sensed at the ECU. When the throttle is gradually opened, this voltage signal will gradually increase until it outputs its maximum value of 8 volts, when it is in a wide open position.

By connecting a voltmeter at either the DG or ECT terminals, as is shown in Fig. 20-25, the acceptability of the TPS can be confirmed. Typical voltage readings for relative throttle angle openings are shown in Fig. 20-27.

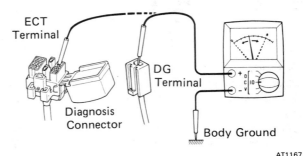

FIGURE 20-25 Voltmeter placement to check the TPS operation. (*Courtesy of Toyota Motor Corporation*)

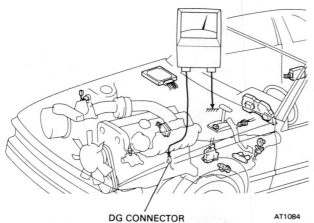

DG CONNECTOR   AT1084

FIGURE 20-26 Non-Cressida/Supra models ECT DG connector underhood location. (*Courtesy of Toyota Motor Corporation*)

THROTTLE OPENING

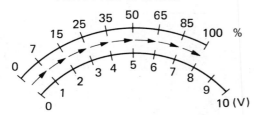

AT1125

FIGURE 20-27 Voltage readings for given throttle angle openings. (*Courtesy of Toyota Motor Corporation*)

Procedure

1. The ignition switch must be on once the voltmeter is connected (Fig. 20-25).

2. If the brake pedal is depressed during this check, a zero voltage reading will exist at all throttle positions.

3. A zero voltage reading as the throttle pedal is depressed could be caused by:

   (a) The brake pedal signal remaining on
   (b) The IDL signal at the throttle switch remaining on
   (c) A problem in the ECU power supply circuit
   (d) A problem in the ECU

Brake Signal Check

To confirm that the brake signal switch is operational, with the voltmeter connected as shown in Fig. 20-26, and the throttle pedal in a wide open position, 8 volts should be recorded on the voltmeter face. This reading confirms that the TPS is OK. Depress the brake pedal, and the voltmeter reading should drop to zero if the brake signal switch is operating correctly.

Shift Timing Check

To check that the ECT transmission is, in effect, shifting at the correct vehicle road speeds, connect a voltmeter to the ECT or DG terminal as shown in Figure 20-25.

Preferably this check should be done by extending jumper wires into the vehicle during a road test. Alternately, the vehicle wheels could be raised while the unit is in the shop, although this is not as satisfactory a test as an actual road test.

When the transmission has shifted to 2nd and 3rd gear positions, the lock-up clutch will come on and off on a regular basis. For this to happen, the throttle pedal must be in a half-open position or greater, since anything less will cause a change to the voltage readings shown below.

GEAR	1st	2nd		3rd		O/D	
Lock-up	—	Off	On	Off	On	Off	On
DG terminal voltage	0	2	3	4	5	6	7

Failure of the ECT transmission to shift as per the voltage readings indicated could signify a possible problem in the shift solenoid valves, or alternately, a mechanical malfunction within the transmission valve body.

ECT Wiring Schematic

Figure 20-28 illustrates the wiring schematic for a Toyota Cressida model car equipped with the TCCS and ECT systems.

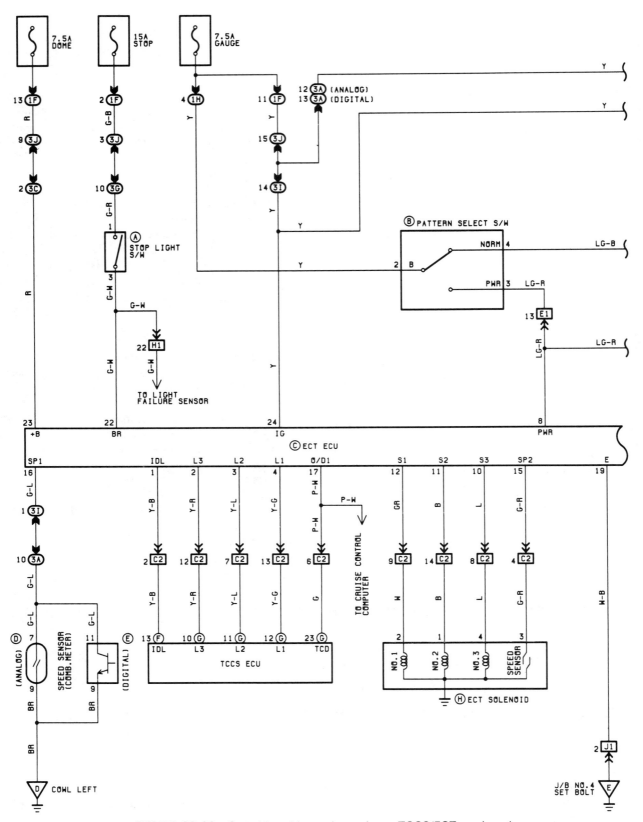

FIGURE 20-28 Cressida wiring schematic — TCCS/ECT equipped.
(*Courtesy of Toyota Motor Corporation*)

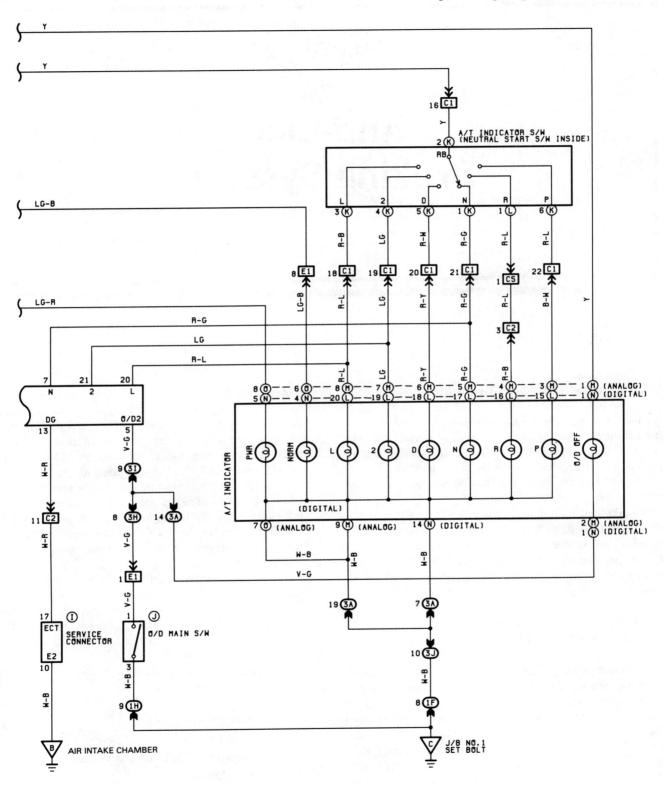

CHAPTER 21

♦

Anti-Skid Braking Systems

SYSTEM CONCEPT AND FUNCTION

A number of passenger car, as well as heavy-duty truck manufacturers, employ anti-skid braking devices on their vehicles. A conventional estimate indicates that at least 10 percent of all accidents occur as a result of the wheels locking up and the driver therefore losing directional stability or steering control.

In addition, during an emergency with wheel lock-up, the braking distances tend to increase because of loss of steering control; tires may blow apart; and if pulling a semi-trailer, jack-knifing is typically the end result. Two major systems are in use in passenger car ABS (anti-brake skid) systems, which are:

1. The Robert Bosch ABS system.
2. The Alfred Teves ABS system.

The Robert Bosch ABS system is used on many European and Japanese manufactured vehicles, notably as standard equipment on Mercedes-Benz models. In North America, it is available on the Chevrolet Corvette. Cadillac uses the Teves ABS system. The Lincoln Mark V11 and Continental employ Lincoln's own ABS anti-lock brake system which Lincoln claims is the most advanced braking system in the world offered as standard equipment.

Since all these anti-skid braking systems are somewhat similar in basic application, there are no major conceptual differences in each system, as you will see from the various descriptions given below.

Anti-brake skid devices are not new and have been in use since the early 1970's as optional equipment on a number of cars, notably on the Lincoln Continental. They have also been used on heavy-duty tractor-trailers in the United States, partly in response to the Federal Motor Vehicle Safety Standard-FMVSS 121 requirements.

A number of prominent manufacturers produced these anti-skid brake systems for use on these heavy-duty vehicles. However, a number of problems with all the systems manufactured in the early 1970's became apparent. Since then, their mandatory use on trucks in the United States has not been required.

They have, however, started to gain prominence once again on passenger cars and pickup-type trucks in the U.S., with both Ford and General Motors offering rear-wheel ABS as an option on their 1987 model pickups. New technology seems to have ironed out many of the bugs that existed in earlier model ABS systems.

ABS systems are now offered as standard equipment on the following vehicles:

1. Audi 5000CS Turbo 4x4
2. All model BMW's
3. Cadillac Allante, DeVille, and Fleetwood
4. Chevrolet Corvette
5. Ford Thunderbird, Mercury Cougar with 2.3 Turbo, 3.8L or 5.OL engine
6. Lincoln Continental Mk V11 LSC
7. All Mercedes-Benz cars with the exception of the 190E

2.3, 2.6, 2.5 and 2.5 Diesel, and 2.5L Turbo Diesel, where it is available as an option

8. Porsche 928S 4
9. Rover Sterling
10. Volvo 760 2.3 Turbo and 2.8L, 780 Model

The ABS system is optional on the following vehicles:

1. Alfa Romeo Milano
2. Buick LeSabre 3.8T Type
3. Mazda RX 7 Turbo
4. Mercedes-Benz 190E 2.3, 2.6, 2.5, 2.5 Diesel and Turbo
5. Mitsubishi Starion 2.6, 2.6 ESI-R
6. Peugeot 505 2.2, 2.2 Turbo, 2.5 Turbo Diesel, 505 2.8
7. Toyota Supra 3.0, 3.0 Turbo
8. Volvo 740 2.3, 2.3 Turbo

The system employs inductive rotational wheel speed sensors at each wheel that send a signal back to an on-board computer to indicate the deceleration rate of each rotating member. The programmed brake system ECM automatically applies and releases the brakes in very rapid succession to prevent a wheel lock-up condition. The rate at which this occurs is of course dependent upon the deceleration rate of the wheel, which in turn is affected by vehicle speed and road conditions.

When the driver applies the brakes, particularly in an emergency or panic-stop situation, the ABS system will regulate the hydraulic brake pressure or air brake apply pressure of the individual wheel cylinders in relation to either the acceleration or deceleration rate.

Although there is a limbo situation in the U.S. regarding anti-skid braking systems for commercial vehicles, in Europe a planned incorporation date of 1988 by the EEC or ECE Regulations has ensured that there will be a growing number of these ABS systems in use on commercial vehicles.

ROBERT BOSCH ABS SYSTEM

The Robert Bosch Corporation has been manufacturing and supplying ABS for cars since 1978, and for heavy-duty commercial vehicles since 1982. One basic system is applied to passenger cars, while three options are available for commercial applications, depending upon the type of application and the number of axles involved. However these fall into one of the following categories:

1. Single axle ABS for a semi-trailer with 1, 2 or 3 axles
2. Two axle ABS for a truck, trailer, semi-trailer, or bus with 2 or 3 axles
3. Three axle ABS for an articulated bus or special application trailer

Passenger Car ABS System

Figure 21-1 illustrates in simplified form the ABS system designed and manufactured by Robert Bosch Corporation, with the major operating components clearly shown. Three major components are employed with the ABS system, and these are:

Antiskid System ABS

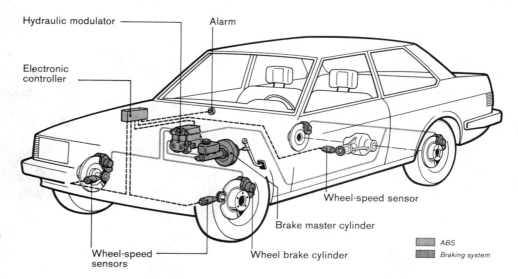

FIGURE 21-1 Basic components of an ABS system. (*Courtesy of Robert Bosch Corporation*)

FIGURE 21-2 Wheel speed sensor and impulse ring. (*Courtesy of Robert Bosch Corporation*)

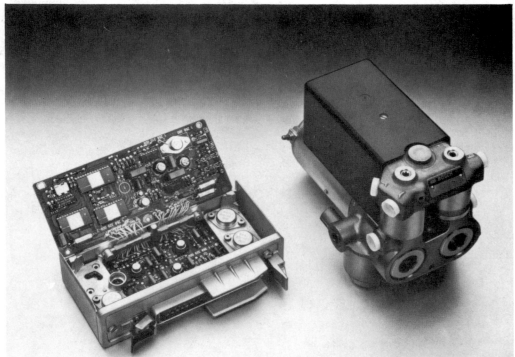

FIGURE 21-3 ABS ECU (electronic control unit) and hydraulic modulator. (*Courtesy of Robert Bosch Corporation*)

1. Wheel speed sensors
2. An electronic controller
3. Hydraulic modulator

In order to monitor the speed of each wheel on the vehicle, a toothed ring known as an impulse ring and shown in Fig. 21-2 is commonly used, although this ring can also be mounted on the differential. The electronic controller and hydraulic modulator are shown in Fig. 21-3 and operate in conjunction with the signal from the individual wheel speed sensors. Figure 21-4 shows a typical wheel speed sensor.

FIGURE 21-4 Typical ABS wheel speeds sensor. (*Courtesy of Robert Bosch Corporation*)

Basic Operation — ABS

The inductive rpm wheel speed sensors are basically magnetic pickups that continuously monitor each individual wheel's rotational speed and relay this signal to the electronic control unit (ECU).

The ECU is programmed for the vehicle. When the wheel speed sensor signals indicate that a wheel or wheels are locking up, the ECU calculates the wheel slip necessary for optimum (best braking) performance and sends out a command signal to the hydraulic modulator magnetically controlled solenoid valves to regulate the required braking.

The solenoid valves within the hydraulic modulator oscillate (open and close) between 4 and 15 cycles per second on average, depending upon the actual road surface conditions. This on again / off again action ensures that no individual wheel can ever lock up and create a skidding condition. The actuation of the solenoid valves by the ECU connects the individual wheel cylinders with either the corresponding hydraulic circuit of the master cylinder, or with the return pump. Alternately, they can close off the wheel cylinder from both the application circuit and pump, depending on whether the brakes are being applied or released. Vehicle stability and steering control are thus ensured at all times.

The Bosch ABS system is available for passenger cars with 3 or 4 hydraulic circuits, in addition to 3 or 4 wheel speed sensors. The system is therefore readily adaptable to vehicles with parallel, diagonal, or other layouts of brake circuits and can be equally applied to a front- or rear-wheel drive vehicle.

A simplified arrangement of a typical three-channel ABS system for parallel brake-circuit division is illustrated in Fig. 21-5, while Fig. 21-6 shows a typical ABS closed-loop control circuit.

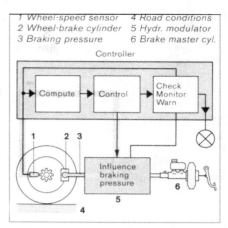

1 Wheel-speed sensor 4 Road conditions
2 Wheel-brake cylinder 5 Hydr. modulator
3 Braking pressure 6 Brake master cyl.

FIGURE 21-6 ABS closed-loop control circuit. (*Courtesy of Robert Bosch Corporation*)

Within the hydraulic modulator are the solenoid valves to control the fluid pressure to each individual wheel cylinder, as well as an accumulator chamber for each brake circuit and the return pump. The accumulators are designed to store energy temporarily by holding the surplus brake fluid, which will occur anytime that there is a drop in system pressure (solenoid valves opening and closing).

The return pump is designed to do just as its name implies; i.e., it carries or returns the brake fluid flowing from the wheel cylinders via the individual accumulators into the correct circuit of the brake system master cylinder.

ECU LAYOUT

Figure 21-7 illustrates the basic arrangement of the ECU, which was shown in its assembled state as Fig. 21-3.

The ECU (Fig. 21-7) consists of four major units, along with seven IC's (integrated circuits). These four major units are:

1. The input amplifier shown as Bipolar IC1. Its function is to simply receive and process the individual wheel speed sensor signals.

2. The computer unit shown as MOS IC2.1 (MOS = metal oxide semiconductor) and MOS IC2.2. It functions to figure out or compute the control signals.

3. The power stage shown as Bipolar IC4.1 and Bipolar IC4.2. Its main function is to activate the individual solenoid valves of the hydraulic modulator.

4. The monitoring circuit shown as MOS IC3. It is designed to detect any faults in the ABS circuit.

The analog signals generated at the individual wheel speed sensors (magnetic pickups) are relayed to the ECU, where they are electrically filtered and processed by the

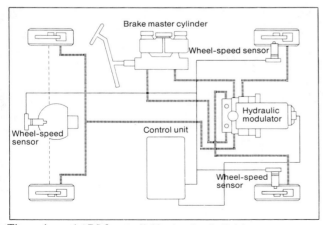

Three-channel ABS for parallel brake-circuit division.

FIGURE 21-5 Three-channel ABS parallel brake circuit division. (*Courtesy of Robert Bosch Corporation*)

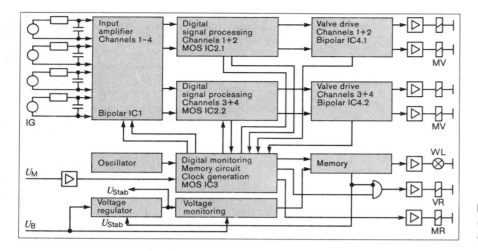

FIGURE 21-7 ECU arrangement. (*Courtesy of Robert Bosch Corporation*)

input amplifier (Bipolar IC1) before being passed on into the computer unit (MOS IC2.1 and MOS IC2.2). The generated signals based upon wheel speed, acceleration, and slip from diagonally opposed wheels are calculated, and the digital signals for the solenoid valves within the hydraulic modulator are created within the valve control unit using a current regulator and power output stage.

The application and release of the solenoid valves that control the steering axle are processed to prevent any torque reaction of the vehicle, which would tend to have the vehicle lose directional stability or produce sideways movement.

The emergency application of the brakes in an ABS system prevents wheel lock-up by this on/off reaction of the solenoid valves within the hydraulic modulator, even while the brake pedal effort by the driver remains constant. This is due to the rapid oscillation of the solenoid valves at between 4 and 15 cycles per second, depending upon road surface conditions.

Basically, when the brakes are applied and a wheel speed sensor triggers a rapid deceleration rate to the ECU, the wheel cylinder pressure is kept constant, rather than being

increased. If the wheel continues to decelerate, the hydraulic fluid pressure in this wheel cylinder is reduced so that the wheel receives less braking effort. This will generally result in the wheel attempting to accelerate again, but the ECU will immediately recognize this action from the generated voltage signal at the inductive speed sensor, and the wheel will again be decelerated by increasing the pressure. The cycle will again be repeated until the vehicle has slowed to a safe speed, or the wheel lock-up condition has been neutralized.

Figure 21-8 illustrates the above-cited actions at an individual wheel as it is controlled by the ABS system.

TESTING EQUIPMENT

In order to test/check performance complaints from the Bosch ABS system, it is necessary that you use a special tester, such as a Kent-Moore J-35890 microprocessor-based diagnostic tool (Fig. 21-9). The tool is used for the ABS system on the Chevrolet Corvette. Major features of this tester are:

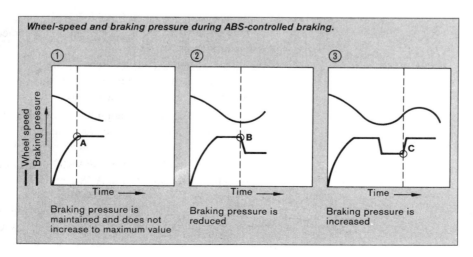

FIGURE 21-8 ABS system action. (*Courtesy of Robert Bosch Corporation*)

J 35890
ANTI-LOCK BRAKE SYSTEM TESTER

The J 35890 ABS Tester is a microprocessor-based diagnostic tool for the Bosch ABS anti-lock braking system used on the 1986 Corvette. The tester is simply connected to the ABS control module harness and will completely perform the following tests:

- Voltage, continuity, resistance and ground checks of the ABS system
- Status test of lateral acceleration switch, ignition switch, brake light switch and anti-lock light
- Dynamic test of pump, two stage valves and speed sensors

System faults are displayed on the 16-character vacuum fluorescent display by a message indicating which circuit or component to check. Two membrane switches are provided to allow the technician to answer messages, select the test modes and wheels to be tested.

Features:

- Identifies and displays twenty fault messages
- Tester is powered through vehicle harness
- Includes 6' harness connector
- Complete comprehensive instructions and diagnostic information

FIGURE 21-9 Anti-lock brake system tester. *(Courtesy of Kent-Moore Tool Group, Sealed Power Corporation)*

1. Identifies and displays 20 fault messages.
2. Tester is powered through the vehicle wiring harness.
3. Includes a 6 foot (2 meter) harness connector.
4. Comes with complete comprehensive instructions and diagnostic information.

This tester is simply connected to the ABS control module harness and completely performs the following tests:

1. Voltage, continuity, resistance, and ground checks of the ABS system.

2. Status test of lateral acceleration switch, ignition switch, brake light switch, and anti-lock light.
3. Dynamic test of the hydraulic pump, two-stage valves, and speed sensors.

System faults are displayed on the 16 character vacuum fluorescent display by a message indicating which circuit or component to check. Two membrane switches are provided to allow the technician to answer messages, and to select the test modes and wheels to be tested.

CADILLAC ANTI-SKID BRAKE SYSTEM

The anti-skid brake system used on Cadillac DeVille and Fleetwood models is illustrated in Fig. 21-10. The system is designed to operate all four wheels through a combined use of the wheel speed sensors with the microprocessor, which determines when a wheel has almost stopped turning or is entering a locked-up mode.

The EBCM (electronic brake control module) or microprocessor, which is located inside the vehicle passenger compartment (driver side), receives voltage signals from the wheel speed sensors. Therefore, should a wheel deceleration condition occur through braking action, the frequency of the sensor signal is changed. The EBCM adjusts brake fluid pressure automatically to each wheel to ensure maximum vehicle deceleration without wheel lock-up, and a dangerous skidding condition is prevented. The EBCM is a separate computer which is used strictly for the control of the ABS system.

System Components

The main components of the anti-skid brake system (illustrated in Fig. 21-10) are the following:

1. Hydraulic pump and motor assembly
2. Hydraulic accumulator
3. Pressure sensing switch
4. Hydraulic fluid reservoir containing an integral filter
5. Hydraulic booster/master cylinder
6. Four-wheel speed sensors
7. EBCM (electronic brake control module)
8. Valve block assembly

System Description

The term ABS (anti-lock brake system) is often used to describe these types of brake systems. In the Cadillac ABS system, the hydraulic unit replaces the conventional vacuum booster tank and the dual master cylinder arrangement that is used in a non-skid type Cadillac power brake system.

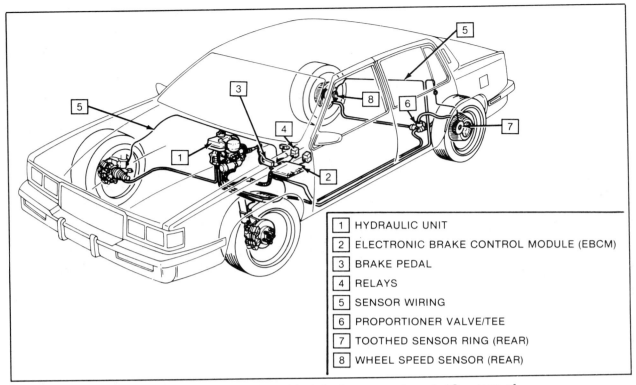

1	HYDRAULIC UNIT
2	ELECTRONIC BRAKE CONTROL MODULE (EBCM)
3	BRAKE PEDAL
4	RELAYS
5	SENSOR WIRING
6	PROPORTIONER VALVE/TEE
7	TOOTHED SENSOR RING (REAR)
8	WHEEL SPEED SENSOR (REAR)

FIGURE 21-10   TEVES Anti-lock brake system layout. (*Courtesy of Cadillac Motor Car Division of GMC*)

Refer to Fig. 21-11, which illustrates the hydraulic unit components, as you read the description of operation of the ABS system. In addition, Fig. 21-12 illustrates the various electrical connector locations used with the ABS system.

Component parts of the hydraulic unit are:

1. An integral master cylinder and booster.
2. Pump and electric motor assembly.
3. An accumulator to store the high pressure fluid which acts upon an internal diaphragm with nitrogen trapped behind it.
4. A pressure switch to energize/de-energize the pump circuit at a predetermined pressure.
5. Reservoir and cap with a fluid level sensor that will signal the EBCM of a low fluid condition. This action will trigger a red *brake* lamp located on the instrument panel, as well as causing the EBCM to disable the anti-lock (ABS) function.
6. A valve block which contains a series of electrically operated solenoid valves to apply/release brake fluid to all wheel cylinders only during anti-skid operation.
7. The system main valve which is solenoid-activated and located in the hydraulic unit. It receives power from the EBCM only when the ABS mode is activated.

The wheel speed sensors (one per wheel) transmit a small a.c. voltage/current signal to the EBCM by creating a voltage which is generated through the process of magnetic induction. A toothed sensor ring rotates past the stationary wheel speed sensor. (See Items 7 and 8 in Fig. 21-10.) This action is similar to that shown in Fig. 21-2 for the Bosch ABS system. The EBCM provides output signals to the hydraulic unit as well as an anti-lock warning lamp, which is located in the left-hand driver information center. As with other computers in the vehicle, such as the ECM and BCM, the EBCM receives its input the instant that the ignition switch is turned on. This action allows the EBCM to perform a series of self-checks on the ABS system, and it enters a "wake-up" mode. Power is sent through the main relay (Item 12 in Fig. 21-12); if for any reason this relay is not energized, then the anti-lock braking system cannot operate.

When the vehicle is moving, the EBCM receives the small generated a.c. voltages from each wheel speed sensor and is therefore able to determine the actual rotational speed at each wheel, based upon the frequency of the signals.

Anti-lock brake protection is inhibited any time that an open circuit is detected on the low fluid/low pressure input circuit, since both of these circuits consist of a continuous loop circuit which runs through the fluid level sensor (Item

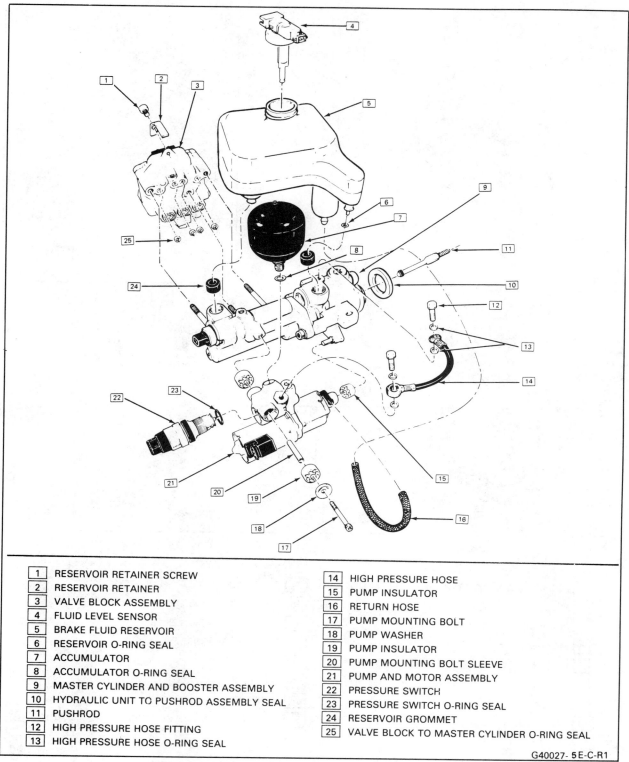

1	RESERVOIR RETAINER SCREW	14	HIGH PRESSURE HOSE
2	RESERVOIR RETAINER	15	PUMP INSULATOR
3	VALVE BLOCK ASSEMBLY	16	RETURN HOSE
4	FLUID LEVEL SENSOR	17	PUMP MOUNTING BOLT
5	BRAKE FLUID RESERVOIR	18	PUMP WASHER
6	RESERVOIR O-RING SEAL	19	PUMP INSULATOR
7	ACCUMULATOR	20	PUMP MOUNTING BOLT SLEEVE
8	ACCUMULATOR O-RING SEAL	21	PUMP AND MOTOR ASSEMBLY
9	MASTER CYLINDER AND BOOSTER ASSEMBLY	22	PRESSURE SWITCH
10	HYDRAULIC UNIT TO PUSHROD ASSEMBLY SEAL	23	PRESSURE SWITCH O-RING SEAL
11	PUSHROD	24	RESERVOIR GROMMET
12	HIGH PRESSURE HOSE FITTING	25	VALVE BLOCK TO MASTER CYLINDER O-RING SEAL
13	HIGH PRESSURE HOSE O-RING SEAL		

G40027- 5 E-C-R1

FIGURE 21-11 Anti-lock brake system hydraulic unit components.
(*Courtesy of Cadillac Motor Car Division of GMC*)

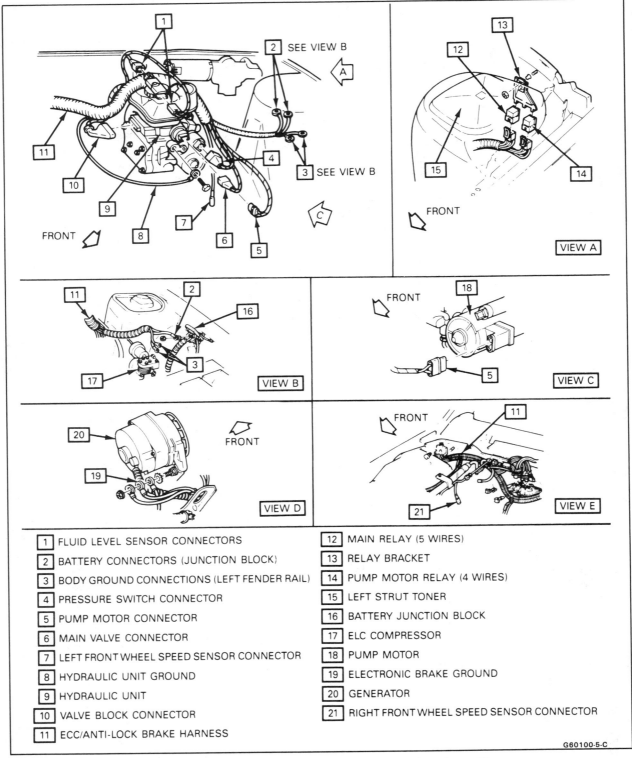

1	FLUID LEVEL SENSOR CONNECTORS	12	MAIN RELAY (5 WIRES)
2	BATTERY CONNECTORS (JUNCTION BLOCK)	13	RELAY BRACKET
3	BODY GROUND CONNECTIONS (LEFT FENDER RAIL)	14	PUMP MOTOR RELAY (4 WIRES)
4	PRESSURE SWITCH CONNECTOR	15	LEFT STRUT TONER
5	PUMP MOTOR CONNECTOR	16	BATTERY JUNCTION BLOCK
6	MAIN VALVE CONNECTOR	17	ELC COMPRESSOR
7	LEFT FRONT WHEEL SPEED SENSOR CONNECTOR	18	PUMP MOTOR
8	HYDRAULIC UNIT GROUND	19	ELECTRONIC BRAKE GROUND
9	HYDRAULIC UNIT	20	GENERATOR
10	VALVE BLOCK CONNECTOR	21	RIGHT FRONT WHEEL SPEED SENSOR CONNECTOR
11	ECC/ANTI-LOCK BRAKE HARNESS		

G60100-5-C

FIGURE 21-12   Anti-lock brake system connector locations. (*Courtesy of Cadillac Motor Car Division of GMC*)

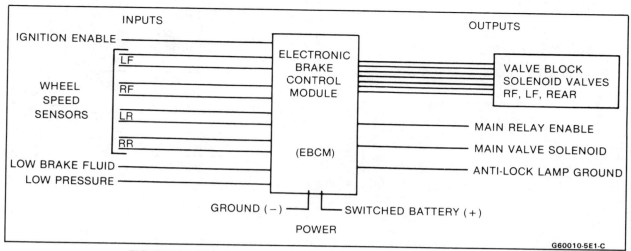

FIGURE 21-13 Electronic brake control module inputs and outputs.
(*Courtesy of Cadillac Motor Car Division of GMC*)

4) and pressure switch (Item 22) on the hydraulic unit (Fig. 21-11).

Each hydraulic brake circuit on the vehicle (namely, the left front, the right front, and the rear brakes) is equipped with two nonserviceable solenoid valves that control the fluid inlet and outlet. During normal braking, the solenoid operated valve block (Item 3, Fig. 21-11) receives no electrical signal from the EBCM. Therefore, the inlet valve is normally open (NO), and the outlet valve is normally closed (NC). The system functions in the same manner as a non-ABS equipped vehicle.

When the EBCM senses a change in wheel speed based upon the input sensor signal from each wheel speed sensor, these inlet and outlet valves for each brake circuit receive a 12 volt signal from the EBCM. These valves can act singly or in combination, since road surface conditions can cause either of the wheels to rotate/decelerate at different speeds. Each wheel cylinder will therefore receive either a fluid pressure increase, hold, or decrease signal to prevent a wheel lock/brake skid condition during the ABS mode of operation.

During ABS operation, the driver may sense a slight oscillation at the brake pedal because the individual brake cylinders are being applied and released very rapidly by the EBCM signal to the valve block assembly (Item 3, Fig. 21-11). In addition, it's also possible to hear a slight ticking or popping sound, which is an indication that the ABS system is in fact operational.

It may take a short time to become used to this different feel of the brake pedal on an ABS equipped vehicle; the slight up and down movement of the pedal is normal. The key is to maintain a steady pressure on the pedal during braking in order to allow the ABS system to operate and provide the shortest possible stopping distance without incurring wheel lock-up and vehicle skidding.

Booster pressure for the rear brakes, and for the front brakes during the anti-lock mode, is provided by an electric pump and motor (Item 21, Fig. 21-11), which pressurizes the accumulator (Item 7). This pump and motor assembly

is cycled on/off by the action of the pressure switch (Item 22, Fig. 21-11) independent of the EBCM.

The pressure switch is designed to engage the pump motor relay any time that accumulator pressure falls below 2030 psi (14,000 kPa), and to deactivate the pump system when pressure rises to approximately 2610 psi (18,000 kPa). Should a leak exist in the accumulator system and the fluid pressure drop to about 1500 psi (10,350 kPa), then the pressure switch will activate the red *brake* warning lamp, and the EBCM will illuminate the amber *anti-lock* lamp on the driver information center.

To prevent excessive running time of the hydraulic pump and motor, an electrical timer flasher module is contained in the pump circuit in the instrument panel behind the glove box. Should the pump be energized for longer than 3 minutes, this module will cause the *brake* warning lamp to flash on the driver's instrument center panel.

SAFETY PRECAUTION: Due to the high pressure fluid stored in the accumulator, should brake service require that hydraulic lines, hoses, or fittings be disconnected at any time, the hydraulic accumulator must be relieved of stored pressure. This can be done by pumping the brake pedal with the ignition switch off. You may have to pump the pedal in excess of twenty times using full strokes to bleed off the system pressure. Once a definite pedal increase is felt, stroke the pedal another two or three times.

ELECTRONIC ABS CIRCUIT

Figure 21-13 illustrates the basic EBCM electrical circuit input and output signals, while Fig. 21-14 (Parts 1 and 2) illustrates the complete circuit wiring diagram for the complete anti-lock braking system. This wiring diagram will allow you to trace the various connections between the major components of the system and may help you to understand more fully the system of operation described earlier.

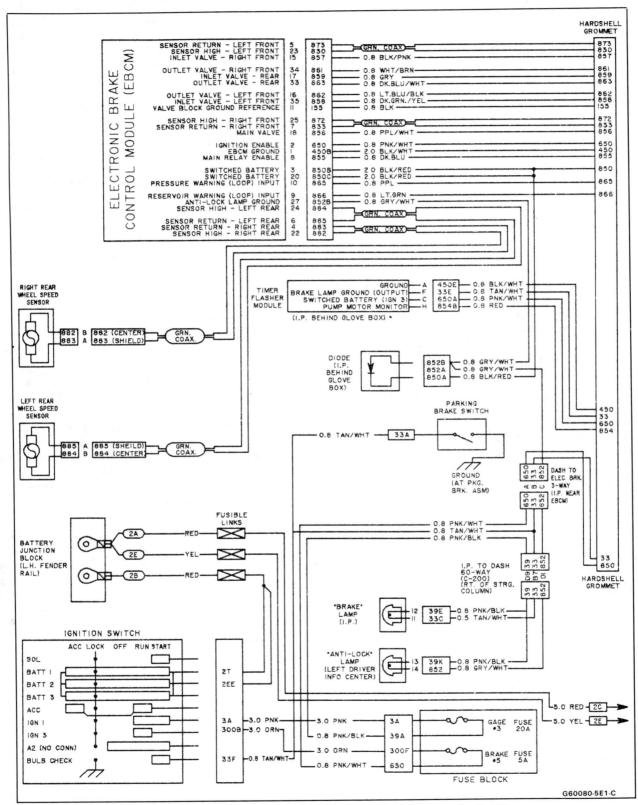

FIGURE 21-14(A). Anti-lock brake system wiring diagram for DeVille and Fleetwood car models. (*Courtesy of Cadillac Motor Car Division of GMC*)

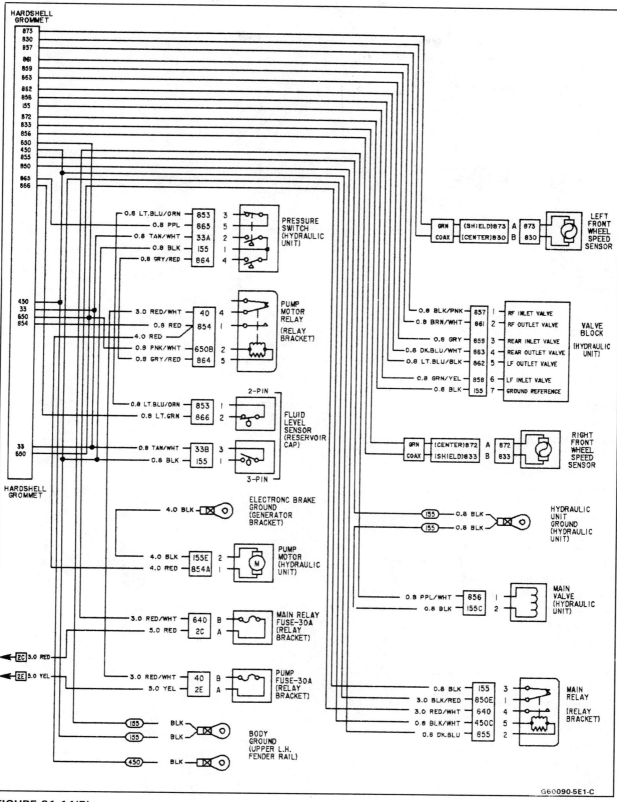

FIGURE 21-14(B)

G60090-5E1-C

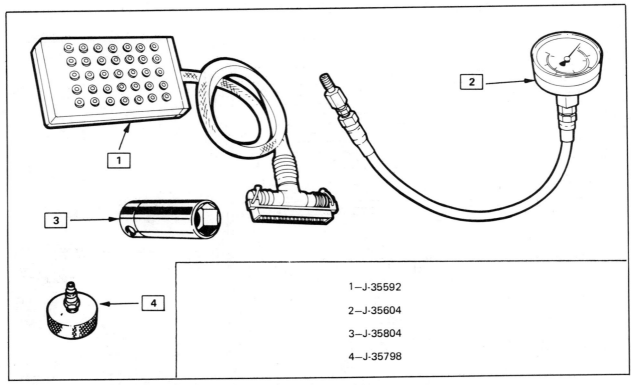

FIGURE 21-15 TEVES anti-lock brake system special diagnostic tools.
(*Courtesy of Cadillac Motor Car Division of GMC*)

1—J-35592

2—J-35604

3—J-35804

4—J-35798

TROUBLESHOOTING THE ABS SYSTEM

To troubleshoot the anti-lock brake system effectively, you must first understand and feel comfortable with the sequence of events involved in its operation.

Secondly, you will require a number of special tools, such as those shown in Fig. 21-15, to monitor the system. These special tools are used for the following purposes:

1. Kent-Moore P/N J-35592, a "pin-out box" that plugs into the controller harness, is used with a DVOM (digital volt/ohm meter) to diagnose the Teves anti-skid brake system. This pinout box can be connected to the EBCM system 35 pin harness connector, as shown in Fig. 21-16.

    A detailed procedure and numerous troubleshooting charts in the vehicle service manual specifies where to check resistance values between various numbered pins and then how to proceed to correct the problem. Using the pinout box, continuity or noncontinuity can be determined. It then becomes a case of tracing each circuit to establish where the problem might be. Refer to Fig. 21-14(a) (system wiring diagram) to identify the various pin numbers on the EBCM. The pinout box is itself numbered; therefore, along with a DVOM, each numbered circuit can be probed at the pinout box.

    Figure 21-17 lists the typical resistance and voltage values that should be obtained when measuring between pin numbers.

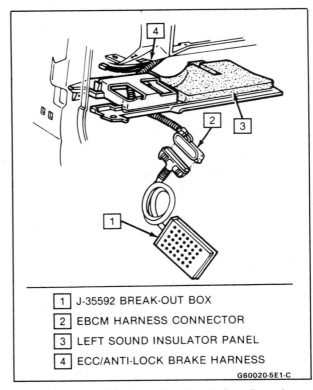

1 J-35592 BREAK-OUT BOX

2 EBCM HARNESS CONNECTOR

3 LEFT SOUND INSULATOR PANEL

4 ECC/ANTI-LOCK BRAKE HARNESS

G60020-5E1-C

FIGURE 21-16 Installing Break-Out Box J-35592 to EBCM harness connector. (*Courtesy of Cadillac Motor Car Division of GMC*)

TEST A
PIN-OUT CHECKS

- CONNECT BREAK-OUT BOX J-35592 to 35-PIN EBCM HARNESS CONNECTOR AS DESCRIBED IN THIS SECTION

- PERFORM CHECKS WITH HIGH IMPEDANCE DIGITAL MULTIMETER J-34029-A OR EQUIVALENT

- ALL CHECKS ARE MADE WITH ENGINE STOPPED

CIRCUIT TO BE TESTED	IGNITION SWITCH POSITION	MULTIMETER SCALE/RANGE	MEASURE BETWEEN PIN NUMBERS	SPECIFICATION	IF RESULT NOT WITHIN SPECIFICATION, SEE CHART
IGNITION ENABLE	RUN	20 DCV	2(+)*,1(−)*	10 V MINIMUM	A-1
MAIN RELAY GROUND	OFF	200 Ω	1,3	CONTINUITY	A-2
	OFF	200 Ω	1,20	CONTINUITY	
MAIN RELAY COIL	OFF	200 Ω	1,8	45-105 Ω	A-3

BEFORE PERFORMING THIS TEST: • REMOVE GAGE FUSE (FUSE #3) FROM FUSE PANEL
• PLACE FUSED JUMPER BETWEEN BREAK-OUT BOX PINS 2 & 8

MAIN RELAY POWER	ON	20 DCV	3(+),1(−)	10 V MINIMUM	A-4
	ON	20 DCV	20(+),1(−)	10 V MINIMUM	

BEFORE PROCEEDING: • REMOVE JUMPER FROM PINS 2 & 8
• INSTALL GAGE FUSE

EBCM SWITCH LOOP	OFF	200 Ω	9,10	LESS THAN 5 Ω	A-5
	OFF	200 Ω	1,9	NO CONTINUITY	A-6
RR SENSOR RESISTANCE	OFF	2k Ω	4,22	800-1400 Ω	A-7
LF SENSOR RESISTANCE	OFF	2k Ω	5,23	800-1400 Ω	A-8
LR SENSOR RESISTANCE	OFF	2k Ω	6,24	800-1400 Ω	A-9
RF SENSOR RESISTANCE	OFF	2k Ω	7,25	800-1400 Ω	A-10
MAIN VALVE SOLENOID	OFF	200 Ω	11,18	2-5 Ω	A-11
VALVE BLOCK GROUND	OFF	200 Ω	1,11	LESS THAN 2 Ω	A-12
RF INLET VALVE	OFF	200 Ω	11,15	5-7 Ω	A-13
LF INLET VALVE	OFF	200 Ω	11,35	5-7 Ω	A-14
REAR INLET VALVE	OFF	200 Ω	11,17	5-7 Ω	A-15
RF OUTLET VALVE	OFF	200 Ω	11,34	3-5 Ω	A-16
LF OUTLET VALVE	OFF	200 Ω	11,16	3-5 Ω	A-17
REAR OUTLET VALVE	OFF	200 Ω	11,33	3-5 Ω	A-18

BEFORE PERFORMING THIS TEST: • REMOVE MAIN RELAY FROM CONNECTOR ON RELAY BRACKET (5 WIRES ATTACHED)

DIODE	OFF	DIODE ─▶⊢──	27(+), 3(−)	CONTINUITY	A-19
	OFF	DIODE ─▶⊢──	3(+), 27(−)	NO CONTINUITY	

BEFORE PROCEEDING: • INSTALL MAIN RELAY

* (+) OR (−) INDICATES MULTI-METER POLARITY
IF ALL TEST RESULTS ARE WITHIN SPECIFICATION, RECONNECT EBCM AND VERIFY CONTINUOUS "ANTI-LOCK" LAMP OPERATION

- IF NORMAL OPERATION RESUMES, SEE NOTE ON INTERMITTANTS

- IF LAMP REMAINS ON, SEE CHART A-20

G60130-5E1-C

FIGURE 21-17 Anti-lock brake system pin-out checks chart. (*Courtesy of Cadillac Motor Car Division of GMC*)

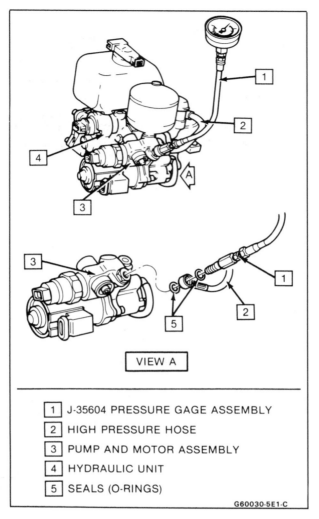

1 J-35604 PRESSURE GAGE ASSEMBLY
2 HIGH PRESSURE HOSE
3 PUMP AND MOTOR ASSEMBLY
4 HYDRAULIC UNIT
5 SEALS (O-RINGS)

G60030-5E1-C

FIGURE 21-18 Installing hydraulic pressure gauge J-35604 to pump and motor assembly. (*Courtesy of Cadillac Motor Car Division of GMC*)

2. Kent-Moore P/N J-35604, which is a pressure gauge. Prior to installing this gauge into the pump and motor assembly, depressurize the system accumulator, as described earlier, by pumping the brake pedal approximately 20 times with the ignition key off. The test hookup for this gauge is illustrated in Fig. 21-18.

3. Kent-Moore P/N J-35804 is a pressure switch remover deep socket. This tool can be used to remove the pressure switch (Item 22, Fig. 21-11). Depressurize the accumulator first as described in this chapter.

4. Kent-Moore P/N J-35798, which is a bleeder adapter.

Only the front brakes should be pressure bled. The rear brakes will pressure bleed without the use of special equipment. Only diaphragm-type pressure bleeding equipment should be used to prevent air, moisture, and other contaminants from entering the system.

The amber and red EBCM indicator lamps on the instrument panel will illuminate under different operating conditions. Figure 21-19 illustrates the sequence of events during which these lamps will or will not illuminate under normal operating conditions.

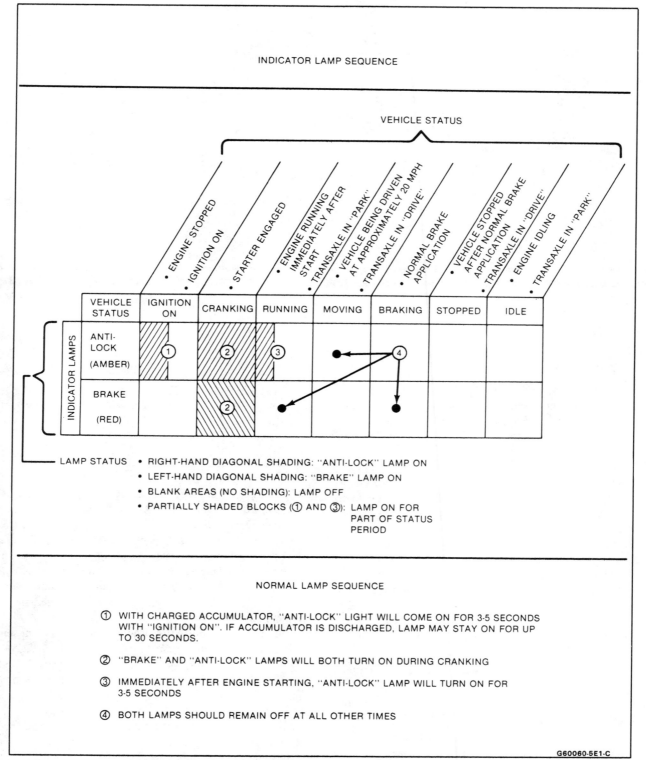

FIGURE 21-19 TEVES anti-lock brake system instrument panel warning indicator lamp sequence. (*Courtesy of Cadillac Motor Car Division of GMC*)

CHAPTER 22

♦

Electronic Level Control

In order to provide optimum ride characteristics and passenger comfort, many vehicle manufacturers offer, as either standard or optional equipment, an automatic levelling control system. Since all of these systems operate on the same general principles, let us consider the system used on General Motors vehicles, such as Cadillac and Oldsmobile.

The ELC (electronic level control) is standard equipment on the Eldorado, Seville, Fleetwood Brougham, Fleetwood Limousine, and the commercial chassis, and is optional on the DeVille. Oldsmobile offers this system on its 88 and 98 vehicles, and on the Toronado as standard equipment.

In addition to the standard rear suspension system, the ELC system shown in Fig. 22-1 uses the following components:

1. A 12-volt d.c. permanent magnet motor air compressor (Fig. 22-2).
2. An air dryer to absorb moisture from the air before it is delivered to the air shocks (Fig. 22-3).
3. An exhaust solenoid located in the compressor controlled by a height sensor (Fig. 22-4).
4. A compressor relay to complete the 12 volt (+) circuit to the compressor motor and dash light when energized (Fig. 22-1).
5. A height sensor mounted to the frame crossmember at the rear of the vehicle (Fig. 22-5).
6. Air adjustable shock absorbers (Fig. 22-6).
7. Wiring, air tubing, and a pressure limiter to maintain

a maximum system ride pressure of 90 psi (620.5 kPa) or 67–74 psi (462–510 kPa) on later model vehicles. (See Fig. 22-7.)

SYSTEM OPERATION

If you are at all familiar with the Neway air ride suspension systems employed on many Class 8 heavy-duty trucks, the basic concept of the air ride system used on passenger cars follows the same general pattern. The major difference is that the passenger car system employs an electric driven air compressor and electric connections at the sensor to monitor height ride conditions of the suspension system. Figures 22-1 and 22-8 show the wiring diagram arrangement for a typical ELC system.

In its simplest form the system employs a height sensor mounted to the frame rear crossmember. (Fig. 22-5) Attached to this sensor is an actuating arm which through a small connecting link is attached to the rear suspension upper control arm. As the vehicle load (passenger and trunk) is altered, the displacement of the vehicle body to suspension system will trigger the actuating link connected to the ride height levelling control valve. The height sensor is an electronic device, as shown in Figs. 22-1 and 22-8, that controls two basic circuits:

1. the air compressor relay coil and dash mounted indicator light circuit; and,
2. the air compressor exhaust solenoid coil ground circuit.

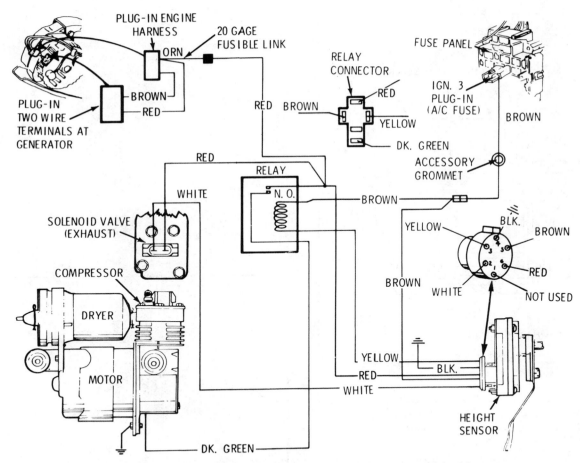

FIGURE 22-1 ELC (electronic level control) components and wiring diagram for the Oldsmobile 88 and 98 model vehicles.

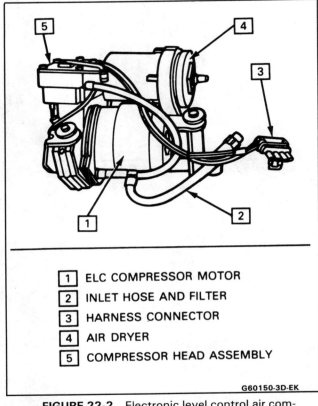

1 ELC COMPRESSOR MOTOR
2 INLET HOSE AND FILTER
3 HARNESS CONNECTOR
4 AIR DRYER
5 COMPRESSOR HEAD ASSEMBLY

G60150-3D-EK

FIGURE 22-2 Electronic level control air compressor. (*Courtesy of Oldsmobile Div. of GMC*)

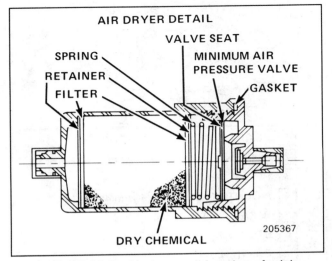

AIR DRYER DETAIL

VALVE SEAT
SPRING
MINIMUM AIR
RETAINER
PRESSURE VALVE
FILTER
GASKET

DRY CHEMICAL

205367

FIGURE 22-3 Air dryer and location of minimum air pressure valve. (*Courtesy of Oldsmobile Div. of GMC*)

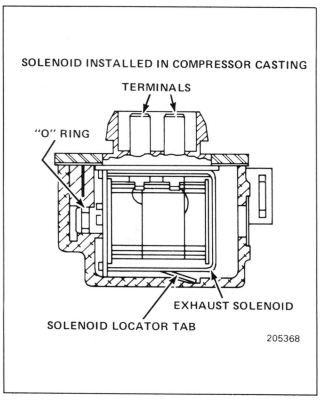

FIGURE 22-4 ELC compressor exhaust solenoid. (*Courtesy of Oldsmobile Div. of GMC*)

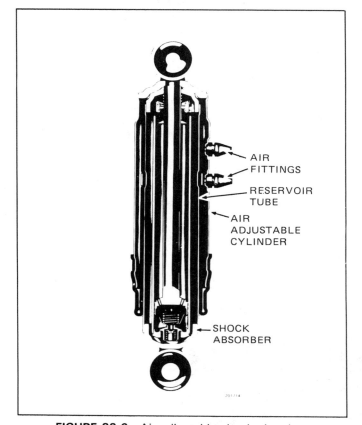

FIGURE 22-6 Air adjustable shock absorber. (*Courtesy of Oldsmobile Div. of GMC*)

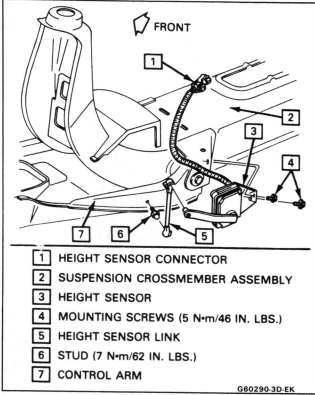

1	HEIGHT SENSOR CONNECTOR
2	SUSPENSION CROSSMEMBER ASSEMBLY
3	HEIGHT SENSOR
4	MOUNTING SCREWS (5 N•m/46 IN. LBS.)
5	HEIGHT SENSOR LINK
6	STUD (7 N•m/62 IN. LBS.)
7	CONTROL ARM

FIGURE 22-5 ELC Height Sensor Mounting. (*Courtesy of Oldsmobile Div. of GMC*)

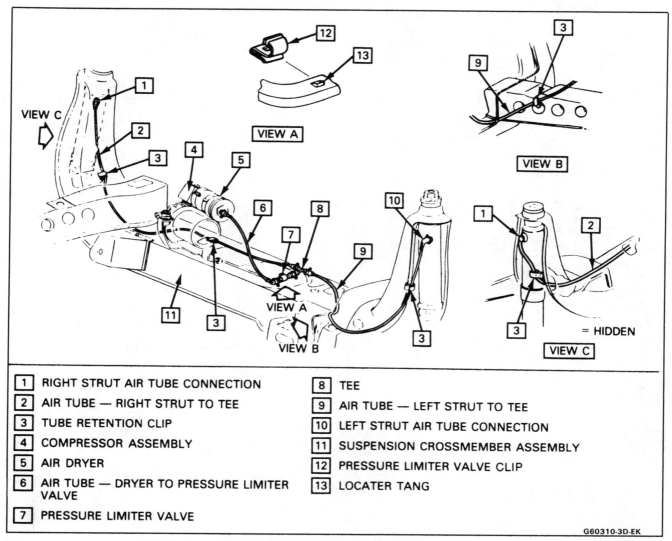

FIGURE 22-7 Air tube routing for ELC components. (*Courtesy of Oldsmobile Div. of GMC*)

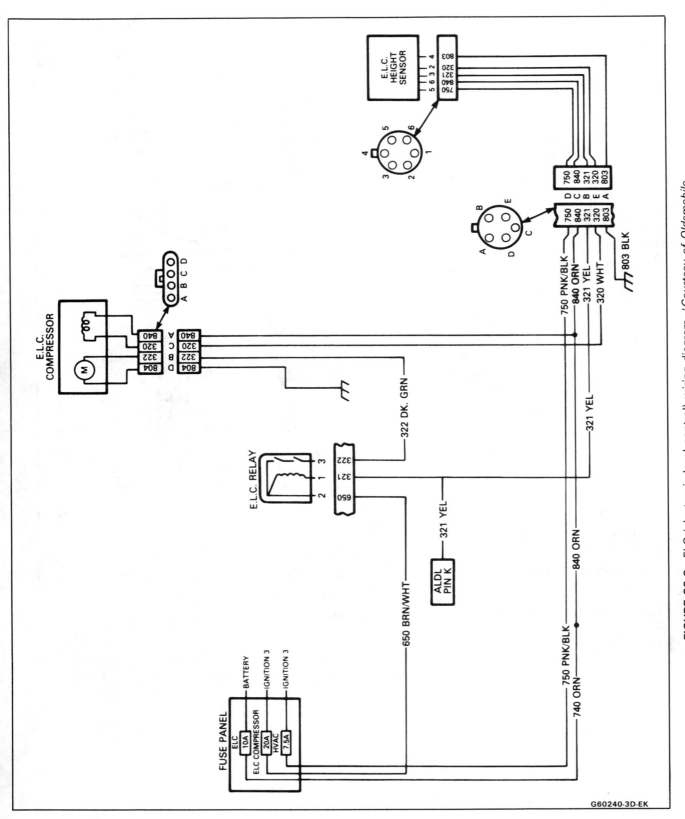

FIGURE 22-8 ELC (electronic level control) wiring diagram. (*Courtesy of Oldsmobile Div. of GMC*)

G60240-3D-EK

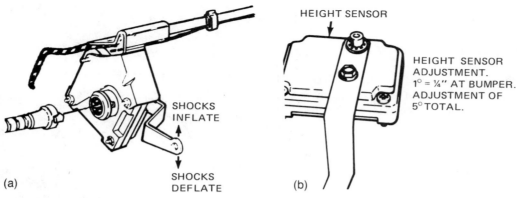

(a)   SHOCKS INFLATE / SHOCKS DEFLATE

HEIGHT SENSOR

HEIGHT SENSOR ADJUSTMENT. 1° = ¼" AT BUMPER. ADJUSTMENT OF 5° TOTAL.

(b)

FIGURE 22-9 Height sensor adjustment. (*Courtesy of Oldsmobile Div. of GMC*)

The load added to the vehicle causes the height sensor actuating arm, shown in Fig. 22-9, to rotate upward and electrically start an internal time delay circuit to actually energize the air compressor relay coil circuit to ground. This will turn on the air compressor and provide compressed air to the vehicle shock absorbers through plastic tubing. Compressed air flowing into the shock absorbers will automatically raise the vehicle body upwards to compensate for the additional loads carried by the vehicle.

This upward movement of the body lifts the height sensor actuating arm back up to its previous position prior to the addition of the extra weight condition. When this position is reached, ± ¾ inch (19 mm) to 1 inch (25.4 mm), the sensor will open the electrical circuit to the air compressor, thereby shutting it off. Anytime that the air compressor is operational, a dash mounted light (level ride) will illuminate.

Removing the load from the vehicle allows the body to ride higher, which causes the height sensor actuating arm to move downward and trigger the time delay circuit as it did when a load was applied to the vehicle. Note that this time delay circuit is necessary to prevent falsely actuating the air compressor relay or exhaust solenoid circuits during normal ride motion which can cause the height sensor actuating link to move. This time delay is between 8 to 14 seconds on the Oldsmobile 88/98 vehicles, while it is between 14 to 28 seconds on the Oldsmobile Toronado and Cadillac vehicles.

After this period of delay has passed, the height sensor completes the exhaust solenoid circuit to ground, and air will vent or exhaust back out of the shock absorber circuit, through the air dryer and exhaust solenoid valve within the air compressor to the atmosphere. This loss of compressed air from the shock absorbers lowers the vehicle body and causes the height sensor actuating arm to rotate towards its original position. When this position is reached, the exhaust valve circuit solenoid will open (de-energizing the solenoid) and prevent any further air loss from the shock absorber system.

The location of the air compressor is generally within the engine compartment, on either the left or right side according to the engine application. An example of the

A.C. mounted on the suspension crossmember assembly is shown in Fig. 22-7, Item 4.

To control the maximum air pressure that can be delivered to the shock absorbers, a pressure limiter valve shown in Fig. 22-7 is used to maximize system pressure at 90 psi (620.5 kPa) while it is kept between 67–74 psi (462–510 kPa) on later models. In addition, to improve ride characteristics when the vehicle is minimally loaded, a minimum air pressure valve located within the air dryer assembly, as shown in Fig. 22-3, is used.

Minimum air pressures of 8 to 15 psi (55 to 103 kPa) are maintained on Oldsmobile 88/98 cars; minimums of 8 to 14 psi (55 to 96.5 kPa) on all Cadillac vehicles, except the Eldorado and Seville which have a minimum pressure of 15 to 20 psi (103 to 138 kPa) in the shock absorbers, while the Oldsmobile Toronado has 14 to 20 psi (96.5 to 138 kPa), or 7–14 psi (50–100 kPa) on the later Toronado model.

ELC HEIGHT CHECK

This check is required to ensure that the system is operating correctly.

1. Park the vehicle on a level floor and measure the distance from either the rear bumper or from the door rocker panel immediately in front of the rear wheel.

2. Turn the ignition switch on.

3. In order to reset the height sensor, place the shift lever into reverse on Cadillac Eldorado and Seville vehicles, and on the Oldsmobile Toronado also cycle the ignition switch from on to off.

4. Apply a load to the trunk of the vehicle or stand on the rear bumper [approximate load between 200 lbs (91 kg) on Cadillac vehicles, and 300–350 lbs (136–159 kg) on Oldsmobile units].

5. The time delay before the air compressor cuts in (starts pumping) should be 8 to 14 seconds on Olds 88/98 vehicles, and 14–28 seconds on Olds Toronado and Cadillac vehicles.

6. The vehicle body should rise to within ¾ inch (19.1 mm) to 1 inch (25.4 mm) of what it was in Step 1 above by the time that the compressor shuts off.

If the vehicle fails to achieve its previous height, then check the compressor and associated wiring for problem areas. Also check for air leaks in the system.

If the system functions correctly, remove the load and after the specified time delay, the body should lower to within ¾ inch (19.1 mm) to 1 inch (25.4 mm) of what it was in Step 1 in less than 3.5 minutes. If the body does not lower, then a problem exists in the exhaust valve solenoid circuit.

AIR COMPRESSOR CHECK

If it is suspected that the air compressor is at fault in the system, it can be checked for current draw, pressure output, and a leak-down test.

These tests can be done on the car or on the bench with the procedure below:

1. Refer to Fig. 22-10 and disconnect the wiring from both the compressor motor and exhaust solenoid terminals.

2. Attach a pressure gauge as shown in Fig. 22-10 to the air dryer fitting.

3. Connect an ammeter into the circuit to monitor the current draw of the system when 12 volts (+) are supplied.

4. The current draw to the compressor should not exceed 14 amperes.

5. When air pressure on the gauge reaches 100 psi (689.5 kPa), shut off the power supply to the air compressor and note if pressure is maintained.

HEIGHT SENSOR ADJUSTMENT

Adjustment of the height sensor can be made by loosening of the lock nut that secures the connecting link to the height sensor plastic arm, as shown in Fig. 22-9.

1986 OLDSMOBILE TORONADO ELC

In later model year upscale vehicles employing ELC (electronic level control) the system operates as described for other vehicles in this chapter. Minor variations exist in the systems employed with these newer vehicles in that compressor operating pressures have been lowered slightly as a

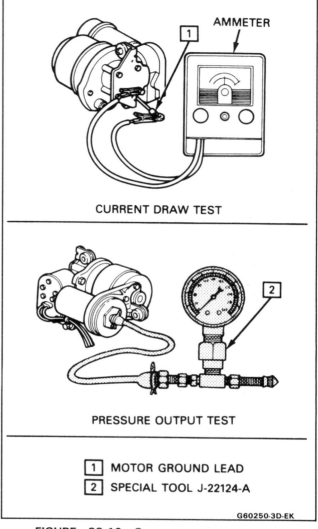

CURRENT DRAW TEST

PRESSURE OUTPUT TEST

| 1 | MOTOR GROUND LEAD |
| 2 | SPECIAL TOOL J-22124-A |

G60250-3D-EK

FIGURE 22-10 Compressor test arrangement. (*Courtesy of Oldsmobile Div. of GMC*)

direct result of the downsizing of the body mass compared to earlier model full-size American family vehicles.

In addition, the swing to front-wheel drive and transaxles from the long used rear-wheel drive design resulted in shorter wheelbases and a re-designing of the suspension system for improved handling and ride characteristics because of the smaller and lighter bodies, as well as suspension systems that have been tuned for exclusive use with radial tires. These lower operating pressures of the compressor for the ELC system, along with minor changes to the time required for the ELC to respond to a change in load, are the only differences in the basic operation of the ELC system described and featured in this chapter.

An example of an ELC system circuit for a 1986 Oldsmobile Toronado fitted with a 3.8L V6 multiport fuel-injection engine system is shown in Fig. 22-11.

ELECTRONIC LEVEL CONTROL

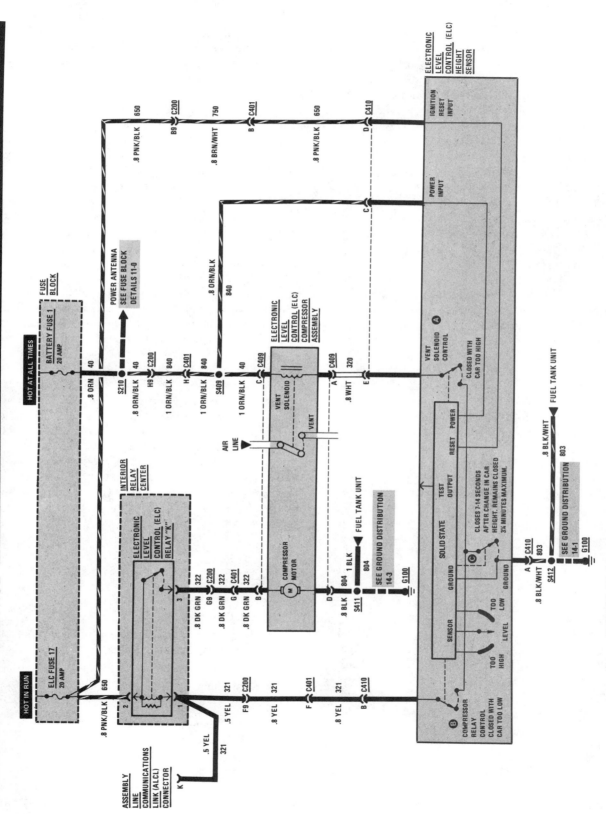

FIGURE 22-11 Electronic level control wiring diagram for a 1986 Oldsmobile Toronado. *(Courtesy of Oldsmobile Div. of GMC)*

1986 Oldsmobile Toronado ELC System Operation

This system contains the same basic components described earlier in this chapter for other such ELC systems.

As the vehicle height changes due to load increases or decreases, or due to road surface irregularities, the ELC actuator arm which is connected between the rear axle control arm and the ELC height sensor will rotate. This relative motion of the actuator arm is sensed by a "solid-state" unit (Fig. 22-11) that will operate switches to control the air flow either into or out of the air-bag type shock absorbers.

If, for example, the vehicle ride height is too high, switch A in the ELC height sensor closes, followed 7 to 14 seconds later by switch C doing the same thing. The major purpose of such a delay system is to prevent the up and down motion of the vehicle from triggering the action of the level control system.

With both switch A and C closed, a ground path exists from the Battery Fuse 1 to the vent solenoid in the ELC air compressor assembly. This action energizes the solenoid and it opens a valve to exhaust air from the ELC air shocks until the vehicle obtains a level ride height condition once again.

Once the vehicle is level, then the height sensor, which is mounted on the rear suspension support assembly, will open switch A. Within the ELC height sensor, a solid-state timer ensures that switch C will remain closed for about a three-minute period to allow the system to adjust for any load changes, but it prevents any continuous attempt by the system to operate and correct for an air leak, for example.

The timer resets automatically to allow a further 3 minute operation any time that the ignition switch is turned off (reset input) and then on again.

After cycling the ignition from off to on, the timer will activate the air compressor for about 3 to 4 seconds to quickly recharge the system, and after another 40 seconds, it will operate once the ignition key switch is placed into the run position.

If the vehicle ride-height is too low, then switch B is closed, followed 30 seconds or so later by switch C doing the same thing. This combined action provides a ground path for the coil of the ELC relay, which then closes and allows battery voltage to the air compressor electric motor in order to supply air to the air activated shock absorbers and therefore raise the vehicle ride-height. Switch B will open once the vehicle has attained a level ride-height condition again.

AUTOMATIC RIDE CONTROL

The latest advancements in automatic ride level/quality control have now moved to rapid control of the vehicle ride quality in direct response to changes in the road surface.

Both Ford and General Motors Delco products now offer advanced suspension systems that command top performance on the road.

Both systems employ a computer command ride system available with automatic road sensing to detect the type of road surface being travelled, and both adjust for optimum suspension damping characteristics.

A control switch is provided inside the vehicle so that the driver can select either a cushioned ride home from the office, or tighten up the suspension for a firm, high-speed drive on a twisting country road. An example of this type of system is illustrated in Fig. 22-12; the system was designed for the 1987 Ford Thunderbird Turbo Coupe.

As shown in Fig. 22-12, the driver can select either an auto or firm ride control position by manipulation of the selector switch that is located to the right of the steering column. In the auto mode, the system provides soft-ride suspension characteristics, until such time as input signals from one or more of the various sensors indicates to the computer that a firmer ride is required.

The computer will trigger all four suspension system actuators, which in turn will alter the vehicle's individual shock absorber rebound rate by changing the fluid restriction flow rate of its shock absorber piston or shock strut piston. This action will alter (stiffen) the vehicle motion rebound/bounce rate to between two to three times that which existed during the soft-ride mode. Since electronics are employed as the sensing and trigger mechanism, the change from one ride mode to another can occur within milliseconds (thousandths of a second).

If the firm mode is selected by the operator, then the system will remain in this setting under all operating conditions and road surfaces that are encountered. In addition to the mode selector switch that the driver can operate as desired, the system includes:

1. A speed sensor
2. Steering sensor
3. Brake application
4. Acceleration force input
5. Shunt motor actuators on the top of each shock strut and rear vertical shock absorber
6. Electronic control module
7. Interconnecting wiring harness

During the auto selector mode of suspension system operation, if the driver attempts to torque-up the drive line by placing his foot on the brake while revving up the engine, the torque transfer through the transmission to the drive line will tend to make the rear end of the vehicle "squat." Once the vehicle acceleration sensor detects a change in either longitudinal or lateral motion of 0.3 g or more, the computer will activate the shock absorber valving

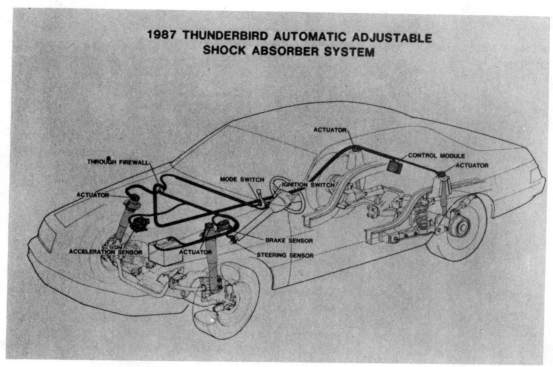

1987 THUNDERBIRD AUTOMATIC ADJUSTABLE SHOCK ABSORBER SYSTEM

FIGURE 22-12 1987 Ford Thunderbird automatic adjustable shock absorber system layout. (*Courtesy of Society of Automotive Engineers, Copyright 1986*)

to the firm ride setting in order to counteract the tendency of the vehicle to squat.

Although a torque-up example is used here, rapid acceleration from a standing position causes the same firm-ride condition. In addition, a heavy brake application from speed causes the nose of the vehicle to want to dive; therefore, the brake application sensor would send a signal to the computer, and it would switch the suspension system valving to the firm-ride position within milliseconds.

If a corner is turned at high speed and if the lateral acceleration exceeds 0.3 g, then again the computer stiffens up the ride quality. Firm-ride valving also occurs as a result of acceleration under conditions that produce more than 8 psi of turbocharger boost or for any wide-open throttle movement. The only time that the suspension system does not switch into the firm-ride mode with the selector switch in the auto mode is when a vehicle corners at speeds under 15 mph.

SPECIAL TEST EQUIPMENT

Figure 22-13 illustrates an electronic level control tester to assist you when troubleshooting and checking the system. Available from Kent-Moore under P/N J-34825, this tester easily connects to the system at the height sensor. Four LED's (light emitting diodes) and 3 switches on the tester face panel allow the system to be manually cycled and monitored. In addition, a bench test of the height sensor can be performed with the included 12 volt battery leads. Instructions come with the tester.

J 34825
ELECTRONIC LEVEL CONTROL TESTER

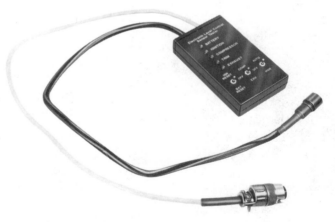

The J 34825 is a valuable test unit for technicians who want to quickly diagnose the electronic level control system on 1978—current General Motors vehicles (except manual height control valve systems). The tester troubleshoots and checks the system quickly eliminating time consuming diagnosis with tree charts and pin-to-pin voltage/resistance testing. The J 34825 easily connects to the system at the height sensor. The four LED's and three switches on the tester face panel allow the system to be manually cycled and monitored. A bench test of the height sensor can also be performed with the included 12 volt battery leads. Instructions are attached to the tester.

FIGURE 22-13 Electronic level control tester, Kent-Moore J-34825. (*Courtesy of Kent-Moore Tool Group, Sealed Power Corporation.*)

CHAPTER 23

Trip-Computer Recorders

SYSTEM PURPOSE AND FUNCTION

Many upscale model passenger cars offer an optional trip-computer system that allows the driver to access quickly desired information regarding such items as:

1. Fuel consumption (average and current)
2. Miles to empty on existing fuel supply
3. Average vehicle speed
4. Outside (ambient) air temperature
5. Elapsed time on a trip or acceleration performance
6. ETA (estimated time of arrival) at destination
7. Time of day (clock with a stopwatch function)
8. Time and date reminder (special meeting or occasion)
9. Distance since last fuel tank refill
10. Calculator function for general purposes, including an English to metric conversion capability, and vice versa.

With the desire for greater driver information in this modern era, many vehicle manufacturers offer either a simple trip computer or an auto-calculator option in their vehicles. Some of these devices are more complex than others. With the technological advancements in electronics, these units continue to offer the most discerning buyer almost every conceivable option you can imagine. Several examples of trip-computer systems are discussed and illustrated in this section.

ROBERT BOSCH TRIP COMPUTER

The trip-computer system offered by Robert Bosch Corporation fits in a space not much larger than that required by the instrument panel clock. This trip computer, available as a basic model and shown in Fig. 23-1, offers six functions that can be called up at the driver's command; Fig. 23-2 illustrates an optional 12 function trip-computer system.

The display unit employs a four-digit 7-segment readout of LCD (liquid crystal display), which indicates the driver selected information. To activate the trip computer, the driver must depress a button on the small keyboard unit shown alongside the trip computer in Figs. 23-1 and 23-2. The keyboard contains a function selector switch, a temporary clock selector for a time check, an illumination but-

Our basic computer has six functions plus time of day.

FIGURE 23-1 Six function trip computer. (*Courtesy of Robert Bosch Corporation*)

482

The premium computer: 4 x 3 functions with quadratic controls.

FIGURE 23-2 Twelve function trip computer. *(Courtesy of Robert Bosch Corporation)*

ton, and a start button. The displayed functions on the display unit can be selected one after another, as desired by the driver.

SENSORS AND INPUTS

An outside or ambient temperature sensor is usually mounted below the front bumper of the vehicle so that it can sense the drop in temperature towards the freezing level and so alert the driver to the danger of ice on the roads. This is particularly important for wet or snowy road conditions. The temperature is measured using an NTC resistor, and its range is between $-40°C$ to $+70°C$ ($104°F$ to $158°F$) and can be displayed in one-half degree increments.

In addition, a fuel line flow sensor is installed in the fuel line to the carburetor or fuel-injection throttle body distributor as a means of monitoring fuel flow and, therefore, consumption rates.

For example, on Bosch's K-Jetronic continuous mechanical injection system, the quantity of fuel used is determined using the position of the air-flow sensor plate, while in the L-Jetronic intermittent/electronically pulsed fuel-injection system, the injector pulse-width time is used as a basis for this calculation. If the trip computer is used on a diesel vehicle, then the sensor is mounted on the fuel-injection pump control lever or control rod as a means of determining the amount of fuel injected.

A voltage signal from the fuel-level gauge and the time function of the clock and stopwatch, which is generated internally inside the trip computer, are used together with other signals to calculate the average fuel consumption, the average speed, and range. The actual average fuel consumption per 100 kilometers, or miles per gallon, is computed on the distance/fuel pulses counted/monitored from the start of the trip, while the average vehicle speed is determined using the distance pulses which are a measurement of the speed and the driving time. Vehicle speed is monitored by a Hall-effect sensor or an induction-type sensor on the speedometer for an immediate readout when required. (See Chapter 4 on sensors for more information.)

The stopwatch function of the clock can be started, stopped, and reset to zero using the start button for the trip computer.

The fuel range is established by monitoring the fuel level gauge signal as well as the calculated fuel consumption in liters per 100 km or in miles per gallon. The fuel tank level gauge output voltage is checked and read every two seconds, and fuel tank quantity is achieved by using a scale of 256 equal measurements. Only an average consumption is given, and this is based upon the last 15 miles (25 km) of driving; however, once the fuel tank is filled up, a new voltage signal is sensed immediately and a new reading is indicated.

TRIP MICROCOMPUTER

The trip computer is a solid-state electronic device and is shown in schematic form in Fig. 23-3, while Fig. 23-4 illustrates a view of the actual trip computer with the protective cover removed.

A total of 32 input/output channels is employed in the microcomputer used with the trip recorder system, and the various inputs to the system are constantly being monitored by the various sensors which create an analog (sine wave) output to the computer.

Since the computer can only understand digital (either on or off) signals, an analog to digital converter using multiplexing (a method of serially switching more than one input on the same feeder line to a single output) is employed, with all inputs to the trip computer being protected against incorrect polarity and electrical interference.

Digital input signals originating from the keyboard, the fuel-injection control unit, and the distance-travelled sensor are all fed into the trip computer after first passing through the input/output channels of the trip computer.

Current draw is only 5 mA (milliamps); therefore, battery power is not greatly affected by use of this system, even if the voltage of the battery drops to the 5 volt level.

The RAM (random access memory) acts as the scratchpad for the trip computer and carries out all the necessary calculations for immediate updating of desired information by the driver using the keyboard switches. The RAM memory contains stored information that is immediately available when addressed, regardless of the previous memory address location. Since the memory information can be selected in any order (random), there is equal access time to all selections.

The ROM (read only memory) contains predetermined information which is stored in the computer at the time of manufacture. It is a memory that allows reading of a predetermined pattern of zeros and ones. (See Chapter 3 for the basics of on-board computers.) A ROM is similar to a dictionary in that a certain address (word) results in a predetermined information output.

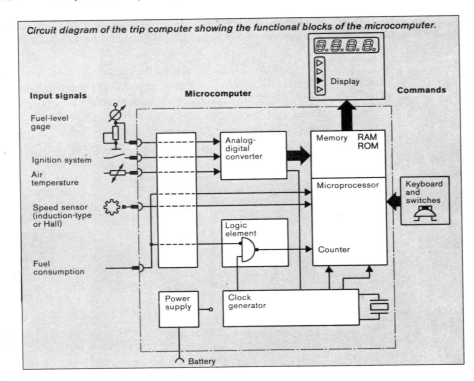

FIGURE 23-3 Trip-computer operational diagram. (*Courtesy of Robert Bosch Corporation*)

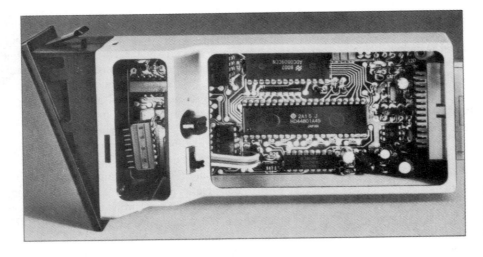

FIGURE 23-4 Trip computer with protective cover removed. (*Courtesy of Robert Bosch Corporation*)

AUTO-CALCULATOR

An optional auto-calculator, available on certain models of Oldsmobile products starting with the 1984 model year, is shown in Fig. 23-5. This component, which is mounted on the console between the two front seats, is designed to provide travel information on fuel economy, time, and distance, and functions as well as a clock/calendar and a four function calculator (add, subtract, multiply, and divide).

There are nine control buttons on the left-hand side of the auto-calculator, as shown in Fig. 23-5, and there are ten numeric buttons that are located underneath the LCD display. The brightness of the display varies with the degree of outside sunlight. When it is dark (night) and the headlights or parking lights are on, the brilliance of the display is controlled manually by the driver from the small serrated/knurled wheel next to the headlight switch. Once the auto-calculator is turned on, the control buttons feel warm to the touch, and this is a normal condition.

Available Displays

Pushing the MET display button allows you to change a given readout value from the customary U.S. measures of gallons, miles, and miles per gallon to metric equivalents such as liters, kilometers, and liters/100 km.

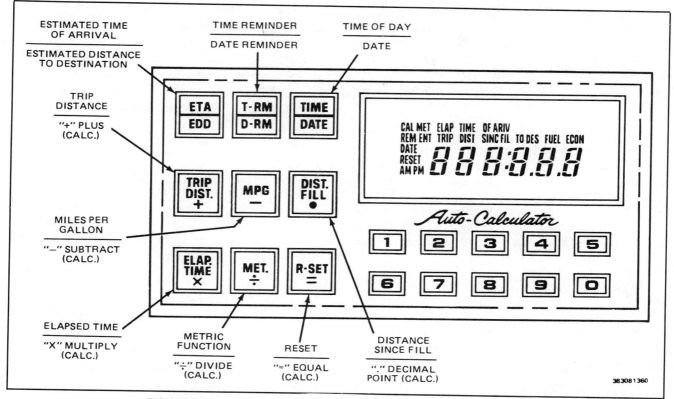

FIGURE 23-5   Auto-calculator. (*Courtesy of Oldsmobile Div. of GMC*)

Pushing the MET button again allows the readout to return to the nonmetric display value.

The clock/calendar allows you to read the time by pushing the time/date button once; pushing this button twice will display the month and day. In addition, a date reminder such as an important meeting, dinner engagement, anniversary, etc., can be programmed into the auto-calculator on any day of the year except February 29th (leap year). This reminder is activated at one minute past midnight on the set date. When the ignition key is turned on for the first time afterwards, the words REM DATE will flash, and then the display will flash the actual date. To cancel this message, you simply push the reset button.

The date flashed up on the console unit can be checked by pushing the T-RM/D-RM button twice, and the month/day currently set in the memory will be shown. If no date has been set, then a number of zeros will illuminate.

When the ignition is on, the auto-calculator can be used as a stop-watch to measure elapsed time by pressing the ELAP.TIME/X button. During the first hour, the display shows the time in minutes and seconds; however, after the first hour, only the hour followed by the minutes is shown. A maximum of 99 hours and 59 minutes can be recorded on the indicator, after which the counter automatically resets to zero.

For travel information, the auto-calculator can determine the estimated distance to your destination, the ETA (estimated time of arrival), the average fuel economy in miles per gallon, or liters per 100 km, the distance driven since the last fill up of the fuel tank, and the total distance driven since the trip feature was last reset.

The auto-calculator determines the approximate time of arrival at a given destination by computing the time of day, the average car speed for the last minute travelled, and the estimated distance to the destination. In order for the computer to do this, the vehicle *must* be travelling in excess of 15 mph (24 km/hr) for at least a one-minute interval before such information is called up.

The trip distance acts like a conventional odometer in that it measures the distance travelled since activation of the auto-calculator system. It will display the trip distance in U.S. or metric up to 1/10 increments to a total distance of 9,999.9 miles or kilometers. By pushing the TRIP DIST./ + button, the distance the car has been driven since the feature was last reset is shown.

To reset four trip features simultaneously (ETA, estimated distance to destination, trip distance, and elapsed time), push the ETA/EDD button once. When the DIST.FILL/. button is pushed, the display shows the words DIST.SINC.FIL, and it displays the distance driven since this feature was last reset up to 9,999.9 miles or kilometers.

For the average fuel economy feature to work, the

DIST.SINC.FIL. button must be reset each time you add fuel to the tank, since the average fuel economy is not a continuous display. Once the tank has been filled, you have to press the MPG/− button; the display illuminates with the words *Ent Fuel*, at which time the driver must use the numbered key buttons to enter the amount of fuel that was just added to the tank to the nearest tenth of a unit (liters or gallons).

Pushing MPG/− again allows the auto-calculator to determine the average fuel economy since the last fill up. Then the reset distance since fill button must be pushed so that the auto-calculator can determine average fuel economy the next time the car is filled up.

To use the auto-calculator as a calculator, simply push one of the numbered key buttons. The word CAL appears on the display, and the six control keys are set for calculator operation. The control keys are:

1. TRIP DIST./+ — Addition
2. MPG/− — Subtraction
3. DIST.FILL/. — The decimal point will not appear when this button is pushed; it will appear when you push the next numeric key button, and the decimal point will move to the left for tenths or hundreds.
4. ELAP.TIME/X — Multiplication
5. MET./ — Division
6. R.SET/ — Equals

To clear the calculator, simply push either the Reset button or the TIME/DATE button.

With the desire for advanced electronics in passenger cars and trucks, more and more of these types of options will be making their presence felt in future new models of vehicles.

CHAPTER 24

♦

Driver Guidance and Data System

LAYOUT AND OPERATION

Although not in wide use at this time, several automobile and electronic component manufacturers have tested and installed various types of driver guidance systems in cars as an optional device. Several different concepts have been tried, with one relying on a number of ground receiver/transmitters mounted at strategic locations on high buildings; in other systems, induction loops are buried in the roadway and transmit driver guidance information to a graphic display center mounted on the vehicle instrument panel.

In the version produced by the Japanese, a small CRT (cathode ray tube) mounted inside the vehicle is used to display a coordinated map layout of a small section of a city; the display can also be reduced in size to show a much larger area, such as a district.

In the concept used by Robert Bosch Corporation, a test area was selected in the Ruhr area of West Germany covering approximately 60 miles (100 km) of freeway. A total of 83 measuring and transmission sections of roadway with 199 induction loops was installed along with the necessary street units. For an example of this system, see Fig. 24-1.

In the system shown in Fig. 24-2, the automobile contains both a transmitter and a receiver device (Items 3 and 4), an antenna mounted in the rear bumper, and a video display unit mounted on its instrument panel, shown in Fig. 24-3.

The street system shown in Fig. 24-2 requires both an inductive loop unit as well as a control unit, with the loop unit containing the transmitter and receiver. The modules of the measurement section of roadway are located in a roadside-mounted weatherproof cabinet fixture. A central processing unit receives the information from the street units. Illustrated in Fig. 24-5 is a schematic of the vehicle and street unit components used with the driver guidance system.

When an automobile enters the monitored section of roadway, its presence is immediately detected by the in-road induction and circuit loop. The driver of the vehicle enters the destination address (Fig. 24-1) in the form of a seven-digit decimal number from the on-board display unit and keyboard, as shown in Figs. 24-3 and 24-4.

This information is automatically picked up by the induction loop buried in the roadway and is relayed to the street unit and roadside-mounted measuring cabinet. The memory circuit of the microcomputer in the street unit sends back to the vehicle via the same induction loop the recommended direction for the desired destination asked for by the driver when he/she first entered the monitored roadway system.

The density and speed of traffic using this same highway is picked up by this same loop arrangement as vehicles pass by in the same direction. This flow of traffic information is monitored and transmitted every five minutes to the central unit microcomputer, which analyzes this data and deter-

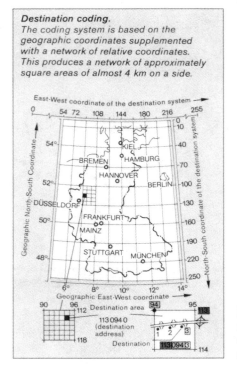

FIGURE 24-1 Destination coding map for a driver guidance and data system. (*Courtesy of Robert Bosch Corporation*)

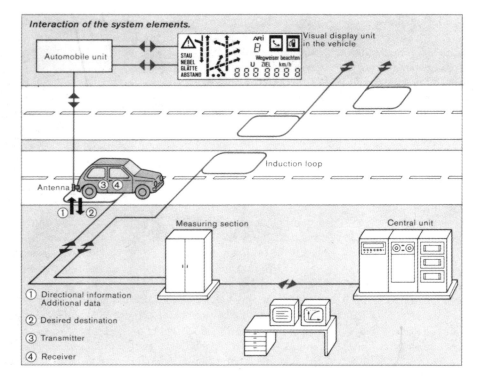

FIGURE 24-2 Driver guidance and data system arrangement. (*Courtesy of Robert Bosch Corporation*)

mines the best route for the destination asked for by the vehicle driver when he/she first entered this highway.

The central computer can do this by continually receiving input data from the 83 measuring and transmission sections on this particular roadway. As well as the best direction/route to take, the computer also flashes up on the display unit in the vehicle the recommended speed, plus any information regarding known traffic jams and road conditions affected by weather.

FIGURE 24-3 Actual driver guidance system display unit and keyboard. (*Courtesy of Robert Bosch Corporation*)

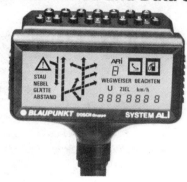

FIGURE 24-4 Schematic of driver guidance display unit and keyboard. (*Courtesy of Robert Bosch Corporation*)

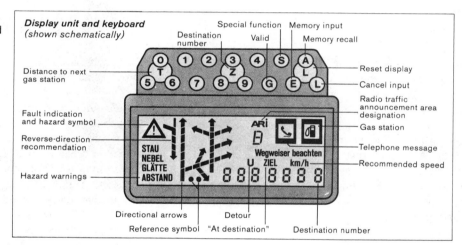

FIGURE 24-5 Schematic of vehicle and street unit componentry for a driver guidance and data system. (*Courtesy of Robert Bosch Corporation*)

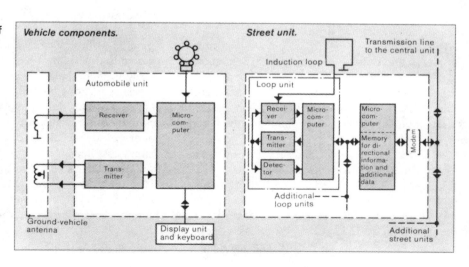

CHAPTER 25

♦

Airbag Restraint Systems

The mandatory use of air bags for passenger car occupant protection has been lobbyed for many years in the United States. Although not yet a mandatory requirement on mass production cars, it is now a viable and optional extra on a number of models. As of 1987, Ford Motor Company offered airbag protection as an optional extra on its midsize Tempo and Mercury Topaz models at a per unit cost of approximately $800. It has sold about 11,000 of these through the end of 1986. Plans call for production of about 12,000 airbag-equipped cars in 1987; about 30,000, in 1988; and between 500,000 and one million, in 1990. This places Ford in the forefront of domestic automakers offering this safety feature. Plans are that the cost per airbag will eventually drop to about $300 per vehicle. Ford plans to offer airbag protection as standard equipment on some of its more expensive models, and as an optional feature on less expensive models.

Chrysler Corporation also plans to offer airbags soon on its LeBaron models; and General Motors Corporation will install this device on some models over the next few years. Honda has also announced that it will offer airbags on its next generation of Accura cars, beginning in the 1988 model year.

Legislation in the United States appears to be heading towards the mandated use of airbags or automatic safety belts on the passenger side of a certain percentage of cars produced in the next few years. The success of electronics in being able to provide a reliable activation system has improved the functional operation of these devices. An example of such an airbag restraint system with automatic safety belts is offered by Mercedes-Benz and BMW. It is known as an SRS or Supplemental Restraint System.

This system, which is a Robert Bosch designed and manufactured unit, offers airbag protection for the driver and passenger, along with a knee bolster system, and emergency tensioning retractors for both front seat belts. The chief purpose for using airbag protection is to provide a soft cushion for the human body in the event of a serious collision. Although there is no guarantee that the airbag will prevent injury, it does offer additional protection to the driver of a vehicle, particularly in the event of a head-on or frontal collision accident.

BASIC ARRANGEMENT

Figure 25-1 illustrates the basic layout of the components required to trigger the airbag and to provide automatic tensioning for both the driver and passenger seat belt restraining systems. Along with the airbag itself, the restraint system incorporates an automatic seat belt tensioner, an electronic triggering device that includes an integral acceleration sensor, a voltage converter, and a power standby and system check lamp.

The system is designed to inflate the airbag automatically at any time a front-end collision occurs. (See Fig. 25-2, which shows the airbag folded inside the padded steering wheel.) This triggering speed can be as low as 11 mph (18 km/hr), although it is more generally set for all collision speeds of 15 mph (25 km/hr) or higher.

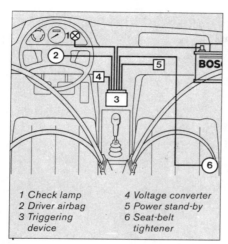

FIGURE 25-1 Basic layout of an airbag restraint protection system. (*Courtesy of Robert Bosch Corporation*)

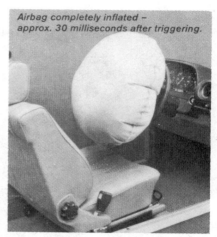

FIGURE 25-3 Completely inflated airbag within 30 milliseconds after triggering. (*Courtesy of Robert Bosch Corporation*)

This sudden deceleration causes a sensor to trigger an electrical pulse to a firing pellet located inside a gas generator. The pellet ignites a solid propellant and detonates it. This action completely fills the airbag within approximately 30 milliseconds (30 thousandths of a second), as is shown in Fig. 25-3. It protects the driver from coming into direct contact with either the steering wheel or the windshield. Within an additional 100 milliseconds (one tenth of a second) (Fig. 25-4), the gas inside the airbag has escaped through slots around the periphery of the bag, causing it to collapse almost as quickly as it was filled. The energy of the driver's body being thrown forward has now been absorbed and dissipated successfully.

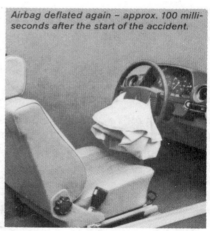

FIGURE 25-4 Deflated airbag within 100 milliseconds after collision impact. (*Courtesy of Robert Bosch Corporation*)

SYSTEM ELECTRONICS

The airbag and automatic seat-belt tensioner system relies upon a compact electronic trigger unit which is generally installed within the passenger compartment of the vehicle, such as in the center console unit. [See Figs. 25-5 and 25-1 (Item 3).] A spring-mass oscillator located within the airbag trigger unit senses and measures vehicle deceleration on a continuous basis, and its sensed signal is compared electronically with a preprogrammed safety level inside the trigger box.

The deceleration monitor system is designed to know the difference between a knock or blow when a vehicle is being repaired in a garage, or even the shock of the vehicle

FIGURE 25-2 Actual view of an airbag folded out of sight in the steering wheel padded center. (*Courtesy of Robert Bosch Corporation*)

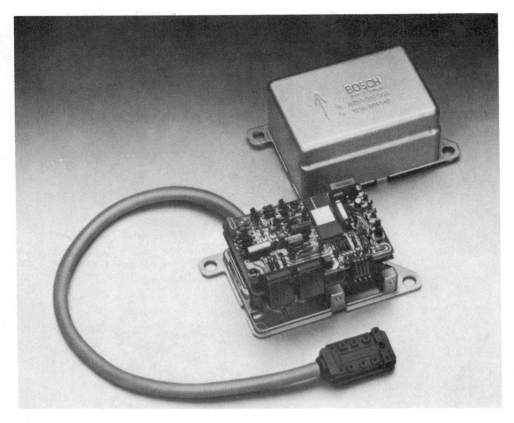

FIGURE 25-5   Airbag restraint system trigger unit. (*Courtesy of Robert Bosch Corporation*)

hitting a pothole or curb. Small indentations caused in a parking lot scrape will not normally trigger the system, unless the speed of the vehicle and its succeeding deceleration rate are adequate to energize the system.

When the vehicle engine is started, the electronic system will quickly run through a self-check to ensure that the system is operational. A test lamp will illuminate on the instrument panel for about a 10 second time period during this phase; if the system is OK, the light goes out, or otherwise, it will remain illuminated.

In addition, should the vehicle's electrical system fail during the course of an accident, then a capacitor which is used as a power stand-by will always ensure that the system will trigger and be able to activate both the airbag and seat belt tensioner systems. Also a voltage converter device ensures that even if the battery voltage were to drop to a 4 volt level, that full power would be available to the triggering unit.

In order to sense rapid deceleration of a vehicle when a front end collision occurs, it is necessary to employ a sensor that can inform the trigger unit ahead of time, so that when impact does occur, the airbag will inflate within approximately 30 milliseconds in order to protect the driver from serious injury.

Figure 25-6 illustrates the acceleration sensor that is employed to sense vehicle deceleration characteristics. How this sensor ties into the overall airbag restraint system can

be seen by referencing both Figs. 25-7 and 25-8, where it is shown on the top left-side of each diagram.

This sensor employs a simple weight suspended below a spring that employs four resistors in a bridge circuit, as is shown in Fig. 25-6. When rapid deceleration occurs, the

Basic illustration of the acceleration sensor.
In the event of a vehicle collision, a weight bends the strain gages on the spring. This changes the resistance of the gages and the current flowing through them.
1 Contacts, 2 Mount, 3 Insulation, 4 Spring, 5 Strain gage, 6 Weight

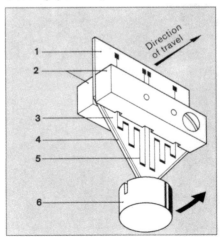

FIGURE 25-6   Acceleration sensor. (*Courtesy of Robert Bosch Corporation*)

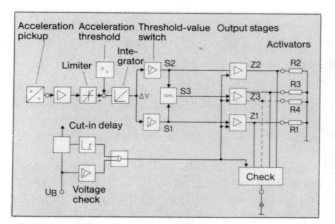

FIGURE 25-7   Basic airbag system schematic.
(*Courtesy of Robert Bosch Corporation*)

Therefore, this voltage signal is passed on into the trigger system shown in Figs. 25-7 and 25-8.

A simplified schematic of the electronic trigger system, with its acceleration sensor, integrated circuits, and control and monitoring functions, is shown in Fig. 25-7. Figure 25-8 illustrates an expanded schematic of the system.

ELECTRONIC TRIGGER UNIT OPERATION

The operation of the electronic trigger unit (shown in Fig. 25-5, as well as in schematic form in Fig. 25-8) is that it receives the generated voltage signal from the deceleration sensor and directs it through a high-pass filter first in order to filter out high-frequency signals and allow them to pass on to the voltage amplifier. The amplifier will, of course, increase the intensity of the signal and direct it to the limiter stage, which acts to isolate the signal from any high frequency vibrations.

A summing circuit or acceleration threshold circuit then calculates, by subtraction, an acceleration limit equivalent

mass of the weight moving forward deflects the spring and causes a change in the resistance value of two of these four resistors. The voltage signal generated from these resistors is directly proportional to the rate of vehicle deceleration.

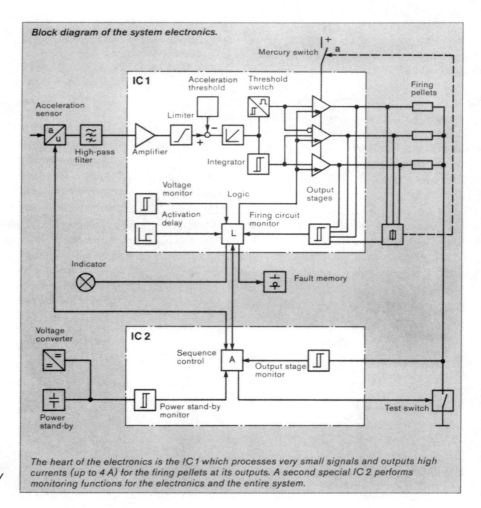

FIGURE 25-8   Expanded schematic of an airbag restraint system triggering unit. (*Courtesy of Robert Bosch Corporation*)

The heart of the electronics is the IC 1 which processes very small signals and outputs high currents (up to 4 A) for the firing pellets at its outputs. A second special IC 2 performs monitoring functions for the electronics and the entire system.

to approximately 4 g's. This value corresponds to typical acceleration characteristics encountered during normal driving routines, and it has been established, of course, through exhaustive and detailed testing factors.

This safety factor of approximately 4 g's ensures that false triggering of the airbag system will not occur during normal everyday driving practices. The deceleration signal generated from the weighted sensor is compared within the acceleration threshold unit to two preprogrammed values, which are S1 for the seat-belt tightener and S2 for the airbag system. Both S1 and S2 are shown in Fig. 25-7.

Should the signal exceed the preprogrammed safety limit, then the restraint systems would be activated. However, the seat-belt tightener is triggered at a lower speed than for the airbag system, with a front-end collision of approximately 15–18 km/hr (9–11 mph) being required.

The airbag system, on the other hand, will not trigger until a front-end collision of approximately 25 km/hr (15 mph) or higher is obtained. When either situation occurs, however, the trigger system output stages will initiate the firing pellets which will cause a reaction within the gas generators for both systems. The system of detonation for the seat-belt tightener is shown in Fig. 25-9.

AIRBAG KITS

Recent legislation in the United States requires that automatic restraint systems be installed in 10 percent of all 1987 production cars. A number of insurance companies and corporations are presently investigating the adoption of airbags to passenger cars as an after-market option in kit form.

If fitted as standard equipment at the factory level in mass-produced domestic model vehicles, the airbags would cost approximately $200.00. In kit form, however, this price escalates to about $1000.00, which is a substantial amount of money.

Crash sensors similar to those used in Mercedes-Benz

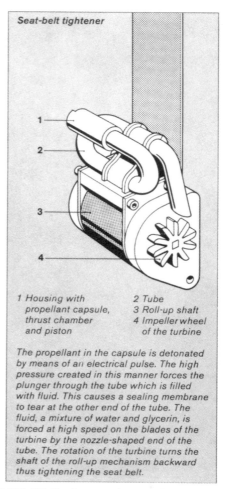

Seat-belt tightener

1 Housing with propellant capsule, thrust chamber and piston
2 Tube
3 Roll-up shaft
4 Impeller wheel of the turbine

The propellant in the capsule is detonated by means of an electrical pulse. The high pressure created in this manner forces the plunger through the tube which is filled with fluid. This causes a sealing membrane to tear at the other end of the tube. The fluid, a mixture of water and glycerin, is forced at high speed on the blades of the turbine by the nozzle-shaped end of the tube. The rotation of the turbine turns the shaft of the roll-up mechanism backward thus tightening the seat belt.

FIGURE 25-9 Automatic seat-belt tightener system. (*Courtesy of Robert Bosch Corporation*)

cars would trigger the ignition of 76 grams of gunpowder in the steering wheel kit. This action would automatically ignite the chemical, sodium azide, which would produce nitrogen gas and inflate the bag within 1/25th of a second.

CHAPTER 26

◆

Cellular Mobile Telephone

CADILLAC SYSTEM

The mobile telephone is one of the most widely used accessory items in passenger cars today. In many cases, the customer rents the device from a local telephone company on a monthly basis. One of the options in the 1986 and later Cadillac DeVille and Fleetwood models is a cellular mobile telephone system.

Major components of the system are:

1. A handset assembly, as shown in Fig. 26-1.
2. A transceiver located in the vehicle trunk (Fig. 26-2).
3. An antenna assembly (Fig. 26-3).
4. A microphone assembly for hands-free calling (Fig. 26-4).
5. Radio mute module and wiring harness (Fig. 26-5).

Figure 26-1 illustrates the location of the telephone handset, which is concealed within the center armrest and held in place by a hang-up cup.

Another major component of the system is the "transceiver," which houses all of the circuitry required to receive and initiate calls. This unit is located in the trunk and mounted on a plate on the rear panel. Two cables connect to the transceiver, which are the antenna cable and the telephone harness that sends and receives information to and from the handset and radio mute control. This unit is shown in Fig. 26-2.

Also required with the cellular telephone system is an antenna assembly, which is illustrated in Fig. 26-3. It is located on the upper left-hand corner of the rear window. A coupling box is mounted on the inside window directly opposite the antenna mount. This box is capacitively connected to the antenna mount through the rear window, without any holes required in the window itself.

This antenna should always be perfectly vertical and can be adjusted by loosening and tightening the two screws in the base of the unit. It should be removed when the car is driven through a carwash. Therefore, to facilitate this removal, the antenna has a threaded adapter which screws into the antenna holder. To remove the antenna, simply grasp the antenna at its adapter and rotate it CCW, applying firm but moderate pressure. To reinstall it, twist it CW by hand until snug.

To provide the driver with "hands-free" telephone operation, a microphone located in the maplight assembly can be used along with the front sound-system speakers (Fig. 26-4). During this procedure, only one party may talk at a time. The first person to speak controls the conversation until he/she stops talking. The voice-actuated electronics switches fast enough so that pauses during normal conversation allow either party to "break-in" on the conversation. The microphone may be muted (turned off) during a call while in the hands-free mode; however, the speakers will remain active. This muting feature is accomplished simply by pressing the mute button on the handset. To reactivate the microphone feature, simply press mute again.

The radio mute module shown in Fig. 26-5 is located under the left-hand side of the instrument panel and to the right of the steering column. It interfaces with the radio

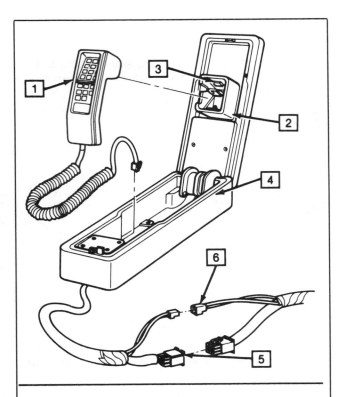

1 HANDSET

2 HANG-UP CUP

3 HANG-UP CUP LIGHT

4 ARMREST

5 ARMREST PIGTAIL HANDSET CONNECTOR

6 ARMREST PIGTAIL HANG-UP CUP LIGHT
CONNECTOR

G60060-9E-C

FIGURE 26-1 Mobile telephone components location. (*Courtesy of Cadillac Motor Car Division of GMC*)

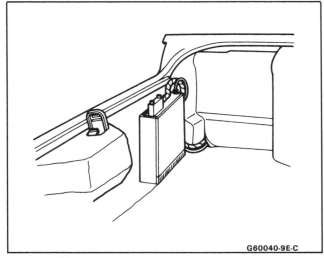

G60040-9E-C

FIGURE 26-2 Location of telephone transceiver in car trunk. (*Courtesy of Cadillac Motor Car Division of GMC*)

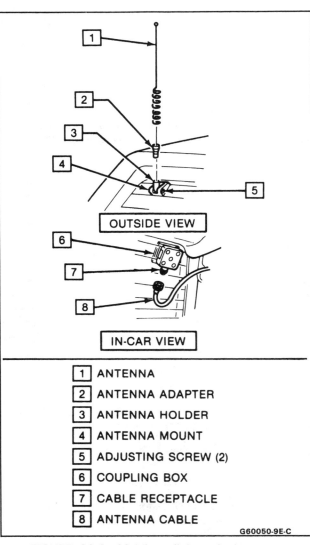

OUTSIDE VIEW

IN-CAR VIEW

1 ANTENNA

2 ANTENNA ADAPTER

3 ANTENNA HOLDER

4 ANTENNA MOUNT

5 ADJUSTING SCREW (2)

6 COUPLING BOX

7 CABLE RECEPTACLE

8 ANTENNA CABLE

G60050-9E-C

FIGURE 26-3 Mobile cellular telephone antenna assembly. (*Courtesy of Cadillac Motor Car Division of GMC*)

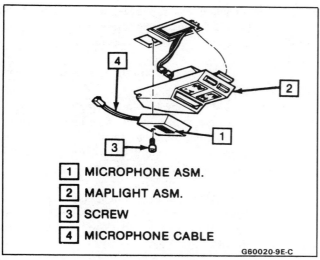

FIGURE 26-4 Mobile telephone microphone assembly. (*Courtesy of Cadillac Motor Car Division of GMC*)

[1] MICROPHONE ASM.
[2] MAPLIGHT ASM.
[3] SCREW
[4] MICROPHONE CABLE

G60020-9E-C

system to mute the sound system's front speakers and lower the volume on the rear speakers during a telephone conversation. The volume will again increase to its original level after a call is terminated, or alternately once 4 seconds have passed without the telephone keypad being used, or without a call being initiated.

SYSTEM OPERATION

In order to place a telephone call, the vehicle *must* be in a geographic location which is serviced by a cellular telephone site and should not be in an enclosed area, such as an underground parking lot, etc. Otherwise, poor reception will occur.

The handset must first be turned on. (See Fig. 26-6.) If the radio is on and the PWR button on the handset is pressed, the front speakers will mute (turn off), and the rear speakers will have their volume level decreased for 4 seconds, unless other keys on the handset are pressed.

Each time that the driver turns on the handset, the following sequence of events occurs:

1. Fourteen 8's will appear briefly in the display.
2. Each of the status messages illuminates briefly.
3. A short tone will be heard over the front sound-system speakers.
4. Normally, the red NO SVC (no service) message will illuminate temporarily.

The driver next dials the telephone number on the handset as it sits in its mount (numbers facing up), and then presses the SND button. The *In Use* indicator will now illuminate, and the call is processed.

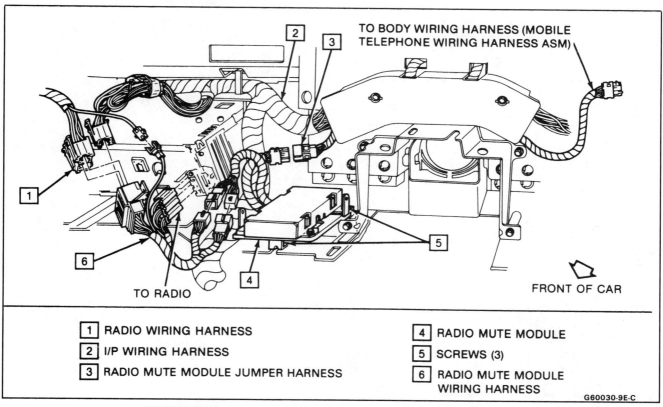

TO BODY WIRING HARNESS (MOBILE TELEPHONE WIRING HARNESS ASM)

FRONT OF CAR

TO RADIO

[1] RADIO WIRING HARNESS
[2] I/P WIRING HARNESS
[3] RADIO MUTE MODULE JUMPER HARNESS
[4] RADIO MUTE MODULE
[5] SCREWS (3)
[6] RADIO MUTE MODULE WIRING HARNESS

G60030-9E-C

FIGURE 26-5 Mobile telephone radio mute module and wiring harness. (*Courtesy of Cadillac Motor Car Division of GMC*)

To switch back and forth between a "hands free" and handset operation, the driver performs the following actions:

1. Lifts the handset to switch from "hands-free" to handset operation.
2. Either presses the mute button, returns the handset to its cradle mount, or presses the mute button a second time to switch from handset to "hands-free" operation. Failure to use the mute button in the first option in this sequence results in a call termination.

SAFETY PRECAUTION: Before attempting to jump-start or charge the vehicle battery of a cellular telephone-equipped vehicle, always remove the main power fuse located in cavity 10 of the fuse panel.

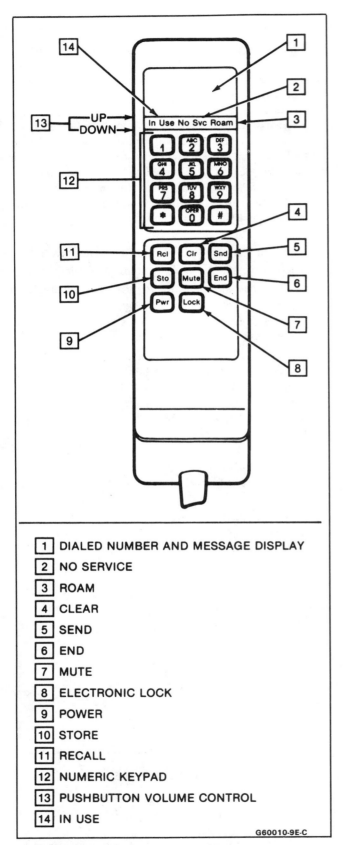

1	DIALED NUMBER AND MESSAGE DISPLAY
2	NO SERVICE
3	ROAM
4	CLEAR
5	SEND
6	END
7	MUTE
8	ELECTRONIC LOCK
9	POWER
10	STORE
11	RECALL
12	NUMERIC KEYPAD
13	PUSHBUTTON VOLUME CONTROL
14	IN USE

G60010-9E-C

FIGURE 26-6 Mobile telephone handset controls. (*Courtesy of Cadillac Motors Car Division of GMC*)

Glossary of Automotive Electronic Terms

Access motion time The time taken between the initial request for information when reading or writing data, and the instant that this information is available.

Accumulator The arithmetic and logic operations are commonly stored in the accumulator, which is the basic work register of a computer, and the result of the operation becomes the new data.

Active display A display capable of emitting light, such as incandescent and gas discharge.

Active element A component of an IC unit such as a transistor, tunnel diode, or a thryristor capable of producing power gain.

Active filter A device which employs passive network elements and amplifiers used to transmit or reject signals in certain frequency ranges, or alternately for controlling the relative output of various signals in certain frequency ranges. In addition, the device can control the relative output of signals as a direct function of frequency.

Active transducer A unit whose output signal waves are dependent upon power sources separate from those supplied by any of the actuating waves, whose power is controlled by one or more of the waves.

Actuator A transducer whose output is a force or torque involving motion in response to an electrical signal.

ADC Analog to digital converter that produces a number proportional to the analog voltage level input.

Adder A switching circuit that combines binary bits to generate the "sum and carry" of these bits.

Address A numerical expression which designates a specific location in a storage or memory device of the computer system.

Address format This can best be explained in two ways, which are: (a) The layout and arrangement of the address component parts relative to a specific instruction. For example, an expression of "plus-one" is often used to imply that one particular address

specifies the location of the next instruction that is to be executed, which might be "one-plus-one," or "two-plus-two," possibly "three-plus-one," and so on; (b) In a single specific address, the information or parts must be arranged in such a way that they can be readily identified as to particular information required.

Address register A specific register that contains the memory location of a particular instruction that is to be executed from that address.

Algorithm A systematic sequence of defined processes and operations required to ensure the solution of a problem.

Alphanumeric code A code whose set of information is made up of letters, numbers, digits, or all three combinations.

Alphanumeric display A visual display which presents stored information within the computer, such as trouble code letters and numbers used in automotive on-board computer systems to indicate to the mechanic/technician what system has logged-in a problem complaint. Only visible once the system memory has been activated in most cases, although a warning light can be made to flash automatically on the instrument panel to warn the driver of a problem situation.

ALU Shortened version for "Arithmetic Logic Unit," which is the part of the computer containing the necessary designed circuitry to carry out the computational information requirements such as addition, subtraction, multiplication, division, and comparing of operations of a digital system.

American wire gauge (AWG) Accepted standard system of assigned numerical designations for electrical wire size related to its circular mil area. The system starts with the number 4/0 (0000) as the largest size, reducing to 3/0 (000), 2/0 (00), 1/0 (0), 1, 2, 3, and on up to 40 and beyond for the smaller sizes.

Ampere The accepted standard unit of measuring the quantity/volume or strength of an electric current. Technically referred to as the actual rate of flow of the charge quantity in a conductor, such as in a wire for example, or similar conducting medium of one coulomb per second.

Amplifier   A unit, device, system, or circuit that is designed to increase the output signal of its input.

Amplitude modulation   System designed to regulate or tone down the amplitude of a wave to a desired characteristic.

Analog   A device or circuit whereby the output varies as a continuous function of its input. The representation does not have discrete values, but is continuously variable. Similar to the sound of the human voice, which fluctuates up and down. Is represented as a wavy line.

Analog circuits   Electronic circuits designed to actually amplify, reduce, or change a voltage signal of the analog type.

Analog computer   A computer that is designed to receive electrical and physical input variables and measure them, such as conditions of speed and height; then it manipulates these variables, usually converting them into numbers, in order to accomplish solutions to mathematical problems.

Analog output   Continuous transducer output which may be modified by the resolution of the transducer.

Analog transmission   The ability to transmit informational data as a continuous wave pattern.

AND gate   A combination logic element whereby its output signal channel is in one state, only if each input signal channel is also in one state. In other words, there are two input points, but only one output point.

Angstrom   Unit of length for light wavelength measurements equal to 10 to the power minus 10 meter. Nanometer is the more preferred and widely accepted SI unit of measurement.

Annunciator   A device used to sound an alarm to indicate what particular monitored circuit has developed a specific problem.

Anode   The positive pole of a battery, galvanic cell, or plating device, or the positive lead of a diode in an electronic solid-state circuit.

Array logic   A configuration of logic circuits forming a rectangular network shape of intersections of its input/output leads, and which has some elements connected at some of these intersections. This arrangement, or network system, is generally designed to function/operate either as an "encoder" or a "decoder."

Artificial intelligence   The ability of a computer to respond systematically to information fed to it by reacting in a human manner to such things as reasoning and the ability to learn.

ASCII   A shortened version that stands for "American Standard Code for Information Interchange." It is a 7-bit code that is widely used to represent informational data for processing and communications.

Assembly language   Accepted language that people use to program computers, normally by taking information and converting it into "binary form" or "notation."

Asynchronous device transmission   A device in which the speed of operation is unrelated to any frequency in the system through which it is connected. Data can be transmitted over a line one character at a time, with each character being preceded by a "start bit," and then followed by a "stop bit."

Avalanche breakdown   In IC circuits employing semiconductor diodes, for example, this is the nondestructive breakdown point that is created when the cumulative multiplication of carriers is subjected to field-induced impact ionization.

Avalanche diode   A term which is sometimes referred to also as a "silicon breakdown diode" that has a high ratio of reverse-to-forward resistance up to a certain level, after which, avalanche breakdown occurs and the voltage drop across the actual diode itself is basically constant, but is dependent upon the current flow. Such diodes are found in systems where either regulation or voltage limiting is desired. At one time, this type of diode was often referred to as a "zener diode," until it was discovered that this zener effect played no major role in the actual operation of these particular types of diodes.

Base   The region when referring to a transistor that actually lies between the "emitter" and the "collector," and into which minority carriers are injected.

Battery backed   A means of using battery power to maintain essential information data when the normal power source has been interrupted or disconnected.

Bias   The condition existing that influences or disposes to one direction, for example with applied direct voltage or with a spring. It can also be described as the persistent positive or negative deviation of the method average from an accepted reference value.

Bidirectional diode thyristor   A thryristor with two terminals that have basically an equal switching behavior in both their first and third quadrants of the principal voltage/current characteristic.

Binary coding number system   In digital computers which employ solid state electrical devices, these components can operate in either an *ON* or an *OFF* state, meaning that current is available or is not available. This is sometimes referred to as clockwise or counterclockwise. The on state is usually attributed a numeral of "one" (1), while an off state is issued a number zero (0). Generally, the binary numbering system for coding decimal numbers is in groups of 4 bits, with the actual binary value of these 4 bit groups ranging from 0000 to 1001, with the decimal digits running from 0 to 9. Therefore, to count up to a value of 9 requires 4 bits; up to 99 requires two groups of 4 bits; up to 999 requires three groups of 4 bits and so on as the value required is increased.

Bipolar   This is a term used to describe a specific type of IC construction whereby both the majority and minority carriers are present. The two most widely used IC constructions involve both bipolar and MOS types.

Bit   Refers to the smallest element of information in binary language that the computer can manipulate, such as a number 0 or 1, with the 0 representing an off condition, and the 1 an on condition. Computer word length and its memory capacity, for example, can be expressed in the number of bits of its information capability. Bits are most often assembled into "bytes" and words when they are placed in a storage address.

Bleeder resistor   Once an IC has been de-energized, this resistor is used to discharge a filter capacitor. In other words, it is a resistor that can be used to draw or absorb a fixed current value.

Blocking   A collection of continuous records combining two or more records in order to conserve storage space and to increase computer processing efficiency. Blocks per se are generally separated by what is known as "block gaps."

Borrow   Describes the action of an arithmetically negative carry during a CPU action.

Branching While a particular program is in progress, the next operation to be executed is already being selected, based upon the incoming or stored results.

Break point A condition during computer operation whereby an interruption or a stop command can be issued upon request.

Breakdown voltage (rating) During operation, the point or value at which a disruptive voltage discharge occurs, either through or over the surface of the insulation. Therefore, the breakdown voltage level is kept below this point in order to prevent arcing or conduction above a specified current value across the insulated portions of a transducer.

Buffer Within the computer itself, buffers are employed to store physical records so that logical analysis may be processed faster when transmitting information from one device to another. A buffer can also be an isolating circuit employed to avoid a reaction of a driven circuit on its corresponding driver circuit. When used as a temporary storage area, it operates to balance the speeds of the two devices.

Bug An error or fault in a computer program or system.

Bus A path or paths over which computer information can be transmitted.

Byte A technical term developed by IBM that indicates a specific number of consecutive "bits" that are grouped to form a single entity. A byte normally consists of either 7 or 8 bits that are used to represent a single character of information, or alternately two numerals.

Capacitance In an electronic or electrical system, it refers to that property which allows the storage of electrically separated charges when potential differences exist between the system conductors. Generally, its actual value is expressed as the ratio of a quantity of electrical charge to a potential difference.

Capacitor Sometimes referred to as a condenser, since it is a device that is constructed of two electrodes which are physically separated by a dielectric or insulator that may be simply in the form of an air gap to introduce capacitance into the electrical circuit.

Carrier An a.c. (alternating current) voltage with a suitably high frequency that can be modulated by electrical signals.

Carry When an arithmetic operation is initiated within the CPU portion of the computer, one or more digits may be forwarded (carried forward) to another digit place for processing there.

Carry look-ahead Within the computer CPU, this is a type of "adder" whereby the actual input signals to more than one stage can be examined; then the correct number of carries can be produced simultaneously, instead of initiating the outcome through a series of operations.

Cascade When two or more similar circuits or amplifying stages are arranged so that an output signal or value from one becomes the input for the next.

Cathode ray tube (CRT) A cathode is a negative electrode; therefore, a CRT consists of an electronbeam tube where a luminescent display can be projected, such as your home television screen. The beam is focused onto the screen where it can be varied in position and intensity to produce a desired display.

Character Basically a symbol that is used to describe a specific bit of information. In microcomputers, such as those used in au-

tomotive applications, the numerals 0 through 9 are used singularly or in combination to address a piece of information contained and stored within the computer. In addition, the letters of the alphabet can also be used, as well as any other desired symbols, to allow identification of stored pieces of information.

Check bit To check on and validate data within the computer memory system, a parity bit or binary check digit is employed.

Chip The actual unit on which all the desired active and passive elements of a specific electronics circuit have been manufactured. Generally, in automotive applications, chips used within the computer have terminals extending from them that are then attached to the desired control system and operating components. In some hybrid circuits, however, such as IAR and TFI, this is not necessary. Similarly, items such as a resistor or capacitor that are to be surface-mounted onto a printed circuit board or film hybrid substrates can be leadless and simply soldered into the system.

Clock Within the computer system, this unit is used to generate periodic signals that are used for purposes of synchronization of various stages. The clock times the changing state of a circuit response, for example, from a high to a low level. Such timed waveforms can be used for counting, for generating other timing pulses, and for determining timed sequences.

Closed loop The situation that exists when an engine is running, and the exhaust gas oxygen sensor is sending a voltage signal to the computer, which accepts this signal (rich/lean) and uses it along with other sensor inputs to maintain both the ignition timing and the stoichiometric air/fuel ratio. (See open-loop description for the exact opposite condition.)

Collector That part of a transistor through which the primary flow of the charge carriers leaves the base.

Collector amplifier Sometimes referred to as the emitter-follower of a transistor, or a grounded-collector amplifier. Basically, the collector element is common to both the input and the output circuits.

Combinational logic Digital system logic circuits that do not utilize memory elements, but whose outputs depend strictly on the existing logic input signals.

Comparator (analog) The electronic device that compares the voltage applied to an input.

Compensation A supplemental device used to modify and improve the performance or sources of systematic error in a circuit or system.

Computation The actions that are conducted within the CPU of the computer system that involve addition, subtraction, multiplication, division, and so forth.

Computer The computer is the electronic device that performs all the necessary computations of input data and provides desired output information to control various system operations.

Often referred to as the ECM (electronic control module), the ECU (electronic control unit), the CPU (central processing unit), etc., by various passenger car manufacturers. True computer systems must contain a provision for input data, a control unit, a storage or memory capability, an arithmetic logic section, and an output system.

Concentrator Concentrators are communication devices combining the features of both controllers and multiplexers. They also have the capability to store and forward information from several low-speed devices prior to sending this information forward at high-speed to another device.

Conditional branch   Any instruction that might cause the computer to actually execute an instruction other than the one that would normally follow the designed program.

Controller   A digital device that is responsible for supervising and implementing communications traffic and how the system is to function, thereby relieving the computer of an otherwise heavy processing burden.

Control structure   The pattern or design of the computer system that allows a systematic flow of logic to ensure an order of priority to more than one control system, particularly when coming from more than one source. Basically, this follows three control structures, which are sequence, selection, and looping.

Counter   Somewhat similar to a ''clock'' in that within the digital circuit it counts the number of input pulses, and when a predetermined number have been received, it allows an output pulse to flow.

CPU (central processing unit)   Often referred to as the computer itself in general discussion, since it is the actual component part of the computer system that is delegated to interpret and execute the arithmetic functions through the logic and control circuits. The CPU communicates with the input, output, and storage devices at all times. The CPU may contain the memory unit, as well as an operator's console.

Cutoff   The condition or operating mode of a transistor whereby very little current flows between the collector and emitter.

Cycle   A series or set of events conducted in a set time period. A good example is the sequence of events performed in an alternator when the voltage flows first to its maximum value (positive), then reverses itself in the opposite direction (negative) during which time one cycle of events is performed. Illustrated by the use of a sine wave when shown graphically.

DAC (digital analog converter)   Digital to analog converter is an electronic device capable of producing a voltage that is proportional to the digit input number or magnitude.

Darlington amplifier   A circuit consisting of two transistors where the collectors are tied together, and the emitter of the first transistor is coupled directly to the base of the second transistor. This produces a condition whereby the emitter current of transistor one is equal to the base current of transistor two. Such a connection between two transistors is regarded as a compound unit with three terminals.

Data   Unorganized informational facts that are collected from the various engine and vehicle sensor devices, but which have not yet been processed into logical information.

Data access   The ability of the computer to read or write data onto a device in either a sequential or direct format.

Database   A collection of integrated informational data which is stored within the computer on a direct-access storage device.

Databus   The path along which the transfer of data to and from the CPU, storage, and peripheral devices flows.

Deadband   A fairly narrow range through which a measured signal can be varied without actually initiating a response from a component.

Decibel   Scale of noise (sound) used to indicate loudness. Also in electronic systems, it is a measure of the amount of power, with the number of decibels denoting the ratio of the amounts (two) of power.

Decoder   A component in the system which allows acceptance of digital input signal information, such as in the case of a memory address decoder or a binary address information system. The decoder selects and activates one line of a large number of output lines in order to act as a conversion circuit.

Demux   Shortened version of a demultiplexer which is a type of electronic switch that is used to select one of several output lines.

Diagnostic sensor   A unit or component that is employed to sense specific operating conditions and then transmit this information to the computer system.

Dielectric   A component or medium in which it is actually possible to maintain an electric field with little or no energy supply from an outside source.

Digit   Generally, a decimal or alphabetical notation that represents a specific character of information, although other identifying notations can be employed.

Digital computer   A computer system that is designed to operate and recognize input information that is usually in numerical form, such as number of people or dollars for example. These digital computers normally employ and use binary or decimal notation and process this information by repeated high-speed use through an arithmetic logic process that includes addition, subtraction, multiplication, and division. Constructed to recognize an ''on'' signal as a number 1, and an ''off'' signal as a zero.

Digital circuits   Electronic circuits whose output signals can change only at specific instances and between a limited number of varying voltages.

Diode   A semiconductor device that acts like a current (ampere) check valve. Sometimes referred to in its simplest form as a two-electrode electron tube which contains both an anode and a cathode. As a semiconductor, it also has two terminals and exhibits an operating characteristic of nonlinear voltage-current. If the diode is used in a restricted mode, it will exhibit an asymmetrical voltage-current characteristic exemplified by a single p-n junction.

Diode transistor logic (DTL)   Used in typical computer logic circuits to obtain the desired output signals and values required to operate the system successfully. It consists of diodes at the input which are employed to perform the desired electronic logic function required to activate the circuit transistor output. When used in a monolithic circuit, the DTL diodes operate as a positive level logic/function, or alternately as a negative level or function. Therefore, the output transistor acts as an inverter which causes the circuit to become either a positive NAND (combination NOT/AND gate), or alternately a negative NOR (combination OR/NOT gate) operating system.

Dip   Shortened wording for a simple ''dual in-line package.''

EBDIC   Means Extended Binary Coded Decimal Interchange. EBDIC actually employs an 8-bit byte and is used to represent up to 256 characters.

E-cycle   The sequence of the computer cycle whereby data is located, an instruction is executed, and the results are stored in memory.

Eddy currents   Currents that exist as a direct result of inducing voltages in the body of a conducting mass through a variation of magnetic flux.

EEPROM Electrically Erasable Programmable Read Only Memory. A computer using an EEPROM module over a straight PROM unit can have its contents altered while plugged into a peripheral device. Computers using straight PROM's must physically be changed out for another in order to change the operating characteristics of the computer.

EEROM Electrically Erasable Read Only Memory. Can have the contents of memory electrically altered similar to that described for an EEPROM (above). The EEROM is sometimes referred to as EAROM or, simply, electrically alterable ROM. EEROM cannot be erased by users or programmers.

Electromotive force (EMF) The electrical force that can cause current to flow any time that a difference in potential exists between two points.

Electron The basic negative electrical charge which is one of the natural constituents of matter.

Emitter That part of a transistor from which current is conducted and flows to the collector in an npn transistor only when the base and collector are positive with respect to the emitter. In a pnp type transistor, the emitter current will flow to the collector only when the base and collector are negative with respect to the emitter.

Error The discrepancy that exits in a system between the computed or observed and measured quantity, with the true and specified theoretically correct value.

Execute The operation that is conducted during the normal computer cycle, in which a selected control word or instruction is actually carried out or completed.

Exponent The mathematical power to which the base number is raised in a floating point representation.

Feedback The ability of a closed-loop system circuit to recycle some percentage of the output signal back to the input side. This feedback signal may pass through an amplifier first in order to modify the performance of the amplifier.

Fiber optics Consists of cables composed of thousands of hair-thin transparent fibers along which informational data can be passed from lasers as light intensive waves.

Field effect transistor (FET) When a voltage is applied to a logic gate terminal, a field is produced to create a resistance between the source and the drain terminals of this semiconductor device.

Filter In digital instrumentation systems, a filter can be employed to improve the visual characteristics of the display, while in other electronic circuits, it can include resistors, inductors, capacitors, or active filter elements that offer minor opposition to certain frequencies. Can also be used to direct current flow, while at the same time blocking or attenuating undesirable additional frequencies.

Fixed-length word approach Each computer address is designed to hold/store a word composed of a certain number of characters.

Fixed binary point number Each binary number is represented by a sign bit and one or more numbered bits, with a binary point placed somewhere between two neighboring bits.

Flip-flop The capability of a storage element consisting of two stable states that has the capability of changing from one state to another when a control signal is applied to it. It will remain in this state after signal removal.

Flux The total amount of all of the actual lines of magnetic force crossing a unit area in given or unit time period.

Font The term used to describe a set of symbols which a typical CRT (cathode ray tube) display can present.

FORTRAN Means Formula Translating System, and it indicates a programming language that is used primarily to express computer programs by arithmetic formulas.

Frequency and assorted terms The term natural frequency signifies basically how many times an action occurs (angular speed or flow rate) within a given time period. Can also be expressed as the number (frequency) of free oscillations (without force) of a sensing element in a fully assembled transducer.

The resonant frequency refers to the measured frequency at which a transducer will respond with maximum output signal amplitude. Therefore when one states a frequency response, it is a statement of measure of the gain or loss of a circuit device/system based upon the frequencies applied to it.

Full-adder A logic-circuit that incorporates the provision for a carry-in from a preceding arithmetic calculation addition.

Full-duplex transmission The ability of the computer to send informational data/messages in two directions simultaneously along a bus or communications path.

Gain Very simply put, gain is the ratio of a system's output magnitude to its input magnitude. An example of gain can be found in a transistor which provides an increase in power when a signal is transmitted from one point to another. The gain is then expressed in decibels.

Gate The term used to describe a device or element used in solid-state system circuits to either allow or alternately prevent the flow of a signal, depending upon one or more specified inputs. Typically used GATES in electronic logic circuits are the AND, NOR, OR and NOT gate types.

GCS Simply an abbreviation for a Gate Controlled Switch.

Half-adder Compare with the "Full Adder" described earlier. However, the half-adder is a logic gate circuit device that is capable of adding two binary numbers, but it does not have the capability for a carry-in from a preceding computer arithmetic function such as a preceding addition.

Hall-effect A magnetic element employed in both solid-state ignition systems and various engine sensors achieved through the development of a transverse electric potential gradient in any current carrying semiconductor or conductor when a magnetic field is applied to it.

Heat sink A heat conducting or radiating device that is employed extensively in most solid-state semiconducting systems to prevent overheating and the resultant damage that would occur. The heat sink is usually made of a metallic compound and is finned/ribbed to increase its heat radiating efficiency.

Hertz The technical term used to describe the unit of frequency, which is accepted as one cycle per second. For example, the electrical frequency of the electrical components used in your home in North America is 60 cycles per second, while in other countries it is often only 50 cycles per second. This frequency is obtained by employing a number of windings and magnetic poles in power generators and spinning them at a fixed speed to maintain the designed frequency.

Hexadecimal In certain types of computers, it is the term used to identify the number system encompassing sixteen possible states, namely that of 0, 1, 2, 3, 4, 5, 6, 7, 8, 9, and A, B, C, D, E, and F.

Hybrid circuit A system with circuits employing either "thin" or "thick-film" semiconductor technology, with the passive components made with thin-film, and the active components by the semiconductor technique.

Hysteresis The response difference that exists in a circuit whereby the hysteretical reaction is characterized by its inability to perform exactly as it did on the previous swing regarding its input/output signal conditions.

I-cycle The sequence reaction within the computer whereby the CPU control unit fetches an instruction from main memory and subsequently prepares it for processing.

Inductor A component or device that is magnetic and therefore capable of storing energy within the magnetic field produced by current flowing within it.

Impedance This is the total opposition expressed in ohms (resistance) presented by any component or circuit in response to the flow of an alternating or varying current source. Impedance generally infers that it is an a.c. circuit which is opposite to the accepted resistance value of a d.c. circuit. The impedance value can be calculated from the formula $Z = E/I$, where E is the applied a.c. voltage, and I is the resulting a.c. current flowing in the circuit.

Indexed address A reaction that occurs prior to or during computer operation when an execution is being performed to modify an address through the content of an index register. Simply a method of address modification.

Indexed register During or prior to the computer carrying out an instruction, this register's content can be added or subtracted from the operand address.

Indirect address The computer program is set up so that the initial address is designated as the information storage location of a certain word that itself contains another address. Once this second address is identified, it is then used to obtain the stored data that is to be acted upon.

Inductance In an electric circuit when a varying current is passed through it, it creates a varying magnetic field which itself then induces a voltage in the same circuit or in a nearby circuit. Measured in a term known as henrys.

Inductor Any device with one or more windings that may or may not contain a magnetic core.

Infrared The term used to describe the fact that a portion of a light spectrum has a wavelength greater than the naked eye can visibly see.

Instruction counter A counter device within the computer, whose job it is to indicate the location of the next computer instruction that should be interpreted.

Instruction register That device within the computer that stores an instruction and prepares it for execution. Basically, it tells the computer what to do next.

Insulator A device made from a material that will not allow electron flow (offers high resistance to flow); therefore it is employed in electrical and electronic circuits to separate conductors (allow electron flow) to prevent any flow of current between them or to any other circuits.

Integrated circuit A solid-state (semiconductor) device that actually contains numerous circuit functions etched on a single silicon chip. The IC can contain diodes, transistors, logic gates, etc.

Interface A computer hardware device that links two components, or alternately it can be a portion of storage or registers accessed by two or more computer programs.

Interrupter A method whereby the computer's attention can be quickly drawn to a specific external event.

Inverse voltage During the half-cycle when current does not flow in an a.c. circuit, it is the effective voltage across the rectifier.

Joule The unit of energy in the SI system of measurement. For example Joule's Equivalent states that 1 BTU will produce 778 foot pounds of energy.

Keep-alive memory Computer memory system that must have continuous power in order to retain memory information. If power is lost, then the stored memory information is also lost; therefore, in this type of system, battery back-up power can be used when main power is lost.

Kilobyte Represents 1024 bytes in a computer. The primary memory on smaller computer systems is generally measured by its kilobyte capability.

LSI (large scale integration) A term used to describe the fact that an integrated circuit has a high density of chips in it. Compare to "SCI" or small scale integration.

Latch In a symmetrical digital electronic circuit employing, for example, a "flip-flop," the latch acts as a feedback loop to ensure retention of a given state. Locks in a state in other words.

LCD Means liquid crystal display, which is a passive display whereby the light transmission or polarization is changed by the influence of an electric field.

LED Means light emitting diode, which is an active display with the degree of light emitted based upon the current flow in a semiconductor circuit. LED's consist of a pn junction that will emit light when it is biased in the forward direction.

Limit cycle An action of the control system operation whereby the controlled variable actually cycles between extreme limits, with the average being near the predetermined desired value.

Linear region The mode of operation of the transistor when the collector current is proportional to the base current.

Logic element An element within the IC that is used to ensure/provide circuit functions inside the computer, such as an AND, OR, NOT, and NAND gate. These devices employ a mathematical approach in order to solve complex situations through the use of symbols that define these basic concepts. The logic gates allow addition, subtraction, division, and multiplication to be carried out.

Look-up table A table that is contained in computer memory, and which is employed to convert an input value from a sensor, for example, into a related value in order to execute that technique.

Loop A repeated sequence of instructions that is executed until a terminal condition exists. Compare with the terms "open loop" and "closed loop."

Luminosity The term used to indicate the brightness or intensity of an electronic display.

Magnetic bubble storage Computer memory that uses magnetic bubbles to indicate both the 0 or off, and 1 or on bit states.

Magnetic particle display This is a passive display that operates on the basic principle of orienting permanently magnetized particles under the influence of an applied magnetic field.

Magneto resistive effect The application of a magnetic field to a conductor or semiconductor will alter its resistance value.

Mainframe It implies that within the computer the processing portion (CPU) contains storage capability, as well as the arithmetic logic unit, and a group of registers.

Majority carrier In n-type semiconductors, there are a greater number of electrons than holes; therefore, the electrons become the majority carrier. In a p-type semiconductor, however, there are more holes than electrons; therefore, the holes become the majority carrier in this case.

Mask A mask can act as a type of filter to control the retention or elimination of portions of another pattern of characters within the computer information system.

Mass storage unit Simply a computer storage device that is capable of storing literally billions of bytes of on-line informational data.

Matrix In computer systems, this refers to the logic network in the form of array or input and output leads with logic elements connected at some of these intersections.

Measureand The term used to describe either a physical quantity, property, or a condition that is being measured.

Megabyte Consists of about one million bytes of information and is generally used to express the secondary storage capacity of many computers.

Microcomputer Describes the smallest type and usually the cheapest style of computer system available.

Micron A term used to describe the physical size of a particle, with one micron being equal to one, one-millionth of a meter. This is shown as 0.00003937″ as a decimal, or simply 10 to the power minus 6.

Microprocessor The digital CPU (central processing unit) on a chip that is allotted the task of performing both the arithmetic and control logic functions.

Microsecond Denotes time as being one millionth of a second.

Microwave An electromagnetic wave that occurs only in a high-frequency range, such as that employed in a home microwave oven.

Millisecond Denotes time as being one thousandth of a second.

Minicomputer A computer that is a step up from a microcomputer, but not as advanced as a mainframe computer.

Minority carrier Compare to the term, ''majority carrier,'' described earlier.

Mnemonic symbol Simply a chosen symbol to assist the human memory by using an abbreviation (such as ''MPY'' for multiply or multiplication) that can easily be remembered.

Monitor A device that can warn either visually or by sound by monitoring and comparing a measured value against a set stan-

dard. In effect, it is the supervising program within an operating system.

MNOS An abbreviation for metal-nitride-oxide semiconductor unit.

MOS An abbreviation for a metal-oxide semiconductor unit.

Multiplexing Advances in electronics are aimed at reducing the number and bulk of wires and harnesses used in automotive applications. By multiplexing, several measurements can be transmitted over the same signal wire path or bus, either through a time-sharing process or simultaneously. However, multiplexing uses either a time division (sharing) method, or a frequency division process, with the time sharing employing the principle of actual sharing amongst measurement channels, while the frequency process utilizes the sharing process amongst information channels whereby the informational data from each channel is used to modulate sinusoidal signals known as subcarriers. This results in a signal which represents each channel and contains only those frequencies within a narrow range.

NAND and NOR logic gates In the CPU section of the computer, when an AND gate is followed by an inverter, it is referred to as a NOT AND or NAND gate. In this arrangement, should all the inputs have a value of 1 (on), the output will be 0 or off. If any of the inputs have a value of 0 (off), then the output will be 1 (on). Used extensively in binary circuit functions.

Nanosecond A time expression that is measured in one billionth of a second.

Negative logic The situation whereby the logic is the more negative voltage signal, and it therefore represents the 1 or on state, with the less negative voltage representing the 0 or off state.

NMOS Simply, MOS devices constructed on a p-type silicon chip, with the active carriers being electrons flowing between n-type sources and drain contacts.

NVM (nonvolatile memory) Computer memory that is not lost when the main power supply is disconnected or interrupted.

NOR logic gate In the CPU system of the computer, it is an OR logic gate that is followed by an inverter in order to form a binary circuit whereby the output is logic 0 (off), as long as either of the input signals is 1 (on) and vice versa.

npn transistor A type of transistor using a p-type base and an n-type collector and emitter.

n-type material A crystal of pure semiconductor material, such as silicon, which has been doped by adding an impurity to produce electrons that serve as the majority charge carriers.

Ohm The unit of resistance whereby one ohm is created when one volt will maintain a current of one ampere.

Operand The term used to describe a device that is operated upon, and is normally identified by an address part of an instruction.

OR logic gate Within the CPU section of the computer, the OR logic gate consists of a multiple input circuit whose output is energized any time that one or more of the input signals is in a predetermined state.

Oscillator An electronic device employed to generate a.c. (alternating current) power at a frequency determined by the value of certain predetermined constants designed into the circuits.

Output Processed informational data within the computer from the various input signals output after processing as usable information.

Parallel operation   The simultaneous computation of instructions by a computer having multiple arithmetic logic functions, or the transmission of data whereby each bit in a byte has its own path.

Parity bit   A check or extra bit that is added to an array of binary digits or to the byte representation of a character to ensure that all of the binary digits including the check bit will always be either an odd or an even number of 1 bits transmitted with each and every character.

Passive display   Both liquid crystal and electrochromic systems are passive displays whereby the transmission or reflection of external light is modulated.

Peripheral equipment   The secondary storage units, as well as the input and output devices, within a computer system.

Photocell   A solid-state device that exhibits photovoltaic or photoconductive effects.

Piezo-electric   The ability of certain crystals either to produce a voltage when subjected to a mechanical stress or alternately to undergo mechanical stress when subjected to a voltage.

PMOS   Abbreviation for a p-type MOS which is manufactured on an n-type silicon chip for example, with the active carriers being holes flowing between p-type sources and drain controls.

pnp transistor   A transistor that is made up of two p-type elements separated by an n-type element or region.

pnpn diode   A semiconductor regarded as a two-transistor structure that has two separate emitters feeding to a common collector.

Polarizer   Material that is employed to generate polarized light from a nonpolarized source or supply.

Potential   The difference in voltage that exists between two points in any circuit.

PROM   Abbreviation for Programmable Read Only Memory, which is the software in the hardware module that is capable of being programmed. However, once the PROM has been programmed, it cannot be altered or erased. When a permanent PROM is used in a system, it is called nonvolatile since it is not erasable when the power supply is disconnected or temporarily lost. The PROM module basically contains specific informational data that applies, for example, to a specific model of car related to its engine size and power, the transmission and axle ratios, tire size, etc. Therefore, such a PROM cannot be interchanged and placed into another vehicle having different characteristics; otherwise, serious performance complaints would result. Refer to the abbreviation EEPROM for a PROM that can be erased electronically.

p-type material   Doped semiconductor material that produces free holes from an excess of acceptor impurity atoms.

RFI (radio frequency interference)   The interference that exists in electronic equipment as a direct result of frequency energy emitted from a radio signal.

RAM (random access memory)   This type of memory is continually being updated as the computer is operating, based on information it receives from changing sensor signals. It is, in effect, the working scratch-pad of the computer unit. Temporarily stored information is always immediately available, regardless of the previous memory address location. Since memory information can be accessed in any order, equal access is assured to all bits of data.

Rectifier   A device to convert alternating current into unidirectional current.

Register   A temporary storage device for digital informational data.

Relay   A device designed to respond to specific input signals and information. Sometimes, more than one unit is assembled into a relay to provide a wider scope of operation whereby these unit combinations together will provide a predetermined output.

Resistivity   When electric current is applied through or on the surface of a material (conductor), this is a measurement of that resistance.

Resistor   A device that is inserted into an electrical or electronic circuit to slow down, by resistance, the flow of current in that circuit.

RCTL (resistor-capacitor-transistor logic)   Within the design of a particular logic circuit, the use of a resistor and a speed-up capacitor that are in parallel for each input signal of the logic gate. A transistor is also employed with its base connected to one end of the RC arrangement. When a positive voltage is applied to the RC input, this energizes the transistor unit, turning it on to provide almost a zero output voltage signal. Such a circuit design is commonly known as a positive NOR gate, or negative NAND whenever npn type transistors are employed in the actual circuit design.

RTL (resistor-transistor logic)   Another type of logic gate circuit design that employs a resistor as the input signal unit that is also attached to the base of an npn transistor. The transistor acts as an inverting element as it does in the RCTL circuit design to produce a positive NOR gate, or alternately, a negative NAND gate logic functioning system.

Response time   The actual time required for a computer actually to respond to a specific input command.

ROM (read only memory)   Part of the software in the actual hardware module that can, in fact, be read, but cannot be written upon, such as the RAM can. The ROM allows reading of a predetermined pattern of zeros (off) and ones (on). The memory in ROM is hardwired at the time of manufacture and cannot be altered. ROM memory is not lost when power is disconnected, such as in the case of RAM.

Sample-and-hold circuit   The system is capable of looking at a voltage level, then storing that reading for a much longer time period.

Saturation voltage   The condition that exists in a circuit when a self-limiting feature comes into being. In other words, the circuit is unable to respond to excitation in a proportional manner.

Schottky barrier   A metal to semiconductor interface that exhibits a nonlinear impedance.

Self-generating   A component such as a piezo-electric, electromagnetic, or thermoelectric transducer that is capable of providing an output signal without applied excitation.

Semiconductor   Semi implies that it is a component capable of conducting some electrical qualities, but also of offering some insulating effect. Therefore, it is an electronic conductor wherein the electric-charge-carrier concentration will increase with a rise in temperature over a specified tolerance range. It is possible, depending upon the type of semiconductor material used, to produce a unit that has two types of carriers, namely that of negative electrons and positive holes.

Sensitivity   How fast a device or electronic element can react or respond to a change at its input.

Sensor   A device that is designed to respond to the value of a measured quantity, such as a throttle position sensor, oil pressure sensor, vehicle speed sensor, etc.

Sequencing   The method or structure of control that is designed into a computer system to ensure that the various informational operations will occur in a predetermined order.

Sequential logic systems   The operating mode in a digital computer system that relies on a number of different design memory elements, such as the various logic type gates described in this glossary.

Serial-parallel   The decimal digits are handled in serial fashion, whereas the actual bits that form the digit are handled in parallel.

Serial transmission   A system wherein the informational data transmission in which each and every bit in a byte has to travel down the same path one after the other.

Shift register   Consisting of a logic gate network whereby a series of memory cells and therefore the binary code can shift into the register by serial input to the first cell, or where the stored data can be moved either right or left.

Signal generator   Used for example in a vehicle speed sensor. It consists of a shielded source of power with the output level and frequency being calibrated for a predetermined range of operation.

Silo memory   A system of stored data that is read on the basis of first-in/first-out.

Solid-state circuit or device   Any circuit or component that employs nonmoving parts made up of semiconductors.

Steady-state   The operating condition whereby the circuit values remain reasonably constant.

Storage register   The area where informational data from primary memory is stored immediately prior to processing.

Strain gauge   The ability of a measurement system to convert a strain level into a resistance value.

Substrate   The foundation material upon which an electronic circuit is actually fabricated.

Synchronous circuit   Any circuit that has been designed to ensure that all of its computed informational offerings are sent out through equally spaced signals controlled from a master clock unit.

Synchronous transmission   The transmitting of informational data over or across a line by a block of characters at a time.

Temporary storage register   Memory storage locations that have been reserved for intermediate results.

Thermistor   Used as a sensor in automotive applications as a coolant and air temperature sensor, where a temperature rise causes a decrease in its resistance value (negative characteristic value), versus one with a positive temperature characteristic which would exhibit a resistance value increase as temperature rises. The negative type is more common to automotive applications.

Thermocouple   Simply a device for measuring temperature change whereby two dissimilar conductors are joined at two points to cause production of an electromotive force.

Thick-film   A design of film pattern achieved by applying conductive and insulating materials to a ceramic substrate in order to form conductors, resistors, and capacitors.

Thin-film   A conductive film of insulating material formed in a pattern to produce electronic components and conductors on a substrate, or alternately it can be used as an insulation between successive layers of a component.

Threshold   The minimum driving signal level at which a perceptible change will take place.

Thyristor   A semiconductor device consisting of three or more junctions that can be switched from either the off state to the on state, or vice versa; therefore, often known as a bistable device.

Track   A path on an input/output medium on which informational data is recorded.

Transducer   A device that is capable of transferring energy (flow) from more than one system or media to more than one other system.

Transformer   A device that can be wired in such a way that voltage can be stepped up or, alternately, stepped down to meet a known system demand rating. An ignition coil is a good example of a transformer, since it takes the 12 volt battery supply and steps it up through the primary winding first to a voltage that is proportional to the number of windings in the coil. This voltage is then increased further in the coil secondary winding to about 25,000 volts in a conventional contact breaker point system, while in a solid-state ignition system, the voltage can be as high as 40,000 volts. The ignition coil contains a metal core to enhance this magnetic field buildup, thereby assisting the voltage increase in the coil windings. However, some transformers may not contain a magnetic core for introducing mutual coupling between electric circuits.

Transients   The term transient usually implies that there is a temporary increase or decrease of the voltage or current signal. These transients take the form of what is commonly called ''spikes'' or ''surges,'' since they occur for a very short time period. Discharge control of such spikes or suges is handled through the insertion of capacitors, resistors, or inductors into the circuit, which suppresses these transients that are caused by a switching action within a circuit (on to off and vice versa).

Transistor   This is what is known as an ''active'' semiconductor device, since it is capable of providing ''gain'' in a circuit. It generally contains three or more terminals. Gain simply means that current can be amplified and switched on and off through the action of the transistor. The word transistor is a combination of the words ''transfer'' and ''resist.'' Since a transistor is used at junction points in the electronic system, it is often referred to as a ''junction transistor.'' Therefore, the transistor is designed to operate similar to a current check valve.

The three main parts of the transistor are the base, the emitter, and the collector. Automotive-type transistors employ either a signal-type unit which operates with an input voltage up to 10 millivolts, or a power transistor that functions with an input voltage greater than 10 millivolts.

True binary representation   A commonly employed method in computer construction that represents numerical values as a string of binary bits.

Triac   Within a logic gate circuit, it is often desirable to be able to control a switching action for either polarity of voltage being applied, and to be able to control this action in either polarity from a single gate electrode. Therefore, a five-layer npnpn device, equivalent in action to two SCR's (rectifiers) connected in an antiparallel design with a common gate system, is employed to achieve this action.

Truth table   In a semiconductor circuit, various combinations of logic gates are employed to control effectively the output values based upon such input signals as those coming from the numerous engine/vehicle sensors on a continuous basis to the ECM (electronic control module) or computer. A truth table is a chart that is something like a look-up table, in that this chart tabulates and summarizes all of the possible combinations or states of the inputs and outputs for a given circuit. Such truth tables are discussed and illustrated in Chapter 3.

TTL or T2L (transistor-transistor logic)   This is a logic gate circuit which has some similarities to a DTL or diode transistor logic system, except that the diode inputs are replaced with a multiple emitter transistor.

Twisted wire   This type of wiring simply consists of pairs of wires twisted together, then bound into a cable. A good example of this is the telephone system cabling used to connect your handset to the main system.

UART   Abbreviation for Universal Asynchronous Receiver Transmitter system used in many automotive computer systems.

Ultraviolet   That portion of a light spectrum with wavelengths shorter than are visible to the naked eye, which wavelengths are less than 3900 angstroms.

Unconditional branch   A computer instruction which causes execution of a specific statement other than the one that would normally immediately follow the set sequence of operation.

Unijunction transistor   A type of transistor that contains three terminals and which will exhibit a stable open-circuit with negative resisting characteristics.

VFD (vacuum fluorescent display)   An active display system that operates upon the emission of light provided by a phosphor that is excited by electrons emitted from a filament in vacuum.

VAR (volt ampere reactive)   A unit of reactive-power as opposed to real-power in watts (amps × volts), with one VAR being equal to one reactive volt-ampere.

Variable length word approach   The storage design whereby a single character of informational data occupies a single address. Compare this to the "fixed-word-length system."

Varistor   Consists of a two-electrode semiconductor device having a voltage dependent, nonlinear resistance that falls off or drops significantly as the voltage being applied to the circuit is increased.

Visible   Contrast with ultraviolet light, which is not visible to the naked eye. We can see any portion of light between 390 to 770 nm.

Volatile memory   The word "volatile" implies that should the normal power supply be lost or interrupted, then the electronic memory such as RAM, which acts as the computer scratch-pad during operation, will lose that information/memory any time that the ignition switch is turned off.

Volatile storage   Simply means that any stored data is lost as soon as the ignition key is turned off or the power supply is interrupted.

Volt   The term used to describe electrical pressure existing between two points of a conductor, such as a wire that is carrying a constant current in amperes, when the power dissipated between these points is one watt (amps × volts).

Watt   The term used to describe amps × volts, with 1000 watts being equal to 1KW (kilowatt). Therefore, it is the power required to produce work at an accepted rate of one joule per second, or when one amp of direct current flows through a conductor having one ohm of resistance.

Word   Includes either a group of bits or characters that the computer treats as an entity, and which can be stored in a single memory location.

Write enable   Within the computer, it is the control signal sent to a storage element or a memory location that will activate the write mode for the computer system. Any time that the write mode of operation is inactive, then the read mode of the computer can be accessed.

Zener diode   A special type of diode that, when forward-biased, becomes an ordinary rectifier; however, when reverse-biased, it exhibits a sharp break in its actual current/voltage characteristics. In this state, the voltage remains reasonably constant with any further increase of reverse current on up to the diodes dissipation rating. The accepted norm for a zener diode is a breakdown voltage slightly less than 6 volts; therefore, this type of diode can act as a voltage regulator, overvoltage protection unit, voltage reference unit, or as a voltage level shifter (trigger).

Index